ENCYCLOPEDIA OF GARDENING

Deena Beverley & Barty Phillips

Special photography
by Andrew Newton-Cox

p

ENCYCLOPEDIA OF GARDENING

This is a Parragon Publishing Book
This edition published in 2002

Parragon Publishing
Queen Street House
4 Queen Street
Bath BA1 1HE, UK

ISBN: 0-75258-775-7

A CIP data record for this book is available from the British Library.

Created and produced by
Foundry Design and Production

Acknowledgements
Illustrations: Kate Simunek
Special photography: Andrew Newton-Cox

Special thanks to Jennifer Bishop, Katie Cowan, Josephine Cutts, Dave Jones, Chairworks, Clifton Nurseries, Draper's Tools Ltd, Idencroft Herbs Jardinerie and Queenswood Garden Centre for the loan of plants, props and tools.

Printed in China

CONTENTS

INTRODUCTION

The aim of this book is to help those with relatively little gardening knowledge make informed choices about how to plan and maintain their gardens. The upsurge of gardening as a leisure activity during recent years has been phenomenal and as a result the demand for information on practical gardening and plants to be grown in gardens has developed rapidly.

Everyone has a unique vision for their garden but many people, when confronted with a garden for the first time, feel intimidated by their lack of knowledge and wonder if they will ever succeed in managing their gardening. This book will show you that gardening need not be difficult – almost any garden, whatever its shape or size, can be tailored to suit individual tastes, and as you gain confidence, you will quickly find your gardening horizons widening. Seven easy-to-follow chapters with practical step-by-step instructions will help you maximize the potential of any plot.

The first two chapters of the book will help you work out all your garden needs, from assessing the plot, to the basic techniques you will need to master and the tools required to see your plans come to fruition. The rest of the encyclopedia provides all the practical gardening information that you will need to begin the tasks of designing the structure, adding paths, patios and ponds, laying lawns and creating borders. Sections on propagation, pruning and working with plants and garden DIY contain simple step-by-step text and illustration sequences, and each chapter ends with a selection of garden projects that will enhance the beauty and function of your garden.

Offering advice on all aspects of planning and planting, you will learn how to deal with problems such as pests and diseases, weed control, as well as learning about general plant maintenance, such as watering and feeding.

With inspirational ideas on garden design, you will be able to achieve the perfect look for your garden by following the simple advice, whether you want a modern, romantic or Japanese style. Individual sections show you how to add interest by incorporating stunning features such as patios, decking and water and light features.

When it comes to planting you are in good hands. With advice and suggestions for planting scheme, taking into consideration soil type, aspect and seasonal interest, you cannot fail to find the right plant. Also included are sections on cultivating an edible garden, and pruning and propagating.

Color, form and texture play a vital role in the modern garden, and achieving the right balance of these in your garden is made easy following the clear step-by-step instructions and illustrations. Fourteen easy-to-follow garden projects can be found at the end of the chapters, the results of which will transform and enhance your garden. These range from a bird-box and a windchime to border edging and a wall planter.

This encyclopedia is for anyone who wants to make the most of their outdoor space, no matter if it is large or small, garden or patio, country or urban. Whether you want to establish a herb garden, create a colorful bed of summer flowers or plant a pot of geraniums for your windowsill, this book will show you how.

Whether you're a first-time home owner with a small urban plot or tiny balcony, or have a large rambling garden in need of renovation this book will inspire you to turn your garden into your own personal haven.

GARDEN PLANNING

Your ideal garden might seem far out of reach and unattainable. Don't worry; take your time. A garden can wait and so can you.

❀

The first step is deciding what you want and the second is turning it into reality. A garden is a very personal thing and everybody wants something different.

❀

Do not be afraid to play around with ideas; even the most experienced professional designers will not come up with the correct solution in an afternoon.

❀

Mistakes will be made – and indeed are often made by professionals, too – but you can always change things. Any garden is a living, growing entity; it can always be adjusted.

YOU AND YOUR GARDEN

There are two aspects to the initial decision-making.
One is to think about your ideal garden – the garden you see in your
day-dreams, the equivalent to the Middle Eastern paradise garden.
What are your secret dreams for this small patch of land? The other is to
think about the practical aspects, such as providing storage for garden
tools and a place to dry the washing. It is useful to make a checklist of
what you require. Here are some possible ideas for your dream garden.
You will probably want to add others of your own.

CHECKLIST FOR YOUR 'IDEAL' GARDEN

ENTERTAINING can be one of the most enjoyable uses of a garden. A generous vine-covered patio, a barbecue area or a croquet lawn may be your dream. If you cannot incorporate all these features, some of them should certainly be possibilities. Other than entertaining, consider the following requirements, too.

Privacy and peace

❁ For some people the most important requirement of a garden is to create a private outdoor space. A tall hedge or trellis with climbers may not cut out all sounds but it will certainly help you to be less aware of them and will effectively separate you from your neighbors. A romantic arbor with a comfortable seat within the garden, surrounded by rambling roses, honeysuckle and clematis can provide a secluded, peaceful place in which to relax and enjoy the garden.

BELOW: *The romantic arbor,* par excellence. *This one would fit well in a small garden with its neat shape and simple wooden bench, and its surrounding of white roses and scented lavender.*

❁ Not everyone finds peace the ideal, however. You may prefer to sit in your small front garden and watch the world go by. Here, a hedge would get in the way, so you might prefer a paved area with pots of flowering plants and perhaps two larger shrubs to give the garden an entrance.

LEFT: *A herb border can be an attractive feature of a garden. This one has contrasting leaf sizes as well as scent and color.*

LEFT: *This small garden has been cleverly designed with ponds and interconnecting spaces to create the impression of spaciousness. The white sails are an attractive way of creating shade on hot days.*

Color

❀ The green of foliage on its own can create a garden with a great sense of unity. At the same time, because there are so many different shades of green, and because leaves come in different shapes, rustle in different ways and catch the light differently, a foliage garden is endlessly interesting, without any extra color.

❀ However, many people like bright colors and this is where a knowledge of plants, when they flower and where they will flower best, can be very helpful.

❀ To begin with, it is a good idea to add annuals or bedding plants where there are gaps, but as you become more knowledgeable you will find you like to experiment with all sorts of different color and plant combinations.

Scent

❀ This is one of the most evocative aspects of a garden. It is worth trying to introduce as many scented plants as possible. In general, the scent from plants is most noticeable in the evening, so think of putting plants such as honeysuckles, scented roses and philadelphus where you are most likely to be sitting with an evening drink. Remember that some scents are more pleasing than others – privet, for example, has a rather overbearing scent, even during the day. Most of the scented flowers are also those that attract wildlife, and worth planting for that reason alone.

Water

❀ Water has a refreshing quality in any garden. Whether you want a quiet, still pool that will reflect the sky or take on an almost black mysteriousness, or whether you prefer the lively gurgle of a fountain or cascade, some form of water feature will give the garden an added dimension. Pools do not need to take up much space; a tiny pool with a miniature jet in a lined barrel on the patio, or a small basin with a narrow jet of water pouring into it from a lion's head on the wall can be effective. Place your water feature where you will enjoy it most, so that you can hear it without straining or gaze into it from a comfortable chair. You may even want a swimming pool and that may not be an impossibility in a moderately large garden.

CHECKLIST OF GARDEN FEATURES

Before starting on your design, it is useful to make a list of all the requirements for your ideal garden. Some of these will be necessities, while you may have to compromise on others. Use this checklist at the planning stage.

BARBECUE ☐

BIRD-BATH ☐

COMPOST HEAP ☐

TRASH CAN AREA ☐

GARAGE ☐

GRAVELLED AREA ☐

GREENHOUSE ☐

HERB GARDEN ☐

HERBACEOUS BORDER ☐

LAWN ☐

PATIO ☐

PERGOLA ☐

PLAY AREA ☐

POND ☐

RAISED FLOWER BEDS ☐

SANDPIT ☐

SHRUB BORDER ☐

SUMMER-HOUSE ☐

SUNDIAL ☐

TERRACED AREA ☐

TOOL SHED ☐

VEGETABLE PLOT ☐

CHECKLIST FOR PRACTICALITIES IN YOUR GARDEN

HAVING pinned down your emotional feelings about the garden and what would make it your personal ideal, you then have to look at the practical aspects. Again, it is sensible to make a checklist, including all the things you need for the garden to make it function well for you. When finished, you will have to make compromises, but you will have the basis for dovetailing the practical with the ideal for a result that you can really savor and enjoy. Below are some possible ideas for your practical checklist.

Somewhere to sit

❀ It is useful to have a patio near the house, where food and drink can be carried in and out. However, if the sun shines best in another part of the garden at the time when you usually want to sit out, it would be better to make a patio there. It may even be a good idea to have two sitting areas, one for the sun in the morning and another that will catch the evening sun. Single seats can be dotted around in various places where they will be inviting at different times of day.

Sunbathing area

❀ This needs to be a hot spot, where the sun shines for most of the day. It also needs to be secluded. In a small garden the patio near the house is often the best place. Remember that if you grow tall plants or climbers to screen off neighbors, they may also screen the sun.

ABOVE: *Attractive in its own right, this miniature log cabin makes a playing area that will entertain young children for many hours.*

Somewhere to play

❀ Children may take up the whole garden for their play, in which case all you can hope to do is plant sturdy but decorative shrubs around the edges and wait until the children are older before planning a more subtle garden. If your garden is big enough and you can provide an interesting enough play area, you may get children to concentrate on that area, leaving at least a little space in the garden for your own pursuits.

❀ A climbing frame and swing can keep children happy for hours. Put plenty of bark underneath to cushion any falls. For younger children it may be more sensible to keep the play area near the house where you can keep an eye on them. A sandpit or a small pool can be located near the garden door and covered when not in use.

❀ By the time children go to school, they often become interested in gardening themselves. Giving them a little plot of their own with sturdy, quick-growing plants and workmanlike garden tools can encourage them to enjoy the garden in all sorts of ways.

Garden buildings

❀ Every garden needs a storage area of some kind. A large shed can be the answer but if you are short of space, there are many smaller sheds available. Using dual-purpose seating/storage units means you do not have to give up so much of the garden.

LEFT: *A secluded paved area offers peaceful shade for a quiet retreat. The planting is also subdued – mainly anemones and grasses.*

❀ A garden room can be something as slight as an open-sided summer-house or as sturdy as an insulated work-room, as decorative as a Swiss chalet or as basic as a garden shed with windows. If it will be very much part of the 'viewed' garden, a decorative shed may be best, but remember that modern paints can cheer up most buildings and careful planting can camouflage them.

ABOVE: *This neat trash can cupboard takes up little space, has a waterproof roof and is stained an attractive dark green so that it melds in well with the garden.*

Somewhere to grow and propagate

❀ A vegetable plot need not take up too much space and can be given a small, sunny corner of its own, perhaps behind a hedge or fence or through a flower-covered arch. Composting goes with food production. It is a way of using up waste material usefully and of getting rid of annual weeds and grass clippings. However, you should be aware that no small garden will be able to provide enough compost for its own requirements. You will have to supplement any you make with organic matter from elsewhere.

❀ A greenhouse is a good idea only if you are really going to have time to use, water, clean and generally care for it. Cold frames and cloches may be enough for beginners or somebody who has little time.

Accomodating wheelchair gardeners

❀ Remember that if you are making allowances for wheelchairs, you must provide not only paths wide enough for the wheelchair to negotiate but also turning spaces. Gravel is difficult for wheelchairs but bricks or paving are ideal. Raised beds can make gardening easier and more fun, while raised pools and water channels are more interesting, too.

BELOW: *This hexagonal summer-house adds a contemporary touch to the garden, with its cheerful blue painted woodwork.*

GETTING TO KNOW YOUR GARDEN

❦

You have made checklists of your own needs and it is now time to assess the plot itself. There is a tremendous amount you need to know before you can confidently begin to design and, unlike a room within the house, the garden will repay you if you have patience and live with it for a year before making any drastic changes.

WHAT TO LOOK FOR

WHATEVER time of year you move into your new home, give yourself 12 months to observe the garden. It will almost certainly surprise you with unsuspected spring bulbs, dead-looking twigs that turn into splendid clematis or herbaceous plants appearing seemingly from nowhere.

❧ Use a notebook to jot down the interesting things that happen over the year, particularly those that are worth keeping.

❧ Look at the garden from the windows of the house and note where views are blocked or eyesores are open to view.

❧ Note where the sun shines for most of the day, which part of the garden gets sun in the morning only and which only in the afternoon. Note how the garden behaves in different weather; what suffers if there is a drought and what gets knocked flat in strong winds. Note whether noise comes from a particular quarter.

ABOVE: *Cheerful little hardy cyclamen can brighten up the garden in fall or winter, depending on which species you choose, they cover the bare ground under trees.*

ABOVE: *The tall bearded iris is a late spring plant. This yellow and mauve one catches the spring sunlight and is seen here growing in a wild garden designed for low maintenance.*

❀ Note if there is any wildlife. Lots of insects and worms mean the garden is fertile and plants should grow well. A complete lack of insect life – except, perhaps, whitefly and greenfly – means the soil badly needs air and compost or other organic matter. If you displace any frogs and toads while clearing out moist patches around drains, try to provide other sources of water because these are among the gardener's friends.

In spring

❀ Notice what bulbs come up that you didn't know about. Are they pretty and in the right place? Are there some missing that you would like to have? Snowdrops are an absolute blessing in the early spring garden and if they feel at home will multiply quickly. Are there any spring-flowering shrubs? Do not remove any dead-looking stalks at this stage. Many clematis and hardy hibiscus, for example, look like pieces of old sticks or string until they start to put out surprisingly sturdy leaves and buds early in the summer.

In summer

❀ Look for dull shrubs that are not pulling their weight; branches of trees that have grown too large and are cutting out necessary light. Few people realise how much light is excluded by overgrown trees and how this stunts the growth of other plants in the garden. Look for

ABOVE: *Spring in a woodland garden with the heavenly blue of the Himalayan blue poppy (*Meconopsis betonicifolia*) and a speckling of varnished yellow buttercups.*

unexpected perennials poking through the soil – are they too leggy, or riddled with perennial weeds? Or are they a delightful surprise? Summer bulbs such as alliums and lilies may appear, too.

In fall

❀ Watch for leaves that turn a wonderful color or for brightly colored berries that liven up the shorter days. Pyracanthas, so often used as hedging plants, are good 'security' shrubs because of their thorns but they also have pretty white flowers and spectacular berries in fall. Bulbs often come up with surprises: look for autumn crocuses and, in later summer, tiny hardy cyclamen under trees. If you do not find these, put them on your wish list of plants. They are all exquisite.

In winter

❀ Look at the framework of the garden. Does it still look good when the flowers are all over? Are there any deciduous trees? If so, do they mean the garden looks rather bare, or do you like the feeling of light that this gives for a few months? Remember that spring bulbs and early flowers can grow under deciduous trees because of the light they receive early in the year, whereas many will not thrive under evergreens.

Front gardens

❀ In the front garden have a look at any trash cans. Are they well concealed behind a wall or a clipped hedge? Could they be better placed? Do people throw drink cans and chip bags into the garden? A closely clipped, prickly evergreen hedge might stop this happening.

ABOVE: *This garden backs on to a field, which allows the snow-covered trees at its perimeter to catch the late evening sun with a warm pink glow.*

INTERIM ACTION

ALTHOUGH it is best not to do too much planting or redesigning during the first year in a garden, there is plenty to be getting on with in the meantime.

Clear rubble and garbage

❦ Many gardens have areas where the builders have tipped rubble rather than carry it to the dump. It is important that this is removed because bits of brick and cement are not conducive to growing things and often contain lime, which many plants do not like. If you have to carry rubble through the house, try to get old builders' bags, which are large, very tough and will shed less dust as you pass through. If the garden contains electrical items such as a microwave oven or refrigerator, it is usually possible to call the local authority and ask for them to be removed.

Clear bramble and weed patches

❦ If a patch of ground is infested with troublesome weeds like brambles, ground elder, nettles or the infamous Japanese knotweed, take the opportunity to clear it now. There is no point in protecting any plant that may be growing among them. It is best to get rid of everything and start again.

❦ Nettles have shallow roots and it is usually possible to pull or dig them out. Brambles can be killed with brushwood killer but ground elder and Japanese knotweed are weeds of a tougher sort. It is best to use glyphosate in spring, when they are growing most vigorously, because the chemical runs through their sap and down into their roots. With both weeds you will

BELOW: *Do not be afraid to prune. The annual cutting back of these trees has encouraged new shoots and produced a wonderful display of contrasting color without taking over the whole garden.*

probably have to give a second application when they come into vigorous growth again in late summer. To be on the safe side, you should apply the herbicide again the following spring. The chemical is no longer active when it reaches the soil, so if you are sure you have killed the weed, you can plant when you want.

Prune trees

❀ Most people are reluctant at first to have trees pruned but, in fact, once pruned, they will spring into growth better than before, and letting light into the garden is absolutely essential if you want to grow healthy plants. However, trees may be protected and in some areas all trees are protected so you need to find out whether you need permission before you go ahead. You should check that the arborist is fully insured before you allow him or her to go up your tree and that the removal of all branches is part of the deal.

Mend fences and walls

❀ Unless you think you might alter the existing fences and walls, this is a good time to get them mended or replaced. Once you have done any planting, it will be difficult to get at fences without damaging the plants. Check that any fences are secure with good strong upright posts and that any trellis is solidly built and firmly fixed. Trellis often has quite a weight to bear if you grow an evergreen clematis or a vigorous climbing rose against it.

Provide temporary color

❀ Even if the garden surprises you with unexpected treats, a neglected garden is unlikely to provide enough color during the first summer. But there is plenty of temporary planting you can do to brighten up the garden for one season. Mallow plants are not expensive and one plant will grow to 7 ft (2 m) in a year and be covered with open pink flowers, giving a good display throughout summer and fall.

❀ You can let yourself go with plants and containers. Geraniums will brighten up sunny places, *Impatiens* are happy in light shade and abutilons will create an exotic

atmosphere against warm walls. You can place pots with brightly colored flowers throughout the garden. Of course, annuals and bedding plants will fill gaps. Petunias, verbenas, *Salvia splendens* and pelargoniums can provide plenty of color.

Use the time

❀ It is good to use this year to inspect as many other gardens as you can. Look at their layouts, the details of their paths and steps and, of course, their planting. If something intrigues you, take a photograph and make a note of it. It may be useful when you are trying to solve a problem later on.

BELOW: *Containers can provide plenty of interest while you are waiting to tackle your garden. Here, various terracotta pots and a galvanised can give a brave display of green and mauve that will be attractive all winter.*

HEART-SHAPED BIRDBOX

This pretty birdbox started life as an offcut of wood and a few empty tin cans. Enjoy watching the birds using it in the knowledge that you have produced something ecologically sound, as well as a place for birds to raise their young. Make sure you wear sturdy protective gloves for working with the cut edges of the tin cans, which are very sharp.

TOOLS AND MATERIALS

⊤ Pencil and paper, for template
⊤ Scissors
⊤ 2 pieces of old floorboard or other offcut of 12 mm (½ in) planed wood, approx. 150 x 200 mm (6 x 8 in)
⊤ Coping saw or jigsaw
⊤ Drill and 32 mm (1¼ in) holesaw
⊤ Chisel
⊤ Can opener
⊤ 4 empty 400 g (14 oz) size tin cans, washed and dried
⊤ Sturdy protective gloves
⊤ Tinsnips
⊤ Hammer
⊤ Small tacks or molding pins
⊤ Exterior wood glue
⊤ Twig, for perch
⊤ Small paintbrush
⊤ Exterior woodstain
⊤ Florist's stem wire
⊤ Staple gun

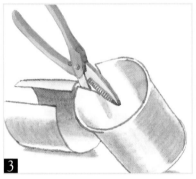

1 Draw a symmetrical heart shape on a piece of paper. Cut it out and draw around the template to transfer the outline to

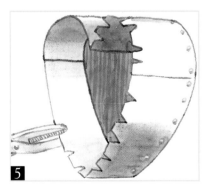

two pieces of wood. Cut out the two wooden hearts, using a coping saw or jigsaw.

2 Drill a 32 mm (1¼ in) diameter access hole through the face of one wooden heart, which will become the front of the birdbox. Chisel a rough angled edge all around this piece, to insure the tin folds over it neatly in Step 5.

3 Remove the ends of the tin cans with a can opener then, wearing protective gloves, cut down the side of each, using tinsnips, to make four sheets of tin.

4 Shape and fit the sheets of tin against the edges of the wooden

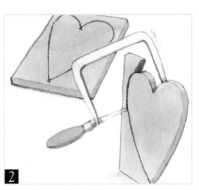

heart that will be the back of the box. Hammer small tacks or pins through the tin sheets into the wood, insuring the sheets overlap where they meet each other.

5 Cut 'V' notches into the front edge of the tin. Place the wooden heart for the front of the box inside the notched tin.

6 Fold the pieces of tin between the notches down over the angled edge on to the front of the birdbox and secure all round with pins or tacks.

7 Glue a small twig, just below the access hole on the front of the birdbox, to act as a perch. Paint a non-toxic exterior woodstain over the outside of the front and back of the box.

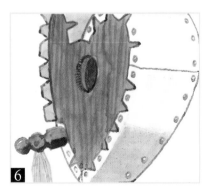

8 To hang the box, twist a length of florist's stem wire into a loop and fix it to the back wall of the box with a staple gun.

CAT SCARER

❦

Cats chancing upon the glittering eyes of this feline intruder lurking in your herbaceous border may think twice before taking up residence in your lovingly tended flowerbed. This simple, folk-art-influenced design has been in use in cottage gardens for many years, its effectiveness is unmatched by more complex and expensive cat deterrents. It is certainly much more decorative and makes a charming gift for a gardening friend.

TOOLS AND MATERIALS

- ⊤ Pencil and paper, for template
- ⊤ Glass or plastic beads, for eyes
- ⊤ Scissors
- ⊤ Offcut of 12 mm (½ in) planed softwood
- ⊤ Jigsaw
- ⊤ Drill, plus flat and small drill bits
- ⊤ Clamp
- ⊤ Dark grey acrylic paint
- ⊤ Small paintbrushes
- ⊤ Exterior acrylic varnish
- ⊤ Florist's stem wires, for whiskers
- ⊤ Floristry scissors
- ⊤ Contact adhesive

1 Roughly draw half a cat head shape against the folded edge of a piece of paper, which will enable you to produce a perfectly symmetrical shape. The size and shape of the cat head will be determined by

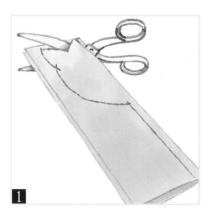

2 the size of beads you use for the eyes. Cut out the cat head shape, allowing for a long 'stalk', which will be inserted in the ground.

2 Draw around the paper pattern to transfer the cat shape to a piece of softwood. Cut out the shape, using a jigsaw. Drill the eye sockets using a flat drill bit of the appropriate size for the beads you are using.

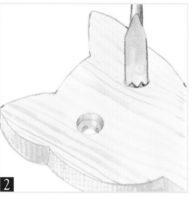

3 Secure the cat in a clamp if you find it easier and paint it dark grey, with two coats of acrylic paint. Apply two coats of varnish when the paint is dry.

4 When the varnish has dried, drill a series of parallel small holes on each of the cat's 'cheeks' to hold the whiskers. Push florist's stem wires through pairs of whisker holes, working from the back towards the front of the cat's face. Trim the whiskers with floristry scissors to length if necessary.

5 To finish the cat scarer, glue the bead eyes securely in place and leave to dry.

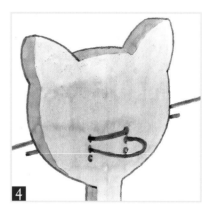

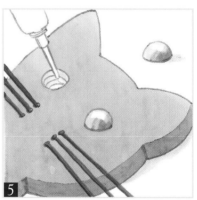

BEFORE YOU BEGIN

To become a gardener is to embark on an exciting journey. Your garden will reward you for taking the time to understand its needs.

❈

Gardening is such a huge subject that it is easy to be daunted by it. Don't be put off. Gain experience by reading about the subject and simply by gardening.

❈

Do not be overwhelmed by all the information within this book. Dip into it to solve particular problems or to check the best way of handling something before you start planning a project.

❈

Reading through the relevant section before you visit a garden center could save you a lot of money. The more informed you are, the wiser your gardening choices will be.

BASIC TECHNIQUES AND EQUIPMENT

In the rush to embark on the planting aspect of gardening, the non-planted elements (the 'hard side') are often overlooked when it comes to garden planning and implementation. However, these play a massively important supporting role. They form a constant backbone that should be installed and maintained properly if the garden is to look presentable from all angles throughout the seasons. Fences, paths, driveways, steps, shed, summer-house, pergolas, arches, gazebos, arbors, cold frames, greenhouses, path edging, seating and tables ... the list is extensive, and it is easy to see that if these elements are not properly considered and cared for, the overall look of the garden will suffer.

WHEN YOU DON'T 'DO IT YOURSELF'

Even if you will not literally be 'doing it yourself', it is well worth appraising yourself of the tools and techniques involved, so that you can plan works in the garden, choose materials and supervise work confidently, as well as make provisions for any future maintenance and upkeep, such as re-treating timbers before, not after, they start to deteriorate.

❀ Read about a project, and carefully consider what is involved, before setting out to the do-it-yourself (DIY) store. Most DIY tasks, even the smallest, benefit from at least some forward planning so that you do not end up wasting time, effort and money.

❀ Gauge how realistic it is to embark on a project yourself. For example, laying a large patio is hard, physical work. If you have a bad back it is not sensible to undertake such a strenuous task unaided, so call in a professional.

❀ Ask friends and neighbors for recommendations of reputable

RIGHT: Unusual fencing materials are increasingly widely available, making it simple to create a highly individual garden style.

contractors, and obtain a variety of comparative quotes before settling on a price. The more informed you are, the more in control you will feel. This is particularly important if you are employing someone to undertake a large-scale project, such as a circular driveway, which will temporarily render your entire front garden a muddy building site. Having this sort of work done is undeniably stressful, as well as expensive, and you will feel much happier if you have an overall awareness of what is happening and why.

HOW MUCH TO SPEND

HARD-side garden projects serve a variety of purposes, from fences that shelter you and your plants from the wind to barbecues beneath pergolas, which provide delightful opportunities for alfresco dining. The level of emphasis you place on these projects, and how much you spend, will depend on a number of factors.

❀ Economic necessity is obviously one, but you should also consider the importance of a particular feature – in relation to the garden as a whole, and to you.

❀ A flimsy, tubular rose arch is undeniably temptingly cheap, leaving you with money to spend on planting. However, if it occupies a prominent place in your front garden, straddling the path leading to the front door of your picturesque cottage, it will add little in terms of visual appeal and may never be really satisfying,

especially when the flowers have bloomed. Far better, in this instance, to invest in a really attractive structure in sympathy with its surroundings.

❀ Careful choice of hard-side items will add not only to your enjoyment of the house and garden, but can prove a sound financial investment should you come to sell your home. Conversely, choosing unwisely can detract from the resale value of your home.

❀ Think about whether you will want to take items with you when you move. If you know that you will be leaving your current home in a year or so, choose portable options unless installing them as investments, such as a wheeled, rather than brick-built, barbecue and a self-contained pond rather than a permanent one.

BELOW: *Adding sympathetic color to the non-planted elements of a garden adds year-round interest.*

TOOLS

THE list of tools required for DIY applications seems extensive, but you need not invest in all of those suggested. A basic tool kit comprising robust, good-quality tools will be sufficient for most requirements. Check carefully through what is involved in a project before you start work. It is very annoying to get half-way through a job, only to find that you need a small but important tool to complete the task.

A BASIC TOOL KIT

Always use the tool appropriate to the job. It is just as pointless and dangerous to use a huge hammer to try to knock in a tiny nail, as it is to try and break up an old patio with a claw hammer. Pay attention to basic safety guidelines; choose the right tool for the job and you will save yourself a lot of frustration and minimise the risk of injury and damage. Large, infrequently used tools, such as cement mixers, are generally hired rather than bought.

Hammers

❀ Claw hammers are useful for levering out nails or tacks, particularly helpful if you are reusing wood from a previous project that has old iron still present. The hammer part is obviously indispensable for a multitude of hammering tasks, but especially for driving in nails.

❀ A club hammer is great for heavy work, such as breaking up old paving, or knocking pegs into the ground. Sledge hammers are for heavier work still, such as knocking in posts or smashing up concrete.

claw hammer

Measuring tools

❀ A tape measure is indispensable and a level is essential for setting and checking levels. Various sizes are available to suit different applications. Obviously, it can be quite difficult to fit a full-sized builder's level on top of a tiny hanging basket bracket in a confined space, so a small level is a useful addition to the tool kit.

❀ Combination squares are useful, with the facility to measure angles and short lengths. A plumb line is handy for finding true verticals. Beyond providing a visual guide for building level brick walls, a brick line has many garden uses, such as providing a level for installing fences.

wire

Saws

❀ A general-purpose panel saw is a good all-round investment as it will be suitable for cutting lengths of timber, the most common garden DIY wood-cutting task. Sheet materials are best cut with a tenon saw. You will need a hacksaw for cutting metal.

saw

Power drill

❀ Do buy a drill of appropriate power for the job. Cheap drills can be incredibly frustrating. If you are slightly built, and unfamiliar with DIY, you may feel that an inexpensive, low-powered, lightweight drill is the best choice. However, the opposite is true. The reason for using a power drill is that the motor should be doing the work, not you. Obviously, you will need to be able physically to hold and control the drill, but a good model will have a motor of sufficient power that you will actually be holding the drill for far less time than if you are trying to force a weak drill to undertake a heavy drilling job, which may end up breaking the motor, as well as exhausting you. Cordless drills are a great innovation for garden DIY. Make sure you have sufficient batteries so that your power does not run out half-way through a job. Look for a drill with a reversing action and variable speed setting, which is very helpful when putting in screws.

power drill

Bucket

❁ The humble builder's bucket is useful for all sorts of mixing jobs. Buy the most substantial you can find.

bucket

Paintbrushes

❁ Buy the best quality you can afford. Cheap brushes that shed their bristles as you work are incredibly infuriating.

paintbrush

Screwdrivers

❁ You will need a selection of screwdrivers, some for slot-, some for cross-headed screws.

Shovel

❁ A shovel is required for the easy moving and mixing of loose materials.

shovel

cross-headed screwdriver

slot-headed screwdriver

Flat trowel

❁ A flat trowel is needed for grouting, pointing, laying bricks and smoothing cement.

flat trowel

Wire cutters

❁ These make light work of cutting through the various types of wire used around the garden, and prevent you from using and damaging your other cutting tools.

wire cutters

Portable workbench

❁ This innovative bench enables you to work on a stable surface, even when in the middle of the garden. A basic workbench offers a facility for clamping pieces of wood firmly in place for cutting, as well as providing a range of measuring guides.

portable workbench

GARDENING TOOLS AND EQUIPMENT

❧

Care of even the smallest garden requires some specialised tools and equipment. Confronted with the range available at hardware and garden stores, it is easy to be bewildered into inappropriate purchasing, so spend some time considering your needs before venturing to the shops. The range of tools required will depend on the size of your garden and the type of gardening you plan to undertake. For example, a garden with a huge lawn may prompt the purchase of a sit-and-ride mower, while a tiny lawn will have far more modest mowing needs. Similarly, a keen vegetable grower will benefit from a range of cultivation tools, while a topiarist will need special shears.

A BASIC GARDEN TOOL KIT

WHATEVER the size of your garden, quality is of paramount importance when selecting tools – be they for cultivation, digging, pruning or cutting. These tools will be in regular use for many years and it is worth investing in the best quality available. A cheap fork that bends on contact with compacted soil is frustratingly useless and a complete waste of money. It can be galling to spend large sums on basic tools when there are so many other, more immediately exciting temptations on sale in the garden center, but sturdy, comfortable and effective tools really will turn basic gardening functions into much more pleasurable tasks.

Spades and forks

❀ You will be using spades and forks regularly so it is vital to select models that are comfortable for you to handle. Great demands will be made on both items in terms of lifting and leverage, so look for designs that combine lightness with strength.

❀ Consider the material of the head carefully before purchase. Stainless steel does not rust but is expensive; coated steel blades are more affordable and will last well if kept clean, but beware of inexplicably cheap tools – the coating is likely to be so thin that it will lift away almost immediately.

❀ Non-stick coatings are available, and undoubtedly make cleaning the tool and working the soil easier, but may wear off after lengthy use.

❀ As with all tools, check that all the joints are secure – particularly where the head of the tool meets the shaft, as this joint will be under a lot of pressure in use.

ABOVE: A well-stocked and well-ordered garden shed with neatly stored tools is pleasant and efficient to use.

✿ For optimum strength ensure that the head and neck are molded from a single piece of metal. Shafts may be of wood or metal, possibly covered with plastic. Both are generally strong. Wooden shafts have the advantage of being easy to replace and warmer to handle in winter than even plastic-coated metal. Ensure that the tines or blades are smooth, for ease of working and cleaning.

✿ Handle shapes differ so don't be afraid to experiment with the varying types – D and T-shapes – in the shop, until you arrive at a model that feels right in the hand. The Y-shape, formed by splitting the shaft wood, may not be as strong as the D-shaped hilt.

✿ Although there are various sizes of spade and fork available – for example border (small, sometimes called 'ladies'), medium and digging (generally the largest) – do not feel that you need a whole selection for different tasks. A fork is useful for turning heavy soil, dividing or transplanting plants, spreading mulch, applying manure and lifting root vegetables.

✿ The addition of a tread on a spade makes digging easier, and less hazardous to footwear, but also adds weight and cost, which it may not be necessary to incur if you have only minimal digging requirements. Be guided by the head size, length and weight that feels most workable for your stature and strength.

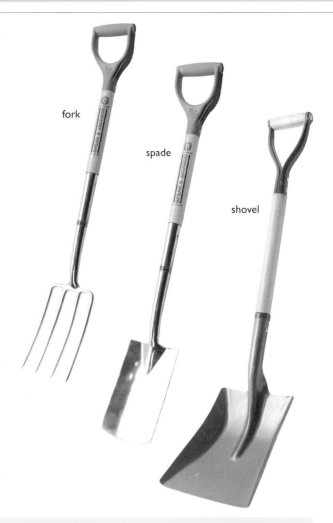

fork

spade

shovel

EARLY GARDENS

THE earliest gardens we have pictures of are Egyptian ones, created over 3,000 years ago. In Egypt the narrow fertile stretch of the Nile is surrounded by desert. The idea of paradise was centred on an enclosed green oasis full of water and fruitfulness. In fact, water became the most important aspect of the garden, both for irrigation and as a symbol of the River of Life. All the irrigated gardens of Persia, Arabia and India developed from these Egyptian gardens. Their influence could be seen in ancient Roman gardens and was brought to medieval Europe by knights returning from the Crusades, and to Spain through the Moorish invasions from North Africa.

The Hanging Gardens of Babylon, built in 605 BC, were different. They consisted of a series of steep terraces planted with trees and shrubs, created by Nebuchadnezzar II for his Persian wife, who was homesick for the green hillsides of her home. They

ABOVE: *This picture of a man and woman ploughing and sowing seed shows the typical boundary of tall trees that lined ancient Egyptian gardens. It comes from a tomb in Thebes, dated about 1200 BC.*

were, basically, the first roof gardens and for many centuries they were considered to be among the Seven Wonders of the World.

Hand forks and trowels

❀ Essentially miniature spades and forks, these tools are used for small-scale jobs like light weeding, cultivating in rock gardens, raised beds and containers, and dividing small bulbs and plants. As before, choose the best quality you can afford, making sure the tool feels comfortable to hold.

❀ Hand forks have either wide and flat, or narrow, round prongs. The flat prongs are more suited to weeding since the weeds are more easily trapped and held between them; the round, narrow prongs are better for cultivating as they pass freely through the earth. A single, flat-pronged hand fork will be adequate for most gardeners.

hand fork
and trowel

Hoes

❀ Hoes are used for weeding around plants and cultivating topsoil. There are several types. The popular 'Dutch' hoe is used like a sharp-bladed spoon to skim along the surface of the soil, loosening weeds, which may then be sliced through. Turned so that the blade is at right angles to the ground, it may also be used to break up and aerate topsoil.

❀ The small, sharp head of the hoe is useful for making seed drills and marking out lines. Swan-neck, or draw hoes, used in a chopping motion for weeding, are less commonly used; other, specialised hoes include onion and triangular hoes.

Garden rakes

❀ A general-purpose cultivation tool, the garden rake can be used with its prongs facing down to break up the surface of the soil and collect stones, leaves and other debris. Inverted, it is used to level the ground. Choose a rake with a head of suitable width for both your own size and the scale of raking job you will most commonly undertake.

❀ Choose shaft length carefully, too. To avoid back strain, you should be able to rake without bending. A 5 ft (1.5m) shaft suits most people, but taller gardeners may need a longer handle. The strongest rake head is made in a single piece, unlike the cheaper, riveted head with its individual nail-like prongs, which are more liable to distortion and loss. A lawn rake is an entirely different tool (see p. 38).

see p. 38

Gardener's knives

❀ The general-purpose gardener's knife is possibly the most essential garden tool. Use it to open bags of compost, cut twine and cane to length, and for taking cuttings, pruning small plants and deadheading. A plastic or wooden handle is not as cold to handle in winter as a metal one. Choose a carbon-steel blade for longevity, wiping it dry and rubbing it over with an oily rag after use.

❀ Specialist knives include budding and curved pruning knives; multi-purpose knives have several different types of blade folded into one handle.

garden rakes

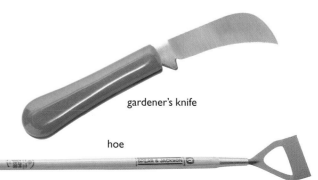

gardener's knife

hoe

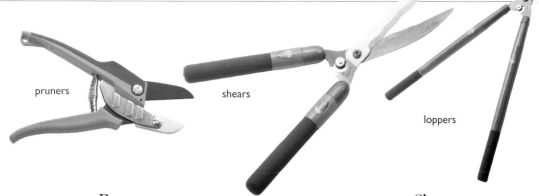

pruners

shears

loppers

Pruners

❀ For cutting that is slightly more demanding than deadheading and harvesting, a pair of pruners is essential. Good ones will cut cleanly and easily through woody stems up to approximately $\frac{1}{2}$ in (1 cm) in diameter. It is vital that the blades are sharp or you will achieve either a ragged stem, which will encourage disease in the plant, or a crushed stem.

❀ There are a confusing range of pruner types available. As always, your hands are the best guides. Select a pair that suits the hand you use most, since both left- and right-handed pairs are available.

❀ Bypass pruners are a good, multi-purpose pair. They have a convex upper blade, which cuts in a scissor motion against a narrow, concave lower blade, and are comfortable for general use. If your hand span is small, or you do not have particularly strong hands, opt for ratchet pruners, which make pruning thicker stems infinitely easier as the ratchet action makes the cut in several small stages, rather than requiring all your strength to make one powerful cut. However, the ratchet action is frustratingly slow if used for general cutting tasks.

❀ Other options include parrot-beak pruners, which use a scissor action, and anvil pruners, which have a sharp upper blade that cuts against a flat anvil. All pruners have a safety catch, which should be easy to operate single handed.

❀ When choosing any pair of pruners, consider how easy it will be to sharpen or replace the blades. Clean the blades after use to remove dried sap, and rub them with an oily rag.

❀ To use pruners correctly, always place the stem to be cut well down at the base of the blades. This holds the stem securely, making an accurate cut much simpler to perform. It also preserves blade life as the blades are less likely to be pushed out of alignment.

Shears

❀ Shears are used for topiary, cutting back herbaceous plants and trimming hedges and small areas of long grass. Although some shears have a notch at the base of one blade to facilitate the cutting of the occasional tough stem, shears are best reserved for their specific, light 'hair cutting' work. Use proper pruning tools to tackle heavier stems and branches.

❀ A good pair of shears will be light, strong and comfortable to operate. Check their balance before purchasing, to ensure that the blades are not much heavier than the handles, which makes them tiring to use.

❀ As with all cutting tools, clean and lightly oil after use, and sharpen regularly. Specialist shears, such as topiary shears, are also available.

Loppers, tree pruners and pruning saws

❀ Cutting branches and stems thicker than about $\frac{1}{2}$ in (1 cm) quickly damages pruners and shears, and is dealt with most effectively by specialist tools.

❀ Loppers (long-handled pruners) are essentially pruners with additional leverage and reach, making it easy to cut stems up to about 1 in (2.5 cm) thick and branches that are difficult to reach. Loppers should be well balanced so that you can use them comfortably at full stretch and overhead.

❀ Tree pruners also cut branches up to 1 in (2.5 cm) thick. The cutting device, operated by a lever or cord, is housed at the end of a long pole, sometimes an extending or telescopic one.

chainsaw

pruning saw

❀ For branches more than 1 in (2.5 cm) thick, use a pruning saw. A general-purpose pruning saw will be sufficient for most needs. Its small blade, usually no more than 18 in (46 cm) long, means that it may be used even in confined spaces.

❀ A Grecian saw has a curved blade, which cuts on the pull stroke only – particularly useful for pruning in a tight area. A small, folding pruning saw is ideal for those with limited storage space and pruning needs. However, it is not as strong and effective as a bow saw, which will cut through even thick branches quickly.

❀ All types should have heat-treated, hard-point teeth, which are tougher and stay sharper for longer than regular saw blades, although they still need regular sharpening to remain fully effective.

OTHER GARDENING EQUIPMENT

IN addition to basic cultivating, digging, pruning and cutting tools, you will need equipment for carrying, such as trugs and buckets, for watering and for propagating, for example a garden sieve, flowerpots, string, plant labels and canes.

Carrying equipment

❀ A folding wheelbarrow is useful where storage space is limited, although not as sturdy as a conventional barrow and its canvas can be damaged by careless handling.

❀ Choose a barrow that is well balanced, where the load is distributed chiefly over the wheel, rather than towards the handles, for good maneuverability. Metal barrows are more durable than plastic ones; a galvanised traditional barrow is a good all-round choice for most gardens.

❀ For very heavy loads, or for use on uneven ground, a builder's ball-wheeled barrow cushions the load and is easier to push, but the ball is susceptible to punctures.

❀ Bulky but light materials such as hedge trimmings can be easily collected and transported on ground sheets and in large bags, which can be conveniently folded flat for easy storage. Look for those made of woven mesh plastic material and with sturdy handles, which wear better than ordinary plastic.

Hose and watering can

❀ The humble hose is a vital piece of garden equipment. If not stored neatly on a reel it is vulnerable to kinks and punctures, as well as posing a tripping hazard.

❀ Many variants of hose are available, including the convenient flow-through type which allows water to be run through it even while it is stored on the reel. Always drain a hose fitted to an outside tap and bring it inside for the winter.

hosepipe

wheelbarrow

watering can and spout

LAWN EQUIPMENT

THE tools you purchase for your lawn will depend on its size and structure, whether it is sloping or flat, has intricate shapes to cut around or is a simple rectangle, and what type of lawn you require – be it a wild meadow or an elegant, striped putting green-type lawn. For the former, which needs trimming only once or twice a year, a sickle or a power trimmer may be all you need. Your choice of equipment will also be governed by how much time and money you have available.

Lawnmowers

❀ Scarcely used today, the manual lawnmower is wonderfully quiet in use and easy to maintain, and is still a viable option for a small lawn.

❀ Electric or gas-driven cylinder lawnmowers are heavy and tiring to use, but produce the clean, close cut desirable on a luxury lawn. They require good maintenance and are generally for those who enjoy spending time and energy on their lawns.

❀ One type of power lawnmower is the electric hover mower, which glides above the lawn on a cushion of air. It is light, easy and quick to use but does not cut as closely as a cylinder mower and is not recommended where a really pristine, formal finish is required.

❀ A well-made metal watering can with a detachable spout will last for years. Always use a separate watering can for applying weedkiller, path clearer and other noxious substances that could cause plant damage if allowed to contaminate clean water. It is worth investing in a cheap, plastic watering can solely for this purpose.

Kneeling mat

❀ A cushioned kneeling mat is invaluable for gardeners of all ages and is inexpensive and easy to store.

❀ A more expensive and bulky option is the kneeling frame, which has the added advantage of supportive handles that make it easier to stand up and kneel down.

❀ This sort of frame is an excellent choice for the elderly, or indeed any gardener with back problems; used the other way up, it becomes a handy stool.

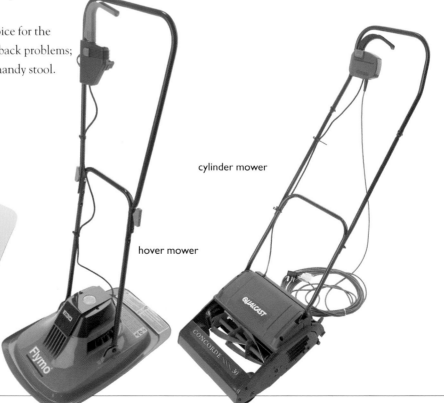

cylinder mower

hover mower

kneeling mat

Lawn edging and maintenance tools

❀ Often overlooked, edging tools add the finishing touch to lawns and are worth investing in.

❀ A lawn edging iron is essential for cutting away any rough edges where the lawn meets the soil of a border. Long-handled lawn edging shears are required for the long, untidy grass at the edges of a lawn.

❀ Power trimmers, driven by electricity or petrol, cut through grass and weeds using a fast-rotating nylon line. They are especially convenient to use in a confined area.

❀ Electric trimmers are cheaper and lighter than the gas-driven equivalents, but need a power source close by and are not suitable for use on wet grass.

❀ A fan-shaped, spring-tined wire-headed rake is useful for removing lawn moss and leaves and also for aerating the lawn.

Tool care

❀ Regular cleaning and maintenance is essential for prolonging the life of tools. In addition, blunt blades will damage vulnerable plant tissues, and dirty tools simply do not function as well as clean ones. A mud-encrusted spade cannot cut into the soil as effectively as a clean one, making digging even more arduous. Similarly, grit works its way into joints and pivot points, causing moving parts to seize up and preventing blades meeting efficiently.

❀ Clean all tools after use and wipe metal surfaces with an oily rag to protect them against rust.

❀ Wipe electrical tools clean, and dry them thoroughly before storing. Have them serviced regularly – a label on the handle, indicating the date of the last service and a reminder of the next one, is helpful.

SAFETY IN THE GARDEN

THE garden can be a dangerous environment if some basic safety guidelines are not adhered to. Eyes are particularly at risk and safety goggles are advisable for jobs such as hedge trimming and lawn mowing, which involve a risk, not only from the tools themselves, but from spiky branches, loose stones thrown up by a mower, and other natural debris, which can move around unpredictably during such tasks.

strimmer

lawnmower

❀ Accidents also occur from tools – especially long-handled ones – left lying around the garden. Stepping on the head of an abandoned rake, for example, causes the handle to fly up with amazing force and speed. A tidy garden is therefore a safer garden.

❀ It is wise to wear sturdy boots when gardening, particularly when mowing. There is a wide range of gardening gloves available and you may need more than one pair – a fairly lightweight pair for light weeding, for example, and a stronger pair for pruning a large prickly, shrub.

Electrical safety

❀ Never use electrical tools in damp weather. Ensure they are scrupulously maintained and serviced, and check cords and connections regularly to ensure they are in good repair.

❀ Fit all electrical tools with a residual current device (RCD), which cuts out the electrical circuit in the event of the power being interrupted, for example by accidentally running over a mower cable.

PREPARING TOOLS FOR WINTER STORAGE

1 *All tools should be properly serviced before winter so that they will be ready for action in the busy spring months ahead. Clean away loose debris and encrusted soil from blades, around mechanisms and on handles.*

2 *Check fixings and moving parts and tighten any parts that have worked themselves loose during the summer and fall months.*

3 *Lubricate any parts that have ceased to move freely. Sharpen tools or have them professionally sharpened.*

BASIC MATERIALS

ALWAYS buy the best-quality materials you can afford. 'Doing it yourself' is an economical and satisfying way of producing the unplanted elements of a garden, but it is not necessarily quick, so value the time investment you are putting in and use materials that will be long lasting and attractive. Treat surfaces with preservatives initially and maintain them appropriately. There is no point spending time and effort creating a marvellous gazebo if you use such poor-quality untreated timber that the whole thing disintegrates in a disappointingly short time.

Wood is an important garden DIY material, used in the construction of fences, gates, outbuildings, plant supports, decking, steps and pergolas, to name but a few applications. Always buy wood that originates from sustainable sources. Salvaged wood, such as railways sleepers, is increasingly popular and an economical and ecologically sound alternative to buying new timber.

Softwood

✿ Softwood, such as spruce or pine, is generally softer and lighter than hardwood. It is cheaper and easier to work because its texture makes it simpler to cut and nail. It is available in rough or smooth planed finishes, and in a wide variety of thicknesses and widths. Always use tanalised softwood for exterior uses. This has been pressure treated with preservative, which is a much more effective weatherproofing than simply brushing on a non-penetrating preservative.

BELOW: *The use of vivid color can make a bold and dramatic statement in a children's play area.*

✿ Some softwoods, such as larch and western red cedar, are inherently more rot resistant than others, and are correspondingly more expensive.

Hardwood

✿ Hardwoods are cut from deciduous broad-leaved trees such as teak, mahogany or oak. Generally, hardwood is denser and harder than softwood, which makes it more difficult to cut and fix. It is also much more rot resistant and durable than softwood, so is an excellent choice for external applications – particularly those where the beauty of the wood grain is an important design feature, as in a pergola or a garden table. Iroko is a popular hardwood, as hardwearing as teak, but much cheaper, although not quite as smooth textured.

Manufactured board

✿ Manufactured boards, formed from wood chips or dust mixed with resins or glues that bond the fibers together, have become increasingly popular in recent times for their strength and value for money. Take care to use grades specifically designed for exterior use.

TREATING WOOD

SOFTWOOD is vulnerable to rot when used in the garden, particularly when it is in prolonged contact with the soil. Always buy pressure-treated timber if using softwood. If this is not possible, apply your own treatment. Choose from a weatherproof paint system or a preservative. Preservatives

BELOW: *Pergolas are dramatic garden features even when unplanted, yet are relatively easy to build and install.*

are available in many colors and finishes, including transparent and imitation hardwood colors, as well as shamelessly synthetic, but none the less attractive shades, such as blue and lavender.

Applying treatments

❀ Most treatments are simply brushed on, but new wood will benefit from immersion in an appropriate treatment for at least an hour. Makeshift treatment baths are easy to improvise, using plastic sheeting supported on piled-up bricks.

❀ Always check that the preservative you are using is not hazardous to plants if you are applying it in a situation where it will be in direct contact with plants. Take appropriate safety precautions when applying treatments that are toxic and/or flammable. Work in a well-ventilated space. This may seem like unnecessary advice since you are working in the garden, but inclement weather may force you into an enclosed garage or other outbuilding, where it is all too easy for fumes to build up to a hazardous level.

❀ Wear gloves, goggles and a face mask when dealing with noxious substances, and have a good throughway of fresh air. Do not eat or drink while using chemicals.

❀ Ecologically friendly, water-based products are available but, unfortunately, most of the products that do a really effective, long-lasting weatherproofing job are still oil or spirit based, with the attendant problems of smell and toxicity.

BELOW: *Treating wooden fences not only makes them look better, but also protects your investment agains the elements.*

KNOWING THE CLIMATE

The climate in your garden is of critical importance in determining what you can grow, and how well it will do. Although some plants may tolerate a climate for which they are not ideally suited, they will never really thrive in it. For example, growing a sun-loving plant in a less-than-sunny spot will produce a plant that does not flower profusely, and may become straggly as it stretches out in an attempt to find the sun. It is far better, if you have a shady garden, to plant accordingly. Climate, of course, is not just about sunlight, but a complex blend of temperature, air humidity and wind, all of which affect the gardener's choices.

General climate

❀ The general climate is literally the climate general to your area. General climate is governed by latitude, altitude, proximity to the sea and the direction of the prevailing wind. Latitude affects temperature, thus gardens in the south are warmer than those in the north. As altitude increases, so the temperature drops, and rainfall and wind speed increase at high altitudes. Proximity to the sea increases rainfall and moderates temperature.

Local climate

❀ The local climate is a term used to describe the climate within your garden. The general climate may be modified within your own garden by a number of factors. For example, if you are generally in a very windy area but your garden is surrounded by bushes and trees, the level of wind within your garden is very much reduced from that outside it.

Microclimate

❀ Microclimate describes climate modified still further within your garden – the climate specific to particular areas of your garden. Although 'understanding and manipulating the microclimate' sounds quite technical, the concept is really very basic. Plan your planting according to existing microclimatic conditions for best results. For example, train fruit trees up a sunny, south-facing wall or fence. Having absorbed the sun's heat, a heat which is further retained by the wall and possibly added to by the heat generated from the house itself, the plant will flower and fruit well. A shade-loving plant would not flourish in this situation.

❀ As well as planting in harmony with the microclimate, it is possible to adapt and exploit it. For example, the sun may fall in one particular part of the garden only, perhaps in an awkward place and not on to the ground itself. Building a raised bed, possibly with a support behind it to further reflect and absorb the heat, will give you the opportunity to grow sun-loving flowers and food crops successfully.

BELOW: *If you live in an area of high snowfall, choose suitably sturdy plants that can withstand winter's worst.*

ABOVE: *Plants naturally accustomed to hot environments will need similarly sunny, dry conditions in order to flourish in the garden.*

Temperature and humidity

❀ Temperature and humidity are important factors in plant growth. Some plants need high temperatures and humidity in order to thrive. Dry, hot sites should be planted appropriately for best results. In very hot weather, some seeds will not germinate and plant transplantation is difficult as the soil dries out rapidly. Low temperatures bring their own problems, the most serious of which is frost.

Frost

❀ Frost is a weather condition that most gardeners quickly become aware and wary of. Late spring frosts are especially cruel to gardens. Just as the plants are starting into active growth and tender new shoots and buds are appearing, an unexpected frost can annihilate or very severely damage them. Ice crystals form within the plant cells. When the cell sap thaws, it expands. If the expansion is rapid, the cell walls split. Obviously, plants that are known to be tender (i.e. not frost resistant) will suffer most, and may be killed altogether. Half-hardy plants are of less certain frost resistance. They may or may not withstand frost conditions. To guarantee the survival of a half-hardy species in your garden, either protect it *in situ* or bring it under cover. Propagation is often undertaken to produce extra plants as an insurance policy against frost loss. Even supposedly frost-hardy plants may come under attack as their emerging, tender new top growth appears. In very severe frosts, woody plants may split their bark.

❀ In spring, every keen gardener watches the weather closely, trying to ascertain the magical moment in the season when the risk of frost has truly passed, so that bedding and tender vegetables can be safely planted out. It is soul destroying to see your healthy young plants, whether bought from the garden center, or lovingly raised from seed or cuttings, blackened and shrivelled, possibly killed entirely, by a single brutal late frost. The only comfort is in knowing that every gardener gets caught out like this at least once. After planting out, pay attention to the local weather forecasts and keep a close eye on the weather, particularly as night falls. If frost is predicted, protect your plants accordingly. A general piece of advice is to delay planting for at least one week after you feel that it is really safe to plant out.

❀ Frost can affect plant roots, loosening the soil and lifting plants out of the ground, where their exposed roots are vulnerable to damage from low temperatures and drying winds (wind chill). Check for frost loosening and refirm affected plants.

BELOW: *Tropical plants require moist, fertile, sunny conditions that mimic their natural habitat.*

ABOVE: *Getting to know your garden in all seasons is vital: what may be a cool shady spot in summer may be prone to frost pockets in winter.*

ABOVE: *A beautiful garden equals a well-watered one, so be prepared for some hose-work if there is a sustained dry period.*

Frost pockets

❀ Because it is heavy, cold air falls so frost collects at the lowest point it can reach. This forms a frost pocket of air – an area particularly prone to all the risks associated with frost. Low sites, such as valleys and the land at the bottom of slopes, are potential frost pockets. If the cold air that forms in a valley cannot move freely away it will be forced back up the slope, increasing the area of potential damage. If the cold air descending a slope meets a solid barrier, such as a fence or a row of closely planted trees, it will form a frost pocket in front of it. Thinning out the trees or removing the obstacle altogether will allow the cold air to pass through. Vulnerable plants should not be grown in frost pockets unless you are prepared to protect them.

Rainfall

❀ Water is essential for plant survival. It is the main component of cell sap and is necessary for photosynthesis, the process by which plants manufacture food and transport nutrients. Seed germination and the development of shoots, roots, fruit, flowers and foliage all need a steady supply of water. Most garden plants depend largely on rainfall for their water requirements.

❀ Along with frost, drought is the other weather condition that gardeners will probably be most aware of and vigilant about in terms of plant care. A drought is a prolonged period – generally considered in the US to be 15-30 consecutive days – without rain. However, plants can suffer in a much shorter time than this, particularly if they have been recently planted, so throughout the summer in particular, water your plants adequately in dry conditions. Some plants found in areas of low rainfall, such as cacti with their succulent, water-retentive tissues, are naturally adapted to drought conditions and are good choices for places where drought is a regular occurrence, or in particularly arid parts of the garden.

Wind

❀ Some wind in the garden is useful. It discourages disease, distributes pollen and seeds and reduces humidity. However, wind can also cause problems. On exposed sites, plants may be susceptible to damage such as wind scorch, which can kill new buds and blacken and wither leaves and stems. Of course, in very high winds such as in gale conditions plants can be partially broken or literally lifted out of the ground. Coastal sites are particularly prone to windy conditions and the wind from the sea is salt laden, which can further damage plants, even killing them if it reaches their roots.

❀ When planning a windbreak to ease the potential of plant damage, the temptation is to install a tall, solid barrier. However, this is counterproductive. A down-draft is caused in the lee of the barrier, resulting in increased, not reduced, turbulence. The solution is to allow approximately 50 per cent of the wind to permeate the windbreak. On a very exposed site, plan a series of windbreaks spaced approximately 10 times their height apart.

❀ Plant sympathetically. Harsh winds are very drying, so choose plants for a windy site that are well adapted to drought conditions. Plants of low-growing habit, planted closely together for more protection, will fare better on exposed sites than tall, vulnerable, willowy plants.

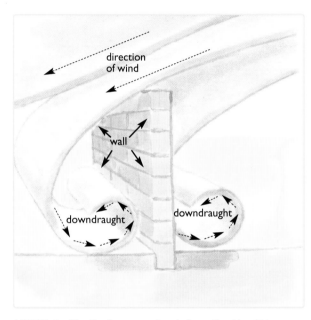

ABOVE: *A solid wall or fence creates downdrafts on either side, which can harm plants.*

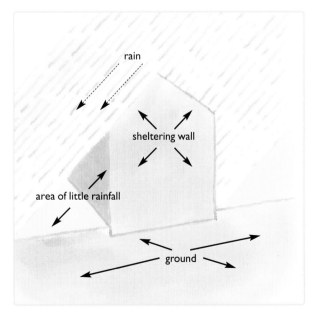

ABOVE: *Potentially damaging frost pockets can occur on either side of a solid barrier on a sloping site.*

ABOVE: *The area beside a sheltering wall receives little rain – this is the rain-shadow effect. Choose drought-tolerant plants for such a site.*

KNOWING YOUR SOIL

Spend time assessing the type of soil that prevails in your garden. Some plants will positively thrive in particular types of soil, while others grown in the same soil will merely survive. Although you can alter your soil to suit particular plants by adding different topsoils, this is not generally recommended, particularly on larger areas of garden. It is expensive and labor intensive to implement and maintain. Contemporary garden thinking leans more towards planting in harmony with pre-existing conditions rather than artificially adapting them.

Soil types

❀ The character of soil is determined by the proportions of clay, sand and silt present within it. Sandy soil is virtually clay free, and composed of large, gritty particles, which make it free draining and easy to dig. Sandy soil warms rapidly in spring, but dries out quickly in drought conditions and both water and nutrients drain away freely.

❀ Silty soil also has a low clay content, but is more moisture retaining and fertile than sandy soil. It tends to compact, which means that water can run off its surface, making it difficult to feed adequately.

❀ Clay soil retains water well and is rich in nutrients, but becomes easily compacted. A dried-out clay soil is virtually brick-like and quite impossible to work. Even when not compacted, clay soil is heavy to work and slow to warm up.

BELOW: *Growing plants in conditions similar to their natural habitat leads to healthy specimens. These lupins are growing in well-drained, sandy soil, which mimics the conditions in which they grow wild.*

❀ Medium loam is the most desirable soil type for gardening, as it comprises approximately 50 per cent sand and 50 per cent silt and clay mix. It has a good crumb structure and holds food and water well.

Soil structure

❀ A cross-section of garden soil reveals three layers (or horizons) – topsoil, subsoil and a layer derived from the bedrock (parent rock).

❀ Generally, topsoil is dark because of its high organic content and is full of useful soil organisms.

❀ Subsoil is lighter in color. It contains far fewer nutrients and less organic matter than topsoil and should not be brought to the surface when digging.

❀ If subsoil and topsoil are similarly colored, the topsoil may be organically deficient.

❀ Some plots may have a soil pan, a hard horizontal layer on or beneath the surface of the soil, which prevents air and water moving freely to the area below.

❀ This impermeable layer can be caused by a number of factors, such as heavy rain on silty soil. It needs breaking up by double digging.

Soil pH

❀ The abbreviation pH stands for parts hydrogen and is used to indicate the level of acidity or alkalinity in soil – measured on a scale from 1 to 14. A reading of 7 indicates neutral soil; above 7, alkaline; below 7, acidic soil. It is important to ascertain the pH value of your soil, since pH affects the solubility of nutrients and therefore their availability to your plants.

❀ A good pH range for most plants is between 5.5 and 7.5. If your soil is dramatically acidic or alkaline, it is possible to adjust the pH, for example by adding lime to acidic soil.

❀ However, since maintenance of this adjustment is ongoing, it is more practical to select plants suited to extremes of soil pH, such as rhododendrons, which thrive on acidic soil, or fuchsias, which enjoy alkaline conditions.

TESTING FOR SOIL TEXTURE

1 *Rub a handful of soil between your fingers. A sandy soil will feel gritty and granular and is impossible to form into a ball, even when moistened slightly.*

2 *A soil that feels smoother and more solid, and easily retains a shape pushed into it, has a high proportion of clay present.*

3 *Between these extremes fall the soil types that contain various minerals in differing proportions. Sandy clay is gritty and granular yet sticky and easy to mold.*

TESTING SOIL pH LEVELS

1 *Soil pH testing kits are in-expensive and easy to use. Add water to a small amount of soil in a test tube and shake well.*

2 *As the soil settles, the water changes color to revel the level of acidity or alkalinity.*

3 *It is worth taking samples from various areas of the garden, as pH can vary within a single plot.*

IMPROVING YOUR SOIL

Having assessed your soil, you will be aware of its properties and possibly its problems. You will know its pH and its texture. Even if you are not making drastic changes, but want to improve drainage or moisture-retaining conditions, as well as create a fertile environment for plants, soil improvement is an important ongoing task.

IMPROVING SOIL STRUCTURE AND TEXTURE

DIGGING will improve soil structure, but for a significant improvement that will doubly repay the effort of digging over soil, add appropriate organic and inorganic matter at the same time.

The importance of humus

❋ Humus describes the partially decomposed organic matter that is full of micro-organisms. There are millions of bacteria and other organisms in a handful of earth, which break down leaves, dead roots and insects and transform them into nutrients, which feed living plants. Without humus, soil is essentially finely ground rock. Humus promotes good air flow through the soil and improves soil texture. It makes light soils more moisture retentive and heavy soil more workable. The humus balance is largely unchallenged in uncultivated soil, but garden planting makes demands on the humus content, which need to be regularly redressed.

Organic soil improvers

❋ Organic options include leaf mold, well-rotted farm manure, garden compost, peat, composted shredded bark and seaweed. All improve moisture retention and soil aeration. Some contain valuable nutrients and also stimulate the bacterial activity, which makes organic material into accessible plant food.

❋ Generally, matured organic matter is used since raw humus makers can damage plants: fresh manure emits ammonia and can burn plants; fresh leaves and straw increase bacterial activity, robbing the soil of nitrogen. Raw matter is best used before planting, or in areas well away from plant roots.

RIGHT: Well-made garden compost is a fantastic soil conditioner, adding workability and fertility to the soil.

Compost

❋ The satisfaction of applying your own garden compost to the soil is immense. Even the smallest garden should find room for a compost bin. Ecologically and economically sound, these may be constructed from scratch or purchased ready-made. Rotating bins are ideal for the smaller garden.

❋ Compost bins should never be regarded as rubbish dumps. Aim to produce a non-smelly, crumbly brown mixture that will enrich and improve your soil texture. Do not create problems for yourself by returning perennial weeds, diseased plants or plants treated with hormone weed killer to the soil.

Leaf mold

❋ Leaf mold is best composted separately as it breaks down slowly. It is not high in nutrients and is generally acidic so is not ideal for every soil or plant type, although acid-loving plants such as camellias and rhododendrons will love it. It is a good source of humus, improves soil texture and moisture retention, and is easy to make. Collect fallen leaves in fall, particularly oak and beech leaves since these decompose quite fast. Store in a wire mesh bin or black plastic sack punctured with air holes and the leaf mold will be ready to use the following fall.

Inorganic soil improvers

❀ Inorganic soil additives such as grit, gravel and coarse sand are useful for improving the workability and drainage of heavy soils.

❀ Fine sand can aggravate drainage problems by blocking soil pores, so use a coarser aggregate.

❀ Lime is often used on heavy clay soil to help bind the tiny particles together to a workable texture. It also contains nutrients and acts on humus.

❀ Apply the soil improver in carefully measured doses, according to the manufacturer's directions, and only after testing the pH of your soil to assess whether lime is needed at all.

A COMPOST HEAP

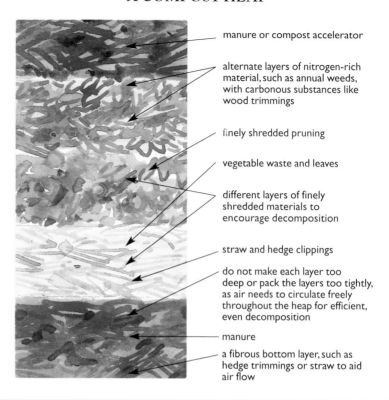

manure or compost accelerator

alternate layers of nitrogen-rich material, such as annual weeds, with carbonous substances like wood trimmings

finely shredded pruning

vegetable waste and leaves

different layers of finely shredded materials to encourage decomposition

straw and hedge clippings

do not make each layer too deep or pack the layers too tightly, as air needs to circulate freely throughout the heap for efficient, even decomposition

manure

a fibrous bottom layer, such as hedge trimmings or straw to aid air flow

MAKING A COMPOST BIN

The front of this box has removable sliding planks to give easy access to the front of the heap.

1 *You will need four 33 in (85 cm) and two 31 in (80 cm) battens, plus ten 39 in x 6 in (1 m x 16 cm) and ten 24 in x 6 in (60 x 16 cm) planks, plus nails or screws. The wood should be water resistant.*

2 *To create the first side panel, place five of the 1 m x 16 cm planks across two of the 85 cm battens. Ensure the sawn ends of the plank are flush with the outside edge of the battens. There should be a 2 in (5 cm) gap between the bottom plank and end*

of each batten. Using two nails or screws for each, attach the planks to the battens. Repeat to make the second side panel.

3 *To create the back panel, hold these two side panels upright, 39 in (one metre) apart, by nailing scrap wood to straddle their tops. Starting at the top, nail or screw five of the 60 x 15 cm planks onto the side panels, as shown in step 3. For the front panel, nail or screw the two 80 cm battens just inside each front upright to*

create a housing for three of the 60 x 16 cm sliding planks, ensuring the planks fit between the battens.

4 *To ensure stability of the structure when the front planks are removed, nail the two remaining 60 x 15 cm planks to the top and bottom of the front panel. You may want to nail a small piece of wood into the bottom in the space between each of the front battens to hold the sliding planks securely in place.*

DRAINAGE

Adequate drainage is of vital importance in maintaining a healthy garden. Soil that drains too readily will require strenuous efforts to keep it adequately watered and fed, while very badly drained soil can actually kill some plants – their roots starved by a lack of oxygen caused by immersion in stagnant water. Healthy bacterial activity is slowed down in these conditions, while harmful organisms multiply readily, leading to diseases such as clubroot. Even if the roots are not killed by poor drainage, they will not be able to flourish. Root growth will be restricted and the resulting shallow root system will not be able to tap into deeper water sources in the event of drought.

ASSESSING DRAINAGE

THERE are varying levels of drainage problem, many of which may be remedied without recourse to major building works. Of course, there are some plants that thrive in both extremes of drainage condition. For example, alpines enjoy very freely drained soil, while bog plants love moist, marshy conditions. Thus you could choose to leave drainage conditions unaltered and plant accordingly.

❀ There is a simple, standard test for assessing the current drainage condition of a plot. It is worth performing at the planning stages of a garden. You will need to dig a hole approximately 24 in (60 cm) deep and 24 in (60 cm) square, and leave it exposed until heavy rain has fallen.

❀ If there is no water in the hole one hour after rain, your soil is excessively drained and you will need to take steps to conserve water, such as applying mulch. If there is no water in the hole a few days after rain, you have good drainage and need take no remedial action. If some water remains at the bottom of the hole a few days after rain, drainage is poor and you will need to take action to improve it, such as double digging and applying organic top dressings.

❀ If, after a few days, the hole is still quite full, even with additional water seeping in from the surrounding soil, drainage is impeded. Also observe the color of the soil, especially towards the base of the hole. Soil with a blue-grey or yellow tinge, possibly with rust brown marks and a stagnant smell, indicates very poor drainage.

ABOVE: *Rather than trying to retain moisture in a naturally dry site, choose plants that enjoy arid conditions for the best results with minimal effort.*

DRAINAGE PROBLEMS

Excessive drainage

❀ Adding humus (partly decomposed organic matter) to the soil will help reduce water loss, as will non-organic mulches such as pebbles. The type of humus you choose depends on what you have available and what you want to grow. For example, mushroom compost is too high in lime to use on areas planted with rhododendrons.

Poor drainage

❀ Adding organic matter generously to the soil will improve conditions where drainage is not too severely restricted. Digging in lots of coarse sand or gravel will also help. Double digging breaks up the soil, producing a more readily drained soil structure. If surface water is the problem, it may be possible to shape garden surfaces so that water can run away freely into simple ditches or drains. You could also consider introducing raised beds, or adding more soil to heighten the soil level generally, to keep roots drier.

Impeded drainage

❀ Drainage will be severely restricted if your garden has non-porous rock close to the surface, a very high water table (the level at which water is held naturally within the ground) or a soil pan (hard layer below the surface). Artificial drainage methods then become necessary. There are several

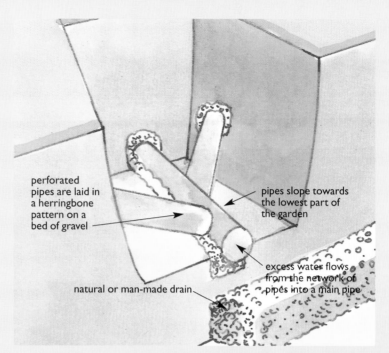

perforated pipes are laid in a herringbone pattern on a bed of gravel

pipes slope towards the lowest part of the garden

natural or man-made drain

excess water flows from the network of pipes into a main pipe

ABOVE: *If surface water is a serious problem in your garden and the water table is close to the surface, you may need to install a submerged drainage system.*

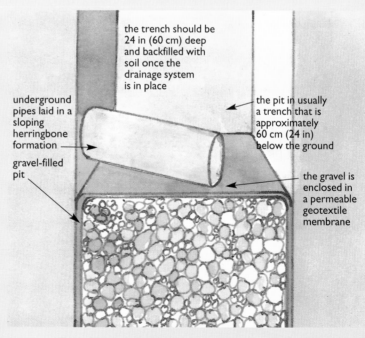

the trench should be 24 in (60 cm) deep and backfilled with soil once the drainage system is in place

underground pipes laid in a sloping herringbone formation

gravel-filled pit

the pit in usually a trench that is approximately 60 cm (24 in) below the ground

the gravel is enclosed in a permeable geotextile membrane

ABOVE: *A French drain is an unobtrusive solution to the problem of a badly waterlogged site.*

possibilities; the simplest is a French drain, a gravel-filled trench. More elaborate piped systems are generally best installed by professionals. If a piped system is planned on a flat site, the pipes will need to slope to allow water to flow away easily.

WATERING

❧

All plants need water and the various watering requirements of different plants need to be considered when planning a garden. For example, if you live in an area of low rainfall or are gardening on a roof terrace exposed to drying wind, it is wise to consider planting to suit these conditions. Some plants cope well with dry conditions, for example succulents, which store water in their tissues, and silver-leaved plants, which are covered with fine hairs to help reduce evaporation.

Existing conditions

❀ Planting sympathetically to dry conditions significantly improves your chances of growing healthy plants, without necessitating an undue investment of time and effort in watering systems.

❀ Although it is possible to develop irrigation systems to deal with whatever conditions you face, it is more sensible to work on conserving the moisture available – for

BELOW: *A sprinkler is invaluable for watering wide areas such as lawns and herbaceous borders evenly and gently.*

example, surface mulching, adding moisture-conserving organic matter to your soil, and planting according to the level of moisture prevalent in your garden.

Effective watering

❀ Watering is a critical gardening task, so an accessible water supply is vital. Although an accessible kitchen faucet and watering can will answer the needs of a very small plot, a garden faucet is invaluable, along with a hose of sufficient length to reach the furthest part of the garden. Make sure that the faucet and any exposed pipework is protected from frost in winter.

❀ Most novice gardeners water little and often, but this actually encourages shallow root growth and germination of weeds. Even a small garden will require a significant amount of watering in dry weather and a hose makes light work of this task. As a guide, an adequate level of watering in midsummer, on a fast-draining soil, would be approximately 2–4 gallons per sq yd (10–20 litres per sq m) – roughly two watering cans full. This demonstrates that simply sprinkling over the border with a single watering can full is inadequate, and will lead to plant problems. Never water in full sun as you risk leaf scorch, and the water will evaporate very quickly from the soil's surface.

Watering container plants

❀ Plants in containers lose water rapidly through evaporation. Group containers together to help conserve moisture. Make plans for watering if you are going away in summer or, at the very least, move containers to a shady place; otherwise you may arrive home to a collection of dead plants.

❀ Incorporating water-retaining granules into the compost at planting time is useful. These granules swell to form a gel capable of holding large quantities of water, which is gradually released into the compost. This is particularly useful for containers especially prone to rapid moisture loss, such as hanging baskets with their large exposed surface area yet small amount of soil, and terracotta pots, whose porosity allows for quick evaporation. Applying a surface mulch will also help retain moisture.

Automated systems

❀ If you garden on a particularly dry site and wish to grow thirsty plants, such as vegetables, or if you wish to simplify your watering duties, consider installing a permanent watering system.

❀ Drip-feed systems comprise tubes fitted with drip heads to trickle water on to particular areas, such as shrubs in a border or growing bags. Unless fitted with a timer, drip-feed systems can waste water, and they need regular cleaning to keep the tubes and heads clear.

❀ Seep hoses are another option. These are flattened hoses punctured finely along their length. They are useful for watering large areas such as lawns, and are ideal for watering rows of vegetables evenly.

ABOVE: A watering can is a perennial gardening essential, and it is worth investing in a good quality metal one for long-term use.

PLANTING A CONTAINER USING WATER-RETAINING GEL

1 *With the addition of a liner and drainage holes, an old basket can be used as a container for plants. To reduce the need for watering, mix water-retaining gel with the compost before you begin, following the manufacturer's directions regarding quantities. Place a layer of drainage pebbles over the base of the container, followed by a layer of compost.*

2 *Add the shrubs and larger bulbs of your choice to the basket.*

3 *Backfill with compost before adding smaller bulbs. Firm the compost gently and water.*

4 *For instant color, fill the basket with some flowering plants.*

PLANT FOODS

Plants need a balanced diet of nutrients in order to thrive.
Plants use the essential elements in soil more quickly than they can be
replenished naturally, for example by the gradual decomposition of
fallen leaves. Substantial amounts of potassium, phosphorus and
nitrogen are lost when ground is cultivated. These major nutrients
are needed in large quantities to maintain good growth, so additional
feeding is required. Potassium promotes disease resistance and
produces healthy fruits and flowers. Phosphorus is needed for
good root development, and nitrogen for healthy growth and foliage.
The amount of nutrients required depends on the plants grown and
how intensively the soil is used. For example, an alpine rock garden
is much less hungry than a densely sown vegetable border.

Organic fertilizers

✿ Organic fertilizers are essentially matter derived from
living organisms, be they animal or plant in origin, such as
fish meal, bone meal or dried blood. They are natural
products, generally slow acting, and not as likely to scorch
foliage as inorganic fertilizers might if inappropriately
used. Organic fertilizers generally provide plants with a
steady supply of food over a long period.

growmore

natural
manure

Inorganic fertilizers

✿ Inorganic fertilizers are not necessarily unnatural. Some
are derived from earth minerals, such as Chilean potash
nitrate; others are synthetically manufactured. Inorganic
fertilizers are very concentrated and fast acting.
Overdosing can result in scorched plants, so great care
must be taken to follow manufacturer's directions
accurately when applying. Inorganic fertilizers are often
used to give plants a quick boost of nutrients.

Soil conditioners

✿ Fertilizer feeds the soil, but does not alter the soil
structure. For example, it cannot make a heavy soil more
open. Soil conditioners such as animal manure add
nutrients, but the amount of food is minute in
comparison to the quantity of material which will need
to be applied. The benefit of adding manure and compost
to the soil is that in addition to their soil nutritional
qualities, they can improve moisture retention and soil
workability. In the longer term, they decompose to form
humus, the dead and live bacteria within soil which is its
life force, facilitating the effective absorption of plant
foods, promoting air flow and improving drainage.

bone meal

TYPES OF FERTILIZER

FERTILIZERS are available in different forms, including liquids, powders and pellets. The form chosen will depend on the type of plant, the season of application and the soil type.

Dry fertilizers

❀ These are nutrients in a dried form – granules, pellets or powder – which are sprinkled directly on to the soil. They are very concentrated and it is critically important to apply them evenly and in appropriate quantities, following the manufacturer's directions, to avoid plant damage.

Liquid fertilizers

❀ These may be bought either in liquid form, or as powder which is to be diluted in water before application. They are generally safer and easier to use than dry fertilizers, and are usually quick acting. Some liquid fertilizers are designed for foliar feeding. Application to the leaves means that the nutrients enter the sap stream quickly, which can be a useful technique if you are trying to resuscitate a sick plant.

Feeding container plants

❀ Container-grown plants need particular feeding care. The amount of soil in a container is limited, so any available nutrients are quickly exhausted by the plant. Regular watering also washes away nutrients through the drainage holes. Slow-release fertilizers worked into the compost when planting, or added as top dressing, are a good solution. If additional feeding is needed, for example if the plant shows visible signs of deficiency, this longer-term feeding program may be supplemented by foliar feeding or by adding a quick-release fertilizer. Fertilizer spikes, small sticks that gradually release nutrients into the soil, are a convenient way of feeding container plants.

ABOVE: *Organic fertilizers include compost made from coconut husks, which can be used for potting and seeding.*

food released into soil in dilute form

water penetrates pores

polymer coat

ABOVE: *The food-releasing pattern of slow-release fertilizer is hard to assess as it is affected by the soil's moisture content, pH level and temperature. However, it is an undeniably simple way of feeding plants and is becoming increasingly popular.*

ABOVE: *There are many general-purpose fertilizers on the market; these are suitable for most conditions and uses.*

DIGGING

Digging may not be the easiest or most exciting garden task, but it has many important functions, particularly on soil that is being newly cultivated. Digging improves the texture and workability in two ways. The spade physically breaks up compacted soil initially. Frost and drying winds further break up the exposed clods. Digging also offers an opportunity for incorporating substances into the soil that can help its fertility, humus-making ability, drainage and moisture retention. What you add will depend on the type of soil you have (see 'Knowing your Soil' on p. 46 and 'Improving your Soil' on p. 48). Digging also makes it easy to remove perennial weeds and bury annual ones.

HOW TO DIG

I T IS all too easy to injure your back when digging. Digging is hard physical exercise and needs to be taken as seriously as any physical workout. Digging is usually done in fall, when the weather has become colder; yet each year, thousands of gardeners embark on a bout of heavy digging without warming up their muscles gradually. Combine this sudden shock to the chilled body with a careless digging technique and you have a recipe for severe back pain.

❀ Wrap up warmly for digging. Acclimatise your body to exertion gradually by embarking on some more gentle gardening tasks before starting to dig. Do not overestimate the amount you will be able to dig, especially on your first session. You could all too easily hurt your back so badly that you will not be able to complete the task at all. Finally, and crucially, take care to use the correct posture when digging, treat your body with respect and never lift more weight than you can comfortably handle.

USING A SPADE CORRECTLY

1 Press one foot down evenly on the blade and insert the spade vertically into the soil. The handle of the spade will be sloping slightly away from you if the blade has been inserted at a true vertical, giving you valuable additional leverage.

2 Pull the handle towards you. Slide one hand down the spade towards the blade. Holding the spade on the ferule with this hand, and

with the other hand still at the top of the spade, bend your knees and evenly lever out the soil. Work smoothly, not with jerky, sudden movements, which can jar your back.

3 Gradually lift the soil on to the spade, taking the strain by gently straightening your legs, not jerking your back up suddenly. Never lift more soil than you are comfortable with at one time.

DIGGING TECHNIQUES

FALL and early winter are the best seasons for digging. At this time of year the soil is generally in an ideal condition – neither baked hard dry by the sun, nor saturated with water. The turned clods will also gradually be broken down by the elements over winter, to improve soil texture. Never dig when the ground is frozen or waterlogged as this will severely damage the structure of the soil, and always use the correct tool for the job. Your spade should be comfortably sized, so that it is not an effort to lift it, and an appropriate length for your height, to reduce the risk of back strain.

Although digging has many significant benefits, its role has gradually been viewed as being of diminished importance in recent times. For many years, garden experts prescribed complex and labour-intensive digging methods such as trenching (digging three spade depths deep). Simple, single and double digging are the techniques widely used and recommended today. Contemporary thinking generally veers towards double digging newly cultivated soil only once. Keen vegetable gardeners may repeat this double digging every few years, but most gardeners will use the single digging technique in subsequent years.

Simple digging

❀ Simple digging is the easiest and quickest digging technique. Since it does not involve any trench work, it is the only really practical way of digging in the sort of confined space created in a garden border filled with many permanent plantings.

❀ Simple digging literally involves simply digging. A spadeful of soil is picked up and turned over back on to its original position, then briskly chopped up with the spade.

❀ When you have dug the soil, leave it alone for approximately three weeks before growing anything in it. This will allow newly buried annual weeds to die, and give the soil time to settle. The weather will act on the soil surface to break it down into smaller clods. The soil will then be much easier to cultivate to the fine tilth needed for planting or sowing.

ABOVE: *As you lift the soil from the trench, slide your hand towards the blade and straighten up slowly without jerking your back.*

Single digging

❀ Single digging is a methodical way of ensuring that an area is cultivated evenly and to a specific depth. The ground is dug to a single spade's depth as you work systematically to produce rows of trenches. As each trench is dug, the soil being lifted is placed in the neighboring trench.

❀ Although a spade is generally used, a fork may be a more comfortable choice when working on heavy soil.

RIGHT: *Digging over the soil before planting improves soil structure and allows you to incorporate the humus-making substances, such as manure, which are so beneficial to plants.*

SINGLE DIGGING

1 *Starting at a marked line, drive the spade vertically into the soil to the full depth of the blade. Remove the soil and place in a wheelbarrow, ready to carry to the opposite end of the plot.*

2 *Dig along the line to produce a trench 12 in (30 cm) wide, and the depth of the spade.*

3 *Dig a second trench parallel with the first. Fill the first trench with the soil from the second trench, incorporating organic matter as required. Twist the spade to aerate the soil as you place it in the first trench.*

4 *Continue digging trenches until you reach the other end of the plot, filling the final trench with the soil from the first trench.*

Double digging

❀ This deep form of digging improves drainage by breaking up any hard subsurface pan in the soil. Double digging is generally regarded as necessary for previously uncultivated soil prior to sowing or planting, and wherever drainage is poor. In double digging the soil is literally dug to double the depth of the spade or fork, and the trenches are twice as wide as those produced for single digging.

❀ It is critically important not to bring subsoil to the surface, as this will adversely affect soil fertility. You will need to ascertain the depth of the topsoil before starting to double dig. If the topsoil is more than two spade depths deep, then you have no problem. You can simply transfer the soil from one trench to the other as for single digging.

❀ If the topsoil is only one spade deep, you will need to ensure that the topsoil and subsoil are kept separate and distinct so that the subsoil goes back on the bottom of the neighbouring trench, with the topsoil on top – not mixed together or the other way around.

❀ You will need both a spade and a fork for double digging. Always dig at the right season for your soil. Dig medium and heavy soils in fall and early winter; dig over very heavy soil before winter sets in.

❀ Sandy soil may be dug in winter or early spring. If you dig too early you may encourage a fine crop of weeds. Always make sure that the soil is not saturated with water, nor frozen solid, before planning to dig. Similarly, it is not prudent to dig when the soil has dried hard after a prolonged period without rain.

DOUBLE DIGGING

1 *Mark out the plot with a garden line. Dig the first trench approximately 24 in (60 cm) wide, and as deep as the head of the spade. As with single digging, collect the soil from this trench in a barrow, ready to take to the opposite end of the plot when the barrow is full.*

2 *Standing in the trench, break up the soil at the bottom of the trench to the depth of the fork tines. Incorporate organic matter such as manure if required.*

3 *Mark out another trench parallel to the first. Dig out this trench, placing the soil from here in the first trench.*

4 *Fork the bottom of the new trench and continue to the next trench. Work your way across the plot until you reach the opposite end. Fill the final trench with soil removed from the first trench.*

TOP DRESSINGS AND MULCHES

Top dressing describes the superficial application of fertilizer and other additives, such as sand, to the surface of the soil or lawn. It is also used as a general term, encompassing any sort of superficial dressing of the soil, including mulching. Top dressings and mulches are applied to the surface of the soil for several reasons. They all help plant growth in one or more ways. All help reduce moisture loss by evaporation. Some add nutrients to the soil, enrich the humus content of the soil and improve soil texture and workability. Some, such as gravel, have no nutritional value but are used to aid drainage, regulate soil temperature, deter pests such as slugs, and suppress the growth of weeds, moss, lichen and other undesirable organisms on the surface of the soil. In addition, a simple gravel top dressing is also very decorative in its own right.

USING TOP DRESSINGS AND MULCHES

Top dressings and mulches may be the unsung heroes of the garden border. They don't look terribly exciting in the garden center, but they have an immense amount to offer every gardener – from the apartment dweller with a solitary window box dressed with an attractive, moisture-retaining, weed- and pest-deterring aggregate, to someone with a large vegetable garden using plastic sheeting for purely practical reasons.

ABOVE: *A natural mulch, such as shredded cedar bark, helps suppress weed growth and conserve moisture, yet is an attractive, unobtrusive material.*

Applying mulch

❀ Always apply mulch to warm, moist soil. If mulch is applied to a frozen or dry soil, you will find that it just works against you, simply sealing in the problems. Similarly, if organic mulch is applied to a soil rife with weeds, the weeds will benefit as much as the desirable plants, reaping the benefits of an enriched soil and improved moisture retention, and growing even more profusely than in an unmulched soil. The overall guiding principle of applying mulch, therefore, is to think carefully before using it, taking care not to seal in any problems, which will be aggravated by the insulating properties of all mulch.

❀ Apply a generous layer of mulch, approximately 3 in (7.5 cm) deep, spreading it out from the plant to cover roughly the same area as the potential growth spread of the plant itself. Apply up to, but not touching plant stems, as this can encourage rotting.

woodchip mulch

ORGANIC MULCHES

MULCHES can be divided into organic and inorganic types. They share many attributes, some organic mulches having the added benefits of nutritional value. This is not always desirable, however, as described above. For example, garden compost has many good properties, but it also provides a perfect environment for germinating weeds. It is therefore not the best choice for weed suppression.

leaf mold mulch

Bark

❀ Available in a variety of scales, from finely shredded to large chunks, bark is a popular mulch. It improves surface drainage and suppresses weeds. Coarsely shredded bark takes a long time to break down, repaying the initial investment, as it should last two years before it needs replacing.

❀ Bark is also sufficiently heavy not to blow about the garden. It is very attractive, and is often used to top dress borders. Bark is slightly acidic, a quality that diminishes when it begins to decompose, so only apply composted (matured) bark as a mulch. Soil dressed with bark will need supplementing with a nitrogenous fertilizer.

dried bark mulch

Cocoa shells

❀ Cocoa shells smell wonderful, as if applying a blanket of grated chocolate to the soil. Apart from this sybaritic benefit, a cocoa shell mulch is very attractive, making it the next most popular ornamental border mulch after bark. Cocoa shell's are slightly acidic, so soil dressed with them will need to be supplemented with fertilizer. Until cocoa shells settle, they are also very lightweight and susceptible to being distributed around the garden by wind and birds. They are also quite expensive.

cocoa shells

Farmyard manure

❀ Once popular, farmyard manure has lost popularity as a mulch in the flower border. It does help the humus content of the soil and has some nutritional benefit, as well as its moisture-retaining and soil-texturising properties. However, it is not attractive, is often smelly, and its fertility promotes weed growth. It must be used only when well rotted, or it may damage your plants.

farmyard manure

woven black plastic

ABOVE: *Mulching helps keep weeds at bay while young plants are becoming established.*

INORGANIC MULCHES

INORGANIC mulches, especially sheet types, are excellent at retaining soil moisture. They are also superb at suppressing weeds because light is excluded totally from the soil, preventing weed germination. Obviously, they do not assist humus production or add nutrients to the soil. If you do need to enrich the soil beneath sheet mulch, pierce it and apply soluble fertilizer through the holes.

Woven black plastic

❀ Excellent for mulching between rows of vegetables, this is initially expensive but it is reusable.

Fiber fleece

❀ Used mainly to raise soil temperature, this is often used as a 'floating' mulch and pest barrier. It is used almost like a cloche – applied over, not around, crops.

fiber fleece

Black plastic

❀ This cheap mulch raises soil temperature and suppresses weeds, but is not attractive unless covered with a more decorative substance such as gravel. It is popular in vegetable plots.

Grit

✤ Grit is useful for improving drainage and is very attractive. To keep weeds at bay, grit is best applied over plastic sheeting. Coarse grit is often used as a slug and snail deterrent, since these creatures dislike moving across its sharp surface.

grit

Pebbles/gravel

✤ This is an attractive and popular inorganic choice. Choose well-washed products, free of soil particles that might bind the stones together, hosting weeds.

gravel

pebbles

TOP DRESSINGS

Some materials are used on the soil around plants, or on lawns, not for their mulching properties, but to improve the soil nutritionally and texturally. Always follow the manufacturer's directions precisely when applying top dressings. Keep solid dressings off foliage and plant stems, since fertilizer can scorch.

Lime

✤ Lime is available in many forms, such as chalk, ground limestone and magnesium limestone. The most popular form is hydrated (slaked) lime. Lime is a plant food, and makes other plant foods available by acting on humus to free the elements necessary for good plant growth. Lime removes sourness from the soil by neutralising acidity. Few plants thrive in very acidic conditions. Lime also breaks up heavy soil and encourages beneficial bacteria and organisms such as earthworms to flourish. A pH test will determine whether or not you need to lime your soil. Even a neutral soil will benefit from reliming every few years, since rain washes lime from the soil. Alkaline soil must not be limed, as it already has sufficient lime. Lime is generally applied after digging, in the fall.

Fertilizer

✤ Fertilizers contain one or more nutrients in a concentrated form, and are added to the soil to feed plants. They must not be confused with humus makers, since they do not share their important attributes. Fertilizers should not be used in isolation. Without humus makers, the plants cannot utilise the food provided by the fertilizers. Fertilizer as a top dressing is usually applied in the spring.

Humus makers

✤ Bulky organic matter is used as a top dressing to improve soil texture and build up the bacterial population,thereby releasing nutrients to the plants. Humus makers do not have a significant amount of nutritional value compared with their bulk, and so need to be used in conjunction with fertilizers for optimum benefits. Organic top dressings are usually applied in the fall.

PLANT PROBLEMS AND WEED CONTROL

❦

Viewed as a whole, this section can appear daunting – depressing even, with its litany of weeds, pests and diseases. However, with careful planting and garden maintenance there is no need to suppose that your garden will play host to all the ailments and problems listed here. Good-quality, healthy plants, given optimum growing conditions, will stand an excellent chance of resisting disease and throwing off pest problems. Practise careful hygiene and vigilant observation, so that you can tackle problems as soon as they occur.

PREVENTION

THE maxim 'prevention is better than cure' applies particularly to gardens. Increasingly, gardeners are turning away from the chemical control of problems, recognising that to rely on chemicals, for example in pesticides and fungicides, can create more problems than they cure. Helpful predators may be eradicated along with the pests, leading to an even worse pest problem.

❀ You may be a gardener who has diligently sprayed your garden against aphids for years, and wonder why, one long hot summer, your garden is plagued with aphids, while your neighbor's unsprayed plot is aphid free. The reason is that you have gradually wiped out the predators who are now so obligingly policing your neighbor's unsprayed garden. Of course, the wider global issues of pollution and the potential dangers from chemicals, as well as the matter of slowly destroying the ecosystem within your own garden, are also of concern when thinking about how to tackle plant problems.

Keeping problems in perspective

❀ The first thing to consider, before becoming hysterical about pests and diseases and automatically reaching for the nearest chemical spray, is to get matters into perspective. Some pests may be unsightly, but are actually not as hazardous to a plant as other threats, such as inclement weather. In fact, in general, weather issues are a much bigger risk to plant health than individual pests – something it is worth bearing in

ABOVE: *Some diseases, such as clubroot, can quickly affect an entire crop, so it is worth being vigilant about plant health.*

mind when you first spot a single caterpillar perched on your precious cabbages.

❀ The second biggest plant enemy is bad gardening practice. For example, overcrowding your plants leaves them prone to infection. Poor hygiene is another plant hazard. If you do not remove diseased material and burn, deeply bury or compost it well, you are inviting further plant troubles.

❀ This gives you some idea of the responsibility you have as a gardener. Your aim should be to maintain plant

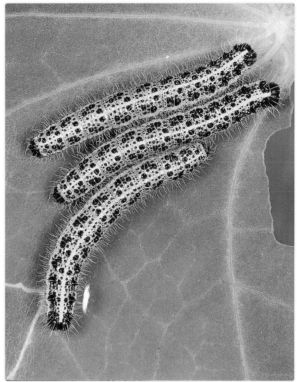

ABOVE: *A group of honeysuckle aphids cluster on the denuded axial of a leaf.*

ABOVE: *Large white butterfly caterpillars, pictured here on a damaged nasturtium leaf, are pests common to brassica crops and some ornamental plants.*

health, rather than allow problems to occur and get out of hand; and then curse the pests, who are in fact way down in the ranks of plant difficulties.

Minimising problems

❀ Keeping your garden healthy by careful and consistent adherence to gardening basics will go an enormous way towards preventing pests and diseases from overwhelming your plants. With the huge variety of plants on offer, it makes sense firstly to choose healthy looking specimens of disease-resistant strains, and plant them appropriately.

❀ A plant grown in the particular type of soil it needs, and where it can receive the amount of light it requires, has much more of a chance of surviving without problems than a plant grown without respect for its natural demands. Take care to provide the appropriate level of water, remembering that too much can be just as injurious as too little.

❀ Spacing is an important consideration. Plants grown too close together will compete for nutrients, and the congested, humid conditions will encourage fungal disease. Follow the guidelines for optimum spacing that appear on individual plant labels.

❀ Garden hygiene is a factor often overlooked as being of serious concern in preventing problems. After all, muck is muck – at least visually. However, it is all too easy to transfer disease through poor hygiene, for example by planting in uncleaned pots, which may carry disease spores, or by propagating using a knife that has not been sterilised.

COMMON PESTS

THERE are a number of common pests that are a widespread problem for gardeners and attack a wide variety of plants.

Aphids

❀ Aphids are widely thought of as the ultimate garden scourge. They suck sap and excrete the excess as a sticky residue, which falls on foliage where it can turn mouldy. Emerging shoots and leaves can be damaged, and affected plants can become distorted and disfigured. Aphids can spread viral diseases between plants such as roses, lilies and tulips. Sooty mould often accompanies aphid attack, since the fungus lives on the 'honeydew' secreted by aphids.

❀ Ladybirds and hoverflies are the best organic control for aphids. Attract them by planting poached egg flowers (*Limnanthes douglasii*) and *Convolvulus tricolor*. Physically place ladybirds on affected leaves.

❀ Companion planting can help in other ways. You could plant sacrificial crops. For example, nasturtiums planted near broccoli are likely to suffer from aphid attack, leaving the broccoli clear. Chives deter aphids and are a pretty edging plant, making them an excellent choice for the herbaceous border.

❀ Spraying with a soft soap – not detergent – solution works well, too. In the greenhouse, parasitic controls are useful. In all cases, simply removing the aphids by hand is also effective and organically sound.

❀ The non-organic approach, possible on vulnerable non-food crops, uses selective systemic insecticides, which leaves beneficial insects unharmed.

Earwigs

❀ The distinctive pincers of the earwig are not generally seen during the day, since they feed at night. They shred the leaves and eat the flowers of plants such as dahlias, chrysanthemums and clematis. Earwigs are not all bad, however. They do eat quite a number of aphids, so if your plants are not being damaged, do not automatically operate a 'search and destroy' mission. To check whether earwigs are responsible for decimated flowers and leaves, investigate by torchlight.

❀ Inverted flowerpots, stuffed with straw and suspended on canes, will attract and trap earwigs, which can then be removed and disposed of.

Slugs and snails

❀ Slugs and snails attack many types of plant, including bulbs, herbaceous perennials, vegetables, strawberries,

ABOVE: *Earwigs shred the leaves of certain ornamental plants such as dahlias and can also attack food crops, but since they eat some aphids and codling moth eggs they are not generally considered a serious garden pest.*

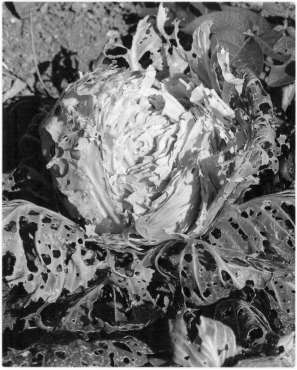

ABOVE: *Aphids are a garden scourge, wreaking havoc on a wide variety of plants by damaging and distorting new leaves and shoots, as well as weakening the plant as a whole.*

ABOVE: *A shiny red lily beetle (Lilioceris lilii) on a damaged lily leaf.*

ABOVE: *An adult cock chafer (Melolontha melolontha) devours fresh green buds on a leaf.*

climbing plants and young seedlings. Although most live on top of the soil, some attack the underground parts of plants such as bulbs, as well as tubers like potatoes. Slugs and snails feed primarily at night or after rain.

❀ Some plants are particularly susceptible to slug and snail attack, such as hostas, delphiniums and all young seedlings. Plants known to be vulnerable should be protected with physical barriers, such as crushed eggshells, sawdust, wood ash or sharp sand.

❀ Slugs have sensitive skin and do not like crawling over these surfaces, but be aware that the barrier is only effective as long it is unbroken. Rain can easily break down these barriers, so either check regularly and replenish or choose a very effective (though not very attractive) barrier method – a ring 10 cm (4 in) high, cut from a plastic bottle and pushed 2.5 cm (1 in) into the ground.

❀ Slug 'pubs', containers of tempting fermenting beer sunk into the soil, are also a popular way of disposing of slugs without recourse to chemicals. However, these traps also drown beneficial creatures, unless you provide twiggy ladders in each one for ground beetles and the like.

❀ Inverted grapefruit skin halves are also used. The slugs congregate within, ready for you to dispose of as you see fit – either by removing them to a distant place, or drowning them. However, you will need quite a number of traps to catch the quantities of slugs that congregate in most gardens, especially in moist conditions. Dedicated gardeners may be driven to seeking out slugs by torchlight, before giving them a burial at sea.

❀ Apart from mechanical and barrier methods, another organic option is a parasitic nematode, which can be watered on to the soil to kill slugs and snails.

❀ Methiocarb or metaldehyde slug pellets can affect animals higher up the food chain, such as birds and cats, and should be regarded as an absolute last resort. Aluminium sulphate pellets should harm only slugs and snails, but could leach aluminium salts into crops. Organic gardeners would not use these types of control.

BELOW: *Slugs are notoriously hard to eliminate but any effort to do so is worthwhile since, like snails, slugs cause damage not only to seedlings, but to all parts of a wide variety of mature plants.*

ABOVE: *Caterpillar damage on cabbage leaves.*

ABOVE: *This cabbage is displaying classic club root symptoms.*

Caterpillars and chafers

❀ There are many types of caterpillar, the most notorious of which is the caterpillar of the cabbage white butterfly. Caterpillars eat foliage, stems, flowers and fruits. Some caterpillars conceal themselves by curling up in young leaves or protecting themselves in a silk-like webbing, so if you see curled leaves and webbing, unroll them to investigate further. Leatherjackets are greyish-brown caterpillars, the larvae of crane flies. These soil-dwelling caterpillars eat the roots of young seedlings, immature plants and lawn grass.

❀ Remove any caterpillars by hand as soon as you notice them. There is an organically acceptable bacterial control, *Bacillus thuringiensis*, suitable for cabbage white caterpillar attacks. Alternatively, you can use special sticky bands of grease designed to prevent flightless pests like caterpillars climbing up the plants.

❀ Although, if left unchecked, caterpillars can munch their way unattractively through ornamentals, such as nasturtiums, as well as food crops like cabbages, the problem is not always critical. Nibbled leaves may look less than lovely, but often, only the external leaves are affected, the caterpillars having departed before the cabbage starts its main growth spurt.

PLANT DISEASES

THE general guidelines for good garden hygiene apply particularly to keeping disease at bay. Remove potential sources of infection by disinfecting pots, trays, canes and other equipment at the end of each season. Diligently remove and dispose of decaying, diseased or dead material by pruning out problem areas. Clear away plant debris that falls naturally, as these leaves and twigs may harbour fungal spores, which would reinfect plants the following spring.

❀ Practise crop rotation. This means not growing the same bedding plants or vegetables in the same spot each year. Overwintering pests and diseases emerge in spring to find that their target has vanished.

❀ Choose disease-resistant plant species where possible and plant them at the appropriate spacing. Keep the garden weed free, well watered and mulched.

Mildews

❀ These fungal diseases attack stressed plants, particularly those that have become dry at the roots and are in stagnant air conditions. Avoid overcrowding plants and keep them consistently watered and mulched in order to prevent this disease, which devours affected leaves and shoots from the outside. Downy mildew is more serious than powdery mildew, as it can penetrate the leaves and eventually kill the plant.

❀ Planting alliums in generous quantities near plants known to be susceptible to mildew is said to offer increased protection. Since alliums look spectacular paired with roses, this is a companion planting suggestion well worth trying but, as always, careful attention to spacing and watering of vulnerable plants is of prime importance.

❀ Remove affected areas to reduce the spread of mildew. There are some organic sprays available, such as those made of nettles or garlic, which claim to improve mildew resistance.

❀ The non-organic approach is to spray with a chemical fungicide, in addition to following the general guidelines on plant hygiene and care.

Grey mold *(botrytis)*

❀ Another fungal disease, which thrives in cool, damp conditions, *botrytis* is an unsightly grey mold, which covers leaves, stems and fruit. Poorly ventilated conditions, such as inside inadequately aired greenhouses or cloches, encourage the condition, as does overcrowding. Strawberries are particularly vulnerable to grey mold. Improve air flow and provide drier conditions to prevent and arrest the problem. Remove and destroy all affected parts of the plant.

❀ In addition to these measures, fungicides can also be used to control *botrytis* – there are organically acceptable ones available.

Rusts

❀ Rusts are a collection of fungal diseases that discolor leaves and encourage them to drop prematurely. They flourish in similar conditions to those that harbor mildews – that is, dank, overcrowded environments. Prevention guidelines are similar to those given for mildew. Take care to provide good ventilation and plant at appropriate spacings. Remove affected areas. Organically acceptable fungicides are available.

Wilts and rots

❀ Soil-dwelling organisms can cause plants to wilt – particularly chrysanthemums, clematis, tomatoes and carnations. Good plant hygiene and garden husbandry will help prevent wilt, which affects weak and generally unhealthy plants. Use fresh, sterile compost for seeds and cuttings, as wilt often attacks new seedlings. In the border, incorporating good quality garden compost will help plant health as the beneficial organisms it contains will help control any bad ones.

COMMON PLANT DISORDERS

1. *Uneven germination caused by damping off in lobelia seedlings.*

2. *A shot hole caused by bacterial canker on cherry leaves.*

3. *A viral disease on a* Pelargonium, *causing leaf venation.*

4. *Coral spot fungal fruiting bodies on the dying wood of an ornamental tree mallow.*

5. *Grey mold damage on the leaves of a* Pelargonium *plant.*

6. *Powdery mildew affecting the foliage of Achillea ptarmica 'The Pearl' in late flowering.*

7. *Close-up of the underside of a rose leaf, showing black teliospore pustules.*

PLANT DISORDERS

SOME plants may appear to have suffered pest or disease damage, but are actually displaying signs of nutritional deficiency or a physiological disorder. Common sense plant care will go a long way towards preventing these problems. For example, planting an acid-loving plant such as an azalea in a heavily alkaline soil is not going to produce a happy, healthy plant, unless the soil local to the plant is regularly adapted to its needs. Such a plant, grown in an alkaline soil, would show stunted growth and yellowing leaves, the symptoms of lime-induced chlorosis (manganese/iron deficiency). Protecting plants from weather damage, be it frost or drought, is also a basic element of garden practice that will give your plants the best possible chance of healthy growth. You will do well to learn to recognise the common plant disorders.

Nitrogen deficiency

❦ Pale green plants that eventually turn yellow, with weak, thin, pinkish-colored stems and stunted growing tips can indicate a nitrogen deficiency. Older leaves turn yellowish-red along the veins and die off. The whole plant will have its growth checked and generally become spindly and unhealthy looking. Growing plants in restricted conditions where they are inadequately fed, or in poor, light soil can cause nitrogen deficiency. This is the commonest plant disorder as nitrogen is so readily leached out of the soil. Make sure your plants have a soil that is adequately fertile, regularly dressed with well-rotted manure and balanced fertilizers. As an emergency remedy where deficiency has been noticed, a high-nitrogen fertilizer or liquid feed can be applied.

Waterlogging

❦ When plant roots suffer a lack of oxygen, the plant becomes waterlogged (unless it is a bog plant). Although there is obviously plenty of water, the plant will wilt as if it was being under watered and its leaves will yellow. If you lift the plant, you may see black, even rotten roots, as the plant starts to die back. To prevent this condition, provide adequate drainage by regularly digging in plenty of organic matter to improve the soil structure. If the problem occurs in containers, there may be inadequate drainage holes, or they may have become clogged with debris. If you have localised areas in the garden that are particularly prone to waterlogging, then you might want to consider growing plants in raised beds. If the problem is more widespread, consider installing drainage pipes, or grow plants suited to boggy conditions.

ABOVE: *Potato plants, showing the effects of drought in a dried-up vegetable patch.*

ABOVE: *The effects of leaf scorch on daffodil plants, causing fused leaves and flowers.*

Drought

❧ When plants suffer a prolonged water shortage, they wilt and collapse, with dried out, curling leaves. Eventually, the plant will die. Container-grown plants are especially vulnerable, as are young plants on light soils. To reduce the potential for drought damage, incorporate plenty of well-rotted organic matter into the soil, and add water-retaining granules to containers. Water really adequately each time, rather than watering little and often, as this can lead to surface rooting, which will only aggravate the problem.

Frost damage

❧ Frost damage is sickeningly familiar to many gardeners. The blackened, dying remains of what was fresh new growth all too often serve as a reminder of how a late spring frost can take the gardener, and the vulnerable young plants newly planted out, unawares. In especially cruel frosts, even woody plants can split their stems. Almost any plant can suffer from frost damage if conditions are harsh enough – even plants that are generally accepted as being hardy. If particularly low temperatures are anticipated (below 32°F/0°C), protect vulnerable plants using fleece, cloches or cold frames. If you live in an area where frosts are common, plant accordingly, using plants that can usually survive in harsh weather conditions.

Manganese/iron deficiency

❧ This deficiency is commonly seen where lime-hating plants such as camellias or rhododendrons have been grown in a very alkaline soil. The leaf veins remain green, but the rest of the leaf turns pale and yellow, and the leaves may brown along the edges. The plant will generally have checked growth and will fail to thrive. The simplest form of prevention is to plant according to the particular soil requirements of a species. If you have a burning desire to grow a plant that would not do well in your garden soil, then restrict yourself to growing it in a container, where you can provide the acidic conditions it needs, using ericaceous compost. If beds or borders are showing this deficiency, you could correct it in the short term using sequestered iron. In the longer term, apply good-quality compost and well-rotted manure regularly.

ABOVE: *Very cold weather can cause damage to vulnerable plants. Protect precious specimens and knock heavy falls of snow off plants before it freezes.*

ABOVE: *The tell-tale symptoms of manganese deficiency showing on a rose leaf.*

WEED CONTROL

WEEDS are simply plants growing in the wrong place. This is worth remembering before you automatically reach for the weed killer or scythe. Some plants are considered weeds by one gardener, who works hard to eradicate them, yet are admired by another, who may propagate them from seed, or buy them as fully grown plants at the garden center. Mind-your-own-business (*Helxine soleirolii*) and poppies (*Papaver*), for example, are plants that can be viewed as attractive, desirable cultivars or irritatingly pervasive weeds, depending on their location and the preference of the individual gardener. Mind-your-own-business can enliven dull paving with its lush, low-growing green carpeting effect, but can wreak havoc in what is meant to be a perfect lawn.

❀ The organic gardener appreciates the value of weeds as free sources of fertility, and works with weeds, rather than directly against them. Weeds are mineral accumulators, rendering minerals accessible to crops. For example, nettles accumulate potassium. Nettles have many other useful attributes, particularly in association with fruit and vegetables. In a large garden the keen organic gardener will find an appropriate place to give over to nettle growing – as good companions for plants such as redcurrants and blackberries, as hosts to many species of butterfly and to make into nettle sprays, which protect leeks from leek flies and moths.

❀ These positive attributes aside, good weed control undoubtedly has a vital role to play in maintaining a healthy garden. Weeds compete with desirable plants for nutrients, water and light, and can play host to diseases, which can spread to other plants. For example, groundsel often harbors greenfly, mildew and rust. Weeds are often extremely tough and pernicious, and can quickly colonise cultivated areas if left untamed.

Annual weeds

❀ Common annual weeds include groundsel, chickweed, nipplewort, shepherd's purse, annual nettle.

❀ Annual weeds grow from seed when the soil is moist, warm and exposed to light, thus mulching (covering the soil in order to block out the light, as well as for other reasons) or deep burying will prevent germination of annual weeds.

❀ Hoeing is often recommended as a control for annual weeds. The roots are severed from the stems to prevent further development. Walk backwards when hoeing, so that you do not tread the weeds into the soil. Hoe before the weeds have set seed. Allowed to germinate, the resulting weeds are quite easy to kill, but if left unchecked they can become more resilient.

Perennial weeds

❀ Common perennial weeds include ground elder, bindweed, dandelion, stinging nettle, horsetail.

❀ Mulching is less effective at controlling perennial weeds. Many perennial weeds such as dandelions have long, fleshy roots, which ensure the survival of the plant even if the top growth is killed off. These weeds will need to be dug out entirely. Some will regenerate if even a tiny portion of the root is left in the soil. Systemic weed killers are often used to control perennial weeds – particularly those that are very difficult to dig out completely, such as horsetail, which can develop roots that grow to depths of at least 6 ft (1.8 m). When a system weed killer is applied to leaves and stems, it is gradually absorbed by the weed and transported through the entire plant via the sap, eventually killing the whole weed.

ABOVE: *Regular hoeing is an efficient way of controlling annual weeds.*

Mulching for weed control

❀ Covering the soil around desirable plants with material that blocks out light and moisture has grown in popularity as a way of controlling weeds without recourse to chemicals.

❀ Although organic mulches have the added benefits of improving soil fertility and structure, they are not as effective as inorganic mulches at suppressing weed growth. Organic mulches need to be at least 4 in (10 cm) deep in order to be effective. Black plastic, however, is a very effective weed-suppressing mulch. Simply cut a cross in the plastic and plant desirable specimens through it. Conceal the unattractive plastic with bark or gravel.

Planting ground cover for weed control

❀ Ground cover plants will help keep weeds down by competing with them. However, they will not win the battle unless they are given a head start, by being planted in weed-free soil in sites suited to their individual needs. Planting ground cover through a plastic mulch, and concealing the plastic with gravel or bark, is an excellent and attractive way to keep weeds to a minimum.

❀ Good ground cover plants include periwinkle (*Vinca*) and lady's mantle (*Alchemilla mollis*).

COMMON GARDEN WEEDS

1. *Young nipplewort plant.*

2. *Annual nettle plant in flower.*

3. *Groundsel in flower.*

4. *Thistle in full bloom.*

5. *Flowering dandelion in grass.*

6. *Bindweed choking other plants.*

7. *Young ground elder plant.*

8. *Field buttercups in full flower.*

CANDLE POTS

❧

These terracotta flowerpots gain a shot of glamor with a
shimmering of gold around their rims. Not only does the candlelight
add sparkle to outdoor entertaining, but a generous dash of citronella
essential oil in the candle wax deters annoying insect invasion
as dusk falls.

TOOLS AND MATERIALS

☦ Small paintbrushes
☦ Acrylic gold size
☦ Terracotta flowerpot
☦ Scissors
☦ Gold-colored metal leaf
☦ Soft bristled brush
☦ Amber shellac
☦ Modelling clay
☦ Wick
☦ Pencil or thin twig
☦ Candle wax
☦ Double boiler
☦ Candle colorant (optional)
☦ Citronella essential oil

1 Brush acrylic gold size around the rims of the flowerpot and leave to dry until transparent, but not so dry that it has lost its adhesive property. The length of time this takes will depend on the ambient temperature and humidity and may be anything between 10 and 30 minutes – some acrylic size has an indefinite 'open' or working time, making it foolproof to use.

2 Cut the metal leaf into manageable pieces. Place the metal leaf on the sized area and gently ease into place using a soft bristled brush. Gently brush away excess leaf. Continue until all of the sized area has been gilded.

3 Apply a coat of amber shellac to the gilded area to form a protective seal. Leave to dry, following the manufacturer's directions.

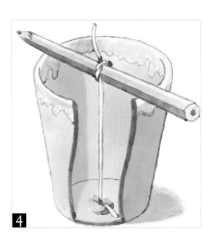

4 Push a small piece of modelling clay into the drainage hole at the bottom of the flowerpot to seal it. Suspend the candle wick centrally in the pot by attaching the upper end of the wick to a pencil or twig laid across the top of the pot. Embed part of the bottom of the wick in the modelling clay, allowing the remaining part to lie across the bottom of the pot so that the finished candle will burn for as long as possible.

5 Melt the candle wax in a double boiler. Add candle colorant if desired, and a few drops of citronella essential oil.

6 Pour the molten wax into the flowerpot and leave until set, then snip the wick with scissors.

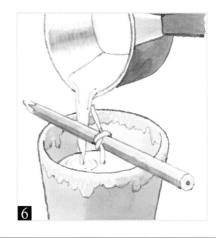

WIRE HOOP BORDER EDGING

Wire hoop edging is sold commercially on a roll, but is generally too flimsy to serve any real purpose as a border edging. Its color range is very limited and, if single hoops are available, the cost of edging an entire garden with them is prohibitive. These hoops solve the problem. They are economical and quick to make, using a reel of fencing wire and spray paint in a soft pastel shade to complement planting.

TOOLS AND MATERIALS

- Tape measure
- Small length 6–8 in (15–20 cm) of hardwood or metal, for twisting handle
- Drill and ⅛ in (3 mm) drill bit
- Stout protective gloves
- Wire cutters or hacksaw
- ⅛ in (3 mm) galvanised fencing wire
- Bench vice
- Small metal floristry bucket (optional)
- Spray can of exterior primer
- Spray can of light grey exterior paint
- Sheets of newspaper
- Protective face mask

1 Measure the length of the hardwood or metal bar that is to be your 'handle' for twisting the wire, and drill a ⅛ in (3 mm) hole at the halfway mark. Drill two more holes, 1¼ in (30 mm) from each side of the central hole. Wearing

protective gloves, cut three 39 in (1 m) lengths of galvanised wire and secure one end of each in a bench vice. Pass the free end of each wire through one of the three holes in the drilled bar and secure by twisting it around itself.

2 Holding each end of the bar and maintaining an even tension on the wires, twist the bar clockwise until all three wires become a single twisted piece – there will be ¼–1½ in (30–40 mm) at each end that you are unable to twist.

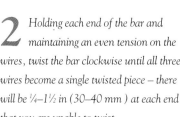

3 Remove the wire from the vice and drilled bar and make more twisted lengths of wire in the same way. Trim each twisted wire to the same length, removing the untwisted sections.

4 Bend the trimmed, twisted wires into open-ended hoops, using a former such as a small metal floristry bucket.

5 Spray priming and painting can be done before or after the hoops are 'planted'. Protect the surrounding areas from overspray with sheets of newspaper. If working indoors, work in a well-ventilated area and wear a face mask.

6 'Plant' the hoops at the edge of the border by pushing them into the earth at a uniform height.

GETTING STARTED

If you are feeling daunted by the amount of work required to get your garden into shape, follow these basic steps to see what is possible and what is not.

❀

First of all assess your site. Take into consideration which way the garden faces, where the sun reaches, privacy factors and soil type.

❀

Take the time to make a plan. Explore all the style, color and planting possibilities, and refer to the checklist of features you want in the garden.

❀

Create a framework for your garden, taking into account your preferred style.

❀

Work out a seasonal workload plan so that you know what needs doing from month to month.

SURVEYING THE SITE

Begin by making a site plan. It should be an accurate record of the boundary of your garden and the main items within it – the house, existing buildings, trees and ponds. It should show where the ground rises, where there are steps, which way the garden faces and where there are eyesores to be concealed or views to be enjoyed. Note on the plan those areas of the garden in the sun and those in shade. You should also note the type of soil and whether it is extremely dry, well drained or boggy, or whether it is dry in summer and soggy in winter, as are many gardens that have a heavy clay soil.

THE PLAN

IT IS best to do your survey on graph paper, which helps to get the measurements accurate. Measure the boundary of the garden first. You should use a 100 ft (30 m) measuring tape, and you will find measuring easier with two people to hold the tape.

ABOVE: *This pastel-painted seaside home needs plants that are able to withstand the salt-laden breezes. Ceanothus and wisteria do well, and there is a shelter belt of hawthorns further down the hill.*

House

❀ Mark where the house is in relation to the garden, and its size and distance from the boundaries. Show the position of the ground floor windows and doors and make sure you indicate which side faces north.

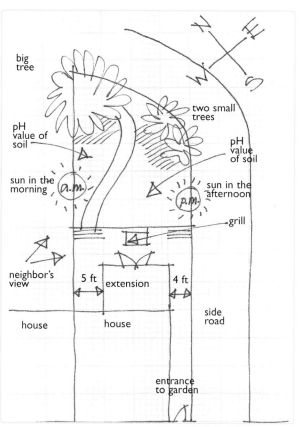

ABOVE: *A rough sketch of your garden need not be a beautiful drawing. Provided the measurements are correct and more or less in scale, you can sketch the garden several times, trying out different ideas. Here, the house is shown with its extension into the garden and its relationship to the road. The north/south aspect should be shown, as should all big trees, sheds and other structures; you can try different placings of paths, areas for barbecues and so on.*

Alterations in level

❀ Show where the ground level alters and measure the width of any existing steps. It can be difficult to work out accurately the rise and fall of ground without special equipment. On a difficult site it is best to get a level survey done by a professional but if you do not need complete accuracy, you can use fences, walls and steps for guidance.

Aspect

❀ Mark which way the garden faces. This will enable you to decide on the best positions for seating and play areas, vegetable plots, flower and shrub borders and many other features that need to be either sheltered or sunny.

Trees

❀ Show all existing large trees and indicate where your neighbors' trees cast shade into your garden. If a tree is in the wrong place or has grown too large, consider getting rid of it and replacing it with something more suitable.

LEFT: *Terracing a garden is a good way of dealing with steeply rising ground. The terraces can be very attractively planted, with each level offering a different type of garden. It is best to get such a site professionally surveyed.*

Shade

❀ Mark areas that are in shadow for most of the day. This may be a good area for a dog kennel or for a play area, although a little sun will be welcome, of course. Areas in deep shadow will require careful planting because only a limited number of plants will thrive in them.

Soil type and drainage

❀ Find out whether your soil type is basically clay, sand or loam. Clay is heavy, difficult to work and clogs into mud that comes indoors on your boots. It warms up slowly in spring but with lots of organic matter added it will become workable and more nutritious than other soils.

❀ Sandy soil is light, easy to work and drains easily, which means that nutrients are likely to drain away, too. Loam is probably the ideal. It is dark and sweet smelling, crumbles in the fingers and holds water well. Very dry soil can be given additives to help it retain water. Draining boggy soil can be expensive. Instead of draining you could create a specialist bog garden where suitable plants will thrive.

❀ An analysis of your soil will tell you whether it is acidic, alkaline or neutral (which is best for most gardens). The pH of a soil – its degree of acidity/alkalinity – is important as some plants require an acidic soil and others require an alkaline one. The pH can range from around 5 (acidic) to 8 (alkaline), 6.5 being neutral and suitable for a great many plants. Soil-testing kits are inexpensive and available from garden centers. Test the soil in several parts of the garden, since the pH may vary within quite a small area.

ABOVE: *The paved area in front of the house has been designed in a semicircular arrangement of bricks leading towards the house. The brick color blends in well with the roof tiles.*

RECOMMENDATIONS AND PRACTICALITIES

YOU have noted on your plan the salient points of the garden as it is, using the notes you made during the first year and the measurements taken during the survey.

You should now be thinking about how you want to alter the garden, what you want to remove and what you want to add. There are a number of practical considerations that will make creating the actual plan easier. For example, it is useful to know that the clearance needed for a swing is 23 ft (7 m).

Remember that everything should be in scale with the house. A very tall house will require a larger patio, taller trees and arches, and larger spaces. A bungalow will need everything on a slightly smaller scale if the garden is not to look pretentious.

Conservatory

❀ It is not good to have a conservatory on the south side of a house where it is too hot most of the time. A better position is the east or west side for sitting, or the north if the important thing is growing plants. As with other structures, a good conservatory will be in keeping with the house. A modern, simple building will suit a modern house, whereas a gothic creation will look fine added to a red brick mansion.

BELOW: *Similar bricks have been used here for both the paving and the wall to give a sense of unity to the design. The paved area is surrounded by a luxurious planting of pinks and purples.*

Steps and paths

❀ Steps should be comfortable to climb up and down. A leisurely scale is right for a garden. They are not like house stairs, which are designed to go up quickly. The slope should not be more than 40° from the horizontal, otherwise steps appear unwelcoming.

❀ The minimum safe riser (the vertical part) for steps in a garden is 4 in (100 mm). If they are shorter, someone might trip on them. The maximum is 8 in (200 mm). The tread should ideally be 12 in (300 mm) deep. A good proportion for garden steps is a 6 in (150 mm) riser with a 15 in (375 mm) tread, although in a small garden that may not always be possible. Steps do take up more room than is generally realised. Six steps, 6 ft (1.8 m) wide with treads 18 in (450 mm) deep, will take up 54 sq ft (4.8 sq m). This could take up a very significant proportion of a small garden.

❀ With stone or brick steps it is best if the tread projects slightly over the riser at the front to create a shadow line. This not only looks good but also helps to define the steps in poor light.

❀ If you are creating a long flight of steps, remember that you will need a 'landing' every 10 or 12 steps, which should be twice as deep as the steps.

❀ Paths can be wide or narrow, as scale or space permits. A wide path allows two people to walk along in conversation but may take up more space than the garden can easily allow. A narrow path will keep your feet dry in wet weather and may be all that is needed.

Pergolas

❀ A pergola is an important garden structure. The design and materials will affect the whole look of the garden. Supporting piers of brick or stone need large solid crossbars to be in scale. Wooden uprights with slender beams make a more elegant construction, suitable for smaller gardens and lighter climbers such as clematis and less vigorous roses.

❀ The height of your pergola is critical. The bar at the top will have something climbing on it, which will make it slightly higher, so 8 ft (2.4 m) is a good height. In a very small garden you could go down to 7 ft (2 m) and in a very large garden up to 9 ft (2.7 m).

❀ With any sort of opening, including arches, the wider and more generous it is, the more welcoming it will be.

Paving

❀ This also has an important structural role in the garden. It should always look good. Paving can be used for anything from patios and parking spaces to paths and steps; in small and urban gardens it can take the place of a lawn.

❀ Natural stone, concrete, brick, tiles, pavings and wood can all be used in different combinations. Do not try to use too many materials at once, however, or you will end up with an uncoordinated result. It is best never to use more than three different materials. This will help to create unity throughout the garden.

❀ Remember to make the patio large enough. You need room not only for a table with chairs tucked in neatly around it, but for people to pull the chairs out and sit in them. Any patio should therefore be at least 10 x 12 ft (3 x 3.5 m).

ABOVE: *A slightly curved flight of gravel and timber steps has wide treads and shallow risers, which give it an unhurried, relaxed quality.*

ABOVE: *Even the smallest space can be packed with interest by the clever use of different media, textures, colors and shapes.*

THE CONCEPT PLAN

This is where you get to fit all your requirements into your actual garden. You should have decided by now whether you want to bulldoze the whole garden and start again from scratch, or whether there is enough of a sensible outline to allow you to work round what you already have. Consider how you can make the transition from garden to house as smooth and pleasant as possible. French windows or patio doors are ideal and can be made secure with double-glazing, laminated glass and good locks. If you are not able to change the door, you can design the garden so that the view from the windows is enticing.

EXPERIMENTING WITH IDEAS

MAKE lots of copies of your initial survey sketch and try out ideas in pencil on these. Decide on the most important of your requirements and sacrifice the others, allowing a few generous spaces in your garden rather than too many slightly mean ones. This will make the garden less fussy and ultimately give more pleasure.

ABOVE: *Any ordinary garden shed can become an integral part of the garden by concealing it with ivy or creeper. Both are used here, with the creeper turning a bright red in fall.*

Using photographs

❀ Your plan or 'map' is useful for getting a feeling of the balance of the different areas within the space, but will not give you a picture of the three-dimensional reality of the garden. For this it is useful to look at your photographs and try out some of your ideas on them. A good way of doing this is to lay pieces of tracing paper over them and sketch out different ideas – the more you do, the better. You will find you begin to revert to a particular idea. When your ideas begin to firm up, make a new plan with everything on it that you want to retain and everything you want to change.

❀ One of the most difficult things is imagining how the plants will look when they have matured and grown, particularly trees and shrubs. This is where your overlay and photographs can help. If you know a shrub is eventually going to become 7 ft (2 m) tall, you can see what effect this will have on the garden plan in a few years' time.

❀ On your initial sketches think of how you can make the garden more interesting and effective. There are several ways in which you can entirely change the appearance of a garden without too much outlay.

Alterations

❀ You might want to move a path nearer to a fence, or further from it, to provide a wider border, or take it diagonally across the garden to create two separate spaces. Diagonal lines across a narrow garden can make it look wider (see p. 87).

❀ You can move a small shed, instead of getting rid of it, to a place where it is less obtrusive and can be concealed behind climbers. Paint can give dull little buildings a more cheerful look.

Extending

❀ You can continue a straight border around in a curve to conceal a shed or surround the shed with shrubs. A greenhouse that is not particularly pretty can also be surrounded by low-growing shrubs. They cannot be too tall or they will cut out too much light and things inside the greenhouse will grow spindly in their attempts to reach the light.

Enlarging and dividing

❀ You can enlarge an existing patio or make it circular instead of rectangular; you might want to make a path wider, to emphasise its direction and lead people on. Using a tall, sturdy trellis fence to divide the patio and the garden can give privacy without completely cutting off the view. This gives an extra place for growing climbers.

BELOW: *In this garden, the patio has been extended into a pathway with planted borders to lead people through the garden.*

MORE IDEAS AND POSSIBILITIES

GARDENS are made up of spaces and shapes for various activities; the bits in between are your planting spaces. When you have sketched in the shapes for, say, sitting, paths, shed, pond, play and vegetable garden and you have eliminated the least essential, go through the whole process again until you have spaces that will fit well into your garden.

Thinking ahead

❀ If your basic framework works well, later on you will be able to change how you use it. For example, if you build a brick sandpit, butting on to a brick-edged lawn, as the children grow older, you will be able to exchange sand for water and have a garden pool. A playhouse can be a marvellous place for children to play in. If you have chosen a solid one you can have it insulated and eventually take it over as a retreat or even a serious workroom.

❀ One early decision, especially in a small garden, must be whether you want a lawn or would prefer to have paving. A small lawn can be a refreshing source of green in an urban winter. Some gardeners derive enormous pleasure from mowing a pocket handkerchief of greenery but a very small garden may not have room to store a lawnmower. Moreover, if the lawn is too overshadowed or impoverished, it will just look sparse and sad. In that case, it will be best to have it all up and lay paving slabs or a pattern of bricks or cobbles for a crisp and clean surface, which may better suit the urban environment or the busy working person.

Features beyond the garden

❀ Mark any good views on your plan and lead the eye to them by creating a gap in the hedge or a circular 'window' in a wall. A path leading in that direction and a seat facing the view will encourage people to enjoy it. Similarly, mark any bad views on your plan so that you can conceal your neighbor's rusty swing or ugly shed with trellis and climbers or a well-placed columnar tree.

❀ Make the best use of any attractive trees and tall flowering shrubs in neighboring gardens. Doing this will not only provide extra color in your own garden but also help extend the sense of space. Hedges can be cut a little lower to allow a view of a neighboring blue ceanothus or pink camellia.

ABOVE: *A sense of spaciousness is achieved in a small area by narrow borders along the fencing and several unimposing features including a seat, trellis and central plant arrangements.*

ABOVE: *This miniature lawn will never need mowing, since it is made of camomile. Although only tiny, it provides a welcome touch of fresh green within this charming seating area.*

A feeling of space

❀ Small gardens can be made to seem much more spacious by designing in diagonals. A path running diagonally from one side of the garden to the other and then back again at an angle will divide the garden into three. The spaces made in this way can be separated by tall or low planting and will make the garden seem larger because the eye cannot see exactly where the garden ends and is intrigued by the planting between.

❀ Arches create a feeling of space by implying that there is more happening beyond them. Arches should always lead to something or the result is disappointment. A small gate under the arch will enhance the feeling of entering into a different domain.

A sense of unity

❀ When you have an idea of what you want, stick with it throughout the whole garden. This will give the garden cohesion and a sense of unity, which is one of the hallmarks of all successful gardens. Decide whether you want the garden to be formal or informal, or asymmetrical with overlapping squares and geometric shapes.

THINGS TO AVOID

❀ Avoid mixing formal with informal. You lose harmony by moving from one to the other. Informal gardens are much more difficult to design than formal ones. The symmetry of a formal garden really designs itself – you can hardly go wrong – whereas the curves and shapes of an informal design require a balance that may not always be obvious.

❀ Avoid mixing different styles. This creates an uncomfortable feeling and diminishes the impact of any one style.

❀ Avoid combining curves and straight edges. Sometimes a circle can be satisfactorily placed within a square but, in general, curves and straight edges are difficult to combine. Try to create generous curves with serpentine paths or borders. These should flow, not wiggle, so that the curves are in wide sweeps rather than worm-like kinks.

ABOVE: *A yew arch takes some years to grow to its full height and maturity, as here. Drawing in ink on a photograph of your garden will give you an idea of what an arch like this would look like when fully grown.*

CREATING A FRAMEWORK

❧

For different parts of a garden to combine into a satisfying whole, a cohesive structure is needed. Decide on your priority spaces and create the framework around them. Keep everything simple. Boundaries and divisions should have a unity that will provide a clear background for the planting and join up the spaces harmoniously. For example, walls should all use similar bricks, or all be rendered and painted the same color. Hedging plants should be compatible – either all native shrubs or trees or one type of clipped evergreen. The lines of the framework, whether straight, curved or squared, should be clear and firm. This is one of the most important factors in garden design.

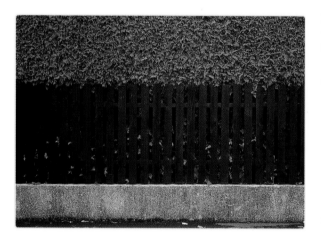

LEFT: *Where garden meets roadside, this neat picket fence is backed by a rigorously clipped conifer hedge, both of which are very much in keeping with the feel of the garden as a whole.*

❀ In gardens by the sea or on a hill, where strong winds and salt spray can damage all but the toughest of plants, the best sort of boundary is a hedge of mixed shrubs such as hawthorn, *Olearia*, escallonia, hazel and holly. This will act as a very effective shelter belt, within which more tender and colorful plants can be grown successfully.

THE PLANTED FRAMEWORK

IF YOU use only deciduous plants all the framework shape will be lost in winter when the leaves fall. Some deciduous plants have interesting trunks and branch shapes but you should include some kind of evergreen planting that will stand out clearly in winter.

Dividing the space into separate areas is a good way of preventing a long, narrow garden from looking like a ribbon, but the technique is also invaluable in many larger gardens to provide a variety of areas for different uses.

Boundary framework

❀ In small gardens, pyracantha and privet are often used as hedging plants along boundary walls. They provide good nesting sites for birds but they are greedy for space as well as water and nutrients, and in urban areas it is probably better to have trellis with climbers and evergreens, interspersed with the occasional evergreen shrub as a contrast and to break the straight line.

ABOVE: *A clipped yew archway makes an attractive gateway to the front path and frames the view of a solid red brick house with its small portico.*

❀ If the garden is bounded by a road, a clipped hedge often looks as neat as a wall and quite in keeping with the defined lines of the road. Beech makes a good and unusual hedge because, although it is not evergreen, it holds on to its leaves after they have turned color and continues to provide protection and privacy throughout the winter.

Separating areas

❀ The framework for a formal garden is perhaps the easiest to design. You need a regular and level site. Once you have that, everything about the formal – its symmetry, regularity and mirror imagery – is in itself a framework. Low clipped hedges of box, taller clipped hedges of yew, clipped pairs of bay in tubs, a formal central fountain and paths crossing at right angles all reinforce the basic shape of the design. Everything adds

ABOVE: *There are many different ways to give a garden form. A trellis is a practical and attractive method of creating an enclosed area.*

ABOVE: *This narrow border of deep red roses and cotoneasters allows space for the pale old stone wall to be seen above the plants.*

up to a disciplined framework and, if it snows in winter, the whiteness emphasises the structure. An informal garden also needs its evergreens to create the framework, but the designer must be have an understanding of proportion and balance and trust his instincts.

❀ The most restful spaces are those with equal proportions, such as a circle or square. They make good seating areas or places in which to pause and relax. Long, narrow spaces, on the other hand, are an invitation to move on.

❀ Your framework should always define spaces that are there for a purpose. A circle should have entrances and exits. A path should lead somewhere; if it curves it should curve around something – a fountain, perhaps, or a feature shrub or sculpture. If it is straight, it should lead the eye to something intriguing.

THE BUILT FRAMEWORK

GARDEN structure consists of areas shaped by the vertical elements that surround and divide them. We have looked at ways in which planting can create divisions and surroundings. Now we can look at how built structures can reinforce and add to these areas.

❧ If you are dividing a playing area from a patio, you may want to be able to supervise what is going on in the sandpit or by the swing. You will therefore need to be able to see. Here you won't want a dense hedge, which would restrict your view, but you can create the effect of division by building a low wall or simply a pergola-type gateway. This will give the impression of entering a different area but you will still be able to supervise the children playing. Climbing roses or honeysuckle will soften the structure.

❧ An arch can be used to connect areas or to divide one area from another. It can be flanked on either side by a hedge or fence, but that is not always necessary. It will, all on its own, give the impression of a gateway into a different environment. There are many different types of arch. Tall, wide arches can be built at regular intervals, rather like a pergola but not so enclosed. If widely enough spaced, they will not cut out too much light and summer-flowering plants such as lavender can be grown beneath them so that you have a walkway to be enjoyed at leisure.

❧ The view through any arch should lead the eye to something interesting further down the garden – perhaps a sculpture, a gateway or a decorative shrub or urn.

❧ If you don't want to divide the garden with too many tall structures, low fences of trellis, provided the supporting uprights are sturdy and good looking, can provide elegant divisions while keeping an open vista at a higher level.

❧ Arbors and niches can divide up spaces, particularly if used on a corner where two paths intersect.

❧ Terraced gardens create good opportunities for structured framework. Long, shallow terraced gardens were popular in the 1920s and 30s. They had wide steps, balustrading and stone or brick cross paths and were often bounded by clipped box or yew on either side. The balustrading was often made of molded concrete and it is very easy today to create a similar result with walls of concrete blocks, rendered and then painted. The walls should be no more than 18 in (45 cm) high so that people can sit on them.

Linking the compartments

❧ Having divided up the garden with a framework of planting or built structures, it is necessary to link the compartments or there will be no feeling of being one complete entity that a good garden needs. Use the same paving or brick for patios and paths throughout the garden. Walls should be topped with coping stones to match the paving, all of which will bring a sense of co-ordination and unity to the whole.

❧ When building pergolas, arbors and arches, again try to use similar materials throughout. If you start off with a simple metal arch use the same metal for any more arches and for arbors. With their clean lines and simple shapes, these are particularly suitable for urban gardens. Similarly, if you start off with a wooden pergola, follow through with wooden furniture, wooden gates and so on.

ABOVE: *This unusual cherry lined pergola has a double row of lavender at its feet, leading the eye to the gate and lake beyond.*

❧ A rustic pole screen can be used to divide a vegetable garden from the pleasure garden, but it should be in keeping with other divisions in the garden. Rough-cut wood would not be particularly suitable in conjunction with a sophisticated curved brick wall, for example, but would be perfectly acceptable if trellis or other wooden fences or evergreen hedges were used elsewhere.

The horizontal and the vertical

❧ When working out the structure, don't forget that you want a contrast between vertical and horizontal surfaces. Low hedges should be interrupted occasionally by a tall, conical tree or shrub. Expanses of open lawn should also have vertical interruptions here and there to keep the viewer interested.

RIGHT: *The multi-colored brickwork on this terrace creates a pattern that is echoed by the careful planting.*

BELOW: *A rendered Italianate wall leads from a woodland garden through a rounded arch, giving an intriguing glimpse into the densely planted area beyond.*

SEASON-BY-SEASON WORK PLANNER

The following planner is designed to make garden maintenance easier, by providing a guide to the optimum times throughout the year for undertaking particular tasks. Climate has a huge bearing on when some jobs may be undertaken wisely. There is no point planting out too early, just because the calendar proclaims it is the first day of spring, if the weather is so frosty that your plants have no hope of survival. Be guided by your prevailing local weather conditions for optimum chances of success.

SUITING YOUR REQUIREMENTS

DO NOT be put off by the number of tasks listed here – they will not all be relevant to every gardener. Use the planner to suit your personal gardening needs and priorities. For example, if you have many tender plants that you enjoy throughout the summer, propagating back-up stocks and overwintering the existing plants safely, all the guidance on this area of planting will be of note. However, if water gardening is your passion, then you will probably prioritise tasks related to this.

ABOVE: *Mulch the soil in borders and beds with compost in spring to encourage healthy plant growth.*

SPRING

SPRING is a busy time for gardeners. Daylight hours increase noticeably and the sun shines more. The garden leaps into life; trees unfurl new foliage and bulbs give a cheering burst of color after the grey of winter. Much sowing, planting, pruning and fertilizing is undertaken, and attention is paid to weeds and pests such as slugs, which are particularly active now. Do not be deceived by early breaks in the weather into spending too much money – and time – on tender plants that have little hope of survival should wintry conditions return. When the weather looks sufficiently kind to risk planting, keep a careful eye on the forecast – a sudden late frost can annihilate plants at a stroke.

ABOVE: *A wild woodland garden in spring is vibrant with color, with tulips and honesty groundcovers.*

General tasks

❀ Feed any plants that have been heavily pruned over winter and apply a generous layer of mulch.

❀ When the soil is moist and weed free, mulch borders and beds.

❀ When the soil is not too wet, prepare it for planting by digging appropriately, removing and disposing of perennial weeds.

❀ Clear weeds from driveways and paths.

❀ When the weather warms up, be vigilant in attending to watering requirements throughout this important growth period, especially during dry spells.

Annuals and biennials

❀ When the soil has warmed sufficiently, sow seeds of hardy annuals such as sunflowers and candytuft (*Iberis*) directly into their final planting sites.

❀ Sow biennials in a seed bed, ready for next spring.

❀ When the threat of frost has passed, plant out half-hardy annuals such as morning glory and *Impatiens*.

❀ Plant out sweet pea seedlings that were sown last fall.

Perennials and bulbs

❀ Apply slow-release fertilizer to flowerbeds and borders and rake in.

❀ When the weather and soil conditions allow, plant perennials.

❀ Deadhead tulips and narcissus when they have gone over, removing the flower head only, not the whole stalk. Leave the foliage to die down naturally, as it produces the food reserves necessary for good flowering next year. Move the bulbs to a less prominent position in the garden while the foliage dies down if the unsightly yellow, withered leaves are too conspicuous. Do not tie the foliage in knots.

❀ When the flowers of aconites and snowdrops have faded, lift, divide and replant.

❀ Divide perennials as soon as new growth begins.

❀ Stake tall perennials such as delphiniums while they are still at an early stage of growth.

❀ Lift and divide ornamental grasses such as bamboo and purple moor grass.

❀ Plant summer-flowering bulbs, dahlia tubers and nursery-grown plants.

❀ Divide summer-flowering alpines.

❀ Protect plants from slugs, paying particular attention to those especially attractive to slugs, such as delphiniums. Take immediate, appropriate action, especially in warm and humid conditions.

❀ Weed.

ANCIENT ROMAN GARDENS

IN AD 79 Pompeii was buried by volcanic ash from the eruption of Vesuvius. Wall paintings of gardens found during excavations show how the buildings were placed to take full advantage of the wider view – including that of Vesuvius – and how box and other green shrubs were clipped into disciplined shapes.

About 40 years later, the Roman emperor Hadrian had a villa built for himself at Tivoli, on ground lying between two valleys. In it he aimed to re-create the many famous buildings and sites he had visited on his travels, reinforcing the idea of the garden as an imaginary place. The site was enormous and the buildings were all linked along straight lines.

RIGHT: *A fresco found at Pompeii of a Roman garden scene with bird, fruit tree and lattice fence, from around AD 2–40.*

Shrubs, trees and climbers

❀ Remove winter protection when weather allows.

❀ In early spring, prune slightly frost-sensitive plants such as lavateras.

❀ In mid- to late spring, take softwood cuttings.

❀ Layer climbers and shrubs, particularly those that do not root easily from cuttings, but which produce new plants naturally from layering, such as magnolia and rhododendrons. Their flexible stems make this a simple procedure.

❀ Regularly guide climbers along their supports and tie in to protect against wind damage. Handle fragile stems, such as those of large-flowered clematis hybrids, gently.

❀ Check and adjust ties.

❀ Remove suckers.

❀ To produce colorful winter stems on *Cornus* and *Salix*, cut back last year's growth almost to ground level.

❀ Prune large-flowered clematis.

❀ Cut out flowering shoots of winter-flowering shrubs such as jasmine.

❀ Plant hedges.

Roses

❀ If stems were earthed up for winter protection, remove this extra soil from the base of the stems.

❀ When the ground is warm and dry enough, plant bare-rooted roses in early spring. Spring, along with fall, is also a good time to plant container-grown roses, although it is possible to plant them at any time.

❀ Prune repeat-flowering climbers, bush, shrub and miniature roses in mid-spring. Burn prunings. Do not prune ramblers and weeping standards.

❀ Lightly rake rose fertilizer into the topsoil in mid- to late spring.

❀ When the ground is warm and moist add an organic mulch.

❀ Remove suckers. Remove enough soil to trace the sucker back to its origin on the root and pull it off at this level. If you cut suckers off at ground level, their growth will be encouraged.

❀ Be alert for pests and take prompt action in the event of attack. Greenfly attack is a particular threat in late spring/early summer.

❀ Weed.

Lawns

❀ Lay turf or sow seed to make new lawns when weather conditions allow.

❀ Rake over and reseed bare or worn patches.

❀ After mid-spring do not cut summer-flowering meadows.

❀ In late spring, weed, feed and, if necessary, apply moss killer.

❀ As soon as grass starts active growth on established lawns, start mowing, with the blades set approximately 1 in (2.5cm) high.

Herbs

❀ Clear away dead growth and debris from the soil.

❀ In frost-free weather, plant out hardy herbs grown indoors from seed.

tulips

narcissus (*pseudo-narcissus*)

✿ Sow hardy annual and biennial seed directly into the soil if it is not too wet.

✿ Most herbs can be divided now.

✿ Cut back lavender and rosemary to encourage bushy new growth.

✿ Plant nursery-bought container-grown herbs.

✿ Pinch out the growing ends of young shrubs to produce a neat shape.

✿ Apply a mulch of compost or other organic fertilizer.

✿ Begin weeding the herb garden.

✿ Stake and support trailing plants.

✿ Towards the end of spring, move tender and half-hardy plants to a sheltered place to harden them off.

Vegetables

✿ Prepare the soil for sowing by digging. Apply fertilizers and manures.

✿ Apply slow-release fertilizer to perennial vegetables.

✿ In warm, moist soil, sow maincrop vegetables. Accelerate soil warming by covering them with cloches, fleece or plastic film.

✿ For a continuous, rather than glut production, sow small quantities of vegetables in succession.

✿ Sow tender vegetables such as sweetcorn and outdoor tomatoes under protection.

✿ As the weather gets warmer, start to sow salad vegetables outdoors.

✿ Protect germinating vegetables with floating mulch or fleece.

Fruit

✿ Apply slow-release fertilizer.

✿ In frosty weather, cover early fruit blossom with fleece.

✿ Mulch early-cropping strawberries and protect them against frost with fleece.

✿ Continue pruning top fruit and soft fruit.

Pools and water features

✿ Remove pool heater and reinstate the pump after its winter service.

✿ Clean out overgrown or dirty ponds and pools in late spring.

✿ Remove decayed foliage that may have been left on marginal plants for winter protection.

✿ Plant aquatic plants.

✿ Lift and divide aquatic plants as necessary.

Under glass and indoors

✿ Plant containers for summer displays.

✿ Sow perennials, tender vegetables and half-hardy annuals.

✿ Harden these off towards the end of spring.

✿ Take softwood cuttings of tender perennials for container displays.

✿ Sow half-hardy annual seeds.

✿ Harden off earlier-sown half-hardy annual seedlings in a cold frame, protected against frost by additional insulation.

snowdrops (*Galanthus elwesii*)

daffodils and hellebores

SUMMER

WATER conservation and attending to the watering needs of all plants becomes the key gardening concern as temperatures rise. Consider how your plants will fare while you are on holiday. Move containers to a shady place and, if possible, arrange a mutual holiday water watch with a gardening friend.

General tasks

❀ Plant up containers in early summer. Move containers prepared in the greenhouse outside.

❀ If not using a slow-release fertilizer, feed your containers regularly.

❀ To encourage new flowers and reduce the spread of disease, deadhead spent blooms regularly.

❀ During prolonged dry spells, water plants that have not yet become established, including shrubs and trees planted within the previous two years. Be observant and water plants that are showing signs of stress, such as rolled leaves, wilting and leaf fall.

Annuals and biennials

❀ In early summer, sow a second batch of annuals in the form of plant plugs, to ensure a good display once the first sowings have started to fade.

❀ Deadhead regularly to keep annuals flowering.

❀ Weed.

❀ Sow biennial seeds in a nursery bed ready for next year's display.

❀ Plant geraniums (*Pelargoniums*) for summer bedding.

❀ Sweet peas will flower continuously if picked regularly and not allowed to form pods.

Perennials and bulbs

❀ Do not be hasty to remove bulb foliage. Allow it to die back naturally.

❀ Remove spring bulbs from containers, where their dying foliage is unsightly, and allow them to die down in a less conspicuous part of the garden.

❀ Lift, dry and store tulip bulbs when the foliage has died down.

❀ As soon as bearded irises have bloomed, lift and divide.

❀ Collect seeds.

❀ Deadhead lilies.

❀ Remove yellowing foliage from perennials and dead-head regularly.

❀ Take softwood cuttings of plants that may be under threat during the winter, such as penstemons.

❀ Order spring-flowering bulbs. These will arrive in the fall.

Shrubs, trees and climbers

❀ Prune late spring- and early summer-flowering climbers and shrubs when they have finished flowering.

❀ Check climbers regularly. Tie in any straggly growth.

❀ Trim topiary, coniferous hedges and evergreens. Remove dead or damaged shoots.

❀ In late summer, take semi-ripe heel cuttings of trees, evergreens and shrubs.

❀ In late summer, order the shrubs and trees required for winter planting.

Roses

❀ Look out for mildew and black spot, and for signs of greenfly or other pest attack. Treat appropriately.

beech hedge with summer flowers

rose garden at the height of summer

❀ Deadhead faded blooms to encourage new growth.

❀ Apply a summer dressing of rose fertilizer.

❀ Order new roses for the fall.

❀ Weed.

Lawns

❀ In very dry weather, raise mower blades and remove the grass-collecting box so that the clippings act as a moisture-conserving mulch.

❀ Feed lawns regularly.

❀ Make the first cut of a spring-flowering meadow.

❀ Mow regularly, and trim lawn edges after each cut.

Herbs

❀ Begin to harvest.

❀ Trim dwarf hedging.

❀ Towards the end of the summer, harvest and preserve.

❀ Collect seed as it ripens, label clearly in envelopes.

❀ Continue to weed.

Vegetables

❀ If a slow-release fertilizer was not applied in spring, feed regularly.

❀ Continue successive sowings.

❀ Plant out vegetable seedlings.

❀ Look out for pests, such as root flies on carrots and onions and blackfly on broad beans. Treat appropriately.

❀ Hoe to keep weeds in check.

❀ Lift onions and shallots when tops have died down.

❀ Harvest regularly.

❀ Feed tomatoes regularly. Remove side shoots and yellowing leaves from tomato plants.

❀ Thin out vegetable seedlings.

❀ When runner beans reach the top of their supports, pinch out the growing points.

Fruit

❀ Protect fruit against birds.

❀ Harvest regularly.

❀ Tidy up strawberries after fruiting.

❀ Towards the end of summer, harvest fruit for winter consumption.

❀ Summer-prune trained fruit trees.

Pools and water features

❀ Plant, or lift and divide aquatic plants such as water lilies.

❀ In hot weather, keep a close eye on water levels and fill up if necessary.

Under glass and indoors

❀ Keep a close eye on plants for signs of pest attack. Treat appropriately.

❀ Be vigilant about providing adequate and appropriate shade and ventilation.

❀ In late summer, thoroughly clean, disinfect, fumigate, tidy and, if necessary, paint the greenhouse and any frames in readiness for fall. This will reduce the risk of pests and diseases becoming a problem over the winter.

mallow shrub in full flower

Lilium 'Journey's End'

FALL

ALTHOUGH the days are growing shorter and the plants are starting to look tired, in many ways fall marks the start, not the end, of the gardening year. Planting bulbs, roses and shrubs is a forward-looking task, when most of the work in the garden revolves around tidying and disposing of dead and decaying plants.

General tasks

✿ Turn the compost heap.

✿ Spread well-rotted compost over borders and beds for winter protection.

✿ Dig heavy, clay soil and leave the clods unbroken. Winter frost will break these up to improve the soil texture.

✿ Collect fallen leaves for making leaf mold.

✿ Clear summer bedding from containers and plant up winter containers.

Annuals

✿ When annuals have finished flowering, clear them away, leaving ornamental seed heads in place.

Perennials and bulbs

✿ When perennials become straggly and unsightly, cut them back. Shred or chop the debris and add it to the compost heap. Lift, divide and replant perennials.

✿ Protect perennials of uncertain hardiness against the worst of the winter weather by applying a thick organic mulch.

✿ After the first frost has blackened the foliage of dahlias and other tender, bulbous plants, trim back the stems to 6 in (15cm) and gently lift the tubers. Discard damaged roots and excess soil. Invert the tubers for a week or so to drain away excess moisture. Store them upright on a layer of peat that covers the roots, not the crowns, in a dry, cool, frost-free environment.

✿ As soon as your order of spring-flowering bulbs arrives, plant them in pots or in the garden.

Shrubs, trees and climbers

✿ Before the soil is cold, take hardwood cuttings, just after leaf fall.

✿ As the dormant season begins, plant trees and shrubs.

✿ Screen slightly tender woody plants with matting, conifer branches or bracken for winter protection.

Roses

✿ Continue deadheading roses, which are generally still blooming as fall commences.

✿ Prune rambling roses and weeping standards.

✿ Dig to prepare soil for new plantings.

✿ Continue to observe and treat disease appropriately.

✿ Take cuttings of all rose types except hybrid teas, which do not transplant satisfactorily.

✿ Plant bare root roses. Although container-grown roses can be planted at any time of the year, fall, along with spring, is a particularly good time.

✿ Tidy up rose beds, hoeing mulch and collecting up and burning fallen leaves and debris.

Hamamelis x *intermedia* 'Sunburst' and 'Diane'

Hydrangea anomala petiolaris 'Hilbam House'

❀ Prepare plants for winter. Cut back long stems to avoid damage by wind if your garden is very exposed. In particularly cold areas, earth up stems with approximately 4 in (10 cm) of soil.

Lawns

❀ Scarify, spike and top dress lawns.

❀ If the weather is sufficiently mild, a new lawn can be established from turf or seed.

❀ If lawns have suffered during the summer due to heavy use or drought, apply fall feed early in the season.

❀ Cut spring- and summer-flowering meadows.

Herbs

❀ Fork over the soil and fertilize permanent plantings.

❀ Plant container-grown herbs.

❀ If you are planning a new herb bed on previously uncultivated soil, prepare by double digging.

❀ Plant hardy herbaceous herbs.

❀ Plant invasive herbs in sunken containers to prevent undesirable spreading.

❀ Transfer tender herbs such as basil and pineapple sage to a conservatory, windowsill or greenhouse.

❀ Grow chives and parsley in pots. Overwinter under glass for a good supply throughout the winter.

❀ Cut back larger shrubs such as rosemary.

❀ Plant low hedging such as rue, lavender and hyssop.

❀ Protect herbs that will be spending winter in the garden by earthing up a generous layer of straw, soil or compost around their roots.

Vegetables

❀ Continue to harvest.

❀ String up onions for winter storage.

❀ Sow green manure.

❀ Clear away, clean and store redundant stakes.

❀ Cut down asparagus.

❀ Earth up celery and leeks.

❀ Protect outdoor tomatoes with cloches to help hasten ripening.

Fruit

❀ Continue to harvest and store for winter consumption.

❀ Prune summer-fruiting raspberries and soft fruit bushes.

❀ Plant strawberries, fruit trees and bushes.

❀ Apply bands of grease to fruit trees to protect against pests.

❀ Take hardwood cuttings of currants.

Pools and water features

❀ Remove the pump in late fall; clean, service and store until spring.

❀ Clear away dying foliage. Skim off fallen leaves and other debris.

Under glass and indoors

❀ Before the frosts arrive, bring tender plants inside.

Aster amellus 'King George'

Aster 'Grandchild'

WINTER

PROTECTION is the chief concern of the gardener in winter. Frost, heavy snowfalls, gales and hail storms all threaten. Make sure that plants are protected accordingly. Even in winter, there is work to be done in the garden, such as some weeding and planting, but the load is much diminished. Take this time to plan next year's garden. Observe the garden without its lively summer colors and consider the overall structure. If there are large areas that seem bare, plan next year's winter color as well as thinking about the broader picture. Changes of height and the general dynamics of the garden design are much easier to plan when you do not have the distraction of too much color.

General tasks

* Take root cuttings of fleshy-rooted perennials.
* Replace faded, broken and absent plant labels.
* Prepare for spring sowing. Clean propagators, pots and seed trays.
* While plants are dormant, maintain paths, trellis, fences and other garden structures.
* Continue to tidy up flowerbeds and borders, cutting back spent plants and clearing away debris.
* Continue to collect fallen leaves.
* Plan any major changes to the garden.

Perennials and bulbs

* Check stored bulbs for rot and mold. Discard affected bulbs.

Shrubs, trees and climbers

* Even if the weather is slightly frosty, prune roses, shrubs, trees and climbers.
* Inspect woody plants for diseased and dead wood. Remove and destroy infected or dead branches and stems.
* Knock heavy snow from conifers and hedges before it turns to ice and breaks or distorts branches. It may also cause top growth to blacken and die.

Roses

* Check that the roots of fall-planted roses have not been loosened by frost and firm up if necessary.
* Check that the supports of climbing roses are in good condition.

Lawns

* Rake up leaves.
* Service mowers and trimmers. Ensure that blades are sharp, ready for the first spring cut.
* Keep off the lawn in frozen conditions.

Herbs

* Remove soggy herbaceous growth and annual growth

Asplenium scolopendrium hit by frost

ornamental cabbage

as it dies back. Leave healthy perennial growth to provide winter protection for other plants.

❀ Keep the herb garden neat and tidy.

❀ Consider next year's planting. Order seeds.

❀ Plan new herb gardens or consider whether alterations are necessary to existing ones.

❀ Towards winter's end, sow seeds of tender herbs indoors.

❀ Pot-grown hardy herbs may be planted out in frost-free weather.

❀ Keep an eye on bay trees. Move them inside if the temperature dips below 5°F (-15°C), as bay is particularly susceptible to frost, which scorches the leaves.

Vegetables

❀ Order seeds for planting next year.

❀ Plan the rotation of crops for the vegetable garden.

❀ Lift parsnips and leeks.

❀ Cover soil with cloches to prewarm it, ready for early plantings in spring.

❀ Plant garlic.

Fruit

❀ Prune fruit trees.

❀ Mulch established fruit trees.

❀ Disinfect canes before storage.

❀ Force rhubarb.

❀ Plant container-grown fruit trees and bushes.

Pools and water features

❀ Install a pond heater or float a plastic ball on the surface of the water to keep an area free of ice. If you have fish, this is essential to their survival.

Under glass and indoors

❀ If you have not brought tender plants inside, do so now.

❀ Bring in tender container plants.

❀ Insulate cold frames against frost, using layers of burlap or old carpet, secured with ties or heavy pieces of wood. These opaque materials will need to be removed during the day so that the plants are not deprived of light. Transparent materials such as several layers of clear plastic sheeting may be left in place day and night. While not totally clear, the plastic does transmit some light.

❀ Insulate the greenhouse using plastic bubble wrap, which allows a reasonable amount of light through. Add polystyrene base cladding – polystyrene panels placed along the lower glazing panes to significantly reduce heat loss. These will need to be removed before planting summer border crops as polystyrene does not allow light transmission.

❀ Continue to ventilate the greenhouse to prevent a build-up of stagnant air.

Hamamelis 'Zuccariniana'

Eranthis hyemalis

WIRE BASKET WALL PLANTER

It is easy to make a whole collection of wall planters that are cost effective and also easily outclass their plastic-coated, mass-produced counterparts. The gentle tones and textures of wire and burlap are a natural, understated partner to any planting. You should always wear stout protective gloves when working with chicken wire, which has very sharp edges.

TOOLS AND MATERIALS

⊤ Pencil and paper, for template
⊤ Scissors
⊤ ½ in (12 mm) exterior-grade plywood
⊤ Jigsaw
⊤ Stout protective gloves
⊤ Protective eye goggles
⊤ Floristry scissors or wire cutters, for cutting chicken wire
⊤ Chicken wire
⊤ Burlap
⊤ Netting staples
⊤ Staple gun or hammer
⊤ Length of wire

1 *Draw a symmetrical basket shape on a piece of paper, slightly shallower than a semicircle. Cut out the paper template. Place it on your piece of plywood and draw around it. Cut out the wooden shape, using a jigsaw.*

2 *Wearing protective gloves and eye goggles and using floristry scissors or wire cutters, roughly cut out a piece of chicken wire to fit the plywood, allowing plenty extra to wrap around behind the wooden shape, as well as sufficient to make a pocket at the front. Cut a piece of burlap to the same size as the chicken wire.*

3 *Cut a second piece of burlap large enough to wrap around the plywood. Wrap it around one face of the shaped plywood and staple it in place on the back, tucking the edges of the burlap under neatly as you work. (The stapled side will be inside the back of the basket.)*

4 *Take the remaining piece of burlap and fold under one long edge twice to form a neat 'hem'. Fold the raw edge of one long side of the chicken wire around the folded edge of burlap to produce a tidy, firmly rolled 'hem', which will be the top edge of the basket.*

5 *Shape the burlap and chicken wire roughly to produce a pocket of the desired size ion the front face of the plywood (i.e. the one that is not completely covered by*

burlap). The bare plywood will be inside the basket and therefore concealed as the pocket is filled with compost.

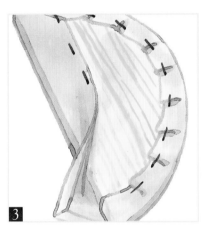

6 *Secure the pocket in place by stapling the edges of the burlap and wire on to the wooden shape. Keep placing your hand inside the pocket as it is formed to ensure that you produce an even, symmetrical shape.*

7 *Trim away excess burlap and chicken wire. Staple the ends of a length of wire to the back corners of the basket to make a loop for hanging the planter on the wall.*

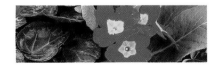

WINDCHIME

This pretty, seashore-inspired windchime makes a softly musical sound with each passing breeze, and is incredibly simple to make from odds and ends. The terracotta shapes used here were Christmas decorations bought from a garden center. Floristry supply shops are also a good source of unusual objects that would work well, for example miniature flowerpots, shells and seashore shapes intended for inclusion in pot pourri. The antiquated-looking piece of 'driftwood' used here is actually an old hammer handle, found while digging over a garden border. Be inventive and cast a careful look over your button booth, garden shed, bathroom and garage shelves before stepping into a shop. You probably have almost everything you need for this project already, and searching for alternatives is a major part of the fun. Some objects will need small holes drilled in them – the type of drill sold for miniature work is inexpensive, widely available and easy to use.

TOOLS AND MATERIALS

- Jute twine
- Clothes peg
- Instant bonding glue
- Scissors
- Piece of driftwood, branch, well-worn hammer handle or similar
- Selection of objects for hanging, such as shells, terracotta shapes and old buttons
- Drill and small drill bit

1 *To make lengths of jute twine easier to thread through objects, grip one end of the twine in a clothes peg and twist the twine tightly to reduce its diameter close to the peg. Drip instant bonding glue on to this tightly twisted end and hold the peg for a minute or so until the glue has dried and the twist is secure. When the glue is totally dry, cut through the glued twist and you will have a rigid, neat, unfraying end, which will thread smoothly through your chosen objects.*

2 *Tie the un-neatened ends of several lengths of twine on to the piece of driftwood, branch or hammer handle that is to form the top support of the windchime. Tie a further length of twine to the wood to form a loop for hanging the finished chime.*

3 *Drill a small hole in each object to be threaded as necessary – for example in the bottom of each miniature flowerpot and in any shells that do not have naturally occurring small holes.*

4 *Thread your chosen objects on to the lengths of twine, knotting them in place to secure. Knot collections of shells and buttons suspended from the pots to produce 'bells'.*

5 *Continue threading objects on to the twine until you have a well-balanced windchime. Add new lengths of twine to the wooden support, if necessary, checking that they are sufficiently well spaced to appear uncrowded, yet close enough together to knock gently into each other when the wind blows.*

1

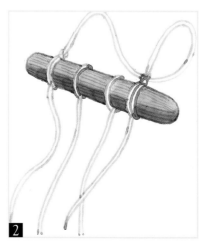

2

GETTING TO WORK

Even the smallest garden has a high proportion of non-living elements. All the 'hard-side' elements need to be as carefully considered, installed and maintained as the plants in your garden if it is to work well.

✿

Before embarking on any major projects, research your options thoroughly to avoid making costly mistakes.

✿

Make an assessment of your garden, your practical requirements and the style of the house, then read the relevant sections in this chapter before you start work.

✿

If you choose well, your plot will look well-integrated; if you choose badly, the resulting mishmash may be a disappointment.

FINDING SOLUTIONS FOR PROBLEMS

Every garden, large or small, has problem areas that irritate or embarrass its owners – be it a shady dry spot where plants steadfastly refuse to grow, a corner of the garden overlooked by an unsightly building or a compost heap that dominates the otherwise perfect potager. Some problems are immediately obvious, such as a garden with a steep slope or incredibly boggy area, while others become apparent with time, or as a garden metamorphoses with changing use. Perhaps your garden was perfect when you had no children, but now that you have toddlers with excess energy to run off, and play things to store, it no longer suits your needs.

Assessing the situation

❀ Every now and again, perhaps in fall, which is the start of the dormant season, take time to look at the garden without the distraction of a multitude of flowers. Take a long, dispassionate look at what worked, and what did not, during spring and summer.

ABOVE: *Al fresco eating generates a diversity of difficult-to-store items, such as barbecues, tables, chairs and parasols.*

❀ Assessing which plants grew well, and which ones suffered, will help you build an increasingly accurate picture of the conditions that prevail in the microclimates around your garden. You can then plant accordingly, or shift the environment subtly to suit. For example, add windbreaks to areas where plants have otherwise flourished, but have suffered due to wind exposure.

ABOVE: *Trellis forms an effective yet inexpensive screen that also provides an excellent support for colorful climbing plants.*

The garden room

❀ You can also assess how well your garden has worked for you as a whole during the warmer months. Was there anything that became a constant annoyance, like a pile of outdoor games that slowly accrued, but which had no storage place, leading to a permanent fruitless attempt at tidying up.

❀ Did your city hall install new wheeled trash cans, which now dominate the front garden? Perhaps you bought a barbecue and ate outside almost every night, but had nowhere to accommodate the barbecue itself, the charcoal, insect-repellent candles, lanterns, table, parasol and chairs that gradually took over the patio.

❀ The garden is increasingly regarded as an outside room, an additional living space, and it deserves to be planned as much with comfort and function in mind as your kitchen or any other room within your home.

Hiding an ugly view/adding privacy

❀ Privacy is an important garden attribute. A garden should be a sanctuary, a place where you can recharge your batteries away from the stresses and demands of the outside world. It is never going to be easy to relax if your garden is overlooked, or has an unsightly view.

❀ The solution is to screen out the problem, while retaining as much light within the garden as possible. In some situations, it may be possible to erect quite a high barrier without affecting the amount of light transmitted, but if your garden is already quite shady, use baffle screens, which diffuse rather than totally occlude, instead of solid screens.

❀ Trellis is a brilliant way of adding instant height, without excluding light totally, and is available in many shapes, sizes and designs – from rustic, twiggy panels topped with arching branches for a pretty, rural look, to elegantly formal geometric shapes in smooth, painted wood, perfect for a smart urban courtyard.

❀ Always support trellis properly, and use a grade appropriate to the task. Thin, expanding trellis may be temptingly cheap, but will quickly collapse under the weight of a heavy climbing plant like honeysuckle, and will look skimpy. It will also need constant propping up and repair, which are difficult things to do when the trellis is clothed with foliage.

❀ Where trellis is installed as a major feature, either as a freestanding screen or on top of a fence or wall, buy the best quality you can afford, pretreated with preservative; install it well and maintain it properly for a screen that will be as attractive as it is functional. Planting will further soften the effect. Scented plants will add another dimension.

ABOVE: *The effect achieved by the use of wooden decking and the wooden struts of the pergola is of a contemporary living area with a Japanese feel to it.*

THE ART OF CONCEALMENT

SOME elements of the garden are necessary, but not particularly attractive. With a little careful planning, every part of the garden can be visually acceptable, even appealing in its own right. All hard-working areas of the garden deserve to be as well thought out, installed and maintained as the purely decorative elements.

Compost areas

❀ Compost areas are an essential part of the well-maintained, ecologically sound garden, but their contribution is definitely functional rather than ornamental.

❀ The compost heap offers so much to the garden that it should be treated with more respect than it tends to receive in most gardens. All too often, the compost heap is just that – a literal heap, not of sweet-smelling, rich brown earth, but of rotting household waste, as well as old branches and weeds.

❀ Consider the functionality of any problem area first, and consider concealment later. Putting a fence in front of a badly installed and maintained compost area will only shield the problem.

❀ Perhaps install a proper compost container, or pair of containers, appropriate to the size of your garden and the amount of composting you feel able to do. A shredder might be a worthwhile investment, since it will enable you to cut prunings into manageable pieces that degrade more quickly, and also take up less space in the compost area. Put only appropriate materials on the compost pile. Maintain the compost heap well, turning it regularly and keeping it covered, and you will have much less of a problem to conceal.

Concealing unsightly areas

❀ Assuming your compost area, cans and other functional, but unappealing, areas are in good general repair, and are designed and used properly, all you need to do is conceal them from view.

❀ The type of concealment used will depend to some extent on the purpose of the area. If you regularly need to wheel your trash can from its usual

RIGHT: A neatly kept trash area will look tidy and reduce the possibility of vermin attack.

resting place to the front gate, you will need a permanent housing for the can, that also allows easy access. A three-sided brick area is a popular way of hiding a large trash can, and can be softened externally by planting.

❀ Obviously, a compost area will require sufficient access around it so that you can turn the heap, and add to or remove the compost, but the whole heap stays in one place, so all-round access is not so critical. Trellis clothed with climbers, hurdle fencing or another natural barrier could all be used to screen the area prettily, effectively and inexpensively.

Planting in difficult areas

❀ Always work with the natural garden environment, not against it. Although you can adjust some conditions, for example by planting windbreaks to shelter plants in exposed sites, some areas will never accomodate certain plant types with any real success.

❀ Respect the various microclimates around your garden and plant accordingly (see opposite). Although your choice of plants may be limited in some areas, sympathetic planting will mean that what you do grow, thrives.

❀ A thriving collection of plants, even in a limited range, will always look more attractive than a diversity of straggly, sick, struggling plants.

ABOVE: A functional corner of the garden between fencing and the door of the garden shed becomes a pretty nook to sit in, with the help of a strategically planted climbing rose.

ABOVE: *Euphorbia enjoy dry, shady conditions.*

ABOVE: *Succulent plants will thrive in hot, sunny conditions.*

Plants for moist, shady sites

- ✿ Astrantia
- ✿ Camellia
- ✿ Dicentra spectabilis
- ✿ Hamamelis mollis
- ✿ Helleborus
- ✿ Hosta
- ✿ Mahonia aquifolium
- ✿ Rhododendron
- ✿ Sarcococca humilis
- ✿ Viburnum davidii

Plants for dry, shady sites

- ✿ Anemone japonica
- ✿ Aucuba japonica
- ✿ Bergenia
- ✿ Euphorbia
- ✿ Ilex
- ✿ Pachysandra terminalis
- ✿ Pulmonaria
- ✿ Skimmia
- ✿ Vinca

Plants for dry, sunny areas

- ✿ Achillea
- ✿ Agapanthus
- ✿ Cistus
- ✿ Echinops ritro
- ✿ Geranium
- ✿ Iris germanica
- ✿ Nepeta
- ✿ Santolina
- ✿ Senecio
- ✿ Verbascum
- ✿ Yucca

Plants for acidic soil

- ✿ Azalea
- ✿ Camellia
- ✿ Pieris
- ✿ Rhododendron
- ✿ Skimmia

Plants for alkaline soil

- ✿ Buddleja davidii
- ✿ Clematis
- ✿ Cotoneaster
- ✿ Dianthus
- ✿ Lavandula
- ✿ Paeonia
- ✿ Scabiosa
- ✿ Syringa
- ✿ Verbascum

Pollution-tolerant plants

- ✿ Aucuba japonica
- ✿ Berberis
- ✿ Chaenomeles
- ✿ Cotoneaster
- ✿ Ilex
- ✿ Philadelphus
- ✿ Syringa
- ✿ Weigela florida

BELOW:. *Many plants will thrive in shady and dry areas of your garden.*

BELOW: *Choose plants that enjoy acidic conditions rather than trying to permanently modify the pH of the soil.*

INTEGRATING HOUSE AND GARDEN

The entrance to your garden is important. An interesting and inviting environment should greet you when you step out of the door. Not every door will open directly on to the garden, of course, but a row of well-tended pots could point the way to the garden, or perhaps a trellis-trained flowering climber on the wall. Remember that a level garden seen from the ground appears foreshortened and shorter than it really is. Individual compartments will seem shorter too; so if you are planning a circular lawn, the circle will seem squashed unless you make it more of an oval, with the longest part facing the house.

DOORWAYS AND WINDOWS

THE ideal entrance to a garden is through French doors to a patio. This really makes the garden into another 'room', and even when the weather is cool or rainy the garden 'picture' can be appreciated through the protective glass.

Single doors

❀ If a large entrance is not possible, the garden door can still be given glass panels, which will make it seem less remote from the house. A scented shrub next to the door and pots or containers of summer-flowering plants will also be welcoming. Scented-leaved geraniums directly by the door will release their aroma as people brush against them. Lavender and rosemary will do the same.

Side entrance

❀ Some gardens can be reached only through a side entrance. Even if a side entrance is narrow and tunnel-like you can make it seem more spacious by painting the walls white.

ABOVE: An arched entrance leading from shadow into sunlight is one of the most romantic ways to approach an outdoor space. The wrought iron gates give the impression that you are entering a secret garden.

ABOVE: *These garden doors lead directly on to lush borders overflowing with flowers and fruit.*

❀ White reflects what light there is and always seems to enlarge a space. At the end of the alleyway you could install a wrought iron gate or arched entrance with climbers over it so that there is a hint of the promised garden before you get there. Always keep side entrances clear. There is nothing so off-putting as having to clamber over bags of compost or old prunings.

Windows

❀ Windows overlooking the garden should not be wasted but should look out on to a pleasant garden view. If the living-room window overlooks the garden, try to make sure the garden can be seen when people are sitting down.

❀ If this is not possible, you should at least ensure that some climbing plant or flowering tree is visible through the window. This is especially important for disabled or elderly people, who spend more of their time sitting down than others might.

Transitional entrances

❀ Porches, pergolas and conservatories all have very different functions but in one respect they are alike: they act as transitional areas between the house and the garden. Porches are usually erected as insulation from the weather. If they are very small they sometimes seem to act more as a barrier between house and garden than as a lobby joining one to the other. However, if they are glazed, they can be used to grow tender houseplants and become almost like miniature conservatories.

❀ A pergola by the garden door can complement the architecture of the house, while the planted elements can relate to the garden. A conservatory is also a meeting point between house and garden, relating both to the architecture and to the hardier plants outside.

ABOVE: *A narrow iron gate and enormous hydrangea entice you along the gravel path at the entrance to this garden.*

Proportion and scale

❀ Anything in the garden that is very large in relation to the house will seem excessive. Many a tree that is nicely in proportion when planted will grow far too large for its allotted space and not only prevent other things from growing but will diminish the house by its size. This is just as true of patios, terraces and paths.

❀ In a garden belonging to a small house, or a house with a narrow frontage, a grandiose patio will look out of place. A small patio with a carefully designed pattern of bricks or other paving and a concentration on the detailing and workmanship will look charming and could be surrounded by plants or a trellis, giving more of a courtyard effect.

❀ In a large house, on the other hand, elements that are too small will give a trivial, fussy effect. A broad terrace by the garden door will give the house a more suitable visual base. Use large paving slabs, and have the terrace or patio running the length of the house, particularly if the house has large windows and patio doors. It should be wide enough to take a dining table and generously proportioned chairs.

❀ Courtyards offer good opportunities for brickwork or paving. Again, the materials and patterns should be in keeping with the house, and any flowerpots and containers should be of similar shape and color.

The view towards the house

❀ Remember that when you are at the far end of the garden, you will get a different view of its relationship to the house that is just as important as the view from the house into the garden. The house becomes a focal point and you will be much more aware of materials that do not match or co-ordinate with those of the house and be pleasurably aware of those that do.

ABOVE: *The tall plants of* Romneya coulteri *here break the hard line of the window frame, creating a softer look.*

ABOVE: *On the street side of this house, a burgeoning* Ceanothus *softens the brickwork and anchors the house to the ground.*

Anchoring the house

❧ Planting evergreen shrubs near to the house helps to anchor it to the ground. This is especially true of new or modern houses, which can seem rather bleak and unrelated to their surroundings. Climbers are another excellent way of anchoring the house. Those that cover the whole house are good for buildings that have no particular architectural interest. Virginia creeper, which turns the most astonishingly bright red color in fall, does the job well.

❧ A traditional house with some architectural interest will be better with climbing roses around the windows and nothing else to hide the materials and design. Interesting modern buildings, some of which are sculptures in their own right, may not need anything clambering over them but could benefit from groups of bold architectural plants nearby to act as anchors.

Paths

❧ Paths leading directly from the house should be as wide as you can make them; narrow paths are less inviting. Two people should preferably be able to walk together in conversation. This is not always possible in small gardens but it is something to aim for. Paths can get narrower as they lead into the remoter parts of the garden, but near the house the path is acting as a gateway to the whole garden and should reflect that fact.

Security

❧ The way in which the garden relates to the house can influence security quite seriously. The street door should not be concealed by tall, dense shrubs, which would prevent a burglar being seen while trying to force the lock. Low planting is advisable here, which would make anyone trying to break in much more visible.

❧ At the back, avoid growing trees and shrubs near the house that a burglar could use as a ladder. If you want to clothe the house in greenery, stick to thorny plants such as the unfriendly climbing roses 'Mermaid' and 'Albertine', or a *berberis* or *pyracantha*.

❧ Make sure you have a place where you can lock up ladders and heavy garden implements such as spades and forks. Padlocking a ladder to the wall is better than leaving it lying about, and certainly never leave one propped up against a wall as an invitation to intruders.

ABOVE: *In the garden of this modern single-storey building, a wide gravel walkway takes you at a leisurely pace back to the house.*

ABOVE: *This small garden is made to seem much larger by the divisions and cross-axes. Here, a brick path leads to a blue seat as the focal point, with the view interrupted only by a large copper planter.*

ESTABLISHING BOUNDARIES

Boundaries are an important consideration in garden planning.
Not only do they mark the limitations of your property, they also
provide the opportunity to screen out noise and unsightly views and
to afford privacy. Conversely, your garden may enjoy a wonderful
view and have no issues of privacy or noise pollution. Thus, marking
the boundary may consist of a visually minimal delineation, such as
sinking a line of stones into the soil that terminate at ground level,
or installing a chain-link fence. Within the garden itself, fences,
walls and screens offer a way of marking out distinct zones of activity,
such as play areas and vegetable plots, as well as providing vertical
surfaces for planting and concealing ugly but necessary parts of
the garden, such as compost containers and recycling areas.

BOUNDARY TYPES

THE issues to consider when choosing a type of
boundary are straightforward, and governed by
common sense as well as visual preference.

Tall, solid boundaries

❀ If you need to enhance the level of privacy in your
garden, you will be considering solid, tall options, such
as high walls or closeboard fencing. Walls will block out

noise, as well as prying eyes, better than fences. In both
cases, remember that tall, solid screens also block out
light and can seem claustrophobic in small areas, so
plan carefully before purchasing and installing.

❀ There may also be local, as well as national, planning
restrictions on the type and height of boundary
marking that may be placed on your property, so do
research any such limitations at the outset.

❀ A final point of consideration is that, contrary to popular
belief, a solid wall or fence does not offer the best
protection on an exposed site, and can even lead to
problems such as the creation of a plant-damaging frost
pocket, instability of the barrier itself, and turbulent, plant-
harming wind conditions on either side of the barrier.

Partially open boundaries

❀ Where a solid wall or fence would be inappropriate,
a partially occluded screen may be the answer. For
example, a wattle fence appears almost solid but actually
allows some air to penetrate, and so makes an effective
windbreak in exposed situations where an impenetrable
barrier would cause problems.

❀ Certain types of partially open boundaries also offer a
degree of privacy and security, while allowing some light
to pass through them, for example walls topped with
screen blocks, or fences headed with decorative trellis.

LEFT: *A partially occluded screen such as a decorative trellis can be used to
create a boundary without building a solid wall or fence, and serves as a
decorative feature as well as creating a feeling of space.*

Open boundaries

✿ Some boundary markings are just that – a way of delineating the extremities of your property, without affording marked additional degrees of privacy, sound reduction or security. There are various options available, some more decorative and practically useful than others.

✿ Prices also vary widely. For example, a cast-iron fence can be highly ornamental and offers some security enhancement if it is sufficiently tall and of an intricate and pointed design that is off-putting to the casual fence-climbing intruder. Such fences can be expensive and will need ongoing maintenance in order to retain its elegant good looks, whether purchased new or from a specialist in architectural salvage.

ABOVE: *Fencing materials define the borders of a plot and need to be sympathetic to the overall theme of the garden, such as this bamboo, used to reinforce a Japanese style.*

RIGHT: *A tall, solid boundary such as closeboard fencing can be used to enhance the privacy of your garden, but remember that it will also block out light.*

WALLS

WALLS are more permanent structures than fences and, correspondingly, need thorough planning before building begins. They are very effective at noise reduction, and of course offer maximum privacy. High walls may seem to offer an increased level of security, since it is obviously more difficult to climb over a wall than to step over a chain-link fence. Bear in mind, however, that an intruder can work unseen and unheard behind the useful concealment of a high wall, so a lower wall may be a better option where security is a more important consideration than privacy.

ABOVE: *Walls can be prettified considerably with planting. Here, the fan-trained pears are attractive as well as productive.*

Choosing a wall

❀ Walls are generally made of brick, concrete or stone, and may be solid or pierced, as in the case of a wall made of screen blocks. Always choose materials that are sympathetic to those used in the construction of your home, and appropriate to the style of wall prevalent in your area.

❀ For example, an old cottage built of stone would look very uncomfortable surrounded by a wall of concrete blocks. Similarly, a stark, modern home would look very awkward partnered by an overly rustic stone wall. Observe the materials and styles used in other gardens around your own, and make a note of what works and what is less successful.

BRICKS

❀ Clay bricks are attractive, and are available in a wide variety of colors, textures and degrees of weather resistance. Ordinary facing bricks are fine for most garden walls, but 'special' quality bricks will be required for applications where increased water resistance is needed, such as on exposed walls in coastal regions.

❀ Salvaged bricks are not necessarily a cheaper option than new bricks, but may be the best choice for producing a wall that tones in well with the brickwork of your home.

ABOVE: *The severity of a solid brick wall is softened by a round window and arched doorway.*

❀ If you have any spare house bricks available to take to the builder's merchant for matching, so much the better. Always obtain a sample to take home to assess whether the tone, texture and coloring really work well *in situ*. Building a wall is a costly investment in terms of time and money, and mistakes are all too glaringly obvious when replicated in row after row of inappropriate brick.

BLOCKS

❀ Blocks are obviously quicker to lay than bricks, since they are so much larger. However, the foundations of a block wall are just as important, so do not regard building a block wall as any less serious an undertaking as laying a brick wall.

❀ The all-too-common garden sight of a shoddily built collapsing concrete wall bears testimony to the fact that block walling is seen by many people as a speedy and inexpensive alternative.

Natural blocks

❀ Stone walling is very attractive, and indigenous to some areas. Indeed, some districts even have planning regulations that necessitate the use of local stone for new walls. Granite, limestone and sandstone are all used for wall building. Flint and slate are also used, often in combination with other materials.

❀ It makes economic sense to buy from a local quarry or salvage company. Garden centers often have a selection of appealing stone, but to buy there the sort of quantities needed for a run of walling, rather than isolated pieces for a small rockery, would be prohibitively expensive.

Concrete blocks

❀ Standard structural blocks are inexpensive and easy to lay, although they are not attractive and their use is generally limited to areas where they will be later disguised by a coat of rendering or plastering. A zigzag pattern on their surface provides a key to encourage adhesion of these materials.

❀ Facing blocks have a decorative face and end, and are used for the external surface of cavity walls, backed by plain, structural blocks. They are available in a wide range of finishes to tone in with local stone, are cheaper than reconstituted stone blocks or natural stone, but much less visually convincing than either.

❀ Reconstituted stone blocks use crushed stone in place of aggregate, and are molded into a range of shapes from smooth to rough hewn, and in colors to suit most local stone types. Although more realistic than facing blocks, they do not have the same lack of uniformity that characterises natural stone.

❀ Screen blocks are concrete blocks pierced with a decorative pattern, and are generally used to form walls produced in a stack-bonded pattern – literally piled up in columns rather than being offset. This produces a weaker wall than traditional bond patterns, so screen walls need supporting piers at each end for additional strength.

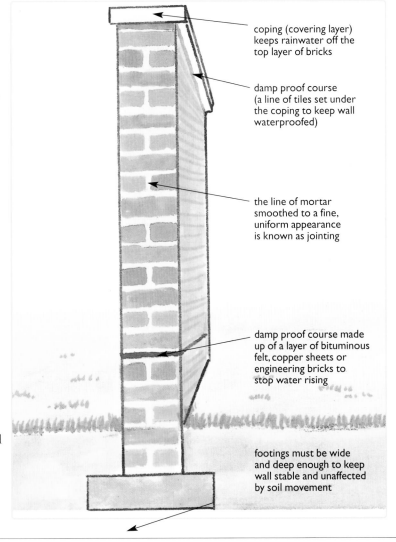

coping (covering layer) keeps rainwater off the top layer of bricks

damp proof course (a line of tiles set under the coping to keep wall waterproofed)

the line of mortar smoothed to a fine, uniform appearance is known as jointing

damp proof course made up of a layer of bituminous felt, copper sheets or engineering bricks to stop water rising

footings must be wide and deep enough to keep wall stable and unaffected by soil movement

TYPES OF FENCE

FENCES come in a wide range of styles and use a variety of materials, namely wire, concrete, plastic and timber. Forms of fencing available include such options as two or three lengths of sturdy wire threaded through upright posts, chain link fencing and ready-made wooden panels, among many others; and prices vary considerably, according to the type of fence chosen.

Post and chain fencing

❀ Post and chain fencing marks a boundary and deters people from straying from a path on to a lawn or flowerbed, but affords no additional privacy or enhanced security.

❀ Lengths of metal or plastic chain, which are available in several link types and colors, are suspended between wooden or metal posts. The most commonly used arrangement is a black-painted metal chain of oval links, alternating with diamond spikes, hung from white-painted posts.

Trellis fencing

❀ Trellis fencing has become increasingly popular in recent years. Used to divide the garden into separate areas, conceal unsightly views or top a solid fence, trellis is comparatively inexpensive, easy to install, wonderfully compatible with planting and suitable for many situations, since it allows light and air to pass freely through it.

❀ Trellis comes in many styles, sizes and variants – from rustic larch poles, which give a quaint, country cottage feel, to sophisticated shapes in smooth wood.

❀ The method of installing trellis will depend on the type used. Insubstantial concertina-fold trellis needs to be housed in a stout holding frame for added stability, whereas split larch poles, nailed on to sturdy posts and rails properly installed in the ground, produces a stable and attractive fence.

Closeboard fencing

❀ Closeboard fencing consists of vertically overlapped wooden featherboard strips, nailed on to horizontal rails. Cedar is the best quality wood for this, and is correspondingly expensive. Softwood is the more affordable option.

❀ Both types are attractive and strong and provide a high degree of privacy. Because the strips are vertical, the fence is not easy to climb, deterring children from attempting to scale it. Closeboard fencing is a good but expensive option for adding privacy to a sloping garden. It can be erected *in situ* – or made from 'off-the-peg' panels.

Picket fencing

❀ Picket, or palisade fencing, particularly when painted white, immediately conjures up images of country cottages and old-fashioned charm.

❀ Narrow vertical pales are spaced approximately 2 in (5cm) apart, attached to horizontal rails. The tops of the pales may be pointed, rounded, or cut into decorative shapes such as Gothic-style finials. This fencing is highly decorative and is used primarily as an ornamental way of marking a boundary rather than to provide privacy, since it is open, and is also usually no more than 4 ft (1.2m) high.

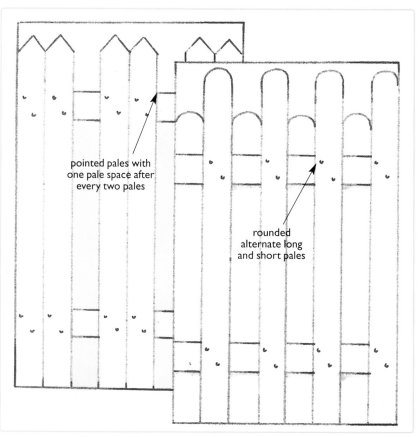

pointed pales with one pale space after every two pales

rounded alternate long and short pales

Ranch-style fencing

❀ As its name suggests, ranch-style fencing brings to mind the wide open spaces of the American plains. It is simply constructed from wide horizontal rails attached to stout boards. Made in soft- or hardwood, it may be painted or simply treated with weatherproofing.

❀ Low-maintenance plastic ranch-style fencing is also available. Removed from a large-scale, ranch-style context of bordering a field, this type of fencing can look somewhat oversized and municipal, and affords no privacy.

❀ This style of fencing is also irresistible to children as a ready made climbing frame and to passing adults as a convenient leaning post and makeshift seat; these are points worth considering if your boundary lies next to a bus stop or telephone booth. Finding that you have spent a considerable amount of time and money in installing what is in effect a public bench could prove very irritating.

ANATOMY OF A FENCE

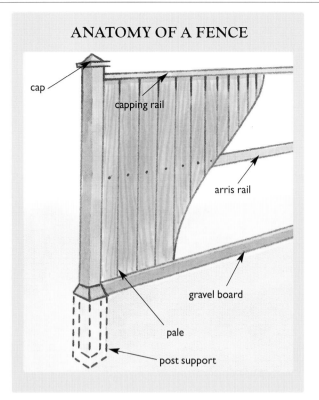

cap

capping rail

arris rail

gravel board

pale

post support

BUILDING A PICKET FENCE

Fence posts must be extremely sturdy and firmly positioned when constructing a fence.

1 Sink each post at least 24 in (60 cm) into the ground for good stability. Metal post spikes remove the need for digging and concreting as they are simply hammered into position, but are suitable only for firm ground. If you are not using metal spikes, you will need to dig a hole, fill the bottom with compacted hard core, then concrete the fence post in place. Chamfer off the concrete just above ground level.

2 Fix the arris rails to the fence posts. Fix the pickets to the arris rails, taking care to place them evenly.

3 Use a picket to act as a spacing guide. Keep the top of the pickets level by working to a string line suspended between the fence posts.

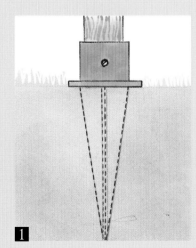

1

2

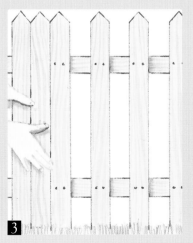

3

PANEL FENCES

FENCES made from ready-made panels nailed between wooden posts are popular because they offer a reasonable level of privacy at relatively little expense, and are quite simple to erect. Various types are available.

Interwoven panels

❀ These are made of thin wooden strips woven between vertical stiffeners to produce a closed, but not totally occlusive fence. Choose good-quality interwoven panels with strips that fit tightly against each other, since the wood may shrink back in the summer and leave unsightly gaps.

Hurdle fencing

❀ Hurdle fencing is another type of interwoven panel, made from strips of flexible branches such as willow woven horizontally around sturdy upright wooden poles. It is an effective windbreak, since some air is allowed to pass through it.

❀ Hurdle fencing has become increasingly popular in garden design because it gives instant rustic appeal at comparatively low cost, and is made from natural materials from renewable sources.

ABOVE: *Ready made panel fences are a popular choice, since they are reasonably cheap to buy and easy to erect.*

❀ Although not as permanent an investment as a brick wall or closeboard fence, hurdle panels will last for several years, and make very pretty garden screening. Short hurdle fences are perfect for edging borders, and can be made *in situ* or bought ready-made.

Horizontally lapped panels

❀ Slightly more expensive than interwoven panels, these are more durable and offer greater privacy, since there are no gaps for prying eyes to peep through. Strips of wood, usually larch, are overlapped horizontally, and held between a sawn timber frame.

❀ The strips may have a smooth, straight edge or, for a more informal feel, are available with undulating edges with or without the bark attached.

Vertically lapped panels

❀ Self-descriptive, these panels of overlapping vertical strips, attached to a frame, make a durable, peep-proof fence, which mimics closeboard fencing. Choose good-quality panels that are well overlapped so that gaps do not appear as the wood shrinks with changing weather conditions.

Interlap fencing

❀ Interlap fencing consists of square-edged boards nailed to horizontal rails, and fixed on alternating sides. It is a popular choice for an exposed site, as it is sturdy, yet wind is allowed to pass through the gaps between the boards.

LEFT: *The appearance of panel fencing is greatly improved by sympathetic planting.*

❀ Where wind is not a problem the boards may be spaced as you wish – overlapped for more privacy, or spaced more widely to allow light to pass through. The construction method means that interlap fencing is equally attractive on both sides – another reason for its popularity.

Chestnut palings

❀ Sold by the roll, this consists of a series of parallel chestnut stakes, fixed together top and bottom with lengths of twisted wire to form a cheap fence.

❀ Attached to sturdy posts at 6 ft (1.8 m) intervals, chestnut palings produce an effective barrier, but do not offer increased privacy. Although not particularly attractive, this type of fencing is light, easy to transport and install, and blends quiet inconspicuously into its surroundings, especially if softened by planting.

Post and wire fencing

❀ Post and wire fencing comprises two or three lengths of sturdy wire stretched between strong posts of wood, concrete or steel and kept taut by straining bolts.

❀ The posts must be firmly fixed and well supported. The end posts will need supportive struts. Although privacy and security are not improved by this type of fence, it is an inexpensive, unobtrusive way of marking a boundary while a hedge is growing, as it also offers good support for the hedge itself.

Chain link fencing

❀ Chain link fencing comprises plastic-coated or galvanised wire mesh, attached to firm posts of wood or concrete. Choose a mesh color that tones in with its surroundings.

❀ This fence type is familiar in municipal settings. Not the most attractive boundary option, it does offer optimum light transmission, some measure of additional security and is comparatively cheap and easy to install.

Wire picket fencing

❀ Plastic-coated wire hoops are linked together and fixed on to posts to make a discreet fence, which does not improve security or privacy but is a popular, inexpensive way of marking out boundaries and, in particular, flower borders and beds.

❀ The posts need to be sturdy and well fixed, and the wire panel held taut between them. Miniature versions are available for edging borders and paths at ankle height.

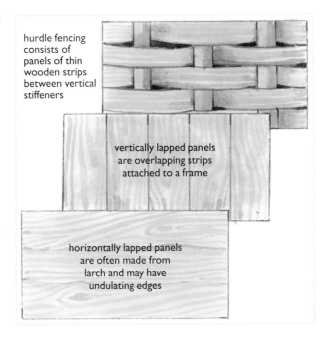

hurdle fencing consists of panels of thin wooden strips between vertical stiffeners

vertically lapped panels are overlapping strips attached to a frame

horizontally lapped panels are often made from larch and may have undulating edges

Concrete fencing

❀ This fence is a popular choice in municipal applications, valued for its minimal maintenance requirements and ease of installation compared with a brick wall.

❀ Slabs of interlocking concrete are slid horizontally between grooves in pre-formed concrete posts to make a solid, masonry wall that does not need foundations as brick walls do. It is difficult to climb, so enhances security, but blocks out light, is brutally unattractive and is also quite expensive.

BELOW: *A white painted heavy wooden wall can reflect the light in strong sunshine.*

ARCHES AND PERGOLAS

ARCHES and pergolas offer great opportunities for adding height to a garden, as well as providing additional planting surfaces and helping to divide the garden visually, so that the whole vista is not taken in at a glance.

Which to choose

❀ Arches are comparatively narrow, while pergolas are essentially a single wide arch, or several arches linked together to form a garden corridor.

❀ Both arches and pergolas can encourage the eye to move through the garden more slowly by offering varying heights and making much more of the available space. These versatile structures can also encourage the eye to linger when appropriate, giving added visual impact, for example by placing a statue beneath an arch placed in front of a hedge.

Siting arches

❀ Always place arches so that they appear to have a definite purpose. All too often, an arch is purchased as an impulse buy, with little thought given to its appropriate site, and it ends up placed awkwardly in the middle of a lawn.

❀ As a rule, arches look most natural if they appear to lead somewhere, such as from a flower garden into a vegetable plot. Alternatively, arches can be used as a kind of picture frame, emphasising a particular feature, for example an arch fronting a scented flowering hedge, with an attractive seat placed thoughtfully below it.

ABOVE: *A pergola clothed in flowers adds height, drama and a valuable additional planting surface to the garden, as well as providing shade on hot days.*

BELOW: *The simple shape of the pergola can be greatly augmented by planting flowering climbers at each of the four corner bases.*

Siting pergolas

❀ Pergolas need to be placed with equal sensitivity. A large pergola in the middle of nowhere can simply look like the skeleton of an unfinished building, instead of the striking garden feature you envisaged.

❀ Used for centuries to adorn long pathways, and often clad in wisteria or roses in large-scale formal gardens, pergolas have enjoyed a recent renaissance in more domestic settings. This is partly due to the increased availability of do-it-yourself pergola kits and because pergolas provide the sort of semi-covered environment ideally suited to al fresco eating.

❀ Lean-to pergolas are increasingly popular, as they form a visual link between the house and the garden and, when planted, can shade a patio used for entertaining.

Choosing arches and pergolas

❀ There are many materials and styles of arch and pergola available, including simple, inexpensive tubular metal curves, more ornate wrought-iron structures in Gothic-style shapes, and a variety of natural materials such as willow and the ever-popular rustic arch, consisting of split lengths of wood fixed to wooden poles in a trellis formation.

❀ Wooden arches and pergolas are also available in kit form. These are not expensive, and they save a considerable amount of laborious calculus. The selection of wooden components at most garden and do-it-yourself stores can be quite bewildering, and it

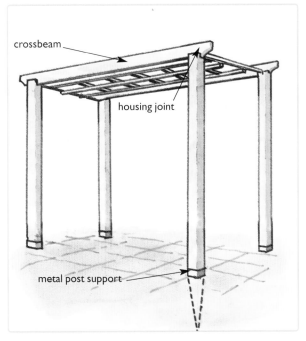

ABOVE: *Although imposing, pergolas are essentially very simple structures comprising vertical posts linked by cross beams, using halving joints at each intersection.*

can be difficult for the busy gardener to plan and translate such pieces into a single three-dimensional structure.

❀ Plant arches are very attractive, but obviously take time to become established – for example box hedging cut into archways, or willow planted and trained to form a living arch.

❀ Moon gates are circular arches popular in Oriental gardens, which are slowly becoming fashionable internationally, especially when used in conjunction with water as a striking visual feature. Brick and stone archways usually form part of a wall, and are often seen in large, formal gardens. They are an expensive and permanent option.

❀ Always make sure that you choose an arch of sufficient width to allow for a smooth passageway through it, even when it is covered with mature planting. As a rough guide, a reasonable internal height is 7 ft (2 m), and 4 ft (1.2 m) will be a sufficient internal width.

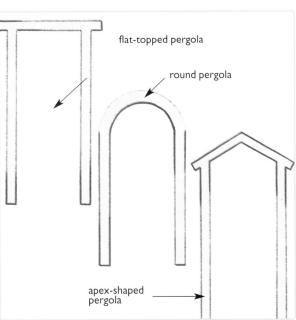

LEFT: *Pergolas are usually flat-topped, because this shape is simple to manufacture, but rounded and apex-shaped pergolas are also available, and can look much softer than the square profile.*

PROTECTIVE FINISHES, CLEANING AND MAINTENANCE

Fences and other boundaries can be such a dominant part of a garden that it is important to maintain them properly. A collapsing, rotten fence is not the sort of visual highlight you want to draw attention to. Happily, if care is taken at the time of installation and, where appropriate, maintenance is carried out routinely, most fences and walls should remain attractive and functional for many years.

WOODEN FENCING

Fences are often neglected until a problem occurs, for example parts of it blowing over in a gale. Careful installation obviously helps to prevent such accidents. Ensuring that a fence is properly supported by appropriately secured posts at the outset will save a lot of remedial work.

Choosing a fence

✿ Choosing a fence that suits your needs will also determine the level of maintenance needed. For example, with an inadequately supported solid fence on an exposed site, it is almost inevitable that, sooner or later, panels are going to get damaged and displaced by high winds, which cannot move freely through the impenetrable barrier.

ABOVE: *The increasingly wide range of paints and preservatives available for exterior use has made it possible to unleash your wildest flights of decorating fancy in the garden as well as on the living-room walls.*

Stopping the rot

✿ Rot is the chief enemy of wooden fencing. Treat wood with an appropriate preservative annually, or at least every two years. Well-maintained wood should last for between 15 and 25 years. Softwoods, such as pine or larch, are obviously not as durable as more costly hardwoods like oak and beech.

✿ Water-based treatments should be chosen where the fence is in contact with plants. Manufactured fences and panels are generally sold already treated with preservative, but if you are creating your own fence from bare timber, you will need to treat it yourself.

✿ Pay special attention to particularly vulnerable areas, such as post ends, end grain and all parts of the fence that are at, or will be below, soil level. It is worth soaking the parts of the fence that will be below ground in

LEFT: *Applying the right protective finish to a well-prepared surface can prevent your garden buildings from becoming unsightly and unstable.*

preservative for at least 10 minutes, and preferably for an hour or so. To immerse whole lengths of timber, use an old bath, or make a temporary bath out of heavy-duty polythene sheeting supported by piled-up bricks.

Types of preservative

❀ As well as the preservatives in colors designed to replicate the shades of pricy hardwoods on inexpensive softwoods, a wide range of other colors is now available.

❀ Gardeners have increasingly come to consider the garden more as an outdoor room than as a separate entity, and judicious use of color on hard surfaces, as well as in planting, can harmonise the soft and hard elements of the garden, as well as linking the garden visually with the house.

❀ Soft blues work surprisingly well in combination with planting, and the whole spectrum of greens is obviously a natural and discreet choice. Clear preservatives are popular, too, allowing the natural grain of the wood to show through. Most preservatives offer protection against insect attack, as well as warding off fungal disease.

Brick and stone walls

❀ If you are planning to paint masonry, always leave at least three months after installation before applying any further treatment, so that the wall has a proper chance to dry out. Impatience may lead to all your carefully applied paint or plaster falling off the wall as it dries.

Efflorescence

❀ Do not be alarmed if you see white deposits defacing the surface of new brickwork. This is the water-soluble salts within the bricks coming to the surface as the wall dries out. The salts crystallise and form a white film on the wall's surface. Simply brush the deposits away with a wire brush or a piece of old sacking. Do not use water as this will bring new salts to the surface, aggravating the problem.

❀ Efflorescence will generally be a problem only for a couple of years on a new, freestanding wall, but the moisture behind a soil-retaining wall may cause a recurrence of the salts over many years. If you want to paint a wall that has been efflorescing with oil-based products, wait until the wall has dried out completely, and treat with an alkaline-resistant primer to neutralise the effects of the soluble salts before painting.

❀ Alternatively, use a paint specially formulated for this purpose, and which includes a primer. Water-based products are not adversely affected by alkaline salts, so the priming step can be omitted if such products are being used.

BELOW: *Always leave a newly constructed wall for at least three months before applying any treatment and brush any efflorescence off with a brush for a perfect finish.*

MAINTAINING LAWNS

A good lawn is an attractive feature but a poor one can
be a real eyesore. On clay soils in wet districts, for example, a really
green, healthy lawn is difficult to achieve. Many people tend to take up
unsatisfactory lawns and lay bricks or paving instead. However, if you
garden on clay and really would like to have an area of lawn, you can
lay new turfs on rafts of sand and rubble to ensure good drainage.
Lawns should be very slightly sloping to prevent waterlogging.
Aim for a minimum slope of 1 in 80 and a maximum slope of 1 in 4.
Steeper gradients are better terraced.

ABOVE: *A tiny tree in a lawn should not adversely affect the grass growth. This maple makes a stunning contrast against a green backcloth of foliage.*

Grass for lawns

❀ There are different mixtures of grass for different
situations. For example, some will stand up to bikes and
ball games, some will grow satisfactorily in light shade
and some will produce the sort of velvety green suitable
for putting greens but are not so resilient as the others.

Lawn shape

❀ Although a rectangle is probably the most common
shape for lawns, it is often more pleasing to have an oval,
circular or irregularly shaped lawn. Avoid small and fussy
curves and awkward corners, which are very difficult to
maintain and mow.

❀ If you want to include island beds, make sure the verges
are wide enough to take a mower. When deciding where
the lawn should go, remember that all parts of a lawn
need to receive some direct sunlight during the day so
try not to choose too shady a part of the garden.

Access to the lawn

❀ You should be able to reach the lawn from several
angles. If you approach the lawn along only one path or
one small entrance or gateway, the soil will become
compacted and the grass worn and brown. Paths should
run alongside the lawn rather than across it, unless you
choose to lay concrete stepping stones.

ABOVE: *Lawns do best under lightly canopied trees. This lawn is flourishing under silver birches.*

❀ A path between a lawn and a flowerbed can be useful in wet weather, and summer flowers tumbling over a path do look attractive. Lay paths and stepping stones below the level of the lawn and leave a narrow grass-free mowing edge between the lawn and path to make mowing and edging easier.

❀ Avoid using loose chippings as a material for paths next to a lawn. They inevitably get kicked on to the grass and will damage the mower blades.

Lawns under trees

❀ Lawns will not thrive beneath a dense canopy of leaves. Shortage of light and water and the dripping from the edges of the trees will make it difficult for the grass to grow. It will end up thin and wispy and moss will soon encroach.

❀ Cutting the lower branches and shortening the higher ones may help a little but you are still never likely to achieve a good lawn. The best thing is to remove the turf completely from around the tree trunks and create a large bed for bulbs such as hardy cyclamen and crocuses and shade-loving plants such as periwinkles (*Vinca*) and dead-nettles (*Lamium*).

ABOVE: *A well-situated lawn can be used as an outdoor room with judicious use of sunlight and shade and comfortable garden furniture.*

❀ Specimen trees can look marvellous when planted in a large expanse of green lawn. If you want to plant a tree in a small lawn, choose a small tree such as the cut-leaf Japanese maple (*Acer palmatum* 'Dissectum'), which will take 20 years to grow to 5 ft (1.5 m). *Acer japonicum* 'Aureum' will grow to 10 ft (3 m) and has attractive leaves, which provide color from early spring to early fall.

The non-grass lawn

❀ Although grass is certainly the most reliable material for a lawn, you can create small areas of lawn with other plants such as camomile or thyme. They do not have the resilience of grass and should not be walked on too much.

❀ A good place might be at the base of a fountain or in the center of a circular herb bed. A popular plant for this kind of use is *Anthemis nobilis*.

BUILDING HARD SURFACES

The garden floor can be a very dominant element in a garden design, yet its planning is all too often neglected in favor of perhaps the more exciting part of gardening –planting. Although most gardeners take great pride in their lawns, which are, essentially, living, green garden floors, the same attention is not lavished on hard-floored areas. An expanse of grey concrete, interrupted only by the odd weed, is not going to enhance any garden. The visual impact of hard flooring, particularly in large-scale applications such as driveways and patios, is often not considered until installation is complete, by which time it is too late to change your mind.

The planning stage

❀ Take home as many samples of hard flooring as you need, and view them *in situ* for several days before making a decision. Since hard surfaces are a critical part of the permanent structure of a garden design, highly visible even when most of the plants are dormant, you need to choose the material according to the style of your garden and house, as well as for practical and economical reasons.

❀ A path of modern grey slabs will clearly do nothing to enhance a 18th-century red-brick house. Equally, a herringbone path of weathered old paving bricks would look wildly uncomfortable in an austere urban setting.

❀ As well as being a prominent visual feature, hard surfaces are important practical components within the garden. They work hard for their keep, yet are often ignored until problems occur, such as frozen puddles in a pathway which trip up the unwary

ABOVE: *Plan your terracing carefully to maximise sunlight and create different flooring patterns and levels to add interest to the area.*

ABOVE: *Cobbles are uncomfortable to walk on, so stepping stones provide a welcome contrasting surface.*

ABOVE: *Gravel is an inexpensive yet elegant garden flooring material.*

pedestrian. Proper planning at the outset, choosing materials appropriate to the situation and purpose, and simple routine maintenance, will give you a garden floor to be proud of.

❀ The type of material you choose for a path or drive will largely depend on its primary function. For example, a path intended chiefly for decoration, which will barely be walked on, will have quite different demands placed on it than the walkway that leads to your front door.

Practical matters

❀ Consider whether your preferred material is suitable for the design of your path, drive or other hard surfaced area. For example, gravel or flagstone paving can easily be used to make an intricately winding path, but to produce an undulating narrow shape in large paving slabs would involve a lot of tedious calculation and cutting, and would not necessarily look natural or comfortable on completion.

❀ It may sound obvious, but make sure that your hard surfaces are adequately sized for their function. As a rough guide, paths need to be at least 3 ft (1 m) wide to allow comfortable access. Do not assume, if you are replacing an existing hard surface, that you automatically lay a new surface the same size as the old one. It is all too easy to have a driveway or parking space professionally, and expensively, laid only to find that it is too small for your car, or too cramped to allow room for your vehicle and pedestrian access around it.

❀ Mark out your proposed design with rope or a hose, or by dropping dry sand through a funnel to leave a trail. Check out the area from every angle, preferably over a period of a few days. This is especially important in areas like patios, which are garden rooms as well as hard surfaces.

❀ You will want to make sure that the area you are planning to use for entertaining receives the kind of light you want, at the time of day the patio will most commonly be used. For example, if you are installing a patio chiefly for early evening dining, there is no point placing it next to the house if the sunlight is at the other end of your garden at that time.

TYPES OF HARD SURFACE

THERE are a number of options to choose from, when it comes to creating a hard floor in your garden.

Bricks

❀ It is tempting to economise on bricks for paving, but the shortcomings of using ordinary house bricks for this demanding function become clear all too quickly. Their porosity means that as water penetrates, freezes, then expands, it cracks away the layers of brick, creating an uneven, flaky, broken surface. This is unsightly and can also be dangerous to walk on, particularly when used as steps.

❀ Engineering bricks are often specified for paving instead, as they are much denser and impervious to water. However, they can become slippery when wet, so 'special' quality bricks are the recommended choice. These are also weather resistant, but are not so prone to weather damage.

❀ Second-hand bricks make a very attractive path, which tones in well with old buildings, but always check that you are buying proper pavers, not simply old house bricks sold as pavers. Insist on a written description if possible. Reliable architectural salvage companies are generally quite happy to provide such a guarantee, since they should be aware of the provenance of the salvaged material.

Stone

❀ Natural stone, once the first choice in path making, has been superseded in popularity by cast alternatives, due to the high cost of the real thing.

❀ Flagstones of slate, limestone or sandstone are exceptionally beautiful, as well as hard-wearing, and can be chosen to complement the local stone. Being of natural origin, they also harmonise wonderfully with plant, water and other organic garden elements. Their irregular surface and random patterning can never truly be mimicked by cast alternatives, but the difficulty of cutting them and their expense place them firmly in the luxury bracket.

Cobblestones

❀ The naturally rounded surface of cobblestones makes them uncomfortable to walk on, so their use is best restricted to ornamental applications. You could break up an expanse of paving slabs by interspersing the slabbed area with areas of cobblestones. They provide an interesting shift in texture, and complement planting well.

❀ Cobbles may be laid loose, or set in concrete or mortar for a more permanent, formal effect. Always ensure that the tops of the stones are level for an even finish for walking on.

Wood and bark

❀ Natural materials are particularly appropriate and attractive in a woodland, or semi-wild setting, which would look uncomfortable paved with a harsh, non-organic surface such as concrete. Sawn rounds of timber are surprisingly hard-wearing as pavers if they are well treated by soaking in preservative prior to installation, then laid on a bed of sand on top of perforated polythene sheeting.

❀ Fill the gaps between the circles with a sand and gravel mix or chipped bark. Bark needs refilling up every few years as it slowly degrades. Wooden decking is increasingly popular as exterior flooring, and looks equally good in urban or country locations. Wooden rounds are also often used as stepping stones across a lawn.

ABOVE: *Decking is a decidedly contemporary flooring material, ideally suited to modern urban gardens.*

Concrete

❀ Concrete may not be the most attractive hard garden surface, but it is probably the most durable, relatively inexpensive, maintenance free if properly installed and suitable for awkward shapes such as winding paths and driveways.

❀ Essentially, concrete consists of cement combined with an aggregate (fine particles of stone). These dry ingredients are mixed with water, which reacts chemically with the cement and binds the stone particles into a firm, compacted material capable of withstanding tough treatment.

❀ Various mixtures of concrete are used, incorporating, for example, PVA to enhance frost resistance, and/or pigments to produce colors other than the usual grey.

❀ For small jobs, concrete can be mixed by hand, but for more extensive areas, it is well worth hiring a concrete mixer, or having ready-mixed concrete delivered direct to the site. Careful preparation of the site is critical. All too often, concrete is seen as the easy paving option, but if added to an unstable, inadequately prepared surface, the results will be unsatisfactory.

❀ Concrete is also available formed into cast slabs, which can mimic real stone. These provide a popular, affordable alternative to real stone paving.

Gravel

❀ Gravel is another popular, affordable and versatile material. It can withstand heavy use on a driveway, yet is equally suited to small-scale settings such as walkways through a herb garden. Gravel is easy to install, even in curved situations, but for best effect needs to be placed on a proper bed of consolidated coarse gravel.

brick patterns

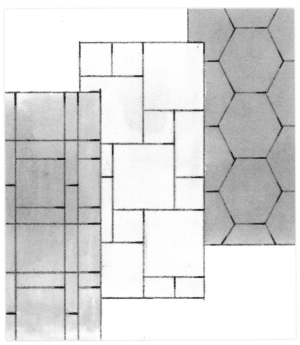

paving slab patterns

decking patterns

PATIOS

ALTHOUGH, technically, a patio is an area paved with flagstones, enclosed by walls, it has come to be used as a generic term for a hard-surfaced area, usually, but not always, adjoining a house, which is used for relaxing and entertaining. Installing a patio is quite a major undertaking, and needs extremely careful planning and preparation. Mistakes are costly, and permanent.

Customising an existing patio

❀ You may have inherited a patio that is technically sound, and performs its practical function perfectly, but which is bland and uninspiring. Sympathetic planting can do much to improve matters, without extensive structural work.

❀ Container plants look thoroughly at home on patios, and can be changed seasonally. Choose the style and materials of the containers to link the patio with the house.

❀ Removing some of the slabs and replacing them with planting, and/or other surfaces, such as cobbles, broken slate, gravel or colored aggregate, will also enliven the overall scheme. You could also introduce vertical elements to break up an overlarge expanse of paving, for example trellis, a pergola, raised beds that incorporate seating, or simply a stunning table, chairs and parasol.

ABOVE: *This colorful patio appears at first glance to be stone, but it is decking interwoven with blue strips of wood and small clumps of herbs.*

ABOVE: *Although patios were originally made up of stone flags, nowadays more and more people are opting for wooden decking.*

PLANNING A PATIO

THERE is a surprising amount to think about when planning a patio, if you want to create a feature that will be as visually attractive as it is practical. It is easy to be swayed into buying a load of paving because it appealed on one sunny afternoon in the garden center, or was on special offer, only to find that it is quite unsuitable when installed.

Site

❀ Of course, a patio adjoining the house is ideal. Food, drinks, books and cushions may be easily transported between house and garden, particularly if you are fortunate enough to have French doors that lead directly on to the patio.

❀ However, if the area that initially suggests itself as the patio site is very shaded at the time of day that you plan to use it most, you may want to think about having an additional hard-surfaced area elsewhere in the garden. If the problem is one of light shade, caused by overhanging foliage, then the answer may be as simple as pruning back unwanted growth.

❀ If wind is a problem, but the site is otherwise perfect, then consider installing some form of windbreak, for

ABOVE: *The word patio is now a generic term for a hard-surfaced area that is used for relaxing and entertaining.*

example a semi-permeable natural screen such as hurdle fencing, bamboo or an interwoven fence. Privacy may also be an important issue, particularly if you plan to sunbathe and relax on your patio, yet your garden is exposed. Again, natural or artificial screens can come into their own here.

Size

❀ It may sound obvious, but check that the size of patio you are planning is adequate for your needs. If you just want to sit outside and read occasionally, then technically you will need only a quite limited space, but if you enjoy container gardening, you may want to increase the patio to accommodate significant numbers of sizeable plants.

❀ If you plan to cook outside frequently – perhaps on a large gas-fired barbecue or outdoor stove – and entertain on a regular basis, your requirements will be quite different. You will need space for a table and chairs that will comfortably accommodate your guests, together with space for food cooking and preparation.

Patio surfaces

❀ Once you have established what the patio is mostly going to be used for, where it is going to be, and how big it needs to be, you can at last turn your attention to how it is going to look. The general guidelines on the previous pages on choosing materials still apply.

❀ Choose a surface to suit your home. Patios are a dominant visual feature, and can just as easily detract from the beauty and value of your home as they can add to it. Do not be tempted to mix too many types of surface in an effort to add interest. By the time a patio has dining seats, sun loungers, perhaps more than one table, possibly lighting, screening, maybe a water feature, together with a barbecue and all the other paraphernalia that tends to accumulate on a patio, it will quickly become very busy looking and is unlikely to need much in the way of added interest underfoot.

❀ Two surfaces are probably the most you will need to create a dynamic, but balanced and restrained patio, for example slabs interspersed with pebbles and planting, or wooden decking bordered by gravel.

PATHS

PATHS are hard-working surfaces. They carry not only foot traffic, but often wheelbarrows, heavily loaded sack trolleys and bicycles, too. They may also be required to permit the regular use of wheelchairs or a stroller. If planning a garden from scratch, these individual needs can be catered for.

Choosing a path

❀ Always make the path sufficiently wide for its purpose. Ideally, two people should be able to walk along a path, side by side, without any sense of being cramped.

❀ Choose materials suited to the surroundings, as well as to the practical requirements placed on them. For example, a asphalt path may be inexpensive and hard-wearing, but will be an unforgiving feature leading up to your front door. It may be worth investing in a more attractive surface for such a prominent position.

Gravel paths

❀ Washed gravel is an attractive and inexpensive paving material. The ideal size of stone is approximately $^3/_4$ in (2 cm) in diameter. This generally presents the least problems in terms of stones being brought into the house via shoes.

ABOVE: *Paths should always be planned according to individual requirements; consider what your needs are before deciding on the style of walkway that would suit you best.*

ABOVE: *Here the blue of the sea and gentle pink of the flowers in the background are reflected in the soft colors of the paving on the terrace.*

Brick paths

❀ Brick paths are particularly attractive and, if created using bricks sympathetic to those used for the house, provide a strong yet unobtrusive visual link between the house and garden. They may be laid in a variety of patterns, including straight or angled herringbone, basket weave and stretcher bond.

Concrete paving

❀ Concrete is an enduringly popular choice for paving. It is relatively inexpensive, yet very durable. Concrete is only hard-wearing if it is installed properly, so careful planning is essential before starting to prepare the path.

❀ Concrete is a much maligned surface, decried for its bland grey appearance. However, a well-laid concrete path can, in some cases, be more attractive than a more showy surface of ill-proportioned, poorly installed, over-bright imitation stone slabs, which may have cost much more.

Textural possibilities

❀ You can vary the surface texture of a finished concrete path for added visual interest. The natural surface that results from the tamping process, which completes the path laying, is practical and non-slip, with a slightly rough texture.

❀ The setting concrete may be dragged with a broom to create a subtly striped, rippled finish, or swept with a wooden float for a smooth finish that works well in stark, modern settings. Another option is to mimic the effects of flagstone paving by marking the surface of the concrete with a stick to resemble irregularly shaped slabs.

✿ Embedding a decorative aggregate in the surface of the concrete is another option. Scatter dampened pebbles on to the newly laid concrete and tamp with timber until flush with the surface. When all surface water has evaporated, gently wash away cement from around the pebbles until they protrude. An alternative textural finish is achieved by simply washing away the fine surface of the setting concrete to reveal the gravel below.

LAYING A BRICK PATH

Brick paths need to be laid on a 3 in (7.5 cm) thick, compacted hard core base, topped with a 2-in (5-cm) thick layer of sharp sand.

1 *Support the bricks with a permanent edging such as timber or a row of bricks set on end into concrete.*

2 *Set the bricks with fine sand and water well. Ensure that the sand packs down between the bricks. Repeat until the cracks are packed.*

LAYING A GRAVEL PATH

Prepare a site for gravel well. Edging, to contain the gravel, is very important. Bricks laid on their edge and set in concrete are popular edgings.

1 *Thoroughly compact the hard core surface for the path, then top it with a 2-in (5-cm) deep layer of coarse gravel.*

2 *Follow this with a layer of clay binder, spread it to fill any cracks, then roll it. Finally, add a 1–1½ in (2.5–4 cm) layer of washed gravel and roll this, too.*

LAYING CONCRETE PAVING SLABS

Paving slabs are widely available. Choose a finish sympathetic to your garden style for best results. Laying heavy slabs is simple but hard work.

1 *Take care to set out the slabs and lay them properly for best results. Try to use only whole slabs to avoid the need for cutting slabs.*

2 *Lay paving slabs on a firm, level base of hard-core topped with sharp sand and tamp them down. A slight, even slope will be needed to allow water to run off the surface. Paint with mortar after a couple of days*

DRIVEWAYS

DRIVEWAYS have the toughest hard-surface job of all. They need to be able to withstand heavy, continual traffic. Gravel is an attractive, relatively inexpensive material for driveways and makes a satisfying crunch as you park. Concrete is a popular alternative. Commercial contractors can install concrete drives imprinted with patterns. These can be more attractive than flat concrete drives, yet less expensive than specialist individual bricks or slabs.

Planning driveways

❀ It may sound obvious that the first step in planning a driveway or car parking pad is to ascertain how big the area needs to be, yet it is alarmingly easy to underestimate the amount of space that a vehicle occupies. As a general rule, a minimum width of 10 ft (3 m) is required, but this will vary according to your individual needs – you may regularly need to park a much larger vehicle in your garden. Consider, too, the turning circle of your vehicle.

❀ You may not have unlimited space for a drive, but if you do have a little more than the bare minimum available to give over to a drive, life will be very much more convenient for you. Imagine not having to shout at your children about banging the car doors against the wall or fence on a daily basis, and you might resent less having to give over a little of your garden to the car.

❀ A very easy mistake to make is to forget to allow for opening the car doors, which becomes a real problem if the driveway is close to a wall. Ideally, also allow plenty of space for pedestrian access around parked cars. If you know that strollers and bikes are going to be wheeled past your parked car regularly, it is well worth incorporating a little extra space into your driveway to avoid frayed tempers

ABOVE: *Be prepared to cut back on your borders to allow space for your parking area.*

as the paint gets repeatedly scraped away from the side of the car by an exuberant young cyclist.

❀ It is tempting to make driveways as small as possible, since they are not generally things of inherent loveliness. However, if you refuse to move your flowerbed a single inch to accommodate a reasonably sized driveway, you may find your precious perennials destroyed anyway, as people scramble out of the car and across the ornamental borders.

RIGHT: *A hard-working driveway is softened visually by a curved edge and planted border.*

The importance of slope

❀ Parking areas and driveways must have a sufficient slope to allow water to fall away, so that the surface retains enough traction for vehicles in icy conditions. You do not want puddles forming in the drive, so the surface needs to be absolutely even. When a concrete parking area is laid next to a house, it must slope away markedly from the building for good drainage.

❀ As a general guide to the degree of fall-off required, a drive needs a 1-in-40 gradient – 1 in per yard (2.5 cm per metre) to be effective. A hard surface such as a parking area or patio installed next to a house needs a 1-in-60 gradient – $^5/_8$ in per yard (1.6 cm per metre).

PREVENTING CONCRETE FROM CRACKING

TEMPERATURE changes cause concrete to expand and contract. If this motion is allowed to continue randomly, the surface will crack open at its weakest point. Control joints, also known as expansion joints, made of compressible material such as wooden planks, are added at regular intervals to concentrate or absorb the force of the contraction and expansion.

Pathways need control joints at approximately 7-ft (2-m) intervals, while driveways need such joints every 13 ft (4 m). If a parking area is more than twice as long as its width, or its length is more than 40 times its thickness, you will need to divide the concrete into equal sections with control joints. Control joints are also always needed between concrete that adjoins a wall, and where concrete surrounds inspection chambers.

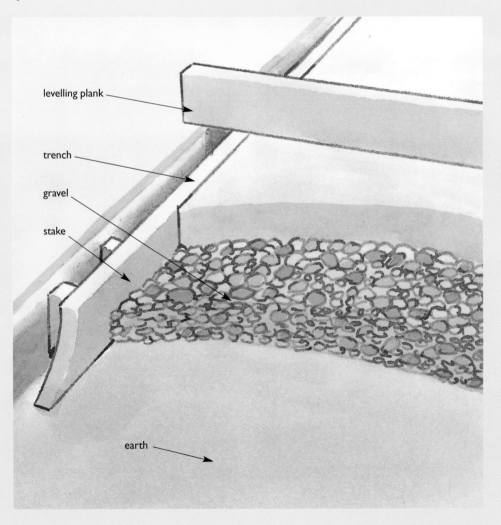

levelling plank

trench

gravel

stake

earth

PAVED AREAS, STEPS AND PATHS

Probably the first step in designing a garden is to incorporate a paved area for relaxation, entertainment and family meals. Paved areas near the house form important transitional meeting places between house and garden. Hard materials carry the architectural feel of the house out of doors. Planted containers and shrubs nearby bring in the garden element. Paths and steps also provide an architectural element and should be carefully planned, as they will become part of the basic framework. Stick to one or two basic materials throughout or the end result will be fussy.

Patio shapes

The shapes you use in all garden spaces will be among the important things that set the style of your garden. A symmetrical arrangement will give the space a formal look, whereas a curving, asymmetrical one will suit a more relaxed style and a geometric asymmetrical one will suit an abstract modern garden.

ABOVE: A small area outside the house has been attractively bricked in a square shape and surrounded by interesting and varied plants. Even the smallest outdoor space can be made into a pleasant spot.

ABOVE: You do not need very much space to create a small oval or circular seating area. This one is gravelled and has mostly green planting with a little seat for contemplation.

❀ If your garden is surrounded by tall buildings, as is likely in an urban setting, straight, geometric lines are likely to work best, as they will complement the lines of the surrounding buildings.

❀ In a small area it is best to stick to one shape, just as it is best to stick to very few materials. It is also best not to try and mix diagonals and curves or squares and circles. Even in larger gardens, there will be better unity and cohesion if you limit the number of different shapes you use.

❀ Once you have decided on the shapes for the paved areas, you can design the patterns for the bricks or paving you are going to use. There is all the difference in the world between well-laid paving in interesting patterns and concrete slabs carelessly placed on the ground.

❀ Paving patterns can be divided into those that are static and those that are dynamic. Static patterns hold the eye within the area and have a peaceful quality. Dynamic patterns lead the eye along a path or paved area with a feeling of movement, an invitation to explore further.

Types of paving

❀ There are numerous forms of paving to choose from. Pre-cast concrete is available in many forms, including slabs that vary in size, shape and thickness. Clay bricks in many colors and dark engineering bricks are suitable

for many areas. Paving blocks and cobbles are ideal for small awkward areas.

❀ Concrete slabs interspersed with small areas of cobbles can break up the blandness of concrete on its own. Some paving materials become slippery when wet; others, like brick, are highly non-slip.

Combining gravel and paving

❀ If you have decided against lawns and soft surfaces in your garden, one paved area can lead to another through a series of enclosures and paths. The whole garden can be given an extended courtyard effect, which will provide plenty of space for sitting and entertaining.

❀ Some of the paving can be given over to gravel, with 'stepping stones' of paving slabs to give a firm foothold and plants growing in the gravel. Many plants like growing through gravel because it drains well but also helps to prevent moisture from evaporating too quickly.

❀ Many alpines and Mediterranean silver-leaved plants flourish and will seed themselves. There are various types of gravel to choose from, including white limestone, white gravel chippings and washed pea shingle, which has rounded edges. It is best not to use white gravel in sunny areas where the light shining on it can make it quite blinding.

ABOVE: *This circular paved area is surrounded by a shady pergola and furnished with folding chairs, which can easily be carried indoors in wet weather.*

DECKING AND OTHER USES FOR TIMBER

TIMBER decking is a natural material with simple lines, which can be practical and attractive in a number of different situations. It is often used as an alternative to paving. The combination of doors, flooring, fencing, furniture and steps all made of wood can help provide a unified look, which is simple and yet stylish. Decking should ideally be made of hardwood, which needs no preservative treatment. Softwood must be planed or it will splinter, and it should be given preservative treatment, which should be repeated at regular intervals. Large areas of decking are not always successful in a cold, damp climate, where the timber may never have the chance to dry out fully and will eventually rot.

Construction

❀ An area of timber decking is not hard to construct. The decking timbers rest on beams and joists supported by posts held in the ground with concrete. This type of construction allows air to circulate, keeping the wood dry unless there are prolonged periods of snow or rain and the atmosphere remains moist.

Raised decking

❀ In the USA older houses were traditionally built with the living area above ground level, leaving space beneath for a cellar and to allow air to circulate. A wooden deck was often built as a way of extending the upper level to create an extra patio area.

❀ Decking is particularly suited to this form of extension because the air circulating around it helps to keep it dry and prevents the wood from rotting. However, it can also be used as a surfacing material at ground level. It is particularly suited to houses with timber clapboarding or shingled roofs and it can give a small space a pleasing look when used in conjunction with wooden fencing.

Decking on roof gardens

❀ Timber is a good material for roof gardens because it is much lighter in weight than other forms of paving. Many flat roofs have not been designed to carry heavy weights and decking will help to balance the weight of people walking on the roof.

❀ Square timber panels, similar in size to paving slabs, can be clamped together to provide flooring. They should be laid on a timber base above the roof finish so that water can drain to a downpipe. Before making any plans for a roof-garden you should find out whether you need permission to use it for this purpose and how much weight the roof can bear.

ABOVE: *Decking tiles in interesting patterns have been used here in geometric arrangements on two levels. Small blue glazed pots hold clipped evergreens that will be attractive all year.*

Decking and water

❀ Timber decking and water always look very natural together and landing stages for river boats have traditionally been made of decking. It can be useful for disguising the edges of artificial pools made with plastic liners and is also ideal for bridges.

❀ A real bridge can be constructed over a small pond or a mock bridge can be built to separate the pond from the water plants, thus making the pool seem bigger than it actually is. A 'landing stage' jutting out over a pond can be finished off with a timber balustrade, giving an attractive bird's eye view of the water. A small hump-backed timber bridge painted rich red is an excellent addition to a Japanese-style garden.

Timber decking in modern designs

❀ The regularly spaced lines created by boards of decking can be used to create exciting and attractive angles and changes of level. Timber decks look good in modern settings and make an excellent foil to plants and containers. Boards can also combine well with gravel, which on its own is not an ideal surface for wheelchairs or delicate shoes.

ABOVE: *This compact and well-stocked roof garden uses decking with rounded sea cobbles to soften it and add interest. A variety of evergreen, variegated and flowering shrubs provide interest all year.*

Wooden paths

❀ Wood is not often used for paths but might be a good choice as a continuation from a bridge or patio made of decking. Discs cut from tree trunks can be set into the ground but these usually look best in a fairly rural setting and are not suitable as a complement to decking used in sophisticated geometrical shapes. Discs are also likely to become slippery in wet weather so could be dangerous underfoot. Coarsely shredded bark can look attractive, although it looks better in a woodland or wild garden setting and is not right for a formal garden.

LEFT: *Decking and water combine well together. Here, decking is used along with brick to surround a pond with its lavish growth of evergreens and windmill-like sails, purposely designed to give shade.*

DEALING WITH AWKWARDLY SHAPED GARDENS

Many gardens are awkwardly shaped. They may be very narrow
or have been awkwardly fitted between buildings.
They may narrow at one end to create a triangular plot.
Basement gardens often have tiny patio spaces with very steep
steps leading to dry gardens overshadowed by neglected trees.
All these problems may be seen as challenges rather than
disadvantages. There are many ways of approaching the solutions.

LONG NARROW GARDENS

GARDENS belonging to row houses are often long and narrow, sometimes almost ribbon-like in shape. The danger with this sort of garden is that it can feel more like a passageway than a garden. The part nearest the house may get used as a sitting-out area, but the rest of the garden is a repository for old furniture, and stinging or prickly weeds. One of the following solutions may suit this sort of garden.

A series of rooms

❀ The most obvious and usually most successful answer is to divide the plot into a series of separate compartments linked by a path. Each compartment can then be filled with a symmetrical design based on a square, a circle or an oval. By dividing the plot in this way you may be able to use the dividing barriers to hide an ugly barbecue or an intrusive large shrub or tree or to disguise a shed or screen a distant telephone pole seen over the garden fence.

❀ The different areas will allow you to do much more with the garden. You might combine a small shrubbery or woodland area in which you could conceal a small shed, with a special play area with a swing and sandpit or a formal water garden with a fountain. If your main interest is in plants and growing things, one of these areas could be a small vegetable plot or could be devoted to growing show flowers.

Geometric divisions

❀ Rather than separating the areas with hedges or shrubs, you could use low walls and paving shapes to create interest and variety. Use diagonal lines, which will help to make the garden seem wider. A diagonal brick-lined pool could face a diagonal brick patio outside the garden door.

❀ A path could lead to the next area, perhaps a small lawn with flowerbeds around it. The path could then lead on to a small barbecue area. To prevent this sort of layout

ABOVE: A raised wooden walkway built about a pond and bog garden allow
the visitor to gaze down on to the water and the spectacular collection of irises.

from seeming too flat, you could add vertical elements at strategic points. These might be small trees or carefully placed shrubs, arches or small pergolas.

❦ Each compartment should invite the visitor in with a visual surprise such as a sculpture, a water feature or an architectural plant and should have some form of seat so that people can stay and enjoy it.

A garden walk

❦ For extra narrow gardens, an alternative to the idea of separate garden spaces is to devote the whole garden to a deliberate garden walk. This will make an advantage of its narrowness. A path leading in gentle curves down the center of the plot will create undulating borders on either side.

❦ Recesses or arbors can be created at intervals, where people can sit and read or relax and savour the flowers and their scents. At the end there should be a reward for those who have made the journey – a pool perhaps, or a fountain or statue. This kind of garden offers opportunities for urns and statuary at intervals along the walk and plenty of opportunities for formal or romantic planting.

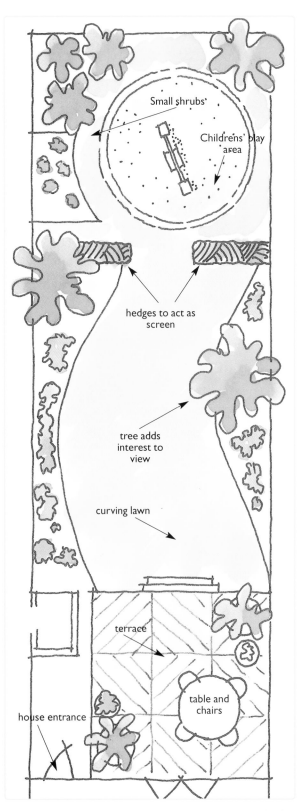

ABOVE: *This garden is long and narrow, like many town gardens. The edges contain plants of varying heights to conceal the edges, and the whole garden has been divided into 'rooms', each with its own character. The patio is near the house, separated from the compost heap by a hedge. The lawn is slightly curved to give a feeling of movement, and the children's play area occupies the end of the garden.*

ABOVE: *Long, narrow gardens can be made to look more spacious by the addition of features such as walkways or recesses and arbors. Perhaps you could place a fountain or a statue at the end.*

TRIANGULAR-SHAPED GARDENS

TRIANGULAR plots are not as unusual as you might think. They are often found where the original building site met a road or a river. This shape can seem limiting and the apex seems to draw the eye uncomfortably, especially if the garden is new and bleak, surrounded by bare fences that exaggerate the awkward shape.

❀ You can use tallish trees and shrubs to conceal the awkward-looking pointed section. A small grove of trees or a group of shrubs at the apex will create a feeling of height and space and conceal the narrowness at the end of the garden. Or you could place a small summer house or arbor there as a deliberate focal point and full stop to the garden.

❀ You can also use false perspective, for example by gradually narrowing a flowerbed as it approaches the narrow end, giving the impression of a larger distance and making the garden seem altogether bigger. You can also suggest that the garden is larger than it really is by placing a smaller-than-usual sculpture or garden building at the end of the garden.

❀ Make sure you have some interesting feature in the center of the plot, which will attract the eye and lessen the emphasis on the awkward point. A hexagonal or paved space or a circular lawn right in the center will do this, especially if there is a central water feature or interesting container or sculpture in the center. If this is reached by a path screened by shrubs, the whole area will be disguised and the triangular point becomes less obvious.

L-SHAPED GARDENS

AN 'L' shape, that is, a plot with two short 'arms', is in many ways not awkward at all but provides two gardens for the price of one. The position of the house is crucial to this sort of garden. It may form the inside corner with the garden on two sides. Or it may sit at one end of one of the arms. Almost certainly, one arm will be generally shady and the other mainly sunny. Careful choice of plants to suit these two aspects will be important and will create its own design to some extent.

ABOVE: The rather awkward narrowing shape at the end of this triangular garden has been planted with a small grove of trees to conceal its odd shape. A narrow patio at the back of the house leads to an asymmetrical lawn with a pretty seat as a focal point. The kitchen garden is behind the garage but conveniently near the kitchen.

ABOVE: A circular paved area acts as the link between the two arms of this L-shaped garden. A paved path leads from one part of the garden into the next under a tall pergola and through a gate.

❀ You can carry the same theme on from one to the other or create two completely different gardens. Whichever you decide to do, the important (and the trickiest) thing to do is to design the meeting point of the two sections so that the transition is comfortable. This meeting point

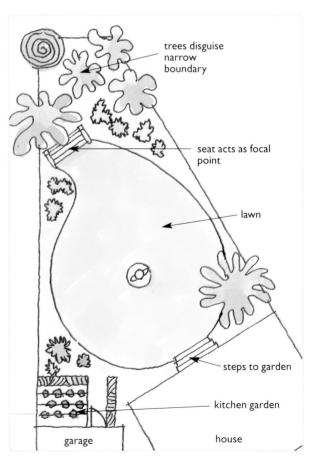

trees disguise narrow boundary

seat acts as focal point

lawn

steps to garden

kitchen garden

garage   house

could be literally that, a place with seats or a summer house where you can pause before moving on to the next area. It could be a third garden, entered from either of the others through arches or along a path bordered by shrubs.

❀ One traditionally successful device is to create a deliberately formal garden near the house, which becomes less formal further away from the house and eventually leads into a shrubbery, woodland area or wildlife garden around the corner.

WIDE AND SHALLOW GARDENS

A WIDE, shallow plot can be surprisingly awkward to plan for. It is generous in one way but its lack of depth from the house can make it difficult. For example, when sitting by the garden door, you may feel as though your nose is pressed against the boundary hedge opposite. However, there are a number of features that lend themselves to this shape of garden and with some careful planning, you can still create a feeling of depth.

❀ One way of tackling the problem is to create a plan of long narrow spaces divided by box hedging or low walls. Carefully detailed brick or stone divisions will emphasise the breadth of the garden and give an impression of space.

❀ Low arches and the occasional topiary feature or urn will encourage the eye to concentrate on the detail rather than the lack of depth. Opposite the house, an interesting detail such as a niche with a sculpture or a fountain will also distract attention from the lack of depth.

❀ Choose colors that will counteract the foreshortening effect. Avoid reds and yellow that will make space seem even narrower. Concentrate on mixing pale colors, for example lavender, santolina, pale blue hardy geraniums, catmint and herbs of all kinds.

BELOW: *This L-shaped garden has been designed with a formal area next to the house leading through a clipped hedge into something completely different – a much more informal lawn with a flower border and a path leading from the house through a small gate to the road.*

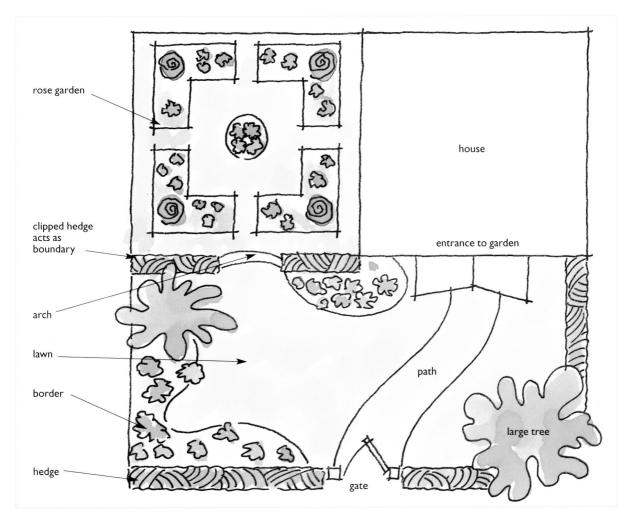

SMALL FRONT GARDENS

Generally, urban front gardens are difficult to cope with because they are often quite heavily shaded and also have to hold the trash cans. It is easy to give up on them completely but thoughtful planning can transform a front garden into a really attractive welcoming feature to the house.

❀ The first thing is to create some structure for the trash can, where it will be easily accessible but concealed from people going in and out of the front door. Something simple, such as a three-sided 3-ft (1-m) tall brick enclosure is a good answer. One open side means the container can be easily removed for emptying. A carefully constructed shed is less useful, being difficult both to keep clean and to maintain.

❀ Front gardens are seldom used for sitting in, being too public, but they do mark the approach to your home and should be well designed and welcoming. It is best to create a garden that will not require too much maintenance. Front gardens are often the forgotten areas of the gardener's domain and receive little watering, feeding or weeding.

❀ An important rule for the tiny garden is not to try to squeeze too many plants into it and it is often best to go for formality. Eliminate all grass, lay paving and install pairs of large pots planted with clipped bay or box. A

ABOVE: *This house sits directly on the pavement but its owners have managed to 'green' the area with planted boxes of ivy and colorful hanging baskets.*

small weeping tree in the center of the plot can create an attractive feature. The weeping pear (*Pyrus salicifolia* 'Pendula') makes an excellent specimen tree in a small space and has a charming arching habit and pretty silvery leaves.

❀ Alternatively, go for a more informal look. This is not always easy in a small space and it is tempting to put in too many plants, which will soon grow out of control.

❀ One answer is to cover the whole area with gravel or pebbles and create a Japanese garden with a rock or two placed at judicious intervals and a silver-leaved plant to balance them. Otherwise, colorful groupings of pelargoniums or *Impatiens* can brighten up a front garden magically. All these ideas will draw the eye away from the walled-off area of the trash can and create a positive impression on those walking by.

ABOVE: *Front gardens should be simple and welcoming. This one has matching blue paint on the front door and planting boxes, which looks spectacular against the white walls. The two miniature willows with their attractive variegated foliage create a light, optimistic mood.*

ABOVE: *This restrained but effective planting scheme with one ivy covered wall and a ribbon of pink in front of a cotoneaster hedge suits this modern house.*

SLOPING SITES

IF YOUR garden is on a slope, you can create a wild meadow or sloping lawn, but other choices are limited because water will drain away quickly and many plants will suffer. In general it is better to terrace the site, using low walls to contain the different levels.

* For retaining walls use materials that complement the house itself. Brick houses look better with their garden walls and paths made of similar colored bricks.
* For stone houses, try to use stone for retaining walls and paths. Rendered or stucco houses look best with concrete walls, rendered and then painted. Modern outdoor paints are available in a wide range of excellent colors. All walls should be topped with coping stones, which overlap the wall by about $1\frac{1}{2}$ in (4 cm). Steps should be as wide and as shallow as the space will allow, using similar materials to the walls and paths.
* Each level of terracing can be treated differently. One level could be planted with yellow and orange plants, for example, while further down oranges, reds and purples could take their place; further down again, misty blues and mauves would seem to disappear into the distance.
* If the site is shady, this color transition will not work so well, because you will not be able to grow the variety of plants necessary. Here a formal terrace could lead down to a less formal collection of mixed shrubs and herbaceous plants or a quiet seating area with a pool or fountain.

BASEMENT GARDENS

BASEMENT gardens often consist of a very narrow patio with steep, narrow steps leading up to the garden, which is normally too high to be viewed from below. The patio itself can feel cramped and dark and is not an inviting place to sit. In such cases, it may be best to sacrifice some of the growing space by making the patio a little larger and the steps a little more generous, giving you the opportunity to make both patio and garden more attractive.

ABOVE: *Steps should be as wide and shallow as space allows when leading from one area of terracing to another.*

WATER AND LIGHTING

Water has a magical quality in a garden. Quite literally, of course, it brings the garden life, since nothing will grow without it. Added to that, the sight and sound of water bring liveliness, light and movement unmatched by anything else. Combined with effective lighting, you can transform your garden into a brilliant and enchanted place. Both water and lighting offer the opportunity for beautiful and unexpected features.

ABOVE: *A long, narrow garden deceives the eye with the creation of a pond and a wooden bridge with a bright red hand rail, followed by a paved seating area beyond. The edges are concealed by evergreen planting.*

STILL WATER

PONDS and pools offer tranquillity. In the open they can reflect the sky with a delightful magical mirror effect of light. Such smooth planes of water can act as a foil to planting either in the water or next to it. A pool should be treated as an integral part of the garden's plan and should be built of materials sympathetic to the shape, size and materials of the garden and house. You can choose to have a natural-looking pool or you can give it a much more formal aspect with hard stone or tiles and a symmetrical shape.

Formal pools

❀ Formal pools look at home in symmetrical gardens, set in paving or some other hard surface and reached by straight paths or set in a terrace or courtyard. They can be sunken or raised and will reflect the stone or brick as well as any water lilies grown in them. They make excellent homes for ornamental fish, which can be observed at close quarters.

❀ Geometric shapes work best for formal pools – it is hard to beat a rectangular pond. A short wide one will look good on a terrace, whereas a long narrow one,

PLANTS FOR POOLS

WATER lilies (*Nymphaea*) are the ideal plants to grow in a formal pool. They like the stillness of the water and their flowers seem to float upon it. Hardy water lilies include *Nymphaea* 'Escarboucle', which is vigorous with large red blooms. *N.* 'Helvola' has dainty, star-shaped canary yellow flowers throughout summer and is good for a tub or small pool; *N.* 'Hermine' has pure white flowers over a long period.

more like a canal, will look good beside a straight path or as the centerpiece in a narrow garden. Small circular, sunken ponds can look very pretty in tiny gardens. Ideally, this sort of pond should form an important feature in the garden and not be tucked away out of sight.

Wildlife pond

❀ You do not need a very large pond to attract wildlife and grow moisture-loving plants. A pond 3 ft (1 m) across is quite big enough to have its own population of water insects, damsel flies, frogs and toads. If you place your pond near a flower border, the plants will provide cover for shy creatures to hide in. A lawn nearby will provide

an open space for birds. If the pond is completely surrounded by lawn or paving, remove some of the turf or slabs so that you can create a bog or rock garden or a wild flower patch, which will give shelter to small creatures. If young children are going to be playing in the garden you may want to avoid open water but you can still create a small boggy area for wildlife by digging a hole, lining it as for a pond, but filling it with soil. As this cannot then drain it is easy to keep it topped up with water.

BOG PLANTS

Marginal plants for the shallow edges include the yellow flag iris (*Iris pseudacorus*), marsh marigolds (*Caltha palustris*) and *Veronica beccabunga*. Leaves that float on the surface provide shade for underwater creatures and help prevent algae. They include water soldiers (*Stratiotes aloides*) and fringed water lilies (*Nymphoides peltata*). Plants for permanently wet soil near the pond include bugle (*Ajuga reptans*), creeping Jenny (*Lysimachia nummularia*) and lady's smock (*Cardamine pratensis*).

ABOVE: *Ponds respond wonderfully well to planting, reflecting tall, elegant plants particularly well in the water. It is always best to keep the planting simple. Here, yellow water irises and water lilies make a spectacular show.*

ABOVE: *Still water gives interesting and beautiful reflections as well as visions of the bottom of a pool. In shallow water, small water-loving plants will grow well around cobbles and over stones.*

MOVING WATER

ADDING movement to water creates a truly magical effect. Reflections are enhanced, the sound of moving water is soothing and musical, and fish benefit from the enhanced oxygenation of the water. Water lilies, however, prefer still water, so are better suited to ponds without fountains, or where a fountain is offset so that part of the pond remains still. Movement can be created by fountains, waterspouts, rills or cascades and is guaranteed to bring sparkle and dash to the garden. As always, it should be planned in scale with the area. A gentle trickle can be refreshing in a small garden, where a large fountain would be pretentious.

ABOVE: *An elegant formal fountain with a tall jet surrounded by smaller ones. The pale adjacent pink brick paving includes beds of lavender.*

Cascades

❀ Cascades have frequently been used in great and grand gardens, especially in Italy, to create spectacular stairs of water. The splendid cascade at Chatsworth in Derbyshire, England was built in 1694 and still amazes visitors with its tumbling staircase of water. It is quite possible to make more modest cascades in keeping with smaller gardens.

❀ On a sloping site, a narrow channel, interrupted at intervals by a short cascade and an occasional octagonal or round pool, can create an enchanted atmosphere not unlike that of a Persian or Moorish garden.

❀ On a flat site, an informal cascade can be built quite easily, the water being circulated by a small electric pump.

❀ An unusual cascade suitable for a small informal garden can comprise a series of watering cans or urns lying on their sides, each emptying into the one below to create a kind of cascade. This idea could be developed in different ways using a variety of receptacles.

ABOVE: *This sculpted glass fountain alters subtly as you walk around it, catching the sun and glittering as the water runs down it.*

Fountains

❀ Fountains have become popular recently, partly because of the availability of comparatively inexpensive reproductions of traditional designs, and partly because of the mass production of small submersible pumps, supplied with a fountain jet and sold in kit form. Installed in a part of the garden that becomes very hot during the day, a fountain has a distinctly cooling effect.

❀ Reproductions and copies of traditional fountain designs such as dolphins and cherubs are widely available. There are also some modern metal fountains in the form of leaves, twigs or birds, in which the water cascades down from one section to another.

OTHER TYPES OF WATER FEATURE

THERE are any number of ways of getting a small amount of water to bubble, trickle, flow or glint in a decorative and refreshing way. You can introduce the sound of running water by running it through a pipe in the wall, using one of the cheapest electric pumps and a small cistern.

Cobbles

❀ Rounded pebbles collected together are popular as a base for water to trickle over. (These are widely available from garden centers so please do not collect them from the outdoors.) A cobble fountain is simple and pleasant and does not need a pool. The effect relies on the sound and movement of water splashing over the stones into a reservoir, which is constantly recycled.

❀ You will need a tank large enough for a submersible pump and holding enough water to cope with evaporation from the surface of the cobbles on a sunny day. The size of the reservoir will depend on how often the system is filled up – it need be no bigger than a plastic bucket.

Millstones

❀ A large millstone has a strong architectural impact so should be carefully placed where it will balance some other strong feature. The water falls over the side of the

stone and is collected in a reservoir below; again, no pool is required. A geyser jet can be used to introduce air if you want a more turbulent effect.

Bamboo spout

❀ In Japanese gardens, bamboo canes are used as spouts. Balanced on an upright, the cane fills up with water, tips it out on to pebbles below, then starts all over again. Some people find the regular filling and emptying peaceful, others find it monotonous.

BELOW: *A traditional Japanese bamboo spout deposits water into a large stone bowl that stands on a craggy rock with cobblestones below.*

INSTALLATION

WATER and electricity are always a combination to be taken seriously where safety is concerned. Low-voltage pumps are available, but are suitable only for small-scale features as they have limited power. Solar-powered pumps are also an option, but are not yet realistic alternatives to electrical systems because of their high initial cost and intermittent power in changing weather conditions.

❀ If you are in any doubt at all about installing an electrically powered water feature, use a qualified electrician familiar with this type of work.

❀ An electrical cable needs to be run through a conduit pipe to protect it from damage. The conduit is concealed beneath the soil, decking or paving. Always fit a residual current device (RCD), which will cause the power to cut out immediately should there be an interruption to the supply.

❀ Alternatively, have armored cable and a weatherproof outdoor box with permanently wired-in cables professionally installed.

BELOW: *Water features can incorporate seemingly humble household materials with style and wit.*

TYPES OF MOVING WATER FEATURE

MOVING water can be incorporated within a pond or pool, or can be a self-contained fountain. Fountains are a particularly useful way of introducing water in difficult situations. Confined spaces that cannot house ponds can almost always offer a vertical surface for a self-contained wall-mounted fountain. In addition, many types of fountains and streams run off over pebbles or slates, so that there is no standing water, which might pose a drowning hazard for small children.

Fountains

❀ There are many different types of jet available, which fit on the outlet on the top of a submersible pump, to produce a variety of effects. Even a pump with no jet fitted will produce an attractive ripple of water. Choose a jet pattern that is suited your chosen water feature and its surroundings.

CHOOSING A PUMP

SUBMERSIBLE pumps are suitable for most applications. They are installed at the lowest part of the system, but not on the bottom of the pond where they would draw in the sediment that collects there and quickly become blocked. An upturned pond basket makes a good support.

Buy the best-quality pump you can afford. The pump included as part of an inexpensive fountain kit may be of such low power that the water cascade turns out to be no more than a dispiriting dribble. If the fountain or water feature itself appeals, and it is reasonably priced, consider buying a better pump to replace the one sold with the kit.

If you are creating your own moving water feature, it is worth buying your pump from a reputable specialist water garden supplier, who is dealing with pumps all the time and will be able to advise you as to the most appropriate pump for your needs. Pumps have differing outputs, and these should be clearly marked on the packaging. The output determines how high the pump can propel the water. Clearly, a small bubble fountain does not need a powerful pump, but if you are planning a large fountain that incorporates a gusher jet, you will need more power.

ABOVE: An ingenious cobble fountain, using large slabs of stone to give a generous flow of water over the cobbles and a lovely splashing sound.

❧ For example, a bell-jet fountain may look very appealing in the quiet shelter of an enclosed garden center display, but the neat, bell-shaped fall of water will not be consistent in an exposed, windy position. A foam jet would be a better choice in this situation. All jets are prone to blockage to some degree, so site your fountain where you can easily access the jets for routine maintenance.

Waterfalls

❧ Waterfalls are not as popular as fountains, largely because they are not generally self-contained and they are more difficult to incorporate within a garden scheme in a convincing way. Ideally, a waterfall should appear totally natural and in harmony with its environment. A good way of introducing a waterfall is to have it linking two streams together. Be especially careful about landscaping a waterfall. Think about how it will look when the water is turned off. It is all too easy to create a concrete edifice that looks like a miniature quarry rather than an idyllic alpine vista.

CHOOSING THE TYPE OF JET

ALTHOUGH narrow jets of water can sometimes be effective spouting from an informal pool, fountains tend to be more suited to formal layouts. Stone fountains suit symmetrical balance, paved paths, clipped hedges and straight edges. Small, enclosed medieval gardens often had paved paths leading to a fountain in the centre.

However, a fountain jet in an informal pond or a terrace pool will help to oxygenate the water. A few hours of fountain operation in a small pool on a hot summer's day will greatly enhance the oxygen level for fish and plants.

You can diminish turbulence on the water surface by using certain types of jet. For example, a bell jet confines the spray to a very small area of a pool's surface, and will not disturb the leaves of water lilies.

BUILDING PONDS

❧

Water, contained or moving, is a fabulous addition to any garden. Even the smallest plot can accommodate a water feature, even if it is as simple as a wall-mounted spout trickling water into a small ornamental trough. The sound of moving water is incredibly tranquil, and gazing into the reflections of a pond is also very calming. Do not be put off by the technical aspects of water gardening. There are ways of incorporating water into a garden design that need no complex wiring or plumbing arrangements. For example, simply adding a bird-bath and keeping it filled with a watering can is a feature that will attract birds to your garden.

Water and wildlife

❀ Many gardeners introduce water features because they want to encourage wildlife to come into the garden. This has many significant benefits beyond the immediate pleasures of watching frogs leaping around the pond, or birds enjoying a morning bath.

BELOW: *A fountain adds interest to a geometric pond.*

❀ Introducing wildlife to your garden moves you closer to an organic gardening style – that is, gardening using all the forces of nature to optimum effect. Birds, animals and insects will be attracted by a ready supply of water, and will repay you by assisting in pest control and by improving soil fertility.

❀ Birds will not only amuse you with their antics in your bird-bath, but also devour pests such as wireworms and leatherjackets and improve soil fertility by adding their droppings, and eventually their bodies when they die, to produce humus. Birds with good access to water will also eat less of your berries and fruits.

CONTAINER PONDS

CONTAINER ponds are a brilliant introduction to water gardening, and are wonderfully adaptable to individual needs. Even if you are gardening outside a fifth-floor apartment, on an area little bigger than a fire escape, you can still have a pond. Another great attribute of self-contained ponds is that they are portable. You can move one around to change the look of the garden, in the same way that you dress it differently throughout the seasons with container plants. You can also take it with you when you move house.

Choosing containers

❀ A wide variety of containers are suitable, such as glazed pots in aquatic tones of cobalt blue or viridian, or half-barrels, which look very comfortable in cottage-style settings. Plants can include miniature water lilies, which prefer still water, combined with marginal and oxygenating plants, while goldfish can dart prettily in

ABOVE: *There is a pond style to suit every gardening taste – this Oriental-looking pond is full of koi carp.*

and out of the foliage. If you are using a metal container, make sure that it is not of a type that will leach rust into the water, as this can harm plants and fish. Painting a galvanised container with black bituminous paint will render it safe.

❀ It may sound obvious, but always choose a container that

is leakproof. Ask to have the container filled with water if you are in any doubt as to its watertightness. Risking momentary embarrassment will save a lot of aggravation later. Small containers look unattractive if you need to line them with something. Although you can drain a leaking container and seal it internally with a proprietary sealant before painting it with bituminous paint, this is not a job most gardeners would actively seek to undertake.

Winter care

❀ Ideally, bring a ceramic container pond under cover for winter, as it may crack if the water in it freezes and then expands. Alternatively, drain and store it upside down if keeping it outside, so that it does not fill with rainwater, which may also freeze and cause cracking.

❀ Barrel ponds are made of wood, which is a natural insulator, so can be left out of doors in sheltered conditions. However, pay attention to the individual needs of the fish and plants in all types of container pond. Even if the wood does not crack in freezing conditions, the fish may not be so resilient.

BELOW: *Here water is piped in steps from a spouting fountain in one ceramic container to a second and on into a third.*

PERMANENT PONDS

SINCE permanent ponds are designed to be just that, it is well worth taking a really careful look at all the factors that need to be considered before starting work. It can be all too easy to be swayed into buying a liner that has been made into an attractively landscaped pond in a garden center, but which may be quite unsuitable in the site available in your own garden, so do plan thoroughly before purchasing.

Size

❊ To keep the water clear, and to sustain a reasonable amount of wildlife such as several different types of fish, you will need a pond with a minimum depth of 24 in (60 cm), with a water surface of at least 40 sq ft (3.7 sq m).

Site

❊ Ideally, site a pond in an area that receives at least six hours of sunlight each day, is sheltered from easterly winds, and not close to deciduous trees, which will shower it with leaves every fall. Decayed leaves produce gases and salts that are hazardous to fish, and encourage green algae.

❊ Ponds can obviously be positioned in shady sites, and the reflections on the surface of the water can light up a dull corner, but most pond plants need good light in order to thrive. A water feature without organic elements, for example a fountain or waterspout, is a better choice in a shady spot.

BELOW: *Blue ceramic pots and blue paving that surround the pond are matched by blue flowers.*

❊ If you are planning to incorporate moving water within your pond, you will need access to electricity. Although you can have an electricity supply installed where it is needed, you may find the cost precludes this option.

❊ Rather than surrender your dream of a cascading fountain entirely, you may reach a compromise by siting your pond close to an electrical power source, such as an outbuilding or the house itself. Solar-powered pumps are another option. At the time of writing, they are in their infancy, expensive and with power that diminishes as light levels drop. However, they are an ecologically

BELOW: *Ponds can be as big or small as the space in a garden dictates.*

sound development, and of particular interest to gardeners without access to external power supplies.

Shape and style

✿ Choose a shape that harmonises with the rest of your garden. A pond that mimics a natural pool, complete with rocky outcrops and alpine planting, is all too often the automatic choice of the novice water gardener; yet it may look hopelessly incongruous in an austere, modern setting. Conversely, a small, cottage-style garden would look very uncomfortable with a ferociously geometric formal pool at its center.

Safety

✿ Any amount of standing water poses a potential drowning hazard, especially to a small child. The only truly child-friendly water features are those with no standing water, such as pebble fountains.

✿ However, it is possible to render a conventional pond childproof by covering the water with a strong metal grid, which may be concealed by growing plants through it. The grid can be removed when your children have grown up, but remember that your uncovered pond is also dangerous to any visiting children, who will be particularly attracted by the novelty of unfamiliarity.

MAKING A LINED POND

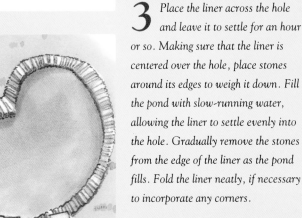

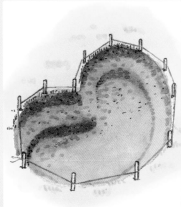
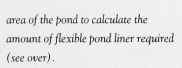

2 Excavate the hole, initially working around the edge to a depth of approximately 12 in (30 cm) to produce a planting shelf for marginal plants. Continue by digging out the central part of the pond, leaving the planting shelf the same width as its depth. Remove any roots, rocks and debris from the base of the pond, since these may puncture the liner.

3 Place the liner across the hole and leave it to settle for an hour or so. Making sure that the liner is centered over the hole, place stones around its edges to weigh it down. Fill the pond with slow-running water, allowing the liner to settle evenly into the hole. Gradually remove the stones from the edge of the liner as the pond fills. Fold the liner neatly, if necessary, to incorporate any corners.

1 Mark out the required pond shape on the ground, using a hose or string and pegs. Measure the area of the pond to calculate the amount of flexible pond liner required (see over).

4 Remove the stones and trim the liner with scissors, leaving a 6-in (15-cm) 'fringe' all the way around. Lay edging stones on a mortar base around the perimeter of the pond to conceal the excess liner.

CHOOSING POND LINERS

TRADITIONALLY, puddled clay was used to retain water in ponds, but it is not a reliable or convenient lining method. Concrete is still used in some commercial applications, but is costly and laborious to install. Most modern water gardeners choose between rigid and flexible liners when installing a pond.

❀ Preformed liners can be expensive, and their 'ready-made' look is deceptive. They are actually more difficult to install than flexible liners, which are brilliantly versatile.

❀ Always buy the best-quality liner you can afford, so that you don't need to replace it in a hurry. This is particularly important if you are planning a large, complex water garden, full of fish and plants, which would be time-consuming and tedious to dismantle for liner repair or replacement.

RIGID LINERS

PREFORMED liners are an extremely popular choice, but the cheaper, more commonly used semi-rigid preformed liners actually move about as you are trying to fit them, making installation very difficult. Any inaccuracy in fitting is soon cruelly revealed as water gathers at one end or, worse still, the liner cracks as it is forced to try and hold a great weight of water at a point that is not sufficiently supported beneath the liner. They are also short-lived, lasting only five to 10 years. They are generally too shallow for overwintering fish, unless you use a pond heater. They are also too shallow for many plants. Truly rigid liners are much more expensive, and do last for 25 years or more if installed properly; but for most situations, a good-quality flexible liner is a better choice.

ABOVE: *A well-maintained pond brings a whole new dimension to gardening.*

FLEXIBLE LINERS

WITH a flexible liner you can create a truly customised pond, shaped as you wish, with appropriate depth for all the plants and fish that you want. Mark out the shape on the ground using a line of sand, a hose or rope to get a feel for your design before you commit to it. To calculate the amount of flexible liner needed, measure the length and width of the desired pond. Add double the maximum depth of the pond to each measurement. For an irregularly shaped pond, follow the same process, first fitting the irregular shape into an imaginary rectangle to determine its rough size.

Butyl rubber

❀ This is wonderfully forgiving and tolerant, easy to install, flexible, and will even adapt over time as the soil beneath it settles. As long as it is not punctured by careless handling or animal attack, it will last for at least 25 years, a major plus if you are installing a complicated water feature.

Long-life PVC

❀ Not as expensive as butyl rubber, this material has been chemically treated to enhance its flexibility so that it will resist cracking in sunlight. Some liners classified as long-life PVC have been nylon reinforced, which does strengthen them, but does not necessarily make them less brittle. Both types should last up to 25 years.

PVC

❀ PVC is really suitable only for lining a bog garden, where the liner will be totally concealed from the sun, since PVC becomes brittle after repeated sun exposure, and will start to crack around the edges where it is not covered with water.

❀ Although punctures in flexible liners beneath the water can be repaired, it is not possible to repair cracks around the pond's rim satisfactorily. PVC is inexpensive and may be an option if you are installing a water feature destined to be very short-lived. The average life expectancy of a PVC liner is between five and 10 years.

Black polyethylene

❀ Do not be tempted to use cheap black polyethylene as a pond liner, not even for a bog garden. It is simply not substantial enough, and will last for only two or three years at the most.

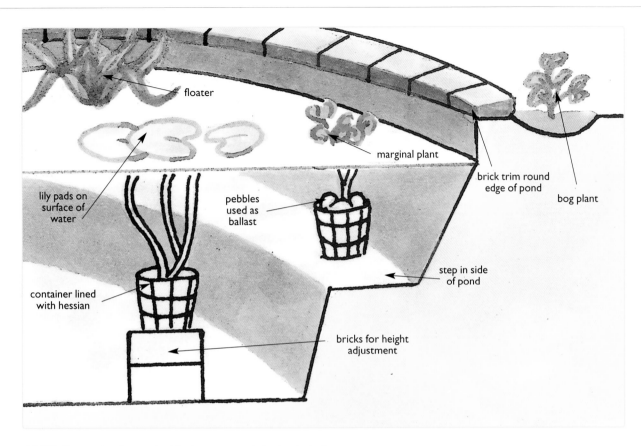

ABOVE: *Cross-section of a stepped and lined permanent pond, showing planting features.*

Labels on diagram:
- floater
- lily pads on surface of water
- container lined with hessian
- marginal plant
- pebbles used as ballast
- brick trim round edge of pond
- bog plant
- step in side of pond
- bricks for height adjustment

PLANTING UP A POND BASKET

1 *Use a container of adequate size for the root system of the fully grown plant. Unless it is of very fine mesh, line the container with hesian. Add moist aquatic soil to the container and place the plant on top. Backfill with more aquatic soil, firming it in.*

2 *To weight down the container and prevent soil dispersing into the water, add a top dressing of gravel.*

3 *Cut away any excess hessian and fix string handles to the rim of the* container to help you lower it into position in the pond. If the plant is too immature and light to stay anchored below the surface of the water, add more gravel or large pebbles as ballast until the plant grows bigger.

1

2

3

MAINTAINING A POND

Your pond will require various maintenance tasks, depending on the season.

Spring

❀ Feed fish according to their individual needs when you notice that they have become active.

❀ Check that all electrical components of your water feature are in good working order.

❀ Remove, clean and store your pond heater.

❀ Reconnect the submersible pump on your fountain or waterfall.

❀ Lift, divide and replant new portions of congested water lilies and other overcrowded plants.

❀ Start to plant new aquatics.

❀ Fertilize established aquatic plants, following the manufacturer's directions explicitly so that you do not inadvertently feed the algae rather than the cultivated plants.

Fall

❀ As long as fish appear active, continue feeding.

❀ Continue planting until the weather begins to grow cooler.

❀ Continue lifting, dividing and replanting new portions of overcrowded plants until the colder weather arrives.

❀ Cut down and remove the foliage and flower stems of plants as they fade, having first checked the individual needs of each plant. For example, marginal plants should not be cut down below the water level.

❀ Remove debris from the pond regularly.

❀ Screen the pond by placing mesh netting over the surface, if necessary, to keep out leaves until neighboring trees are bare.

❀ Remove tender plants and overwinter them in water in a cool, but frost-free environment.

❀ Remove, clean and store the submersible pump.

❀ Install the pond heater.

Summer

❀ Continue feeding the fish, following the food manufacturer's directions precisely.

❀ Continue planting.

❀ Monitor the water level and fill up as necessary. In hot conditions, the level can drop 1–2 in (2.5–5 cm) in a week, which can make a real difference in a small pond, and is obviously hazardous to plants, fish and the pond liner. If you are going away for a long period, have a friend keep an eye on the water level in your absence and refill it if necessary.

❀ Remove blanket weed from the surface of the water using a rake or by winding it on to a stick.

❀ Deadhead faded flower heads before they set seed.

Winter

❀ Stop feeding the fish.

❀ Stop planting.

❀ Take precautionary measures against the worst of the winter weather. Float a ball on the surface of the water if you do not have a pond heater to prevent ice forming. In a small pool, the whole pond can become frozen, which is lethal for fish and many plants. In larger ponds, the ice itself is not a killer, but if the surface of the water is covered with ice for more than a day or so, the toxic methane gas released from submerged, decaying vegetation is allowed to build up and can be lethal to fish. Keeping a small area of the pond free of ice permits the gas to disperse into the air.

Treating leaks

✿ If a pond is losing more water than you would expect from normal levels of evaporation, you will need to investigate further. Temporarily house fish and plants elsewhere during your explorations.

✿ If you have a fountain or other water course fitted, turn off the pump and see if the water level drops, since most leaks occur around the cascade part. If no leak is visible here, or if you do not have a water course fitted, refill the pond and allow the water level to drop naturally until you see the leak. The planting shelf is another common site of leaks.

✿ Sudden, dramatic water loss indicates a major hole, which will need to be fixed in a similar way to repairing a puncture on a bicycle tire. Use a kit appropriate to the type of liner you have.

✿ If all efforts to find the leak prove fruitless, you may need to put a replacement liner over the old one.

Leaks in newly installed ponds

✿ Check that the edges of the pond are level. The problem may simply be caused by gravity – the water flowing out of the pond at its lowest point. Another potential problem, which is easily rectified, is that a fold in a flexible liner may be forming a lip, over which water is running, away from the pond. A quick adjustment will stop the leak instantly.

ABOVE: *Float a ball in a newly made pond to ensure that the edges are level – if they are not the ball will naturally drift to the lower edge.*

MENDING A MAJOR HOLE IN A POND

If water is lost suddenly from a pond, this indicates a major hole has formed in the liner.

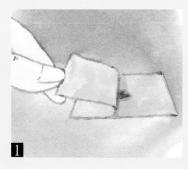

1 *Locate the hole and find a repair kit to suit the lining of the pond. Place glue over and around the hole in the pond liner. Smear the glue on the patch. Allow to firm up.*

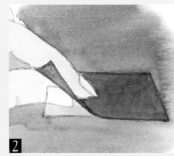

2 *Place the patch firmly on the glue over the hole in the liner, press down and seal. Allow to harden.*

MAINTENANCE

Planted ponds need maintenance to remain healthy and attractive.

1 *Cut away yellowing leaves with a sharp knife.*

2 *Remove blanketweed by revolving a stick in the water.*

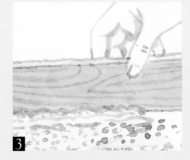

3 *Skim off duckweed by drawing a plank across the water's surface.*

WATERING SYSTEMS

ALL gardens need watering in hot, dry weather. In very tiny gardens, a watering can may be adequate, but most gardens need something more.

Watering by hand

❀ Some people are content to water by hand, using a simple hose on a reel. The reel can be mobile or fixed to a wall, in which case it should ideally be concealed by shrubs or climbers where it will be unobtrusive.

Using sprinklers

❀ Rather than watering by hand, you may prefer to leave a sprinkler on and move it around the garden from time to time. Oscillating sprinklers are the most versatile option for large gardens. Static sprinklers are the simplest and are good for small, confined areas. Pulse jet sprinklers are the most costly but will cover the largest area. Before using a sprinkler, check how far the spray reaches. It can be very annoying for neighbors if they get sprayed unexpectedly!

Using perforated hoses

❀ These are laid among the flowerbeds or around the perimeter wall, which often gets particularly dry. Rather than simply laying them on the soil, you can bury them about 2 in (5 cm) below the surface so that the water will not evaporate so quickly.

Automatic watering systems

❀ These range from simple devices that fit on to a faucet and cut off after a measured volume of water has passed through, to sophisticated programable timers.

ABOVE: *Careful positioning of a wooden barrel in an inconspicuous corner of the garden will look decorative and provide a constant supply of rainwater to water the plants.*

ABOVE: *A sturdy metal watering can will suffice for the watering needs of container gardens.*

ABOVE: *Sprinklers can be an invaluable aid to watering. This one is watering a herbaceous border in the early evening, when the water is less likely to evaporate before it gets to the plants' roots.*

EARLY ENGLISH GARDENS

Dᴜʀɪɴɢ the dangerous and war-torn Middle Ages, monasteries played an important role in preserving the art of gardening. Sadly, there are no remnants of medieval gardens today so we have to rely on pictures and writings.

These describe enclosed gardens, similar in shape to the ancient Persian ones. Right up to Tudor and Stuart times, small enclosed gardens were scattered higgledy-piggledy encircling the house. Features included medicinal and herb gardens, trelliswork, fountains, turf seats and a meadow area planted with tulips, forget-me-nots and daisies. Mounts were also built, from which to view the garden. These might be as high as 30 ft (9m), with a small shelter built on the top.

GARDEN LIGHTING

In recent years the garden has increasingly come to be regarded as an additional living area, rather than an area purely for planting. Lighting may be purely functional or more atmospheric. It can extend the amount of time you are able to spend in the garden, as well as enhance your view of the garden from the house at night and when the weather is less kind. Garden centers and do-it-yourself (DIY) stores have increased the range of garden lighting available, so a beautifully lit garden is no longer the exclusive preserve of the garden designer.

Lighting for safety

❀ The first lighting consideration in most gardens is a practical one. At night you should be able to see your way clearly from the garden entrance to your front door. If there are any steps that are difficult to navigate safely in the dark, good lighting will greatly reduce the risk of accidents.

BELOW: *It is important to ensure that areas such as steps, which are difficult to navigate, are well-lit at night.*

❀ However, do not install intense, isolated lights, such as spotlights, at potential accident spots. As you move from an area of bright light into sudden darkness, your eyes cannot make the adjustment quickly enough to be safe, and you may have unwittingly increased your chances of a fall. Such areas need a broad spread of light so that the whole journey may be made in the same lighting condition. These lights are sometimes called spread lights.

Lighting for increased security

❀ Strong illumination around the home is a proven deterrent to intruders. Floodlights with in-built passive infra-red detectors (PIRs) are widely available. Activated by localised changes in heat, these are automatically switched on when a person or animal approaches.

❀ Think carefully about where you place these lights. Although they are undoubtedly effective close to the door, it can be very irritating for both you and your neighbors if the light is placed so that it is constantly being activated by passers-by. Moving the light just a few feet to one side may mean that you will still be able to see clearly to get your key in the door, and would-be intruders are effectively deterred.

❀ PIR lights are available in many styles, so choose one that fits in with the mood of your home. A high-tech light, for example, would look very incongruous outside a Victorian cottage, where a carriage lamp might sit very happily.

BELOW: *Lighting increases the amount of time you can comfortably spend in your garden.*

Lighting to extend garden use

❀ Al fresco cooking and eating have enjoyed a massive increase in popularity in recent years. Improvements in outdoor cooking methods, such as gas-fired barbecues and even outdoor Mexican-style ovens, have truly turned the garden into an additional room.

❀ When daylight hours grow shorter, there is no need to curtail the pleasures of patio living. Provide adequate light so that cooking and food preparation can continue comfortably, and you will find that outdoor entertaining can start earlier in the year and continue well into the fall.

❀ Although a simple floodlight fitted to the wall of the house will illuminate a wide area, the light given is not intimate or attractive. More appropriate would be specific lighting of the cooking and eating area, together with lighting to highlight particular points of visual interest around the garden. This may be as simple as a spotlight above the barbecue and lanterns around the table, or a more sophisticated arrangement of permanent lighting throughout the garden.

BELOW: *Effective lighting extends the living space of your home out into the garden.*

Lighting for effect

❀ Anyone who has gazed out at the garden when it is illuminated for Christmas, even if the lighting is limited to a few fairy lights strung through a lone tree, will appreciate that lighting can increase your enjoyment of the garden, even when you are inside your home. This lighting for added mood is not the same as functional lighting.

❀ An even wash of light over the whole garden will add nothing in terms of charm or romance. Mood lighting, as in the home, comes from distinctly separate areas of light, positioned carefully so as to illuminate features of particular interest. Less attractive features can be left darkened to recede into the shadows.

❀ Just as too many decorative features in a garden can fight for attention and give an overbusy, cluttered look, care should be taken when planning accent lighting. Too many, different types of light can give a disjointed appearance – more appropriate in a large-scale municipal park than in the generally smaller domestic garden.

❀ A single, silhouetted tree or pond with submerged lights may be all that is required to make an impact. Clear white light is generally best for retaining a naturalistic feel. Reserve colored lights for special occasions, or you may end up with a garden that looks uncomfortably like a grotto instead of a sophisticated idyll.

BELOW: Electrical lighting can be expensive and disruptive to install but the results will be worth the effort and expense involved.

The practicalities

❀ Most garden lighting will necessitate installation of electricity. There are two types of electric lighting used in the garden – low voltage and main electrical.

❀ Main electrical lighting is best considered at the planning stage of a garden, since the cables will need to be laid professionally, at least 18 in (46 cm) underground. This is obviously expensive and disruptive, but is necessary if you want powerful lighting around the garden, if long runs of cable and prolonged lamp life are required, or if you have a broad landscape to illuminate.

❀ Low-voltage lights use a transformer to reduce the voltage, effectively reducing the illumination power available, but also making the lights safer. The main advantage of a low-voltage system is that there is no need to submerge the cables.

❀ Heavy-duty low-voltage cable can even run along the soil surface if necessary, although it is better to submerge cable if possible, and house it in protective conduit to avoid damage while cultivating the garden.

BELOW: Subtle recessed lights are useful for unobtrusive illumination of areas such as walkways and steps.

Lighting patterns

❀ Generally, lighting falls into two categories –
spotlighting and floodlighting. The difference is in
the spread of light. Spotlighting is a narrow beam with
sharp definition at the edges of the beam; floodlighting
is a wide beam falling off softly at the edges. Either type
may be used to create different effects, such as
uplighting, backlighting and downlighting, although
spotlighting is most often used because of its
controlled, narrow beam.

❀ Backlighting is created by placing light behind a
feature, for example a statue, so that it is thrown into
dramatic silhouette. Uplighting entails placing light
at ground level, pointing up at a plant or other
feature. Mature trees look particularly striking lit
in this way.

❀ Downlighting is self-explanatory – literally a light
pointing downwards. This can be functional, such
as wall lights pointing towards the patio, or used for
dramatic effect, as in moonlighting, where lights are
placed in a tree pointing downwards to imitate
moonlight. Just as soft pools of downlight from table
lamps create intimacy in the home, downlighting in the
garden gives a cosy feel.

Types of external lights

❀ Most people will be familiar with wall-mounted
external lights, such as those used to illuminate the
front door or the area around garages and sheds. Post
lights are also popular. In addition to the familiar
carriage lamp-style post lights, there are shorter post
lights available. These have a smaller spread of light
and are a more subtle alternative.

❀ Spike lights may be less familiar, but are well worth
exploring for their flexibility of use. This type of light is
pushed into the lawn or soil, and is available both as a
fixed position light, or one with an adjustable angle, so
that specific lighting effects can be achieved.

❀ Recessed lights, such as those that replace bricks in
walls bordering paths, can be very useful for lighting
walkways safely yet unobtrusively. Whatever the
choice, it is important not to get carried away with the
exciting possibilities of garden lighting. The aim
should be to enhance the garden with lighting, not
dominate it.

RIGHT: *These garden steps are lit by an unusual and attractive lamp.*

LIGHTING SYSTEMS

ELECTRICITY in the garden has made it possible to create effective lighting schemes from the smallest to the largest gardens, and has equally made it possible to water the garden effectively and economically over a long period, even when you are not there. For garden lighting always use lights specifically designed for outdoor use. Any other lighting is dangerous if used outside.

Advantages of garden lighting

❀ Lighting adds another dimension to the garden and should be planned into your scheme from the beginning. A well-designed scheme can turn your garden into a completely different world at night. You can create subtle pools of light with a general illuminating effect or dramatically highlight particular trees, shrubs and garden features.

❀ The eye is intrigued and delighted by small lights nestling among the foliage and flowers of large containers and plants in surrounding beds. It is usually more flattering to light the garden rather than the house, unless your house has unusual architectural features that merit special highlighting.

How much light?

❀ For typical suburban gardens, one or two small floodlight fittings mounted on the back wall of the house will provide enough light for moving about safely and enable a patio area to be used for barbecues. However, much more can be done to highlight aspects of the garden plan or planting and make the garden more fascinating at night.

❀ Focal points such as sculptures and fountains can look particularly effective when well lit. Remember, though, even when aiming for dramatic effects, subtlety is important. It is very easy to be over-enthusiastic and overdo the lighting, ending up with something glaring and uncomfortable.

BELOW: *A handmade ceramic Japanese lamp gives the garden a pleasant glow in the dark and will guide you along a path.*

Lighting the outdoor room

❀ Lighting is particularly important where the garden is small and designed to be used for entertaining in the evening, as well as for displaying the plants. Here you want not only to highlight plants seen from the sitting area, which may be at the far end of the garden, but also to light the path leading to it. This lighting does not need to be as bright as daylight but bright enough to see where you are going, yet leaving the rest of the garden mysterious.

❀ A collection of small candle-lit lamps can light up a table perfectly adequately, casting a becoming light on both objects and people. There are many different and attractive glass and perforated metal holders for candles and nightlights and the flickering of a live flame creates interesting moving shadows.

Lighting seen from the house

❀ If you don't go into the garden at night, but want to be able to admire it from indoors or from the patio, you do not need to light the paths and can concentrate mainly on the 'picture' from the windows.

❀ Highlight decorative foliage, sculptures and other features. You will probably find that individual branches you have not really noticed before will respond like magic to being lit at night and will become positively sculptural when individually highlighted.

ABOVE: *Unobtrusive light sources are by far the most effective for night lighting. Here, the light source is hidden by the trees, giving a dramatic effect.*

Positioning garden lights

❀ A little lighting, if well positioned, can have a tremendous impact. Avoid dazzle and glare by keeping fittings and bulbs hidden. There are all sorts of places where you can do this, such as behind tree trunks or walls or behind plant containers or large-leaved shrubs. Try out their positions by placing lights temporarily and then walk around the garden to check that the source is concealed from all angles.

❀ Spike lamps are useful because they can be moved around but they should be regarded as temporary only and not for permanent installation. The plug should be removed from its socket and the lamp taken into the house when not being used. As with all lamps, it is important to use the bulb recommended by the manufacturer or there may not be a watertight seal and the lamp might shatter.

Lighting trees

❀ The texture and shape of tree trunks, branches, leaves and blossom provide endless opportunities for decorative lighting. Use (tungsten) halogen flood spotlights, positioned to shine upwards into the branches from a garden wall or a lower part of the trunk.

❀ You can fix a light fitting at the center of the tree to create a soft glow. Strings of tiny white Christmas lights strung through the branches give a magical effect. Make sure you use lights designed for outdoor use.

❀ Bulb holders on this sort of lighting should be molded on to the cable; the type with sharp contacts that bite through the insulation of the cable to make connection with the cores are extremely dangerous if used outside.

The magic of light and water

❀ Water and light are a magical combination and at night can provide extra glitter and sparkle. Use wide and narrow beam spotlights on fountains and moving water. When lighting a pond make sure that the source of the light is not reflected in it, which would diminish the mystery.

Lighting for safety

❀ You should always have some lights to show steps and other changes of level and check that these do not cast confusing shadows. There should also be enough lighting near the house so that when you come out of the bright light of the house interior or the patio, you are not blinded by the sudden darkness.

Light fittings

❀ As with all other elements of the garden's design, the light fittings themselves should be in keeping with the garden's style. There are many good-looking functional fittings available, made of high-grade materials to resist corrosion and sealed against the weather. They are therefore not cheap.

❀ Several designs will hold energy-efficient, compact fluorescent bulbs and any fitting designed to use standard light bulbs could take one of these. Several low-level light sources are more pleasing than a few very bright ones but it does mean that the cost can quickly mount up.

BELOW: *Lighting on water can produce a magical effect; here the different colors of the the lights give added interest.*

❀ Light fittings powered by the sun are available. They can make good guiding lights, but the range of fittings available is not very large and some of them look as though they were designed for hotels rather than domestic gardens.

Installation

❀ All outdoor lighting should be installed by an approved specialist electrical contractor. Connections must be properly sealed and wiring must be of a special type, set

ABOVE: *Tiny Christmas lights twisted around the arches of this walkway enhance the flowers.*

in a conduit. Outdoor lighting is not cheap so test your chosen lights and make sure they are in the right places before you call in the contractor. Remember that plants will grow and the garden will change. Permanent lights that are complicated to install should therefore be positioned beneath mature trees and shrubs or sculptural items that are unlikely to change.

GREENHOUSES
AND FRAMES

Greenhouses are often thought of as the exclusive preserve
of the dedicated gardener. However, with greenhouses and frames
to suit every pocket and size of garden, there is no need for even
a novice gardener to feel daunted by the prospect of installing
and running one. Although one normally associates greenhouses
and frames with propagation, which may seem a little daunting and
time consuming to a new gardener, there are other, more immediate
benefits to owning a greenhouse or frame.

THE ADVANTAGES

THE most obvious benefit of having your own
greenhouse or frame is that the growing season is
extended beyond the first frosts of winter and the last frosts
of spring. This is particularly useful if, like thousands of
gardeners every year, you are tempted by the delights on
display at the garden center early in the year, which are too
vulnerable to be put out in the garden until the risk of frost
has passed.

Why choose a greenhouse?

❦ It is simply not practical to protect each individual
bedding plant with fleece, yet if you wait until later in

the season the best plants have sold out. Greenhouses
and frames offer the perfect solution, providing an
environment for hardening off, gradually acclimatising
plants to the elements prior to planting out. Favorite
tender plants may also be safely overwintered.

❦ For most gardeners propagation remains the impetus for
buying a greenhouse. Although it will take time to repay
the initial investment, great savings can be made by
creating new stock in large numbers. The satisfaction in
producing your own plants is immense and the techniques
are essentially very simple.

ABOVE: *The benefits of having a greenhouse are many; young plants can be
protected from frost and the warmer environment is useful for propagation.*

ABOVE: *Greenhouses should have good ventilation systems, with air vents at
ground level, windows in the roof and doors that can be fixed open.*

GREENHOUSE MATERIALS

YOU have a choice of structural and glazing materials when deciding on the type of greenhouse you would like.

Wood

❀ Wood is the traditional material for greenhouse structures and is undeniably very attractive, whether painted or stained, rendering the greenhouse not only a useful addition to the garden, but a striking visual feature in its own right.

❀ Hardwoods, for example oak, teak, or cedar, although expensive, are the optimum choices, as they require minimal attention. Softwoods should be pressure treated with preservative, and will need regular painting or re-treating with preservative.

❀ If an old wooden greenhouse is largely intact, it may well be worth renovating and may require only a little attention to the woodwork and glazing to restore it to its former glory.

Metal

❀ In recent years, aluminum has become the most popular structural material for greenhouses. It is less expensive than a hardwood greenhouse, easy to maintain, and its narrow glazing bars admit more light than wider wooden ones. It does not retain heat at night quite as well as a wooden greenhouse and is not generally considered as attractive, but for most gardeners, the advantages of cost and ease of maintenance more than compensate for these slight drawbacks.

❀ Both plastic-coated galvanised steel and galvanised iron houses will need checking regularly for rust. If rust develops they can require a certain amount of treatment and repainting.

Glass

❀ Glass is not only the most traditional glazing material for greenhouses, it is also the most effective. It is easier to clean and shade than plastic. It also retains heat well and conducts light better. However, it is not the most appropriate choice if the greenhouse is close to a play area or road, as it is obviously more prone to breaking than plastic.

Plastic

❀ Plastic glazing is not as durable as glass, yet is often more expensive. It discolors easily and tends to become scratched over time. This is not only unsightly, but dramatically reduces the amount of light passing through the glazing. Plastic will generally need replacing over time.

❀ Polycarbonate has better insulating properties and is almost unbreakable, making it a good choice for greenhouses close to roads and play areas. However it is expensive, easily scratched and prone to discoloring.

CIRCULATION OF ENERGY IN A GREENHOUSE

Energy from the sun is transmitted through the glass sides and roof of a greenhouse and warms the air inside as it travels round.

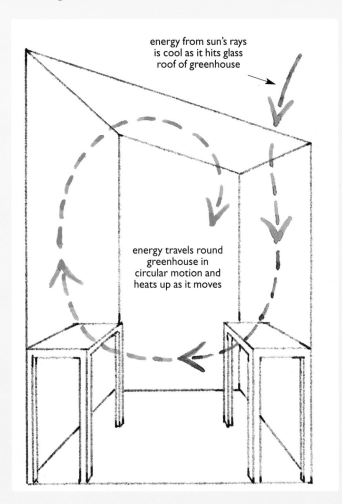

energy from sun's rays is cool as it hits glass roof of greenhouse

energy travels round greenhouse in circular motion and heats up as it moves

TYPES OF GREENHOUSE

THE greenhouse was originally the place in which the 'greens' (clipped evergreen shrubs) were housed over winter. It is is a functional building and should normally be integrated unobtrusively into the garden. When choosing your greenhouse you will find a variety of structural and glazing materials available as well as a wide choice of designs. Your choice will be dictated firstly by your budget and then by the space you have available in your garden. Avoid using climbers as screening for greenhouses, which will cut out much of the light from the roof and produce sickly plants within the greenhouse. A group of well-chosen decorative trees or shrubs placed to one side of the greenhouse will effectively provide an attractive visual barrier instead. Try to make sure that some of these are evergreens so that the hedge will disguise the greenhouse all year round.

The traditional greenhouse

❀ The traditional greenhouse has vertical sides, closed in the lower part, and an evenly spanned roof. It uses space well and the covered lower part conserves heat effectively, making it energy efficient. If you plan to grow a lot of low-growing border plants or use growing bags, a greenhouse without filled-in sides will be a better choice.

❀ A wide range of accessories such as shelves and staging is available to suit this type of greenhouse, making it a good all-round choice. Many sizes are available. Choose one to suit both your garden and the amount of time you plan to spend in the greenhouse. A keen propagator will quickly outgrow a small model.

BELOW: *A lean-to greenhouse can save a great deal of space and, as the wall acts as insulation, it retains its heat well.*

The lean-to greenhouse

❀ A lean-to greenhouse built against a wall is useful for those who do not want to give up precious garden space. You need a suitable wall, of course, so that the greenhouse can be tucked away at the side of the house.

❀ An alternative place would be a high wall at the far end of the garden, where the greenhouse can share an area with a vegetable plot and a compost heap or a propagating area for new plants, all screened off by a hedge or trellis. Because it is situated against a wall, it retains heat well, often benefiting not only from sunlight, but from a certain amount of heat emitted by the heating system of the home.

❀ Lean-to houses can be extremely attractive in their own right and can double up as garden rooms if there is a connecting door to the home. Their reduced glazed surface means that they are less expensive to heat than a conventional greenhouse, although, obviously, they receive less light than traditional models. Watering and heating systems are also comparatively simple to install, there being no need to lay cables to a more distant part of the garden.

❀ Another type of greenhouse attached to a wall, which shares the properties of the basic lean-to greenhouse, is the three-quarter span greenhouse. This is a traditional greenhouse with a quarter of one side removed. This is the side placed against a wall.

The mini greenhouse

❀ Mini greenhouses provide an excellent introduction to growing under glass, invaluable not only to the gardener with limited space, but also to the novice who does not wish to make a costly investment in a more substantial model. Both freestanding and lean-to mini greenhouses are available. The lean-to models are best situated against a south-west, west- or south-east facing wall or fence for maximum light.

Specialist greenhouses

❀ A range of greenhouses in unusual shapes and sizes is available. Some are designed primarily for their decorative properties, such as octagonal greenhouses, others for increased efficiency of heat retention or stability in high winds. A major drawback of a specialist greenhouse is that staging, shelving, glazing accessories and replacements are not standard items. The choice may therefore be both limited and expensive.

LEAN-TO GREENHOUSE

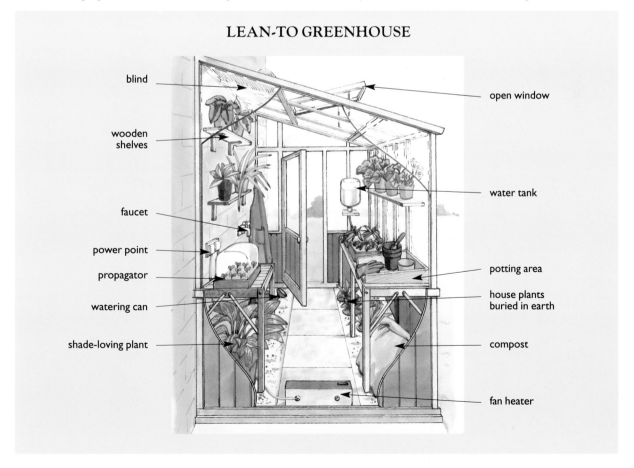

SITING THE GREENHOUSE

❀ Freestanding greenhouses need to be situated away from trees, in a bright but sheltered position, ideally placed so that the central walkway runs from east to west. The greenhouse must not be exposed to wind tunnels or frost pockets.

❀ In exposed areas it may be necessary to erect a wind-protective barrier, although you should take care not to make this fence or hedge so high and close that it blocks out light and makes it difficult to access any part of the greenhouse for maintenance. If possible, try to place the greenhouse near the shed or other utility structure to make a work area in scale with the other garden spaces. This will limit the number of paths required and will make it easier to supply water and electricity.

COLD FRAMES AND CLOCHES

❀ These provide many of the same benefits as greenhouses, extending the growing season, overwintering vulnerable plants and making it possible to grow an increased range of crops. They are obviously on a much smaller scale, making them an excellent choice for small gardens and novice gardeners unwilling to make bigger investments in terms of space and money.

❀ They also provide a useful adjunct to the greenhouse at busy times of the year when space is limited, for example when hardening off plants in the spring. For those gardeners who do not have a greenhouse, plants may be propagated in the home and then hardened off in frames or cold cloches.

ABOVE: *Greenhouses should be situated in a bright spot, with some shelter from wind tunnels or the danger of frost pockets.*

Cold frames

❀ The structure of cold frames can vary in the same way as greenhouse designs; some have filled in sides, some are glazed from top to bottom. The same guidelines on choosing structural and glazing materials apply. Since cold frames are generally at ground level, it is particularly important to install plastic glazing material if young children will be playing close to the frame.

❀ Cold frames are simple and inexpensive to make at home, using either wood treated with preservative or bricks if a supply of old bricks is easily to hand. Aluminum frames have a distinct advantage over these more permanent structures, since they can be moved around the garden to benefit from the maximum light available throughout the year.

❀ All cold frames should be sited in areas of good natural light, in a sheltered area, again following the same guidelines as for siting a greenhouse. Like greenhouses, cold frames may also need shading in summer and

ABOVE: *The structure of cold frames can vary; some are all glazed, others have only glazed sides.*

insulating in winter. They will certainly need adequate ventilation, so read the general care and maintenance guidelines for greenhouses when setting up a cold frame.

❀ Heating may be installed in these frames, although technically it then ceases to be called a cold frame.

Cloches

❀ Cloches are used chiefly in vegetable growing to protect young plants from the elements and predators. Cloches are available in many shapes such as tent-, tunnel- and dome-shaped, and come in a variety of materials. As with greenhouses, the recommended material for best light transmission and heat retention is glass, although the same safety caveats obviously apply and plastic is a better choice for gardeners with children.

❀ Plastic is inexpensive. Although it does not retain heat or allow such good light transmission, this is not of vital importance with all crops. Whatever the material, ensure that the cloche has well-fitting ends, or it has the potential to turn into a wind tunnel, which will quickly damage plants. Simple individual cloches may be made from cut-off plastic bottles. These may not be as attractive as traditional glass cloches, but they are infinitely cheaper and just as effective.

LEFT: *Cloches provide convenient, moveable protection for vulnerable plants.*

IN THE GREENHOUSE

CHOOSING the type of environment appropriate to the plants you wish to grow is at the heart of successful greenhouse gardening. Heat, humidity and ventilation will all need to be carefully considered at the planning stage, and controlled effectively throughout the year in all types of environment, from cold to tropical. Having selected your chosen environment, you will need to plan how it is to be installed and controlled.

The cold greenhouse

❀ A novice greenhouse gardener may be well advised to begin with an unheated greenhouse, while becoming accustomed to the basic principles of greenhouse gardening. These include ventilation, basic shading and insulation, as well as pest and disease control.

❀ Although the range of plants that may be grown in a cold greenhouse is obviously fairly narrow, the unheated greenhouse still has many uses, for example growing alpines, overwintering slightly tender plants and bringing plants on earlier than would otherwise be possible. A heated propagator could be used to increase the potential of this type of environment, although some propagation from cuttings may be possible without this.

The cool/frost-free greenhouse

❀ This type of house is heated just enough to keep frost at bay – a daytime temperature of 41–50°F (5–10°C) is required, with a night-time temperature that does not drop below 35°F (2°C).

❀ As well as providing all the same benefits as the cold greenhouse, frost-tender plants may be overwintered and flowering pot plants and summer crops grown in a cool/frost-free greenhouse. Again, a heated propagator will be useful, particularly for germinating seeds, as will a growing lamp to provide extra light for young seedlings.

ABOVE: A greenhouse needs to be properly maintained in order to be both effective and attractive.

The temperate greenhouse

❀ This environment is slightly warmer still, with a daytime temperature of 50–55°F (10–13°C) and a night-time temperature of no lower than 45°F (7°C). A good range of tender pot plants, vegetables and half-hardy plants will thrive in this type of house. Again, a propagator is needed for best results. Alternatively, boost the regular heating during the required period. A growing lamp is useful in either case.

The tropical/warm greenhouse

❀ The daytime temperature of this house is 55–64°F (13–18°C), falling to no less than 55°F (13°C) at night. An exciting range of plants may be grown in this environment, including ornamental and edible tropical and subtropical plants.

❀ This type of house is also sufficiently warm to propagate seedlings without a propagator, although the additional light provided by a growing lamp would still be useful.

Heating

❀ There are various methods of heating your greenhouse. Electric heaters are convenient, reliable and clean to use; they are also generally energy efficient since most are thermostatically controlled. However, you will need an electricity supply to the greenhouse, which could prove expensive.

❀ Fan, convector and tubular heaters are all possibilities. Fan heaters are particularly versatile; they are portable and can be used as a fan only in summer to cool the greenhouse. Independent gas and paraffin heaters release both fumes and water vapor, which can result in a stagnant, moist atmosphere that encourages disease, so good ventilation is particularly important with these.

❀ Whatever the choice, every greenhouse needs a thermometer to check that the desired temperature is being maintained. A frost alarm is useful in unheated greenhouses, and also in heated ones where a sudden temperature drop due to a power cut, for example, would spell disaster.

Insulation

❀ Effective insulation will conserve heat, reducing heating costs considerably. Double-glazing is too expensive for most gardeners. Plastic bubble wrap, fixed with pins, clips or suction pads, is an affordable and efficient alternative. It also allows a good amount of light transmission. Plain plastic sheeting is cheaper, but does not provide such efficient insulation.

INSULATING AND SHADING

A greenhouse must be protected from heat in the summer and from sudden drops in temperature and frost in the winter.

1 *Plastic bubble wrap is an effective insulator, while allowing good light transmission into the greenhouse.*

2 *Applying a shading wash prevents your greenhouse from overheating in summer.*

3 *Alternatively, fit blinds to keep the greenhouse cool in hot weather.*

Ventilation

❀ Good ventilation is critical to healthy plants. It prevents a build-up of stagnant air, which fosters pests and diseases, and maintains the desired greenhouse temperature. Even the cool greenhouse needs adequate ventilation to keep damp, stale conditions at bay in winter.

❀ Besides the ventilation systems fitted in the greenhouse on purchase, many ancillary options are available, some very sophisticated, such as thermostatically controlled vent openers and extractor fans. If you leave the greenhouse door open in summer, fix netting across the opening to keep out animal intruders.

Shading

❀ Shading also controls the temperature of the greenhouse. Shading washes are inexpensive, effective and simple to apply to the exterior of the greenhouse, although the finished result is not particularly glamorous. The wash allows through enough light for good plant growth and can be rubbed away at the end of the summer. Blinds are effective and attractive but need constant attention. Thermostatically controlled automatic ones are convenient but expensive.

BELOW: *Attractive to look at, this little greenhouse is made of extruded aluminum and can be glazed in tempered safety glass. The finish is polyester, so it requires very little maintenance.*

Watering

❀ In the rain-free environment of a greenhouse, effective watering is critical. A watering can is an option in a small greenhouse but you will probably need to consider other watering methods. Systems where water is drawn up into the plants using capillary action are widely used; these involve placing plants on capillary matting, a part of which is trailed into a water reservoir.

❀ Trickle irrigation is another option. These automated watering systems need careful monitoring to ensure plants are being watered according to their individual needs and the time of year.

Humidity

❀ Humidity is the amount of water vapor in the air. Excess humidity can be reduced by ventilation, or increased by adding water to the air – be it simply spray misting by hand, sloshing down the floor and staging with water during the summer or sophisticated automated spray systems.

❀ Hygrometers measure humidity and are useful in greenhouses. A relative humidity level between 40 and 75 per cent is desirable for most greenhouse plants. Above this, mildew and grey mold may develop.

Greenhouse pests and diseases

❀ The protected environment of the greenhouse provides an ideal breeding ground for pests and diseases. Adequate attention to ventilation and humidity control, plus scrupulous hygiene, will go a long way to maintaining a healthy greenhouse.

❀ Throughout the year, take care to use only sterile compost and clean pots. Regularly sweep the floor to remove leaves and debris, which may contain harmful spores. Clean the greenhouse thoroughly each fall. Remove the plants to a suitable place and disinfect and rinse the greenhouse well, both inside and out.

Pest and disease control

❀ Check the undersides of leaves regularly, as pest infestations can quickly build up here unnoticed. Treat pests and diseases promptly – fumigation is effective against both. Biological controls are another option, and involve introducing parasites and predators that feed on particular pests. Chemical sprays are another, although less environmentally friendly solution.

FRENCH FORMALITY

THE FRENCH took the Italian Renaissance garden and gave it their own brand of formality. French gardens were larger and the terrain flatter. They reflected the absolute power of the king and were strictly regimented and controlled. Versailles, built for Louis XIV, the 'Sun King', is the epitome of such gardens. The enormous palace was an extension of a modest hunting lodge that belonged to Louis's father. The garden stretches away in formal avenues wide enough to take an army and disappears into the distance. Louis's gardener, André le Nôtre, designed the gardens

to the glory of his king and as a vast theatre for outdoor fêtes in which His Highness could make graceful and noticeable entrances and exits. Enormous parterres were planted as intricate garden 'embroideries' whose patterns were best seen from the first-floor windows.

RIGHT: *The Basin d'Apollo at Versailles, France, in all its glory, making use of the flatness of the land and the enormous amount of space to display huge stretches of water, golden sculptures and long, wide avenues stretching back towards the palace.*

CONSTRUCTING OUTBUILDINGS

Small buildings in the garden contribute greatly to efficiency and often to the garden's charm as well. On the practical side, they provide shelter and essential storage space for garden equipment and furniture. They make pleasant places for conversation, shelter and refreshment and can be excellent play spaces for children. Visually they can contribute in an important way to the look of the garden, providing architectural balance to the house or to some other structure in the garden. Buildings of all kinds are potential focal points, used to draw the attention and provide interest and entertainment. They can also be eyesores, of course.

THE BASIC SHED

REASONABLY priced sheds are available in kit form to put together at home. The smallest are large enough to hold garden tools, folding furniture and games equipment. The most basic garden sheds are not particularly pretty, but there are ways in which they can be hidden. It is surprising how often sheds are placed against a wall in the middle of a small garden, where you cannot avoid looking at them.

BELOW: *Garden sheds are available to buy in kit form; they can be as basic or sophisticated as your budget dictates.*

❀ If the garden is not quite rectangular and has the odd awkward corner, this might be the very place to put a small shed. Tuck it away out of sight behind some sort of screen, perhaps a shrubbery or trellis with climbers trained on it.

❀ Try to focus attention on some other interesting feature and away from the shed itself. It should be reached by a path so that it is easy to get to, even in wet weather.

❀ There are many different sizes of shed available and the more robust ones can be converted into workrooms with extra windows put in. They do not make particularly attractive buildings from the outside but should not be difficult to camouflage with paint or conceal with shrubs and climbing plants.

Alternatives for small gardens

❀ If your garden is very small and there is no room for a full-height shed, you can get seats that are also storage units, large enough to hold implements such as spades, forks and trowels, small enough to place on the patio and attractive enough to hold their own with the regular patio furniture.

Brightening up a shed

❀ There have been great steps forward in exterior paints in the last few years. You can paint almost anything now in paint that will withstand the weather and comes in an exciting range of colors, from wonderful sea greens and blues to old rose and sunflower yellow.

❀ With these paints you can customise your shed by painting it in pale blue and white stripes, like a beach hut, for example, or in a really deep blue or green, perhaps outlining door and window frames in a different color.

Garden rooms

❀ As homes become smaller and more people work from home, creating an extra room in the garden to use as a studio or office makes a lot of sense. There are many companies who specialise in building such rooms, so you can get an attractive chalet-type building or a cottage-like 'second home'.

❀ Shop around for different designs and qualities – prices vary enormously. One thing you must be sure of is that it will be weathertight and warm. You can quite easily carry electricity via special cables buried underground so that you can run lighting, heating and computer equipment in the room. You need to make sure that doors and windows can be safely secured and that the room is properly insulated.

ABOVE: *This very basic garden shed has acquired a personality all of its own by being painted a bright sea-blue. This color seems to show up foliage colors particularly well.*

BELOW: *A well-ordered garden shed is a tremendous asset in any garden, however small. It is the perfect place to keep packets and tins, seeds and seed trays and other garden paraphernalia.*

CONSERVATORIES

THE purpose of buildings that use glass is to make full use of the sun and the daylight. The conservatory makes a useful, weatherproof link between inside and outside, but it can also create a magic of its own. In this extension of the home you can enjoy the jungle atmosphere of tender plants with their bright colors and exotic scents. You can use it as a light and airy dining room or a quiet space in which to read or snooze. Cane or perforated metal chairs and tables will emphasise the tropical aspect, and plenty of tropical plants and climbers in containers will add to the 'holiday' feeling.

Conservatory style

❀ Most conservatories are attached to the house and great care should be taken to choose one whose style, proportions and materials are in keeping with the materials and the architecture of the house. This does not necessarily mean that all buildings should be of the same period. In fact, a simple modern construction added to a traditional house can look very much in keeping. Getting the scale and proportion right in relation to the house are by far the most important things.

❀ Many conservatories are made of treated softwood and will require frequent painting, which is tricky and time consuming. Cedar can be used unpainted and will weather to an attractive silver-grey. Aluminum is expensive but almost maintenance free, as is UPVC.

❀ Georgian houses suit simple conservatories with arched windows and square panes, rather like the original English orangeries popular in the 18th century for growing citrus fruits brought back from the Mediterranean. Victorian buildings, which are usually more eccentric and decorative, look good with a more flamboyant conservatory, perhaps with an ornamental metal frame, pointed windows and other Gothic detailing.

❀ Small cottages and houses suit small conservatories, which bridge the transition between house and garden

ABOVE: *This Gothic-style greenhouse/conservatory is firmly based on brick foundations. It blends in well with the garden, while the planting around it also helps to make it 'fit in'.*

RIGHT: *A wrought iron pavilion is a good focal point with its white painted curlicues and decorative seat. The whole effect is enhanced by an evergreen backdrop and a froth of* Alchemilla mollis.

without being too dominating. Simple designs with aluminum or UPVC frames and no frills will often look better than anything more sophisticated.

❀ It is easy to be tempted by the advertisements for 'period' conservatories. Many are over-ornamented, however, with decorative details that are completely wrong for the house. With conservatories, as with so much in the garden, simplicity is usually more effective than too much detailing.

A focal point

❀ A good-looking greenhouse can be a focal point in a small garden. The hexagon is an attractive shape, and hexagonal greenhouses with wood or aluminum frames can look charming. It can be used as a display area for colorful plants such as geraniums, *Impatiens* and tender fuchsias, for example, as well as for growing seeds and cuttings.

Pavilions and gazebos

❀ Pavilions are largely built for romantic atmosphere in larger gardens and to give a sheltered resting place with a view on to the garden. The idea comes from ancient Rome, from ancient Chinese pagodas and Indian Mogul temples or pavilions. A gazebo is a smaller version of a pavilion.

❀ Pavilions are often circular or hexagonal, giving a view on to the garden from all sides. The roof should have a high pitch to give it a more commanding presence and elegance. Wreathed in foliage, it will offer an agreeable contrast between the geometry of the materials and the free form of the planting.

❀ A Chinese pavilion looks marvellous with light bulbs picking out the exaggerated shape of the roof at night. Pavilions and gazebos should be positioned in a sunny part of the garden but with some planting to ensure a certain amount of shade and seclusion.

BELOW: *This Victorian conservatory is very tall and is able to hold quite large trees.*

MAKING SMALL STRUCTURES

Pergolas, arbors, gazebos and other small garden structures
open to the air provide pleasant places for shelter or simply to sit in
and enjoy the view of your garden. They can also provide interesting
and attractive focal points in the garden. Features such as bridges
can transform the style of your garden, whether it is an Oriental or
traditional look you are seeking. It is important to make sure all
these structures are generously proportioned but not too large
or grandiose for the size and style of garden you are creating,
otherwise they will be overbearing and detract from the beauty
of the garden itself.

ABOVE: *A small white gazebo acts as a stunning focal point in this garden of lawns and foliage. It is carefully balanced by lead planters.*

ABOVE: *Small structures such as this little summer house provide welcome spots for shelter and relaxation in the garden.*

Pergolas

❀ Pergolas were used as long ago as 2000 BC, by the ancient Egyptians as supports for vines. They have continued to be a popular design feature of gardens throughout the ages and have many uses in modern gardens as paths, walkways and shelters. They have become particularly popular for their ornamental value. Festooned with climbers, they can be situated anywhere in the garden.

❀ They may run around the perimeter of a garden or straight down the middle of the plot. They can also be used to cover a patio, architecturally unifying the transition between house and garden. They are also particularly effective in joining two separate garden areas.

❀ Pergolas may be made of brick pillars with wooden cross beams or constructed entirely of wood. Once the main pieces of the structure are in position, lighter struts can be added to assist climbers to reach over the gaps.

ABOVE: *This is the epitome of English garden style with a mass of pink, red and white roses rambling over an arched pergola.*

✿ Metal or plastic arches can be linked together to make elegant pergolas that are very suitable for small gardens.

✿ If the supporting pillars seem too light, they can be made to look more substantial by planting evergreen shrubs at the base.

✿ In many gardens a central pergola running right through the garden may be too dominant. It is better to run it along one side, near the wall or fence.

✿ When it is used as a long shady walk, you can place a few seats underneath for people to sit and enjoy the planting. However, it is not necessary for a pergola to be this long; it can also be quite a short structure, simply covering a seat or arbor or the place where paths intersect.

Arbors

✿ An arbor is an open structure, strong enough to support climbing plants.

✿ Traditionally old-fashioned plants such as climbing scented roses and honeysuckle are used in arbors, although there is no need to be restricted by these and there are many other attractive climbing plants that will work just as well.

✿ The arbor usually encloses a seat. Once again, this may be made of wood or metal, or you can be even more creative and make the seat by simply by clipping a niche in an evergreen hedge such as yew.

❀ Arbors make romantic focal points and they, too, mark transitional areas where one part of the garden ends and another begins, or the meeting point of two paths.

❀ An arbor can be a large pergola-like construction, perhaps taking the place of a summer house, or it may be quite small. However, as with other small structures, it is important to ensure the arbor is in scale with the garden and does not take up too much space or detract from the planting.

Bridges

❀ A bridge offers exciting opportunities for design – from a simple timber plank or decking to a hump-backed Chinese or Japanese-style bridge painted a rich red.

❀ Bridges usually look best when seen from a boat on the water or from a path approaching from the side.

❀ As always, the style should match that of the garden. A modest, perhaps rustic style of bridge is best over a small stream; an oriental zigzag bridge constructed from posts and boards makes a suitable walkway over a wildlife pond. If the water is still, the bridge and any planting next to it will be reflected in it with magical effect.

❀ A false bridge next to a small pond can give the impression that the pond is bigger than it looks, perhaps suggesting that it continues beyond the garden.

BELOW: *This simple, but very effective, Japanese-style wooden bridge is complemented by colorful planting and a velvety green lawn.*

USING GARDEN ORNAMENTS

❦

Sculpture, at its simplest, is placed in gardens to provide pleasing forms or a way of marking and emphasising spaces and contrasts, as a focal point or surprise, and to give a sense of movement or stillness. Traditionally, sculpture had a certain symbolism but, in general, this is not so meaningful today. Sculptures and other ornamental objects stand in complete contrast to the forms and colors of plants. Even 'found' sculptures, such as granite boulders, and 'collected' sculptures of piles of pebbles can act as a contrast to the flexible and soft forms of things growing in the garden.

ABOVE: *Bright ornamental glass balls provide a dash of color in a snowy landscape.*

What sculpture?

❀ Many people associate sculpture with traditional western forms such as large stone or lead figures from classical literature. These are too large, too grand and too steeped in the past to look at home in many of today's small gardens.

❀ However, sculpture incorporates many other objects that can add interest, focal points, humor or romance to a garden. During the 20th century sculptors have explored abstract forms and different ways of depicting figures, and many of these are eminently suited to the modern garden.

ABOVE: *These eyecatching stone frogs appear to be sheltering underneath a hanging stone.*

LEFT: *Sculptures do not need to take pride of place. Some are most effective if 'chanced upon', such as this modern head of a young boy peeping out from behind a curtain of ivy.*

❀ A figurative sculpture can look spectacular in an alcove or bower. In general, one piece or a pair should dominate. Too many sculptures will compete with each other for attention and lose their individual impact.

Choosing sculptures

❀ Always use sculptures with discretion. If they are too fussy they will compete with the plants for attention. If they are too big, they will compete with the view. They may be in stark contrast with their surroundings or cunningly hidden among greenery.

❀ Traditional figures of shepherds and shepherdesses, and cherubs and nymphs should be smaller than their classical counterparts for most gardens today. There are many concrete-based copies available, which can look enchanting placed under a tree or hidden in a rose arbor. Modern sculpture is often abstract, lending itself to modern gardens and acting as a marvellous foil to foliage.

Uses of sculpture

❀ A sculpture may be large or small, temporary or permanent, prominent or half-hidden. Whatever its qualities, it should reflect the tastes of its owner and the style and size of the garden. A sculpture can attract attention to the end of an alley or become an integral part of a group of shrubs or trees.

❀ A figure or urn can be used to emphasise a particular aspect of the garden, such as an inviting green path or a pool or enclosed courtyard, or to draw the eye so that visitors are led around the garden to discover what will be around the next corner.

Placing sculptures

❀ Sculptures should be deliberately placed to create an impact. You can commission a piece specially for a particular place in the garden, or choose a piece you like and then find a place for it. You could search for objects such as old glass fishing floats, which look sculptural, and hang them from trees or place them on stones or pedestals.

❀ Sculptures should always be positioned in strategic places – at the end of a vista, grouped in an open grove or balanced by a group of shrubs or other strong planting. A strong piece can be used as a distant eye-catcher to be seen from a rise in the ground. Pairs of urns are effective at the top of steps or as a gateway to a different area of the garden.

ABOVE: *The globe is an appealing shape. This glass globe has the added fascination of water that flows over its surface, altering the flowers seen through it.*

URNS AND VASES

THESE are important as garden ornaments. Like figurative sculpture, a large urn may be used as a focal point at the end of an avenue or vista, or as a terminal feature on a gatepost. Identical urns or vases on pedestals may be used in rows to line a path, with a backdrop of clipped yew to draw attention to their shape. Sometimes they may be planted with some eye-catching plant such as a single palm or a collection of silver and pink bedding plants. Sometimes they look best standing on their own.

❀ Antique urns and vases are very expensive but there are good reproductions in various materials that can give the right impression. Simple terracotta pots are available in many sizes, are comparatively cheap and can look very impressive. Reproduction troughs are also available in cement-based artificial stone and can look imposing on a terrace.

ORNAMENTAL FURNITURE

SEATS and tables take up a fairly large space in the garden. Too often they spoil the effect by being of unsympathetic materials or simply too large for their environment. Putting a group of furniture on a special area of paving helps give it a purposeful look and acts as a framework. Scale is important. It may be a good idea to enclose the area partially so that the furniture's bulk does not intrude visually into the garden.

❀ Plastic furniture, although cheap, lightweight and easy to move about, cannot be said to add aesthetically to a garden. It may be the most convenient sort of furniture to have on a patio, but for permanent seats and benches, which become part of the garden design, there are more sympathetic materials to choose from.

❀ One seat placed in a niche, or angled against a group of shrubs or tall perennials can look very sculptural. Stone seats are undeniably sculptural, although they are best positioned where they will warm up in the sun before you sit on them. Wrought iron can look graceful; treated, painted or stained timber looks particularly good in the context of a country-style garden. A bench can be 'settled' into its place with plants at the sides. This makes furniture look as though it has rooted and gives it a permanent look.

❀ A tree seat can run fully or half-way around a tree, providing a shady place in which to relax and an eye-catching decoration. Cast-iron reproduction Victorian furniture looks particularly good in rather overgrown, informal gardens. Cast-aluminum copies have the advantage of being light, but they lose the detailing of the decoration.

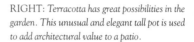

RIGHT: *Terracotta has great possibilities in the garden. This unusual and elegant tall pot is used to add architectural value to a patio.*

BELOW: *A traditional decorated terracotta urn can look good in a formal or informal setting. In a formal setting urns are best used in pairs or rows. Here, the background is somewhat overgrown and informal.*

PLANT CONTAINERS

WELL-grouped plant containers add a touch of luxury to a small courtyard, a porch or front door or the edge of a pool. The plants themselves contribute to the sculptural look so must be chosen carefully to enhance and complement the container. A large container with a short geranium poking out of the top will not look sculptural, no matter how colorful the plant.

❦ A timber half-barrel will hold a fairly large shrub and would look good with a standard clipped bay tree, particularly in country settings. A sophisticated alternative is the Versailles tub, which looks splendid planted with a lemon tree. Stone or tufa troughs can be planted with alpines or annuals.

❦ Metal buckets are unusual but attractive containers and look surprisingly good positioned on decking. Tall terracotta 'Ali Baba' urns with narrow necks are graceful and imposing on their own and best left unplanted.

BELOW: *This stone pedestal carries an elaborate container of helichrysum; a little stone pig sits to one side.*

Placing pots

❦ When using pots in groups try to keep similar materials and shapes together, otherwise there will be a lack of unity and the group will look fussy. Unglazed terracotta pots look good with each other but not so good with color-glazed pots from China, for example. Stone pots look best sitting on stone paving and terracotta is best on brick, while stainless steel or galvanised metal buckets are popular for modern gardens and give a bright, fresh look to roof-gardens. A pair of pots placed on either side of a front door may be planted with well-cared for topiary yew, bay or box and will imply a welcome to visitors. Square pots are a good choice for the entrance to a rectangular area of garden, confirming its shape.

BELOW: *A tall, elegant, squared pot in the brightest indigo makes a striking focal point and co-ordinates with the rather paler grey-blue trellis behind it.*

TIE-ON SEAT CUSHIONS

Folding garden chairs are wonderfully inexpensive and practical for impromptu al fresco dining, but are not always sufficiently comfortable to invite a lengthy stay. This pretty cushion is designed for simplicity of making and laundering. Natural piping cord adds a jauntily nautical feel and removes the need to make and insert fiddly covered piping and fabric ties. The whole cushion may easily be washed with no need to remove the cover.

TOOLS AND MATERIALS

- Pencil and tracing paper, for template
- Garden chair
- Tape measure and/ or ruler
- Scissors
- Pins
- Needle and thread
- Sewing machine and thread to match fabric
- Iron
- Thick wadding
- Piping cord

1 Place a large piece of tracing paper on the seat of the chair and trace the outline of the seat. Mark a 1 in (2.5 cm) seam allowance all around the outline of the seat and cut out the template.

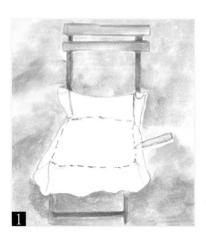

2 Pin the pattern on the fabric and cut out two pieces, taking care to match any obvious patterns such as the large checks shown here.

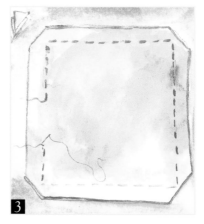

3 Pin the two pieces of fabric together, right sides facing. Tack then stitch along the seams, leaving a gap in the center of one side to allow for turning the cushion cover the right side out. Snip diagonally across the corners of the seam allowance so that the finished cushion cover will have neat, sharp corners when turned right side out. Press the seams open.

4 Turn the cover the right side out and press. Cut away the seam allowance from the paper pattern to leave the original outline of the seat. Cut a piece of thick wadding to this size and insert in the cushion cover. Slipstitch the opening closed.

5 Pin then stitch piping cord around the edge of the cushion. Cut two lengths of cord for the cushion ties. Knot the ends of each length to prevent fraying and fold the lengths in half. Securely stitch each cord at this half-way point on to the rear edge of the cushion, at the point where they will be tied to the chair back.

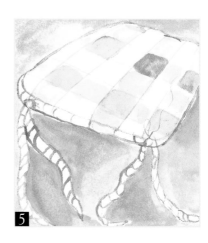

WILLOW OBELISK

A little extra height is always welcome in the garden border, adding another level of interest to large, bland expanses, and providing a valuable further planting surface in a smaller plot. You can use any attractive straight sticks instead of the hazel, their length determined by how tall you want your obelisk to be. Flexible willow stems are increasingly available in do-it-yourself stores and garden centers, as well as being a popular mail order item from specialist growers. If fresh ones are not available, soak older, dried-out willow stems in a large container of water overnight or longer, until pliable.

TOOLS AND MATERIALS

⌶ Hazel or other non-branching straight stems, approx. 5 ft (1.5 m) long
⌶ Twine
⌶ Scissors
⌶ Pliable willow stems, for weaving
⌶ Knife or pruners

1 *Stand an uneven number of rigid hazel poles together – 19 were used here – to form a wigwam shape. Temporarily tie a short length of twine around the poles near the top to secure them while you complete the rest of the process.*

2 *Wrap two or three pliable willow stems around the group of poles approximately 4 in (10 cm) down from their tops to bind the poles tightly to each other. Push the end of the willow securely into the wrapping to fix in place. When a tight binding has been formed, remove the temporary twine.*

3 *Take two pliable willow stems and twist them loosely together before wrapping them around and weaving in and out of the upright poles to make bindings*

1 *about 2 in (5 cm) wide in two places – roughly one-third and two-thirds the distance between the top binding and*

ground level. Trim, and tuck any loose ends of willow to the inside of the obelisk as you work.

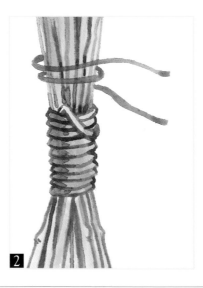

GARDEN STYLE

There are two ways of approaching the design of a garden – the planned and the informal. Most garden styles fit into one of these.

Planned gardens are based on a central axis with cross-axes running at right angles dividing the garden into compartments. Informal gardens are curvaceous and natural looking.

❁

Within these two styles there are many different possibilities. Romantic, wildlife and exotic gardens tend to be informal, while roof gardens or tiny front gardens lend themselves to careful planning.

❁

Decide which effect you want to achieve before you start work on your garden and remember that it is not usually a good idea to combine planned and informal styles.

INFORMAL GARDENS

Informal gardens are characterised by flowing curves, non-symmetrical arrangements of features and spaces, and plants that are allowed to grow into their natural shapes. Traditionally, gardens have always had their most formal areas near the house, gradually becoming more informal as they get further away. This still makes sense today. Whereas in the formal garden you can see the backbone of the garden as part of the pattern, in informal gardens the underlying framework is almost entirely disguised by planting and the garden should look as though it has grown up naturally. Nevertheless, some structure needs to exist or everything will relapse into uncontrolled wilderness.

PLANNING FOR INFORMALITY

INFORMAL gardens are more difficult to design than formal ones. Since straight lines and symmetry rule the formal garden, balance is inherent. But the informal garden is ruled by irregularity and natural-looking planting, so the designer must create a balance through a mixture of instinct, experiment and experience. This is rather like painting a picture or like thinking of the garden as a sculpture.

❀ If you are trying to create informality in a plain rectangular plot, consider planning your design on the diagonal. A path might run from the right-hand side near the house, past an oval lawn and end up on the left-hand side at the bottom of the garden. On the way, trees and other planting will create informal screens.

ABOVE: A medley of shrubs, grasses, fuchsias and low perennial plants make a charmingly informal border next to a large lawn.

❀ On a sloping site you can create winding or zigzag paths and steps down a grassy bank, rather like the 'flowery mead' of medieval times, planted with bulbs in spring and wild flowers in summer. An irregularly shaped site is made for informal garden planning. You can use awkward spaces for creating secret gardens or for more mundane purposes such as hiding a greenhouse or making a play area.

LEFT: Bright purples and pinks are easily found in the plant world and always combine well together. The gravel path gives form to what otherwise might be a rather straggling bed.

Informal shapes

❀ An informal garden has carefully planned spaces but conceals its boundaries. You can create boundaries by using native mixed hedging such as hawthorn, holly and briar roses or, in larger gardens, by planting clumps of trees such as birch or rowan.

❀ Irregularity is achieved by organic-looking spaces and winding curves. A grassy lawn may lead circuitously to a wild garden or a rose garden. Make sure the shapes are generous. Paths should wind gently in large curves, not wiggle up the garden in a worm-like way.

❀ One large curve always looks better than two or three meanly angled ones. Informality implies relaxation, so the whole garden should seem relaxed. There should be plenty of space for slow movement around the garden and plenty of places in which to sit.

❀ At each bend a series of tall plants should conceal what is around the corner, so that there is always a new surprise – a flowering cherry tree, a sculpture half-hidden by ivy or a rural arbor – because this should not be a garden with strict patterns, but a garden of random walks and mysteries.

❀ In very narrow plots you can treat the whole garden as a walk, with undulating borders on each side of a gently curving path leading you down to a seat or other eye-catcher at the end. The path can be made of bricks, stone or even grass, although grass is liable to become worn in summer and soggy in winter, making it difficult to work in the garden.

ABOVE: *A narrow border has been filled with plants with strap-like leaves at the back and low-growing perennials at the front. The mosaic pot gives the bed a focal point.*

❀ At intervals on either side of the path, set back into the planting, you can create seating areas, allowing the visitor to pause and enjoy the plants. The plants themselves should be chosen for their color and scent and they should have interest most of the year. The occasional small tree or large shrub will provide shade and height.

RIGHT: *Even a very small garden can be made to seem larger and be filled with surprises by introducing winding curves, diagonal lines and tall plants to conceal what might be waiting round the corner. Here, a lawn is located fairly near the house and a herb garden at the bottom of the garden; comfortable seats invite the visitor to sit and enjoy the plants.*

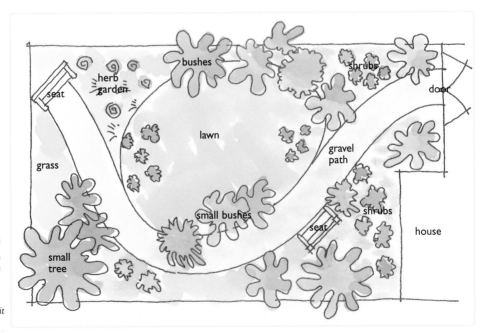

ABOVE: *Willow supports sit attractively in the flowerbed, whether on their own or with flowers growing up them. Here, one is being used as a support for clematis, and the others allow various plants to bloom at their bases.*

Vertical elements

❀ Vertical elements in the garden create a necessary extra dimension. They provide interest, 'punctuation points', contrast with spreading plants and mark the ends of avenues. Used in pairs they can become frames to a wider view or gateways to other parts of the garden.

❀ In general, planting in informal gardens will include tall shrubs to create compartments and secret walkways. You will also need the input of taller trees to add to the vertical dimension and to provide shade. They will also hide the edges of the plot, and nearby buildings, and help give a secluded country feeling.

❀ Sculptures, obelisks and other ornamental features can all add a vertical element in low planting, either prominently positioned or lurking secretively behind foliage.

Flowers for the informal garden

❀ The informal garden revels in color. Where the formal garden often looks best restricted to a variety of shades of green or green and white, the informal garden may revel in the riotous reds and pinks of geraniums and *Impatiens*, in nasturtiums, red salvias and sunflowers.

❀ Alternatively, you may choose silvers, pinks and soft blues. These are all colors that respond so well to a paler sun and a misty atmosphere. An informal rose garden should be filled with old-fashioned roses, sharing the space with complementary plants such as foxgloves, lavender and herbaceous clematis. The important thing is that the garden should have a natural look, as though all the planting had happened of its own accord.

Focal points

❀ Informal gardens do not have the straight walks and avenues that create obvious places for focal points. Their curves and hidden spaces should reveal eye-catching surprises at the last minute. As you round a corner, you should be confronted by something to please, astonish or amuse.

❀ Sculptures should have a sense of movement; this is why animal sculptures often work well. How you place these eye-catchers is all-important because, as they will probably be approached from many different directions, they must look good from all angles. Sculptures will enhance wherever they are situated: they can be hidden behind foliage, hung from the branch of a tree or placed beside a pool or pond.

RIGHT: *If your garden lacks tall trees or bushes, add something to bring height and interest into it, such as a planted obelisk.*

A feeling of movement

❀ You can control the way people move around your garden by the way you plan the spaces. Long, narrow paths will encourage people to walk fairly quickly. If you want people to linger and look, you must provide wide paths of firm, dry material and seats for them along the way.

❀ A path next to a summer border should be wide enough for two people to linger and admire together, whereas a path going to a compost heap can be narrow and hedged. Paths that are too long, narrow and enclosed will make people feel uncomfortable – the higher the sides, the narrower and longer a path will seem.

A feeling of balance

❀ Balance in the formal garden is provided by symmetry. In an informal garden you have to create your own balance. A large, open space such as a lawn can be balanced by a strong upright tree or sculpture.

❀ A white seat, always a very prominent feature, can be balanced by a dark green background or by setting it in an arbor. A group of trees or shrubs can be balanced by an answering bulk of some kind, such as a table and chairs of a strong defined sculptural shape or a small building.

Water

❀ Natural-looking ponds and pools are ideal water features in informal gardens. You will probably get a better shape by digging the hole and lining it with butyl rather than by buying a preformed liner. Planting should include water plants, as well as marginal and bog plants.

ABOVE: *An intriguing and attractive scheme of mound-shaped flowering plants backed by tall spiky plants and, behind that again, a wall of climbing roses. The colors are predominantly red with shades of yellow, and the neutralising white burns in the middle.*

❀ Other water features could include a small stream or a rocky cascade, which can quite easily be created with a collection of rocks, a small reservoir and a submersible pump. Cobble, millstone and wall fountains can all be useful when you want to provide the sight and sound of water without giving up space to a pond.

ABOVE: *A bright, colorful flowerbed containing – among others – Calendula, Ligularia, lilies, delphiniums and roses.*

MATERIALS

GRAVEL is a good material for informal gardens. Concrete slabs set in grass or gravel provide a firm basis for wheelchairs or dress shoes. Bark is good for winding through woodland and will provide a soft landing for children if laid thickly under their play equipment.

ROMANTIC GARDENS

The romantic garden is basically a dream – a garden of bowers and gazebos, of scent and pastel color, where plants grow with soft, arching habits and sweet-smelling flowers that never outgrow their allotted spaces. Birds flit from branch to branch, ferny foliage is reflected in still pools and nearby are the sounds of waterfalls. The sun shines down on flowers of many colors growing in profusion, never clashing, never dominating, and nobody ever seems to do any actual gardening. Pictures of the flowery enclosures of the Middle Ages depict lovers meeting under apple trees and sitting on turf or camomile seats, while gazing tenderly into each other's eyes.

ABOVE: A bench or other seat tucked into a small corner of the garden, or in a shady arbor surrounded with sweet-scented flowers, will create a perfect romantic hideaway.

COLOR AND SCENT

THERE is no reason why we cannot have a romantic garden in a modern setting. The most important things are color and scent. The colors should be soft and gentle; pale pink, buff and white are romantic colors, and the flowers should be prolific. There are many new and old roses with pretty colors and delightful scents, which will flower for long periods and will not outgrow their spaces.

❀ Gazebos, garden buildings, arbors and seats with rounded arches or pointed, Gothic ogee shapes are all easy to come by. Scented flowers can be grown next to seats and walkways and scented climbers can surround shady arbors.

❀ Shrub roses with good color and scent include 'Gertrude Jekyll' with rich pink blooms, 'Constance Spry' whose clear pink flowers continue over a long period, 'Buff Beauty' and 'Felicia'. Climbers and ramblers include 'New Dawn', a light satiny pink rose that will grow over a north wall, and 'Albertine', a popular rose with very pretty dark red buds, warm pink flowers and fierce thorns.

THE VICTORIAN ROMANTIC GARDEN

THE modern idea of a romantic garden follows a Victorian tradition. The Victorians were not only interested in the new plants being imported from all over the world, but they found the idea of the strange countries the plants came from wonderfully romantic, too.

BELOW: This little garden is full of surprises, including the statuette peeping out underneath the rose-covered pergola.

The larger Victorian garden might include a garden devoted to roses of all kinds, including old scented roses; there were also rockeries, streams and ferneries. Then there was the so-called 'cottage garden', portrayed in idealised water colors by nineteenth-century artists, showing cheerfully chaotic beds of rampant perennial and annual flowers, growing cheek by jowl in front of thatched cottages.

TODAY'S ROMANTIC GARDEN

MODERN gardeners are highly imaginative and creative when thinking up romantic gardens that can look natural and still be manageable. Traditionally, the orchard is an important part of the idea of a romantic garden, but the idea is symbolic, of course, and there is no need to have rows of fruit trees. One apple tree, two fruit bushes espaliered against a wall or a 'hedge' of cordoned fruit trees will serve the same purpose and be a marvellous addition to your garden.

ABOVE: *Roses are the most exquisite of flowers, whether they are in bud or full bloom. If adequately fed and watered, many will continue to flower until well into fall or later.*

There are plenty of plants whose common names can give an indication of how romantic a garden was in the old days. Hearts-ease was the name for the purple and yellow viola. Black-eyed Susan, bachelor's button, love-in-a-mist, forget-me-not, sweet Alison, sweet Cicely and blue-eyed Mary are all names used for cottage garden flowers, many of which are still enchanting planted in natural or romantic gardens today.

Today's romantic gardens are liable to be more deliberately designed, with fewer varieties of plants and an easy maintenance bias, but scent and colour, and a sense of timeless-ness are the essence of this style and these things are as attainable today as they ever have been.

LEFT: *The romantic garden is based on curves. Here, a camomile lawn has stepping stones for a path. Its pond is designed to attract wildlife. The pergola is covered with attractive vines, and from the seat you can see the only slightly formal element: a hexagonal summer house as a focal point at the far end.*

small tree

summerhouse

island

pond

camomile lawn

pergola with vine

informal border

paving pathway

seat

door to house

COLOR IN THE ROMANTIC GARDEN

Color depends so much on where, when and how it is seen. In the romantic garden color is one of the most important aspects of the planting so choose plants carefully to look their best in a particular part of the garden. Make sure you design the garden not just to be seen from the house, but to be enjoyed as you walk through or sit in a shady bower. Many plants are best seen close up so provide plenty of seating areas and plant for the pleasure of sitting in these spots.

❀ Dark, rich colors such as purples and reds, and especially deep reds, are exciting when viewed close up with the light behind you. These colors, which include deep red roses and the crimsons, scarlets and loud pinks of geraniums, are best kept near the house. Pale colors look best from a distance and these

are the ones most suitable to the romantic style of garden. The pale blue clematis such as 'Lasurstern' and 'Perle d'Azur' are the most effective of all clematis colors in the romantic garden. The deep, rich 'Royal Velours', 'Ville de Lyon' and 'Niobe' clematises are best kept near the house, although the smaller-flowered *viticella* types with their pagoda-shaped flowers can be grown among paler-colored roses in the main garden very effectively.

❀ Note whether the plants are best seen with the light behind you or behind the plants. The yellow forms of privet (*Ligustrum*), *Philadelphus coronarius* 'Aureus' and *Choisya ternata* 'Sundance' all look best against a dark background and against a north-facing wall. The high sunlight coming over on to the foliage will highlight the yellow beautifully against a dark wall or hedge.

TRADITIONAL PLANTS FOR THE ROMANTIC GARDEN

There are many plants that can add to the romantic quality of your garden. During the nineteenth century at least two dozen varieties of vines or wall grapes were grown as ornamental as well as productive plants. Walls were thickly covered with roses. Large colorful flowers were popular, such as peonies and oriental poppies. Scented flowers are an absolute essential in a romantic garden today, for example honeysuckles, lilies and old-fashioned pinks like the clove-scented white 'Mrs Sinkins'.

Climbing roses

❀ Repeat-flowering climbers are the most suitable roses for training up garden arches and bowers, whereas the vigorous but once-flowering ramblers may need the more substantial support of pergolas. 'Aloha' is one of the best repeat-flowering climbing roses, which will eventually grow to 10 ft (3 m). It is very healthy with lovely rich pink fragrant flowers and can be grown quite satisfactorily as a shrub. 'Golden Showers' is a good one if you like yellow. It is almost thornless but does not have much scent. 'New Dawn' is a beautiful pearly pink, highly fragrant and flowers almost continuously. 'Madame Alfred Carrière' is another almost thornless rose with white, scented flowers and satisfactory repeat-flowering. It will grow on a north-facing wall.

LEFT: *The top of this informal arch is almost completely hidden, as though it were wearing a bonnet of brightly colored roses.*

ABOVE: *A hammock slung under a tree, surrounded by a summer border with sweet-smelling flowers such as stock, makes a truly romantic environment.*

❀ Rambler roses have only one flowering period, which begins about midsummer. They are easier to train than climbers and the flowers are smaller. They are very vigorous and may be difficult to accommodate in a small garden but worth a try if you have a pergola or

wall or even an old tree for them to climb. 'Goldfinch' is a strongly scented pale yellow rose, which grows to 10 ft (3 m).

Old roses

❀ Some of the old Bourbon and Portland roses are very desirable and exactly right for the romantic garden, offering billowing masses of soft color and elegant habits of growth. Most of the old roses are exquisitely scented. 'Mme Isaac Perrière' is a Bourbon with exceedingly fragrant flowers with fully double globular cups and is said to be the most strongly scented of all roses. It can reach 7 ft (2 m) so make sure you allow it plenty of room.

❀ 'Mme Pierre Oger' also has deeply scented globular flowers of pale silvery pink and an arching habit, one of the most beautiful of all roses. 'La Reine Victoria' has a rather lax habit and may need some support. It has beautifully scented globular flowers, which open pale pink and deepen in color on exposure to light.

LEFT: *With so many different roses to choose from you will be sure to find a variety to suit your garden, whatever the size, aspect or shape. Include roses in your romantic garden to add both color and scent.*

WILDLIFE GARDENS

❀

As with all gardens, in a wildlife garden you are not attempting to re-create nature itself, but designing a garden in which native species of plants, birds and animals will flourish. A wildlife garden can be used for human enjoyment as well. It can look well designed and modern without losing any of its attraction to small creatures, who mind not whether it looks rural and 'natural' and just want the plants and habitats they can feel at home with. If the soil near the house is filled with builders' rubble, you can cover it with decking. This will be useful as a 'patio' and also for observing the garden from a slight height.

WILDLIFE HABITATS

WILDLIFE can be enticed into the garden by providing a variety of habitats and sources of food. Ideally, the garden should contain a woodland area, a wild flower meadow and a pond, all features that can be adapted to fit into a small garden successfully. Make the most of the conditions that prevail in your garden. For example, a poor soil is ideal for growing a wild flower meadow, while a damp, shady area will suit many woodland plants.

✿ Other good habitats include a pond and a dry stone wall or a pile of logs. You need plants that will supply pollen, nectar, berries and seeds. Wild flowers will also encourage many small creatures. Give structure to the garden with a natural stone path set in grass or a forest bark path winding through a grove of trees. A slightly raised seating area will give a view over the garden. Surround it with a planting of tall shrubs so that it will offer opportunities for watching small creatures as they move around in your garden.

Planting

✿ You can apply the same ground rules for the design of this type of garden as with any other: creating well-proportioned garden spaces, focal points, areas of interest and varied planting.

✿ A sunny flowerbed is the perfect place for growing some of the old cornfield weeds such as corncockle, corn marigold, cornflowers and poppies. A mixture of poppies alone makes a really spectacular sight in summer.

✿ If you have a fairly large garden, you might like a central meadow with wild flowers and grass seed appropriate to

ABOVE: *A wild meadow in England with yellow daisies, cornflowers, oregano and many different grasses.*

BELOW: *The spectacular sight of a meadow planted with wild flowers in France. Seen here are cornflowers, poppies and daisies, making an astonishing splash of color.*

the soil type. Choose a part of the garden that has rather poor soil if possible. Unlike most garden plants, wild flowers need soil with low fertility. This will help to restrict the more vigorous grasses so that the wild flowers have a chance to compete. Remove any turf and topsoil and replace it with subsoil.

❀ Buy an inexpensive kit for testing the soil so that you know its pH, and buy a mixture of seeds that will grow well on that. There are several seed companies selling appropriate mixtures. The plants should come into flower at roughly the same time, either all in spring or all in summer, so that you can cut the grass when appropriate. A spring-flowering meadow should be cut in midsummer and then mowed as usual until fall or cut once again in late fall. A summer-flowering meadow should be cut in late spring and again in late fall.

❀ A true lawn will have its own wildlife community, too. Do not allow dandelions and plantain in, but you can add seed of white clover to the lawn seed or scatter it on to an existing lawn. You can mow a path through this meadow and around its edges so it is easy to walk round and admire the flowers.

BELOW: *Treating the garden as a wildlife sanctuary means allowing flowers to retain their seed heads. Here, Agapanthus seed heads create interesting structural shapes.*

ABOVE: *The cheerful little marigold Calendula officinalis will fill gaps in the summer garden and associates well with many different flowers.*

BELOW: *A wildlife garden implies a certain amount of "laissez-faire"-or letting things be. Do not try to keep it too neat. A small heap of sticks and prunings may encourage hedgehogs, for example. A pond with overgrown edges will encourage other small creatures to run back and forth. A woodland section will attract squirrels and birds and if you have a boggy area, you can grow a wider variety of plants.*

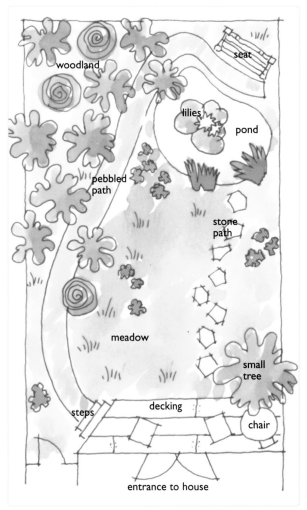

Woodland

❀ A woodland edge provides a rich natural habitat for wildlife and may attract hedgehogs, bats and a range of other creatures. You can re-create this sort of environment even on a small scale to bring a great diversity of creatures into the garden. A woodland area should consist of several layers of vegetation, including tall trees, smaller trees and a lower tier of shrubs. Under these can be planted ground cover plants and early bulbs.

❀ In a small garden, where large trees such as English oak (*Quercus ruber*) and beech (*Fagus sylvatica*) would not be appropriate, plant hazel (*Corylus avellana*), hawthorn (*Crataegus*) or bird cherry (*Prunus padus*), all of which will support wildlife. In a small town garden, use a mixed hedge as the top layer or substitute climbing plants including woodbine (*Lonicera periclymenum*) grown up a trellis. Small shrubs for the intermediate layer could include *berberis* and cotoneaster. Plants such as wood spurge (*Euphorbia amygdaloides*) and wood sorrel (*Oxalis acetosella*), which enjoy damp, shady situations, are good plants to grow in woodland.

❀ Every wildlife garden needs a pond as a home for all sorts of animal, bird and insect life and this should be

ABOVE: *A variety of trees and dense ground cover using ivies, hostas and ferns make this a most attractive woodland walk.*

in the most open area of the garden. It will make an excellent focal point. Boggy and marginal plants will make a natural-looking surround and offer cover for little creatures.

Windbreaks

❀ Fences provide inexpensive instant windbreaks. They can be of woven willow or hazel, or wattle in medieval style. They are all good at gently filtering the wind. Since this is an organic garden you will want to dedicate an area to composting, hidden by shrubs or a hedge or fencing to match that used in the rest of the garden.

❀ Hedges provide food, shelter, nesting sites and a safe, sheltered corridor for travelling creatures. Choose a flowering hedge such as *Rosa rugosa* 'Frau Dagmar Hastrup', which is a pretty pale pink, or the pure white 'Blanche Double de Coubert'. Alternatively, plump for clipped holly or a mixed hedge. Conifers do not mix well with other evergreen shrubs and do not make the best wildlife hedges on their own.

LEFT: *A woodland area can be one of the most attractive parts of a garden, as shown here by the graceful shape and fall color of this small Acer japonicum.*

Shrubs for a mixed hedge

❀ Choose one species as the mainstay of the hedge. The common hawthorn (*Crataegus monogyna*) is an attractive choice, with its sprays of fragrant white flowers in spring, red leaves and purple haws in fall. The blackthorn (*Prunus spinosa*) is another good mainstay hedging plant, with its white flowers in spring and blue-black sloes in fall.

❀ Choose from the following to interplant with your main choice: buckthorn (*Rhamnus catharticus*), which provides food for the caterpillar of the brimstone butterfly; holly (*Ilex aquifolium*); dogwood (*Cornus sanguinea*); wild privet (*Ligustrum vulgare*), which has strongly scented white flowers in summer; hazel (*Corylus avellana*), with pretty dangling catkins; and spindle (*Euonymus europaeus*) which has extraordinary puce and orange berries, beloved by birds.

Variety is the spice of wildlife

❀ The best garden for wildlife is one with the most variety of plants. A bit of grass, some herbaceous plants, some roses, some vegetables, a tree or two, even a few weeds such as nettles and a privet that some caterpillars need to feed on, will make a good start. The garden borders should be wide enough to take several layers of vegetation.

ABOVE: *These cherry trees allow useful ground cover plants such as honesty and periwinkle to carpet the ground beneath them.*

ABOVE: *If you provide the right woodland conditions you may get hedgehogs visiting your garden. They should be welcomed, since they eat slugs and snails.*

❀ Make sure there are some evergreen shrubs for winter cover as well as winter interest, and some deciduous trees and shrubs to let some light through in the spring. Each layer of vegetation provides a habitat for different creatures. Thrushes are at home in the treetops, sparrows and tits congregate slightly lower down and blackbirds like to peck around and listen for worms on the ground. Spiders, beetles and mice will all make their homes in a pile of stones in a secluded corner.

Birdlife

❀ Birds can be encouraged to nest in the garden if you fix nesting boxes to the trees. Put these up in fall or midwinter so the birds have time to go house hunting and explore them thoroughly before the next nest-building season begins.

❀ Nesting boxes with small holes (about $1^{1}/_{4}$ in or 3 cm) will allow smaller birds such as nuthatches and tits to use them. Larger entrance holes will attract a wider range of birds. A box should be fixed high enough so

ABOVE: *A thoughtful gardener has created a colorful spring-flowering garden at the edge of a wood where it meets the road.*

BELOW: *Soft greens and the palest of yellows provide color and texture in a border between a meadow lawn and a hedge.*

that cats and squirrels cannot reach it. The positioning is crucial. It should be sheltered from wind, rain and strong sunlight and away from bird tables.

❀ Birds are attracted by such plants as asters, golden rod, cornflowers, teazel, cotoneasters, violas, fennel, lavender, forget-me-nots, scabious, sorbus, honeysuckle and pyracantha. Insects enjoy *Phacelia tanacetifolia*, a hardy annual with bell-shaped blue flowers with prominent stamens, which seeds itself around the garden even in poor soils. Insects also like thyme, mint, oregano, crocuses and ivy.

Butterfly borders

❀ Butterflies like to sunbathe in sunny, sheltered spots that are protected from the wind. In a perennial border grow *Aubrieta* to attract painted ladies, red admirals, brimstones and small tortoiseshell butterflies. The same butterflies use lavender as a nectar source, as do the small copper, common blue, meadow brown and small skipper. Later in the year they will be attracted by Aster (Michaelmas daisies,) valerian (*Centranthus*), phlox and *Sedum spectabile*, which has fleshy green leaves and flattish heads of tiny pink flowers in late summer and fall. It has thin narrow florets, into which the butterflies can reach for nectar with their long tongues.

❀ Honesty has heads of small purple flowers and is a good source of food for caterpillars of the orange-tip butterfly, and the lilac- or white-flowered buddlejas are well known for attracting peacock and tortoiseshell butterflies, which can absolutely cover the flowers on a sunny day.

Other insects

❀ Flowers are attractive to bees for both their nectar and pollen and they are also important as a continuous food larder from early spring to late fall. Particular favorites are herbs such as thyme, marjoram, mint, lavender and lemon balm.

❀ Beneficial insects in the garden pollinate fruit and vegetables and prey on common garden pests. Between them, anthocorid bugs, ladybugs, hoverflies, lacewings, ground beetles and centipedes will eat caterpillars, midges, weevils, scale insects and red spider mites, slugs, snails, mealy bugs, thrips, scale insects, leafhoppers, aphids and cabbage fly and carrot root fly eggs and larvae. So choosing plants that will attract the beneficial insects is obviously sensible. Fennel (*Foenciulum vulgare*), with its flat heads of yellow flowers above feathery leaves, is a favorite plant of hoverflies. Pollen and nectar-feeding insects also love sunflowers (*Helianthus annuus*).

ABOVE: Gleditsia *trees and* Linaria *provide contrasting colors on the edge of a wooded area.*

❀ Other useful flowers are the annual pot marigolds (*Calendula officinalis*), the poached egg flower (*Limnanthes douglasii*), Californian poppy (*Eschscholtzia californica*), baby blue eyes (*Nemophila*), yarrow (*Achillea*), anaphalis, Shasta daisy (*Chrysanthemum maximum*), sea holly (*Eryngium*), wild strawberry (*Fragaria vesca*) and candytuft (*Iberis*).

Preference for species plants

❀ When choosing flowers remember that single flowers are best for wildlife. The extra petals in double forms are often formed at the expense of nectaries and anthers, which means they provide less food for insects. For example, the common bird's foot trefoil has a yellow pea flower, which produces plenty of nectar, but the double variety has none at all.

❀ In other plants, the extra petals on double flowers often make an insurmountable barrier for insects. This means that often they cannot get in to the flower to find the food at all.

❀ You need to check that nasturtium and columbine flowers have pointed sacs (or spurs) behind the flowers. These are reservoirs for nectar and are important for species like long-tongued bumble bees, an increasingly threatened form of wildlife.

❀ Delphiniums and larkspurs should also have spurs. When in doubt, choose old-fashioned varieties of plant and the nearest to the wild flower or species as possible. They are often more graceful and elegant in any case.

❀ Night-flowering nectar plants include flowering tobacco (*Nicotiana alata*) and night-scented stock (*Matthiola longipetala*). These will attract night-flying insects, which in turn may attract bats.

ABOVE: *A decorative* Rodgersia *stands out against a background of ferns in woodland.*

CONTAINER GARDENS

Pots and containers can be used to provide visual interest throughout the year; the most sculptural ones need have nothing planted in them at all. They can be moved around to fill gaps, rearrange the balance of some aspect of the garden, or add a particular color. Used for tender plants, they can stand outside in summer and be brought inside during cold weather. Pots can also be used to hold climbers to enhance patios, terraces, balconies, courtyards and windowsills. They can be used to revitalise dull areas and introduce interest to the bleakest of tiny alleyways or basement areas.

CHOOSING CONTAINERS

THE range of possible containers is enormous. Almost anything can be used as a container, provided it has drainage holes and will hold enough compost to support the plant. Many are purpose made but there is plenty of scope for using containers not originally intended for plants, and these may be equally effective and cheaper. In Greece, for example, brightly painted old paint cans filled with red geraniums are often ranged along the street wall of whitewashed cottages.

❀ Old chimney pots can be simple in shape or very decorative and will add height where it may be needed.

❀ Wheelbarrows have become popular as containers, although definitely not for formal gardens, and old watering cans, buckets and pails, ceramic sinks and ancient water tanks are all possibilities.

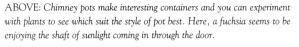

ABOVE: *Chimney pots make interesting containers and you can experiment with plants to see which suit the style of pot best. Here, a fuchsia seems to be enjoying the shaft of sunlight coming in through the door.*

❀ Sinks are very heavy; once positioned you will not want to move one again. Shallow sinks are good for rock garden plants, miniature bulbs and dwarf conifers. White, glazed fire clay sinks can be covered in a substance known as 'tufa' to look just like stone. Alternatively, you can bury a sink in the ground, having first blocked up the plughole, and use it as a miniature bog garden for moisture-loving plants such as primulas.

LEFT: *A brightly painted container garden on different levels provides a colorful entrance to a seaside house.*

LEFT: *Wheelbarrows are often used to display an interesting selection of annual plants. Probably the most attractive barrows are those that have already done their stint in the garden, like this one, whose attractive grey-green paint is showing signs of wear.*

Other choices

❀ Cement-based artificial stone or plain cement planters can look handsome. Large concrete and timber planting cases and barrels can hold enough compost to support a small tree. In the eighteenth century, square or circular wooden tubs planted with orange and lemon trees were placed in rows in formal gardens and taken into an early form of conservatory, or 'orangery', over the winter.

❀ Plastic containers are very much lighter to lift than most other planters, which is a great advantage if you want to move them around. They do not look quite like terracotta but once full of plants and sitting on a patio, the containers themselves will not be very noticeable.

Clay pots

❀ Clay pots and containers come in a great variety of sizes and designs. Small and medium-sized pots are best grouped together because just one can look a little pathetic on its own in an open space. Very large, shapely ones can be used as ornaments in their own right at the end of an axis or some other prominent place.

❀ Clay pots can vary in colour from cream and pale pink to deep red and a rather brash orange. The colour will weather in time. Choose a relatively simple design so as not to distract attention away from the plants.

❀ Elaborate pots are really suitable only for special situations. Chinese-style pots with coloured glazes are available in useful, sturdy shapes. It is best to choose the same type and colour for pots that are going to be placed in the same area. Check that the pots you buy are frostproof.

BELOW: *This small courtyard garden has been laid with flag paving and planted with large and small pots of plants to provide interest all year round. There are clipped evergreens for winter interest, pots of geraniums and busy Lizzies that will need be taken in during the winter, and one or two tall shrubs to soften the edges.*

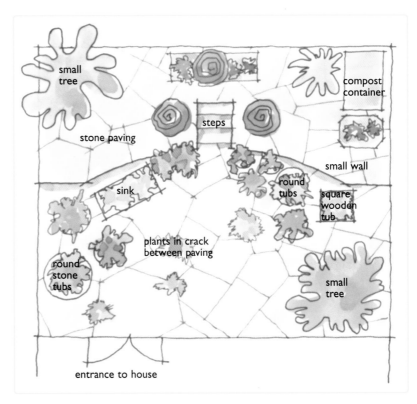

PLANTS FOR CONTAINERS

As with all design, keep your planting schemes simple. Do not try to mix too many different varieties. Opt for just two or three that will bloom in succession to give a long season of color. One variety to a pot often looks best of all. You can juxtapose the containers for their color combinations after planting.

Planting for spring

❀ Fairly shallow containers with wide tops look great with low-growing spring bulbs such as crocuses and scillas. Taller containers can take taller stemmed plants such as daffodils and tulips. A long-lasting and attractive display can be made with crocuses and iris together with later-flowering tulips and daffodils in a container deep enough to take two levels of bulbs.

❀ Plant the tulips and daffodils at the lowest level. The satiny, almost black tulip, 'Queen of the Night', or a group of elegant lily-flowered tulips such as the snowy 'White Triumphator' are good container bulbs. For daffodils you could try 'Minnow', which has delicate creamy yellow flowers, two to four on a stem. 'Hawera', with pretty yellow heads, is one of the latest-flowering daffodils.

❀ Plant *Iris reticulata* and early crocuses higher up in the compost – when these die down, their leaves will not be noticed because the interest will have moved to the daffodils and tulips. These tiny irises have an upright habit and long slender leaves and look very good grown on their own in pots, although their season is not very long.

LEFT: *This bold display of Agaves and cacti in pots works particularly well because the stripy spirals of the pots are repeated throughout the area. The low-growing shrubs at the back create an informal low hedge that softens the fence.*

❀ Wallflowers (*Cheiranthus cheiri*) have the most wonderful scent in the late spring garden. Grow them with tulips and daffodils for a rich tapestry of colors. Tulips also look good underplanted with forget-me-nots (*Myosotis*), scillas and grape hyacinths.

❀ Polyanthus are excellent contenders for pots, too. Plant them with pansies or small trumpet daffodils and grape hyacinths. Their colors are wonderful. You can grow the whole palette of colors together, or try the blues and whites as a combination, or blues and pinks and so on. Double daisies (*Bellis perennis*) make good perimeter plants and associate well with forget-me-nots, wallflowers and pansies.

Planting for summer

❀ There are many interesting and colorful plants for summer containers. Variegated or silvery trailing plants such as small ivies, *Helichrysum petiolare* and *Senecio maritima* 'Silver Dust' can enhance any mixed planting. Useful summer bedding plants include impatiens (for shady places), petunias, verbenas, *Felicia amelloides* and lobelias.

BELOW: *In this peaceful water garden, evergreen plants have been used to provide interest at all times of the year, but the summer planting of brightly colored rock roses in tubs gives it a cheerful feeling in the sun.*

LEFT: *A hot climate is just right for a cactus garden like this one. The garden walls have been painted white and accentuate the shadows of the pots. Even the dog seems to enjoy the sun.*

Acid-loving plants

❀ Containers can be particularly useful for growing plants for which the soil in your garden is not suitable. Acid-loving plants such as dwarf rhododendrons, azaleas, camellias and heathers can be planted in ericaceous compost. Most of these are woodland plants and prefer not to be in full sun. All have shallow rooting systems, which makes them particularly suitable for container planting.

❀ Pots and geraniums might have been made for each other. Use them in window boxes and any other container on their own. Unlike *Impatiens*, geraniums like strong light. Their foliage has an amazing range of scents, from lemon and peppermint to apple, pine and rose so you can place pots where the aromatic foliage will send out its scent as soon as someone brushes against it.

BELOW: *The succulent plants in these terracotta pots introduce a variety of shapes that are set off against the sun's shadow on the painted fencing behind them.*

Planting for fall and winter

❀ All clipped evergreen shrubs look good in winter, providing pattern and structure when everything else is over. The common snowdrop (*Galanthus nivalis*) is a hardy bulb not often grown in containers, but it will make a brave show of white and green from late winter to early spring. Flowering shrubs can provide interest, too, especially near the house, since during winter the garden will mostly be seen only from inside.

❀ The small deciduous shrub *Ceratostigma willmottianum* can be planted on its own in a medium-sized pot. It has bright blue flowers all through summer and well into fall, when its leaves turn red. *Daphne odora* is an evergreen shrub with glossy dark green leaves and clusters of fragrant purplish-pink and white flowers from midwinter to spring. The heather families (*Calluna*, *Daboecia* and *Erica*) contain species and cultivars that will flower all year. Good winter ones include *Erica* x *darleyensis* 'White Perfection', *E.* x *veitchii* 'Pink Joy' and *E. carnea* 'Vivellii' (bright pink).

ROOF GARDENS

❦

A roof garden can be one of the biggest luxuries of city life.
It is a true extension of the indoor living space, offering spectacular
views over rooftops with a feeling of light and space that you cannot
normally get in the urban environment.

HISTORY

THE roof garden has a long history. The Hanging
Gardens of Babylon were really roof gardens, built
over an arcaded palace in ascending terraces. On top of
the arches, bundles of reeds and asphalt were laid and
covered with brick tiles and thick sheets of lead to
provide waterproofing for the decorated state rooms
below. Water was raised up by pump. The whole thing
was planted with flowering shrubs and trees such as larch,
birch, cypress, cedar, acacia and mimosa.

❀ When Derry and Tom's department store was built in
London in the 1930s, permission for a further storey
was refused because the firemen's ladders were too short
to reach it, so a roof garden was built instead. This was
made up of a series of traditional gardens including a
Hispano-Moorish garden, a Tudor garden and a
woodland area complete with a small stream filled with
fish and ducks. There was even a cascade and grotto.
The garden is still open to the public, and although the
introduction of flamingos has led to damage of some
vegetation and loss of fish, it is still a magical place to
visit and hard to imagine you are among the rooftops.

ABOVE: *This tiny roof space is a haven among the chimney pots in central
London. The permanent planting is evergreen, while annuals are grown in tubs
for summer interest.*

Practical difficulties

❀ Recent developments in waterproofing technology and
materials and increased roof insulation have made the
roof garden a possibility for anyone with a flat roof, and
the luxury of extra living space in a small city flat cannot
be overemphasised.

❀ Before you begin stocking your lofty garden with plants,
there are a number of practical difficulties you should be
aware of. Most roofs have a limited load-bearing capacity

LEFT: *This little London roof garden is not only attractive to sit in, but also
pretty when seen from the street and the houses opposite. The planting is mostly
shrubby and provides interest all year round.*

there may be regulations limiting or prohibiting screens or plants being visible from street level, so check with the local authority.

Room-like spaces

❀ High up spaces, open to the sky, can seem threatening, so the best idea is to try and create a room-like space with some sort of enclosure. If there is no low parapet or wall, you will certainly need to put something up anyway, simply from the point of view of safety. The other thing you will find on a roof garden is that the wind is much stronger than at street level and has a dehydrating effect, so plants will need more watering.

❀ You can surround the garden with trellis to act as a psychological barrier and also to help filter the wind to a certain extent. You can plant this quite lightly with ivy or clematis for privacy and leave parts of it unplanted so as not to block the wider view. Choose the most robust trellis you can find and fix it firmly to supports, otherwise the wind will blow it over in a very short time.

ABOVE: *On this extremely stylish roof garden, trellis has been used to form an outdoor 'room', creating a space with a Japanese flavor – open to the sky but concealed from the world.*

and may not be able to support the extra weight of surfacing materials, soil, containers and so on. You may have to have the structure strengthened or you may have to keep pots and plants around the perimeter, close to the structural walls, where the roof is supported.

❀ You must make sure the roof's waterproofing is sound and will not be interfered with. So before you begin, get a structural engineer to check the site for you. In historic or conservation areas,

RIGHT: *The first priority for a roof garden is to establish that the roof is strong enough and waterproof and has planning permission for use as a garden. Paving should be as lightweight as possible – thin tiles or decking are probably the best materials. Any pergola should be sturdily fixed to prevent it rocking in the wind and pots should be ranged around the edges of the roof where it is supported.*

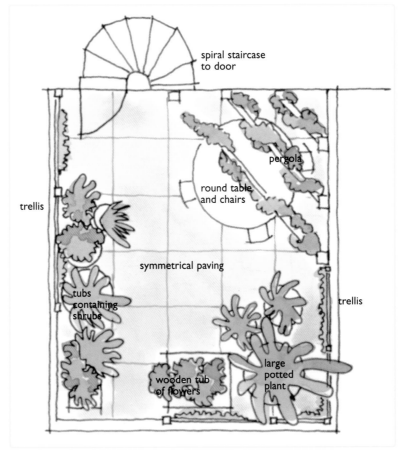

spiral staircase to door

pergola

round table and chairs

trellis

symmetrical paving

trellis

tubs containing shrubs

wooden tub of flowers

large potted plant

Adding a pergola to a roof

❀ You can add to the enclosed feeling by introducing a small pergola for shade and to support climbers. This will also reduce the effect of the possibly rather oppressive area of sky and provide privacy from nearby roof gardens. It should be attached to walls and sturdily fixed seats and planters to ensure stability.

BELOW: *This attractive, sunny little roof garden is protected from the elements and neighbors by ivy and a small bay tree. Evergreen herbs such as rosemary are brightened up with the reds of geraniums and pinks of sweet peas.*

ABOVE: *The plants in this small roof garden are mostly low growing so as not to suffer from the wind. They include a Mexican orange blossom (Choisya ternata 'Sundance'), some low bamboos, variegated hostas, broom, ceratostigma, lavender and, for climbers, solanum and clematis.*

Flooring materials

❀ Lightweight gravel is a good foil to small containers. Decking is comparatively lightweight and therefore suitable for a flat roof. Timber tiles are available, which are easy to lay and convenient to carry upstairs. If you have enough space, you can add a raised area of decking to use as a table or for sunbathing.

❀ Roberto Burle Marx, the celebrated Brazilian garden designer, uses brightly colored mosaic designs as a prominent feature on the floors of his roof gardens and, provided you have a suitable surface, this is an idea that would look cheerful on small roof terraces, too.

Planters and containers

❀ Most flat roof spaces have some unfortunate built-in features such as a water tank or air-conditioning unit that you cannot get rid of. Portable timber planters of varying heights can be used to hide such eyesores. Fill them with lightweight, moisture retentive compost and plant them up with small trees to make an effective screen. You can paint containers to match any trellis or wall. White is always effective, but there are many excellent colors to choose from and you might prefer a pastel color or something bolder like a deep blue.

Plants for the roof

❀ If your roof space is open to the sky, it will probably be best to choose a few carefully placed sculptural plants that will thrive in difficult high-rise urban circumstances, or put containers around the perimeter, planted with wind-resistant shrubs and small trees. Cacti and succulents are sun lovers, and require the minimum of watering. If the temperature is too cold for them, use grasses, which do not need much maintenance and will look very attractive blowing in the wind.

❀ If the space is small and partly enclosed, you could create a bower of flowering shrubs and climbers with a few small conifers for height, variety and shade. Plants that tolerate seaside conditions are often good for rooftop gardens; varieties of *Escallonia*, *Berberis* and *Lauristinus* should all be able to cope with high-rise conditions.

Balconies

❀ A balcony can become a useful visual and physical extension to the living area. A very effective way of integrating the two areas is to stand a few pots on the inside as well as the outside to act as links and make the balcony seem larger. Use identical pots and flowers to emphasise the sense of unity. If your scheme involves structural work, get advice from a structural engineer as to the weight capacity of your balcony, as you would for a flat roof.

Window gardens

❀ If window boxes and hanging baskets are the only garden you have, make the most of them. It is wonderful that English pubs have gone so wholeheartedly for

ABOVE: *This large, sunny roof garden has been treated rather formally, with rows of white-flowered geraniums in black pots along the bottom of the window and purple violas climbing up the steps.*

highly colored hanging baskets and window boxes. Many are truly splendid in their rich and varied plantings, but all the best ones have very deliberate color schemes. They are not simply a chaos of any old colors planted together.

❀ If you like these cheerful displays, note down what plants have been used to create them and do the same at home. However, not every window box gardener wants to be quite so flamboyant. There are plenty of other ways of making the most of window boxes. The mixed colors of red and white geraniums with some trailing ivy will look bright and cheerful all summer.

❀ Herb window boxes can be both charming and useful. Choose herbs that all like the same conditions and that will grow to much the same sort of height or the display won't work or will look unbalanced. Sage, golden marjoram, a dwarf lavender and chives could make an interesting and tasty display.

❀ If the window is on the shady side of the house, you can plant miniature bamboos in window boxes, which will provide a sort of lacy curtain of green. Choose containers that suit the style of the house and make sure the boxes are firmly secured.

PLANNED GARDENS

Planned gardens are precise and often arranged symmetrically around a central axis, which divides the garden down the middle. The central path may have paths crossing it at right angles, dividing the garden into rectangles or squares. A very small and square garden might not have a straight path, just a central feature with paving around it. The positive symmetrical shapes of the garden must be kept very defined and clear. Paths should be carefully detailed, hedges precise and evergreen shrubs clipped into disciplined shapes. Several features have been associated with the great formal gardens of early times. Many can be introduced into small gardens with great success. The style is particularly suitable for square or rectangular level sites where the symmetry fits well into the basic shape of the plot.

Hedges

✿ Because a symmetrical pattern is the important thing, hedges are often used to mark out the pattern like piping on a cushion. Many of these are low so that they emphasise the basic geometry and do not hide one part from another. Box is one of the most popular shrubs for low hedges, as it grows slowly and is easy to clip.

✿ Tall, clipped hedges of yew, privet, hornbeam or beech can create divisions between different areas or mark out the perimeter. Straight avenues can be lined on either side by pleached hornbeam or lime. Pleaching means planting the trees equal distances apart, cutting off the lower branches and intertwining or grafting the side branches to meet at about eye level, making a

ABOVE: A vegetable garden laid out in a carefully planned manner with contrasting stone steps and paths and clipped bushes introducing symmetry.

clipped hedge on tall 'stalks'. In larger gardens two rows can be planted to create a dense double hedge with a tunnel in the middle.

Knots and parterres

✿ Knot gardens were popular in Tudor times and were based on ancient mazes. These developed into small, rectangular, intricate geometrical patterns planted in a continuous, unbroken line. A knot garden may be complete in itself or filled with colors to accentuate

LEFT: Simple geometrical patterns in knots or parterres can enhance any garden – no matter how small.

LEFT: *A small garden showing careful attention to planting, precise patterning in the terracing and formal placing of garden furniture*

triangles, hexagons and octagons. This need not necessarily mean straight lines. An oval shape can be very satisfactory in a rectangular plot and circular shapes have often been used very successfully inside square plots.

❀ Adjacent shapes can touch, overlap or be separated by a gap. It is usually best to choose one shape, such as a square, and then arrange squares of different size in a formal pattern.

Axis paths

❀ When making your axis lines, you can reinforce them by planting clipped hedges along each side. Box is the most popular for this but lavender or rosemary will also make attractive low hedges. If you want something taller, plant standard roses on supports.

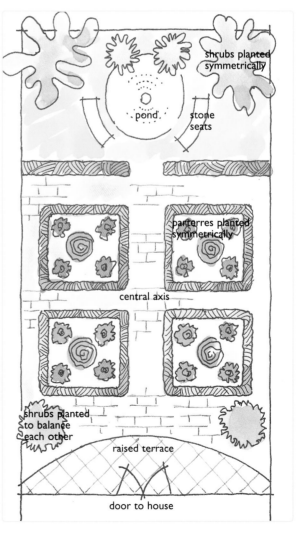

the shapes. Traditionally, different colored gravels and coal or perhaps low-growing herbs such as thyme and lavender were used. Today recycled glass chippings and colored glass pebbles have added to the possibilities.

❀ A parterre is simpler than a knot – often planted in individual squares, not joined up together. Parterres were developed from knots in 17th-century France where they were designed to be viewed from first-floor windows. They are usually larger and more open and the plants grown inside them can be taller, for example shrub roses such as 'Felicia', 'Ballerina' and 'Iceberg'. Parterres can also be used for growing vegetables.

Symmetrical shapes

❀ Symmetrical shapes are those that are regular in outline. Although squares, rectangles and circles are the most common shapes, it is also possible to use

RIGHT: *This garden leads, via two steps, from a curved patio of square slabs to four squares of clipped yew set in brick paving. Each square has a standard small rose or bay tree in the center. A clipped hedge divides this area from a circular pond with seats for peaceful contemplation.*

ABOVE: *The wooden garden chair provides a focal point here, with the eye being drawn from the herring-bone patterned paving by the symmetry of the carefully clipped bushes on either side of the seat.*

BELOW: *Geometrically shaped beds of box make up this parterre. They are divided by narrow brick paths and filled with a variety of white flowers, mainly with silver leaves.*

Vertical elements

❀ Because so much of the pattern in planned gardens is derived from paths and low hedges, it is necessary to bring in some vertical elements to provide height and interest. These can be introduced in various ways. A sundial or bird-bath on a pedestal or a stone fountain can make a good central feature. Yew or box clipped into tall shapes or mop-headed box or bay trees in tubs can be positioned in rows on either side of a path.

Focal points

❀ A focal point is something that attracts attention. It might be a small building or tree on the horizon or a sculpture or urn. A focal point should be deliberate. You do not want the eye attracted towards a washing line or tool shed. The eye likes to go to a focal point in a straight line, so formal gardens are asking for focal points to be positioned at the ends of straight paths and avenues.

❀ A focal point may be a specimen tree, a well-designed bench in an arbor, a small summer house or a white painted seat (white is an instant focal point).

❀ A view could also be a focal point. To do this you will need to frame it with planting or create a 'window' in a clipped hedge through which to see it.

Materials

❧ Formal style is highly disciplined. Paving materials need to be very carefully chosen so that they are in sympathy with any nearby buildings. Even mixing different kinds and colors of bricks can produce a disruptive effect.

❧ All materials should be well defined. It is best to use as few materials as possible so that the overall effect gives a sense of unity. If using paving stones, they should be placed in a geometric manner, not as flagstone paving, which is seldom suited to a formal plan.

❧ When laying bricks you will find that a herring-bone pattern has a softer effect than when the bricks are laid in straight lines. Paths can be edged with small cobbles to give them an 'outline' to reinforce the pattern. Both brick and stone make a warm, static ground cover that marries well with brick walls to give a unified design.

❧ Gravel is not usually a good choice for the symmetrical garden. It is too easily kicked around and does not provide a clear enough outline for the geometric garden. One exception is a very small garden that is more for viewing than for walking around, where gravel can make an effective background for a central clipped shrub or stone sculpture.

Water

❧ Water is very much part of the traditional formal garden. It harks back to the desert gardens of old with their irrigation channels and refreshing central pools.

❧ A central pool of circular or geometric shape, perhaps with a fountain in the center, or indeed any central water feature with a symmetrical shape will look in place.

❧ Narrow channels can run alongside paths and long, rectangular ponds with matching seats on either side will enable visitors to sit and enjoy water lilies and the reflections of the sky. A long, narrow rectangular pond can have a fountain at each end to add interest.

❧ If water is the central element in the garden, it creates an atmosphere of great tranquillity. The reflecting quality of the water in a large pool, plus pale-colored paving, will give the center of the garden a very light, optimistic feeling.

RIGHT: *Graded heights make these yew topiary shapes very intriguing. Combined with the red standard roses and the white shrub rose, they make an impressive sight.*

❧ The pool should of course be symmetrical and balanced. In an enclosed area, more water can be added via wall fountains. Even water plants can be placed symmetrically.

❧ A wide paved path allows the visitor to get near the water, and steps can lead right down to the water's edge. A symmetrical row of small trees or a clipped hedge will act as a framework to the pool, giving a general feeling of privacy and accentuating the formality.

CHILDREN IN THE PLANNED GARDEN

THERE is no reason why young children should not be able to play in a formal garden. Clipped hedges are usually pretty sturdy, particularly in tubs, and the very fact of having paved paths and straight lines means that running and cycling, roller-skating and skate-boarding are made possible. Remember that paths should be wide enough to make all these activities easy and it is a good idea to provide turning circles at each end.

SMALL GARDENS

❦

The key to the formal garden is repetition, unity and geometrical patterns and spaces. Small square or rectangular gardens belonging to urban houses are well suited to formality. The symmetrical shape is good for the geometric division of spaces and for straight lines of plants. Remember that although clipped hedges are a highly finished kind of formality, the mere lining out of identical plants in rows is in itself a formal arrangement. There are several ancient and traditional models of formal garden on which to base a design.

A Persian garden

❀ The first pleasure gardens in Egypt and Persia were based on water and their long narrow canals ran in grid patterns, stemming from the idea of the four-square paradise garden. Where these channels met, there would be a large central pond or tank with fish and water lilies. The royal paradise garden was large, with raised pavilions to catch the slightest breeze. Here you could sit under the shade of trees and enjoy the sound of running water and the scents and colors of flowers.

❀ Although in temperate areas water does not have quite the same significance as it does in desert areas, we still find water soothing and relaxing. Most gardens, large or small, are more interesting if they include a pool, fountain or stream. In city gardens an enclosed garden designed along Persian lines can keep ugly neighboring buildings out of sight. Even in tiny gardens a narrow channel of water can be created, either running alongside a path or taking up the center of the plot.

❀ Narrow flowerbeds can run around the perimeter with seats or spaces for sitting under shady trees. In a small garden you can use paths rather than water as your grid with some formal planting on either side of standard rose bushes and clipped shapes in box or yew. Fastigiate (having erect branches) and mop-headed trees will provide shade without taking up too much light.

A Moorish garden

❀ There are many similarities between Persian and Moorish gardens, for example the shady trees, scented flowers and the idea of water channels. But whereas Persian gardens were enclosed to keep out the desert, in Moorish gardens the rigid and confined lines were opened up to give views of orchards, olive groves and distant hills.

❀ Patios, porticos and arcades made an almost seamless transition between the house and the garden. Similarly, the wall or hedge of your four-square garden could open out to reveal a tree or an interesting piece of

LEFT: A very small space can be given interest by the pots used. Here, a pair of chimney pots has been planted with clipped box, giving a striking and unusual appearance. The box leaves serve to echo the green of the door.

Box-edged borders

❋ An elaborate parterre may be too
large for the smaller garden but
simpler box-edged borders are very
suitable. Although the plants may
take some time to get going, they
will eventually form a solid block
of foliage that is a good foil to other
plants. The variegated varieties,
although pretty, do not create such
a good background and are best
grown as features on their own.

LEFT: *Simple borders – such as this carefully laid
out lavender border, with its attractive cloche at
the center – are often best for a small garden.*

BELOW: *Formality can be achieved with repetition,
unity and geometric lines. A small fountain in the
middle is surrounded by a low hedge and a perimeter
of grass, the width of a lawn mower. Formal seats are
set in niches created by clipped yew hedges and
sheltered by topiary shapes.*

architecture outside the garden
itself. Summer houses could be
constructed with columns, giving a
cloister-like impression to be
reflected at one end of the water.

A parterre

❋ The parterre is basically a 'flat'
pattern, often best seen from a
height, such as a first-floor window
or a raised terrace or mount. Even
where there is no raised area, a
parterre can still be enjoyed while
walking through it. It may be part
of a larger formal garden or can
take up the whole of a small
garden.

❋ The simplest parterre, perhaps
a rectangle or square of clipped
box or shrubby honeysuckle such
as *Lonicera nitida*, makes an
excellent design for a small
front garden, which is usually
viewed in passing, rather than
actually entered.

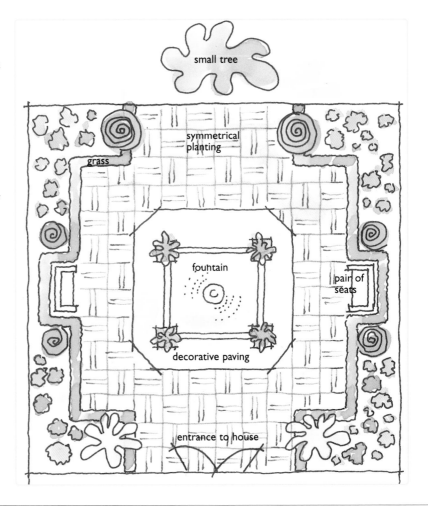

FORMAL FRONT GARDENS

A VERY small garden may not offer much scope for an extended symmetrical arrangement but even one small standard tree in a square bed edged with box will make a charming formal front garden. You could place a clipped bay *(Laurus nobilis)* in a tub at each corner of the bed and use paving slabs or gravel as the surrounding material.

❀ If the site is sunny and you do not want the shade of even a small tree, the silvery leaves of the small shrub *Convolvulus cneorum* in a small sea of gravel will look pretty all year round. In a shady area, grow one bold plant of *Hosta sieboldiana*, whose bluey-green leaves are large and important looking.

Clipped hedging plants

❀ Although box is probably the longest-lasting hedging plant, there are several others that will make attractive edging hedges and you may prefer the silvery look that many of them offer.

ABOVE: *Careful planting, pruning and clipping of bushes such as bay can introiduce a sense of fomality into even the smallest of garden areas.*

LEFT: *This tiny, narrow garden incorporates careful planning in the decorative paving work, the small ponds mirroring each other and the planting along the pathway.*

❀ Lavender, rosemary and santolina were all traditionally used as clipped hedging plants and are still very attractive used in this way. They are not as long lasting as box and if you want them to live for many years, they must all be cut back really hard. They do not like to be crowded and hate any competition for light, moisture and nutrients so make sure there is a gap between the hedge and the planting inside it.

Formal but soft

❀ A very long, narrow plot can seem difficult to deal with formally because its ribbon-like shape already accentuates the straight lines and constricted space. You can soften the lines of straight paths by creating circular areas along the way, planting dome-shaped plants and clipping shrubs into rounded shapes.

Similarly, the path can be lined with round-headed flowers, for example the soft rounded shapes of golden marjoram and alliums, which will produce big round flower heads in summer. Gravel rather than paving or brick will also soften the outline.

ABOVE: *This picturesque old-fashioned thatched cottage is very formal with its neat clipped hedge and white gate. The topiary columns support a clipped shape that echoes tha thatching on the roof.*

Axes and vistas

❀ One of the first decisions to make is the direction of the main axes. This will determine where the main vistas will lie and the garden's relationship to the house. The ornaments and features that close a vista can be added at a later stage. In most cases you will want the main axis to relate to the main door of the house so that garden and house can be seen as one entity in the plan.

❀ Cross-axes should be at right angles, but this is not always easy to achieve if the ground is not level or the plot not rectangular. At Sissinghurst in Kent, England the axes are not always at right angles but this has been cleverly concealed by the planting.

Materials

❀ The choice of material for hard surfaces and how it is laid can make or spoil a formal garden. Gravel is a versatile material, which combines well with other surfaces, including concrete and paving blocks.

❀ Always get the best quality of any material that you can afford. York stone is unfortunately too expensive for most gardeners but there are acceptable forms of reconstituted stone, which can look perfectly good. paving blocks setts make good substitutes, too.

❀ Rounded cobblestones are attractive visually but uncomfortable to walk on, so should be used only for decorative details among other paving. They are useful as a contrast to other materials and as part of a decorative paving pattern. They can also be used to mark transitions between two separate areas or the change of direction of a path. Tiles laid on their edges can also mark changes of direction or provide interesting edging between other materials.

Plants for formal gardens

❀ Edging plants are useful for emphasising the line of a straight border. Choose those that will be of interest over a long season and use one plant along the whole length of the border to give a sense of unity. Possible plants include *Alchemilla mollis*, a pretty greeny-yellow plant that associates well with almost everything.

❀ The catmint *Nepeta cataria* is another good edging plant if your border is wide enough. *Bergenia cordifolia*, otherwise known as elephant's ears, will give a border a striking dark green edging, which turns red in fall.

CONTEMPORARY GARDENS

Many modern buildings have simple, rectangular shapes, repetitive forms and the minimum of applied decoration. It is the shape of the whole structure that is important – the spacing and proportion of windows and doors and the relationship of the different planes. To complement such buildings, we need to design gardens of great simplicity, elegance and style, which will reflect the geometric lines of the house with their own geometric lines, softened by planting.

MODERNIST IDEAS

MODERNIST principles in gardening come from the Modernist style of architecture, which emerged at the beginning of the twentieth century. This made use of the newest technological developments to design buildings that did not have to rely on traditional building techniques. Reinforced concrete could be molded into exciting new forms, creating lighter buildings with bigger, interconnected spaces and uncluttered interiors.

❀ Today there is a new wave of Modernist thinking, which regards the garden as an outside room whose link with the house is paramount. Key elements of the building's architecture such as doors and windows will be repeated as elements of the garden. Wooden floors inside the house can be repeated outside with wooden decking, and stone floors with stone paving. A lawn or rectangular paved area outside can be related to a rug indoors.

❀ Even if your house is not particularly interesting architecturally, you can feel free to interpret a traditional style in a modern way, bringing new ideas to an old theme. Whereas the classical formal garden is based on a central axis, Modernist gardens are always asymmetrical. Nevertheless, they are unmistakably formal. The lines are geometric, the ideas and plants are few but repeated. The angles and spaces are dynamic, implying energy and life, but the uncluttered terraces are also tranquil.

❀ The trimmings are the plants, which include spring and summer flowers, grown in pots and urns or galvanised metal buckets and trash cans. They can be

moved around as desired. Such gardens are designed for minimum maintenance, often for people with busy lives and exacting jobs who want to use the garden for leisure and entertaining, not for propagating and growing. There is no aping nature here; this is an artificial environment and proud of it.

Forms and shapes

❀ All shapes should be simple, functional and unpretentious. If you are designing an exotic garden or one that uses architectural plants, clarity of geometric form is desirable as a balance to the untidiness of plant growth. If you choose to design your garden in the geometric manner, use it confidently.

RIGHT: A tall, curved concrete wall has been painted deep ultramarine and decorated with sea creatures and flying ducks. The mosaic table adds extra color and interest.

LEFT: Square containers and a restricted planting scheme will complement many modern gardens. Here, a galvanised container has been filled with bold and colorful plants using only reds and yellows.

Narrow gardens

✿ The paving in a typically narrow city garden can be done inexpensively with concrete slabs. Along one edge you could cut the concrete to form a generous curve which will leave room for a flowerbed with some depth. This means that at the widest part, you will be able to grow two or three tiers of plants, which will give opportunity for more plant height and variety.

Courtyard gardens

✿ You can modernise the Italianate courtyard style by using a formal pool of water with an elaborate but modern fountain in the center, surrounded by terracotta tiles with brick edging. As for plants, keep to formal, clipped evergreens in very simple containers. Galvanised containers include buckets and trash cans. Just one or two of these planted with architectural palms, for example, will create an outdoor room of great style.

✿ In a small front courtyard, you can paint the walls in any deep color. The introduction of new ranges of outdoor paints has enabled gardeners to paint fences, walls and whole courtyards in colors that will highlight plant forms and leaves to great effect.

✿ The style will suit any modern building, whether made of concrete, brick or timber, and can be used with modern mock Georgian or other brick houses, especially where the gardens are rather squeezed in between buildings. Often, these oddly shaped plots are asking for a geometric solution to the design.

RIGHT: The modern garden takes the idea of the garden 'room' quite literally. The lines are geometric, the feeling architectural, the plants few but sculptural. Modern materials such as engineering bricks or decking can be used, and water is often present in the form of a sculptural fountain, again using modern materials such as stainless steel or glass.

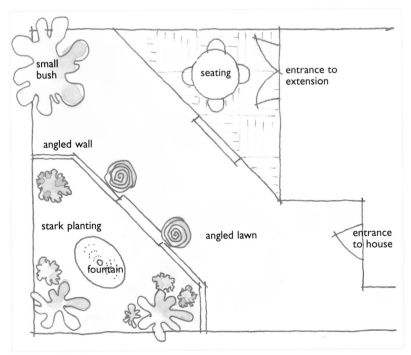

small bush

angled wall

stark planting

fountain

seating

entrance to extension

angled lawn

entrance to house

ABOVE: *In this garden, the owner has painted a curved line on the fence, which leads the eye into the curved line of the actual garden where it turns into woodland.*

Small rectangular gardens

❀ If the garden is very small, you can divide it up diagonally, the long line creating a feeling of more length. Mark the line with a change of level or a change of material, perhaps using gravel for one side and concrete slabs for the other.

Materials

❀ The first consideration in a modern garden is not necessarily the planting. Indeed, there may be very few plants or even none at all. The surfaces of the walls and floors of the garden offer opportunities for decoration. The traditional garden used mostly brick, stone, paving blocks, sand or gravel.

❀ The modern garden designer can add to such materials glazed tiles, mosaic (especially on walls), glass bricks, mirrors, colored glass beads and rubber and reconstituted materials. Glass bricks need some support but can be let into suitable frames. There are also bright stainless metal containers, poles and columns, which can be the supports for 'sails' for shade, rather than the traditional garden umbrella.

RIGHT: *Modern gardens should be functional and unpretentious. The tall and secure fence of this garden is made of simple wooden poles painted in graded shades of blue and purple.*

❀ Traditional materials are often perfectly suitable for the modern garden but used rather differently. Slate can be cut and laid with great precision. Precision cutting suits the spare 'hard-edged' designs of contemporary architecture. Alternatively, it can be sawn in random lengths and laid as a patio, path or surround for a geometrically shaped pool or L-shaped canal.

❀ Green slate is ideal for the modern garden but the surface should be roughened so that it is non-slip in all weathers.

❀ Any paved area should have a unified feeling, and this is especially important to counterbalance any exotic planting.

❀ Timber decking is a good material for many modern gardens, particularly roof-gardens. It can look magnificent with the dark, rough texture of railway sleepers used as retaining walls or with brick, and surprisingly perhaps, it also seems to go very well with modern galvanised containers.

❀ Concrete can be colored with the addition of colored cements. The various stone colors are usually the most popular because they are the 'kindest' and quietest foil to grass and plants.

Vertical elements

❀ Fine timber laths can create elegant vertical structures such as pergolas with a definitely modern look. They can symbolise tree trunks and create the feeling of a small copse or grove, but are very far removed from the deliberately rustic look of the traditional pergola. They will complement the straight lines of narrow decking. Timber obelisks can take the place of fastigiate trees with their erect branches, such as junipers or yews.

❀ Modern lighting can also add to the vertical effect. Globes on metal 'stems' give a modern effect. The stem can rise up from a group of dome-shaped shrubs, which themselves echo the shade's rounded shape.

Paint

❀ Walls, fences, furniture and containers can all be painted. White reflects more light than any other color and will brighten a shady wall. It is also a good color for highlighting foliage shapes.

❀ However, the enormous advances made in outdoor paints and the color ranges now available give the modern gardener a really exciting choice. Blue-green and grey-green seem to be universally attractive colors in a garden and again, most foliage and flower colors

and shapes look well against them. However, the brightest orange and the deepest blue can look right, too, when used with confidence and minimal planting, and many sculptural objects, particularly abstract ones, can look marvellous against them.

The plants

❀ Plants without flowers are ideally suited to the Modernist garden. Ferns such as *Athyrium filix-femina* can be massed together in front of a large-leaved ivy such as *Hedera helix* 'Montgomery'. Groups of three small trees planted together, such as *Betula pendula*, especially those with interesting bark, will remain small and look attractive. Their lacy foliage and narrow trunks will allow you to see the architecture through them.

❀ Large square or rectangular containers will also relate to the architecture and you can grow exotic plants such as palms, hostas or grasses in them.

Color

❀ If you do want to introduce color, it is best to choose restricted color schemes so that the color will not detract from the bold lines and geometric spaces of the garden plan. You can plant in blocks of geometric color using geraniums or bedding plants and you can use foliage color such as the red forms of *Phormium*.

BELOW: *Modern paints are available in a range of colors as bright as garden flowers themselves. Here, panels of a concrete fence have been painted in uninhibited shades of green, red and yellow.*

JAPANESE GARDENS

Japanese gardens have developed over many centuries and have been refined and shaped by religious and philosophical ideas, ranging from Shintoism, Hinduism and Taoism to Buddhism – very different from the classical roots of Christianity and Islam that have shaped European garden traditions. The basic principle behind Japanese gardens is a quest for harmony and an important element is the idea of retaining the spirit of the place and appreciating the beauty of the natural rock.

THE PRINCIPLES

IN early Japanese gardens design principles included the idea that rocks already *in situ* should be respected for their own inner stillness, and that rocks, islands and ponds represented nature and should always be placed asymmetrically. Symmetrical elements represented humans.

❀ The representation of a mountain is essential and refers to the Cosmic Mountain at the center of the universe. The Island of Immortality can be represented by an island or a rock. Rocks are arranged in groups of three. In old Japanese gardening books this is explained as representing three forces – horizontal, diagonal and vertical – which correspond to the structure of the universe – heaven, earth and mankind.

❀ The aim is not to overpower nature but to enter into a partnership with it. The garden is a place for divine spirits and when harmony is achieved, the good spirits will be drawn into the garden while the hostile ones will leave it in peace.

ABOVE: *This is an unusual but attractive and appropriate way to fence off a Japanese-style garden, using bamboo poles knotted together with rope.*

BELOW: *Bright red fish in a still pond are not difficult to keep, and they coordinate with the red paint used on many Japanese bridges.*

ABOVE: *Japanese design is always very disciplined. The black decking and the single shapely plant in a pot very much reflect the Japanese sense of design.*

❋ Everywhere in the garden there should be devices to ward off evil spirits. Trees and stones should be grouped in odd numbers – threes, fives and sevens. Devils are thought to walk in straight lines so garden pathways are made to twist and turn.

❋ In the Japanese garden non-living features are paramount and plants are not the prime ingredients. One of the most important items is water – the Japanese word for gardener means 'He who makes the bed of streams'. Others are stone, sand, gravel, bamboo, aged trees and space.

❋ There is a 15th-century Japanese diagram that shows how a landscape should be deliberately designed to look natural. It has 16 pieces of land and water arranged around a central 'guardian stone'. The design is asymmetrical but carefully balanced, and each piece has a distinct function and importance. The pieces include mountains (near and far), rocks, beaches, islands, a lake and a cascade.

❋ Every item is balanced by something else. Tall plants grow next to bushy ones. Sharp angles are balanced by gentle bends. Any stream should be as natural as possible, moving from the east, going underground and flowing into the 'ocean' at the west. A stylised form of well head symbolises freshness.

❋ Some Japanese gardens have no water but are made up simply of rocks and gravel. This is because in the 15th century the Japanese Civil War put a stop to all gardening except in Buddhist monasteries. Here the monks kept up the tradition but in a very simple form. Sand represented the ocean and was raked daily to create wave forms. Uncut and weathered stones represented gods, mountains and animals.

The boundaries

❋ Japanese gardens are always separated from the surrounding land. Bamboo can be used for boundary fencing and for fencing to divide various parts of the garden. It should be tall and solid enough to conceal distracting views when contemplating the stones. Stepping stones laid on gravel are deliberately spaced to slow you down and leave behind your daily cares.

❋ A typical feature of Japanese gardens is a small bamboo pipe pivoted on a stand. When the pipe is filled it tips forward and then drops back on to a 'sounding stone' with a clack. This device was originally designed as a bird and animal scarer to protect crops.

BELOW: *Simplicity is the hallmark of a Japanese-style garden, as is retaining the spirit of the place. If there are old trees or rocks, try to retain them in your design. Gravel with stepping stones, a regularly shaped pond and characteristic plants such as bamboo and cherry trees are all within the spirit of the style.*

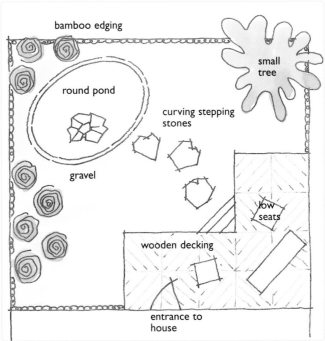

THE TEA HOUSE GARDEN

I T IS thought that the Zen monk Muratushuko (1422–1502) probably originated the tea ceremony. He built a little tea hut in the middle of Kyoto, furnished with simple utensils, and this idea of simplicity and austerity caught on. The main feature of a tea house garden is the path of rough stepping stones preventing the visitor from trampling on the beautiful moss. Stone lanterns light the way at night and a stone bowl stands outside the tea house for cleaning the visitor spiritually and physically before entering the house.

✿ The tea house itself should resemble a small rustic retreat and was based on the traditional Japanese farmhouse. Traditionally, there should be no windows in this little house because there should be no view of the garden from inside. There might be a veranda, from which the shape of the garden can be viewed.

✿ The whole garden is in muted colors with plenty of moss, kept damp and green by watering, sprinkled on paths and stepping stones. Everything should appear totally natural. If there is a pond, it should be sinuous with jutting peninsulas and deep inlets, often shored up with rocks so that you can get a dramatic overview from the tea house veranda. Shrubs and bushes are clipped into shapes suggestive of mountains.

ABOVE: *Rocks are essential to a Japanese garden. They are chosen and placed with the greatest care and balanced by both the planting and other objects in the garden.*

BELOW: *Although appearing to be informal, this is in fact a very formal garden, planted with the utmost discipline so that everything balances and is reflected in the pool.*

THE STROLLING GARDEN

THIS is basically a garden walk in which visitors are taken around a deliberately designed pathway so as to see the various changing vistas and set views designed for that purpose. Artificial hills, artificial ponds, broad winding streams and waterfalls with islands, rocks and topiary emphasise the rustic ideal. There are paths and bridges in great number and variety, with a tea garden tucked away in a small separate garden within the strolling garden.

❀ Bridges can take several forms. The Steep Bridge is arched and usually painted red and black, but bridges are often simple planks laid across a narrow stretch of water. There may be stepping stones across the water as well as in the gravel or moss. Typically, both plants and rocks are rounded bun shapes and vertical elements are provided by trees. The ponds are full of golden carp.

❀ The gateway to the strolling garden is a pergola-like structure with a roof. The whole garden is dotted with trained and shaped conifers and miniature conifers. Ponds have many rocks and grass right up to the edges. This sort of strolling garden can be bounded by bamboo screens or it can merge gradually into natural woodland. Clipped paths and interestingly shaped rocks can show up to advantage against a white-painted wall.

BELOW: *This gravel garden represents the ocean with green islands floating in it. Such disciplined raked patterns are meant to be seen, rather like the parterre, from a window above that looks down on the garden.*

THE DRY GARDEN

THE dry landscape garden can represent a pond or the ocean and is often raked into wave-like patterns. It can look very stylish simply with cherry blossom hanging over it in spring. This sort of garden can be the answer to a small front garden overhung by trees where little will grow and which is more of a viewing garden than a garden to go into. This means the gravel will remain undisturbed and continue to look good for an appreciable length of time. Rocks can be set into the gravel and perhaps a dwarf pine tree such as *Pinus mugo* 'Mops' or an ornamental cherry.

SUITABLE PLANTS FOR JAPANESE-STYLE GARDENS

THE range of trees and flowers is fairly limited. If plants were used the main idea is to make the most of the different seasons. Pine trees, cherries and plums have a special place. Bamboo is an obvious choice of plant, being both natural looking and architectural. *Prunus* x *yedoensis* 'Shidare Yoshino' is a weeping cherry with pink buds ageing to pure white in short racemes. It grows to 13 ft (4 m) in 10 years. *Acer palmatum* 'Dissectum' forms a mound with arching shoots and has finely cut leaves turning gold in fall. It will grow to 6 x 10 ft (1.8 x 3 m).

EXOTIC GARDENS

The exotic can be achieved simply by creating the effect of something foreign. The Victorians were fascinated by foreign ideas and had gardens inspired by many different countries. The nineteenth-century garden at Biddulph Grange in Staffordshire, England – now owned by the National Trust and restored to its original splendor – was designed in separate compartments, reflecting styles of different parts of the world, including a Chinese garden, an Egyptian garden with sphinxes and a Japanese garden.

TROPICAL-LOOKING PLANTS AND CONSERVATORIES

THE Victorians also used tropical-looking plants which had to be taken into conservatories in the winter in their summer borders. No truly tropical plant will survive outside in temperate climates but recent technological advances in propagation have produced a number of tropical-looking plants, which can tolerate a temperate climate even in winter. This gives tremendous scope for creating exotic, jungly gardens, especially in milder areas or in cities where the temperature is always several degrees higher than in the areas surrounding them.

❧ Conservatories expand the possibilities, too, and even the smallest one offers opportunities for creating really flamboyant effects with climbing plants, hanging baskets and epiphytic plants (those that grow on other plants) hanging from branches, as well as orchids and bromeliads.

ABOVE: *The stately yucca always surprises with its tall spire of white bells in summer. It has a good architectural quality and will provide height in a border or stand on its own.*

LEFT: *Bananas and canna lilies are truly exotic and the robinia tree behind them has an exotic look as well. They will all grow in sheltered spots in temperate areas, although you cannot expect the bananas to fruit.*

Creating a hardy jungle

❧ A jungle is lush with foliage, with many large, differently shaped leaves growing at different heights in curtains of green, all overlapping and intertwining. You can create this effect in the garden by using vigorous climbers in association with large-leaved hardy plants. Many plants grow very tall in the jungle, climbing up

ABOVE: A lush and exotic water garden with a small walkway across the stream is positively tropical in feel.

into the trees towards the light. You can simulate the height of a forest canopy by installing tall scaffolding screens. Make sure the scaffolding is robust and firmly fixed because many plants become very heavy when in leaf and need strong supports.

❀ If the site is sunny, the golden hop (*Humulus lupulus* 'Aureus') is a good candidate and perfectly hardy. Any vigorous climber with large leaves will add to the effect. The crimson glory vine (*Vitis coignetiae*) will eventually grow to 80 ft (24 m) and Virginia creeper to 50 ft (15 m). The leaves of both plants turn bright red in fall. The evergreen *Clematis armandii* is another vigorous climber with plenty of large shiny leaves and will make your screen look like a snowstorm in spring with its masses of white flowers. For a shady site, *Hydrangea petiolaris* is a vigorous, hardy climber with handsome, flat, white lace-cap flower heads, which will reach 12 ft (3.5 m) on a wall or 16 ft (5 m) growing up a tree.

❀ For lower plants use *Fatsia japonica*, with its enormous palm-shaped leaves, or phormiums and yuccas. *Yucca glauca* is a mass of straight, thin grey-blue leaves 5 ft (1.5 m) across. Plant it in drifts close together. *Yucca* 'Vittorio Emmanuel II' is one of the biggest and best. It will grow to 6 ft (1.8 m).

RIGHT: This small, sheltered garden relies on a few architectural and semi-tropical plants to give an exotic quality, relying on sculptural shapes and gaudy colors. Tall scaffolding provides a screen for vigorous climbers such as Virginia creeper, providing a jungle-like enclosed feeling. Palms, yuccas and large-leaved shrubs add to the jungle quality and a fountain provides sparkle and life.

❀ For a moist site choose *Gunnera magellanica*, *Zantedeschia aethiopica* and *Rodgersia aesculifolia*. Bamboos are easy to grow and can contribute to the exotic feel of a garden. Choose ones that will not spread, or grow them where you really want a jungle or keep them in pots. *Phyllostachys aurea* is well behaved and will grow to 15 ft (4.5 m).

Creating a tender jungle

❀ Many tropical-looking plants, often from Mediterranean areas, although difficult to propagate, are not difficult to grow. Some prefer an exposed site; others grow best in dappled shade. The hardier eucalypts and the holm oak (*Quercus ilex*) are dense enough to keep the heat in and sparse enough to let light through, especially if you cut off their lower branches. *Eucalyptus aggregata*, *E. perriniana* and *E. parvifolia* all make good canopy trees.

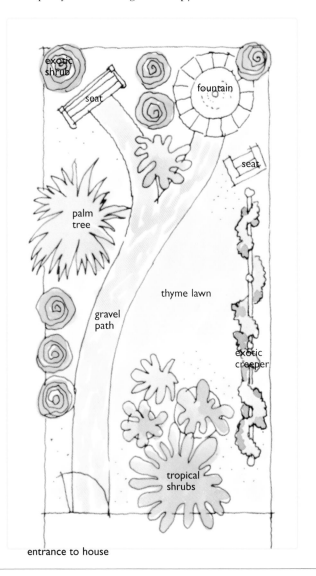

entrance to house

Almost hardy exotic-looking plants

❀ There are some small evergreen trees that can look highly exotic grown on their own. These include mimosa (*Acacia dealbata*) with pretty, grey-green ferny leaves and masses of tiny ball-shaped yellow flowers in spring. *Acacia* 'pravissima' is a small weeping mimosa with triangular leaves, suitable for a small garden.

❀ The monkey puzzle (*Auracaria araucana*) comes from Chile and is strikingly exotic. It is the only one of its family hardy enough to be grown outside in temperate zones. In the nineteenth century it was a fashionable tree to grow in front gardens. Grow it as part of a grove or as a specimen tree near enough to the house so that its fascinating flowers and fruits may be seen from an upstairs window. The red-barked strawberry tree (*Arbutus* x *andrachnoides*) is evergreen, fast growing and winter flowering, as well as having attractive bark.

❀ Bananas are really herbaceous plants but they are tall enough to act as trees in the exotic garden. They look good at the edge of a pond where they are reflected in the water. The hardy banana (*Musa basjoo*) has enormous tattered leaves, which can be used for anything from wrapping paper to picnic plates or

RIGHT: Hedychium densiflorum *is a clump-forming perennial bearing tubular, fragrant orange flowers in late summer. It will grow to 16 ft (5 m). It needs moist soil with shelter from the wind. It may survive outdoors in winter if given a deep winter mulch.*

LEFT: *This is a plant for a desert garden, a rock garden, a raised bed by a sunny wall or a container. Grow in poor, sharply drained soil in full sun. Where the temperature drops below 36°F (2°C), grow it in a cool greenhouse.*

umbrellas! Other bananas, including edible ones, must be kept in a conservatory.

❀ The two hardy palm trees are the chusan palm (*Trachycarpus fortunei*), which will reach 23 ft (7 m). The dwarf palm (*Chamaerops humilis*) has broad green fans on prickly stems and grows to 13 ft (4 m). It is the only native European palm and will withstand wind better than *T. fortunei*. Tree ferns are both stately and feathery, a surprising and attractive combination. *Dicksonia antarctica* has 7-ft (2-m) fronds. You will have to water or spray its trunk in summer and wrap it up in winter, but it is certainly worth it if you have a sheltered spot in which to show it off.

❀ *Melianthus major*, from southern Africa, is a dramatic plant with serrated grey-green leaves. It is actually a shrub but best treated as a herbaceous perennial. It will survive in a warm position in many areas, if protected in winter.

All these exotic plants will add an architectural dimension to the garden and can be grown in association with hardier large-leaved plants such as *Rodgersia*, *Ligularia* and *Astilbe*, or add height to a bed of ground cover plants such as *Sedum* and *Polygonum*.

ABOVE: *The cardoon* (Cynara cardunculus) *is an imposing, statuesque plant that should be grown in fertile, well-drained soil in a sheltered spot in full sun.*

Exotic plants for pots and conservatories

❀ These plants can be placed in the garden during summer, but really need the protection of a greenhouse or conservatory during the winter.

❀ The cannas are exotic in both form and flower. *Canna indica* has banana-like leaves, grows to about 5 ft (1.5 m) and has bright red and yellow flowers in summer. *C. indiflora* is bigger and good for summer bedding or for pots. It has shocking pink flowers and will grow 3 m (10 ft) in a year. *C.* 'Purpurea' is a purple-leaved form with orange flowers. Cannas are best dug up in fall and stored under a bench for the winter, then planted out again in spring.

❀ Agaves are succulent perennials grown for their large, fleshy, sword-shaped leaves. *Agave americana* has curvy-toothed grey-green leaves armed with short spines. It needs to be kept in a pot so it can be moved indoors in winter.

Poolside exotica

❀ Surprisingly few swimming pools have had any attempt made to integrate them with their environment. But why put up with municipal surroundings if you have your own pool at home? Hedges, walls or trellises can all create an enclosed private space that you can make as exotic as you wish.

❀ The pool could be integrated into a spacious patio or terrace with room to stand large pots of citrus fruit or tropical-looking plants, which will be reflected in the water.

❀ The pool itself can be any shape you wish. It can be long and narrow, reminiscent of the Moorish gardens of Spain. Standard clipped mop-headed box trees can stand sentinel alongside the pool. A cloistered Moorish changing room with rounded arches could face one end of the pool. Or you could have a Baroque pool built with scrolls, statues and more clipped plants.

KITCHEN GARDENS

One of the pleasures of vegetable gardening is being able to pick the produce while it is fresh, and cooking or eating it straight away. Many people imagine that a large-sized plot is needed to grow vegetables, but this is not true. A pocket-sized patch in any small garden can be used to grow salad vegetables and a couple of growing bags on a sunny patio will give you a satisfactory crop of your own tomatoes or beans.

VEGETABLE APPEAL

CAREFULLY chosen and imaginatively grown, vegetables can provide a surprisingly aesthetic pleasure garden in their own right. Anyone who has seen the glorious decorative vegetable parterres at the Château of Villandry in France's Loire valley will know that vegetables can be as colorful and appealing as flowers, so there is no need to relegate your vegetables to an unseen part of the garden. The enormous expanse of the lower terrace of this great garden is planted with rows of brightly colored vegetables in great variety inside clipped hedges.

❀ Happily, you do not have to be the owner of a large château to make wonderful use of the fascinating shapes and colors of vegetables in your own garden.

BELOW: *An elegant home-made wigwam has been made for this box parterre potager, to support sweet peas and runner beans. The whole potager is intended to be as decorative as it is practical.*

THE SITE

VEGETABLES should not be planted in heavy shade. An open site is best but they do need shelter, particularly from the wind, so a hedge or woven fence to filter the wind would be ideal. Provided the area is not too shaded, the ideal place for the vegetable plot is near the greenhouse and shed, with space enough to have a compost heap.

❀ This means that the utility parts of the garden are all in one place. It gives unity to what might otherwise be a scattered group of buildings and work areas. The vegetable plot itself does not need to be part of this area. It can be fenced or hedged off but it will be practical to have the working area nearby with a firm path leading from one to the other.

BELOW: *These very attractive rows of vegetables have been chosen for their color and shape, not just for their taste. They include Longbow leeks, and Rubine and Icarus Brussels sprouts.*

LEFT: *This well-organised space uses square wooden tubs and trellis to create a colorful and high-yielding potager, mixing vegetables such as broad beans with climbing red roses.*

❀ A plot can be arranged in a circular pattern divided by radial paths, and the pattern marked out by edging stones. Circles always look elegant. Their outlines can become valuable focal points and need not conflict in any way with an otherwise purely decorative garden.

❀ Vegetables grown in rows within the divisions will give an attractive colored pattern to the design. Square or more complicated geometric shapes can be used if you have the space. Beds with straight lines can be edged with purpose-made edging tiles or you can use wooden boards.

POTAGERS

A POTAGER is a sort of cottage garden where the main ingredients are vegetables rather than flowers. It is a decorative vegetable patch and can be more or less disciplined according to your preference. At its most defined, it is not unlike a parterre, with vegetables growing in spaces delineated by low hedges or brick or gravel paths. Then it becomes a larger, more varied version of the formal herb garden.

The formal potager

❀ Strictly ordered rows of vegetables can be attractive if they are well maintained, but it is not necessary to grow them like this. Build raised beds and surround them with brick paths. They may be square or rectangular, each being planted with one or two varieties to give order to the whole design. Dwarf tomatoes can be grown alongside dwarf beans; leeks next to ornamental cabbages. Globe artichokes in the center of a bed will give height and structure; strawberries provide a decorative edging for some of the beds.

BELOW: *A vegetable plot can be among the most decorative of gardens. This one has been designed rather like a formal herb garden. It has four square beds, each comparatively small so they can be easily reached for garden work, with a decorative bay tree in the center. The greenhouse and the compost heap are both conveniently nearby.*

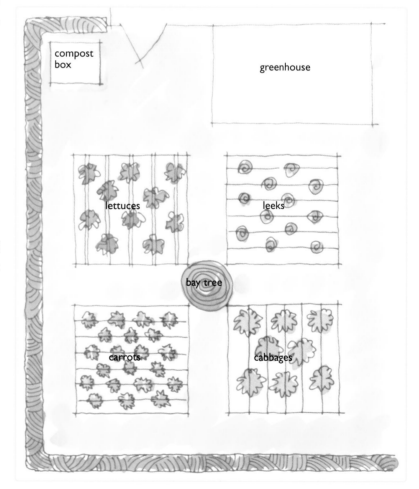

compost box

greenhouse

lettuces

leeks

bay tree

carrots

cabbages

ABOVE: *Some of the most mundane vegetables can look enchanting if they are grown where the sun can shine on their young foliage. This Swiss chard is called Rainbow and ranges in color from green to red and bronze.*

The informal potager

❀ In a small garden, or if you have chosen an awkwardly shaped part of the plot as your potager, an informal vegetable patch will probably be a more sensible option. Here you can allow the plants to grow in a somewhat haphazard, more natural manner than in the formal plot.

❀ You will therefore need a strong framework because, although the luxuriant growth in summer will tend to conceal the edges, in winter you will want the shape to reappear. You can mark out the area with wicker fencing, which will be quite appropriate to the design, or you could use espaliered apple or pear trees whose branches will look attractive when they are both in leaf and dormant.

❀ Give some height to the beds with standard soft fruit bushes such as gooseberries or black and redcurrants, which will be easier to maintain and to pick and will

help give form to the area. Other vegetables can be planted in more or less organised patterns, as you prefer.

❀ Ornamental cabbages, tall and round lettuces of as many different colors as you can find, Swiss chard, leeks and dwarf sugar snap peas can all be interplanted with herbs and standard or shrub roses for extra decorative value. Rhubarb is a dramatic plant in its own right. One plant will be enough to feed a family with rhubarb crumble for a season and its magnificent leaves and attractive pink stems make a good, strong impression and contrast well with other plants.

The basement potager

❀ Basement flats often have tiny patios with steps to gardens at eye level or higher. People generally sit in the patio area because the steep, narrow steps to the garden are uninviting. Such plots are good candidates for vegetable gardens. If you can push the garden out by enlarging the patio area, making the steps wider and shallower, you will lose some growing space but make the whole place feel much more open and spacious.

❀ You can decorate the patio with large flowering shrubs in containers and set up table and chairs there, and concentrate your growing skills in the upper part of the garden. Ornamental cabbages with their round,

LEFT: *Ornamental cabbages are astonishingly decorative. They can be grown with other vegetables in a decorative mixture, but often look best on their own in rows, like this pink and turquoise variety called 'Benihato'.*

brightly colored shapes, the feathery pale green leaves of carrots, chives with their bluey-green spikes, the tall strap shapes of leeks and soft, round spinach leaves will make contrasting patterns on the lower terrace.

❀ Tall, stately vegetables such as cardoons can grow right at the back. Carefully planned and with the addition of some summer-flowering perennials and shrubs, this can become a pleasant place to sit, especially when the sun is on the garden and not on the patio.

VEGETABLES IN MIXED PLANTING

Vegetables can also take their place in the mixed border, along with herbs, perennials and shrubs. This relaxed attitude to growing vegetables allows you to add plants for color and to fill gaps. It also has practical value as the more varied the planting, the more it helps to prevent a build-up of the pests and diseases attracted to particular plants. French marigolds (*Tagetes*), for example, and pot marigolds (*Calendula*) attract beneficial insects and deter harmful ones, so planting vegetables in a mixed border next to them will be beneficial.

RIGHT: *This delightful corner of a flowerbed shows an intriguing piece of mixed vegetable and flower planting, using red and white impatiens with a towering lettuce growing at the center.*

LEFT: *Vegetables can work well in the flower border, a particularly useful characteristic if you want to grow vegetables in a small garden and cannot afford space for a separate kitchen garden area.*

❀ Ruby chard is a coarse, spinach-like vegetable with deep purple leaves and spectacular scarlet stems and veins. It associates dramatically with herbaceous plants at the front of a border. Ornamental cabbages have wonderful winter colors of bright purple and blue-green, sometimes with cream markings and firm, rounded, symmetrical shapes. They are at their best in winter and can brighten up a dormant border in the colder months.

Vegetables and fruit on the patio

❀ Apples on dwarfing rootstocks, tomatoes, runner beans – in fact a complete miniature kitchen garden – can be grown in containers on a patio. The colors, the different leaf forms and the fruit and vegetables themselves can prove an attractive combination. Strawberries look particularly attractive poking out of strawberry pots. A practical advantage is that you can slip out and pick a few fruits or vegetables as needed. You must make sure you feed and water them regularly or the results will be disappointing.

VEGETABLE GARDENS

One of the great joys of gardening is undoubtedly producing your own edible crops. Tomatoes picked fresh from your own plot, still warm from the sun that ripened them, are an incomparable treat. Shop-bought vegetables have often had all the flavor bred out of them in a rush to cultivate the highest possible yield, as well as having possibly been treated with pesticides and fertilizers that you would prefer not to eat. With home-grown produce, you have the security of knowing exactly what has gone into the production of your own crops.

HOME-GROWN IS BEST

WHEN you grow your own vegetables, you can choose varieties that may not be commercially available, because you are growing them for their culinary attributes, rather than for profitability. Vitamin content and taste are also optimised, because you can cook and eat your crops immediately after harvest, unlike the shop-bought equivalents, where the vitamin content has been slowly oxidising away as the produce sits on the shelf.

❀ Although growing your own vegetables can have economic benefits, for most gardeners it is the unique satisfaction of producing food from seed to table that provides the motivation.

ABOVE: *Mixing edible crops with ornamental plants is an increasingly popular way of growing vegetables, especially in a limited space.*

CHOOSING A VEGETABLE GARDEN TO SUIT YOU

THE type of vegetable gardening you do will depend on the size of your plot and the amount of time and energy you intend to devote to growing vegetables. You also need to decide whether you are wanting just a few choice crops that are expensive to buy in the shops and taste so much better home-grown, or enough vegetables to feed your family all year round.

❀ A well-organised plot, approximately 23 x 13 ft (7 x 4 m), should yield enough crops for this. Don't be dismayed, however, if you have a much smaller area. It is possible to grow a considerable quantity of vegetables in even a restricted space, and growing vegetables in containers has become increasingly popular in recent years.

ABOVE: *Maintaining a productive vegetable garden is hard work, but the results are definitely well worth the effort.*

VEGETABLE CROPS

Legumes and pod crops:

Okra
Scarlet runner beans
Lima beans
French beans
Peas
Broad beans

Alliums:

Bulb onions
Pickling onions
Spring onions
Shallots
European Welsh onions
Oriental bunching onions
Leeks
Garlic

Solanaceous, root and tuberous crops:

Sweet peppers
Tomatoes
Eggplant
Celery
Celeriac
Beetroot
Carrots
Sweet potatoes
Parsnips
Scorzonera
Salsify
Potatoes

Brassicas:

Kales
Cauliflowers
Cabbages
Brussels sprouts
Purple sprouting broccoli
Calabrese
Oriental mustards
Chinese broccoli
Pak choi
Mizuna greens
Chinese cabbages
Kohlrabi
Swedes
Turnips
Radishes

THE TRADITIONAL VEGETABLE GARDEN

KEEN vegetable gardeners like to set aside an area of the garden exclusively for vegetables. The entire area can be cultivated, and the primary purpose of the plot is to provide optimum growing conditions for vegetables, rather than gardening for any particular decorative merit. That said, there is something inherently beautiful about a well-maintained vegetable garden. It has natural geometry, because the crops are grown in rows so that you can move freely between them to tend them.

❀ A vegetable plot should not be undertaken lightly, since maintaining one is truly a labor of love. It will need to be dug over every fall, weeded regularly, and the vegetables nurtured tenderly and protected against marauding pests and the elements.

❀ There is also considerable work in planning the plot effectively, in order to maximise the space, prevent gluts and to keep pests and diseases at bay by careful crop rotation. Intercropping is a good way of saving space in a traditional plot, but does need careful planning. For example, sow fast-maturing crops such as saladings, between slow-maturing vegetables like carrots. The fast-growing crop will have matured and been harvested before the other crop needs the space.

Crop rotation

❀ Vegetables should not be grown in the same place each year. Soil-dwelling pests and diseases endemic to a particular crop would steadily increase if repeatedly given their favorite host. Also, continually cropping the same vegetable in the same place can lead to an imbalance in soil nutrients.

❀ Crop rotation can seem so dauntingly complex that some gardeners abandon it altogether. It is far better for the novice vegetable gardener to practise a very simple three-year plan – dividing crops into three types: roots, brassicas and others – than to embark on a complicated regime that may be impossible to follow long term.

❀ A very simple rule is that if a vegetable from one group does particularly badly one year, never follow it the next year with a crop from the same group, unless you are willing to risk having the same poor result.

ABOVE: *Raised beds ease the work of the vegetable gardener and look neat and attractive.*

VEGETABLES IN CONTAINERS

GROWING vegetables in containers has developed from the ubiquitous commercial growing bag of tomatoes that starts many gardeners on the path towards more ambitious vegetable gardening. Even gardeners with extremely limited space to devote to vegetables are able to produce edible crops, which not only taste great, are chemical free, vitamin rich and super fresh, but also attractive plants in their own right. Cabbages, for example, are increasingly grown not only as food crops, but for their ornamental properties. There are breeds of tomato that have a delightful tumbling growth habit, perfectly suited to containers such as hanging baskets and the multi-holed terracotta pots, more usually seen housing strawberries.

❀ Growing vegetables in containers has many other benefits besides maximising space. The soil pest problems, weeding and digging that make vegetable growing in open soil hard work are eradicated. Since container-grown vegetables are portable, you can grow plants that need particular local environments, moving them as necessary to suit the changing climate and their individual needs.

❀ For example, you may be able to grow tender vegetables, which need a sheltered spot, against a sunny wall, far away from the main, exposed vegetable plot where they would perish. Choose containers sufficiently sized to suit the crop. For example, long-

rooted vegetables such as carrots need a depth of at least 18 in (46 cm) to flourish, while a lettuce can thrive in a window box.

DRAWBACKS

A DISADVANTAGE of container growing vegetables is that you will need to pay particular attention to watering and feeding. Another issue to consider is that plastic growing bags are not attractive, and can be quite unsightly if you have a lot of them, undisguised, surrounding your house.

THE ORNAMENTAL POTAGER

PLANNING a vegetable garden that is ornamental as well as productive has become very fashionable. Potager is the French word for kitchen garden, but is now used internationally to describe a garden where edible plants are grown with an emphasis on their decorative potential. Other elements are included to produce an area that is as pretty as it is productive – for example neat pathways of brick or gravel passing between geometric beds enclosed by formal dwarf box hedging, sometimes embellished further with vines, roses and grapes draped over arches traversing the walkways.

❀ Many of the vegetables in the potager are chosen for their visual appeal, for example leaf beet and red lettuces, although even ordinary varieties appear more attractive when displayed in such a charming setting.

VEGETABLES IN THE BORDER

INCORPORATING vegetables within the herbaceous border has also become increasingly acceptable and fashionable. Many gardeners do not have the space to devote a whole area to vegetables, along with the attendant demands on time and the potential production of crop gluts, which can be difficult to handle without wastage.

❀ Gardeners have mixed flowers with edible crops for many years, although historically, cottage gardeners would have been concerned with having herbs to hand for practical reasons, and any decorative effect would have been fairly incidental.

❀ Today, ornamental crops, as in the potager, are often selected in preference to more workaday species.

For example, ruby chard, a variety of leaf beet, has stunning red stalks, worthy of inclusion in the border in their own right. There are also prettily colored, flowering runner beans, which can add height at the back of the border, and zucchini, with their spectacular exotic-looking, edible yellow flowers, in addition to their stripy fruits.

❀ Although growing vegetables in the border is convenient and attractive, as well as producing useful edible crops, the work and thought involved should not be underestimated. The vegetables will compete with the ornamentals for food, light and water, so never overcrowd when planting. Ideally, consider the ornamentals as the adjuncts to the edibles, not the other way around, so that the vegetables are given the best possible growing conditions.

COMPANION PLANTING

FASCINATING work has been done on companion planting, which means growing plants side by side for their positive effects on each other, whether directly or indirectly. It is worth researching this subject further, particularly if you are planning to grow edibles and ornamentals together.

❀ Combining certain flowers and edible crops often has significant benefits, particularly in assisting pest and

disease control. For example, garlic is an excellent friend to roses, since it is reputed to deter aphids as well as improving the roses' perfume. Equally importantly, research on companion planting reveals that some combinations have a detrimental effect on each other, for example garlic planted alongside peas and beans.

ABOVE: *A well-tended vegetable plot can yield a wonderful array of crops that will sustain you throughout the year.*

BELOW: *A neatly planted large growing strawberries, chives and shallots to ripen in the early summer.*

ABOVE: *Neat rows of vegetables have a pleasing symmetry, which bears testimony to the care with which they are tended.*

ABOVE: *A garden planted with vegetables can be as attractive as one packed with purely ornamental plants.*

GROWING VEGETABLES

VEGETABLES grow best in a sunny, sheltered spot, on a loamy, humus-rich soil with a pH between 6.5 and 7.0. Other soils can be improved by incorporating plenty of well-rotted organic matter and by thorough cultivation.

Sowing vegetables and early care

❀ Read seed packets carefully to determine the recommended sowing depth and method, together with anticipated germination and harvesting time, so that you can plan your planting accordingly. General propagation guidelines apply when sowing vegetables. Seed may be sown directly into the soil where it is to mature, into a seedbed, or into pots and trays.

Preparing the soil

❀ The soil needs to be in optimum condition to give vegetables the best possible chance of growing success. Tedious as it may be, digging the vegetable plot is of prime importance. It introduces air into the soil; it raises clods of earth, which can be broken down by frost, thereby improving soil texture; and it encourages the biological activity that is necessary for soil fertility.

❀ In some cases, notably on light soils where digging would disturb rather than improve the soil structure, the no-dig method is used. Generous layers of well-rotted organic matter are spread over the soil as a mulch, and resident worms obligingly incorporate this into the soil, improving soil fertility. Young plants are inserted through the mulch, and new crops are grown between the roots of previous crops, which are allowed to decompose in the soil.

❀ Seeds need good overall contact with the soil in order to germinate so, if you are preparing a seedbed, it is necessary to rake the soil to a fine tilth in the sowing season that follows the fall digging.

Feeding the soil

❀ Intensively cultivated soil needs to be well nourished for best results. This can be achieved with organic or inorganic fertilizers. Many gardeners prefer organic fertilizers, since a desire to eat produce that is uncontaminated by chemicals is the motivation for many gardeners to grow their own vegetables.

❀ Organic manures and fertilizers encourage worm activity, which benefits soil fertility. Higher yields may be possible with chemical fertilizers, but in the domestic setting, as opposed to a large-scale agricultural environment, quality and flavor are generally considered to be of more importance than maximum yields.

❀ The amount of fertiliser required is governed partly by soil type. For example, heavy clay soil retains nutrients for longer than a fast-draining sandy soil. Another factor is the kind of crop grown. Leafy crops like cabbages need lots of nitrogen — approximately one-third supplied on planting, followed by the remaining two-thirds as the plant grows.

❀ An enthusiasm to keep plants well fed needs to be tempered with common sense. Overwintering vegetable crops that have been fed with too much nitrogen in fall are vulnerable to frost damage, as soft growth would be encouraged at a harsh time of year. Respect the individual requirements of each crop. Fruiting crops like tomatoes will need regular feeding with appropriate fertilizers as the plants come into flower, to ensure optimum flowering and fruiting.

Watering

❀ Vegetables have water requirements in line with most other plants. They need particular watering care during germination and at the seedling stage until their roots are established. After transplanting, again take special care with watering until the plants are re-established. Root crops need steady watering from sowing until cropping. Fruiting and flowering crops need most water when they are in flower and as the fruits develop. Foliage crops need thorough watering 12–15 days prior to harvesting.

BELOW: *Regularly incorporating compost with the soil is an important part of successful vegetable gardening, as in this well-tended plot featuring sweet peas, asparagus, broad beans and onions.*

VEGETABLE GAZETTEER

Vegetables are extremely rewarding to grow, and do well on most soils. Pay attention to the individual needs of your crops and the yields will be higher, and your chances of success more consistent. Crop successively to avoid a glut of vegetables that is hard to cope with.

Vegetable	Sow	Plant/Plant out	Harvest	Yield per m²
Asparagus	Apr	Apr	May–Jun	1.5 kg (3¼ lb)
Bean, broad	Feb–Apr	–	Jul–Aug	4 kg (8¾ lb)
Bean, runner	Apr (UG)	May–Jun	May–Jun Aug–Oct	4 kg (8¾ lb)
Beetroot	Apr–Jun	–	Jun–Oct	2 kg (4½ lb)
Broccoli	Apr–May	Jun–Jul	Feb–May	2 kg (4½ lb)
Brussels sprout	Mar–Apr	May–Jun	Oct–Feb	1.5 kg (3¼ lb)
Cabbage	Apr	May–Jun	Aug–Sep	4 kg (8¾ lb)
Calabrese	Apr–May	Jun–Jul	Aug–Oct	2 kg (4½ lb)
Capsicum	Feb (UG)	Apr (UG)	Aug–Sep	1.5 kg (3¼ lb)
Carrot	Apr–Jun	–	Sep–Oct	2 kg (4½ lb)
Cauliflower	Apr	Jun	Aug–Sep	4.5 kg (10 lb)
Celeriac	Mar (UG)	May–Jun	Oct–Nov	3 kg (6½ lb)
Celery	Mar–Apr (UG)	Jun	Aug–Oct	4 kg (8¾ lb)
Chard	Apr	–	Aug–Nov	1 kg (2 lb)
Chicory	May	–	Dec–Mar	0.4 kg (13 oz)
Cucumber	May–Jun	–	Aug–Sep	3 kg (6½ lb)
Eggplant	Feb	Apr	Aug–Sep	5 kg (11 lb)
Endive	Apr–Aug	–	Sep–Feb	1.5 kg (3¼ lb)
Kale	May	Jul	Dec–Mar	1.5 kg (3¼ lb)
Kohlrabi	Apr–Jun	–	Aug–Oct	2.5 kg (5½ lb)
Leek	Mar–Apr	Jun	Nov–Mar	1.5 kg (3¼ lb)
Lettuce	Mar–Jul	–	Jun–Oct	1 kg (2 lb)
Marrow	May–Jun	–	Aug–Oct	2 kg (4½ lb)
Onion	Mar–Apr	–	Aug–Sep	1.5 kg (3¼ lb)
Parsnip	Mar	–	Nov–Feb	1.5 kg (3¼ lb)
Pea	Mar–Jul	–	May–Oct	3 kg (6½ lb)
Potato	Apr	–	Sep–Oct	3 kg (6½ lb)
Radish	Mar–Jun	–	May–Sep	0.4 kg (13 oz)
Salsify	Apr	–	Nov–Jan	1.5 kg (3¼ lb)
Shallot	Feb–Mar	Aug		2 kg (4½ lb)
Spinach	Mar–May	–	Jun–Oct	1.5 kg (3¼ lb)
Squash	May (UG)	Jun–Jul	Oct–Nov	2 kg (4½ lb)
Swede	May–Jun	–	Nov–Feb	2 kg (4½ lb)
Sweetcorn	May	–	Aug–Sep	0.5 kg (1 lb)
Tomato	Mar–Apr (UG)	Jun	Aug–Sep	2.5 kg (5½ lb)
Turnip	Jul–Aug	–	Oct–Dec	1.5 kg (3¼ lb)
Zucchini	May–Jun	–	Jul–Sep	2 kg (4½ lb)

Frost tolerant	Cultivation	Suitable for freezing
yes	difficult	yes
yes	average	yes
no	simple	yes
yes	average	yes
yes	average	yes
yes	simple	yes
yes	simple	yes
no	average	yes
no	average	yes
yes	average	yes
yes	difficult	yes
yes	average	yes
yes	difficult	yes
yes	simple	no
yes	difficult	no
no	average	no
no	difficult	yes
yes	average	no
yes	average	yes
yes	average	yes
yes	average	yes
no	simple	no
no	average	yes
no	average	yes
yes	average	yes
no	simple	yes
no	simple	yes
yes	simple	no
yes	average	no
no	average	no
yes	average	yes
no	average	no
yes	simple	yes
no	difficult	yes
no	average	yes
no	simple	yes
no	average	yes

THE ENGLISH LANDSCAPE GARDEN

Early English gardens had been places of refuge from a terrifying world outside where both nature and men were hostile and aggressive. By the early eighteenth century nature had been greatly tamed and, in addition, many wealthy young Englishmen had travelled to Italy on the 'Grand Tour', taking in the wonders of Renaissance architecture and gardens and the fashionable landscape paintings that idealised natural scenery. They wanted to turn their lands literally into paintings. Rich and powerful landowners were able to get acts through Parliament, allowing them to enclose large areas of common land and even to move whole villages so they would not spoil the view. Lancelot 'Capability' Brown became famous for his designs of landscape gardens, damming up rivers to create lakes, moving earth to create rolling hills and planting clumps of natural-looking trees. Dotted about in the landscape were follies and temples designed to catch the eye.

Earlier gardens had their hedges razed and parterres dug up. Green grass came right up to the house and a combined ditch and sunken wall, known as a ha ha, meant that the eye could gaze right out into the countryside with no apparent hindrance. Perhaps as an antidote to the lack of color and flowers, the *ferme ornée*, or ornamental farm, was invented. This retained the idea of the landscape, but took the form of a sort of landscape walk in which the verges and hedges would be planted with flowering shrubs. Plenty of seats were provided along the route at strategic points for a good view. Small groups of sheep or cows were encouraged to graze picturesquely nearby.

Humphrey Repton, who followed Capability Brown, was largely responsible for turning landscape back into a garden. He produced watercolor sketches for his clients with sliding 'before' and 'after' pictures to demonstrate what he proposed. He created flowerbeds near the house and would often add a new low fence or wall to divide the more colorful part of the garden from the landscape beyond.

RIGHT: *The Gothic temple at Painshill in Surrey, England, one of the most popular and visited gardens of the eighteenth century, was built between 1738 and 1773. It consisted of a garden walk centered around a lake, with a series of 'set pieces' such as a Roman mausoleum, a rustic hermitage and a grotto.*

HERB GARDENS

❦

Every garden needs some herbs, whether they are grown for their charming flowers, aromatic foliage or culinary qualities. During the four centuries of their rule the Romans introduced many herbs to Britain which are still grown and used today. Many of those herbs would have been lost during the war-torn Middle Ages, had it not been for the monks who, safely inside their monastery walls, continued to grow herbs for healing and cooking. In the early years herbs were primarily grown for use as medicinal plants – indicated by the species name *officinalis*. The monks grew them in neat, rectangular beds and meticulously categorised and labelled them.

PLANTING HERBS

THE tradition of herbs grown in ordered beds has survived to the present day, partly because many are neat, low-growing plants, which look particularly good grown in this way. In the 17th century they were grown in formal patterns in parterres, purely for decoration.

❀ In a modern garden, growing herbs in patterned beds is not only visually attractive but also practical because small beds separated by low hedges, paths or stones make tending and harvesting the plants easier.

❀ However, herbs will find a place in any style of garden; the range of possibilities is enormous. They can be grown among other plants in a mixed border or, if you lack space, a few pots can look good on a kitchen windowsill or you can create a little herb garden in a window box.

❀ Ground-hugging creepers such as pennyroyal, some thymes and mints can be planted among paving slabs or bricks; hummock-forming plants such as oregano, common sage, and chives make charming front-of-border plants, and tall stately plants such as fennel, lovage, angelica and sweet cicely can provide structure.

BELOW: *This circular herb garden has been created in the center of a lawn surrounded by hedges to keep out the wind. There is a wide variety of herbs, grown both for their colors and contrasting shapes.*

BELOW: *This herb garden has a formal framework of stone, yet quite informal planting, in which the herbs have been allowed to grow into their own shapes. The small willows and the little fruit tree add height.*

it should be as near to the kitchen as possible. Even if you enjoy a stroll through the garden to reach the herb bed, you may not always have the time (although you can always grow a separate collection of herbs in pots for cooking).

✤ Most herbs will benefit from being grown in an open, sunny part of the garden, since many of them come from Mediterranean areas where the climate is hot and dry. Many herbs smell delicious when walked on or brushed against, so large herbs can be grown by an outside door. Others may be planted along pathways – thyme, eau de Cologne mint, peppermint and cilantro can be planted near paths and creeping varieties of thyme and camomile between flagstones.

✤ The whole herb garden can be enclosed by a clipped yew hedge, or simply divided from the rest of the garden by a clipped hedge. If your garden is on different levels, a circular herb garden at the lower level, sheltered from the elements by walls and shrubs, can make a good sun trap for both plants and people to enjoy.

✤ If your garden is on heavy clay, it may be worthwhile creating raised beds so that water can drain away quickly. Add gravel and sand to the compost, since most herbs prefer a poor soil.

LEFT: *An outsize mortar planted with thyme lends character to this small herb plot. Around it are a selection of artemisias and other feathery plants.*

✤ The well-behaved habit of most herbs (mint is an exception) makes them useful in formal gardens, while their soft foliage colors make them good companion plants in herbaceous borders or in the cheerful disorder of cottage gardens. Many will do well in containers, and a cluster of pots near the kitchen door is both attractive and convenient.

Where to grow herbs

✤ Where to put your herb plot is an important consideration. If you are going to use the herbs for cooking,

RIGHT: *The cartwheel shape can make an attractive and practical herb garden, the 'spokes' dividing different herbs from each other and providing narrow paths useful for planting, weeding and picking. Here, the wheel is the center of a square, sunny garden with roses and shrubs around the edges and a bench from which to enjoy the scents and sights.*

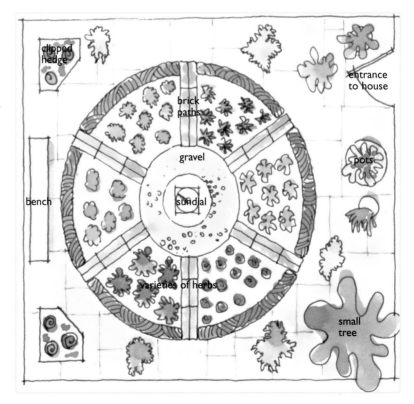

HERB GARDEN STYLES

A FORMAL herb garden is often designed in the form of a parterre with closely clipped low hedges of box, which give a defined frame to the herbs. There are other suitable plants for hedging, however. *Santolina chamaecyparis* gives a beautiful silver frame to the design, wall germander (*Teucrium x lucidrys*) has neat triangular dark green leaves, and the dark green foliage of rosemary and the dwarf lavender 'Munstead Dwarf' can be effective.

❀ Hyssop and thyme will also grow dense enough to be regularly trimmed, and chives can make a very pretty edging during the summer, but will disappear in winter.

❀ Work out your design first on paper and then mark it out on the ground with string or hose pipe before you start planting. Rectangular, circular and square shapes can all look good. Triangular shapes are more difficult to manage but may suit a particular plot. The whole thing can be as large or small, as simple or complex as you like.

❀ In a small garden you can use a cartwheel shape, laid out in stones or bricks, and grow the plants between the 'spokes'. It is best to separate the plants with narrow paths or stepping stones of brick or paving or they will grow into one another and spoil the clarity of the pattern.

❀ Add height by planting standard roses at regular intervals and a vertical eye-catcher in the center of the plot such as a sundial, a fountain or other water feature or a large urn on a pedestal.

Using herbs informally

❀ A formal herb garden does take up space and may not be the best answer in a basically informal garden. Formality is successful when linked to a grand or formal building but does require constant maintenance with frequent clipping to keep it under control.

LEFT: *The pale and interesting stalks and dark seed heads of these Egyptian onions have been allowed to remain to add winter interest to the garden and to feed the birds.*

BELOW: *Even when there is not much room, herbs can be grown very satisfactorily in pots. Here, an interesting variety of herbs, including basil, tarragon and sage, are growing in terracotta pots conveniently situated near the house.*

❀ A more sensible way of herb gardening for those with a busy lifestyle is to incorporate herbs in a mixed border, as you would any other flowering plants.

❀ Rosemary makes a tall, stately shrub with sky-blue flowers all along its branches in spring and summer. It can be used as a structural plant in a border or as a specimen plant, on its own against a sunny wall or freestanding. Angelica, lovage, and sweet cicely, too, are all tall, stately plants, which can provide structural elements in a border. Bronze fennel, with dark feathery leaves, can provide good contrasts with other plants. Chives, sage, golden marjoram and other plants with similar habits can make good companion plants towards the front of a border. Garlic chives have narrow, strap-like leaves with flat heads of small white flowers in late summer and fall.

Paved herb area

❀ You can create a dedicated herb garden in a paved area of the garden by creating square beds between brick paths. Plant masses of the same variety of herb in each square for a deliberate pattern of habit and color. More informal would be a gravel garden with concrete stepping stones in which the herbs can be allowed to grow and spread naturally in a seemingly random manner.

❀ Tall plants like globe artichokes (*Cynara scolymus* 'Green Globe') and angelica can be grown at the back; in front you could grow pot marigolds with their cheerful round orange heads, the silvery-leaved curry plant (*Helichrysum augustifolium*) and varieties of artemisia. Orris root (*Iris florentina*) will provide strong strap-like vertical interest. Add some shrub roses and one or two *Alchemilla mollis* to create pretty associations and a discreetly colorful garden of great charm.

Herbs in window boxes and on balconies

❀ Some herbs such as basil, scented geranium and lemon verbena may do better indoors or in sheltered window boxes and balconies rather than outdoors. Success depends on where the window box or balcony is situated, which direction it faces and whether it gets enough sun and not too much wind. You can introduce a herb corner on a balcony with a few containers of herbs that are easy to grow. You can sow some herbs such as chervil, summer savory, borage and sweet marjoram directly into their containers. Certain perennials such as thyme and lavender can be kept for several years if you keep them dwarfed by clipping them.

BELOW: *A herb garden can be quite dramatic like this one, where the usual central square parterre is filled up with tall spiky seed heads.*

ABOVE: *A mature holy basil (labiatae) has grown bushy and in a wooden half barrel.*

GROWING HERBS

HERBS are enjoying a major resurgence in popularity – both as attractive plants and for everyday use in cooking. Of course, herbs have also been used for centuries to decorate and perfume the home, as well as for their medicinal attributes.

❀ Since harvesting herbs regularly actually helps the plants, by keeping them compact and bushy, and encouraging new, fresh, tasty young growth, herb gardens are best placed within reasonable range of the kitchen. You will feel less like tramping down the garden path in the pouring rain for a handful of fresh herbs, than simply reaching out to a window box or herb garden close to the kitchen door.

❀ Herbs make great container plants, since many of them enjoy the well-drained conditions that containers can provide. At one end of the spectrum, a perfectly useful and decorative herb garden can be planted into small pots which, when placed on a sunny windowsill, will provide you with a an easily accessible supply of herbs all year round.

❀ By contrast, twinned tubs flanking your front door and containing elegant standard bay trees with plaited stems are major herb investments that may need winter protection – and even protection against theft. Whatever size of garden you have, you will always be able to find room for a few herbs.

❀ Concentrate on growing a few varieties well, rather than a diversity of species that can quickly grow untidy. Where possible, separate each herb – perhaps by growing each one in an individual container or, as in a traditional herb garden, in distinct compartments.

❀ Many herbs can be quite invasive and vigorous growing. Separating them helps to prevent one herb overwhelming another, looks neat, and enables you to harvest and cultivate one herb without disturbing its neighbor. Divided containers are available specifically for this purpose, or you may have space to plant a knot garden, or herb garden in a wheel formation, with each spoke delineated by bricks or path edging, to create separate sections.

DIVIDING HERBS AND OTHER SMALL PLANTS

DIVIDING small plants is an excellent way of adding to your stocks at zero expense and with minimal effort. In addition, many perennial plants benefit from being lifted and divided every few years. Left undivided, their middles may start to die out, and the remaining growth can become straggly.

Ease the plant into sections, teasing out the roots gently, rather than tearing them apart. Replant each section and water well. When dividing old plants, discard the weak, old, central section and replant only the fresh young growth around the edges of the plant.

RESTRICTING THE SPREAD OF MINT

Invasive and fast growing, mint is best grown in a container in the ground, which will restrict its root spread yet provide adequate moisture. Use a standard pot or bottomless bucket; some gardeners use slate embedded in the ground to restrict the root run.

1 *Dig a hole large enough for the rim of a generously sized pot to be buried just below ground level.*

2 *Place the pot in the ground and bed it firmly into the soil with your hands. Make sure the rim is level with the soil surface.*

3 *Add a small amount of potting compost to the bottom of the pot.*

4 *Place the mint in the pot and then backfill the pot with compost and firm it around the plant. Water well. Lift, divide and repot the plant each spring.*

STARTING OUT

MANY herb gardens begin with an impulse buy of a healthy, container-grown perennial herb from the wide range of herbs on display at the garden center, and this can be an excellent start. Although many herbs can be grown from seed, if you need only one example of a herb, such as rosemary, it is cheaper, as well as easier, to buy a single plant. Herbs such as chives, which you may want in larger quantities, for example, to use as a decorative edging or as a companion plant elsewhere in the garden, are easily propagated by division; so just a few plants from the garden center will quickly yield many more. Some annual herbs, such as nasturtiums and basil, are quick and easy to grow from seed.

Cultivation requirements

❀ Many herbs are sun lovers, needing at least six hours of sunlight a day in order to thrive. Without good light, they can become thin and straggly, with a poor aroma. Most herbs also dislike being waterlogged, so plant them in well-drained soil. Some, such as thyme, sage and dwarf lavender, are very drought tolerant and actively enjoy sunny, dry conditions. Most herbs prefer warm conditions. Although they can tolerate temperatures of 45°F (7°C), herbs do not thrive in the cold.

❀ Protect cherished perennial herbs such as bay and rosemary against extremely cold or windy weather conditions. A simple way to care for tender herbs is to plant them in containers, plunged into the ground during the milder months and removed for overwintering in a protected environment. Some herbs, such as mint, are very invasive, and are always best planted in containers within the soil so that they do not colonise the garden.

HARVESTING HERBS

PICK leaves at any time during the growing season. Evergreens such as thyme may be harvested at any time, but allow new growth to harden off before winter.

PLANTING A CONTAINER HERB GARDEN

1 Strawberry pots allow many different herbs to be grown in a small space. Place a layer of crocks (for drainage) at the bottom of the pot. Fill up to the first planting hole with compost mixed with water-retaining gel.

2 Taking care not to disturb the root ball, push the roots of the first herb through the lowest planting hole into the pot.

3 Work up the pot, adding more compost and plants until you reach the top. Plant more herbs in the top of the pot. Water slowly and carefully so that the water reaches into every planting pocket.

4 Each spring, lift and divide any herbs that are growing too large or straggly for the pot.

❀ Harvest leaves in the morning, after the dew has evaporated from the foliage. Leaves are at their most flavorsome and tender just before the herb comes into flower. If harvesting the flowers, you should collect these at midday in dry weather, just as the flower is beginning to open fully.

❀ Take care to keep your harvested herbs loose, and with plenty of air circulating freely around them to prevent bruising, crushing or other deterioration prior to use. Traditional trugs are perfect for collecting herbs.

❀ Herb seed may be collected when it is fully hardened and ripe, on a warm, dry day. Roots are generally harvested in fall when the parts of the plant above the ground are starting to die back.

❀ The active components sought by herbalists for medicinal uses will have developed in the root systems of perennials in the second or third year after planting. Annual roots may be harvested at the end of each year. If you are not planning on using the herbs immediately after picking, then prepare them for preservation as soon as possible after harvesting, for optimum results.

STORING HERBS

How you handle herbs after harvesting will depend on the type of herb, and its intended use. Some herbs lose a lot of their flavour if dried. The taste and aroma of such herbs is better retained by freezing or by preserving in oil or vinegar.

Freezing herbs

❀ Freezing is a simple and effective way of preserving much of the flavour, color and nutritional content of herbs. Some of the more delicate herbs produce fresher tasting results when frozen rather than dried. Freeze them in labelled plastic bags or rigid containers. Alternatively, freeze small quantities of finely chopped herbs in individual ice cube trays and top up with water for convenient cooking quantities.

Herb oils and vinegars

❀ Herbs may be infused in oil or vinegar. These are simple to make; they liven up salads and marinades and make lovely gifts, too. Herb vinegars are also popular in cooking and as hair or skin rinses.

DRYING YOUR HERBS

Herbs need to be dried as quickly as possible after harvesting, in order to retain maximum color and scent. It is important that any moisture is removed before the plant material begins to deteriorate – rotting or becoming moldy.

1 *Pick several stems or leaves of your herb, in this case rosemary. Remove any leaves that would crowd together and hold too much moisture so that they would rot rather than dry out. Make small bunches for quick drying. Hang them upside down in a dry, warm, dark or shaded place is needed, such as a cupboard. Allow plenty of air to circulate around the drying herbs.*

2 *When drying is complete, after one to four weeks, the herbs may be rubbed through a sieve to remove the stalks, or shredded by hand, and bottled. Keep the bottled herbs in a dark, dry place until needed.*

GROWING AND USING HERBS

This chart identifies some of the most regularly used herbs. In addition it shows their various uses in cooking and, in some cases, medical treatments and explains how to grow them most effectively.

Herb   Use   Cultivation

Basil

Used in many popular Italian dishes; natural partner to tomatoes. Roughly tear the leaves, rather than chop

Tender annual; cannot withstand frost

Bay

Prime ingredient of bouquet garni; goes well with fish, stews and rice dishes. Tear the edges of the leaf before adding to a dish, and remove before serving the meal

Evergreen shrub; can withstand cold, but benefits from frost and wind protection

Borage

Delicately flavored and pretty addition to long summer drinks

Hardy annual; grow in a sunny position, in any soil type

Chives

Mild onion flavour; partners cheese, potatoes, eggs and butter particularly well. Not as rich in sulphur as onions, thus do not have the same tendency to cause digestive disturbance

Hardy perennial. Chives left to flower are pretty perennial plants, easily propagated by division. For the tastiest flavour, do not allow the plant to flower

Cilantro

Young leaves are deliciously perfumed and widely used in curries, as are the aromatic seeds

Hardy annual; prefers a sunny, well-drained position

Dill

Partners salmon and other types of fish especially well

Hardy annual; grow in a sheltered, cool position in rich, deep soil

Feverfew

Mainly ornamental; medicinal use as a cure for headache – note, herbal remedies should only ever be taken on the advice of an experienced practitioner

Hardy perennial; self-seeds readily. Prefers dry, well-drained soil in a sunny position

Herb		Use	Cultivation
Lavender		Popular culinary ingredient; adds delicate perfumed flavor to honey, and to savory dishes. Popular in pot pourri, sleep pillows and as decorative flower – fresh and dried	Hardy evergreen; grow in a dry, sunny position; clip after flowering
Marjoram		Partners eggs, cheese and tomatoes particularly well	Hardy perennial; grow in moist, sunny position
Mint		Used in mint sauce as essential accompaniment to roast lamb	Hardy perennial; grow in moist soil in partial shade or sun. Very invasive, therefore best grown in a container
Oregano		Widely used in bouquet garni, stuffings and for sprinkling over meat before roasting	Hardy perennial; grow in a well-drained, sunny position
Parsley		Popular garnish; goes particularly well with fish and potatoes	Hardy biennial; grow in slightly sheltered, rich moist soil
Rosemary		Traditional accompaniment to lamb and pork	Evergreen; grow in a sunny position in sandy, well-drained soil, preferably in sheltered position
Sage		Natural partner to onions; popular as a stuffing to counteract the richness of roast meats	Evergreen; grow in sunny site on light, well-drained soil
Thyme		Used in widely in soups and stews, omelettes and salads	Evergreen; grow in light, stony soil in full sun

FRUIT GARDENING

❦

Compared with vegetables, fruit gardening is very straightforward and relatively undemanding. While a vegetable patch needs consistent work and management to be at all productive – digging, feeding, weeding, planning successional sowing, intercropping and crop rotation – most fruits simply need to be planted in appropriate surroundings and will thrive with very rudimentary care. Some fruit trees will crop successfully for years with almost no attention, provided they have been planted properly and cared for early on.

THE ADVANTAGES OF GROWING YOUR OWN

GROWING your own fruit guarantees a chemical-free crop and offers the delicious taste and beneficial vitamins of fruit fresh from the plant. Some commercially grown fruits, for example grapes, are particularly likely to have been drenched in chemicals during cultivation.

❁ It is very easy to grow fruit organically, without recourse to pesticides and fertilizers, since perennial fruit plants do well on quite poor soil, and have a chance to benefit from the full ecological support that builds up in an established area. Companion planting can assist even further, attracting increased populations of predators and pollinators once a plant has settled in.

❁ Fruit can also be an extremely decorative element of garden design. Fruit trees are attractive all year round, even in winter when bare. Fruits can be trained to

ABOVE: *Strawberries are simple and satisfying to grow.*

LEFT: *Fruit trees such as apples thrive in open orchards.*

divide the garden vertically, and enliven or conceal walls and fences. Vines can scramble across arches, trellis, sheds and pergolas.

CHOOSING FRUITS TO SUIT YOU

THE TYPES of fruit you grow will depend on the size of your garden and the amount of time and energy you intend to devote to fruit growing, among other factors.

❁ Some fruit trees can grow to 23 ft (7 m) tall and are clearly unsuitable for a tiny garden, whereas those produced on dwarf rootstock may be suitable for

ABOVE: *Fruit can be grown successfully even where space is extremely limited, by using vertical surfaces to support plants.*

❀ Consider your site carefully, too. Although many fruit trees will do well with very little attention, they will do best if planted with consideration for their growing needs. Most fruits prefer a sheltered, sunny position. The sun encourages ripening and the production of good flavor and color. Shelter helps keep the plants warm and reduces the risk of wind damage. In addition, the insect activity so important for pollination is reduced on windy sites, which will restrict cropping.

❀ Although an entire orchard is obviously the optimum area for growing fruit trees, and a large fruit cage, big enough for an adult to stand in, is great for growing soft fruits, it is possible to grow a reasonable fruit crop even in a restricted space.

❀ Growing fruits in containers, as with vegetables, has become increasingly popular, allowing every gardener – even those who can devote no more than a patio or a couple of large planters flanking the front door to fruit growing – to have the satisfaction of eating fruit fresh from the plant.

container growing. Think carefully about the species and where to grow it, before visiting the nursery or garden center.

GROWING STRAWBERRIES

Simple to grow, strawberries are an ideal introduction to fruit growing. Although they will thrive with little attention, some basic care will improve the amount and quality of the crop considerably.

1 Plant strawberry plants in well-drained, humus-rich soil, spaced approximately 18 in (46 cm) apart.

2 As the ripening strawberries dangle towards the soil, a mulch of clean straw or a rubber strawberry mat will protect the fruit from mud splashes and from rotting. Mulching also retains moisture within the soil in hot weather and suppresses competitive weed growth.

3 To ensure the best crop possible, remove runners from the plants as soon as they appear. These runners can then be grown on to produce new plants.

4 When the strawberry plants have fruited, cut back the old foliage to within approximately 4 in (10 cm) of the leaf stems and remove debris and old straw from around the plants.

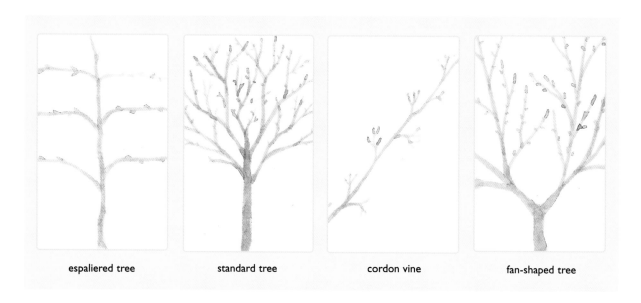

espaliered tree   standard tree   cordon vine   fan-shaped tree

GENERAL CARE FOR FRUIT GROWING

Buy only sound, sturdy plants, especially when selecting trees and bushes, which will be long-term garden residents. Plants of certified 'A' grade stock are guaranteed to be healthy and free of disease. This is a particularly useful guideline for buying good-quality soft fruits, which can be prone to diseases such as mosaic virus, which may not be detectable on a young plant.

❀ Choose cultivars suited to your site, and according to the effect you want – perhaps a tree you can train to an espalier shape to cover a warm wall, or a standard to take pride of place in a lawn. Make sure that you buy a rootstock appropriate to the scale of your plot. Rootstocks range from very vigorous to dwarf, so choose carefully. Remember that most tree fruits need cross pollinating, unless you choose a 'family' tree with several varieties on it, which fertilize each other.

Planting

❀ Fruit bushes and trees are generally planted in late fall or early winter, although container-grown plants can be planted out at any time, weather permitting. Most fruit thrives on well-drained, slightly acidic soil with good water reserves in the subsoil.

❀ To avoid the risk of disease, plant at the correct spacing. Many fruits are susceptible to rot caused by the fungal diseases that thrive in humid, overcrowded conditions. Where plants have sufficient air and light, fungal diseases rarely occur, and do not spread very easily if they do appear at all.

Supporting

❀ Apart from strawberries, bush currants and gooseberries, all fruits need supporting, either by staking or training against a surface. To stake a bare-rooted plant, drive a vertical stake into the planting hole before adding the plant.

❀ Container-grown plants need an angled stake added after planting. Soft fruits such as raspberries and some types of redcurrants and gooseberries need support systems of wires and posts, or wires fixed to walls or fences. Whatever support you choose, it must be well secured.

Feeding

❀ Some plant food will have been added at planting time, and leaf fall will return some more fertility to the soil, but harvesting fruit means that nutrients are being removed permanently from the soil, which will need replacing for best results.

❀ Regular mulching with well-rotted organic matter will aid soil fertility, and adding an organic fertilizer in late winter is beneficial. Although this may seem early, tree roots will just be starting into life again and organic fertilizers take time to be absorbed into the soil and become available to plant roots.

❀ Some fruits have particular feeding needs, so read labels carefully when buying and note any special requirements. For example, redcurrants and gooseberries need potash; stone fruits need calcium.

Watating

❀ The shallow, fibrous roots of soft fruits are especially vulnerable to drought, so be vigilant in attending to their watering needs. Top fruit will generally need watering only if grown against a fence or wall.

Protecting

❀ Most fruiting plants need some form of protection against frost, birds and other pests, and diseases. Barrier protection such as netting, fleece or cages is simple and effective. Try to avoid using chemical sprays as these can kill or deter pollinating insects, and are undesirable products to have in contact with edible crops. Remember to remove coverings used to protect against late spring frosts during the day, so as to allow insects to pollinate the flowers.

COMPANION PLANTING

AS WITH vegetables, growing fruit in tandem with other plants often has substantial benefits, especially in relation to pest and disease control. For example, alliums – particularly chives – are useful to apple trees, as they help prevent apple scab. Planting nasturtiums around the base of an apple tree and encouraging them to scramble up the trunk will deter woolly aphids. Conversely, some planting combinations are actively harmful, for example innocently pretty anemones harboring plum rust and planted near plum trees.

HARVESTING AND STORING APPLES

When to harvest depends on whether the apples are to be eaten immediately or stored long term. For the former, choose apples at their pinnacle of ripeness. Assess this visually, by watching the developing color, and also by twisting the fruit gently on the branch. If the stalk snaps easily under this light pressure and the apple comes away cleanly, it is fully ripe.

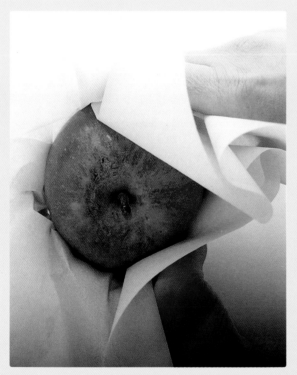

1 *Pick apples for storing just before they are completely ripe. They should be top quality, unblemished and free of any bruising or pest damage, which could contaminate the entire store.*

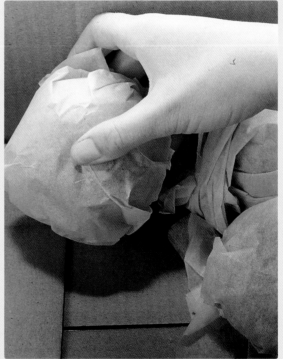

2 *Wrap each apple carefully in wax paper and place in a shallow box. Store in a cool dark place. These harvesting and storage guidelines can be applied equally to pears.*

ABOVE: *Some fruit trees make attractive and productive container plants.*

GROWING FRUIT IN CONTAINERS

Growing fruit in containers has grown in popularity in recent years. Even gardeners with diminutive plots can produce fruit crops that taste wonderful, are free of chemicals, rich in nutrients and absolutely fresh. Most fruiting plants are also extremely decorative as well as productive. For example, apple trees are often grown as much for their ornamental virtues as for their edible fruits. Strawberries possess a convenient tumbling growth habit, ideally suited to hanging baskets as well as the multi-holed terracotta pots that are more familiar as strawberry planters.

❀ Choose your species carefully when planting fruit in containers, especially if growing fruit trees. The plant should be clearly labelled in the garden center or nursery, with full details of its rootstock, how much space it requires, and whether it is self-fertilizing or will

RIGHT: *Strawberries reward even minimal care with generous crops of juicy, ripe fruit.*

need other trees around it for pollination. For example, if you have the space and inclination for only a single apple tree in a container, you will need a dwarf rootstock, such as M27 or M9, with a 'family' of three or four compatible varieties grafted on to it so that no further trees are needed for pollination.

Suitable containers

❀ Choose your container with due consideration to the needs of the plant you are growing. Fruit trees prefer a free root run, so will need generously proportioned containers. Cherries, plums, pears, apples and the like need containers that are at least 38 cm (15 in) deep, preferably much deeper.

❀ Trashcans, although not the most attractive of containers, make perfect homes for container-grown fruit trees. You could choose a galvanised metal one for industrial chic, or wrap bamboo or other natural screening around an inexpensive plastic container. The latter option has the added advantage that you could easily conceal a layer of plastic bubble wrap beneath the decorative natural wrapping for added winter insulation.

❀ There are also very attractive large containers that once served quite different purposes, for example old washing tubs, which look like giant Chinese lanterns made of silvery metal that has softened in tone over the years.

Caring for container-grown fruit

❀ The container fruit gardener needs to pay special attention to planting, watering, feeding and potting on, particularly if growing trees in containers. One useful way of reducing the effort involved in potting on every two years or so is to plant in a container that is initially oversized, lifting up the plant when necessary and adding further layers of compost beneath the first until the plant eventually outgrows the container. Plant with a good organic potting compost.

❀ Ideally, arrange some sort of permanent watering system for containers, to save work and ensure that the compost doesn't dry out. To give an idea of the watering needs of a container-grown fruit tree, you may find that in hot weather it needs a drink three or four times a day! Clearly, it is worth investing in a system that makes this an achievable proposition. Watering is not generally needed during winter.

Fruits for container growing

❀ For the best chance of success, always choose fruits with a good track record as container-grown plants. Strawberries are a perennial favourite and can be grown in all sorts of containers. Even individual small pots of strawberries on a windowsill will produce a good yield. Growing strawberries in containers has the

ABOVE: *Figs thrive in containers, since they like having their roots restricted.*

additional benefit of reducing the risk of slug attack and removing the need for the laborious mulching and weeding that is required when growing strawberries in the ground.

❀ Figs make good container plants, since they like having their roots restricted. Conversely, grapes hate root restriction and never do well in containers. Apples are a better choice than pears, since pears are not available on dwarf rootstocks at the time of writing, and even the smallest grows to at least 2.4 m (8 ft) tall.

❀ Some fruits are perfectly happy in containers, but their growth habit makes them too untidy a choice for decorative planting, for example raspberries, which grow tall and need staking and netting. Chosen well, watered well and placed in a spot sympathetic to their needs, container-grown fruits will be an attractive and rewarding addition to your garden.

LEFT: *Pear trees do not thrive in containers because they are not available in dwarf rootstocks.*

FRUIT GAZETTEER

Many fruits are remarkably tolerant to neglect. Even a fruit tree untended for several years will produce a reasonable crop, but all fruits will benefit from some appropriate care and attention. This will keep the plants healthy, cropping with a good yield and producing well-sized fruits.

FRUIT	Apple	Apricot	Blueberry	Blackcurrant	Fig
NEEDS FULL SUN	yes	yes	yes	yes	yes
HARDY BELOW 18°F (-8°C)	yes	yes	yes	yes	no
HEIGHT x SPREAD	controlled by rootstock	controlled by rootstock	5 x 5 ft (1.5 x 1.5 m)	4 x 4 ft (1.2 x 1.2 m)	8 x 10 ft (2.4 x 3 m)
SOIL REQUIREMENTS	deep, well drained	slightly alkaline	acidic	rich, moist, heavy	slightly alkaline
COMPANION PLANT	chives	garlic	no	nettles	rue
CULTIVATION	simple	average	simple	simple	average

FRUIT	Gooseberry	Grape	Kiwi	Peach	Pear
NEEDS FULL SUN	yes	yes	yes	yes	yes
HARDY BELOW 18°F (-8°C)	yes	no	yes	yes	yes
HEIGHT X SPREAD	4 x 4 ft (1.2 x 1.2 m)	Height 20 ft (6 m)	Height 30 ft (9 m)	controlled by rootstock	controlled by rootstock
SOIL REQUIREMENTS	rich, moist	average	average	acidic/neutral	rich, moist
COMPANION PLANT	Limnanthes douglasii	blackberries	no	garlic	no
CULTIVATION	simple	simple	average	simple	difficult

FRUIT	Plum	Raspberry	Redcurrant	Strawberry	Whitecurrant
NEEDS FULL SUN	yes	yes	no	yes	no
HARDY BELOW 18°F(-8°C)	yes	yes	yes	yes	yes
HEIGHT x SPREAD	controlled by rootstock	Height 6 ft(1.8 m)	4 x 4 ft (1.2 x 1.2 m)	6 x 12 in (15 x 30 cm)	4 x 4 ft (1.2 x 1.2 m)
SOIL REQUIREMENTS	heavy, moist	acidic/neutral	cool, average	rich	cool, average
COMPANION PLANT	garlic	garlic	nettles	onion	nettles
CULTIVATION	average	simple	simple	simple	average

THE JEKYLL/LUTYENS PARTNERSHIP

GERTRUDE JEKYLL was a friend of William Robinson's and the most influential garden designer in England before the Second World War. In 1889 she met a young architect called Edwin Lutyens and they collaborated on many gardens. He worked on the architectural aspects and hard landscaping and she on the planting. She had trained as a painter and was influenced by the sophisticated color theories of the day. She developed single-color and graded color schemes, quite different from the earlier brash bedding colors. Her naturalistic approach was particularly successful within the formal framework of Lutyens' bricks, steps and paving.

ABOVE: *Les Bois des Moutiers in France. The house was designed by Lutyens for the family that still own it today and the planting was very much in line with Gertrude Jekyll's philosophy, with graduated color schemes in the formal section and a grand informality at the back of the house.*

ORGANIC PRACTICES

In recent years, there has been a noticeable swing away from some of the advice previously issued almost automatically by gardening experts. Nowadays, the advice on pest and weed control is not necessarily limited to a directive to buy the strongest chemicals available and apply them routinely. Providing an alternative approach in addition to, or instead of, a chemical solution has increasingly become the gardening norm. This naturalistic approach is not new. It is merely a return to the centuries of gardening wisdom that preceded the onslaught of garden chemicals, which came to be seen as essential horticultural kit in the last hundred years.

THE PRINCIPLES

ORGANIC gardening is not just about reducing a reliance on chemical support. Choosing a 'natural' pest killer is not necessarily much more ecologically sound than using a chemical variant. Organic practice is about considering the garden in a much more holistic way.

❀ Rather than automatically dismissing all garden creatures as pests and all plants other than crops as weeds, an organic approach considers, values and utilises the complex interplay between plants and creatures, the elements and the soil – a series of relationships that can be turned to a gardener's advantage. The organic approach is not a single rule or dictate. It is a way of gardening that is ecologically sound, sustainable, naturalistic and environmentally friendly.

The benefits

❀ Most people have a creeping awareness of the ecological issues that have become of increasing concern in recent years – namely, a desire not to pollute the environment or our bodies with chemicals, and a wish to encourage nature back into our lives on a daily basis, by encouraging birds, butterflies and other creatures to visit our gardens.

BELOW: *Respecting a plant's natural habitat and replicating it in a garden setting is the simplest way to encourage healthy growth.*

❀ These are not just cosmetic concerns or matters of gardening fashion. People have become increasingly concerned about what they are eating – aware, for example, that there is little point in washing fruit in order to remove pesticides and fertilizers from the skin if, as is the case with some commercially grown fruit, the flesh is contaminated with chemicals throughout. Organic produce has therefore become increasingly popular, and many gardeners have started to grow their own.

Valuing the soil

❀ Besides enhancing the quality of food production, an organic approach has much to offer the garden as a whole. Organic gardening centers around protecting and increasing the life blood of the garden – the soil.

❀ For the past hundred years or so, farmers and domestic gardeners have been using artificial fertilizers to encourage plant growth and chemicals to control pests in the soil. Safety issues with regard to the often dangerous chemicals involved seem obvious now, as do concerns over potentially poisoning not only our own bodies directly, but also harming life around us, since chemicals wash out into water supplies and find their way into the diet of wildlife.

ABOVE: *Plant according to the conditions prevalent in your garden, such as the dappled shade of this woodland path, and the plants will grow vigorously with few additional requirements.*

❀ Another, less immediately visible layer of damage has slowly occurred as commercial and domestic gardeners have become reliant on chemicals. Soil, abused and neglected, ceases to live, and without living soil beneath our feet we cannot hope to sustain life above the soil. Healthy soil is vibrantly alive with organisms, which convert inert minerals and water into materials that plants need in order to grow.

❀ Overuse of chemical fertilizers and overintensive cultivation are short-sighted gardening methods, and strip the soil of humus-making organisms. Since soil without humus is essentially finely ground rock on which nothing will flourish, the aim of organic gardening is to introduce and sustain the natural life within garden soil. This raises soil fertility, improves moisture retention and encourages plant health, as well as gradually building up and supporting a wider natural environment. For example, by encouraging worms, which feed blackbirds, not only do you add the sweet sound of bird-song to your garden, but the birds will repay your soil by adding their droppings, feathers, eggshells and eventually their own bodies to further enrich your soil.

ABOVE: *Producing your own compost is probably the single most important step you can take towards gardening organically; a compost heap does not need to be elaborate or expensive.*

GOING ORGANIC: WHERE TO BEGIN

CHANGING the habits of a gardening lifetime to 'go organic' can seem overwhelming, but there are some simple immediate steps, which will have a positive impact on your garden.

❀ Stop using chemical insecticides, fertilizers, fungicides and herbicides. Buy only ecofriendly products; for example, choose not to buy peat from non-sustainable sources, or bulbs gathered from wild sites. Incorporate as many natural control/encouragement techniques as possible – for example companion planting and creating habitats to attract helpful wildlife into your garden.

❀ Since respecting and nurturing the soil is at the heart of organic gardening, producing your own compost is the most important first step in becoming an organic gardener. Organisms are essentially any items that have once lived. Converting

these items back into compost is not only ecologically sound on the grounds of recycling and avoiding waste, but also marvellously helpful to the soil.

❀ Well-balanced, well-matured compost is a perfect plant food, which does not carry the risks of overfeeding or even active damage associated with chemical fertilizers. Importantly, the humus-making organisms present in compost not only convert plant food into substances accessible to the plants, but also gradually help return the soil to its naturally balanced, healthy state. This encourages plants to grow more easily and be more resistant to disease.

Compost making

❀ Garden compost is preferable to farmyard manure, since it contains a wider range of nutrients and micro-organisms. There are many different methods for making compost, but all share the same basic principles.

❀ Generally, good composting comes from using a variety of different substances rather than one material only, and it must be well mixed, aerated and moistened. Getting this balance of materials, air and moisture right is the key to successful composting, together with efficient mixing and effective insulation to retain heat well. The bigger your compost heap, the more efficiently it will heat up and 'cook' to produce compost reasonably quickly.

RIGHT: *Throw all your degradable matter into the compost holder to provide rich mulch for the plants.*

✿ An expensive compost container is not essential. A simple home-made compost heap, an area approximately 1¼ sq yd (1 sq m) contained within a construction of wood, wire or brick will be very effective, if not as elegant as a commercial equivalent. Protect the heap against rainfall and insulate it – although unsightly, an effective lid is a piece of old

ABOVE: Organic vegetables, like these lettuces, chives and spring onions, are full of vitamins and natural goodness.

carpet covered with plastic sheeting. A conventional lid, insulated by plastic bags filled with crumpled newspaper placed inside it out of sight, is a more attractive solution.

WHAT TO COMPOST

✿ A good composting mixture contains moist green matter that will rot fairly quickly, such as grass clippings, together with more brackish materials such as straw and twiggy stems, which break down more slowly but add useful bulk.

✿ Do not squash down huge heaps of grass clippings, which will inhibit a good flow of air. Intersperse thin, uncompressed layers, approximately 6 in (15 cm) thick, with other materials.

✿ Fibrous matter will compost more readily if shredded or cut into small pieces before being added to the heap. Ideally, add a layer of manure every 12 in (30 cm). The nitrogen in the manure will speed up the composting process and contribute beneficial soil organisms.

✿ Kitchen waste, such as crushed eggshells, vegetable peelings, tea leaves and coffee grounds are all suitable, but avoid meat, fish and cooked food, which encourage vermin. Never use the compost area as an extra trash can.

✿ Diapers, pet litter and general household debris will produce a stinking mess, not the sweet-smelling friable brown compost that is your aim. Also, do not create problems for yourself by adding perennial weeds, diseased plant matter and seeding flower heads to the heap.

✿ Compost generally takes about three weeks to reach its maximum temperature, then goes on to mature in around three to six months. The compost will benefit from turning during this time.

THE VALUE OF A
POSITIVE ECOSYSTEM

THIS sounds terrifyingly technical, yet simply describes a garden environment that becomes increasingly self-supporting. By encouraging wildlife into the garden, you can share all the benefits of the natural cycle, which may have been thrown destructively off kilter by contemporary gardening methods. For example, aim to attract predators that live on pests, which live on other pests and so on.

✿ Predators generally breed more slowly than pests, which can create a major problem if you are using chemical pest controls, which can unwittingly destroy useful predators along with the pests. The self-regulating system of pests and predators is thus thrown off-balance and can take years to rebuild. It is important to rethink the way that you regard what you may previously have considered purely as pests. For example, a butterfly, beautiful in its own right, as well as helping to produce more flowers in your garden by pollination, was once a caterpillar, munching its way through leaves.

✿ Aim to control the wildlife in your garden and make it work for you, rather than destroying it unilaterally. A pest by another name can also be seen as wildlife, a pollinator, a predator and ultimately, fertilizer.

RIGHT: *Leaving the seed heads on plants provide valuable seed heads for birds.*

ABOVE: *An organic environment need not be wild and undisciplined. A pond of any kind will attract beneficial wildlife to the garden.*

Not all pests are as lethal to plants as gardeners have

been led to believe over the past century, and there are pest control options available to the organic gardener, that do not involve saturating your garden with hazardous chemicals.

CREATING A POSITIVE ECOSYSTEM

BUTTERFLIES, beetles, wasps and bees are pollinators. They all transfer pollen, which encourages more flowers in your garden, for as long a season as possible. Of course, as the pollinators die, their decomposing bodies make a further contribution to soil fertility.

Attracting pollinators

❀ Some plants are particularly attractive to pollinators. It is important to provide as long a season of nectar for them as possible, so plant a range of plants popular to pollinators – from early spring flowers like bluebells and *aubrieta* through to summer flowers such as buddleja, valerian and lavender.

❀ Hoverflies are superb aphid eaters, and should be encouraged by planting their favorite, the poached egg flower (*Limnanthes douglasii*), a pretty, easy-to-grow annual.

❀ Other plants attractive to hoverflies include broom, marigolds, golden rod and Michaelmas daisies, as well as most other flowers. Lacewings and ladybugs take nectar from the same flowers as hoverflies, but also like dill, yarrow and alliums, which are spectacular ornamental plants to grow in any case.

BELOW: *A predatory ground beetle on a plant stem.*

ABOVE: *Frogs and toads are very beneficial garden creatures, eating the slugs and snails that can cause untold plant damage.*

Encouraging frogs and toads

❀ Toads, frogs and newts eat many pests, notably slugs, and a wise organic gardener provides water and moist areas for these garden friends to inhabit. A pond is the obvious environment, but any moist, sheltered corner may be home to these useful creatures.

❀ Some organic gardeners deliberately create a temptingly moist, overgrown area in the greenhouse, where frogs and toads congregate, so helping to control greenhouse pests such as earwigs, and numerous other insects and grubs. Do allow the creatures access to a pond for mating and breeding.

Beneficial beetles

❀ Beetles comprise a huge group of insects – at least 250,000 species. Although there are exceptions, such as wood-boring beetles, most are garden helpers, eating slugs and soil pests, as well as pollinating in inclement conditions when other pollinators do not fly.

❀ Some beetles are ground dwellers, while others can fly. It is a good idea to help protect useful ground-dwelling beetles from larger predators by providing them with dense-foliaged, dew-collecting plants such as lady's mantle to hide beneath. Propping up some slates and adding pieces of wood, stones, old tiles or brassica collars to the vegetable plot will encourage beetles to dwell there and see off aphids.

ABOVE: *A garden spider on a dewy web formed on a seed head in the early morning.*

Spiders

❀ Spiders are beneficial in two ways. They prey on pests, and also provide food for wrens, robins and other garden friends. Encourage spiders by allowing the natural debris that builds up under hedges to accumulate. Dead twigs and leaves make a perfect habitat for spiders and other useful insects and small mammals.

Birds

❀ Although birds can damage crops, the benefits of attracting them into your garden far outweigh the disadvantages. Thus the organic gardener prefers to protect vulnerable plants against bird attack, while actively encouraging particularly useful birds to visit and live in the garden.

❀ Providing nesting places in which young birds can be safely reared, along with feeding the birds to help them survive the winter and providing an adequate water supply, will all repay you many times over.

❀ Most birds are berry or seed eaters, so growing fruit and other berrying plants will obviously attract them. Leaving the seed heads on plants will also help. Keen organic gardeners often plant sacrificial crops, so

RIGHT: *Birds are great insect eaters and are well worth attracting into your garden.*

valuable are some birds to the garden as a whole. Stop feeding in summer, in order to encourage the birds to devour unwanted pests.

❀ Some birds are especially useful, and it is well worth providing conditions that are likely to attract them by supplying birdboxes designed to replicate their natural preferences, and favoured foodstuffs. For example, blue tits, which devour caterpillars, aphids and leaf miners, nest in small holes in trees, so prefer nesting boxes with a small round hole on the front which mimics this environment; while robins will settle in boxes with wider, open fronts.

❀ However you feed the birds in your garden, be consistent. In winter, a wasted journey to an empty bird table can exhaust what may already be a weak bird. Ideally, feed twice a day during winter.

❀ Site nesting boxes carefully, away from feeding tables, as the feeding birds would disturb the nesting birds. Position nesting boxes approximately 7 ft (2 m) up a tree trunk, pole or wall, facing away from prevailing winds and strong sun. Open-fronted boxes should be placed in thick cover.

Hedgehogs

❀ Hedgehogs are popular garden creatures, eating slugs, caterpillars, beetles and other insects. Contrary to popular opinion, hedgehogs should not be fed on milk. They fare much better on cat or dog food, which may help encourage them into the garden if put out in the fall when they are laying down fat stores for their winter hibernation.

❀ Purpose-built hedgehog houses can be bought or made and installed under hedges or shrubs. Always check a bonfire for hibernating hedgehogs before lighting it. Many hedgehogs perish in this way each year. If you have a pond, supply a rough piece of wood on one side as a ladder, as hedgehogs can drown in steep-sided ponds.

ABOVE: *Hedgehogs are marvellous mobile slug controls.*

ABOVE: *A common long-eared bat hanging asleep from a tree branch.*

Worms

❀ The humble worm is a vital garden creature. The casts that they excrete are a wonderful soil texturiser and fertilizer, and worm burrows assist soil drainage and aeration. Of course, if you are going to encourage birds, you also need worms. Encourage worms by keeping the soil moist and mulched, with plenty of organic matter incorporated. Liming also encourages worms, since they prefer slightly alkaline soil.

Bats

❀ Although unpopular with many people, bats perform useful functions, which make it well worth encouraging them to take up residence in your garden. They eat vast numbers of flying pests, for example aphids and mosquitoes. Many bat species are declining, so providing favorable roosting and hibernating sites for them in your garden is a very worthy undertaking.

❀ Bats are not easy to attract and have very specific requirements, but you could try putting up a bat booth in a suitable place and seeing if any roost. Ideally, have two bat boxes – one facing south for summer, one facing north for winter hibernation – both at least 5 ft (1.5 m), but preferably 16 ft (5 m), off the ground, placed on a tree trunk or under the house eaves.

ABOVE: *Use shears rather than a chemical weedkiller to get rid of unwanted growth in your garden.*

THE ORGANIC APPROACH TO PESTS AND DISEASES

As already described, the organic gardener takes a wider view of garden wildlife than simply eradicating every living creature with hazardous chemicals. By encouraging predators into the garden, some pests are kept under natural control, while taking care of the soil and general good plant husbandry encourages plants to grow healthily and with improved disease resistance.

❀ A very exciting recent development in gardening has been the growing acceptance of companion planting as a valuable horticultural tool. Although this practice has been undertaken for centuries, it has only recently been brought to center stage as a useful gardening technique, rather than being viewed as a quaint mixture of folklore and myth.

Companion planting

❀ Growing particular combinations of plants for specific beneficial effect has long been practised, and a developing trend away from treating pests and diseases with chemicals has provoked a resurgence of interest in this intriguing area of garden science.

❀ The organic approach in general takes a holistic view of the garden, accepting, utilising and maximising all the complex beneficial interconnections of nature, while minimising negative interplay. Companion planting springs from this viewpoint, and works in a number of ways.

❀ Some plants repel undesirable insects, or lure them away from other specific plants. For example, marigolds deter whitefly, so are often grown near plants susceptible to whitefly attack, such as tomatoes grown in greenhouses. Marigolds are particularly well known nowadays as a companion plant, valued for their long-flowering attractiveness, as well as for their ability to kill eelworms and fend off pests.

❀ Some plants help each other directly, by providing shelter from the elements or by less immediately obvious means, such as by positive secretions from roots and leaves. For example, some roots exude substances that render them distasteful to pests, and this useful property can be transmitted through the soil to neighboring plants. Some plants can help the soil, for example legumes, which render nitrogen available to other plants.

❀ While some plants are good neighbors, others are enemy combinations. This may be down to one plant shading another, preventing germination, or to one plant starving its neighbors of soil nutrients, or producing root secretions which inhibit growth. Companion planting notes these undesirable relationships and minimises them.

Organic pest and disease control

❀ You might expect this section to be a list of home-made concoctions for alternatives to chemical pest- and weedkillers, but the organic approach is more wide ranging than simply replacing chemicals with 'natural' recipes.

❀ Organic gardening focuses on a broadly healthy, long-term approach, rather than the quick-fix to gardening problems that we have been taught by manufacturers to regard as the norm. The organic gardener takes care to provide optimum growing conditions for plants, thereby encouraging natural plant health and disease resistance. Good hygiene practices also help keep disease at bay, as does choosing to plant varieties resistant to disease.

❀ Crop rotation is a well-accepted way of protecting plants from pests and diseases. Mechanical methods are also part of the organic pest control lexicon. These include erecting physical barriers to pests, for example protecting food crops with netting to exclude birds, or simply picking off offending creatures, such as plucking caterpillars off brassicas.

RIGHT: *Pulling up weeds by hand is laborious but effective, especially on perennial weeds that hoeing does not remove.*

MAKING EARWIG POTS

The traditional earwig trap is not a thing of great beauty but it is very effective at attracting and trapping earwigs that would otherwise attack particularly susceptible plants such as dahlias. In a cottage garden border the straw-filled pots can even appear prettily rustic. A more unobtrusive option is to leave pieces of rolled-up newspaper on the soil around the base of vulnerable plants. Any kind of trap will need daily checking and emptying.

1 To make a traditional trap, stuff a flowerpot with straw.

2 Invert it and place it on a garden cane in the border. Each morning, check the trap and dispose of any earwigs that have taken up residence overnight.

CHIMNEY POT PLANTER

❦

This elegant planter started life in a much less sophisticated guise –
as an orange-colored plastic chain store bargain. A simple paint
technique transforms the fake terracotta into a deceptively realistic
faux lead finish, which complements plants beautifully.

TOOLS AND MATERIALS

† Medium grade sandpaper
† Plastic chimney pot planter
† Spray can of white
  acrylic primer
† Matt emulsion paint in white
  and charcoal grey
† Paintbrush
† Acrylic glaze
† Plastic carton
† Spray can of exterior acrylic
  varnish, in matt or satin finish

*1 Using medium grade sandpaper,
sand the plastic planter well
so as to provide a 'key' for the
paint, enabling it to adhere well.
Working in a well-ventilated area,
spray the planter evenly with
white acrylic primer – all over the
outside and on the inside at the
top of the planter.*

*2 When the first coat of primer has
dried sufficiently (follow the
manufacturer's directions for drying*

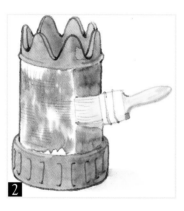

*and re-application times), apply a
second coat of white acrylic primer –
sufficient to cover the planter
uniformly. Leave to dry thoroughly –
preferably overnight.*

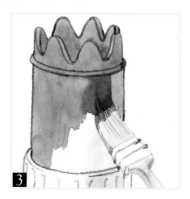

*3 Paint the planter evenly with
charcoal-grey emulsion paint and
leave to dry for at least 3 hours.*

*4 Place a little acrylic glaze in a
plastic carton and tint it with
white emulsion paint. Add water until
the glaze has a runny, milky
consistency. Briskly brush the glaze all*

*over the planter, allowing the glaze to
run unevenly down the surfaces,
forming pools that are opaque in some
areas and watery and translucent in
others. Wash randomly over the glaze
with a little water, taking care not to
dislodge the glaze in areas where it has
formed naturalistic patterns. Leave to
dry for several hours.*

*5 Add more of the same glaze to
some areas of the planter to give
an impression of age-encrusted salts.
Add water to soften any hard,
unnatural lines. Flick splatters of the
glaze randomly over some parts of the
planter to give a further weathered
impression. Leave to dry thoroughly
– preferably overnight.*

*6 Working in a well-ventilated
area, finish the planter by
spraying it with acrylic varnish.
Apply several coats, following the
manufacturer's directions for drying
and re-application times.*

PLANTED BUCKET

Metal complements plants beautifully and it weathers attractively, too. For impromptu entertaining, this hanging bucket can be filled with cut flowers arranged in wet florist's foam to enliven a garden wall, then later planted up for a more permanent display. The project is as ecologically sound as it is pretty, since this bucket has been recycled, now enjoying a new lease of life after its initial incarnation as a candle pot.

TOOLS AND MATERIALS

- Hammer
- Long nail
- Small galvanised bucket
- Wallplug plus masonry screw, or wood screw, as appropriate
- Screwdriver
- Plants and compost or cut flowers and wet florist's foam

1 *Using a hammer and a long nail, punch a hole in the side of the galvanised bucket near the rim for hanging the planter.*

2 *In the same way, punch drainage holes through the base of the bucket.*

3 *Hang the bucket in place, using appropriate fixings – a wallplug and screw for masonry, or just a screw for wood, as here.*

4 *Plant up the bucket or arrange cut flowers in well-soaked wet florist's foam for a temporary, colorful display.*

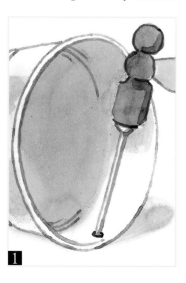

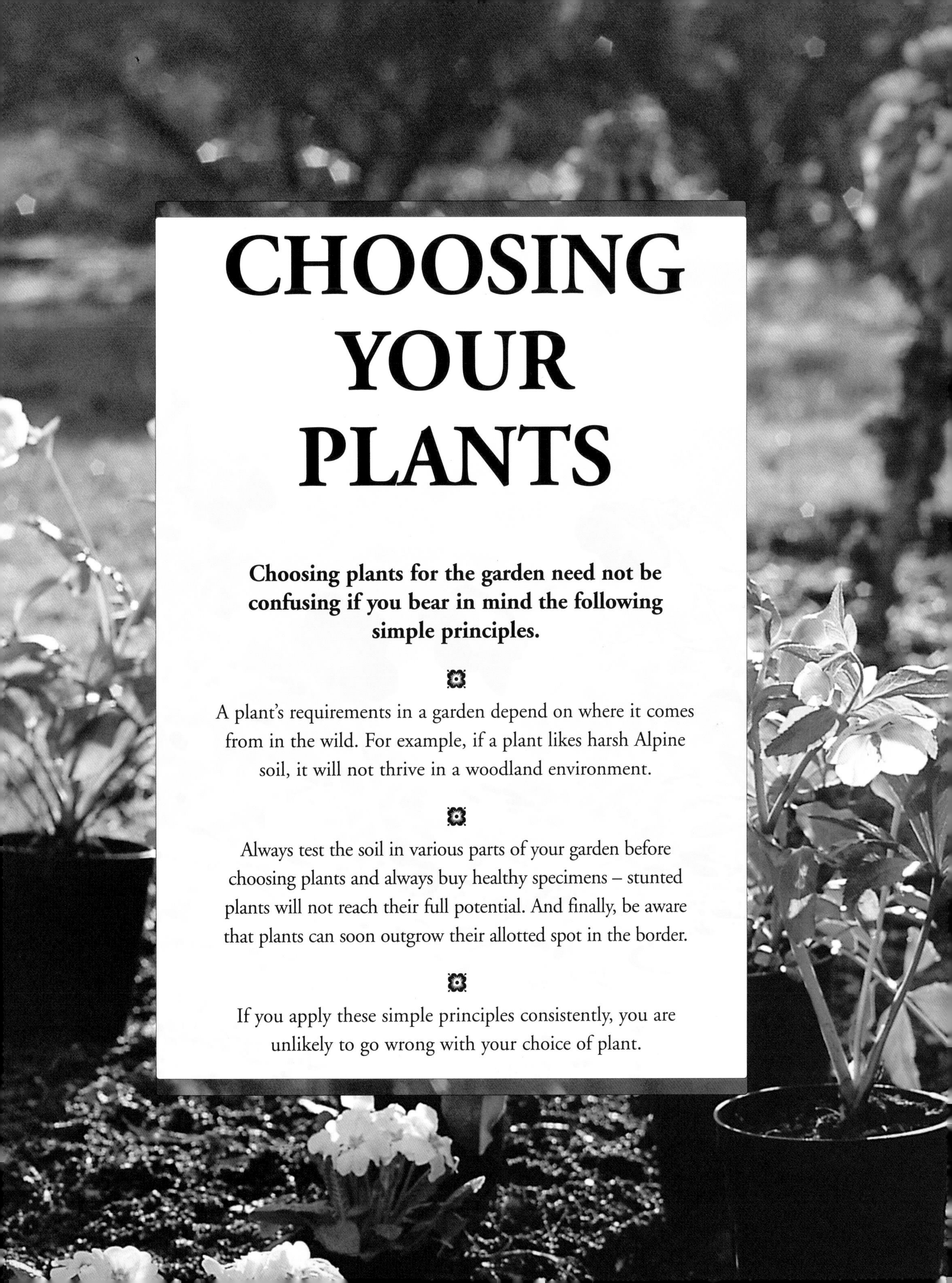

CHOOSING YOUR PLANTS

Choosing plants for the garden need not be confusing if you bear in mind the following simple principles.

✜

A plant's requirements in a garden depend on where it comes from in the wild. For example, if a plant likes harsh Alpine soil, it will not thrive in a woodland environment.

✜

Always test the soil in various parts of your garden before choosing plants and always buy healthy specimens – stunted plants will not reach their full potential. And finally, be aware that plants can soon outgrow their allotted spot in the border.

✜

If you apply these simple principles consistently, you are unlikely to go wrong with your choice of plant.

LEARNING PLANT NAMES

❦

The ancient Greeks and Romans began classifying plants over 2,000 years ago. In the monasteries and universities of Europe where the work was continued, the universal language was Latin. So for centuries Latin names were used to describe individual plants. Each plant needed a long sentence to describe it so that scholars could recognise it. The scientific descriptions were unwieldy and did not always correspond to each other in different parts of the world, so there were many misunderstandings. Common names for plants were not satisfactory either. One plant may have several different common names in different localities and, conversely, the same name can be given to different plants.

THE BINOMIAL SYSTEM

In the 18th century the Swedish naturalist, Carl Linnaeus (1707–78), created a system for methodically naming and classifying the whole living world 'from buffaloes to buttercups'. His system, the binomial system, consisted of two names for each plant.

❀ Since then, the Linnaean system of classification has been developed by scientists so that the entire plant kingdom is divided and subdivided into what amounts to a 'family tree' according to each plant's botanical characteristics. There are now international rules as to the naming of plants.

❀ Linnaeus grouped plants together into families and then divided each family into smaller groups called *genera* (singular genus).

Plant families

❀ All flowering plants are grouped into particular families based purely on the structure of their flowers. The family name always has a capital letter and ends in –aceae or –ae. For example Rosaceae is the rose family; Ranunculaceae is the buttercup family; Liliaceae is the lily family; and the Umbelliferae family includes plants that have clusters of small flowers like cow parsley and angelica.

RIGHT: Twelve pansies and violas painted by Joachim Camerarius the Younger in 1589. He called them 'Little day and night flowers' – Linnaeus did not introduce his binomial system for the naming of plants until the eighteenth century.

Genus and species

❀ Each plant family is then divided into smaller groups called genera. The binomial (two-name) system gives each plant name two words. The first word is the genus name, for example *Ilex* (holly).

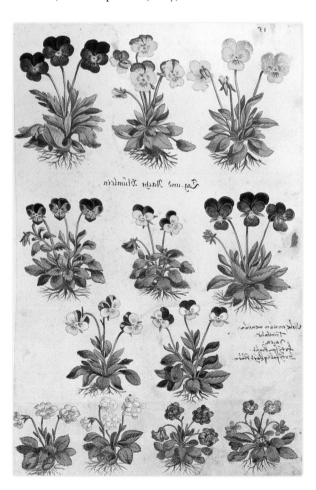

ABOVE: *A row of modern pansies (*Viola wittrockiana*) growing with lavender in front of a clipped hedge of privet.*

✿ The second name is the specific, or species name, (which is equivalent to a person's Christian or given name), for example *aquifolium*, which means 'pointed-leaved'. Thus *Ilex aquifolium* is the name for the common holly tree and means 'holly with pointed leaves', whereas *Ilex platyphylla* means 'broad-leaved holly'. In the binomial system the genus name is always given an initial capital letter, and the second, species name, which applies to that plant alone, starts with a small letter.

✿ A plant may be named after the plant 'hunter' who first discovered it in the wild and brought it back to civilisation. For example, *Dicksonia antarctica* is named after James Dickson, who discovered it in Antarctica.

✿ Subspecies (denoted by 'subsp.') indicates a distinct variant of the species, usually because it has adapted to a particular region.

Cultivars

✿ There are many plants that differ from the normal form of the species. These may have occurred spontaneously in the garden by mutation, or have been created by plant breeding or induced from radiation or chemicals.

✿ These used to be called varieties when naturally occurring in the wild, and cultivars when produced by humans.

More recently, all variants are now described as cultivars. Cultivar names follow the species name and have a capital letter and single quotation marks. For example, *Rosa rugosa* 'Blanche Double de Coubert' is a white-flowered *rugosa* rose and *Rosa rugosa* 'Frau Dagmar Hastrup' has pink flowers.

Hybrids

✿ Hybrids are plants produced by crossing two different parent plants. These are most common between two species of the same genus because they are closely related. For example, *Viburnum* x *bodnantense* is a cross between the two species *Viburnum farreri* and *Viburnum grandiflorum*.

However, there are some crosses between species from different genera, for example the very vigorous x *Cupressocyparis leylandii*, which is a cross between the genera *Chamaecyparis* and *Cupressus*.

✿ Hybridisation and selection have produced many cultivars with similar characteristics. For convenience these are often classified into groups or series, for example Delphinium Pacific Hybrids or Elatum Group.

LEFT: *A delicate watercolor painting of the broad-leaved* Anemone hortensis, *taken from a botanical drawing dating from 1795.*

NAME CHANGES

Sometimes it is necessary to change a plant name, which can be very confusing for gardeners. There are several reasons for this. The plant may have been wrongly identified or an earlier name for it may have been found, in which case the International Code specifies the earliest name should be used. Another reason is that two different plants may have been given the same name.

❀ The reason it is important to know the correct name of a plant is that two different species from the same genus may be very different from one another.

❀ For example, take the spurge family *(Euphorbia)*. These plants have unusual blooms and good foliage and make excellent plants for creating decorative effects or background foliage in the garden.

❀ But you do have to choose the right one. *Euphorbia wulfenii* is a large, shrubby very hardy plant, which forms a loose dome of large yellow flower heads and grows to 5 ft (1.5 m) tall. It is a splendid plant for creating an architectural effect, whereas *E. myrsinites* is only 6 in (15 cm) high and *E. obesa* is a tender ball-shaped succulent requiring greenhouse cultivation.

LEFT: *Scarlet poppy* (Papaver rhoeas) *from a book entitled* Familiar Wild Flowers *by F. Edward Hulme, published in 1894.*

LATIN NAMES AND THEIR MEANINGS

Many genus names and even more species names have a particular meaning, which helps to identify them.

RIGHT: *This detailed watercolor is of a snowdrop anemone* (Anenome sylvestris), *first printed in a botanical magazine that was published in 1796.*

Genera names

❀ Generic names sometimes commemorate classical gods and heroes or famous botanists. For example *Achillea* (yarrow) was named after the warrior Achilles, who was slain by an arrow in his heel; Daphne was a maiden pursued by the sun god Apollo; Iris was the goddess of the rainbow. All come from classical literature.

❀ Plants named after famous botanists include *Aubrieta*, after Claude Aubriet (1668–1743), a French botanical artist; *Clarkia* after William Clark (1770–1838), an American explorer; *Dahlia* after Anders Dahl (1751–89), a Swedish botanist; *Magnolia* after Pierre Magnol (1638–1715), a French physician and botanist; *Mahonia* after Bernard McMahon (1775–1816), an Irish-American nurseryman; *Nicotiana* after Jean Nicot (1530–1600), a French traveller; *Rudbeckia* after Olaf Rudbeck (1660–1740), a Swedish botanist; *Saintpaulia* after Baron Walter von Saint Paul-Illaire (1860–1910), a German traveller; and *Tradescantia* after John Tradescant (*c.* 1570–1638), English royal gardener to Charles I.

Species names

❀ Species names can be even more informative. They may honor people who had a direct connection with the plant. Often a plant used to be named after the plant 'hunter' who collected it or the nurserymen who propagated and sold it.

❀ *Darwinii* after the genus name of a plant, therefore, commemorates the English scientist Charles Darwin

(1809–82); *douglassii* denotes David Douglas (1798–1834), a Scotsman who collected many conifers in North America; *farreri* denotes the English collector and author, Reginald J. Farrer (1880–1920); *fortunei* is for the Scottish collector, Robert Fortune (1812–80); *veitchii* is for the English family nursery firm of Veitch, which flourished in Exeter and London between 1808 and 1914 and which sponsored several successful plant hunters; *willmottiae* is for Ellen Mary Willmott (1860–1934), an English gardener; and *wilsonii* for Ernest Henry ('Chinese') Wilson (1878–1931), English collector and botanist.

❀ Some names refer to the geographical area where a plant originated, although these are not always reliable. Botanists sometimes made mistakes. For example, several plants introduced as from Japan (*japonica*) were later found to be natives of China.

❀ Linnaeus himself regarded Indian (*indica*) and Chinese (*sinensis*) as virtually interchangeable. Geographical names often used include *cambricus* (Cambria or Wales), *capensis* (Cape of Good Hope), *damascenus* (Damascus), *gallicus* (Gaul or France), *hispanicus* (Hispania, Spain), *lusitanicus* (Portugal) and *neopolitanus* (Naples).

❀ There are hundreds of names that simply describe aspects of the plant. Just a few common examples are given in the table above. They are almost all of Latin origin.

LEFT: *These colorful Iceland poppies have the Latin name* Papaver nudicaule, *which means 'naked stemmed poppy'.*

DESCRIPTIVE LATIN SPECIES NAMES

acaulis	stemless	*lacteus*	milk-white
albus	white	*maculatus*	spotted
amoenus	pleasing	*meleagris*	speckled
argenteus	silvery	*nanus*	dwarf
atropurpureus	dark purple	*niger*	black
azureus	sky-blue	*nivalis*	snowy-white
baccatus	berry-bearing	*occidentalis*	western
caeruleus	dark blue	*parviflorus*	small-flowered
citriodorus	lemon-scented	*plumosus*	feathery
cordatus	heart-shaped	*reptans*	creeping
coronatus	crowned	*saggitifolius*	arrow-leaved
dentatus	toothed	*scandens*	climbing
farinosus	floury	*sinensis*	Chinese
flavus	yellow	*speciosus*	showy
floribundus	free-flowering	*spinosus*	thorny
fruticosus	shrubby	*tomentosus*	woolly
fulgens	shining	*tortuosus*	very twisted
glaber	smooth	*uliginosus*	of marshy places
gladiatus	sword-like	*venustus*	handsome
hybridus	hybrid	*vernalis*	of spring
japonicus	Japanese	*viridis*	green

PLACING YOUR PLANT

Plants in the wild have adapted to the soil and climate of the regions in which they grow. If you want to grow plants where they do not originally belong, you have to try and provide the conditions they are used to or they will die. Many plants from the tropics or the deserts will not survive out of doors in a temperate climate. Other plants may be half-hardy and able to withstand a certain degree of cold but will be killed by a hard frost.

CLIMATIC ADAPTATIONS

IN warm temperate regions such as the Mediterranean, plants have learned to grow where the soil is poor and there is a lack of moisture during the summer months. Often they have silvery leaves, the silver due to tiny hairs, which help to protect the plant from the sun.

❀ Plants in the tropics have a plentiful water supply and heat all year round and so grow non-stop – buds, flowers and fruit all out at the same time on the same plant. Succulents and cacti, on the other hand, are used to being in dry-as-dust deserts. They have adapted their stems as plump reservoirs for water and reduced their leaves to spines so that they lose very little moisture through the pores.

ABOVE: *A low bench is used as a display area for a group of interesting small succulents in terracotta pots.*

❀ Between the very warm and the cold, frozen regions, lie the temperate zones where the majority of plants are deciduous. Plants that have evolved in temperate zones have learned to cope with the wide variation of conditions in different seasons, having adapted to grow when the weather is warm and become dormant when it is cold. Deciduous trees drop their leaves and hibernate in winter, evergreens pause in their growth and perennial plants die down completely, sheltering their buds under the ground and not pushing up new shoots until the following spring.

LEFT: *A sunny bench surrounded by succulents, including an imposing agave and pots of smaller succulent plants.*

HARDINESS ZONES

How hardy a plant is depends on the lowest temperature it will have to endure. In the USA, where severe winters are common, plant hardiness zones (zones of consistent annual average minimum temperature) have been mapped out by the Arnold Arboretum of Harvard University.

❀ Zones are numbered and a plant might be described as 'Hardy to Zone 9'. This would mean it would survive an annual average minimum temperature of between 43° to 34°F (6° and 1°C). A similar map has been compiled for Europe.

ABOVE: *Frost can turn winter seed heads and stems into magically mysterious and attractive shapes with sugar icing coatings.*

Local climates

❀ Within each zone are areas with milder or more severe climates. Local conditions can vary considerably and altitude is an important factor. For every 330 ft (100 m) upwards, the temperature drops substantially. Unexpected frosts may kill the new shoots of plants that have survived a severe winter, while dormant and even hardy plants may be vulnerable to frost damage.

❀ Several things can make a difference to an individual garden. The climate in a city can be much warmer than the surrounding countryside, allowing more tender plants to be grown. Aspect is important, too, i.e. whether a garden is facing north or south, or whether it is at the top or bottom of a hill.

❀ South-facing slopes are much warmer than north-facing ones and will bring on growth early in spring. In a hollow, there is always a risk of frost. The stillness of the sheltered air contributes to the risk and what seems to be a sheltered corner of a garden can be far from sheltered in reality. If wind meets a solid wall, the compressed gusts have very high speeds and may damage plants.

LEFT: *Even without leaves, deciduous trees often have interesting forms. This* Acer palmatum *'Oshio Beni' has leaves that turn spectacularly red before they drop.*

SUITING THE PLANT TO THE SOIL

GARDEN soil should be a fertile, well-drained loam, able to retain moisture. Soils have their own characteristics, which will suit some plants but not others. Some are mainly clay and rich in nutrients but slow to warm up in spring; others may be sandy and easily worked but water and nutrients will drain away very quickly; others may be too acidic for most plants.

❀ Soils can be improved enormously by adding organic matter but their basic type will remain the same. You will find it much easier to grow plants suited to the particular soil in your garden rather than trying to alter the soil fundamentally to suit particular plants you want to grow.

THE IDEAL SOIL

THE ideal soil is made up of 22 per cent water, 20 per cent sand, 20 per cent air, 15 per cent silt, 10 per cent clay, 8 per cent 'unavailable' water (that is, water trapped within the soil that the plant cannot use) and 5 per cent organic matter. Soil texture is how the soil feels when you handle it. This is due to the basic rock the soil is made of and cannot be altered. Soil structure is how the particles are held together in the soil. This influences whether the plant can get at the air, water and nutrients in the soil. It can be improved by adding organic matter, ensuring good drainage and digging in autumn to allow the breakdown of clods in heavy soils during winter. It is surprising how much difference adding organic matter can make to almost any soil.

Clay soil

Clay soils feel cold and heavy and can be molded in the fingers. They are often very fertile but they are also heavy and may become waterlogged. They are slow to warm up in spring and may become very compacted when wet and covered with a cap or crust, which reduces the air available to roots and seeds. Plants from hot, dry areas are very unhappy in clay unless it has been much improved with sand, gravel and organic matter. Plants that grow well in clay include day lilies (Hemerocallis), roses, astilbes and peonies.

Sandy soil

Light, free-draining and easily worked, sandy soil warms up quickly in spring, giving plants a good start. Its disadvantages are that water drains through too easily and minerals can leach out quickly. Mediterranean plants and many herbs grow well in sandy soil.

Peaty soil

Very dark brown and often acidic, peaty soil is not very fertile and often poorly drained. Rhododendrons and heathers grow well in it.

Silty soil

This feels silky to the touch but not sticky and you can mold it in your fingers to some extent. It is moderately fertile and holds less water than clay soils but is easily compacted and can acquire a hard cap, which prevents both water and air from getting through to the plant's roots.

clay soil

sandy soil

peaty soil

silty soil

ABOVE: *Many woodland plants prefer a peaty or acid soil. Here,
rhododendrons are growing with other acid-loving plants to make a pretty
woodland scene.*

ABOVE: *Clay lovers include Astilbe, Zantedeschia, Lychnis, evening primroses
(Oenothera), day lilies (Hemerocallis) and foxgloves (Digitalis), all of which are
thriving in this garden.*

ACIDITY AND ALKALINITY

ACIDITY and alkalinity are important when considering what to grow. They are measured on a pH scale numbered 1–14. Acidic soils have a pH value below 7; neutral soils are pH 7 and alkaline pH value is above 7. Adding lime helps reduce acidity, while incorporating organic matter such as compost and manure will lower alkalinity to a certain extent.

❀ However, it is better to select plants that will thrive on the existing soil. Changing the pH radically is very difficult. Many plants prefer neutral to slightly acidic soils, others prefer acidic conditions and hate any alkalinity.

❀ Plants that like acidity are called calcifuges, those that like alkalinity are called calcicoles. Many plants, however, are happy with a neutral soil verging on the acidic or alkaline.

❀ Acid-lovers include heathers (*Calluna* and *Erica*), rhododendrons and camellias. A soil-testing kit will test your soil for acidity/alkalinity in different parts of your garden. It is well worth doing this to save your plants from succumbing to soils they are not suited for.

HELPFUL SYMBOLS

THE following symbols are widely used to indicate the sun and shade requirements of individual plants, their hardiness rating and how large they will grow.

Sun/shade requirements

Sun	☼
Sun or partial shade	◐
Shade	●

Frost tender

Half-hardy	❉	- Can withstand temperatures down to 32°F (0°C).
Frost-hardy	❉❉	- Can withstand temperatures down to 23°F (-5°C).
Fully hardy	❉❉❉	- Can withstand temperatures down to 5°F (-15°C).

Size

Typical height
Typical spread
Typical height and spread

10ft-3m

10ft-3m

LEFT: *The camellia is an evergreen shrub that produces spectacularly beautiful red, pink or white flowers.*

SOME PLANTS FOR PARTICULAR PLACES

THE following suggestions may help you to choose plants for some of the trickier places in your garden. No garden is exactly the same and plants themselves can be curiously reluctant to grow where you think they ought to, so a certain amount of experimenting with your own garden will be necessary.

PLANTS FOR ACIDIC SOILS

Many plants will grow on moderately acidic soil but few will thrive on very acidic soils, which are infertile. Many acid-loving plants are woodland in origin and many of the following plants will grow well in partial shade.

❀ If you do not have an acidic soil but would like to grow some of these plants, you can plant them in peat beds or containers filled with ericaceous compost.

Azalea

❀ See Rhododendron.

Bottlebrush *(Callistemon)*

❀ These shrubs have flowers that look just like bottlebrushes. They come from Australasia and need a mild climate and a sheltered site. *Callistemon salignus* has white flowers; *C. citrinus* 'Splendens' has brilliant red flowers and is probably the most hardy.

RIGHT: *The delicate sky blue bloom of the Himalayan blue poppy (Meconopsis betonicifolia) needs a cool climate in which to flourish.*

Scotch heather, ling *(Calluna)*

❀ This very attractive ground cover shrub is best grown in large masses, together with ericas. It also associates well with azaleas.

Camellia

❀ Extremely beautiful evergreen shrubs with shiny, leathery leaves and perfectly shaped red, pink or white flowers, camellias do well in large containers or can be fan-trained on sheltered walls. Camellias may grow to 10 ft (3 m). *Camellia. x williamsii* 'Donation' is one of the most popular with clear pink flowers, which do not go brown as they die.

Bell heather *(Erica)*

❀ This attractive ground cover plant is good grown in large masses near woodland and in association with calluna. Several species are available.

Dog's tooth violet *(Erythronium)*

❀ This is not really a violet at all but a bulb that produces charming little pagoda-shaped flowers in spring. Keep it moist and cool with plenty of well-rotted compost and it will spread into sizeable clumps.

RIGHT: *This beautiful ornamental rhododendron produces its mauve flowers during the months of spring.*

Gentiana *sino-ornata*
❀ Gentians need deep, acidic soil that never dries out and never becomes waterlogged. Given the right conditions, they will spread into grassy mats.

Lace-cap hydrangea (*Hydrangea macrophylla*)
❀ These hydrangeas look well in natural settings such as light woodland, where they are sheltered from frost damage. They can become large and spreading. *Hydrangea macrophylla* 'Whitewave' and *H. m.* 'Bluewave' are recommended varieties. Blue flowers will turn pink if the soil is slightly alkaline.

Tiger lily (*Lilium tigrinum*)
❀ All lilies are grown from bulbs. Lilies like full sun, good drainage and lime-free soil. Plant several together for a strong effect in a mixed border.

ABOVE: *The bright pink spires of lupins look splendid in combination with a variegated cornus and deep blue columbines.*

Lupins (*Lupinus*)
❀ Lupins are hardy perennials with spectacular spikes of many colored pea-type flowers in summer. They are short-term perennials but will often seed themselves and add height and excitement when grown in swathes in large borders from spring to early summer.

Magnolia
❀ This is a stately tree with spectacular fragrant flowers. Use magnolias as specimen trees or among other trees and shrubs. They like well-drained lime-free soils in sun or partial shade. *Magnolia grandiflora* is evergreen and suitable only for very mild climatic areas. M. *stellata* is a well-loved, exceptionally beautiful small tree or large shrub with star-like white flowers in early spring. Summer-flowering magnolias include M. *conspicua* (pure white, cup-shaped flowers) and M. *wilsonii* (hanging white flowers with crimson stamens).

Himalayan blue poppy (*Meconopsis betonicifolia*)
❀ This beautiful blue poppy needs coolness and moisture. It may bloom just once after several years and then die. Where it has the right conditions, however, it may bloom for many years.

Primula
❀ Many primulas enjoy acidic soils. The common primrose (*Primula vulgaris*) is suitable for a woodland or wild flower garden. Most primulas need moisture.

Rhododendron
❀ This group, which includes large-flowered hybrids, dwarf hybrids, low-growing species and azaleas, is among the most beautiful of the spring-flowering shrubs. Low-growing species relate well to heathers, tall ones make imposing freestanding feature shrubs or may be planted in informal woodland walks.

Flame flower (*Tropaeolum speciosum*)
❀ A hardy, climbing form of nasturtium with the brightest scarlet flowers, it grows well on a north- or east-facing wall and contrasts well clambering up the dark green of a yew hedge.

PLANTS FOR HEAVY CLAY SOILS

There is a wide range of plants suitable for clay soils and you will have a much more successful garden if you stick to growing these. Plants suited to light sandy soils, for example pinks and silvery-leaved plants, will simply sicken and die in clay soil.

Michaelmas daisy (Aster)

❀ Hardy perennials with large daisy flowers in shades of pink and purple, these flower in late summer to autumn and are useful for damp soils.

Crocosmia

❀ These hardy perennials with strap-like leaves and brilliantly colored red, orange or yellow flowers in summer need a sheltered site and good drainage.

Foxglove (Digitalis purpurea)

❀ The foxglove has tall spikes of trumpet-shaped purple or white flowers. It grows well in woodland and likes a moisture-retentive soil.

Helenium

❀ This is another hardy perennial with a daisy flower that will grow well in any garden soil, even if not well drained. The flowers appear in late summer and autumn in strong yellows and reds.

Day lily (Hemerocallis)

❀ The strap-like leaves of this hardy perennial form thick, elegantly arched clumps. The flowers vary from yellow to cream and brick red. They like moisture-retentive soil and will grow by the edges of pools.

ABOVE: *Although strictly speaking a wild flower, forget-me-not does well as a self-seeding ground-cover plant.*

Bergamot, bee balm, oswego tea (Monarda didyma)

❀ This has shock-headed flowers in pinks and purples, flowering in late summer to autumn. It likes moist, fertile soil.

Forget-me-not (Myosotis)

❀ A hardy biennial with sky-blue flowers that will seed itself, this likes moist, fertile, well-drained soil.

PLANTS FOR DRY SHADE

Very dry, very shady places in the garden are hard for most plants to cope with. A few, however, will thrive.

Anemone x hybrida

❀ This hardy autumn-flowering anemone grows to 4–5 ft (1.2–1.5 m) and each plant has many pink or white flowers and is useful in borders, *Anemone.* 'Honorine Jobert' is very effective and has single white flowers.

Cyclamen, sow bread

❀ Beautiful little tuberous relatives of indoor cyclamen, these are perfectly hardy and will grow well under trees. The flowers may be white or shades of pink and may be borne at almost any time of year, depending on the species. The leaves are heart shaped, often with silver markings. *Cyclamen coum* flowers in winter or early spring; *C. hederifolium* (syn. *C. neapolitanum*) flowers mid- to late autumn, before the leaves appear;

LEFT: *The day lily has leaves which grow in arched clumps and flowers in mid-summer.*

C. *purpurascens* flowers in mid- to late summer and prefers alkaline soil; C. *repandum* flowers in mid- to late spring. They may self-seed and turn up in unexpected places.

Barrenwort, bishop's hat *(Epimedium)*

❀ This hardy perennial has wiry stems and delicate foliage with bronze tints in spring and colors well in autumn. The small cup-and-saucer flowers in white, pink, red, purple, beige or yellow are borne in spring to early summer in racemes. Its height and spread are around 20–30 cm (8–12 in). *Epimedium grandiflorum* 'Crimson Beauty' is deciduous; E. *pubigerum* is evergreen with creamy white flowers; E. x *warleyense* has yellow flowers.

Spurge *(Euphorbia)*

❀ This genus includes annuals, biennials, evergreen and herbaceous plants. Some suit dry shady places. *Euphorbia amygdaloides* (wood spurge) has dark green leaves and greenish-yellow flowers; E. *myrsinites* is ever-green with succulent blue-green leaves and bright greenish-yellow flowers; E. *characias* subsp. *wulfenii* is a tall architectural plant with grey-green leaves and yellow-green flowers.

Fuchsia magellanica

❀ This hardy fuchsia is an upright shrub, which produces small elegant pendant flowers of deep red and purple all summer. Once well settled in, it will put up with dry soil.

Dead-nettle *(Lamium)*

❀ This low, ground-covering plant is grown mainly for its foliage but the flowers are worthwhile, too. It can be invasive if grown in moist soils but used in light woodland or among shrubs it is pretty and effective. *L. maculatum* is a low-growing perennial, with silver markings on the leaves. In summer it bears spikes of white or pink flowers.

PLANTS FOR DENSE SHADE

Some gardens, particularly those in towns and cities, have areas of dense shade, which get little sun and are shaded even more by overhanging trees and tall walls. Basement areas, courtyards and corners of larger gardens often pose problems in this way. Few plants will cope well under these conditions so you need to make the most of those that will.

Laurel *(Aucuba japonica)*

❀ This large 5 ft (1.5 m) shrub has shiny leaves and bright red berries. The leaves of the dark green form shine like mirrors in the sun but the variegated form can bring a sunny feeling to a dark corner. It likes moisture-retentive soil but will grow in dry shade.

Privet *(Ligustrum)*

❀ Deciduous or evergreen, *Ligustrum* is often used for hedging but can make pretty small trees. *L. ovalifolium* has golden and silver variegated forms and will tolerate deep shade; *L. lucidum* has some striking variegated varieties.

ABOVE: *Barrenwort comes in many colors, including white, pink and yellow, and flowers in the spring or early summer.*

ABOVE: *Once established,* Fuschia magellanica *can survive in dry soil, producing its pendant flowers in the summer.*

UNDERSTANDING PLANT CHARACTERISTICS

❦

The different ways in which plants have evolved is a fascinating subject in its own right. Understanding the origins and different characteristics of the various main groups of plants is helpful to all gardeners. Conifers are among the oldest plants; flowering plants appeared much later. Flowers themselves are amazingly diverse. Many have evolved to attract various creatures in very specific ways to ensure fertilisation. Others produce millions of tiny seeds that are dispersed by the wind. When you are buying and growing particular flowers, shrubs and trees for the garden, it is useful to have such background knowledge.

THE PLANT KINGDOM

ALL plants are represented in the plant kingdom, which is divided into two main groups and then sub-divided according to shared botanical characteristics, resulting in something rather like a family tree.

❀ Vascular plants have conductive tissue, which circulates water and nutrients. They come under two main divisions – non-flowering seed bearers (gymnosperms) and flowering seed-bearers (angiosperms). Non-vascular plants are those like mosses, liverworts, ferns and horsetails, which do not have conductive tissue and rely on a moist environment to survive. They are widespread in the wild but often not very interesting in appearance.

❀ Gymnosperms include the conifers, which bear seed on their cones. Many, such as yew and cedar, are very tolerant of heat, cold and drought and are therefore extremely useful in gardens.

❀ Angiosperms or flowering plants produce seed in an ovary. There are 300 families of flowering plants and 250,000 species. They may be monocotyledons or dicotyledons according to their seed leaves (cotyledons) and other differences in their anatomy and growth patterns.

❀ Monocots have a single seed leaf, leaves with veins that run along their length, slender non-woody stems and flower parts arranged in threes. They include grasses, bamboos and lilies. Dicots have two seed leaves, a network of veins on their leaves, thick, woody stems and flower parts arranged in multiples of 4, 5, 7 or more.

Family, genus, species

❀ The basic division of all higher plants is the family. All flowering plants are grouped into families based purely on the structure of their flowers. The plants in a particular family may all be clearly related, for example orchids (Orchidaceae), or one family may contain numerous and very diverse plants such as the Rosaceae family, which includes trees, shrubs and garden plants including roses, apples, strawberries, hawthorn and *Alchemilla*.

❀ Within the families, plants are categorised further into smaller groups, according to certain characteristics. Accordingly, they are given defining genus and species names, which are those used in the binomial system to identify plants in gardening encyclopedias and catalogues.

ABOVE: *A floribunda rose with large deep red flowers and a glorious scent, the epitome of what roses mean to gardeners.*

ABOVE: *Although they do not look like roses, the tiny little greeny-yellow flowers on the right of this picture belong to Alchemilla mollis, which is a member of the rose family, Rosaceae.*

ABOVE: *Conifers belong to the division of seed plants called gymnosperms, whose seeds are grown on the outside of the cone.*

THE LIFE CYCLE OF FLOWERING PLANTS

Flowering plants have evolved in many different ways to help them reproduce and survive in a range of habitats. Knowing how plants function and understanding their life cycles will make it much easier for you to grow them satisfactorily and work out an interesting planting plan in your own garden.

There are four steps in the life cycle of a flowering plant.

2. Growth
Seed leaves (cotyledons) appear first, then true leaves grow to build up food reserves for the young plants.

1. Germination
Once the seeds have fallen from a plant, they are stimulated into growth only when they have enough water, light and warmth. Seeds of some flowers such as alpines must experience a period of cold before they will germinate; others may require their seed coat to be nicked or 'sandpapered' to allow the seed to absorb water. In nature this happens when, for example, the seed travels through the digestive system of an animal or bird.

3. Maturity
The first leaves and stem rapidly develop into a mature shoot system. Their initial function is to gather energy from sunlight, essential for photosynthesis, which uses a complex series of chemical reactions to produce glucose from carbon dioxide. The initial growth of the leaves often slows down to allow the plant to put its energy into developing flowers. All the plant's energies are now focused into flowering and reproduction.

4. Seed formation
The flowers have been fertilised and develop into fruit containing seeds, which ripen and disperse.

Flowers

❀ Flowers have evolved innumerable forms to make pollination easy. Some are pollinated by insects, others by birds, wind or water. Insect-pollinated flowers are usually large, brightly colored and heavily scented. Some are adapted to be pollinated by only one particular type of insect or bird. Wind-pollinated flowers are smaller and less conspicuous but there are millions on each plant.

❀ Most flowers contain both male and female reproductive organs. These may pollinate themselves or be pollinated by another plant of the same species. Other plants produce unisexual flowers. Monoecious plants have both male and female parts in separate flowers on the same plant.

❀ Dioecious plants are either all-male or all-female, so both male and female plants must be grown to produce fruit. A few species are polygamous with both bisexual and unisexual flowers.

❀ The parts of all flowers are borne in concentric circles (whorls) or spirals. The outer whorl or calyx protects the bud before the flower opens. It consists of sepals.

❀ The next whorl is the corolla, made up of the flower's petals. The next whorl is the male parts, the stamens, each consisting of a stalk (filament) and an anther containing pollen sacs.

❀ The inner ring is of female parts or 'carpels'. Each carpel has an ovary at its base, a stem (the style) and the stigma. For fertilisation to take place, a pollen grain must be deposited on the stigma.

Leaves

❀ The enormous diversity of leaves – their shapes, sizes, forms and the way they are arranged on different plants – enables the gardener to provide a huge variety of different effects in terms of texture and color.

❀ Evergreen trees and shrubs are among the permanent features of a garden. Among them can be planted bulbs for spring and early summer interest, perennial plants for the summer and autumn border, alpines that brighten up the rock garden and climbers and roses that add magic to the scene.

❀ Understanding the contribution that these diverse plants can offer and the ways in which they may be intermingled to best effect is vital when designing a garden. The ground must always be prepared thoroughly before planting, to give the roots plenty of air, moisture and support.

ABOVE: *Buddleja is called the 'butterfly bush' because butterflies flock to feed on the nectar on warm summer days. Here, a red admiral enjoys the flower.*

BELOW: *Dahlias are among the most exotic-looking flowers, often looking as though they are made of paper. They owe their name to the 18th-century Swedish botanist, Anders Dahl.*

After the water and nutrients have entered the roots, they are drawn up through the plant by 'transpiration', which carries minerals to the leaves where oxygen and water evaporate through the stoma (pores) in the leaf surface. The movement of water allows the cells to remain swollen and upright. Plants soon wilt when they are short of water.

Modified shoots and roots

Many plants have modified shoot and root systems. For example, tendrils of climbing plants are modified leaf stems, which have adapted for grasping supports – ivy is an example. In some plants a large part of the stem develops underground. These include bulbs, corms and tubers, which act as food stores.

They produce baby bulbs called bulbils or offsets, which can be planted to produce new plants. Rhizomes are also stems but grow horizontally close to the soil surface, while 'adventitious' roots grow along the length of the rhizome. Bearded irises have slow-growing rhizomes and some bamboos have very fast and vigorous ones. Knowledge of such growth habits is important to avoid any plant becoming invasive.

Adventitious roots are aerial roots rising from plant stems. They can cling to any surface and penetrate into tiny cracks and crevices, where they expand until they have securely anchored the plant. The

RIGHT: *A fresh and charming spring border of* Crocus vernalis *(meaning 'of spring') and* Helleborus orientalis *(meaning 'from the East').*

LEFT: *The deep lilac flowers of* Vinca minor *(meaning 'small') can brighten up a woodland garden. It can be invasive when grown in a flowerbed.*

climbing hydrangea (*Hydrangea petiolaris*) displays this characteristic, as does ivy.

Many low-growing plants like the periwinkle (*Vinca*) produce adventitious roots from nodes on the stems. This characteristic is used by gardeners to 'layer' or pin the stems down so that they root in the soil and produce new plants.

The whole picture

A garden is made up of many different types of flowering and non-flowering plant, each of which contributes its special quality of height, permanence, texture, color and form.

Trees, shrubs, climbers, perennials, rock plants, annuals and biennials, bulbous plants and aquatics all have their place in a garden, as do the non-flowering plants such as grasses, bamboos and ferns. It is the way in which these types of plants are combined and contrasted that creates the most interesting sorts of garden.

PROPAGATING YOUR PLANTS

Growing your own plants from seed or increasing your stocks from existing plants is undoubtedly one of the most satisfying areas of gardening. It is not only an economical way of filling the garden, but the thrill of stocking your garden with plants that you have produced yourself is incomparable. You can regenerate old, tired-looking plants, and also produce back-up stocks of plants that may be vulnerable to frost damage or disease. Propagation is also a very sociable occupation, since you will often find that you produce many more new plants than you have room for, and so gardening friendships develop as cuttings and seedlings are exchanged.

THE BASICS

THE word propagation somehow conjures up quite off-putting connotations of science laboratories, specialist equipment and in-depth botanical knowledge. However, it simply means 'to breed, to multiply', and applies to every method of increasing plant stocks – from broadcast sowing of annual seeds directly into the soil, to taking and rooting cuttings.

❀ Specialist equipment such as greenhouses and mist benches are useful but by no means essential to many forms of propagation. A bright (but not sunny windowsill), a cold frame and, if possible, a small heated propagator will enable you to grow a very wide range of plants.

ABOVE: *Always use perfectly clean pots and trays for healthy, disease-free propagation and cover them with mesh-wire or netting if there is a danger of something falling on the delicate new plants.*

ABOVE: *Seed can be sown directly into the soil, but the success rate may not be as great as if the plants had been transplanted from pots.*

PROPAGATION EQUIPMENT

THE very simplest form of propagation – sowing seed directly into the soil – needs no special equipment, as every child who has ever grown an abundance of nasturtiums from an inexpertly cast handful of seeds will testify.

❀ However, many gardeners, thrilled by early triumphs from sowing direct into the soil, quickly become more adventurous, and keen to extend the range of plants grown. Just a few simple pieces of equipment will dramatically increase your chances of consistent success.

Pots and trays

❀ There is a wide range of pots and trays available, and the choice can seem quite overwhelming. Since hygiene is a critical concern when propagating, it may be advisable to start your propagating experience with new, single-use modular seed trays, since these will not hold any old, potentially lethal bacteria or fungi.

❀ These trays consist of individual plastic cells, which make it easy to sow seeds singly and avoid any damage when thinning out the seedlings. The trays are flimsy and are held securely in a more rigid tray. This type of tray is generally intended only for a single season's use.

❀ More lasting and expensive trays are available in rigid plastics. These will need to be thoroughly disinfected after each use, and stored out of the sunlight. Novice propagators with limited space and time will probably prefer the inexpensive, labour- and storage-space saving flexible tray option. These trays are usually sold with a useful clear plastic lid, which assists in providing the warm, humid environment necessary for successful germination.

❀ Larger pots are useful for sowing larger seeds, such as climbers or shrubs and, of course, are also needed for potting on all plants. Fibre-based pots are especially good for plants that resent root disturbance. The young plant is simply planted out still in its pot, which

water vapor falls on to plant

ABOVE: *A rigid-topped propagator offers an excellent start to young plants. Water vapor condenses on the inside of the lid and falls onto the plants, so the general atmosphere within the unit is moist. This combination helps the plants to replace the water lost through their leaves.*

will eventually break down into the soil. Home-made biodegradable pots can also be made from simple cones of newspaper.

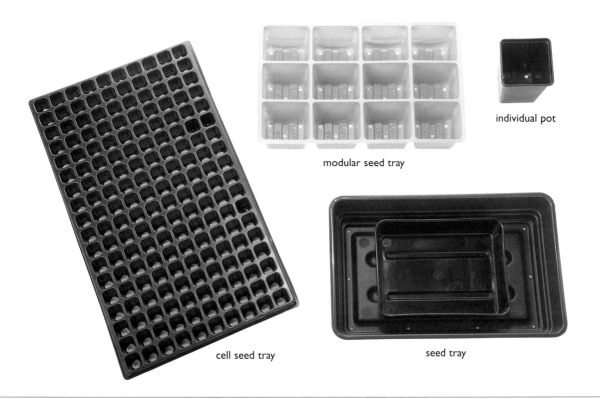

individual pot

modular seed tray

cell seed tray

seed tray

HOME-MADE PROPAGATION EQUIPMENT

PLASTIC bags, simply suspended above pots or trays with canes or with wire twisted into hoops, are a popular and inexpensive way of providing a warm, humid atmosphere that will encourage rapid germination and healthy growth.

❀ Cut-off clear plastic bottles, upended over pots, are another effective, low-cost idea. It is important in each case to keep the leaves of the young plants away from the plastic itself, as they will rot if they come into direct contact with the moisture that collects there.

Heated propagators

❀ A little heat from underneath assists germination generally, and is essential for the germination of some plants. Small, self-contained domestic heated propagators are available, which sit on the windowsill. These are an ideal next step up from the plastic bag propagation technique. Heated bases that fit under

RIGHT: Any size or shape of plant pot can be used for making home-made propagation equipment.

ABOVE: Cold frames provide an excellent introduction to growing under glass. They can easily overheat in summer because of their diminutive size. Propping the lid of the frame open in hot weather allows the rising warm air to escape, as well as keeping the plants inside well ventilated and at a reasonable temperature.

seed trays are also available.

❀ Many gardeners, encouraged by early successes with propagation, quickly run out of windowsills, and spill over into the greenhouse. If propagating in a greenhouse early in the year when temperatures are still low, you will need to invest in a more sophisticated propagator with a thermostat and a powerful heating element. You will probably also need larger units than the domestic models, which house only two or three seed trays.

LEFT: *Growing cuttings under plastic is an inexpensive way to increase your plant stocks.*

❀ The lid should be removed on warmer days to air the plants, and covered at night with additional insulation if extremely cold weather is expected. If transparent insulation, such as plastic bubble wrap or layers of clear plastic, is used there is no need to remove this during the day, as it still transmits light to the plants.

Soil-warming cables

❀ These are designed to warm the compost in unheated propagators, or to heat the soil and air in a cold frame or a mist bench in a greenhouse. They are fitted in an S-shape pattern, with the cable not touching at any point, buried approximately 3 in (7.5 cm) below the surface of moist sand.

❀ The cables are sold with instructions as to what size area they are capable of warming effectively, and it is obviously important to follow strictly all directions concerning their installation and use.

❀ The best cables have a wired-in thermostat. All should be used in conjunction with a residual current device (RCD) in case they are accidentally cut through during cultivation. Most novice propagators will find self-contained propagation units more convenient to install and use than cable systems.

BELOW: *A cold frame propped open to increase ventilation.*

warm air
circulates within
the cold frame

Mist propagators

❀ Enthusiastic propagating gardeners will enjoy the benefits of mist propagators. These incorporate all that plants need for their best possible chance of successful, easy germination and early, healthy growth.

❀ The simplest mist propagators to use are the self-contained enclosed units that include a heating element, thermostat, transparent lid and a misting head.

❀ A constant film of water is maintained on the plant material and, when the misting head operates, the risk of fungal disease is reduced, as spores are effectively washed out of the air and from foliage before they can infect plant tissue. This is a more sophisticated version of what happens in the plastic bag propagator – just on a larger, more convenient scale and with the added benefit of consistent heat from underneath and controlled humidity. The misting head is activated automatically when the plants become too dry. Open misting units are also available.

Cold frame

❀ A cold frame is extremely useful for hardening off plants. The air and soil temperatures in cold frames are warmer than in open soil, making it possible to acclimatise plants gradually to the conditions outdoors after their protected start in the home or greenhouse.

SOWING INDOORS

FINE and medium seeds may be sown by the method shown here. Large or pelleted seeds (seeds specially prepared in a coating to make a pellet for easier sowing) should be sown individually in compartments, degradable containers, or evenly spaced in pans (shallow pots).

❀ Mixing very fine seeds with an equal quantity of fine sand before sowing makes even distribution much easier. Always check the individual germination requirements of your seeds. Some germinate in darkness, others in light. The directions given here are necessarily generalised but apply to most fine seeds, such as many half-hardy annuals, which are popular plants to grow indoors from seed.

PROPAGATION COMPOST

Plants have a much better chance of germination if sown into the correct sort of compost. Fine seeds, in particular, need to be in good overall contact with the soil.

❀ Purpose-made seed compost is finely textured to meet this requirement. It is also moisture retentive and low in nutrients, since salts can damage seedlings. As the seedlings grow, they will need to be transplanted to a soil that can feed them adequately.

Seed compost

❀ A general-purpose seed compost consists of two parts sterilised loam, one part peat or peat substitute and one part sand, plus a small amount of lime. It is advisable to buy a pre-mixed seed compost, as you can then be sure that the proportions are accurate.

Cuttings compost

❀ Cuttings composts are free draining, as they are designed for use in high-humidity environments. A general-purpose cuttings compost comprises roughly one part peat or peat substitute and one part sand (or other free-draining substance such as perlite), plus a small percentage of lime, dried blood, calcium carbonate, potassium nitrate and potassium sulphate.

❀ As with seed compost, buying a pre-mixed cuttings compost will ensure you have the correct proportions of each component.

RIGHT: *Overcrowding and a lack of ventilation can cause 'damping off', a catastrophic scourge, wreaking havoc on plants by damaging and distorting new leaves and shoots, as well as weakening the plant as a whole.*

HYGIENE

Hygiene is critically important in propagation. The moist, humid conditions within a propagator are as perfect for the development of fungal diseases as they are for developing healthy plants.

❀ It is therefore essential to use sterilised containers, compost and tools to reduce this risk. Fungicidal solutions are available, which may be applied to protect seedlings further. Ensure that you follow the manufacturer's directions strictly.

❀ Taking cuttings inevitably exposes bare plant tissue, which is an increased risk of infection. Good hygiene practices will decrease the risk. Clean tools with a methylated spirit solution between cuttings to avoid cross contamination, and keep benches spotlessly clean.

Preventing damping off

❀ Overcrowding causes an overly moist, stagnant atmosphere in which fungi can flourish. These air- or soil-borne fungi can cause the condition known as 'damping-off', whereby roots become diseased, darken and then die. The seedling collapses, and a fluffy growth may be seen on the compost as well as on the seedlings.

❀ There is no cure for damping off, so attention to cleanliness, pricking out seedlings to avoid overcrowding (see below), not overwatering and providing adequate air flow above and around the plants are essential requisites. Keep the surface of the compost clear of any fallen leaves or other debris, which could foster disease.

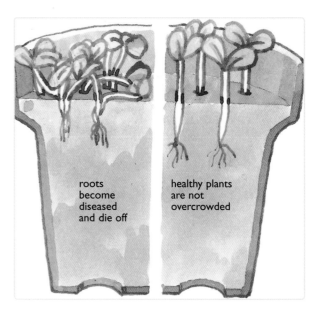

roots become diseased and die off

healthy plants are not overcrowded

SOWING SEEDS IN A TRAY

1 *Fill a seed tray with good-quality seed compost and firm it to within 3/4 in (1.5 cm) of the top, using a presser board. Water the compost and leave to stand for approximately 30 minutes.*

2 *Scatter the seed or the seed and sand mixture evenly across the surface.*

3 *Sieve over a layer of moist compost to produce a covering approximately the same depth as the size of the seeds that you have planted.*

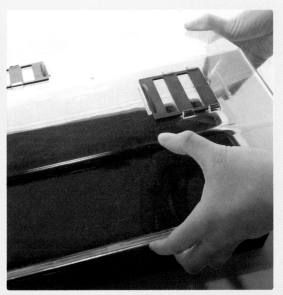

4 *Cover the tray with glass or clear plastic, not allowing it to touch the seeds, and place the tray somewhere warm and bright. If the tray is placed in direct sunlight, shade it with fine netting.*

CARE OF PROPAGATED PLANTS

As well as taking good care of hygiene when preparing compost, containers and cuttings or seeds for propagation, care must be taken of the young plants as they germinate and grow.

Firming in

❀ It is essential that seeds are in good contact with the compost since water is drawn up by capillary action. If air pockets form around the seeds water cannot be transmitted to where it is needed, so it is important to firm the compost gently when planting seed. However, do not compress the soil heavily.

Watering

❀ Propagated plants need a consistently moist, but not wet, environment. An overly saturated compost will reduce the oxygen available to the plants and potentially encourage disease.

Caring for new seedlings

❀ Seedlings must have sufficient room around them to breathe. As soon as shoots appear, remove the propagator lid. Protect the seedlings from drafts and harsh sunlight, but keep them in bright light. Continue to water, ensuring that the roots do not dry out.

ABOVE: *Ensure that your new plants have enough water, but make sure that they are not over-watered, as this may encourage disease.*

Pricking out

❀ When seedlings appear, the plants are still very vulnerable. As well as the risk of damping off, overcrowded seedlings will be competing for light and nutrients. If they do not succumb to disease, they will probably become underfed, weak, spindly plants that will never achieve their full, healthy potential. They therefore need to be thinned out. This planting-on process is known as pricking out.

❀ The initial leaves you see after germination are seed leaves, or cotyledons, which swell on germination, forcing the seed coat open. These provide the initial food reserves for the plant. The next pair of leaves to appear will be the first 'true' leaves, and seedlings may be pricked out when the true leaves are well developed. Discard weak, unhealthy-looking seedlings.

❀ Fill the next appropriate size up of container with good-quality potting compost – a 3 in (7.5 cm) diameter pot or planting compartment will suit a single seedling, while a larger pot may hold three growing plants comfortably.

❀ Knock the container of seedlings gently to loosen the compost. Carefully separate the seedlings, handling them only by the seed leaves to avoid damaging the seedlings. Carefully lift each healthy seedling from the soil, trying to maintain a little compost around its roots if possible. Plant them at the same depth in the soil as they were in the first tray and gently firm the compost around them. Tap the container to settle the compost, and water the seedlings to settle the compost around their roots.

❀ To give the plants a good chance of recovery from the pricking-out process, increase the humidity as for germinating, by covering the container with clear plastic, just for a few days. Ensure that the plastic does not touch the leaves.

Hardening off

❀ Gradually acclimatising plants to the very different conditions outside the protected environment of the propagator should be taken every bit as seriously as the initial, exciting part of the propagation procedure.

❀ Hardening off takes time. The natural waxes coating the leaves of the young plants need to adapt their form and thickness in order to reduce water loss – a process that takes place over several days and cannot be hurried. The pores on the leaves, which control water loss and through which oxygen and carbon dioxide pass in and out of the leaves, also need time to adapt to the harsher conditions outside.

❀ As a rule, hardening off takes about two weeks. When the young plants have become well established inside, they can be moved to an unheated cold frame, where they are still protected by polythene or glass. Gradually increase the amount of ventilation by opening or removing the cover for increasingly long periods until the plants are fully acclimatised. Close the frame at night to begin with, graduating to leaving it open at night, except when frost is anticipated. Insulate the cold frame if the weather is very harsh.

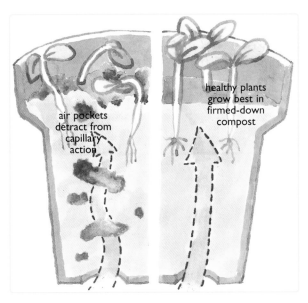

air pockets detract from capillary action

healthy plants grow best in firmed-down compost

ABOVE: *It is important to press down compost evenly before planting seeds, so that water can be drawn up towards the roots of the seedlings by capillary action. Air pockets in the soil will break this action and the seedlings will therefore not flourish as they should.*

PRICKING OUT

All young seedlings are vulnerable so handle them with care as you are replanting them.

1 *Make a hole in the soil with a pencil roughly to the same depth as the seedlings were planted in their old pot or seed tray.*

2 *Place the seedling carefully into the hole, leaving a little of the old compost around the roots to prevent damage, and gently firm the earth around the plant to prevent air pockets.*

Potting on

❀ As the plants grow, they will need more space for the roots to grow uncramped, and will need more nutrients from the soil. The subsequent container needs to be big enough to allow a generous layer of new compost to be placed around the existing rootball, but it should not be too oversized, as this will not encourage good root formation.

❀ Allow the plant to dry out slightly before transplanting, so that it may be easily removed from its container with minimal root disturbance. Fill the new pot with a layer of drainage material and new potting compost. Tap it to remove air pockets and plant at the same depth as before, filling in with compost carefully and firming in gently. Water well and leave to drain.

SOWING OUTDOORS

❀ Hardy perennials and annuals are generally sown directly into the soil in their desired final positions, avoiding any need for transplanting later. This is a particularly useful technique for growing deep tap-rooted plants such as poppies, which do not transplant well. Sowing usually takes place in spring, after the risk of frost has passed and when the soil has warmed, so that the seeds do not rot.

❀ However, precise sowing times will depend on when and where the plants are to flower, and the temperatures they need for germination. For example, some hardy biennials, which are also sown outside, grow quickly and should not be sown until midsummer, while others are slow starters and need to be sown in late spring. Always read seed packets carefully before sowing, and be sympathetic to the requirements of particular seed types best growing success.

❀ There are two methods for sowing outdoors – broadcast and drill sowing. In drill sowing, the seeds are sown in rows. Broadcast sowing is literally casting the seeds broadly on the seedbed where they are to grow. Both types of sowing need to be on properly prepared soil for the best possible chance of success.

The seedbed

❀ Ideally, you will be sowing into a bed that has been dug over the previous autumn, and which benefited from the addition of some mature organic matter at the same time – roughly $1\frac{1}{3}$ cu yd (1 cu m) of organic matter to every $5\frac{1}{4}$ cu yd (4 cu m) of soil. You do not want to sow seed into an overly rich soil, as this will encourage the production of foliage rather than flowers.

❀ If, however, you know that you are sowing into very poor soil, you may fork in a fertiliser dressing at the rate of approximately 2 oz per sq yd (60 g per sq m). If your soil is particularly heavy, you may wish to incorporate grit or coarse sand to open it up and improve drainage.

WATERING PROPAGATED PLANTS

Seedlings need careful watering to encourage growth after sowing outdoors.

1 *To water a large area, connect up a hosepipe to the main water supply. Choose a pipe with a very fine sprinkler.*

2 *Begin to water the area, preventing the soil from becoming waterlogged and rinsing out all the nutrients. Move on to the next area and repeat.*

BROADCAST SOWING

1 *Tread the soil evenly to produce a firm, even surface. Rake the soil to remove stones and retain a level surface with a fine, crumbly texture, so that the seeds have a good opportunity to gain direct overall contact with the soil.*

2 *Sow the seeds finely and evenly over the prepared area. Very fine seeds may be mixed with sand to produce a more consistent spread.*

3 *Rake in the seeds very lightly, working at right angles, first one way, then the other, so that they suffer minimal disturbance.*

4 *Label the area, and water the seed using a watering can with a fine spout.*

Drill sowing

❀ In drill sowing, shallow drills, or rows, are marked out with the corner of a hoe or a trowel tip. The seeds are sown equally spaced along these rows, beneath a fine layer of soil, and are gently watered in and labelled.

❀ Drill sowing has the advantage that, since the seedlings grow in recognisable rows, it is easier to distinguish desirable plants from emerging weed seedlings. Generally, both drill-sown and broadcast-sown seeds will need thinning out.

Thinning out

❀ To prevent overcrowding, and the attendant problems as plants fight for air, light and nutrients, most seedlings will need to be thinned out as they grow.

Working when the soil is moist and the weather is mild, remove surplus seedlings, particularly the weaker, less healthy-looking specimens.

❀ Take care to press gently on to the soil around the seedlings as you work, to minimise root disturbance to those seedlings that are remaining in place.

❀ If the seedlings have grown very densely, you may need to dig up entire clumps and gently separate out healthy seedlings before replanting.

❀ Surplus seedlings can be used to bulk out sparse areas where germination was poor or sowing was patchy. They can also be planted elsewhere in the garden, as well as making wonderful offerings to gardening friends. Firm in transplanted seedlings gently, and lightly water in to settle their roots.

GROWING FROM CUTTINGS

TAKING cuttings from plant stems to produce new plants is a popular way of adding to your stocks at minimal cost. It is a good way of producing additional plants from a parent plant that is of dubious hardiness, and is an economical way of introducing a plant to your own garden that you may have admired in a friend's plot. Many gardening friendships grow alongside the developing cuttings.

✿ Stem cuttings are loosely divided into three groups, according to the season the cutting is taken, and the maturity of the parent plant. Individual plants respond to different cutting techniques, and it is wise to research the needs of a particular plant before attempting its propagation by taking cuttings. As a rough guide, perennials and small shrubs are propagated by softwood cuttings, while trees, roses and many shrubs are propagated by semi-ripe and hardwood cuttings. Once you know which technique a plant prefers, the basic techniques of taking and rooting cuttings are very straightforward.

✿ There are some general rules that apply to all cuttings. Cut only from healthy plants, and take cuttings from non-flowering side shoots, as these generally root more easily than cuttings taken from the main stem. Always use a clean, sharp knife to avoid damaging plant tissue.

TAKING A STEM-TIP CUTTING

1 *Take the cutting from the parent plant then cut straight across the stem, just below a node, so that the cutting is approximately 3 in (7.5 cm) long.*

2 *Gently remove the leaves from the lower half of the cutting. Dip the base of the cutting in hormone rooting powder.*

3 *Make a hole in a container of cuttings compost, using a pencil, and insert the cutting. Gently firm and water it in.*

4 *Create a warm, humid environment by supporting a clear plastic bag above the cutting, not allowing it to touch the leaves, or place the cutting in a propagator. Keep in bright light, but not direct sunlight. Inspect daily for signs of disease or dryness and act accordingly. Pot on when the cuttings has rooted – roughly two to three weeks.*

TAKING A SOFTWOOD CUTTING

1 *From the parent plant, cut a young, vigorous side shoot approximately 4 in (10 cm) long, trimming it straight across, just below a leaf joint.*

2 *Gently remove the leaves from the lower half of the cutting. Dip the base of the cutting into hormone rooting powder.*

3 *Make a hole in the cuttings compost with a pencil and insert the cutting, firming it in gently with the pencil and ensuring that there are no air pockets around it.*

4 *Gently water in the cutting and cover with a clear plastic bag suspended above the plant on canes or wires so that it does not touch the foliage and cause it to rot.*

❀ Plant the cutting as soon as possible after taking it, and ensure that it has excellent all-round contact with the compost when planted. As with all propagation techniques, use compost, containers and utensils that are scrupulously clean to avoid the risk of plant infection. You may wish to water in with sterilised water mixed with fungicide for added protection. Do not check that plants have rooted by tugging at the cuttings impatiently. Look out for new growth instead.

Stem-tip cuttings

❀ Herbaceous perennials that do not divide well are often grown by the stem-tip method. Cuttings may be taken at any time during the growing season, assuming that suitable shoots are available. These need to be healthy and sturdy, with no flower buds. Plant the cuttings as soon as possible after collection.

Softwood cuttings

❀ Softwood cuttings are cuttings of the current season's growth, taken from early spring through to midsummer. Generally, they are literally soft, immature tissue, green from tip to base and, as such, wilt quickly after cutting. If propagating by this method, speed and care when collecting are of the essence. Collect the cuttings in a closed plastic bag, kept away from sunlight.

❀ Prepare the cuttings as soon as possible after collection for the best chance of success. Some softwood cuttings root readily in water, while others need to be put into compost. Research the particular requirements of the plant you are propagating. Some will need the heat from beneath, provided by a propagator or heated mat, for rooting. Some may be placed in a cold frame. As when germinating seeds, keep the cuttings in a well-lit but not directly sunny position.

❀ Once you have planted the cuttings, check the pot or propagator on alternate days to see if water is needed. Most softwood cuttings root in approximately six to eight weeks. When new growth appears, the plant may be gradually hardened off.

Semi-ripe cuttings

❀ Semi-ripe cuttings are also taken from the current season's growth, but are cut later in the year – from midsummer through to early autumn. Again, choose non-flowering, healthy side shoots. These should be soft at the top and just hard at the base.

❀ Because they are slightly harder than softwood cuttings, semi-ripe cuttings are not so susceptible to wilt. However, they do take longer to root, and for this reason they are often propagated from heel cuttings, which means they have the base of the stem 'wounded' to encourage rooting.

❀ Wounding involves making a shallow cut, approximately 1–1$\frac{1}{2}$ in (2.5–3.5 cm) up from the base of the cutting, and stripping away the bark from this point to the base, using a sharp knife, not tearing away the bark. Root production is then stimulated from the wounded edge as well as the base of the cutting. Heel cuttings expose the swollen base of the season's growth, which contains a concentration of growth hormones, thereby assisting rooting.

TAKING A HEEL CUTTING

1 *Pull off a strong, non-flowering side shoot from the parent plant, pulling outwards and downwards so that you bring away a small heel of bark. Tug sharply, rather than peeling the heel cutting away. Take care not to strip away bark from the parent plant, as this could encourage infection.*

2 *Using a clean, sharp knife, cut off the leaves from the lower half of the cutting's stem. Trim away any excess, damaged plant tissue and any long tails of bark.*

3 *Dip the bottom 1 in (2.5 cm) of the cutting into hormone rooting powder. This helps prevent fungicidal attack, as well as assisting rooting.*

4 *Make a planting hole in a small pot of cuttings compost. Gently firm in and water in the cutting. Cover the pot with a clear plastic bag, suspended*

away from the foliage on canes or wire, or place in a propagator. Situate the cutting in bright light, but not direct sunlight.

Hardwood cuttings

❀ Many shrubs can be raised from hardwood cuttings. These are taken from ripe, vigorous, current season's growth – from mid-autumn to early winter. Hardwood cuttings from deciduous shrubs are taken just after the leaves have fallen.

❀ Cuttings propagated in this way are slow to root but, well cared for, will produce strong, resilient plants in about a year. Propagate hardwood cuttings in containers, in a cold frame, or even in open ground.

❀ To grow cuttings on, dip the end of the cutting into hormone rooting powder. Make a planting hole and plant in cuttings compost in a container. Firm and water in gently. Label and place pots in a cold frame. Water well during the growing season. Harden off before planting out.

TAKING A HARDWOOD CUTTING

1 *Take pencil-thick cuttings at the junction of the current, and last season's growth.*

2 *Trim the cuttings to approximately 6 in (15 cm) lengths. At the top, cut just above buds or leaves, and at the base, cut just below buds or leaves. Make an angled cut at the top, cut straight across at the bottom – you will then know which way up to plant the cutting.*

3 *Remove any remaining deciduous leaves. On evergreen cuttings, remove leaves from the lower two-thirds of the stem and cut large leaves in half across.*

4 *If propagating outside, plant cuttings 6 in (15 cm) apart, in a trench 6 in (15 cm) deep filled with compost and sharp sand. Back fill with soil, and water in. Firm the soil after heavy frosts and water during periods of drought.*

DIVIDING PLANTS

DIVIDING plants not only regenerates what might have become quite a sad-looking plant, but is also an incredibly easy and cost-effective way of increasing your plant stocks. Many perennials will deteriorate over time, slowly dying out in the center, unless they are lifted and divided every three or four years.

❀ Division entails literally splitting the old plant into lots of smaller sections, the most healthy of which are replanted. Large divisions made in spring may even flower later in the season – albeit initially with shorter stems than the original, established plants.

❀ If the size difference between the young plants and their neighbors in the border bothers you, plant the new sections in pots or nursery beds until they are of a suitable size to put in their new positions.

Where to begin

❀ Left to their own devices, most plants reproduce themselves anyway. Propagation by division, complex as it may sound, simply involves the gardener taking a more active part in a natural process.

❀ Most gardeners start by dividing perennials since it is usually a reproachfully sad-looking border plant, dying out in the middle and straggly around the edges, that

DIVIDING RHIZOMES

1 *Carefully remove the clump from the ground with a fork, taking care to insert the fork well away from the rhizomes as you do not damage them. Shake away any excess soil.*

2 *Roughly break up the clump with your hands or a fork. Large clumps may need the back-to-back fork technique used on large perennials. Detach fresh new rhizomes using a clean, sharp knife. Each piece should have buds or leaves above it and roots below it. Discard diseased or old rhizomes.*

3 *Trim back long roots by one-third. On irises, cut the leaves into an arrowhead shape, approximately 6 in (15 cm) long to avoid damage by wind rock. Dust the cut edges of the rhizome with hormone rooting powder to help prevent disease and to encourage new growth.*

4 *Plant the new rhizomes at the same depth at which they were originally growing, their leaves and buds upright. Water and firm in.*

provokes some activity. Rather than simply discarding the whole plant, it is well worth taking some healthy sections from the outside of the plant, and producing many healthy, young plants from the single old specimen.

When to divide

❀ Be aware that some plants resent disturbance, so always check the needs of a particular plant before dividing it. Division usually takes place in the semi-

dormant seasons – early spring or autumn – on a day when the soil is moist but not waterlogged.

❀ Some plants have a marked preference for the time of year that they are moved, however, so again, research carefully before moving plants. Rhizomes (plants with fleshy, almost horizontal underground stems), such as bergenias, rhizomatous lilies and rhizomatous irises, are very easy to divide and are generally divided in the late summer.

DIVIDING PERENNIALS

1 *Dig up the overcrowded clump with a fork, disturbing the roots as little as possible. Shake off excess soil locate the best points for division. Discard diseased parts, as well as the central part of the plant. Divisions from the outer section of the clump will grow into new, healthy plants. Wash away excess soil with water if you cannot see the roots and shoots clearly enough for accurate division.*

2 *Divide the plant into sections that have healthy roots and shoots. You divide some plants with your hands, but plants with fleshy, tough roots will need to be cut with a clean, sharp knife. Dust any cuts with fungicide, following the manufacturer's directions.*

3 *Very tough, fibrously rooted clumps may need to be divided using two forks placed back to back in the center of the clump, to provide additional separation and leverage. Hand forks will suffice in some cases; full size garden forks may be needed in others. Always ease the forks apart gently, teasing out the roots to separate them, rather than wrenching them violently apart and breaking the roots.*

4 *Replant the new plant sections immediately after division, at the same depth at which they were already planted, with the roots spread well out. Firm in and water in well.*

Dividing bulbs

✽ After one or two seasons in the soil, most bulbs and corms produce offsets around their base. The offsets of bulbs are known as daughter bulbs; tiny ones are called bulblets. Corm offsets are known as cormels or cormlets. If these are allowed to develop unabated, they become overcrowded and compete for nutrients. The result, in most cases, is a dramatic reduction in flowering.

✽ It is therefore a good idea to lift and divide most clumps of bulbs and corms every three or four years, to sustain a really good show. Apart from preventing overcrowding, propagating bulbs also enables you to increase your flowering display at no cost, and with relatively little effort. Since the bulbs are increasing themselves naturally below the ground, it is simplicity itself to separate the developing bulbs from the parents and increase your stocks.

✽ Most popular bulbs and corms, for example narcissi, snowdrops, crocuses and lilies, will respond extremely well to division. Flowering will be increased and you will be able to plant over a wider area with your additional numbers of bulbs or corms. However, it is highly recommended that you check each plant's individual preference before planning division, as there are a few exceptions to these rules. For example, the Scarborough lily (*Vallota*) flowers well when overcrowded, while the autumn daffodil (*Sternbergia*) and cyclamens hate disturbance.

When to divide bulbs and corms

✽ Dividing is best done when the plant is dormant. However, it is obviously much easier to locate the bulbs when they have visible foliage, so division is usually undertaken when the leaves have almost entirely died down. Some bulbs have slightly different needs. For example, snowdrops are best divided when they are in full leaf, so again check each plant's individual requirements before you begin.

DIVIDING BULBS

1 *Gently lift the clump with a fork.*

2 *Shake off the excess soil and separate the clump into smaller, more manageable portions.*

3 *Pull away the individual bulbs with your hands. Discard soft, dried out, damaged or diseased* bulbs. *Clean the bulbs that you wish to replant, removing any loose tunics (the papery membrane enveloping bulbs).*

4 *Plant the offset bulbs at the correct depth and spacing in prepared soil. This is generally between two and three times the size of the bulb, but check the requirements of the individual species before dividing.*

INCREASING BULBS BY SCORING

Towards the end of the dormant season, hyacinths may be increased by scoring.

1 *Use a sharp knife to make cuts through the basal plate of the bulb. Dust the cut areas with fungicide and store the bulb in damp perlite, mixed with fungicide, in a warm place. The injury caused by the cutting will encourage small bulbs (bulblets) to develop along the cuts.*

2 *When bulblets have formed, plant the bulb upside down in gritty compost. The bulblets will grow above the parent bulb and may be carefully separated from the old bulb for replanting. A simpler method is to score the parent bulb, plant it again immediately and wait for bulblets to form.*

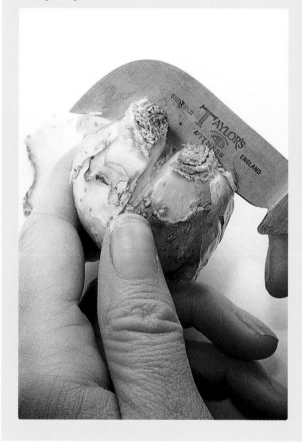

Scaling bulbs

❀ Scaling is a straightforward method for increasing the stocks of bulbs that consist of scales, most notably lilies, which are quite simple to propagate in this way. Propagating lilies is particularly satisfying since the bulbs are comparatively expensive to buy. A bonus is that, after scaling, the parent lily may be replanted to continue flowering as normal.

❀ Most lily bulbs comprise concentric rings of scales, joined at their bases to a basal plate. To scale lilies, work in early fall, before root growth begins. Lift the bulbs, or scrape away soil from around the bulb and work *in situ*. Remove a few scales from the bulb, taking care to remove a little of the basal plate tissue when you detach the scales. This will greatly increase your chances of success.

❀ Coat the scales with fungicide and place them in a tray of two parts damp peat substitute and one part coarse sand. Keep them moist in a warm, shaded place for approximately two months. In spring, move them to a cold place for two months, to encourage good leaf development. Pot on the single bulblets and grow on for another year before planting out.

LAYERING

LAYERING offers the novice gardener a superb introduction to propagation, since the young plants are not separated from the parent plant until they have formed roots and are growing independently. This is obviously not as challenging as raising plants from seed or cuttings, where the new plants are very vulnerable until established and need particular care to ensure strong rooting and vigorous growth, and require vigilant attention to ensure disease is kept at bay.

❀ Layering is such a simple propagation method that some plants even layer themselves, for example strawberry plants and shrubs with low branches like the smoke bush (*Cotinus coggygria*). Others attempt to layer naturally (self-layering plants), and can be easily encouraged in their efforts by pegging or weighing down branches until they root.

❀ Many climbers, such as ivy, have trailing shoots that develop roots on contact with the soil. The propagation in this case has already taken place. All you need do is gently ease the new plant from the soil without damaging the roots, and cut it away from the main stem before replanting the new plant.

❀ Layering is also a very useful technique for increasing stocks of plants, such as some shrubs and climbers, that do not root easily from cuttings. Layering is not necessarily a rapid propagation method, but the plants produced are strong, already well adapted to the soil in which they are to grow to maturity, and the technique is not labor intensive.

❀ In addition, it needs no specialist equipment, can be done at any time of the year, and does not take up any space on your windowsill or in a greenhouse. Thus, every gardener could start their propagation experience with a little layering.

❀ There are essentially three types of layering: air layering, where the growing medium is brought up to the plant stem; a range of techniques where soil is mounded over a stem, for example French, trench and stool layering; and the basic range of techniques in which the stem is brought down into the soil, namely tip, serpentine, natural and simple layering.

❀ This is all easier than it sounds, and most amateur gardeners will find the last techniques mentioned, which capitalise on the plant's own desire to root when it reaches the soil, sufficient for their propagation needs.

Planting self-layered climbers

❀ You may spot several places along a trailing stem where the plant has taken root. It is easy to see where the stems have produced new root systems as there is abundant healthy young growth at these points.

❀ Gently ease these areas of the stem away from the ground, bringing the roots up carefully. Using sharp pruners, cut away this section of stem from the parent plant. Cut the stem into sections, each with a good root system. Remove any leaves growing close to the rooted areas. Plant each portion of rooted stem in compost or directly in the garden, watering in well.

BELOW: *As the shoots of ivies (such as this* Hedera helix *'Goldheart') tend to produce roots naturally when they come into contact with the soil, the propagation is already done.*

INCREASING PLANTS BY LAYERING

1 Although many plants layer themselves, some will benefit from a helping hand. Choose a healthy, flexible stem that may be easily bent to touch the soil. Cut off any side shoots.

2 Make a shallow hole in the ground at an appropriate point, and enrich the area with compost. For an increased chance of success, make a short slanting cut on the underside of the stem at the point where it is to be layered. The concentration off carbohydrates and hormones at the point of the wound, together with the plant being slightly stressed in the area, helps to promote root growth.

3 Twist the shoot to open the cut. Apply hormone rooting powder to the injured part, to discourage disease and further encourage rooting.

4 Place the injured part of the stem in the soil and secure it firmly with a metal peg or piece of bent wire, making sure that the cut remains open. Backfill with soil, firm and water in using a watering can fitted with a fine spout. Keep the area moist throughout the growing season. After about a year, scrape away the soil to check for new roots. If all is well, sever the new plant from the parent and leave it in situ to establish for another season before moving it to its final site

GROWING TREES AND SHRUBS

❦

Trees are woody perennial plants, usually with a single stem or trunk, and may grow to 300 ft (90 m) tall. Evergreen trees keep their leaves all year round while deciduous trees lose their leaves in winter. Shrubs are also woody perennial plants but produce several stems, which branch out from soil level. Most shrubs do not grow taller than 15–20 ft (4.5–6 m). Larger shrubs such as cotoneasters and lilacs (*Syringa*) can be grown as small trees. Subshrubs are plants that are woody only at the base, like *Perovskia* and *Fuchsia*, and which die back annually. They are often cultivated as herbaceous perennials. Trees and shrubs provide a good structural basis for a garden design and should be planted first before other plants.

TREES

BOTH conifers and deciduous trees grow in many different shapes and sizes. Conifers have distinctive shapes, regular branches and needle-shaped leaves. They can be useful both as specimen trees and as hedging.

❀ Deciduous trees have an extremely varied range of leaf shapes and sizes and many can be chosen for the interest afforded by their branch shapes or by their bark in winter when the leaves have fallen. Many of the birch family have peeling bark of interesting colors.

❀ Trees can introduce height and grandeur into the garden. They are also useful for introducing contrasts in size and form with other plants. A tall columnar tree can make a punctuation mark in the environment, whereas a spreading tree offers a more sheltering and protective view. Their leaves are often very decorative, and vary greatly in effect, depending on their size, shape, color, surface texture and the way they are held on the twig. Poplar leaves are held so that they shake and rustle as they move in the wind, making a sound like the sea.

❀ Good specimen trees for large gardens include beech. All the beeches are beautiful, tall trees with smooth grey bark and fine foliage. The common beech tree is *Fagus sylvatica*, the weeping beech is *F. s. 'Pendula'* and *F. s. 'Roseomarginata'* is smaller than other beeches but still a big tree.

❀ Striking foliage color can be important but try not to overdo it. Yellow can look marvellous, especially when placed where the leaves catch the low sun in the

LEFT: *Conifers of different varieties associate well together, as demonstrated by the tall shapes and varied colors of this mixed conifer border.*

Trees for the smaller garden

❀ For the smaller garden *Aesculus pavia*, one of the horse chestnut family, is smaller than most, with interesting flowers, and can be used as a large shrub. *Aamelanchier canadensis* is a small, pretty tree for any size of garden, eventually growing to 21 x 16 ft (6.5 x 5 m). It is covered in white blossom in spring and the foliage turns brilliant orange-red in fall.

❀ Silver birches are delightful small trees, which can be planted individually or in close groups to form a coppice. The white-stemmed varieties are spectacular. *Betula papyrifera* (paper birch) has large leaves and peeling, paper-like bark. *Catalpa bignonioides* is the Indian bean tree and has attractive large leaves and panicles (heads of tiny stalked flowers) of white bell-shaped flowers with frilly edges and purple markings. It is exotic and makes a good shade tree.

morning or evening, but too much can be tiring to the eye. It is best to balance the foliage colors and not go for too many in a small area. Evergreens should be placed to create balance when the rest of the garden is dormant. Pines are best seen against the sky, where their interesting trunk shapes will stand out.

❀ Many of the maples are graceful and attractive. Snake bark varieties have good fall foliage color and very attractive trunks and branches.

BELOW: *The weeping pear* (Pyrus salicifolia 'Pendula') *is a small, highly decorative tree, which can be grown very successfully in a small garden. This one is underplanted with white tulips.*

SHRUBS

SHRUBS constitute an enormous range of plants suitable for gardens of any size and style. They are immensely varied in size, color, shape and the interest they provide at different times of the year, and are therefore invaluable for giving shape and substance to the garden and for providing a framework.

✤ The smaller shrubs are good for bringing body, form and texture to summer flower borders. Larger ones can be used to create mystery or to screen off unsightly parts of the garden and many can be used as features in their own right. They are also useful hedging plants.

✤ Alternatively, use just one variety, such as box in a parterre, lavender to edge a rose bed or yew as a backcloth to a border. Use a mixture of varieties to create informal divisions or as a windbreak. Groups of compatible shrubs can be grown together to create a shrub walk or border, but bear in mind that a mass of unrelated shrubs can be most unsatisfactory, providing no unity or harmony at all.

RIGHT: Lavendula augustifolia, *the lavender shrub will look well edging a rose bed, but remember that a haphazard mixture of shrubs will lack harmony and look careless.*

LEFT: *Planting rhododendron shrubs such as this en masse can create a stunning and vivid display and can be found in a variety suitable for most types of garden and soils.*

✤ Choose a theme for your planting, perhaps a specific color range or a choice of shrubs with similar shape or habit. Acid-loving plants often relate well to one another and rhododendrons planted *en masse* can look spectacular. Two of the most useful contributions that shrubs can make to the garden are leaf color and interesting berries in fall.

Deciduous, evergreen or semi-evergreen

✤ A deciduous plant sheds its leaves every fall, while an evergreen plant retains its leaves throughout the year. A shrub is described as semi-evergreen if it sheds some but not all of its leaves during the colder months. A plant's ability to retain its foliage varies according to the weather.

✤ During a mild winter, a normally deciduous shrub may keep some of its leaves, and in particularly harsh conditions an evergreen may shed more leaves than usual. Where the form of a shrub is an essential part of the framework of your garden, you should choose an evergreen unless you think the shrub's branches and twigs are interesting enough on their own to provide an imposing silhouette in winter.

Ornamental shrubs

❊ Shrubs that are important to the basic structure of the garden may also be highly ornamental with colorful, scented flowers, variegated foliage or attractive berries or stems in winter. But beware – it is easy to be seduced by individual plants and end up with too many varieties or simply too many shrubs, which will soon outgrow their welcome.

❊ Among things to consider are compatibility with the growing conditions, eventual height and spread and compatibility with other shrubs. Deciding where to place a shrub and, indeed, if it is really suitable for the garden at all, are important considerations.

Size and habit

❊ Shrubs differ enormously in size. There are mat-forming plants such as the creeping thymes, which will grow in a rock garden or between paving stones; there are small upright shrubs such as the lavenders, which can be used as part of a flower border or as low hedges, perhaps as a framework for a herb garden.

❊ There are also many silver shrubs, which contrast well in both habit and color with pink, purple and red flowers. The curry plant (*Helichrysum italicum*) is good in this respect and easy to grow, as is *Artemesia* such as A. 'Powys Castle', with feathery leaves.

❊ Medium-sized shrubs can be used either as punctuation marks in a border or as features. The larger salvias make interesting medium-sized shrubs in

ABOVE: *An informal placing of an 'Easter Island' sculpture within a planting of a yellow azalea and the large leaves of a tree peony.*

milder areas. *Salvia microphylla* is an evergreen, which needs a sheltered spot and has deep crimson flowers at the tips of its branches right through summer into fall. *Senecio laxifolius* is an easy-to-grow silver-leaved shrub with yellow daisy flowers. In sunny places it forms an upright bush 3 x 3 ft (1 x 1 m) and in shade it will scramble along the ground.

❊ The giants of the shrub world include smoke bush or burning bush (*Cotinus coggygria*), which can be used as a feature shrub or to divide up the garden. The cotoneasters are a versatile family, ranging from horizontal varieties, which look good stretching out in a sunny courtyard, to *Cotoneaster* 'Cornubia', which grows to 16 ft (5 m) tall and has the brightest of red berries in fall.

LEFT: *A very pleasing combination of clipped, rounded shapes and contrasting spiky leaves in front of a tall, dark green clipped hedge.*

ABOVE: *Successful contrasts of foliage shape and color can be seen in this shrub border, with the crinkled leaves of Swiss chard in the foreground.*

Features of interest

❀ The shapes, bark and stems of shrubs vary enormously, quite as much as their size. Some shrubs have a sprawling habit. They can be useful as ground cover but may look better trained up a wall. *Ceanothus prostratus* is one of these. It will form a mound of bright blue flowers in spring, but will take up less space if trained on a wall.

❀ The low-growing forms of willow (*Salix*) can be very pretty for rock gardens or for use by small pools. They have attractive foliage and catkins. A rounded form of shrub such as *Daphne collina*, an attractive dwarf, is ideal for a medium-sized rock garden, providing softness among the rocks. An arching form such as *Buddleja alternifolia* can provide a canopy over lower-growing plants at the back of a border.

Focal points

❀ Focal points or eye-catchers are important in the garden. Shrubs can do the job but they need to be of interest all year round. Many *Cornus* varieties make excellent feature plants, as do *Cotinus*, *Corylopsis* and hydrangeas.

❀ Phormiums have strong, strap-like leaves, giving a highly architectural, even tropical, effect. Yuccas, which grow to 7 ft (2 m), are useful for providing vertical interest and have elegant, creamy white flowers.

Links

❀ Shrubs are invaluable for providing links between one part of the garden and another, and between plants that otherwise do not relate to each other. They can mark an entrance to the house from the garden and, grown in groups or rows, they can flank a drive or a door. The shrubs chosen should be in sympathy with the style, scale and color of the building.

❀ Evergreen shrubs are often chosen because they are continuously in leaf and are always good for a formal setting. Varied planting that includes deciduous shrubs, such as *Magnolia stellata* with its hundreds of white starry flowers, as well as evergreens will add interest in spring.

❀ Lilac (*Syringa*) is a good example of a plant to mingle with others because once its flowers are over it can look uninteresting and leggy. Spreading shrubs such as *Hydrangea quercifolia* can provide links between more upright plants.

Shrub borders

❀ Shrubs can be grown to great effect on their own in borders. Choose ones that will suit the soil and climate of your garden and provide a succession of color and interest throughout the year if possible. Balance the shapes, heights and forms of the shrubs, and leave plenty of room for their ultimate spread.

❀ You can choose shrubs with interesting color combinations or concentrate more on the textures. A border of mainly variegated shrubs with variations in the greens and yellows and the occasionally single color to provide contrast should do well in a slightly shaded position.

❀ Evergreen and deciduous shrubs can be mixed together, provided you balance them well. Taller shrubs should be at the back, creeping ones at the front. Some shrubs will give months of interest while others tend to

mature and fade quickly. When planning the border, make sure the short-term shrubs are camouflaged by long-term ones. Fast-growing shrubs will probably need to be thinned out as the border matures.

❀ A larger shrubbery or shrub walk can be planted in grass. Here the shrubs should not be grouped closely as in a smaller border, but each should be given room to grow into its natural shape and still leave room for walking around it and standing back to admire it.

Shrubs in the mixed border

❀ Borders of herbaceous perennials only were popular at one time. Today it makes more sense to combine a framework of shrubs interplanted with a variety of herbaceous perennials to give all-year interest and a much more labor-saving border.

❀ Many shrubs act as ground cover, keeping down weeds and preventing moisture from evaporating. A mixed border can be planted next to a wall and can include wall-trained plants as a backdrop, as well as climbers.

❀ Other plants are positioned between the shrubs to present a balanced, colorful composition. It should be interesting from late winter to late fall. In an island bed, shrubs can be planted with the tallest in the middle surrounded by other plants in clumps and drifts.

ABOVE: *A decorative wall forms the backdrop for a well-planted mixed border featuring roses, begonias,* Achillea *and* Coreopsis.

BELOW: *A low shrub border with great variety produced by the dark purple* Berberis, *variegated* Euonymus, *purple* Salvia *and pink-tipped* Spiraea.

TRAINING ROSES

There are about 100 naturally occurring species roses and many natural hybrids growing in the wild. People have been growing roses in their gardens for over 2,000 years, however, and there are now thousands of cultivars, ranging from tiny ground cover roses to large shrubs and climbers, all of which have a part to play in modern garden design.

THE HISTORY OF ROSES

THE first garden roses probably occurred in the Middle East and spread via ancient Greece and Rome to the rest of Europe. These are the gallica, damask and alba roses. They are robust and highly scented but bloom only once a year. In the seventeenth century Dutch and French breeders crossed albas and damasks to produce large-headed roses with over 100 petals.

❀ In the 1780s merchant ships began to come home with roses from Chinese gardens, derived from two wild species – the 'giant' rose, a huge climber with big yellow flowers and *Rosa chinensis* found in the Ichang Gorge of the Yangtse river. Rose breeding between European and China roses has continued ever since and rose catalogues today include an enormous variety of rose types, both old and new.

ABOVE: *Roses and lavender always make a good combination, the lavender helping to conceal the bare 'legs' of many roses in the summer. This rose is called 'Cameo'.*

Rose groups

❀ Roses can be divided into several groups. Wild, or species, roses and their hybrids are large, arching shrubs flowering once only with single, five-petalled flowers in spring or midsummer. They have decorative hips in fall and are useful for wild gardens.

❀ Old garden roses are best suited to informal gardens and include the gallica, damask and alba roses. Modern garden roses are best for formal rose gardens and include the patio and miniature roses.

❀ Climbing roses have long, strong shoots and large flowers borne singly or in small clusters. Some flower in summer only, but most will repeat-flower in fall. Rambling roses are vigorous with long, flexible shoots, which bear small flowers in large clusters, mostly in early summer.

LEFT: *A seaside rose garden, heavily protected against the wind by a succession of clipped hedges and shrubs.*

TYPES OF GARDEN ROSE

The many thousands of species and cultivars available all fall within one of the categories below.

Old garden roses

Gallica: *Probably the oldest rose type. Usually forms small shrubs around 4 ft (1.2 m) high with strong, upright growth and many small bristly thorns. Flowers range from deep pink to purple and have a faint fragrance.*

Damask: *Also ancient but more elegant than the gallicas with open, arching branches, long elegant leaves and richly scented pink and purple flowers.*

Alba: *Closely related to the wild dog rose (Rosa canina). Large stately shrubs, once known as 'tree roses', with grey-green foliage and soft pink or white flowers.*

Centifolia (Provence): *Lax, open growth, big rounded leaves and globular flowers with a rich fragrance.*

China rose: *Much lighter in growth than European roses, with thin stems and sparse foliage giving them a twiggy look.*

Portland rose: *Short, upright habit; beautiful, strongly scented flowers with the invaluable ability to repeat-flower.*

Bourbon roses: *Similar to Portland rose but more lax and taller.*

Hybrid musk: *Vigorous, repeat-flowering shrub with abundant foliage and trusses of fragrant double flowers.*

Hybrid perpetual: *Vigorous, sometimes repeat-flowering; flowers borne singly or in threes in summer and fall.*

Moss rose: *Lax shrub with furry, moss-like growth on stems and calyx. Flowers once only.*

Noisette rose: *Repeat-flowering with large clusters of flowers and a spicy scent.*

Sempervirens: *Semi-evergreen climber with numerous flowers in late summer.*

Tea rose: *Repeat-flowering shrubs and climbers with loose, usually double, fragrant flowers.*

BELOW: *An attractive mixed floribunda rose garden enclosed within a wall. The roses have been carefully chosen to grow to the same height and flower simultaneously.*

Modern garden roses

Large-flowered bush (hybrid tea): *Upright, repeat-flowering shrub with a single, large flower to a stem or in small clusters, summer to fall.*

Cluster-flowered bush (floribunda): *Upright, repeat-flowering shrub with large sprays of flowers, summer to fall.*

Dwarf cluster-flowered bush (patio rose): *Similar to cluster-flowered bush but with smaller, neater habit.*

Miniature rose: *Tiny counterpart of large- and cluster-flowered roses.*

Ground-cover rose: *Low-growing trailing or spreading rose.*

Modern shrub rose: *Varied group, ranging from low, mound-forming cultivars to spreading shrubs and giant, cluster-flowered bushes.*

Roses on their own

❀ The traditional way to grow roses is in a bed on their own. This is especially recommended for the large- and cluster-flowered bush roses, whose large and perfect flowers seem to ask for special attention.

❀ Avoid multi-colored or undefined backgrounds. Most roses grown on their own look best against a smooth green setting – either a lawn or a clipped hedge as the background. They can also look attractive grown next to a paved, brick or gravel courtyard or path. The large- and cluster-flowered bushes become very bare and leggy, especially later in the year, and planted with only bare earth as the background can take on a somewhat moth-eaten look.

❀ The whole look of a bed devoted to roses can benefit from an edging of plants such as clipped box. Silver-grey plants seem particularly compatible with roses, and plants such as *Nepeta* and lavender also make very good low hedges that help to conceal the roses' bare 'legs', while providing a raised frame for the whole bed. It is important to choose plants that will last at least as long as the roses.

CHARACTERISTICS TO LOOK FOR

ROSES offer a great variety of flower shapes and colors. Flowers may be single (4–7 petals), semi-double (8–14 petals), double (15–20 petals) or fully double (over 30 petals). As for shape, they may be flat, cupped, pointed, urn-shaped, rounded, rosette-shaped, quartered or pompom. About the only color you cannot have in a rose is blue.

Hips

❀ Some roses will not set hips but the ones that do can provide clusters of really wonderful fall color. The rugosa roses with single or semi-double flowers have bright red decorative hips. Some of the species roses have yellow, red or purple hips.

Foliage

❀ Foliage is important where a rose is being used as a hedge or as a dividing feature in a garden. *Rugosa* roses have wrinkled, bright green foliage. *R. glauca* has feathery foliage of a dusky greenish-purple color and deep red hips. Its arching habit makes it a most attractive plant as a specimen or as part of a shrub or large mixed border. The foliage of the large-flowered hybrids is often very attractive in spring when the young leaves are deep purple or bronze, although the leaves become sparser later in the year, but this can be concealed by other plants.

BELOW: Rosa 'New Dawn' is a popular silvery-pink climber, which flowers prolifically in summer. It can be grown up a wall or over a pergola or arch.

Roses in association with other plants

❀ In smaller gardens especially, it seems a pity to segregate roses or devote a part of the garden to one type of plant only. Roses are sociable and mingle well with smaller plants that do not compete for light or nutrients.

❀ Bedding plants are not usually very successful grown in association with roses, but many of the smaller geraniums, especially those with blue flowers such as G. 'Johnson's Blue', make very good bedfellows with roses, growing tall enough to conceal the angular lower rose stems in a mist of blue flowers. Clematis can be grown as companions for roses, too, adding color during the summer when the roses are flowering less vigorously.

The formal rose garden

❀ In formal rose beds, as with any formal garden, it is best to restrict the colors to just a few in one bed. Too many different bright colors draw attention away from the beauty of the individual roses and confuse rather than please the eye. An all-white rose garden can be attractive.

❀ You can have a rose garden made up of different beds, each with its own color combination: a bed of whites and pinks for example, another with shades of red, another with yellows and oranges. Yellows and whites can look good together, too.
A bed of mainly low-growing roses can be made

RIGHT: 'Paul's Himalayan' musk, a deep pink with a glorious scent, and 'Blessings', a white floribunda, make a pleasing combination.

ABOVE: Shrub roses are among the most suitable for surrounding a seat. Their abundant flowers are prettily shaped and their strong scent wafts through the air.

more interesting by introducing a vertical element in the middle or at the four corners. Standard roses can be used in this way very effectively.

❀ Remember that not all roses will flower at exactly the same time, so mixing too many different varieties together may result in a patchy display. Cultivars also reach different heights, another thing to bear in mind at the early planning stage. Choose plants of the same height for a flat, open bed. A bed backed by a wall or hedge should have the taller roses at the back and the smaller ones in front.

A more relaxed formality

❀ A formal rose garden can be created in a more relaxed way by dividing the plot into formal paths, by using water to enliven the space and covered seats to encourage the visitor to spend time there. Small rectangular pools with fountains can make the meeting places of paths delightful places to stop and rest.

❀ Standard roses or large- and cluster- flowered roses can be accompanied by climbers and ramblers growing over arches and arbors. Although such a garden has all the formality of the ancient Islamic gardens, the strict geometry is less rigid, with old roses and climbing roses creating height and a sense of freedom. Choose the most scented roses you can to add to the enchantment of this sort of garden.

Roses in containers

❀ Roses will grow quite well in containers, provided they are watered and given nutrients regularly – they require generous amounts or they will soon begin to suffer. They can brighten up a courtyard or patio and the tiny ones will even grow in window boxes.

❀ There are some excellent bushy plants in this category with prettily formed miniature flowers. Choose compact modern cultivars, which will form bushy mounds over the top of the pot.

❀ Miniature roses look charming in tubs or troughs. For pink, try R. 'Silver Tips', which is bushy with abundant, many-petalled flowers with a silver reverse, or R. 'Stars 'n' Stripes', a very pretty little rose with red and white striped flowers.

❀ For white you could use the ivory-colored R. 'Easter Morning' and for something brighter, R. 'Little Flirt', a small, double orange-red flower with gold at the base and on the reverse of the petals. All these grow to about 12 in (30 cm).

❀ Patio roses are hardy, repeat well and are particularly useful for larger containers. They are larger and more robust than miniature roses but not as large as the cluster-flowered group. They have charming rosette-shaped flowers and a neat, bushy habit of growth. Ideal for sunny courtyards and patios, R. 'Bianco' has pure white pompom flowers in great profusion and bushy growth; R. 'Festival' has clusters of semi-double crimson-scarlet flowers with a silver reverse, R. 'Queen Mother' has semi-double soft pink flowers against glossy dark foliage and a slight scent.

BELOW: *Roses often look better in association with other plants than on their own, their angular stems softened by the form of many perennial plants. Here, Rosa 'English Miss' is grown with lavender and lavender-blue pansies.*

RIGHT: *The pale buff rose 'Alchymist' growing up the wall and around the diamond-paned window is set off beautifully by the* Centranthus ruber *growing at its feet.*

❀ Even quite vigorous climbers can be grown in large tubs or half-barrels and trained up a wall. Plant and train them as you would other roses but be sure to water and feed them regularly and replenish the topsoil, as it will be difficult to repot them. *R.* 'New Dawn' is one of the best and most vigorous modern climbers, with silvery-pink flowers in clusters, *R.* 'White Cockade' is a rather slow grower, which is advantageous in a pot. *R.* 'Danse de Feu' has repeating, semi-double brilliant orange-scarlet flowers and is suitable for a north-facing wall.

Roses as ground cover

❀ Most roses recommended as ground cover roses are not truly ground covering in the sense of plants that creep along the ground. They may be better described as dense, low-growing shrubs. They are usually very hardy and disease-free.

❀ Those that do spread along the ground form a dense carpet covered in flowers in summer. They are excellent for hiding the trunks of felled trees, manhole covers and other unsightly features you cannot actually remove. They can also scramble down a steep bank.

❀ There are several roses to choose from. Some cover the soil well but may grow too tall to look like a carpet. Others are too vigorous for a small garden, spreading rapidly and requiring constant control.

❀ The taller ones can be used to fill gaps in a mixed border where their healthy foliage and small flowers can blend in with many other plants. *R.* 'Max Graf' is prostrate with dense, glossy foliage and non-repeating single pink flowers with an apple scent. *R.* 'Raubritter' is a sprawling low mound with clusters of cupped pink flowers, which can be used to trail over a bank or low wall. *R.* 'Running Maid' has single pink flowers and a dense, low spreading growth that covers the ground well.

LEFT: *The beautiful climbing rose 'Adelaide d'Orleans' clambers happily over this metal pergola with a medley of perennials and bedding plants growing at its feet.*

PLANTING CLIMBERS

Climbing plants are the dressing-up clothes of a garden. They provide great scope for the imagination and can bring color to a garden in great profusion. They can be used to clothe unsightly buildings – from the standard garden shed to a concrete garage. Many are also sweetly scented and from their height on a support can waft fragrance through the whole garden. Some plants are not true climbers but can be trained up a wall, producing a curtain of flowers or berries. For example, the red berries of *Pyracantha* are a fantastic sight in fall and the bright blue flowers of *Ceanothus* will cover a wall in spring or summer.

SOME POSSIBILITIES

SOME plants, like the beautiful single yellow rose 'Mermaid', are vigorous and will cover a whole wall or, like 'Kifsgate' with its profusion of tiny white flowers, will climb to the top of the tallest tree. These are not for small gardens. The stately wisterias, brilliant red Virginia creeper and *Hydrangea petiolaris*, with long-lasting flowers, will also cover a large expanse of wall. The large-flowered clematises will gently creep through the branches of supporting shrubs to produce wonderful large, colorful flowers in summer. They are then cut back in spring the following year.

Climbing methods

❀ Climbers have adapted in many different ways to raise themselves up towards the light. Some, such as the ivies (*Hedera*), are self-clinging and will attach themselves to their supports by aerial or 'adventitious' roots. Others, like Virginia creeper (*Parthenocissus quinquefolia*), adhere by tendrils. They cling to walls and tree trunks, needing no other support. Twining species all need permanent support.

❀ A few climbers attach themselves by curling leaf stalks. Others, like sweet peas (*Lathyrus odorata*) use tendrils. Passion flowers twine their axillary shoots around supports, while vines use terminal shoots.

❀ *Bougainvillea* species and jasmines produce long, arching stems, which need to be tied into their supports. Some species have hooked thorns to help them scramble through host plants. Blackberries are notoriously difficult to remove because of their ability to cling in this way.

ABOVE: Virginia creeper (Parthenocissus tricuspidata) *will cover a large wall and has leaves that turn a truly spectacular deep rich crimson color in the fall.*

Climbers on buildings

❀ Use plants to emphasise the good elements of a building. If it is built of pleasant materials and architecturally pleasing, you may want to keep to low climbers that will help anchor the house to the ground without concealing its shape or any architectural detailing. A boring-looking building, however, can be made more attractive by allowing climbers to cover the walls.

❀ *Actinidia kolomikta* has decorative variegated green and pink leaves with white tips and will cover red brick satisfactorily. Golden or yellow foliage plants such as *Humulus lupulus* 'Aureus' will complement red brick. A pale-colored wall makes an effective background for deep red blooms such as *Rosa* 'Climbing Ena Harkness'.

ABOVE: *There are many beautiful and scented honeysuckles and this one, Lonicera 'Graham Thomas', is slightly unusual, with pale lemon-yellow flowers.*

Climbers for low walls and fences

❀ Low walls can be heightened by growing climbers up trellis. This will conceal unwanted views and create more privacy. If you are going to grow a vigorous climber, remember they can become very bulky and heavy so you will need a strong fence and the most robust form of trellis, otherwise the climber will pull it all down in a year or two.

❀ If you want to cover a fence quickly, use a quick-growing ivy. Some grow particularly fast and create an attractive 'curtain' of green. *Hedera canariensis* is a vigorous climber with large, glossy leaves. *H. c. algeriensis* has yellow-green leaves on smooth wine-red stalks. *Hedera* 'Dentata Variegata' has light-green leaves, mottled grey-green with broad, cream-white margins. Remember, however, that the quicker growing a climber is, the more likely it is to get out of hand and you will probably have a lot of cutting back to do eventually.

BELOW: *Hedera helix 'Goldheart' is an attractive variegated ivy with a very yellow center to the leaf. It can be used to hide a garden shed, as it does here very successfully.*

Sun lovers

❀ Many climbers love the sun. Clematis love to have their flowers in the sun and their roots well shaded. If on a sunny wall, they can be shaded by a shrubby plant in front of them or by a large slab of stone laid above their roots.

❀ Many roses prefer full sun, although some will tolerate a little shade. In sheltered areas and very often in cities, where the temperature is several degrees warmer than in the surrounding countryside, you can often grow exotic climbers.

❀ The bright yellow *Fremontodendron californicum* really catches the eye. *Eccremocarpus scaber* has red tubular flowers with yellow shading and will scramble to a good height. The common passion flower (*Passiflora caerulea*), with its jellyfish-like flowers, looks spectacular in a sheltered spot. Other passion flowers are tender and need to be grown in a greenhouse.

Climbers for north walls

❀ There are several plants that will tolerate north-facing walls, including *Hydrangea petiolaris*, the pretty, white repeat-flowering rose 'Madame Alfred Carrière' and the deep black-red rose 'Guinée', which has a delicious perfume and dark green leaves on a well-branched stem.

❀ For shady and north-facing walls or walls exposed to cold winds, use vigorous, hardy climbers. Many ivies are good for this. If the wall is heavily shaded, use green-leaved varieties; you can use variegated or yellow leaves where there is no danger of frost damage. Some honeysuckles will do well in these conditions, too.

ABOVE: *This is an exciting combination of* Clematis tangutica *and* Clematis *'Perle d'Azur', grown on either side of a sky-blue door.*

BELOW: *This absolutely enchanting rose 'Phyllis Bide', with chameleon-like flowers of pale to deep pink and masses of small blooms, looks particularly good against a brick wall.*

Climbers for pillars

❀ Freestanding supports such as pillars and even old tree trunks allow climbing plants to be viewed in the round and contribute a strong visual and stylistic element to the garden. The plants must therefore be carefully chosen and trained.

❀ Depending on the materials and design of the support, the climber may be formal and disciplined, or cottage-garden style and rambling. Metal obelisks look good in a formal rose or herb garden and their shape makes them easy to train climbers on to. They must be strong enough to bear what may be the surprisingly heavy weight of the climber chosen. Small obelisks are particularly good for summer-flowering clematis, sweet peas and honeysuckles.

❀ Pillars add a strong vertical element to a mixed herb border. A pillar can also be used as a focal point or at the end of an axis, at the corners of a border or at the top of steps where the garden level changes.

❀ A series of pillars alongside a path can be linked by rope swags with the climbers trained along them. Roses are probably the most popular climbers to use for this. A stout post with wire mesh fixed around it will provide good tying-in support for many climbers. If the supports you are using are particularly attractive, why not choose deciduous climbing plants such as the golden hop (*Humulus lupulus* 'Aureus'), together with the dusky summer-flowering *Clematis* 'Madame Julia Correvon'? Even when both plants are cut back, the support will still be a feature on its own.

Climbers for arbors

❀ An arbor covered with climbing plants provides privacy, a sense of relaxation and opportunities for growing spectacular climbing plants and letting them grow to their full potential. Arbors are used most in the summer, seldom in winter, so you can concentrate on summer-flowering climbers. Choose those that have fragrant flowers, as they will ensure that the arbour becomes a particularly enchanted and sweetly scented place, particularly in the early mornings and the evenings.

❀ *Rosa* 'Félicité Perpétue' has enormous heads of creamy-white double pompom flowers, whose petals are sometimes tipped with red. Its small, dark leaves are plum-red when young. It is vigorous and shoots freely from the base.

ABOVE: *Sweet peas like a rich, deep loam and plenty of water. They will then flower copiously up any support. This home-made bamboo wigwam is an excellent way of allowing the flowers support and plenty of sunlight.*

❀ If you prefer pink for your arbor, the old-fashioned, rich pink flowers of R. 'Bantry Bay' are highly decorative and a great favorite. Many honeysuckles have a glorious scent and very pretty flowers. *Lonicera* x *americana*, for example, has fragrant pink and cream flowers from summer to fall. It is evergreen and needs a sheltered place in either sun or shade; L. 'Donald Waterer' has red and cream fragrant flowers in summer, followed by red berries.

LEFT: *Roses and apples come from the same family and associate really well in the garden. Here, a buff-yellow climbing rose and a deep pink one have been encouraged to grow into an ancient apple tree.*

foliage. All are twining, woody and deciduous. They climb vigorously and need plenty of room to look their best. A pergola gives them all this.

❀ Most wisterias are hardy but prefer a sunny, sheltered position. It is important to prune them correctly to get them to flower well. *Wisteria floribunda* has fragrant, violet-blue flowers; W. *f.* 'Alba' has white flowers tinged with lilac; W. x *formosa* 'Kokkuryu' is strongly fragrant with double purple flowers; W. *sinensis* is fast growing and vigorous with dense trails of slightly fragrant violet-blue flowers.

Pergolas

❀ Pergolas are often built over a patio near the house or in a prominent situation over a path that can be seen from the house. Because of this it is sensible to try and choose climbers that will retain some attraction in winter. Of course, if the structure itself is attractive enough, this is not always necessary.

❀ Make sure the cross beams on the pergola are high enough to allow the flowers to trail without touching the heads of people walking underneath.

❀ Wisteria varieties, although their flowering season is short, are among the most beautiful of climbers, and a pergola gives them the opportunity to hang their great trailing flowers elegantly and to show off their feathery

Growing climbers through supporting plants

❀ Many climbers will grow happily through other plants, although it is important to choose climbers that are not too vigorous for their hosts and that will not become so entangled in them that you cannot prune them effectively. It is important, too, to choose host plants that are not so vigorous that you will need to prune them while the climber is in flower.

BELOW: *This grapevine* (Vitis vinifera) *obviously makes the most of the sun reaching the small balcony and associates well with the pale pink and red geraniums peeping through the ironwork.*

LEFT: *Wisteria is perhaps the monarch of climbing plants with its enormous hanging heads of purple pea flowers. Here,* Wisteria sinensis *softens a red brick house and patio.*

❀ Other vigorous spring-flowering clematis such as C. *montana* can also be allowed to grow naturally; C. *m.* 'Mayleen' is an attractive variety with very dark leaves and single pink flowers smelling of vanilla. Another attractive *montana* type is C. *chrysocoma*, with large single white flowers tumbling in waves down its dark green leaves.

❀ In summer *Rosa* 'Kifsgate' (a famous one grows in the garden at Kifsgate in Gloucestershire, England) will reach right up into a very tall tree. *R.* 'Albertine' is another vigorous and much-loved rose that enjoys being allowed to grow to its full potential on a large pergola. *Vitis coignetiae* is one of the vine family with enormous, velvety leaves that will grow all along a pergola, offering shade. The Virginia creeper (*Parthenocissus quinquefolia*) really needs a large area to make the most of its hanging curtains of brightest red.

Climbers in small gardens

❀ For small gardens choose climbers that will not grow too tall. These can be grown in containers and will lend height to groups of other container plants. You can make a tripod out of bamboo canes, or alternatively you can buy small metal or cane obelisks to train the climbers up.

❀ Many clematis will grow well in pots. They can be used to brighten dull parts of a concrete yard area or along the walls of buildings. It is important to choose clematis with this in mind. C. *alpina* and C. *macropetala* can be grown in pots but their flowering period is limited to spring.

❀ Early, large-flowered clematis will flower in early summer. Good ones include C. 'Miss Bateman' (white with green anthers) and C. 'Pink Champagne'. Both are compact and ideal for training in pots. Slightly later-flowering clematis include C. 'Nelly Moser' (pink and white stripes) and C. 'The President' (deep purple and red).

❀ The grapevine (*Vitis vinifera*) is another wonderful plant to grow over a patio and the bunches of grapes will hang down invitingly.

❀ Climbers to use with shrubs include the large, summer-flowering clematises that are cut nearly down to ground level each year. *Clematis viticella* varieties can be grown through medium-sized shrubs. C. *v.* 'Polish Spirit' has rich purple flowers, which associate well with golden shrubs such as *Choisya ternata* 'Sundance' and silver-leaved shrubs such as *Senecio laxifolius*.

Climbers in large gardens

❀ In a large garden where pergolas can be long and wide and space is not restricted, you can choose the most vigorous and spectacular climbers. The early spring-flowering evergreen, *Clematis armandii*, will cover long lengths of wall or fence, looking like snowdrifts at a time when little else is in flower.

CLIPPING PLANTS

Any evergreen plants can be trained or clipped to create garden architecture such as hedges and arches. They can also be used to create living garden sculpture. Topiary, or the training and pruning of trees and shrubs in this way, has been popular since Roman times and many traditional gardens in Europe, particularly in France, Italy, Portugal and Spain, depend largely on clipped evergreen trees and shrubs for their planting. Color is rarely used, except perhaps for the ubiquitous deep red rose used around front doors.

TIPS AND TECHNIQUES

TRAINING and clipping is suitable only on plants that have small leaves growing close together so that they will keep a clear shape. The technique offers scope for special effects, both in large gardens and the very tiniest of plots. In fact the modern garden relies more and more on such plants to create a strong skeleton to the garden and the architectural effects they can achieve can be used effectively to complement geometric modern buildings.

❀ Most hedging and clipping is carried out in yew or box because these respond particularly well to the technique and grow into close shapes with good definition. You can use many other evergreen shrubs, however. For example, the Portuguese laurel (*Aucuba japonica*) can be clipped into an imposing hedge whose large and shiny dark green leaves catch the sunlight like mirrors. The shrubby honeysuckles such as *Lonicera nitida* also clip well; the variety 'Baggesen's Gold' is much more interesting than the ordinary green one.

BELOW: *This elaborate garden includes a box parterre, clipped yews and roses of one variety only, giving the impression of unity and variety at the same time.*

ABOVE: *The garden sculptures in this cottage garden provide a dramatic contrast to the rest of the plants, as well as forming a striking centerpiece at the front of the house.*

❀ As always, hedges should be of a height in keeping with the size of the garden, and trees should be shaped in a way that relates to their surroundings. It is nearly always a mistake to have many highly elaborate topiary sculptures because they will conflict with each other and diminish other aspects of the garden.

❀ Simple, rounded umbrella shapes can look good in association with each other and clipped ball shapes can look effective when repeated in pairs or multiples in a larger garden.

❀ The common yew (*Taxus baccata*) grows much faster than is often supposed if fed and watered generously. Box is slower growing but will still mature acceptably if cared for in the same way. The common yew is good for hedges, whereas Irish yew (*Taxus baccata* 'Fastigiata') has upwardly pointing branches and is therefore better if you want a narrow silhouette.

Maintenance

❀ If you are going to clip and train many shrubs in your garden, bear in mind that they require constant maintenance. Clipped evergreen shrubs should be fed with slow-release fertilizer in spring and watered during dry spells until the plants are well established – about two or three years. You will have to clip a formal hedge at least twice a year in order for it to maintain its shape.

❀ Hedges are mostly cut with shears or an electric trimmer. Use a straight edge or garden line as a guide. Informal hedges need regular pruning to remove untidy growth; cut back as far as you think is necessary. Flowering and fruiting hedges should be pruned only at the appropriate season, which will vary according to the species. Use pruners to avoid damage to leaves, which would look unsightly.

❀ Old, neglected topiaries do not always need to be grubbed up to start again. They can sometimes be renovated. Hornbeam (*Carpinus*), honeysuckle (*Lonicera*) and privet (*Ligustrum*) will all respond well to pruning if they have become overgrown. Yew, in particular, can be pruned back hard and will sprout from what looks like dead wood. It is best to clip in stages over three years, cutting only one side of the plant at a time.

ABOVE: *The glowing red stems of Cornus alba are best planted in a group, where their massed branches can be seen in sunlight during the winter months.*

CLIPPED PATTERNS

PLANTS have been used since time immemorial to create patterns on the ground. Mazes were among the earliest patterns. The parterre became popular in France during the seventeenth century. They were often so complicated they became known as *parterres de broderie* or embroidered parterres. They were designed to be seen from first-floor windows or from raised terraces. In level gardens, a mount was often built with a little building on top from which to look down on the pattern.

❁ The knot is a complicated parterre pattern, which uses a continuous line of planting. This is usually made with box but other plants can be used such as marjoram, rue, lavender, rosemary, santolina or germander. You can use one plant interlaced with another, contrasting the silver foliage of santolina, for example, with the dark green of rosemary or box.

❁ A parterre does not interlace in a continuous line and is therefore easier to design and maintain. It is made up of separate patterns, often squares, and the middle is traditionally filled with colored sands and gravels or flowers.

❁ Such designs can provide a unified design for spaces of almost any size. They are not too difficult to maintain and clip if the area is quite small. Colored recycled glass beads are sometimes used instead of gravel. Bedding plants can also provide a brave show of color. Perennial flowers such as small shrub roses mingled with foxgloves (*Digitalis*) or a mixture of herbs can be used inside the patterns.

HEDGES

WHEN choosing plants for hedging you need to choose the variety carefully for the particular place you have in mind. Yew can be burnt by the wind when young and will not tolerate boggy ground, while some conifers such as cypresses cannot regenerate from old wood so cannot be cut right back if they become too large. *Thuja* and *Lonicera* both grow fast and require much more clipping than yew.

❀ The best deciduous plants for formal clipped hedges are beech and hornbeam because they are easy to clip and they stay tight and compact. A hedge of beech (*Fagus sylvatica*) will hold on to its attractive brown leaves until new growth starts in spring. Good evergreens include *Aucuba japonica*, *Chamaecyparis lawsoniana* 'Pembury Blue' (an evergreen conifer with silver-blue foliage) and holly (*Ilex*). There is also a good hawthorn with polished dark green leaves (*Crataegus laevigata*).

❀ Informal ornamental hedges can be created with roses. *R. rugosa* 'Frau Dagmar Hastrup' has silvery pink flowers and big red hips and *R.* 'Mundi' makes a very pretty hedge with striped white and pink flowers. *Eleagnus pungens* 'Frederici' has dark green, glossy leaves with silvery borders; *Osmanthus delavayi* has evergreen, dark green rounded leaves.

Functional hedges

❀ If you are looking for security as well as ornament, try *Berberis* or *Pyracantha* varieties with long and unkind thorns, which are very difficult to break through. The flowering quince (*Chaenomeles*) has long, sharp thorns as well as pretty apple blossom-shaped flowers and it, too, can make an attractive and effective security hedge.

BELOW: *Pleaching takes a little effort but can create a formal division or avenue of great style. This pleached hornbeam avenue leads the eye to an arched exit at the far end.*

PLEACHING, POLLARDING AND COPPICING

Pleaching is a method of planting trees in rows and training the side branches to meet in horizontal, parallel lines. Other growth is cut back or interwoven to form a vertical screen. Beech, lime, hornbeam and plane trees are all suitable for pleaching. This technique is particularly effective in a formal setting and often used to line paths or avenues in larger gardens.

❀ In smaller gardens it can make an elegant division between two adjoining areas. A pleached avenue automatically leads the eye to what lies at the end so it is important to make sure there is something worth looking at, such as a sculpture or a decorative seat.

❀ Pollarding, very popular in France, involves regularly lopping back the entire crown of a tree to short stumps, so producing many thin branches and a single mop head of foliage. It can be useful in small gardens where a natural crown would produce too much shade. Some shrubs such as willow (*Salix*) are pollarded to encourage colorful young shoots.

❀ Coppicing involves cutting a shrub such as dogwood (*Cornus*) down to ground level, again to encourage colorful young shoots. Eucalyptus trees can be coppiced to provide a constant supply of juvenile foliage and a more shrub-like effect.

LEFT: *These admirably sculpted yew chocolate pots at Great Dixter in the south of England guard the entry into another part of the garden and are echoed by the great battlemented yew hedge beyond.*

✿ Do not choose to have topiary in the garden unless you have time and patience, or a gardener, to care for it well. Every time you clip it, you are removing all the young, strong new shoots and leaves, which weakens the plant. Feeding, watering and weeding are therefore of the utmost importance. Use a slow-acting organic manure, which will improve the structure of the soil as well as provide nutrients.

TOPIARY

TOPIARY is a way of making sculptures from living plants. By training and clipping you can make bold, often imposing structural shapes, including 'walls' and arches. You can also create birds and animals, trains, chess sets or simply cones, ball shapes and spirals, which can create formality or points of interest in even the smallest garden.

Using topiary

✿ There are many types of evergreen shrub that can give shape and solidity to a design, whether formal or informal, or anchor the corner of a bed to a neighboring path or the house itself to its surroundings. Most evergreens have a distinct habit. Some are naturally tall and slender, such as *Cupressus sempervirens* 'Green Pencil', which can add height without taking up too much precious space or light.

✿ Others can be clipped into various shapes. If you want to use topiary next to the house, you could echo some architectural feature of the building with your topiary shape. Topiary goes well with almost any

BELOW: *Pillars of box and juniper provide a variety of textures and add height to this attractively planted border of pink flowers.*

ABOVE: *The topiary evergreens here give a disciplined finish to this marvellous burgeoning border of roses, ferns and the exotic growth of the tree fern,* Dicksonia antarctica.

paving material and in gravel. If growing your topiary in containers, it always looks best in very simple ones. The main interest should be in the shape of the plant, not in the container.

❀ Single plants can make individual points of emphasis in the overall plan; pairs of plants can form or identify a gateway, or you can use rows of clipped plants to line a path or avenue.

❀ Plants clipped into similar or contrasting shapes can be grouped together to make a dramatic show against a plain background such as a stone or brick wall. One garden in the south of England has a complete chess game in clipped yew. The opposing pieces are ranged along either side of a green lawn and from there the eye is taken to a view of the distant countryside.

Simple topiary shapes

❀ Simple geometric shapes are the easiest to create. Box is particularly good for these because new shoots develop from the center of the plant. Yew and shrubby *Lonicera* also respond well. To create a standard topiary shape – a round head on a bare stem – you can train a single leader up a cane then pinch out the top growth regularly until you have created a firm, rounded shape. This is usually quite easy to do by eye. The culinary bay tree (*Laurus nobilis*) turns into a neat little mop-headed shrub, which looks good in a tub.

❀ Trees that naturally grow into a conical shape, such as yew and *Cupressus macrocarpa*, can be shaped easily into geometric cones by making a wigwam of canes and placing it over the plant before cutting, to use as a guide.

❀ To make a spiral shape from an established cone, choose a plant at least 1 m (3 ft) high. Tie a length of string to the top of the plant, wind it in a wide spiral around the bush and secure it to the stem at the base. Following the spiral marked by the string, cut away the outer branches with pruners. Try to keep the tiers even all the way round.

Topiary on hedges

❀ In some gardens you can treat the top of a hedge as topiary. It can be clipped into spheres, cubes, castellations or birds and animals. Simple scalloped shapes can be effective too. Always use string or wire to measure and mark out the pattern before you cut.

❀ Columns and buttresses can be created in large hedges with an interesting architectural effect. You must allow the sides of the hedge to grow out at regularly spaced points and take up to three years to trim it into shape. Round windows in a hedge can act as peepholes into the view beyond. They can be created by training pliable young branches around an iron frame on a rod firmly fixed into the ground.

PRUNING PLANTS

❀

Pruning describes the act of cutting away unwanted growth – unwanted because it is diseased, old, or simply in the way. It is a subject that many gardeners find daunting. Individual plants have individual pruning needs, which means that any book covering pruning necessarily contains a large amount of information. Do not be put off by this. Once you understand the chief principles of pruning, together with the pruning requirements specific to the plants in your own garden, you will be equipped to enhance dramatically the look and health of many plants.

ABOVE: *Renovating a neglected plant by pruning is a simple yet very satisfying task.*

THE USES OF PRUNING

Pruning can maintain a balance between growth and flowering. It can restrict growth, which may be necessary should a plant encroach on a walkway or into a neighbor's garden. It can train plants, encouraging a neat habit and profuse flowering or fruiting. Pruning can also help to maintain healthy plants, with good-quality stems, foliage, fruit and flowers.

❀ Pruning falls loosely into three categories – renovative, regenerative and formative pruning.

RENOVATIVE PRUNING

There are a number of specific conditions that can be treated or prevented by pruning.

Rubbing or crossing shoots

❀ Where shoots repeatedly rub against each other, they will eventually become damaged by friction, forming open wounds that expose the plant to disease spores. Crossing shoots also look untidy and prevent the plant from growing into a pleasing overall shape.

Removing dieback

❀ When young shoots die back towards the main stem, you need to cut them out. Otherwise 'dieback' can continue unabated, affecting healthy tissue, too. To prevent this spread, prune back as far as the healthy part of the stem, cutting just above a bud.

Halting disease

❀ Cut out rot and disease before they spread and affect the rest of the plant. Remove dead shoots, as these not only harbor disease, but also look unattractive. Cut back as far as healthy wood.

Pruning to retain variegation

❀ Pruning is also used to prevent variegated plants from reverting – that is, becoming plain once more. If you see mature green leaves appearing on an otherwise variegated plant, cut them back to the point of origin, as they will tend to grow vigorously and gradually

RENOVATIVE PRUNING

RENOVATIVE pruning is pruning to remove problems such as damaged and diseased parts of a plant. It is always preferable to prune to avoid problems in advance, rather than after they have occurred. Careful pruning can help stop plant troubles before they begin. For example, pruning to keep the plant uncongested, allows plenty of light and air to travel through the plant, keeping it growing well and discouraging pests and diseases.

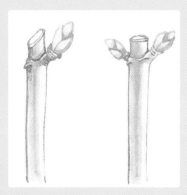

ABOVE: *Two examples of correct pruning; on the single shoot the cut is angled away from the bud; on the double shoot, the distance of the cut from the buds is just right.*

ABOVE: *Example of cutting incorrectly, from left to right: too far away, too close, with blunt pruners, or sloping towards a bud. Bad techniques cause plant problems such as 'dieback', rotting and disease.*

dominate the plant. Some plants develop variegated leaves only as the foliage matures, so check the individual characteristics of your plant and wait until you are certain before pruning.

REGENERATIVE PRUNING

Some plants benefit enormously from hard, yearly pruning. Plants such as dogwoods and willows require this heavy pruning so that they will produce strong, large leaves and healthy, colorful new stems. Other plants, notably shrub roses and fruit, grow much more vigorously and flower more profusely, with better-quality blooms, if pruned annually.

FORMATIVE PRUNING

Formative pruning is literally pruning so as to achieve and maintain a desirable form. It is always preferable to start creating the desired form early on in a plant's life, rather than trying to impose a shape on a plant once it has been allowed to grow unchecked for a long time.

PRUNING TECHNIQUES

ABOVE: *Removing badly crossing shoots encourages good air circulation throughout the plant.*

ABOVE: *Pruning variegated plants is vital to stop them reverting, in which case plain leaves will soon dominate the plant*

ABOVE: *Cut out 'dieback' and damaged stems, which may otherwise cause infection and continue to die back.*

ABOVE: *Remove rotten stems, which could cause disease throughout the plant.*

PRUNING BASICS

CARELESS pruning can do more harm than good. It is critically important that you do not damage the plant when pruning. Use clean, sharp tools, and respect the natural growth pattern of the plant.

❀ For plants with leaves that grow alternately up the stem, cut at an angle, approximately 1/4 in (5 mm) above an outward-facing bud. Make sure that the cut slopes away from the bud so that moisture runs away from it, not towards it, which would encourage rot.

❀ For plants with leaves that grow in pairs, cut straight across, just above a pair of buds.

❀ In both cases, you need to cut quite close to the buds, as stem tissue heals much better close to growth buds. If the cut is too high, the stem will probably die back to the bud, which renders the plant susceptible to disease, and also looks unsightly. Conversely, do not cut right up against the bud, as you could damage the bud itself, or introduce infection.

❀ Always make a clean, sharp cut. A ragged cut or a bruised, torn stem is very prone to disease.

PRUNING TREES

THE individual requirements of a tree must be taken into account before pruning. Some trees will require minimal pruning or may even be harmed by pruning, for example the mulberry tree, while others, like tree of heaven (*Ailanthus*), will relish hard pruning in order to check growth and produce luxuriant foliage.

Evergreen trees

❀ Evergreens are generally pruned in late spring, but always check the individual needs of your particular evergreen before you prune.

❀ With young trees, train the main or leader stem upwards to establish a strong main stem and a good basic form for the tree. Prune out leader shoots that are competing with each other, as well as badly crossing or rubbing stems.

❀ Mature evergreens need little pruning, apart from removing any dead, damaged or diseased branches. Cut back to a healthy shoot or remove the offending branch altogether. Remove crossing lateral shoots and competing leader shoots. Do not be tempted to simply hack away at the top of a conifer that is too tall, as this can leave a very ugly shape. If possible, dig up the tree and start again.

Deciduous trees

❀ Most deciduous trees are pruned when dormant, in late fall or winter. However, as always, check the individual requirements of your tree before pruning, since some trees need to be pruned in spring or summer.

❀ The aim of pruning and training a young tree is to produce an attractive and stable framework. The central stem should be straight, and the branches nicely spaced. It is particularly important to prune trees that bud in pairs, such as ash. If the central stem is allowed to develop into a fork, it may even split. Other trees, if allowed to fork too soon, will not have an attractive overall shape.

❀ To create a vertical stem on an ornamental tree remove competing shoots, as well as weak or crossing laterals. Remove all lateral shoots from the bottom third of the tree in the first spring after planting, and reduce the lateral shoots in the middle section of the tree by about half. In late fall/early winter completely remove the lateral shoots on the middle section that you reduced in the spring. Continue this process over the next two years until you have produced a vertical stem reaching approximately 7 ft (2 m) in height.

Mature deciduous trees

❀ Established deciduous trees should need little pruning, other than to maintain the pleasing shape that has hopefully been created over the years. Remove congested branches from the center of the tree, as these will block light and air flow. Retain the overall shape of the tree by removing any branches that have become too dominant and unsightly.

BELOW: *This elegant, sweeping avenue of trees should now only need pruning to keep the pleasing shape created by expert management over the years.*

PRUNING ORNAMENTAL TREES

There are basic rules for pruning young ornamental trees, but check on the individual requirements of each plant first.

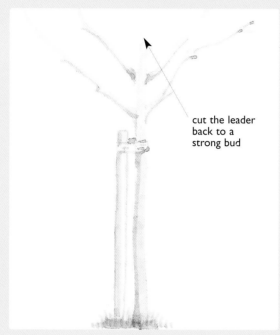

cut the leader
back to a
strong bud

1 *Three years after planting, cut the leader back to a strong lateral or bud, 12 in (30 cm) above the required length of clear stem.*

allow unchecked
growth in
summer of
fourth year

2 *During the summer of the fourth year, allow laterals and sublaterals to develop without pruning.*

prune out
crossing or
crowded laterals
and sublaterals

3 *In the fall of the fourth year, prune out crossing or crowded laterals and sublaterals to leave between three and five evenly spaced laterals.*

remove branches
that spoil the
symmetry of
the tree

4 *In the fifth and subsequent years, remove young branches that spoil the tree's symmetry, as well as shoots that appear on the main stem.*

POLLARDING AND COPPICING

POLLARDING describes the act of pruning a tree back to its main stem, so as to produce new shoots at this point. Coppicing, similarly, involves the regular pruning of a tree close to the ground. Both techniques were traditionally employed to produce accessible and regular supplies of pliable wood for firewood, fence and basket making. Nowadays, coppicing and pollarding are generally done to produce colorful stems, or to restrict the size of a tree.

❀ Both pollarding and coppicing are generally done in late winter or early spring. When the trunk has reached the desired height, cut the branches back to approximately 2 in (5 cm) away from the main stem. This brutal-looking treatment will encourage a mass of new shoots to be produced during the summer. Ideally, repeat the process annually, and feed and mulch the tree after pruning.

HOW TO POLLARD AND COPPICE TREES

Pollarding and coppicing are generally done to provide colorful stems or to restrict the size of a tree. Both methods promote healthy regrowth.

ABOVE:*Pollarding means cutting stems hard back to the trunk to produce vigorous new shoots.*

ABOVE: Coppicing involves *pruning back almost to ground level to encourage basal shoots to develop.*

Cutting large branches

❀ The pruning of very large, mature trees is best dealt with by professional arborists. There may be judicial constraints on cutting certain trees in certain situations, so always check the legal position before planning major work on mature trees.

❀ Smaller trees, or overgrown old shrubs may have thickish branches that you are able to remove yourself safely. Use a pruning saw and cut in three stages, starting with an upward cut, so that the weight of the branch does not cause it to rip away from the plant in a ragged, uncontrolled way.

PRUNING SHRUBS

THE general rules and reasons for pruning trees apply equally to shrubs. Some shrubs require virtually no pruning other than a light 'haircut', but the majority will eventually deteriorate if left unpruned. For most shrubs, pruning encourages strong, healthy growth and vigorous flowering with well-sized, good-quality blooms.

❀ As a rule, flowering shrubs are pruned soon after the last of their flowers have died off. There are notable exceptions, however, such as some late summer-flowering shrubs like buddleja and hydrangea, which would be susceptible to frost damage if pruned at this time. Wait until spring before pruning these. As always, for best results, always check the individual requirements of a shrub before planning pruning.

Hard pruning

❀ Hard pruning on the right sort of shrub can produce really rewarding results. Tall, straggly flowering shrubs are a depressingly common sight in front gardens everywhere – mean, spindly stems topped with a few, small flowers that are so high they are not even at eye level where they can be enjoyed.

❀ Ideally, plan your shrub's pruning needs while the plant is still young, starting your pruning program the first year after planting. It is always preferable to create and maintain a good pruning routine, rather than to attempt to resuscitate a shrub that may have become unhealthy, out of shape and congested as a result of having been left unpruned for many years.

❀ You can try cutting this sort of neglected shrub back to just above ground level, as it may produce basal shoots, but the results are not predictable. Most hard pruning

HOW TO PRUNE SHRUBS

As with trees, it is important to understand the requirements of each indvidual shrub to avoid inflicting heavy damage or not getting the best out of a shrub by pruning too lightly.

ABOVE: *Hard pruning is advisable only for certain shrubs. It stimulates vigorous new growth and encourages a good floral display on appropriate plants.*

ABOVE: *Ungainly shrubs can be persuaded into more pleasing shapes by careful pruning, which provides a better framework of stems.*

ABOVE: *Some shrubs, like this dogwood (Cornus), are pruned hard in spring to produce colorful stems.*

is done in spring, to encourage vigorous growth, but always check the individual requirements of any shrub before pruning, since pruning at the correct time of year is of crucial importance.

❀ Hard pruning seems very drastic, but on shrubs that flower on shoots produced in the current year, it is easy to see how, left unpruned, the stems would simply continue to grow, with the flowers appearing at the very ends only. You will need to cut back all the previous summer's growth to within approximately 2 in (5 cm) of last year's stem. Although the result looks brutal, the plant will generate healthy new shoots at this point.

❀ Cut back to a point just above a bud, outward facing if possible, to give the plant a good overall shape. In general, cut the plant back as far as new growth, but

to regenerate a very bushy old shrub that has become crowded and out of shape, cut a few stems back almost to ground level to improve the overall shape.

Deadheading

❀ Many plants, such as heathers and lavenders, need deadheading as soon as the flowers have died back. Check if each plant needs deadheading before doing so automatically, as there are a few exceptions.

❀ Using shears, trim away the dead blooms to a point just below the flower spike. Take care not to cut into the old wood, as some shrubs do not flower well, or at all, on old wood, and you will be left with unattractive bare brown areas if you cut too enthusiastically.

BELOW: *Pruning shrubs at the right time will help to increase flower production next season.*

PRUNING CLIMBERS

CLIMBERS grow in several different ways. Clinging climbers such as ivy attach themselves to their supports by aerial roots or suckers, and do not require a supplementary support systems like trellis.

❀ Twining climbers, such as honeysuckle and clematis, entwine around a support by means of tendrils, stems or leaf stalks, and benefit from a support. Scrambling plants, for example some types of rose, hang on using hooked thorns. Scrambling, rambling plants will need tying on to a support. A guide to pruning scrambling climbers is given in the section on pruning roses that follows. For pruning twining climbers, see the section on pruning clematis.

Basic principles

❀ Climbers have different pruning needs, depending on their flowering season and the age of the wood on which they flower. As a guide, climbers that flower on the previous season's growth need pruning when flowering has finished. Climbers that flower on the current season's growth are pruned in early spring or at the end of winter, so that they have adequate time to produce new flowering shoots.

❀ Having checked that you are pruning at the right time of year for the plant concerned, there are general rules to follow for all pruning. Use sharp tools and make clean cuts, removing damaged or weak growth.

❀ Cut out branches that are rubbing, or that have become congested. Prune just above a bud or healthy shoot; on climbers that grow in an opposite-facing pattern, cut straight across above a pair of buds. On climbers that grow with an alternating pattern, make a cut that slopes away, just above a bud pointing in the direction that you want the new shoot to develop.

Pruning to control growth

❀ Although clinging climbers are easy to grow and establish, they can overwhelm a structure. Ivy, in particular, can inflict severe structural damage. Roots can penetrate mortar and, as plant stems thicken, guttering can be forced away from the building.

RIGHT: *To retain a well-shaped, wall-trained climber, prune and train diligently from the start.*

ABOVE: *Vigorous climbers, such as honeysuckle, need careful pruning to keep them in check.*

❀ Vigorous climbers like this can creep under and loosen roof tiles and wooden cladding. Once they have taken hold, removal is difficult, so it is important to keep a watchful annual pruning eye on these plants to ensure a balance between attractively cloaking growth and unwelcome invasion. Remove as much growth as you need, at the time of year appropriate to the plant.

Pruning for good coverage

❧ Pruning clinging climbers early in their life also promotes an even growth pattern with a well-spaced framework of new shoots. Although self-clinging climbers do not technically need tying in and supporting, they will grow to cover a surface more evenly if trained laterally while still young and pliable and pruned to encourage budding from side shoots.

❧ In order to do this successfully, you should either tie or peg down the young stems. In the second spring after planting, cut back the plant's side shoots to a point just above a bud near the main stem. As each new stem develops, cut back the tip the next year so that the shoots branch out and create better coverage of the support. Cut back other new shoots to within two buds of the nearest stem.

RENOVATING NEGLECTED CLIMBERS

A NEGLECTED climber is a rather depressing sight. Not only does the plant bulge unattractively from its support, but it may start to pull the support away from the wall or fence altogether.

❧ Neighboring plants may be forced into deep shade, affecting their growth adversely, too. A tangled, congested mass of mostly dead or dying stems can be a daunting prospect. However, tackle it with confidence, since, in most cases, even severely overgrown climbers can be regenerated with appropriate pruning.

❧ Some climbers will grow again even if cut back almost to the base. As with all pruning, check the individual needs of your plant before picking up the pruners. If the plant's ability to withstand drastic pruning is uncertain, tackle renovative pruning over a two-year period.

❧ Gradually, fresh, vigorous growth will replace what you have removed. Be methodical if you are undertaking renovative pruning over a protracted period; otherwise, new shoots will grow and become entwined with the old stems, which will make pruning extremely difficult.

❧ Although the plant will look unbalanced during this time, it is best to cut down one side of the plant only in the first year of renovation. A very neglected plant may take several years to recover from this treatment, so do not be hasty to dismiss the success of your work if the plant does not flower for two years or so, even after both sides have been pruned. Be patient.

prune any crossing or rubbing stems, which can cause plant weakness and disease

woody stems will need lopping, rather than trimming with pruners

remove very tangled, matted growth for a neat, healthy climber

PRUNING ROSES

ROSE stems grow and produce flowers for only a few years before becoming exhausted and starting to develop flowers lower down the stem. Pruning is therefore needed to prevent the plant becoming an ungainly tangled mass of dying and living wood, with inferior blooms.

Rambling roses

❧ Rambling roses have diminished in popularity over the years. They bloom only once a year, albeit with a spectacular show of flowers, but are not generally disease resistant, and do need regular pruning.

❧ Flowers grow on new wood, so you will need to prune each year for a good show of flowers all over the plant. However, rambling roses are a good choice in some areas, where their natural talents can be exploited. Their long, flexible stems will clamber enthusiastically up dead trees that would otherwise be an eyesore, or scramble riotously along the soil to produce unusual ground cover.

Climbing roses

❧ Climbing roses have much less flexible stems than ramblers; many are more disease resistant, and some are repeat-flowering. Since flowers develop on a framework of established wood, pruning climbers is much less demanding than pruning ramblers. Essential pruning is restricted to removing dead, weak or diseased growth.

❧ Deadhead as much as is practical during the summer, and prune in the fall, after flowering. If you also shorten the side shoots that have flowered, taking them back to approximately three buds, you will encourage a good coverage of flowers next year.

Regenerating an old climber

❧ If a climbing rose has been neglected, and lateral growth not encouraged by regular training and tying in, there may be many bare stems visible near ground level. You can encourage new, basal shoots to develop by cutting down some of the old bare stems almost to ground level.

SHRUB AND MINIATURE ROSES

The term 'shrub rose' covers many old varieties of rose, which predate the floribundas and hybrid teas roses so popular today. Shrub roses generally have a much shorter flowering period than their contemporary rivals, and often produce much bigger bushes, so are not as popular as they once were. However, there are notable exceptions to these rules. Some shrub roses are repeat-flowering; some do grow in smaller bush sizes and some, although they do flower only once in a season, flower spectacularly and over such a long period that they are still excellent choices. Shrub roses do not generally have very demanding pruning needs, an attribute shared by miniature roses. Pruning of these roses is generally limited to controlling the size of the bush, as well as removing dead, diseased or weak growth. Miniatures may be pruned with scissors, instead of pruners.

light pruning is not recommended, except for very vigorous hybrid tea roses

hard pruning is recommended for newly planted bush roses, and to renovate neglected plants

roses respond wonderfully to efficient pruning, producing a multitude of flowers

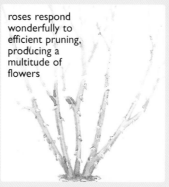

miniature roses only need scissors to cut off spent blooms and diseased or damaged stems

Cutting out suckers

❀ Where plants have been produced by grafting, suckers may develop. These shoots grow from the original rootstock, not the required variety grafted on to it. If left unchecked, these suckers will eventually overwhelm the plant completely, reverting it to the rootstock variety.

❀ It is vital to remove the sucker properly at its source. You will probably need to remove some soil, before pulling off the sucker where it has developed on the rootstock. If you simply snip suckers off at ground level, they will thrive on this pruning and develop even more.

ABOVE: *Most hybrid tea and established floribunda roses require moderate pruning.*

Hybrid tea and floribunda roses

❀ Hybrid tea and floribunda roses are popular garden choices, and have broadly similar pruning needs.

❀ Hybrid teas have been used for around 100 years. Their flowers have what is often seen as a 'classic' rose shape. They are available in an amazing range of colors and are often well fragranced. However, there are drawbacks with some varieties.

❀ Many hybrid tea bushes are quite rigid in shape, producing a slightly stiff appearance that does not suit every garden, and hybrid teas generally bloom less frequently than floribundas. They are also more susceptible to rain damage, and are not tolerant of less-than-perfect conditions; so choose your breed carefully.

❀ Floribundas have been popular for around the last 50 years. Although the individual blooms may not be as choice as their hybrid tea counterparts, floribundas are chosen for their ability to flower continuously for long periods, for their increased disease resistance, their ability to thrive in less-than-ideal conditions, and for their rain tolerance.

❀ Prune these roses in early spring, when growth is just beginning, but to avoid the possibility of damage by wind rock cut back long shoots in fall. Cut stems back to approximately half their length, and remove damaged, weak or diseased stems. For floribundas, hard prune some old stems close to the ground to encourage new basal shoots, while pruning last year's new shoots only moderately. This variable pruning will encourage a good coverage of flowers over the whole plant.

REGENERATING OLD CLIMBERS AND DEALING WITH SUCKERS

Suckers spoil the look and shape of any rose and should be dealt with firmly. Likewise, a neglected rose needs firm attention to encourage healthy and shapely regrowth.

shorten side shoots to just above a bud, facing in the direction that you want the rose to grow

when hard pruning, cut out unwanted stems close to their base for a good overall framework

remove suckers at thir point of origin on the root, not at ground level

PRUNING CLEMATIS

THERE is a great deal of intimidating mystique about how to prune clematis correctly. In fact, there are just three basic methods. The choice of method appropriate for a particular clematis is the most important part of pruning this plant.

❀ Clematises are divided loosely into three groups, based on when they flower. These groups are widely referred to as Groups One, Two and Three type of clematis. When buying a new clematis, you will save yourself a lot of pruning indecision later on if you take the time to find out and note the group that your clematis falls into. Getting the type right is important. If you make a mistake in identifying the type of pruning required, you could unwittingly remove the next flush of flowers.

GROUP ONE: MINIMAL PRUNING NEEDS

THESE vigorous clematises flower in spring or early summer, directly on last season's ripened stems. They typically have quite small flowers. Clematises in this group need to be pruned hard when planted, but subsequently need only minimal pruning. If the plant becomes tangled, untidy and congested, you can prune it after flowering to control it.

❀ Popular Group One cultivars include *Clematis montana, C. macropetala, C. alpina* and *C. armandii*.

ABOVE: *Group One clematises, such as C. Montana, are very lightly pruned after flowering.*

GROUP TWO: LIGHT PRUNING NEEDS

THESE clematises produce large flowers early in summer or in midsummer. Some varieties continue flowering through into fall. Group Two clematises flower on short stems produced in the current season, which grow on last season's ripe wood, and need only a light pruning in spring, before the plant starts active growth. Both Group One and Two clematises are sometimes referred to as 'old-wood' flowering clematis.

❀ Given their attributes of large flowers and an often prolonged flowering season, it is no wonder that Group Two contains many of the most popular hybrid clematis cultivars such as 'Nelly Moser', 'The President', 'Mrs Cholmondely' and 'Lasurstern'.

ABOVE: *Lightly prune Group Two varieties, such as 'Nelly Moser', in early spring.*

GROUP THREE: HARD PRUNING NEEDS

GROUP Three clematises flower late in the season – from mid- to late summer, and possibly through to fall – producing blooms on the current year's stems. In early spring, before the plant starts active growth, cut back all last season's growth to just above the lowest pair of healthy buds, approximately 12 in (30 cm) above soil level. Tie in the new stems as they grow in late spring and summer. Take great care when training, as the stems are extremely brittle and prone to breakage.

❀ Group Three clematises include 'Ernest Markham', 'Jackmanii', 'Ville de Lyon', 'Perle d'Azur' and 'Gipsy Queen'.

RIGHT: *C. 'Jackmanii' and other Group Three clematises need hard pruning in early spring.*

CLEMATIS GROUPS

GROUP 1

ABOVE: *Prune Group 1 clematis if needed after flowering, removing a minimal amount of foliage.*

GROUP 2

ABOVE: *Prune Group 2 clematis only if the plant needs neatening up straight after flowering.*

GROUP 3

ABOVE: *Prune Group 3 clematis in late winter or early spring, taking them back to the lowest healthy shoot.*

Pruning and training clematis and other climbers on an arch or pergola

❀ Any climber looks best on a pergola or arch if it has been encouraged to produce a good, even coverage, with flowers over the whole plant, not just a few at the top, out of range of eye level. The key to producing a good climbing display is to train horizontally while the stems are flexible, and to prune main stems to encourage side shoots to develop.

❀ Always take care to tie in shoots gently, leaving room for movement and growth. Prune at the time of year appropriate for the type of clematis grown, removing diseased, damaged or dead wood. When the main shoots have climbed to the top of the support, prune them – again at the appropriate time of year – so that they do not become congested, untidy and susceptible to windrock.

BELOW: *Climbing flowering plants need careful pruning in order to keep the whole plant in bloom.*

PRUNING HEDGES

THE type of pruning a particular hedge requires depends on two things – the type of overall effect you are trying to create and the individual requirements of the plant.

❀ A dense, formal hedge like privet will need regular pruning if it is to maintain its neat good looks, whereas an informal flowering or fruiting hedge such as snowberry will need much less attention in order to achieve a desirable look.

Shaping a hedge

❀ A common mistake in trimming hedges is to produce a straight-sided form, or one that tapers towards the bottom. This will eventually yield the type of hedge that is an all-too-common sight in front gardens everywhere – the hedge that is leafy at the top and bare, twiggy and brown at the base. The reason is simple. The foliage at the base of the hedge has died due to a lack of light from being in the shade of the upper leaves and stems. Happily, there is a simple technique for preventing this.

❀ Always trim a formal hedge into a slightly pyramidal shape – so that it is approximately one-third narrower at the top than at its base – so as to allow plenty of light to reach all parts of the plant. This sloping angle also encourages greater wind resistance and helps the plant shed snow. In areas of high snowfall it may be advisable to make a more exaggerated A-shaped sloping cut at the top of the hedge, to further discourage snow from settling and ice forming on the plant.

❀ When the hedge has grown to the desired height, make yourself a cutting template from plywood to give you a clear, easy-to-follow guide to the shape and height required.

❀ When you start work from the base of the hedge, make sure that you work upwards so that clippings are discarded from the path of progress. A power trimmer makes light work of what can otherwise be an arduous task if you are dealing with hedges on a large scale. Always use the correct safety precautions and equipment, including gloves, goggles and, if using an electric trimmer, a residual current device (RCD).

Informal hedges

❀ Informal hedges are much less demanding than their neatly clipped formal counterparts. They generally need pruning only once a year, and maintaining a precise finished shape is not necessary for their visual success. These hedges are generally pruned in order to control their size and spread, to cut out any disease or decay, and to encourage new shoots to appear.

❀ Pruning is usually done after the plants have flowered, but do check the needs of individual species before pruning. For example, berrying hedges are generally left unpruned until the berries have finished fruiting, or the birds have eaten them. As a rule, simply cut out any congested or weak areas, shorten old shoots and cut back some shoots almost to the ground in order to encourage basal shoots.

FORMAL HEDGES

Formal hedges – ones that are clipped into precise shapes – need regular trimming to maintain a good appearance. A neglected formal hedge is a very depressing sight. Just as unkempt hair on an otherwise well-dressed person gives a generally scruffy impression, an untidy formal hedge transmits an air of neglect throughout the whole garden. The aim of pruning a formal hedge is to produce a dense mass of compact shoots that will form a bushy hedge, which grows evenly within its desired shape. Clipping side shoots will remove the growing tip of each shoot to promote this bushy growth. Many formal hedges can be trimmed when they look untidy – between spring and fall – but always check the individual pruning needs of any hedge before picking up the trimmer. Fast-growing hedges may need several cuts a year; slower growing types will look perfectly respectable with just one or two trims during that time.

a pointed top helps shrug off heavy snowfall in especially vulnerable sites

shape hedges to be narrower at the top than at the base in order to produce even leaf coverage

HEDGE-PRUNING METHODS

Decide which tools to use for cutting a hedge according to the area that needs trimming.

1 *Pruners will suffice for lightly trimming the occasional shoot.*

2 *Sharp shears are adequate when quite small areas of hedge need trimming.*

3 *Power tools make light work of hedge trimming. Always use the appropriate safety equipment when using power tools in the garden.*

RENOVATING A NEGLECTED HEDGE

It is tempting to ruthlessly prune a very unsightly, neglected hedge, but severe cutting can over stress the plant and recovery will be slow. Initially, working at the time of year appropriate to the plant, trim only one side hard to encourage new growth from the center of the hedge. You may repeat this drastic pruning in the following year on the other side of the hedge, and only lightly trimming the new growth on the other side.

the following year, trim new growth on the opposite side

in year one, trim one side of the plant hard

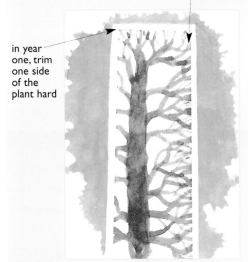

MAKING A HEIGHT GUIDE

A string line gives an accurate cutting guide for trimming a formal hedge. Fix a taut, brightly colored line at the required finished height of the hedge as an easy-to-see guide for level.

colored string line for easy viewing

desired height of hedge

poles holding sting line

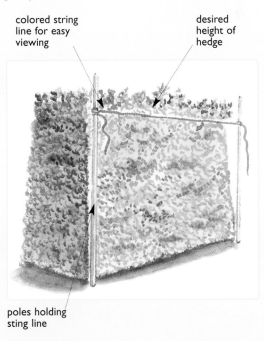

TOPIARY

TOPIARY is pruning elevated to an art form. Plants have been trained and cut into artificial shapes for decorative effect since Roman times. Topiary has a place in many gardens, not only the grand, formal settings with which it is normally associated.

❀ Topiary can visually anchor a more informal setting and provide valuable, year-long structure and color in a garden. Even the smallest garden, perhaps little more than a flight of steps leading to a doorway, can look more imposing when embellished with a neat pair of clipped, container-grown plants.

TOPIARY SHAPES

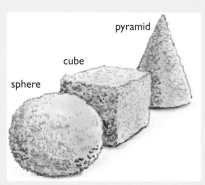

NOVICE topiarists are advised to start with a simple, geometric shape. Rigidly geometric shapes, such as cubes, are less forgiving of inaccurate cutting than slightly softer forms, like pyramids and spheres. More figurative shapes, such as teddy bears and peacocks, are not necessarily difficult to produce, particularly if you form them using a ready-made rigid frame as a guide. However, they can take many years to reach a size at which they can attain a recognisable shape, because the plants are generally slow growing, and are therefore not for the impatient topiarist.

Initially, young plants are snipped to shape by eye to form a loosely geometric shape. As the plant grows in subsequent years to a sufficient size, place a cutting guide over the plant and trim to shape. Canes, held together with wire at the top, make a simple and inexpensive pyramid 'template'. When the plant has reached the required shape and size, simply clip it lightly at intervals appropriate for the topiary shape and type of plant used, to maintain a crisp, outline and dense growth pattern.

❀ Low box hedging has long been used to contain herb gardens, which can, by the very nature of the plants, be quite unruly. Not only does the clipped hedging define and neaten the overall appearance of the area, but it also helps to protect the plants within its borders from the elements, and contains and intensifies the fragrance of the herbs in the local environment.

❀ Topiary can consist of very simple geometric shapes, such as spheres and cubes, or it can be extremely fanciful, such as chess pieces or a whole menagerie of animals. It can be used to add interest to a long run of hedging, or as stand-alone pieces of living sculpture. Slow-growing plants are generally chosen for topiary – species that can withstand regular clipping, but do not grow so rapidly that they lose their outline overnight.

The technique

❀ Topiary is not a low-maintenance form of pruning, although many of the plants used for topiary are chosen for their resilience and dense growth patterns. With just a little attention to some basic guidelines, successful topiary is not difficult to achieve. The results are impressive and extremely satisfying to produce.

❀ Always use very sharp, clean tools for topiary, as the soft shoots you are cutting are sappy and will be vulnerable to disease if torn. It is also very difficult to make decisive, accurate cuts on this flexible growth with blunt tools.

❀ Sheep-trimming shears are excellent for producing a light, accurate cut, but are not suitable for heavy work. Cutting little and often is the key to successful topiary. Dramatic, inexpert cutting can create an unbalanced shape, which will take at least a season to settle, and it is all too easy to cut inaccurately when making severe cuts. Cut large-leaved evergreens, such as laurel, with secateurs to prevent the unsightly halving of leaves, which can occur if clipping with shears.

Frequency of cut

❀ How frequently to clip topiary depends on the speed at which the plant grows, the intricacy of the topiary shape and the degree of finish required. Simple shapes in slow-growing plants will need relatively little clipping. For example, a yew pyramid will need only an annual trim, whereas a complex abstract geometric shape in box may need cutting at four- to six-weekly intervals during the growing season, in order to maintain its definition.

SIMPLE TOPIARY FRAMES

There is no need to buy purpose-built frames to produce topiary shapes.

1 *Canes secured together at the top to form a pyramid make an inexpensive and effective guide.*

2 *Trim back excess growth until the plant is level with the guides.*

3 *Wire spheres look attractive even partially covered with foliage. Tie in shoots to encourage even coverage of the shape.*

✿ As always when pruning, check the individual needs of a particular plant before planning clipping. Clipping times will also depend on your local climate. In cooler climates, do not clip after early fall as the young shoots produced will not be tolerant of low winter temperatures. Milder environments, in which the plants grow almost continuously, may necessitate regular clipping throughout the year. Most topiary plants should be clipped as thier summer growth begins, however, the exceptions to this are hornbeam and beech, which should not be clipped until the late summer.

SHAPING A HEDGE CORRECTLY

EFFECTIVE topiary needs even leaf coverage, which is hard to achieve on shapes that have a lot of leaf shade shielding the lower parts of the plant. Do not allow hedges to become top heavy, flat-topped or tapering towards the bottom, with a twiggy base. Slope the hedge from a narrow top to a wide base for greatest ease of pruning, healthy growth and an attractive appearance.

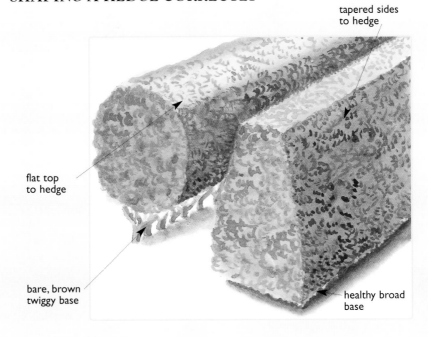

tapered sides to hedge

flat top to hedge

bare, brown twiggy base

healthy broad base

Acacia

Laurel

Bottle brush

PRUNING ORNAMENTAL PLANTS

GIVEN below are the pruning requirements of some popular plants, with advice on timing and the best method to employ to make the most of the plants.

Mimosa (*Acacia*)

❀ No regular pruning is required for mimosa except cutting back the dead wood after a severe winter. If you need to restrict the height of the shrub cut it right back to a third of its size following flowering.

Laurel (*Aucuba japonica*)

❀ No regular pruning is needed for laurel unless it grows beyond its allotted space, in which case it can be cut back in spring.

Bottle brush (*Callistemon*)

❀ No regular pruning is needed but it is sensible to thin out the old branches and shoots at the base of the plant from time to time.

Scotch heather, ling (*Calluna*)

❀ Heather quickly becomes straggly and untidy if left unpruned for any length of time. Luckily, it is easy to prune, merely requiring a quick clip over with shears in the early months of spring. Do not cut right back into the old wood, as bare patches will appear.

Camellia

❀ No hard pruning is required for camellias; any straggly shoots can be taken off following flowering in mid-spring. Deadheading on varieties with masses of blooms will increase growth for the following year.

Scotch heather

Camellia

Convolvulus

Dogwood

Convolvulvus

✿ To create a bushy appearance, remove about two thirds of this shrub annually in late summer. This will encourage new growth of the pretty silvery leaves and flowers the following year.

Dogwood (*Cornus*)

✿ Dogwoods grown for their colored stems need pruning regularly to promote new growth. For winter color, the stems should be cut right back to the basal level in late spring.

Daphne

Daphne

✿ No routine pruning is required for any of the many species of *Daphne*, but cut the straggly shoots out in early spring to keep a pleasing and neat appearance.

Bell heather (*Erica*)

✿ Clip off dead flowerheads to encourage new growth aand prune during the spring months when new growth is about to start.

Bell heather

Fuchsia magellanica

✿ The hardy fuchsia dies back in the winter as the top growth is killed by frost and low temperatures. Cut it right back almost to ground level in the spring and a profusion of new shoots will soon appear.

Fuchsia

Hebe

Helianthemum

Laburnum

Lace-cap hydrangea

Shrubby veronica (*Hebe*)

❀ Some varieties of these plants are not very hardy and will need attention after the winter. Do not prune the plant until spring, even if the leaves are brown and the stems bare, as they offer some small protection against the elements. Cut the damaged shoots off when the new growth begins to appear and cut back for shape if needed after about a month.

Rock rose, sun rose (*Helianthemum*)

❀ Cut two-thirds of the new shoots in the summer months to encourage new growth the following year.

Tree hollyhock, Tree mallow (*Hibiscus*)

❀ Very little general maintenance is required for this hardy species. Remove old branches to restrict size and prune back any frost-damaged shoots in early spring.

Lace-cap hydrangea (*Hydrangea macrophylla*)

❀ Leave the dead brown heads on many varieties of hydrangea during the winter months to protect flower buds from damage. Instead, remove the dead heads in spring, when the weather is warmer and the first green shoots appear. Remove straggly shoots at the same time.

Laburnum

❀ As these plants grow so abundantly, train them into shape when they are young. If necessary, remove crossing or over-large branches in the later summer, but in general it is preferable not to prune them, as the wounds tend to bleed excessively.

Lavender

Peony

Lupins

Lavender (*Lavundula*)

❀ Prune lavender to promote a neat appearance, since it can quickly become straggly and untidy. Cut right back to the new shoots in early spring as soon as the new shoots begin to appear. Keep lavender beds tidy by pruning them lightly with shears after flowering. Take cuttings for propagation in the summer.

Cistaceae

Lupins (*Lupinus*)

❀ Lupins are short-term, fast-growing perennials that should be deadheaded after flowering to prevent reseeding. For bushy growth, cut one stem in three.

Oleander (*Nerium*)

❀ Oleander is not a hardy plant and should be placed in a greenhouse in winter. Remove half of the year's new growth after the plant has flowered in early summer. As Oleander is poisonous, always wear protective gloves when pruning.

Oleander

Peony (*Paeonia*)

❀ Remove all dead wood in mid-summer and cut off dead pieces of stem once the fruit-bearing shoots have died back.

Rhododendron

❀ This spring-flowering shrub requires no regular pruning until it is fully grown, which takes around 10–15 years. At this point, cut one stem in every three in the summer to promote healthy growth and an attractive shape. Deadhead the flowers anually.

Rhododendron

CARING FOR BORDERS

A well-stocked, colorful border is one of the chief pleasures of a garden. Think about border color only when the rest of the garden has been planned and given its basic spaces and framework. Perennials, annuals and biennials are the plants that bloom in spring and summer, then fade and die down during the winter months; these provide most of the color for borders. There are innumerable varieties, and flowers in thousands of color combinations. Some will last in the garden for years; others will flower and bloom in the same year and then die. Between them, they can provide color from late spring until well into fall.

PERENNIALS

PERENNIALS are non-woody plants, which live for at least two years and sometimes many more. Most of them are herbaceous, dying back in fall to ground level. From roots thus safely protected from frost, they send up new growth in spring. There are varieties of most perennials suitable for almost any garden, and they can provide riotous color or more subtle shades for a long season.

BELOW: Many border plants can be grown near the sea, provided they have protection from salt-laden winds. Here, poppies, pinks, santolina and other low-growing perennials are thriving behind an evergreen hedge.

✿ A few herbaceous plants are evergreen and provide valuable ground cover and color during winter. These include the hellebores, including the Christmas rose (*Helleborus niger*). In some places this does, in fact, flower at Christmas, but in many areas and in heavy soils the flowers will not appear until spring.

Choosing perennials

✿ Perennials can range in height from the creeping bugle (*Ajuga reptans*) and dead-nettle (*Lamium*), which grow well at the edges of borders, especially if allowed to flow over on to brick or stone paths, to the regal delphiniums, which can reach 7 ft (2 m).

LEFT: *With its deep black centers and orange-yellow petals, Rudbeckia 'Marmalade' – grown here in a large trough – provides enough interest growing on its own.*

whereas *Iris sibirica*, which has more grass-like leaves, will begin to look untidy after flowering.

❀ Some perennials flower in later summer or fall, bringing a welcome revival to the border after the difficult, dry summer period. The hardy chrysanthemums (*Dendranthema*) can bring a sprightly feeling to the fall garden. *Dendranthema* Korean hybrids have pretty little flowers in shades of purple or rust and will flower from midsummer right up until the first frosts; *D. rubellum* hybrids such as 'Duchess of Edinburgh', a single bright red variety with a large yellow center, are excellent.

BELOW: *Campanulas, Thalictrum, veronica and day lilies (Hemerocallis) grown in swathes rather than clumps, make up a varied, interesting and long-lasting summer border*

❀ Low-growing perennials can be grown in containers but tall, statuesque plants will thrive better on their own, presiding at the back of a border over the lowlier inhabitants. Many of the taller plants need staking or they may lean untidily over the smaller plants in order to reach the sun. This will hide the smaller plants from view and also stunt their growth. Staking should be done early in the season when the plants have begun to sprout. Trying to tie them in later creates an untidy look and you will find their flowers facing the wrong way.

❀ Because there are so many beautiful perennials beckoning to you from garden centers and nurseries, it is tempting to 'buy and try'. But, as with all plants, check that the ones you choose are appropriate for your growing conditions – the soil, the aspect and the microclimate should all be favorable, otherwise they will probably die and will certainly become poorly.

❀ When choosing perennials remember that, in general, the foliage lasts much longer than the flowers. For example, peonies will give a really breathtaking display of flowers for perhaps three weeks in spring, but their foliage is so handsome that they still add 'body' and good looks to the border after the flowers have faded.

❀ The splendid early summer-flowering bearded irises have strong strap-like leaves and give definition to a border, especially among more rounded plants,

DESIGNING BORDERS

HERBACEOUS borders can be designed to emphasise the particular style you have chosen for your garden. In a formal garden, straight, geometric borders look appropriately well ordered and are best ranged in opposite pairs along a pathway, for symmetry. They should have a restricted color scheme because in a formal garden the pattern of the garden as a whole is more important than color. In an informal garden irregular, curved borders and freer, more adventurous planting is more in keeping.

❀ Always be generous with paths. If two borders are divided by a path, make sure the path is in proportion to the width of the beds and allows room for flowers to spill over on to it.

HERBACEOUS AND MIXED BORDERS

A TRUE herbaceous border is one that has only perennials in it – no shrubs, bulbs or other types of plant. This kind of border is very labor intensive and plants that are over before others are ready to flower leave unsightly gaps, so true herbaceous borders are seldom planted these days.

ABOVE: *This carefully designed border demonstrates the restricted color scheme necessary in a formal garden. The border is made up of* Lupinus texensis *'Texas Blue Bonnet' in brilliant pinks and purples.*

❀ A mixed border uses many herbaceous plants, but in association with shrubs, bedding plants, bulbs and perhaps even vegetables. In small gardens, where space is limited and precious, a mixed border is certainly the most satisfactory. During the growing season gaps are filled by shrubs with ornamental foliage and when the herbaceous plants die down in fall and winter, evergreens and bulbs will still provide color and interest.

❀ Formality asks for large, distinct groups of one type of plant. Indeed, more plants of the same variety generally look better, especially in small gardens, rather than one plant each of many varieties. Informal borders can be arranged in drifts rather than clumps so that groups of plants dovetail into one another.

❀ A completely unplanned medley of herbaceous plants will produce a traditional cottage garden effect of color and variety, whereas a mixed border provides more structure and a sense of order. Every gardener is part plants person, part designer and the two will always be at odds, so it is usually necessary to come to some sort of compromise between too many plants and too austere a look.

Invaluable perennials for the border

❀ Plants characteristic of the traditional herbaceous border are the tall, white shasta daisies (*Chrysanthemum* x *superbum*), the pale mauve scabious with its pincushion flowers and the wonderfully fragrant, heavy-headed, sugared almond-colored varieties of *Phlox paniculata*.

❀ All associate well with other flowers and have a good long season. Day lilies (*Hemerocallis*) and agapanthus have strap-like leaves, which contrast well with feathery or less well-defined plants.

Useful associations for the mixed border

❀ Yarrow (*Achillea*) has feathery leaves and flat heads of tiny daisy flowers. *Achillea filipendulina* 'Gold Plate' is a tall favourite with spectacular bright yellow flowers most suitable for large gardens. A. 'Moonshine' has gentler yellow flowers and a hummock of silvery-green leaves, retained throughout the winter. The genus associates well with many other herbaceous perennials including varieties of geranium such as G. 'Buxton's Blue', which will behave like a climber and

peep out from among the achillea leaves. *Astilbe* x *arendsii* has ferny foliage with spires of tiny feathery flowers lasting throughout summer. A. 'Fanal' is a very dark red and contrasts well with the spiky leaves of day lilies (*Hemerocallis*).

❀ *Astrantia major* is an invaluable plant for shady borders. Its tall stems rise above coarsely dissected leaves, and the flowers are rosettes of tiny papery petals with a long flowering season. It associates extremely well with *Geranium psilostemon*, which grows to a similar height, has similar leaves and uses the astrantia for support. Its brilliant purple flowers with stylish black centers are startling among the ghostly mass of astrantia blooms.

❀ Lady's mantle (*Alchemilla mollis*) is a beautiful low-growing plant with downy green leaves and clouds of tiny green-yellow flowers throughout summer. This good-tempered little gem will harmonise with many other plants and grow in sun or shade. Try it as an edging plant all along a path or growing under rose bushes. It will seed itself freely and may know, better than you do, where it will look most at home.

BELOW: *Although this border is wonderfully bright, the colors have been limited to reds and yellows so that it is not too confusing to the eye. The nasturtiums at the front of the border are backed by the bright red stems of Swiss ruby chard.*

ANNUALS AND BIENNIALS

THESE are short-lived but valuable plants in the garden, often known as 'bedding plants' because they are used in beds for one season and then discarded.

❀ An annual is a plant whose entire life cycle, from germination to seed production and death, takes place within one year. Those that are able to withstand frost are known as hardy annuals. Those that are not frost hardy are known as half-hardy annuals. These have to be raised under glass and are planted out only after all risk of frost is over. Many of the most popular plants we use as annuals come originally from the tropics.

ABOVE: *A beautiful and confidently planted border, in which the colors have been carefully combined to provide a simple yet elegant feel; the garden bench offers a pleasant place to sit and admire the view.*

❀ Hardy annuals include forget-me-nots (*Myosotis sylvatica*), pot marigolds (*Calendula officinalis*), cornflowers (*Centaurea cyanus*), candytuft (*Iberis umbellata*), the very useful wallflowers (*Cheiranthus*), which provide cheerful color and scent in spring, sweet peas (*Lathyrus odoratus*) and the majestic sunflower (*Helianthus annuus*).

❀ Half-hardy annuals include *Begonia semperflorens*, a perennial from Brazil grown as an annual, with clusters of flowers during the summer, petunias, lobelias, *Convolvulus tricolor* and *Cosmos bipinnatus* in a range of colors from blue-purple to crimson, single flowers and feathery foliage. *Dianthus chinensis* is a popular annual pink with some beautiful colored forms, and *Dimorphotheca sinuata* has lots of daisy flowers with dark brown centers and a variety of petal colors, mainly in the orange and salmon pink range.

❀ A biennial plant takes two years to complete its life cycle. During the first season after sowing, it produces leaves. It then overwinters and the following year produces flowers. Examples of biennials useful in the garden are foxgloves (*Digitalis*) and hollyhocks (*Alcea*), which are in fact perennials but treated as biennials.

LEFT: *Hollyhocks, shown here growing attractively against a cottage wall, are actually perennials, but are treated as biennials.*

Characteristics of bedding plants

✿ Most bedding plants have rather feathery, soft foliage and are neat and low growing rather than imposing. Some hardy annuals will seed themselves over the garden and can be allowed to remain, only being removed where they will smother other plants or where they are not wanted.

✿ Forget-me-nots can resemble a blue mist over the whole flowerbed in spring, but should be removed if they start getting the better of some other plant.

How to use bedding plants

✿ A complete border may be devoted to annuals and biennials and it may be a useful way to treat a new garden not yet planted, as they quickly produce a lively show of color. In an established border they are invaluable for filling spaces left by early-flowering plants.

✿ They make pretty 'edging' plants and add extra color to containers on a patio. Plants with many small flowers, such as diascia, lobelia and verbena, form low mounds or carpets and grow well under tall flowering plants such as shrubby salvias or fuchsias.

✿ Many provide a contrast of color or foliage or a link between different perennials. Silver-leaved bedding plants such as *Senecio cineraria* look very pretty planted under roses or provide a link between blue and pink geraniums or the brighter colors of *Rudbeckias* and the

ABOVE: *A striking border of warm yellow and reds is created using* Rudbeckia, *tobacco plants (*Nicotiana*),* Tagetes *and* Dendranthemums.

smaller asters. *Echeveria elegans* is another useful silver-leaved plant to use in this way.

✿ Many bedding plants are true annuals and die down at the end of the season. Others are perennials but are treated as annuals because they produce the best displays in just one year, or else they are not frost hardy.

✿ Pansies are hardy perennials but are treated as annuals or biennials. They are well loved as cottage garden flowers and can give a brave display of color in winter and spring when the rest of the garden is looking a bit bleak. They are usually more effective if just one or two colors are used together rather than if all the colors are jumbled into one bed.

Bedding in containers

✿ Half-hardy and hardy annuals are ideal as container plants. Many have a drooping habit just right for hanging baskets. Some pelargoniums are good for this.

✿ Always plant generously, getting as many plants in as possible. The rootballs of the plants can touch, provided the container is deep enough to allow a little compost beneath them. The silver-grey foliage of *Helichrysum petiolare* acts as a good background and contrast to almost any container display, as do small evergreens such as ivies.

USING BULBOUS PLANTS

🌹

Bulbs, corms, tubers and rhizomes are perennial plants in which part of the plant has evolved into a below-ground storage unit where food created one year is used to nourish the plant in the next. They are valuable in the garden for many reasons. Spring bulbs appear early, before most perennials have properly started to grow again after the winter. They can also add color to containers when other plants are not ready to face the danger of frost. In summer, bulbous plants such as alliums and lilies can provide stately interest, while autumn crocuses and tiny hardy cyclamen can cheer up the garden towards the end of the season.

WHAT IS A BULBOUS PLANT?

A TRUE bulb is formed from fleshy leaves or leaf bases, and often consists of concentric rings of scales attached to a basal plate. The outer scales form a dry, protective skin. True bulbs include the daffodils, reticulata irises and tulips. If provided with enough nutrients, they will often flower for many years.

✽ A corm is formed from the swollen base of a stem and is replaced by a new corm every year. They are common in crocuses and gladioli and usually have a protective skin formed from the previous year's leaf bases.

✽ A tuber is a swollen stem or root used for food storage. *Corydalis* and some terrestrial orchids such as *Dactylorrhiza* and cyclamen species are tubers.

✽ A rhizome is a swollen stem, usually lying horizontally almost above ground, and is found in the bearded irises and in some lilies. In general, all these bulbous storage larders are referred to as bulbs.

Spring bulbs

✽ There are bulbs for all seasons of the year but their glory is in spring when they epitomise the regrowth of a world that has seemed dead all winter. Among the first are the snowdrops (*Galanthus*) with snowy-white flowers and trim clumps of leaves.

✽ Daffodils, with their sunny yellows and oranges, can flower over a long period if the varieties are carefully chosen; the bold blue, pink or white heads and heavy scent of hyacinths are another spring delight, and the heavenly blue of swathes of scillas and *Anemone blanda* look good in flowerbeds or woodland settings.

RIGHT: A striking annual border curving around a lawn uses reds and purples to give a warm low edging to a stone wall. Plants include Impatiens, *petunias, Swiss chard and salvia.*

Bulbs are particularly useful under deciduous shrubs and trees, where they make use of the light available when the trees are bare and then die down when the trees begin to come into leaf. The bulbs then die down themselves and begin the process of storing and preserving nutrients for the following year.

Summer and fall bulbs

In summer bulbs can provide color and texture in a mixed border without taking up too much space. An advantage of growing them in a border is that when the leaves die down other perennials will conceal them as they bulk out their leaves.

Bulbs such as the allium family can provide interest with their often completely round heads of tiny flowers, while lilies and gladioli can add height and stateliness.

In fall there are the hardy cyclamen species with their heart-shaped, attractively marked leaves and exquisite, swept-back pink or white flowers.

In late winter or early spring, the aconites appear, with cupped yellow flowers framed by a green ruff. They like woodland glades and can multiply well if they like their position but are often difficult to get started.

ABOVE: *This charming little blue* Iris sibirica *'Swank' likes a damp position and will associate well with ferns and other moisture-loving plants. These sit under the shade of the large leaves of a* Lysichiton.

Spring bulbs can be lifted and stored after flowering if they threaten to get in the way of other plants. Many bulbs will spread and increase naturally over the years in many parts of the garden. Crocuses, daffodils, snowdrops and spring-flowering anemones such as *A. blanda* usually increase rapidly.

BELOW: *This delightful grouping of spring bulbs combines pale and darker yellow varieties of narcissi, tulips and fritillaries with a carpeting of bluebells.*

NATURALISING BULBS

BULBS can be allowed to grow under specimen trees, in grass and in woodland. When left undisturbed, many will increase to form natural-looking drifts, lending interest to many parts of the garden.

Bulbs in grass

❀ Many spring bulbs look marvellous scattered in broad sweeps in a lawn. However, since the leaves should not be cut until at least six weeks after the flowers have died, it is best to plant them in a part of the lawn that can be left unmown for that period – perhaps under a small specimen tree.

ABOVE: *The very early flowering* Crocus tomasinianus *has naturalised here to create carpets of freshest violet in otherwise bare woodland. Shafts of sunlight through the tree branches light up the color magically.*

❀ Species bulbs are more delicate in color and form than most cultivars, and should be planted where they will not be dominated by other plants. Tiny little species crocuses such as *Crocus tomasinianus* always cause surprise by appearing overnight in early spring. Their pale lilac or white flowers show up well in short grass and soon increase to create a star-spangled patch of carpet.

❀ Some bulbs like moisture. The snake's head fritillary (*Fritillaria meleagris*) grows well in moist grass bordering a stream and, unlike some others of its family, will tolerate fairly heavy soils.

Woodland bulbs

❀ In light woodland, bulbs can be naturalised in informal groups. Many bulbs enjoy woodland conditions and blend well with other woodland plants such as ferns. Snowdrops, scillas, the wood anemone (*Anemone sylvestris*) and lily-of-the-valley (*Convallaria majalis*) can all spread and colonise beautifully.

LEFT: *Snowdrops are the most welcome of winter flowers. These* Galanthus elwesii *have larger leaves and they flower earlier than the common snowdrop.*

❧ The English bluebell (*Hyacinthoides non-scripta*), one of the most beautiful of woodland plants with blue carpet of flowers, is best planted on its own in woodland because it will invade and overcome other plants. The Spanish bluebell (*Hyacinthoides hispanica*) is less invasive in woodland, although not so elegant, but can be invasive in small gardens.

Bulbs under specimen trees

❧ Bulbs and deciduous trees or large deciduous shrubs can make good partners, if the trees have deep roots and a light canopy. Apple trees, magnolias, ornamental cherries and small weeping trees such as the weeping pear (*Pyrus salicifolia* 'Pendula') all look good with bulbs scattered under them in spring.

❧ Yellow shines out well from beneath a tree and the bright yellow 'Cloth of Gold' crocus is a good spring flower for underplanting. In general it is best to keep the yellows separate from the blue and purple shades of crocus. Fall-flowering bulbs such as the sharp pink *Cyclamen coum* or soft pink autumn crocus (*Colchicum autumnale*) will flower when the tree is losing its leaves.

❧ If you have newly planted a small tree, use only dwarf cultivars under it for the first few years, such as species crocuses or species tulips. Rapidly increasing and large bulbs such as daffodils will reduce the available nutrients for the tree.

Bulbs in the alpine garden

❧ Many of the smaller bulbs like very well-drained soil and will thrive in a rock garden in sun or partial shade. Dwarf bulbs look attractive when planted in small gaps in the rock. They also look good in gravel or grit used as top dressing on a bed of alpines.

❧ The grit acts as a mulch and stops flowers from being deluged by mud in wet weather. *Fritillaria acmopetala*, *Narcissus bulbocodium* (the hooped-petticoat daffodil), *Muscari macrocarpus* (a tiny grape hyacinth) and *Crocus* 'Cream Beauty' are all delightful. The upright habit and spear-like leaves of bulbs contrast well with the low, mat-forming habit of many alpine plants.

Bulbs for a water garden

❧ Few bulbs flourish in damp, poorly drained soils but those that do can be well worth growing. Their strong shapes have a striking effect reflected in the water. The stately arum lily (*Zantedeschia aethiopica*) has large white flowers above arrow-shaped leaves and grows well in pond margins.

❧ Two plants that like moist but well-drained soil are the splendid purple *Iris kaempferi* and the arched sprays of *Dierama pendulum*. On a smaller scale, there is the delicate summer snowflake (*Leucojum aestivum*).

Bulbs in containers

❧ Bulbs can also be grown in ornamental pots, troughs and window boxes. Tufa troughs look good planted with dwarf bulbs and alpines. Grow the smaller fritillary species for their curious flowers. Larger bulbs, such as *Lilium regale*, can be grown in imposing containers outside a front door or on a patio where their strong fragrance can be enjoyed.

LEFT: *The elegant drooping head of the snake's head fritillary (*Fritillaria meleagris*) will brighten up any moisture-retaining position. These are among the few bulbs that do not seem to mind a heavy clay soil.*

LEFT: *These bright puce-colored cyclamen with pretty silvery leaves stand out spectacularly among the variegated ground cover of ivy. Only the species cyclamen are fully hardy, although some half-hardy ones will survive well in warm areas.*

TULIPS

THESE, too, are invaluable in the spring garden. The tall varieties can march in formal rows, their straight stalks standing stiffly to attention. They can just as well be used informally, intermingling with other flowers in a spring border.

❀ They have an astonishing range of flower forms – from the simple upright 'goblets' that look so well in formal situations, to the frilled and fringed petals of parrot tulips and the open, double blooms of peony-flowered tulips. Their colors are clear and bright and include the black-purple of *Tulipa* 'Queen of the Night', as well as vivid reds, clear pinks and the curious mixed colorations of the parrot tulips.

Botanic tulips

❀ These have developed from tiny species originally found around the Mediterranean. They are small with star-shaped flowers, often several to one stem. The hybrids developed from these dainty little bulbs are the *kaufmanniana* and *fosteriana* species, which flower in early spring, and the *greigii* species, which flower a few weeks later. They have large flowers and a variety of shapes and colors.

DAFFODILS

DAFFODILS are invaluable in spring, with their cheerful upright stems and sunny colors. They range from the tiny cyclamen-shaped species and hybrids such as *Narcissus triandrus* and *N.* 'Jumblie' with petals swept back away from the trumpet, to the great yellow giants such as 'King Alfred', ubiquitously planted in public parks but rather overpowering in a small garden.

❀ Daffodil flowers vary from those with long, short and hoop-shaped trumpets to swept-back or straight petals. Most have large single flowers but a very few are double. There are many small varieties, which can be planted in profusion in the small garden, varying in color from white and very pale yellow to deep yellow and orange. The old favourite, the strongly scented 'Pheasant's Eye' (*N. poeticus* var. *recurvus*) has white petals and a tiny bright red trumpet.

❀ Chosen carefully, daffodils can flower over a long period in spring, starting very early in the gardening year with those like 'February Gold', a neat cheerful yellow, and *N. romieuxii*, a pretty, pale yellow hooped-petticoat type. Both are suitable for rock gardens and raised beds.

❀ The larger daffodils look best in large gardens or in formal beds. Smaller daffodils will grow in grass but it is important to wait for the leaves to die down before mowing, so choose a wilder part of the garden. They will grow well on grassy banks and look wonderful generously planted along a drive. In these situations they usually look best when one cultivar is planted *en masse*.

ABOVE: *Many spring bulbs will grow well in deciduous woodland, making the most of the light before the trees come into leaf. Here,* Helleborus orientalis *and pale-colored* Narcissus *brighten up the bare ground.*

❀ The *kaufmanniana* tulips are only 6–8 in (15–20 cm) tall; 'The First' is white with carmine red, while 'Giuseppe Verdi' is carmine with yellow edging. The *fosteriana* tulips are taller, 8–16 in (35–40 cm); *T. f.* 'Red Emperor' is scarlet and *T. f.* 'Purissima' pure white.

❀ The *greigii* tulips are medium-sized, 8–12 in (20–30 cm) tall, and include the popular 'Red Riding Hood' and 'Cape Cod' (orange). All these tiny tulips make a brave display early in the year and have an innocent charm, unlike their more sophisticated soldier-like relatives.

❀ Larger-flowered hybrids used for general garden display look good with forget-me-nots or in clumps among herbaceous plants.

LILIES

THERE are short, tall and sweetly scented lilies, white ones and brightly colored ones. Some look good in pots, others in the company of other plants or growing in the dappled shade of trees or shrubs.

❀ Tall lilies at the back of a border provide not only a vertical presence but also a sense of grandeur. Plant them in blocks of single color because mixed colors or different cultivars within a block are confusing.

❀ Suitable lilies for the back of the border include *Lilium martagon* 'Album', a white Turk's-cap lily with masses

ABOVE: *Lilium regale* is one of the stateliest of lilies and is very strongly scented. It will grow well in woodland or in any partly shaded border in the summer.

of ivory-white flowers from early summer; 'Fire King', which has dense open clusters of purple-spotted bright orange-red blooms and *L. regale*, with trumpet-shaped clusters of very fragrant white flowers streaked with purple.

❀ Some lilies prefer dappled shade. These include *L. Henrii*, with tall arching stems and gently nodding spikes of small, black-spotted orange-red flowers from midsummer; *L. longiflorum*, with sweetly scented white trumpet-shaped blooms from midsummer; and *L. speciosum* var. *rubrum*, with its large, very fragrant spikes of deep carmine Turk's-cap flowers from late summer.

LEFT: *One color will often be more telling than many colors together, as shown by this trough of Tulipa 'Big Chief'. In this case a touch of blue is added by the low-growing forget-me-nots.*

CULTIVATING GRASSES AND BAMBOOS

Grasses have become popular in gardens over the last few years for very good reasons. They have elegant and architectural forms, long seasons of interest and need little attention. They can also cope with a certain amount of drought, an invaluable quality in the modern garden. They bring movement and a luminous quality into garden planting as they sway in the wind and their leaves catch the sunlight.

THE GRASS FAMILY

MEMBERS of the grass family (*Gramineae*), which includes bamboos, have rounded, hollow stems with regularly placed swellings or nodes from which the leaves appear. The flowers of grasses are small but are often held in large, showy panicles, spikes or plumes or stiff poker-like heads, well above the leaves.

❀ Although they lack bright colors, their golds, browns, greens and yellows catch the sun, producing beautiful subtle effects. Their arching stems, feathery flowers and subtle coloring can create marvellous displays, whether used as individual specimens or grouped together. Many have attractive flowers and seed heads that appear in midsummer and last well into winter.

The tall and the short

❀ Large grasses are admired for their statuesque quality and feather-duster plumage. Unfortunately, the overuse of the very tall and stately pampas grass (*Cortaderia selloana*) has given grass a bad name. It is undeniably beautiful in the right setting but at one time it seems to

BELOW: *The strap-like leaves of this purple phormium and the narrower leaves of the grasses go particularly well together, providing interesting movement and light for those sitting on the bench.*

ABOVE: *Although the leaves of the grasses* Imperata cylindrica *'Rubra' and* Roscoea scillicifolia *have a similar strap-like quality, variety is provided in good measure by the colors, which light up when the sun shines on them.*

have been planted in almost every suburban garden as a matter of course, where it was out of proportion, out of keeping and badly maintained. It is indeed a regal plant but only for a very large garden or for planting in quantity by a lakeside or as a feature.

❀ *C. selloana* is the hardiest pampas grass but there are many more rewarding grasses to choose for the smaller garden. Choose *Miscanthus sinensis* 'Silberfeder' (silver feather), or M. *'Zebrinus'*, whose arching green leaves are intriguingly striped yellow. *Pinnisetum alopecuroides* has brown, caterpillar-shaped flower heads and can be grown in clumps under deciduous trees. Smaller grasses are more useful for their foliage effect, both in form and color.

❀ Varieties of *Festuca, Milium, Elymus* and *Carex* are all excellent foliage plants and extremely useful in a border. They associate well with small perennials, dwarf conifers and shrubs, contributing a hedgehog roundness but feather softness that contrasts well with the upright shape of many perennials. Most are evergreen and so provide interest for the whole year.

RIGHT: *The tall, feathery stems of* Stipa gigantea *with the lower-growing* Miscanthus sinensis *'Silberfeder' and the fiery red of* Crocosmia *'Bressingham Blaze' make a really striking combination.*

CHOOSING GRASSES

IT is important to choose the right grasses for a particular effect. Clump-forming upright growers, such as varieties of *Calamagrostis*, will preside over lower-growing plants but lose all impact if crowded by plants of equal height. More open grasses, such as *Paricum virgatum* with loose flower and seed heads, can be used with taller perennials because of their almost transparent quality.

❀ Color is important, too. If you grow the luminous green *Milium effusum* 'Aureum' in front of a bed next to the lawn, it will simply look like another bit of green grass. Choose the blue grass *Festuca glauca* instead, and it will contrast with the lawn grass very effectively.

Grasses by the sea

❀ Almost all grasses are invaluable grown in coastal or seaside gardens. Their ethereal quality seems to match that of the sea; they can cope well with wind and salt spray and are at home in a sandy and pebbly environment. The taller ones can be used for structure, the smaller ones for foliage, color and for filling gaps.

ABOVE: *Grasses can look especially picturesque in a winter border after a heavy frost; they can lend a magical quality to an otherwise bland and colorless area.*

Grasses in the mixed border

❀ Many mixed borders will benefit from grasses grown among the shrubs and herbaceous perennials. *Stipa gigantea* is useful because its pale yellow stems and flowers make a significant shape but it is sparse enough for other plants to be seen through it. Its pale straw-like color goes well with many of the later summer flowers such as *Echinaceae purpurea*, *Crocosmia* 'Lucifer' and *Aster amellus* 'King George'.

❀ Low-growing grasses look good at the front of mixed borders. Choose the tufted ones that build up slowly from a central crown. *Festuca glauca* 'Elijah blue' is evergreen and has vivid blue, needle-like leaves and blue-grey plumes of flowers in early summer. Vigorous, creeping grasses are not suitable for borders. *Phalaris arundinacea*, for example, will simply smother weaker plants growing nearby and will require endless weeding.

Grasses in winter borders

❀ When many flowers have died down for the winter, the grasses can come into their own, keeping a border alive when it has lost its summer and fall color. They can look spectacular when caught by a heavy frost so that their seed heads and leaves are outlined with a sugar icing coating.

❀ Taller grasses associate well with the sea hollies such as *Eryngium agavifolium*, whose seed heads continue to be attractive in winter, and also with *Sedum* 'Autumn Joy', whose flat plates of heads last well into winter, too, and contrast with the feathery heads of grass. In a large border the larger grasses look great with the seed heads of cardoons (*Cynara cardunculus*).

Grasses for paved areas and patios

❀ Some of the smaller grasses are suitable for growing between paving slabs. Purple moor grass (*Molinia caerulea*) has slender green upright leaves, which form into mounds with open panicles of purple flowers in summer. It will tolerate acidic, boggy soils, so can be used near pools.

❀ For a warm patio area try *Helictotrichon sempervirens* in a bed sheltered by a wall. Its slender blue leaves are upright and radiate stiffly so it looks suitably architectural next to a building.

Water's edge grasses

❀ *Glyceria aquatica* 'Variegata' has an attractive form, tolerates shade and spreads slowly. *Phragmites australis* is a tall species. It needs moist soil and will grow well by a pond or stream.

ABOVE: *The tall, feathery plumes of pampas grass* Cortaderia selloana *'Sunningdale Silver' give a spectacular display, which contrasts with the paddle-shaped leaves and bright red flowers of* Canna *'President'.*

Areas dedicated to grass

❀ If you have enough space, you might like to have a grass garden, creating your own area of American prairie. Varieties of *Cortaderia* and *Miscanthus* make a striking display. They are best grown in an open position where they will get the benefit of sun on their foliage and flowers and the wind will set them swaying.

SEDGES, RUSHES AND CAT'S TAILS

THESE plants are often confused with grasses but each belongs to a separate family. Although they will grow in sun or shade, they must have moist soil and are mostly useful for the bog garden.

❀ Sedges are grown for their attractive foliage. They thrive in bog conditions but are often tolerant of dryer sites. The flowers are grouped into spikelets, which may be richly colored.

❀ The variegated species can offer good color contrasts in a border. Members of the *Carex* family form dense mounds of evergreen hair-like leaves. *Carex* 'Bronze Form' has matt brown leaves, while those of *C. elata* 'Aurea' are bright yellow with narrow green edges.

❀ The rush family (*Juncaceae*) includes the rushes and the woodrushes, all of which have attractive leaves. Like sedges, they should be grown in a bog garden or a bed whose soil is reliably moist. The rushes prefer shade and make good ground cover plants. *Juncus effusus* 'Spiralis' has tiny brown flowers in loose clusters. Snowy woodrush (*Luzula nivea*) has light green leaves in loose tufts with clusters of white flowers in summer and will tolerate sun.

❀ Cat's tails are deciduous with invasive rhizomes. *Typha latifolia* is the common bulrush or reed mace, whose brown flower heads are poker shaped and topped with thin spikes. It is often seen growing in rivers or streams but it can be invasive. *T. minima* (dwarf reed mace) is less so and has dark brown flower spikes in summer.

BELOW: *Grasses and sedges are particularly striking when the frost catches them on a bright winter's morning. The grassy meadow by this wooden bridge has a silver frosty sheen, against which the dark pokers of the bulrushes stand out strikingly.*

BAMBOOS

BAMBOOS belong to the grass family (*Gramineae*). They are evergreen with woody hollow stems called culms and narrow, handsome foliage. Bamboos make excellent architectural plants; even when used as screens or hedges, they make a dramatic statement in any garden.

❀ They will grow in any dry, sheltered, shady spot and can create a lush tropical effect together with other evergreen shrubs. The tall vertical culms make interesting contrasts with the fronded foliage of ferns. Japanese anemones can be grown nearby, especially white ones such as *Anemone* x *hybrida* 'Honorine Joubert'.

❀ Most bamboos need plenty of space, since the larger ones will grow up to 13 ft (4 m) tall and many arch over 20 ft (6 m), but there are also some dwarf species.

❀ Some bamboos form clumps and make good specimen plants or focal points. Others have running rhizomes and need to be contained, unless grown in a wild garden or as ground cover. Canes can be green, brown, black, yellow, pink or purple, mottled or streaked. Do not expect bamboos to bloom, however. It may take 100 years for flowers to appear. On the whole, the flowers are untidy anyway and bamboos look better without them.

❀ Bamboos need a sheltered spot, protected from the wind, or they will lose excessive water. Although fully hardy, a bamboo in a container can suffer from drought in winter and it is wise to insulate the pot with fleece or plastic bubble wrap.

❀ Bamboos grow strongly in most soils once they have become established, and some spread very quickly. Many are tropical but plenty are hardy in temperate regions. They can be grown in beds in the garden or in tubs on roofs or in container gardens. A grove or specimen plant of bamboos can transform a prim garden into a much more mysterious and interesting area.

Bamboos in containers

❀ Bamboos can look superb when well grown in large containers. Terracotta and glazed Chinese pots are suitable but the plants can look just as stately grown in galvanised cans and buckets. The invasive, running types of bamboo are certainly best grown in pots, particularly in small gardens, otherwise they may spread and become a nuisance.

ABOVE: *Bamboos can be grown very effectively in pots and it is one way of making sure the invasive types do not spread. This small version sits well near a formal Japanese-style pond.*

❀ Bamboos are thirsty, hungry plants. Failure to water them sufficiently will cause the leaves to turn brown and even loss of nearly all the leaves. Once this has happened, they will be slow to recover. More vigorous and invasive species will fill up their containers in no time with rhizomes and roots and will then use up water and nutrients at an alarming rate.

❀ Such plants should be repotted every year but there are species that are more suitable for containers. These are slower growing and some may be kept in the same pot for five years or more. *Chimonobambusa marmorea* grows to 5 ft (1.5 m) and is a semi-dwarf Japanese variety with tightly bunched leaves. *C. marmorea* 'Variegata' has thin reddish stems and yellow striped leaves.

ABOVE: *This very Japanese scene includes a bamboo fence with the slim, black-stemmed bamboo* Phyllostachys nigra *growing against it, a stone lantern and two small hummocks of the low-growing blue grass* Festuca glauca *'Elijar Blue'.*

Bamboos in a Japanese garden

❀ Bamboos are more or less essential in a Japanese garden. Tall varieties such as *Fargesia murieliae*, which grows to 13 x 5 ft (4 x 1.5 m) and is particularly elegant as a specimen plant, can conceal the edge of a small garden, making it look much larger.

❀ A gravel area with a stone lantern on it will be given extra atmosphere by this arching plant. *F. m.* 'Simba' reaches only half the height or less and might suit a small garden better.

Interesting stems

❀ Some bamboos have striking stems, which are as much of a feature as their leaves. Plant these where the stems will really be noticed, rather than in some forgotten corner of the garden. They will look good in containers in a small area or as focal points and can be used as screens where they will please the eye while concealing what lies behind.

❀ Such bamboos include *Phyllostachys edulis*, whose distinctive culms are covered in a waxy white powder, which makes them look white. *P. nigra* has elegant, narrow ebony-black stems and is a very good variety for smaller gardens.

Ground cover bamboos

❀ A few bamboos can be used for ground cover. *Pleioblastus pygmaeus* (syn. *Arundinaria pygmaea*) is a dwarf bamboo with fern-like leaves with very slender culms. It looks attractive grown in a shallow container.

LEFT: *Bamboos have many uses in the garden and the canes, or culms, can provide as much interest as the foliage. This one is* Clusquea couleou, *which forms dense clumps of yellow-green to olive-green canes and will grow to 20 ft (6 m) tall.*

GROWING FERNS AND MOISTURE-LOVING PLANTS

❧

Ferns are among the most delicate-looking of foliage plants. They grow in many different shapes and sizes and can add texture and atmosphere to many parts of the garden. They can enliven and cheer places the sun seldom reaches, act as foils to flowering plants and look very much at home grown in drifts as ground cover in woodland areas. They are particularly at home by streams and in damp, shady corners, and are therefore good for small courtyards. All in all, ferns offer an enormous variety of plants of invaluable use in a modern garden.

CHARACTERISTICS

FERNS may be evergreen or deciduous and they have leaf-like fronds, which usually begin to appear in spring. The young fronds, known as crosiers, are tightly curled and unfurl with great grace and beauty as they grow.

❀ The fronds of most ferns grow from rhizomes. These are coated in a furry, scaly covering, which may be black, brown or silvery white. Most rhizomes extend above and below ground, sometimes for a long distance. *Matteuccia struthiopteris* produces crowns of fronds at intervals along its rhizomes.

❀ Rather than producing flowers or seeds, ferns release tiny spores from capsules on the undersides of their fronds. You can often see these as brown markings on the backs of the fronds. These will germinate if given the right conditions.

❀ Some ferns, such as *Asplenium bulbiferum*, also reproduce by growing little plantlets or bulbils on their fronds. This particular fern needs a very sheltered position out of the sun and needs protecting in winter with a covering of straw or old fronds. It is probably better grown in a conservatory.

❀ Epiphytic ferns grow on trees, rocks or walls and draw their nutrients from rotting vegetation, which collects in the crevices.

RIGHT: *The feathery flower heads of the pink* Astilbe *'Erica' associate well with the tall and stately* Osmunda *and* Matteuccia *ferns, growing happily in a semi-woodland situation.*

❀ Almost all ferns require damp conditions if they are to thrive. A very few genera such as *Dryopteris* and *Osmunda* will tolerate dry conditions but only if well shaded. Many, such as *Allyrium* and *Osmunda*, die down at the first touch of frost so should not be grown in a winter interest garden. Some of the *Dryopteris* retain their fronds until well into winter. Leave the old fronds on the plant until early spring to protect the crown from frost but remove them as soon as the young fronds begin to unfurl.

LEFT: *This very natural-looking woodland planting scheme has tiny alpine-type plants growing from crevices in the wall and a mixture of wild flowers and ferns against the hedgerow.*

❀ There are lance-shaped fronds, such as those found in the shuttlecock or ostrich fern (*Matteuccia struthiopteris*), whose fronds turn brown in late summer and persist for over a year, creating a striking display. These are among the most graceful of ferns and they deserve a prominent position in a shady part of the garden, perhaps at the top of steps or as an eye-catcher in a paved corner.

❀ Simple strap-like fronds are found in the hart's tongue fern (*Asplenium scolopendrium*), a very hardy evergreen fern with a crown of mid-green fronds. The crosiers look intriguingly like small green cobras when the dead fronds have been removed.

❀ Antler-shaped fronds are seen only in the staghorn ferns such as *Platycerium bifurcatum*, whose basal fronds are shaped like kidneys and reach up to 24 in (60 cm) and turn brown when fully grown. They form a shield around the base of the antler-like fronds, which grow up to 32 in (80 cm) long and remain green. These are tropical plants and suited only to greenhouse, conservatory or indoor cultivation.

Fern shapes

❀ Fern fronds comprise several basic shapes. There are triangular ferns, such as the five-fingered maidenhair fern (*Adiantum pedatum*), which has upright, lime-green fronds that die down in winter. They look attractive grown with other ferns in a shady border or woodland setting.

BELOW: *This congregation of shade-loving plants includes the small bleeding heart* (Dicentra formosa), *the* Dryopteris *fern, a large blue-green hosta and a purple* Cotinus.

THE RIGHT CONDITIONS

FERNS are very tough and require the minimum of care and maintenance once established. Most ferns prefer neutral to alkaline conditions, and well-dug soil with added organic matter will suit most species.

❀ There are one or two that prefer acidic soil and which should be used in areas where other acidic soil lovers, such as rhododendrons and azaleas, grow. For example, the hard fern (*Blechnum spicant*), which has evergreen, leathery ladder-like fronds, is easier to grow in acidic soils, loves shady borders in woodland areas and associates well with acid-loving shrubs.

❀ The large ferns such as *Matteuccia* varieties will thrive in the damp conditions near ponds or streams. They associate well with large-leaved plants that love moisture, too, such as *Gunnera* and *Rodgersia* and reflect very prettily in still water.

Ferns in formal settings

❀ Ferns can be used successfully in formal settings. For example, they can be planted in clumps or rows behind a very low clipped hedge of golden box bordered by woodland.

❀ The dark trees will highlight the feathery outline of the ferns, while the ferns themselves soften the hard edge of the box. They also look good when they are used formally in a courtyard or paved area in the corner of a garden that gets little sun.

❀ If growing ferns in pots you must make sure they are kept moist at all times. They look good grown near formal water features, especially where a little water is allowed to escape into the surrounding soil.

ABOVE: *Most ferns and primulas prefer soil that will not dry out. Here, the large shuttlecock fern (*Matteuccia struthiopteris*) mingles with a cerise candelabra primula (*Primula bulleyana*) to make a delightful combination.*

BELOW: *An enormous, clipped shrubby* Lonicera *hedge, shaped like a pillow, is brightened and enlivened by the bright green feathery leaves of a large clump of* Dryopteris.

Ferns in rock crevices

❀ The lance-shaped fronds of the semi-evergreen *Ceterach officinarum* contrast well with the hard surfaces of the rock or brick that provides shelter and nutrients for them.

❀ If you build a double wall at the edge of a patio or front garden with a space in the middle for plants, these little ferns can be grown there, too, but remember that they should be in the shade.

Naturalising ferns in woodland

❀ Although woodland may sound a bit grand, in a small garden one good-sized silver birch or a small clump of deciduous trees planted close together can count as woodland. Where ferns are concerned, the woodland needs to be moist most of the time.

❀ Ferns planted in drifts in woodland look very pretty but they need not be grown on their own. They associate very well with lilies and also with groups of broad-leaved hostas and spring bulbs such as wood anemones and bluebells.

❀ The male fern (*Dryopteris filix-mas*), which keeps most of its fronds throughout winter, is a very accommodating plant and thrives in shade but will tolerate full sun. It will even grow at the foot of a privet hedge. Like most hardy ferns, it forms solid clumps and looks very pretty grown in drifts among trees and woodland shrubs.

❀ The common polypody (*Polypodium vulgare*) is drought tolerant and adaptable. It spreads easily and makes good ground cover. It will also grow on rocks and trees. It has dark green, lance-shaped, deeply lobed fronds and spreads via green rhizomes, which eventually form mats. It prefers an acidic soil, as does *Blechnum spicant*, a fern with a distinctive rich green color.

Ferns as specimen plants

❀ Many ferns deserve a prominent position where they will be noticed and appreciated for some special quality. The Japanese painted fern *Athyrium niponicum* var. *pictum* is one of the prettiest, with metallic silver-grey fronds and purple midribs. It does not grow very tall, but put it in a moist, fertile soil and a sheltered position and it will thrive and look very pretty, particularly with small spring bulbs such as *Anemone blanda* and the charming little blue scillas and other small woodland plants.

❀ The royal fern (*Osmunda regalis*) is a large, stately fern growing to 5 ft (1.5 m) tall. It particularly likes waterside conditions in sun or shade. It makes a good container plant but must be regularly watered. It is best located near the house where it can be in a prominent position and its watering needs are less likely to be forgotten.

BELOW: *Foxgloves and ferns both grow in woodland conditions and associate well together under the canopy of deciduous trees.*

USEFUL PLANT ASSOCIATIONS

ELEPHANT'S ears (*Bergenia*), with large, shiny, rounded evergreen leaves, can be a little dull on their own when not in flower.

They look much more interesting planted next to ferns, especially the feathery ones, such as the beech fern (*Phegopteris connectilis*), whose lime-green fronds contrast with the dark green of the *Bergenia*. *Bergenia* 'Silberlicht' has loose white flowers and is a more elegant and interesting variety than the more usual pink-flowering ones.

LEFT: This beautifully designed modern garden has a formal rectangular pond with a stone sculpture as a focal point. Water lilies float serenely on the calm surface of the water, and irises and other water-loving plants have been planted in the corners.

❁ Even in the smallest plot you can have a trough with dwarf water lilies floating in it. In a larger garden a formal or informal pond can create a strong focus and set the garden's style. It may incorporate a fountain or waterfall to create movement, sound and liveliness and water lilies will complete the scene.

❁ Floating plants, marginal, deep water and bog plants all add to the interest of a garden but need to be catered for carefully. Ponds should be made with shelves at different heights so that pond baskets can be put at the heights best suited to the various plants.

Plants for formal ponds

❁ Plants with floating leaves and flowers, such as water lilies, are the obvious choice for formal pools. *Nymphaea* 'Froebelii' has deep red, starry flowers and

WATER PLANTS

Water in the garden – whether a formal pool, a small stream, a short cascade or a wildlife pond – will allow you to grow many plants that do not thrive in any other conditions.

BELOW: This thoughtfully designed pond at the edge of a patio is planted with variegated hostas, which contrast with the large green-purple leaves of Rodgersia, *the white and green strap-like leaves of* Phormium *and the slender leaves of a water iris.*

purple-green rounded leaves; *N. 'Marliacea Chromatella'* is a yellow-flowered variety with olive green-streaked leaves.

- Arum lilies do not float but stand upright and look marvellous at the edge of a pond where their arrow-shaped leaves and pure white flowers can be reflected in the water. *Zantedeschia aethiopica* is the hardiest and will withstand several degrees of frost.

Marginal plants

- Marginal plants are, in the main, very attractive plants grown at the edges of pools in shallow water about 3–6 in (7.5–15 cm) deep, but sometimes up to 12 in (30 cm) deep. Some species, such as water mint (*Mentha aquatica*) and *Veronica beccabunga*, also help to oxygenate the water.
- Ferns will grow well at the borders of informal pools and can form a good transition between a stream and the garden. Plants grown at pond margins also provide shelter for wildlife. *Iris laevigata* is tall and stately with fans of green, sword-like leaves and lavender-blue flowers.
- *Butomus umbellatus* has clusters of pale pink flowers in summer and early fall and twisted bronze leaves. Purple loosestrife (*Lythrum salicaria*) has spires of reddish-purple flowers and lance-shaped leaves. The water forget-me-not (*Myosotis palustris*) has sky-blue flowers with yellow eyes all summer long.

- All these plants are valuable for breaking up the hard outline of a pond. In deeper marginal water you can grow the water flag (*Iris pseudacorus*), a tall, bright yellow variety of iris, but it may be too vigorous for smaller gardens.

Bog and moisture-loving plants

- Numerous colorful plants will grow happily in soil that is kept permanently wet. The water violet (*Hottonia palustris*) has pale lilac flowers and likes full sun; *Anemone rivularis* has blue or white flowers from spring into summer; and ragged robin (*Lychnis flos-cuculi*) is a very pretty sharp pink flower with ragged petals, which used to be common and now seems to be rare in the wild.
- If you have room you could grow something on a grand scale such as *Gunnera tinctoria*, which has enormous, rhubarb-like leaves up to 5 ft (1.5 m) wide. Spikes of greenish-red flowers are followed by red or purple fruits.
- *Rodgersia aesculifolia* is another tall, stately plant with leaves like the horse chestnut tree and plumes of tiny, fragrant white flowers tinged with pink. *Rheum palmatum* also has large, handsome foliage and unusual flower spikes on reddish-purple stems.

WATER GARDENS IN CONTAINERS

In a small garden or a patio you can still have a pool without doing any construction work. Appropriate containers might be a sealed and lined half-barrel, a metal cauldron or a ceramic sink with the plughole stopped up. Although you will be able to grow only a few selected plants, the presence of even a little water can give great pleasure.

- Metal containers should be sealed with rubber paint or liner, otherwise the metal may be harmful to the plants and any fish you might want to keep. (If you do keep fish, they should be brought indoors over winter.) One suitable plant would be the tiny water lily, *Nymphaea pygmaea* 'Helvola', with pretty miniature yellow flowers. *N. tetragona* has white flowers no more than 2 in (5 cm) across and heart-shaped, dark green leaves.

LEFT: *The white skunk cabbage* (Lysichiton camtschatcensis) *is a marginal aquatic perennial, which flowers in early spring. Here, it is reflecting beautifully in the water.*

INTRODUCING EXOTICS

Exotic plants are usually thought of as those from tropical and subtropical climates that find it hard to survive in temperate conditions. However, in mild areas such plants may grow quite happily in a sheltered part of the garden and, even in colder areas, many survive outside if protected over winter. Some are so tender that they need the protection of a greenhouse or conservatory even in the summer. However, some exotic-looking plants are perfectly hardy and not actually tropical. Exotics include many handsome architectural plants grown as focal points for their height and interesting shapes and foliage. They also include plants with highly colorful and unusual flowers and evergreens with a jungly look.

CACTI AND SUCULENTS

CACTI and succulents come in an extraordinarily varied array of sizes, shapes, colors and textures. Many come from desert regions, where there is little rainfall and it gets very hot during the day and very cold at night.

❀ Some come from warm, humid rainforests. They have all adapted to their particular extreme conditions, turning their leaves, stems or roots into water storage tanks to help them withstand long periods of drought. Cacti differ from other succulents in having cushion-like growths on their stems from which spines, flowers and shoots develop.

❀ Succulents may have plump, smooth surfaces, a covering of silky hair or colorful spines. They may be symmetrical rosettes in shape or squat and globular or fluted like candlesticks. Many flower for only a short time and have large, brightly colored flowers. Others flower for longer with many tiny blooms.

❀ In cool-temperate climates most cacti and succulents have to be grown in a conservatory or as houseplants, although there are some hardier species, which can make interesting garden displays. Nearly all need good drainage and will grow well in raised beds where the water can drain freely.

BELOW: *This secluded seating area has a wealth of container-grown succulents for color and interest. Scented-leaved geraniums are fronted by the strong, spiky shapes of the* Agave.

ABOVE: *A row of succulents in terracotta pots sitting on a sunny wall by a patio will get the best of the daylight and warmth of the sun and will flourish accordingly.*

❀ Attractive collections of succulents can be grown outdoors in a relatively cool climate if you choose your varieties carefully. *Sedum* cultivars are often grown in mixed borders, although they usually look much more striking grown in a row or in swathes against a stone wall. There are some excellent deep purple varieties such as *S. spectabile* 'Abendrot'.

Succulents in containers

❀ Most succulents have shallow roots and are therefore ideal for growing in containers. Wide, shallow containers are best for low-growing and creeping species such as the hardy *Sempervivum montanum*, a variety of houseleek, which makes neat little rosettes and is ideal for a trough garden.

❀ *Lewisia* varieties have brilliant little blooms on delicate stalks and also grow well in a trough or gravel garden, given a sheltered spot. Troughs are good for creating mixed planting of different sizes and habits.

❀ Large pots or urns are better for large plants with strap-like leaves such as *Agave attenuata*. A raised bed with shallow soil and plenty of gravel is also a good place to grow mixed succulent plantings.

Succulents as focal points

❀ The agaves are spiky and statuesque. Grown in regions where the temperature seldom drops below freezing, *Agave parryi* has plump symmetrical rosettes of grey-green leaves and *Opuntia polyacantha* has brilliant yellow flowers. Each of these makes a splendid focal point on its own.

Trailing succulents

❀ Several succulents have a trailing habit and can be stunning planted in hanging baskets. *Ceropegia woodii* produces waterfalls of brightly colored flowers and can be used in warm, sunny courtyards or in conservatories.

RIGHT: *Bananas are satisfyingly exotic with their enormous, shiny green leaves, which become tattered as they grow older. This young banana,* Musa acuminata, *requires a sheltered spot.*

ARCHITECTURAL EXOTICS

THERE are many splendid plants that can be grown for their architectural interest, to use as focal points and eye-catchers. Many are hardy; others can thrive in temperate climates, if they are given due care, attention and protection.

Tree ferns

✿ Tree ferns are true ferns, and come from tropical forests. They have enormous upright rhizomes, which look like tree trunks and which can grow up to 4 m (13 ft). They are so stately that just one could be the only plant needed in a city courtyard.

✿ The Tasmanian tree fern (*Dicksonia antarctica*) will certainly not survive several cold winters in succession but, given a shady position where it is protected from the wind by a tall evergreen hedge, it may well survive many years.

✿ Temperate climates are not really humid enough for tree ferns so in summer spray the trunk or rig up an automatic system to water it. In warmer areas, winter protection may not be necessary but it certainly will be in cold rural areas.

✿ Overwinter your fern by surrounding the trunk with convenient insulating material such as polystyrene plant trays tied around the trunk. Fill the crown with straw and fix a hat of polystyrene on top. Stack straw bales around the trunk and fronds as high up as possible.

✿ Tree ferns become hardier the taller they grow so buy the tallest one you can find. Young plants with no trunk are not suitable to overwinter outdoors except in very sheltered spots.

Yuccas

✿ Yuccas bring height and very exotic white blooms to the garden. Most are hardy enough for hot sunny sites in temperate climates. Use them as focal points in a border or on their own, or as effective eye-catchers on steps and terraces or in courtyards.

✿ If you want lots of lush growth, remove the yucca's spent flower spikes before they have fully faded as well as any dying or dead leaves. Some yuccas form a trunk and branch after flowering.

BELOW: *These purple phormiums, although they certainly look exotic, are reliably hardy in many temperate areas if grown in sheltered areas. In most places bananas should be taken indoors in winter.*

❀ These include *Yucca floribunda*, *Y. gloriosa* (Spanish dagger), *Y. g.* 'Variegata' and *Y. recurvifolia*. Some form a clump of several plants without trunks. When one individual in the clump flowers, it dies and is replaced by a new plant from underneath. *Y. whipplei* may take many years to flower so grow it only for its leaves.

Phormium

❀ These evergreen perennials come from New Zealand. They form striking clumps of large, strap-like leaves, ranging in color from yellow-green to deep purple. They create spectacular focal points in a border, next to a building or at the edge of a lawn.

❀ They give a truly jungly feeling, although many are perfectly hardy. *Phormium tenax* 'Dazzler' has arching bronze leaves with red, orange and pink stripes and looks strong in a mainly red border. *P.* 'Sundowner' has bronze-green leaves; *P.* 'Variegatum' is light green with cream and lime stripes and looks good against darker foliage plants or a clipped hedge.

Palms

❀ These stately trees always look wonderful swaying on the skyline in tropical countries. There are only two hardy palms and both can add an exotic feel to a garden. Grown in a border, they can give a truly splendid touch, or they may be grown as specimens on their own.

LEFT: *Despite its exotic, glamorous appearance, the yucca is surprisingly hardy and makes a spectacular statement, particularly as a feature in its own right.*

❀ *Trachycarpus* (fan palm) is a family of six species of evergreen palms from the temperate forests of subtropical Asia. They have a very attractive habit of growth with fan-shaped leaves and cup-shaped flowers. Fan palms are small enough to be grown in a courtyard but make splendid specimen trees in any garden. They like full sun or dappled shade and should be sheltered from cold, drying winds.

❀ The Chusan palm (*Trachycarpus fortunei*) is a single-stemmed palm with a head of fan-shaped, dark green leaves 18–30 in (45–75 cm) long, and small yellow flowers. Female plants have blue-black berries. It needs shelter, particularly from north and east winds.

❀ The dwarf fan palm (*Chamaerops humilis*) is a shrubby palm, which grows in Mediterranean regions. It has rosettes of long, graceful, finger-like leaves and tiny three-petalled flowers. It is a good specimen plant for a small garden. If there is danger of frost it is best grown in a pot and taken into a conservatory or indoors for winter.

ABOVE: *These gardens at Tresco in the Scilly Isles have a remarkably mild climate, and many semi-tropical plants grow here that will not grow on the British mainland. Here, a tall palm gazes out over the other islands and an agave presides over smaller plants lower down the hill.*

ABOVE: *The strawberry tree* (Arbutus unedo) *is a spreading, sometimes shrubby tree with fascinating shredding, red-brown bark, white flowers and exotic round, warty red fruit.*

EXOTIC FLOWERS

Pride of Madeira (*Echium candicans*) is a wonderfully exotic, enormous woody perennial with cylindrical blue flowers 30 cm (12 in) long, on stems that reach 1.5–2.4 m (5–8 ft) and flower for a long time. It may survive for years against a sunny, sheltered wall. In colder regions grow it in a cool greenhouse.

❀ The large *Abutilon* family comprises deciduous shrubs and small trees from tropical and subtropical regions. They are not especially stately and they need staking, but their flowers are both showy and delicate.

❀ In frost-prone districts grow them in pots against a wall and bring them indoors for winter. *Abutilon* 'Ashford Red' is evergreen with red flowers from spring to fall, while *A. megapotanicum* (trailing abutilon) has slender, arching shoots and bell-shaped flowers with astonishing yellow petals and purple stamens from red calyxes in summer and fall. *A. pictum* 'Thomsonii' has interesting leaves mottled with yellow and salmon-pink flowers flushed with orange.

❀ *Fremontodendron* or flannel bush has spectacular showy yellow flowers, dark green leaves and hairy young shoots covered with scales. Grow it against a warm, sunny wall or at the back of a border, associated with something like ivy. The foliage and shoots may irritate the skin.

LARGE-LEAVED PLANTS

Often best planted as individual specimen plants, some of these are good-natured enough to associate with smaller-leaved plants in a shady corner of the garden.

❀ *Fatsia japonica* is grown mainly for its huge, shiny, dark green leaves and sturdy habit. There is a bonus of creamy-white flowers and small round black fruit. It is ideal for a shaded courtyard, will perk up a dark corner of the garden and can be used in a shrub walk. *Fatshedera lizei* has a splendid jungly look for a shady position. It is a cross between an ivy and a fatsia and looks like it. It is evergreen and easy to grow.

LEFT: *The canna lily is usually grown for its brightly colored, red and orange flowers but this,* Canna striata, *has exotic striped leaves. Grown with dark-stemmed red Dahlia 'Bishop of Llandaff' and fiery Crocosmia 'Lucifer', it helps to create a striking 'hot' display.*

❀ Actually evergreen perennials, banana trees are stately and full of character. The Japanese banana *(Musa basjoo)* is the only hardy one. It grows to 5 m (16 ft) tall and has leaves 3 m (10 ft) long. The yellowish-green fruit are not for eating.

❀ *Gunnera manicata* looks like a giant, hairy rhubarb plant, and makes a superb architectural plant at the edge of a pond or stream. Protect the crowns in winter by folding the leaves over the top and covering them with straw.

SOME EXOTIC TREES

THERE are many interesting trees suitable for small or medium-sized gardens and some splendidly exotic ones, which are not often enough tried.

❀ *Acacia dealbata* is the mimosa tree, which has the prettiest grey-green ferny leaves and is covered in a mass of bright yellow flowers in spring. It grows fast but is really only for mild climates or a conservatory.

❀ The foxglove tree *(Paulownia tomentosa)* is hardy, deciduous and a summer-long jungle plant. If you cut it down in spring it will grow 10 ft (3 m) tall and produce soft, velvety leaves 30 in (75 cm) across, in one season. It has fragrant pinkish-white flowers.

❀ The strawberry tree *(Arbutus)* is well worth growing. *Arbutus* x *andrachnoides* is a beautiful evergreen, which flowers in winter and has interesting, peeling red-brown bark. It is excellent for large shrub borders, in woodland garden or as a specimen, and can also be grown against a wall. It will grow to 25 ft (7.5 m).

❀ All the magnolias are exotic and there is one for every garden, large or small. M. *grandiflora* is evergreen with big glossy leaves and huge scented white flowers, to be used as a freestanding wonder, not as a wall shrub. M. *stellata* is covered in small, star-like white flowers in spring and is very good for a small garden.

❀ *Photinia serratifolia* is an aristocratic evergreen, which grows to 12 ft (3.5 m) with an exotic habit, bronze-colored new leaves in late winter and interesting peeling grey and brown bark. It is good among other trees and shrubs in a grove, shrub border or walk.

❀ The loquat *(Eriobotrya japonica)* is a large-leaved small evergreen tree. It has pale green shuttlecocks of flowers from spring to fall and large and wrinkled leathery leaves. It can withstand drought and if its pale orange fruit ever ripen, they are edible.

BELOW: *The brilliant oranges and vivid reds of dahlias look even more striking when complemented by the strong purple of annual or perennial verbenas.*

BELOW: *All the magnolias are spectacular and make good specimen trees. This is* Magnolia x soulangeana, *which will grow to 20 ft (6 m) and has large goblet-shaped flowers in mid- and late spring.*

LOOKING AFTER LAWNS

The lawn is the centerpiece of many gardens. It remains green when much else in the garden is dormant, and sets off plants and hard surfaces beautifully. It unites diverse garden elements, harmonising planted and unplanted elements. As a practical garden floor, as well as a major visual feature, we make huge demands on our lawns. It is often a children's play area, family recreation area and hardworking everyday surface, trampled on regularly as we hang out washing or walk across it to reach the shed.

ATTENDING TO YOUR LAWN

CONSIDERING how demanding we are of our lawns, and how prominent they are in the design of most gardens, it is surprising that most gardeners expect lawns to perform at their best with very little attention, save mowing and perhaps an occasional weed or feed treatment when problems arise.

❀ Perhaps it will help to remember that a lawn is not a solid material, but is composed of millions of tiny plants, all of which need air, food, light, moisture and good drainage as much as any other garden plant.

❀ The list of tasks required to keep a lawn at putting green perfection is rather daunting, and probably too time consuming for all but the most perfectionist lawn owner to undertake. However, most gardeners will find that increasing the level of lawn attention from mowing alone to include just a few more specific tasks will not be too onerous, yet will reward them with a much improved lawn.

BELOW: A lush green lawn can be as rich and welcoming as a deep pile carpet if it is well maintained.

TYPES OF LAWN

THE type of lawn you have is determined by the type of grasses it contains.

The luxury lawn

❀ Luxury turf comprises fine-leaved, compact grasses – bents (*Agrostis*) and fescues (*Festuca*). It is free of broad-leaved grasses such as perennial ryegrass. Luxury lawns are kept closely mown in order to prevent coarse-leaved grasses colonising the lawn. Although undoubtedly a thing of great beauty, a fine, ornamental lawn is not easy to achieve or maintain.

❀ Getting luxury lawns off to a good start is neither cheap nor quick. Turf and seed are more expensive than utility grades, turf particularly so. Starting such a lawn from seed requires meticulous preparation, as the closely cut finished lawn cruelly reveals any discrepancy in level. Fine grasses are also slow to germinate, so establishing this sort of lawn is a lengthy process.

❀ Luxury-grade grass will not withstand heavy wear, so is definitely not recommended as a lawn for gardeners with children. Nor can this type of lawn tolerate neglect, so unless you are a lawn hobbyist, choose a grade of grass that you can realistically maintain.

RIGHT: *To keep your lawn in good shape in the warm summer months, invest in a good sprinkler system.*

The utility lawn

❀ Most gardeners will find utility-grade grass a far more user-friendly option than the luxury choice. The utility lawn contains broad-leaved grasses, combined with some fine-leaved varieties, which will withstand the rigors of family life.

❀ Most of us use the lawn as an extended living area, not merely as a showpiece to be viewed from a distance. Utility lawns cope admirably with the requirements of modern living, such as being regularly walked and played on.

❀ Very importantly for the busy gardener, utility lawns will also tolerate a certain amount of neglect without suffering irreparably. Utility-grade grass, whether seed or turf, is less expensive than luxury grades, and also establishes much more easily and quickly. The broader leaves also conceal the sort of coarse grasses that frequently invade lawns, and which would be very visible and unsightly on a luxury lawn.

❀ The chief disadvantage of a utility lawn is that it needs regular mowing from spring through summer. However, since this necessity springs from its resilient, fast-growing nature, most gardeners would agree that it is worth putting up with being moderately enslaved to the mower in order to escape the petulant demands of the luxury lawn.

SEED

SEED is an economical and popular way of producing a new lawn. Unlike turf, seed does not deteriorate quickly after purchase, so you have more flexibility about when you sow.

❀ On the downside, however, preparation of the ground is especially critical, and is a time-consuming process. In addition, lawns are best sown in spring or early fall, which are already busy times in the garden. All weeds must be removed, and the emerging lawn seedlings are vulnerable to attack from new weeds, birds, disease, overly dry or wet weather and cats.

❀ You will need to keep a watchful eye on the new lawn for a few weeks as it germinates, in case it needs watering, so do not sow a lawn and go on holiday, expecting a faultless sward on your return. It might have died entirely if the weather is too dry. Another drawback of growing from seed is that the lawn is not ready for normal use for approximately 9 to 12 month.

TURF

TURF is very much more expensive than grass seed, particularly if you are buying luxury-grade turf. Turf laying is also heavy work. However, it has several advantages over growing a lawn from seed.

LEFT: *Most gardeners would not be too happy if weeds such as common sorrel appeared in their lawn; however, through regular lawn maintenance such occurences can be kept to a minimum.*

❀ Turfing is usually done in late fall to winter, or in early spring, which are not especially busy times in the garden. It is therefore comparatively easy to incorporate turf laying into the gardening schedule. The most significant advantage over seed is that turf produces a mature-looking lawn almost immediately, and is generally well established within two to three months.

❀ Turf is not as vulnerable to problems as germinating seedlings and so requires much less attention after laying than a seeded lawn. Finally, although good ground preparation is important when laying any sort of lawn, there is no need for the time-consuming finely tilled seedbed when laying turf.

Choosing standard turf

❀ Hopefully, you will need to buy lawn turf only once in the life of your lawn, so it is worth considering the choices carefully before purchasing, and worth buying the best quality you can afford, from a reputable supplier.

BELOW: *Daisies are one of the most common weeds to grow in lawns, although many people do not mind, as they give the lawn a natural look.*

✿ Economising at this stage could create problems for years to come. For example, some cheap turf looks healthy enough, but may be rough, farmland meadow turf, containing a high proportion of weeds and coarse grasses, which will never look good, despite a lot of attention. Specialist turf suppliers have their reputation to protect, so it is well worth paying a little extra for their products.

✿ Turf needs to be laid as soon as possible after receipt, as it degenerates quite quickly. If you have turf delivered, intending to lay it at the weekend, but the weather is unsuitable, you need to be able to make time during the next week to lay the turf as soon as the weather allows.

✿ For busy, working gardeners, this may simply not be feasible. If, for example, the weather causes delays and you cannot rearrange your schedule, make sure you have a contigency plan. It may be that you have to get someone else to help you lay the turf.

✿ If a delay of more than three days is expected, you can unroll the turf and keep it damped down in a shady place, but it is much better to arrange to lay it promptly after delivery.

✿ Order approximately five per cent more turf than the exact amount required, to allow for wastage. Before delivery, remember to plan and clear the area where the turf will be stacked until needed.

Seeded turf

✿ Professional landscape gardeners have used seeded turf for many years, and it has become an increasingly popular method of producing a new lawn domestically. A major advantage of seeded turf is that it has been produced to a specific 'recipe' and should therefore be of uniformly high quality, whereas it is very hard for the lay person to ascertain the content and quality of standard turf.

✿ Particularly desirable lawn grasses are sown on to a substrate, so you know exactly what you are buying, and the turf is weed free. Seeded turf is also much lighter and easier to lay than standard turf. It may even be cut with ordinary scissors.

✿ However, seeded turf is more expensive than standard turf. It is also less forgiving of undulations in the underlying surface, so more careful site preparation is needed before laying to ensure that the soil is absolutely level.

BELOW: *Three of the most common lawn weeds (from left): dandelion, greater plantain and white clover, all of which can require a great deal of effort to remove permanently.*

ESTABLISHING A
NEW LAWN

PREPARATION is the key to a good-looking lawn that will be easy to maintain – no bumps and hollows to distort mowing, no perennial weeds to deal with, just even, level, healthy green grass. Keep this image in mind as you embark on the laborious, but very necessary process of preparing the site.

❀ Site preparation is essentially the same, whether you are sowing from seed or are laying turf. You should follow the general directions given below until you reach the individual directions for seed sowing and turf laying (see p. 406).

❀ Ideally, you should start preparing the site for a new lawn at least three months before seeding or turfing. There is quite a lot of initial work to be done, and you need to allow the soil time to settle.

Clearing and grading the site

❀ Clear down to bare earth. Remove tree stumps and roots, seeking professional help if necessary. Dig out perennial weeds and treat the area with weedkiller.

❀ You may need to alter the contours of the site to reach an approximate final level for the lawn. Whether the site slopes or is almost horizontal, there should be no bumps or hollows in its surface, as these will naturally lead to problems in the finished lawn – both visually, and when you eventually come to mow it.

❀ When correcting bumps and hollows, always keep the topsoil and subsoil in consistent positions. For example, to level a major bump do not be tempted to scrape away the topsoil only. You will need to remove the topsoil, put it to one side, then excavate the subsoil to the required depth, before replacing the topsoil.

Levelling the site

❀ To produce a level surface, take some wooden pegs – their length dictated by the degree of unevenness of the ground – and make a mark on each, 4 in (10 cm) down from the top. Insert the pegs in the soil at 6 ft (1.8 m) intervals in a grid formation.

❀ Place a length of wood, topped with a spirit level across each pair of pegs and hammer until level. Add or remove soil from between the pegs to bring the soil surface level with the marks you made on the pegs.

Draining the site

❀ Lawns need good drainage. Most sites can be sufficiently prepared by digging that incorporates soil improvers.

❀ Heavy clay soils may need more intensive consideration. The topsoil will need to be removed, and layers of drainage material added on top of the subsoil, starting with a 6-in (15-cm) layer of rubble, progressing through to a 6-in (15-cm) layer of small stones, coarse sand or grit, to the top layer of topsoil.

❀ Very waterlogged soils with impervious clay subsoils may need proper drainage systems installed if you are intent on having a lawn.

Preparing the soil

❀ Digging an area big enough for the average lawn is extremely hard work, and you may find it worthwhile to hire a mechanical rototiller. Remove large stones and perennial weeds. Dig when the soil is reasonably dry. Incorporate sand if the soil is heavy, well-rotted organic matter if the soil is light.

Firming and raking
the site

❀ On a dry day tread the soil evenly, using tiny steps with your weight on your heels. Rake the soil level and remove stones and debris. Alternately you can tread and rake until the site is level, with a fine, crumbly surface.

Leaving the site fallow

❀ When sowing seed, it is vital to prepare a weed-free seedbed. Turf will also benefit from a weed-free site, but this stage is not as critical for turfing as it is for seed sowing. Leave the site until annual weeds germinate, then apply weedkiller. After a few days, when the weeds have died, rake them off, taking care to remove all the roots.

Fertilizing the site

❀ A few days before sowing or turfing the site, lightly rake in a good-quality compound fertilizer, following the manufacturer's directions precisely.

LAWN DISORDERS

Some of the most frequently found lawn problems are illustrated below. Regular care and maintenance of your lawn can help avoid these problems.

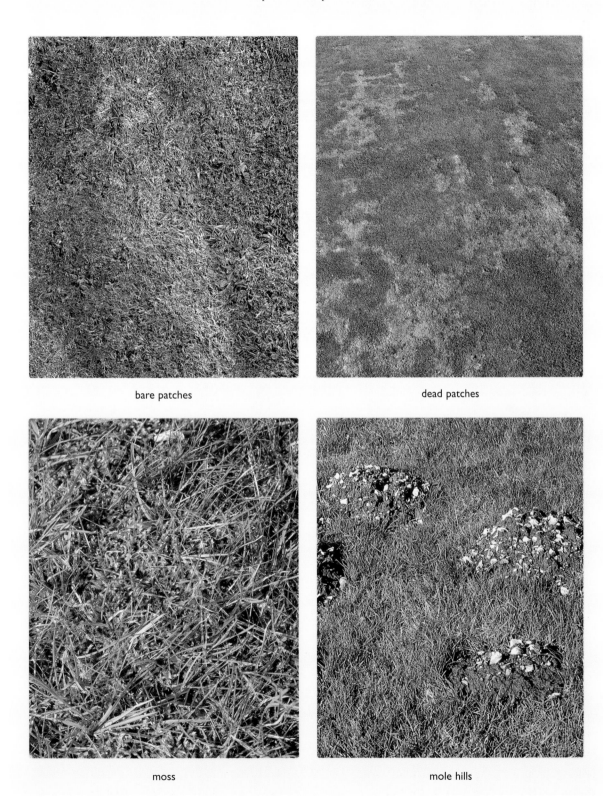

bare patches

dead patches

moss

mole hills

SOWING BY HAND

If sowing by hand, begin by marking out the site into equal areas.

1 Divide the amount of seed accordingly and sow as evenly as possible, working first in one direction, then at right angles to this, as for sowing by machine.

2 Lightly rake in the seed and water with a sprinkler to avoid disturbing the seed.

GROWING A LAWN FROM SEED

FOLLOW the manufacturer's directions regarding sowing rates. Too much seed can encourage damping off in the emerging seedlings; too little will produce an uneven effect, and will allow weed seedlings through to compete with the emerging grass.

❀ Always shake the seed container well so that the different types of seed are evenly mixed before you start sowing.

Sowing by machine

❀ A mechanical seed distributor is very helpful in sowing a medium to large lawn accurately. It is very important to sow evenly and at the correct rate for the area covered. The most even spread will be achieved by using half the seed to sow in one direction, then sowing the second half at right angles to the first.

Caring for a seed-sown lawn

❀ Water the site regularly with a sprinkler if conditions are dry. Cover the site with netting to protect the emerging seedlings against birds. Shoots should appear in approximately one to three weeks.

RIGHT: *Turf produces a neat lawn quickly and with comparatively little effort.*

Cutting a seed-sown lawn

❀ When the grass is approximately 2 in (5 cm) high, cut it to about 1 in (2.5 cm), using a rotary mower. If you have sown the seed in fall you will not need to cut again until spring. If you have sown in spring, continue mowing regularly throughout the growing season, gradually lowering the mower's blades.

LAYING TURF

Laying turf is labor-intensive and more expensive than sowing a lawn but produces a mature-looking lawn much more quickly.

1 Start laying the turf along a straight edge, ensuring that each new turf butts closely to its neighbor. Stand on a plank as you lay the next row, gently but firmly tamping down each turf using the back of a rake head. This ensures that there are no air pockets below the turf.

2 Stagger the joints between the turfs in the second row equally between the joints in the first row, like brickwork. Never finish rows with very small pieces of turf, which will be unstable and vulnerable to damage and drying out. Instead use as large a piece as possible at the end of a row, filling in any gap between this turf and the next with a small segment of turf.

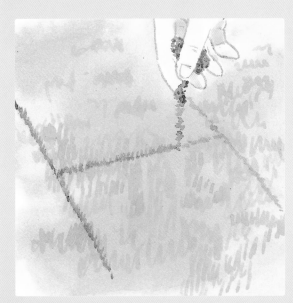

3 Sprinkle a top dressing of sieved sandy loam into the joints to help bind the turfs together.

4 Water the turfs in using a fine spray. Ensure that you keep the turfs moist so that they will root properly in the topsoil.

EDGING A LAWN

Crisp edges make a huge difference to the overall appearance of a lawn. Shaggy edges on lawns may be rectified with sharp edging shears or a power edger. To create neat edges on a new lawn use a clean, sharp half-moon edging iron driven vertically into the turf. Do not be tempted to use a spade, which would produce a scalloped effect.

1 Always protect newly laid turf from undue compression by standing on a plank to distribute your weight evenly as you work. To cut a straight edge, use the plank as a guide. Align the plank with a string held taut in the required position. A long nail driven through the plank into the lawn will help keep it in position as you work.

2 A hose or rope secured in place with bent wire pegs assists in marking out a curved edge.

3 Trim any ragged edges with shears. Always remove clippings after edging, so that grass does not start to take root in your flowerbed.

LEVELLING A BUMP

Uneven bumps or hollows in the lawn quickly become unsightly. Raised bumps become scalped by the mower, causing bare patches to develop on the lawn, while hollows do not drain freely, causing an increased risk of disease and producing patches of grass that are greener than the rest of the lawn.

1 Make an H-shaped cut across the bump or hollow with a half-moon edging iron or sharp spade.

2 Gently peel back the turfs. Add soil to raise the level of a hollow or remove soil from a bump. Tread down the soil evenly. Roll back the turf and check that all is level before treading down the turf. Sift soil over the cracks created by cutting.

NATURAL LAWNS

SOME sites may be more suited to a less manicured look than a traditional lawn. For example, if your garden backs on to fields, you may want to visually blur the transition from your garden to the surrounding countryside by allowing part of your lawn to grow longer so that a more natural effect is achieved.

❀ Natural lawns are alive with wildlife and are low maintenance. However, if planted in the wrong place, such as a small, otherwise formal front garden, a natural lawn can easily look unkempt, as dying bulb foliage rots down in the shaggy grass. Natural lawns are generally best reserved for quite large areas, away from the house, where their wild beauty looks most at home.

NATURALISING BULBS IN A LAWN

1 *Scatter the bulbs randomly across the lawn in the sort of drifts that they would naturally grow in. For larger bulbs make planting holes using a bulb planter, which neatly removes an appropriately sized piece of turf.*

2 *Plant each large bulb, roots down, at the recommended planting depth, making sure there is no air pocket beneath it in which water could collect. You may wish to add a shallow layer of grit or moist peat beneath the bulb to assist drainage. Replace the removed soil.*

1 *Small corms and bulbs are easily planted by partially lifting an area of turf. Make an H-shaped incision and fold back the turf. Lightly fork a little slow-release fertilizer into the exposed topsoil.*

2 *Scatter the small bulbs or corms randomly on the soil, root side down, and replace the turf. Gently but firmly tamp down the turf and ensure that the ground is level. Do not allow the cut edges of turf to dry out.*

MAINTAINING A LAWN

Established lawns need regular attention, and not only from the lawn mower. There are specific tasks you can do, according to the season.

Spring

❁ As soon as the grass starts growing and the weather allows, rake the lawn to remove leaves and other debris.

❁ Give the lawn its first cut with the mower blades set high so that only the very tips of the grass are removed.

❁ Use a half-moon edging iron to neaten the edges of the lawn.

❁ Feed and weed the lawn.

❁ As spring turns to summer, gradually lower the blades of the mower to produce a closer cut.

Summer

❁ Apply summer feed.

❁ Weed the lawn.

❁ Continue mowing once a week. Ideally, rake before mowing to keep clover under control.

❁ At the height of summer, when the grass is growing vigorously, cut it twice a week.

❁ Keep the edges of the lawn neatly trimmed.

❁ If the weather is very dry, water the lawn and cut only once a week.

❁ As summer draws to a close, gradually increase the height of the mower blades for a longer cut.

Fall

❁ Early fall is an excellent time to sow a new lawn.

❁ Reduce the mowing frequency to once a week with the mower blades set high.

❁ Kill moss a couple of weeks before scarifying the lawn.

❁ Scarify the lawn to remove debris and promote good grass growth.

❁ Spike any compacted areas to aerate, and top dress the area.

❁ Top dress the lawn with a mixture of loam, sand and peat or peat substitute.

❁ Brush fallen leaves from the lawn.

❁ Returf or seed bare patches.

❁ Trim the edges of the lawn ready for winter.

❁ Clean and lubricate equipment ready for winter storage.

❁ Late fall/early winter is a good time for turf laying.

Winter

❁ Stay off waterlogged or frozen turf.

❁ Check that mowing equipment is in good repair ready for spring.

BELOW: *Drifts of flowers in a natural lawn add irresistible spring color.*

VICTORIAN FLAMBOYANCE

VICTORIAN GARDENS

WITH the Industrial Revolution, power and money moved from the landowners to the industrialists, who became the new creators of grand gardens. But the up-and-coming prosperous middle classes all wanted gardens, too. Numerous nursery gardens sprang up to supply the new demand. A spate of new gardening magazines appeared, many written by head gardeners. Although these were somewhat dictatorial in their approach, they were certainly widely read.

❧ The most striking aspect of Victorian gardens was 'bedding', which meant filling flowerbeds with patterns of brightly colored annuals and exotics. Head gardeners had to propagate all the necessary plants in enormous greenhouses, and often had to plant a completely new scheme overnight to surprise weekend guests. Meanwhile, a man called E.E. Budding invented the lawn mower, giving rise to the closely cropped, highly groomed, green English lawn.

Growing flowers naturally

❧ The extravagant Victorian floral displays inevitably brought a reaction – in the form of William Robinson, a cantankerous Irishman who started off as a gardener and ended up a journalist. His philosophy was to plant 'perfectly hardy exotic plants under conditions in which they will thrive without further care'. He insisted on informality and introduced the idea of naturalising bulbs in grass. He used color with great sensitivity and preferred permanent planting to the labor-intensive 'bedding' system. Not surprisingly, his ideas are incorporated into many of today's gardens.

The Jekyll/Lutyens partnership

❧ Gertrude Jekyll was a friend of Robinson's and the most influential garden designer in England before the Second World War. In 1889 she met a young architect called Edwin Lutyens and they collaborated on many gardens. He worked on the architectural aspects and hard landscaping and she on the planting. She had trained as a painter and was influenced by the sophisticated color theories of the day. She developed single-color and graded color schemes, quite different from the earlier brash bedding colors. Her naturalistic approach was particularly successful within the formal framework of Lutyens' bricks, steps and paving.

LEFT: *Cartoon of the architect Edwin Lutyens, whose partnership with Gertrude Jekyll produced some of the most influential gardens in the late nineteenth and early twentieth century.*

HURDLE BORDER EDGING

Modern border edging is a quick and simple way of containing soil and providing a neat mowing line, but the unnatural tones of pre-formed concrete edging are not always compatible with a romantic garden style. This rustic miniature fence adds definition to a garden border, and is as pretty as it is practical. If fresh willow stems are not available, soak older, dried-out ones in a large container of water overnight or longer, until pliable.

TOOLS AND MATERIALS

⊤ Mallet
⊤ Hazel sticks, 16–18 in (40–45 cm) long, ³/₄–1 ¹/₈ in (2-3 cm) in diameter
⊤ Long pliable willow stems, for weaving
⊤ Knife or cutters

1 Hammer hazel sticks firmly into the ground approximately 6 in (15 cm) apart along the border, so that the tops of the sticks protrude from the ground level with one another – approximately 12 in (15 cm). Hammer them into the ground only moderately firmly if a removable panel is desired.

2 Working with a handful of willows – about 10–12 – at a time, weave them in front of and behind alternate hazel uprights.

3 When you reach an end upright, go around the stick and back to the next, as in a figure of eight. Keep the willows compacted towards ground level as you work.

4 Continue adding bundles of willows until you reach the top of the uprights, always starting and finishing each bundle at the rear of the panel, trimming ends and tucking them in as necessary.

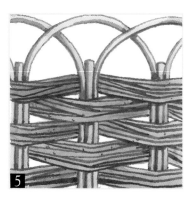

5 Cut single willows to lengths of about 36 in (90 cm). Starting at one end of the woven panel, push the ends of the single willows into the gaps beside alternate uprights to make the decorative overlapping hooped top.

VERSAILLES-STYLE PLANTER

Supermarkets and do-it-yourself stores are great places to pick up inexpensive growing kits, which come complete with compost, bulbs or seeds and even a planting diagram to ensure a naturalistic display with minimum effort. However, the containers supplied with these kits are all too often unsightly orange 'terracotta-effect' plastic. This attractive wooden cover pops neatly over the cheap and cheerful container, has just enough space left around the base for excess water to drain away and is sturdy and attractive enough to use year after year. If using paint rather than woodstain, use an all-in-one formulation, which combines primer, undercoat and topcoat.

TOOLS AND MATERIALS

⊤ Tape measure
⊤ Plastic planting trough
⊤ Pencil
⊤ Straight edge
⊤ Panel saw
⊤ ½ in (12 mm) exterior-grade plywood
⊤ Exterior wood glue
⊤ 2 x 2 in (50 x 50 mm) planed softwood
⊤ 8 corner joining blocks
⊤ ½ in (32 x 12 mm) No. 6 wood screws
⊤ Screwdriver
⊤ Carpenter's square
⊤ 2 in (50 mm) diameter turned knobs
⊤ Hot melt glue and glue gun (optional)
⊤ Medium/fine sanding block and sandpaper
⊤ Damp rag
⊤ Exterior paint or woodstain
⊤ Paintbrush

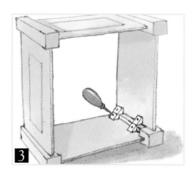

1 Measure the height and width of the plastic planter to be disguised. Cut four plywood panels ⅜ in (10 mm) wider and ¾ in (20 mm) taller than the plastic planter. Cut four plywood panels smaller than the first panels by 4 in (100 mm) all round and glue these in the middle of the first panels, using exterior wood glue.

2 Cut four corner posts of 2 x 2 in (50 x 50 mm) planed softwood, 2⅜ in (60 mm) taller than the height of the plastic planter.

3 With the smaller decorative plywood panels facing outwards, fix the panels to the corner posts, using corner joining blocks and wood screws. Align the bottom edge of the panels ⅜ in (10mm) up from the bottom of the corner posts, to leave a small gap at the base of the planter so that the water can drain away.

4 When all four panels and corner posts have been assembled, glue a decorative knob on the top of each corner post, using hot melt glue or exterior wood glue.

5 Sand all surfaces lightly and smooth off any rough edges with a sanding block. Rub off sanding dust with a damp rag.

6 Paint the planter using exterior paint or woodstain. Apply at least two coats, allowing drying times between coats according to the manufacturer's instructions.

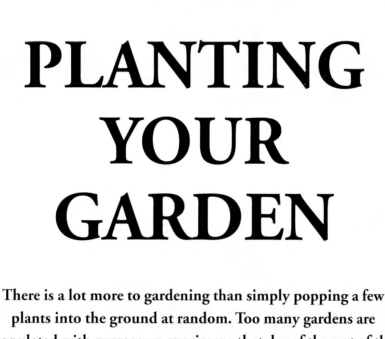

PLANTING YOUR GARDEN

There is a lot more to gardening than simply popping a few plants into the ground at random. Too many gardens are populated with overgrown specimens that dwarf the rest of the plants. Other times plants are placed in the wrong position and become straggly and neglected-looking.

❁

To create an interesting garden you need variety of color, height, form and texture as well as balance and simplicity. It is vital to consider the overall structure of your garden before you buy so much as a packet of seeds.

❁

Take a little time to choose the right place for the right plant and pay some attention to its planting requirements and your garden will reward you magnificently.

STARTING TO PLANT

Planting is one of the most enjoyable areas of gardening.
Placing something in the ground and watching it grow and
change with the seasons is incredibly satisfying, whether you are
planting seeds, shrubs, food crops, decorative perennials or trees.
Choosing the right plant for the right situation is at the heart of good
gardening practice. Every plant has its own individual feeding,
pruning and soil requirements. Some are easier to maintain than
others, but whatever you are growing, take time to absorb some basic
information about the needs of the plants in your garden.
This will enable you to enjoy consistently successful results.

Planting shrubs

❦ Deciding exactly where to plant shrubs is the most important, yet often overlooked, part of the planting process. Shrubs are the backbone of the garden, and deserve very careful consideration in positioning. What looks like a charming small plant in the garden center may quickly reach a size that will dwarf your garden, so take care to research predicted size before purchasing.

❦ Shrubs are often planted far too close together, their eventual spread having been disregarded at the planning stage. The result is a messy jumble of intertwined plants.

It is far better to plant at the recommended planting spacing, and fill in any initial bareness with perennials, which can be moved as the shrubs grow.

❦ Naturally, also plant according to the type of soil you have and any particular demands of the individual shrub. There is no point planting a sun-loving shrub in a shady spot for example, or a shrub that needs very rich, moist soil on a dry, rocky site.

BELOW: *Shrubs can provide as much texture and interest as perennials and annuals if chosen with care.*

Preparing the soil

❀ Although container-grown shrubs may be planted at any time of the year, they are easiest to establish in fall or spring. These are the ideal times for planting bare root shrubs, when the ground is warm and moist. If planted in very hot weather, your shrubs will need vigilant watering after planting.

❀ Shrubs are hopefully destined to live in the garden for a long time, so the soil needs to be adequately prepared to give them their best chance of survival. It is not sufficient simply to dig a hole the same size as the pot and drop in the plant.

❀ You must encourage the roots to spread into the surrounding soil by avoiding a sudden change between the environment in the pot and the garden soil. Container-grown roots will be reluctant to grow from the peat in the container into mineral soil, so add organic matter to an area approximately 4 in (10 cm) bigger than the pot all round to counteract this.

MOVING SHRUBS

Occasionally it may be necessary to move an established shrub. Some shrubs, such as gorse, particularly dislike being moved, so try to avoid doing so if at all possible. If overcrowding is the problem, move a neighboring, more resilient plant instead.

PLANTING A CONTAINER-GROWN SHRUB

1 Water the plant thoroughly at least an hour before planting. Fork over the soil where it is to be planted and remove any weeds. Incorporate a slow-acting fertilizer in the soil.

2 Dig a hole at least 4 in (10 cm) wider and deeper than the rootball. Mix organic matter such as compost with the removed soil, and replace a layer of this planting mixture approximately 4 in (10 cm) deep in the base and around the sides of the hole.

3 Place the plant in the hole while still in its pot, to check the planting depth. A cane or stick laid across the top of the pot should lie flush with the soil surface.

4 Ease the plant from its pot and place it in the hole. Backfill with the planting mixture, taking care to firm the soil sufficiently as you fill, to avoid air pockets forming.

5 Firm the soil around the plant with your hands, and water thoroughly, before adding a layer of mulch approximately 3 in (7.5 cm)

deep and 18 in (46 cm) wide around, but not touching the stems of the shrub, as this would encourage rotting. Mulching helps conserve moisture and control weed germination.

2

3

4

5

Staking shrubs

❀ Most shrubs do not need staking, but where a shrub has been planted in a new border, and does not have the benefit of other plants to support and protect it from wind rock, it may be necessary to provide additional support. This is particularly important when planting a top-heavy standard shrub. If the wind rocks the tall, vulnerable stem, the rootball may move, severing the roots as they try to spread out into the surrounding soil.

❀ By anchoring the base of the shrub, the top of the plant is permitted to move in the wind, encouraging the plant to grow stronger. Whatever staking method you use, consider it at an early stage, rather than when you notice damage or movement. Any instability you notice above the ground will probably indicate movement and possibly damage to the roots below the ground.

Staking when planting

❀ It is always advisable to stake when planting. Some stakes may be removed after they have performed their initial supporting role. For example, when a bushy shrub has been protected with short stakes while it settled into a new, exposed border, the stakes may be removed after a year or so when the roots are established and surrounding plants have grown to protective sizes. Very top-heavy shrubs, such as standard roses, are best left staked, as they are too vulnerable to breakage without support.

Staking established plants

❀ Staking an established plant may inadvertently cause root damage. If it is necessary to stake an established shrub, do not be tempted to knock in a stake close to the stem. The risk of damage to the root system is too great. Instead, knock in two stakes a good distance from the stem and connect them to the stem with heavy-duty rubber ties, to avoid chafing damage to the stem.

Types of support

❀ Tall standard shrubs will need sturdy wooden stakes made of rot-resistant timber, or wood treated with preservative. A selection of purpose-made plastic or wire supports is available in garden centers, alongside the traditional staking supports, canes. Twiggy sticks, simply pushed into the ground around a shrub, are also simple and effective.

❀ Purpose-made ties are available and, although it is possible to use string, these ties are a worthwhile investment. They incorporate spacers, which hold the stake taut against the stem, but which prevent chafing and can easily be adjusted as the plant grows.

BELOW: Most shrubs will not need staking, but if it has been planted in a new border it may need additional support.

STAKING A STANDARD SHRUB

1 *Prepare the planting hole as normal. Use a rot-resistant, thick timber stake, or one of wood treated with preservative. Place it firmly in the hole and knock it in until it is stable.*

2 *Plant the shrub as normal, in planting mixture lining a generously excavated area. Push the rootball up against the stake. The stake*

and rootball should now be approximately 4 in (10 cm) apart and the top of the stake level with the lower branches of the shrub.

3 *Firm the plant into the soil with your hands or your heel.*

4 *Fix a proprietary tie with spacer to connect the stem to the stake approx 6 in (15 cm) above soil level.*

5 *Fix a second tie around the stake and stem, just below the head of the shrub. Water in the shrub well and apply mulch as usual, taking care not to apply the mulch right up to the stem as this will encourage rotting.*

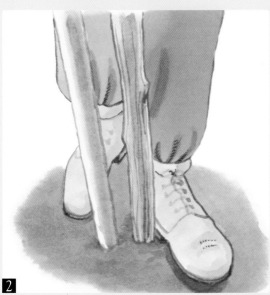

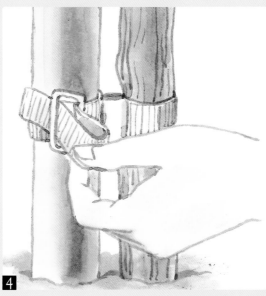

PLANTING TREES

TREES have a place in every garden. Even a tiny garden will benefit from the added height, color and shape of a small tree. Some, like acers, are even happy in containers. Since trees are generally intended for permanent planting, it is critical to research the anticipated final height before purchasing. You will need to find out the expected height of the tree after 10 years before committing yourself.

Siting a tree

❧ Careful positioning will save much heartache later, and may help keep you on good terms with your neighbors. Consider carefully whether that adorable 'miniature' conifer will in fact grow to block out large amounts of light from your or your neighbor's home.

❧ Also, check that you are not planting too close to the house. Some trees, such as poplars, are particularly notorious for damaging foundations and lifting paving, so research your choice carefully. Plants grown in the lawn look attractive, but deciduous trees will shed leaves, which will need to be raked up each fall.

❧ Planting a tree towards the back of a border, where leaves are allowed to slowly decompose and add to the organic content of the soil, is a lower maintenance option.

BELOW: *Trees provide year-round structural interest as well as seasonal color.*

STAKE HEIGHT

For many years, the advice given on staking a tree was to have the top of the stake level with the base of the head of the tree. However, contemporary thinking is that a shorter stake, which allows the head of the tree to sway in the wind, encourages better root growth and a sturdy trunk. You should therefore use a stake that reaches only one-third of the height of the tree.

❁ However, you may still wish to remove some of the fallen leaves if the tree is particularly large and the leaf fall significant.

❁ Research the degree of spread and coverage the mature tree will provide, as this will obviously affect the amount of shade beneath its canopy, and the type of plants that you will be able to plant under it.

Planting a tree in a lawn

❁ The same general guidelines that apply to shrubs apply equally to tree planting. The planting hole must be sufficiently deep and wide to allow a good amount of planting mixture to be incorporated into the hole. Most young trees will need support for at least the first two years of their life, particularly in windy areas.

❁ The stake should be applied vertically, close to the stem of a bare-rooted tree, but at an angle of 45° when planting a rootballed or container-grown tree. The guidelines here apply only to newly planted trees. If you are considering moving a mature tree, it is advisable to consult a professional tree surgeon.

PLANTING A TREE IN A LAWN

1 *Using sand, mark a circle approximately 4 ft (1.2 m) in circumference on the grass in the desired position. Cut into the turf with a spade and remove approximately 6 in (15 cm) depth of soil with it. Dig a planting hole deep enough to be at or just below the existing soil level on the tree stem, and wide enough to allow the roots of a bare root tree to spread out well. If you are planting a container-grown tree, plant at the same depth as the tree when in its container, and allow an area approximately half the diameter of the container all around the rootball.*

2 *Mix plenty of organic matter, such as well-rotted farmyard manure or compost, plus a general-purpose fertilizer with the soil removed from the hole.*

3 *Securely place a sturdy, rot-resistant stake in the hole, just to the windward side of where the tree will sit. Add a layer of planting mixture to the base of the hole. Place the tree in the hole, gently spreading out the roots if you are planting a bare-rooted tree. Use a* cane or spare stake to check that the soil level on the stem is level with the surrounding soil – approximately 2 in (5 cm) below the grass. Adjust the planting height by excavating further or adding more soil as necessary.

4 *Backfill the hole and firm in the tree with your heel or hands. Secure the stem to the stake with a tree tie. Water the tree in thoroughly and add a generous mulch around the stem to suppress weed growth and help conserve moisture in the soil.*

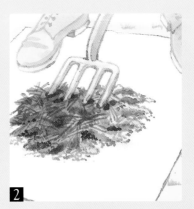

PLANTING CLIMBERS

THERE is a vast variety of climbers available, suitable for disguising or enhancing any number of vertical surfaces – from fast-growing Virginia creeper covering an unsightly old garage, to delicate annual sweet peas that can scramble prettily up a willow obelisk.

Siting a climber

❀ As with all planting, it is important to consider positioning carefully. Check that your intended climber will suit the soil, will receive the sunshine it needs and is appropriately sized for its location, support and your gardening habits when fully grown.

❀ Wisteria, for example, is very vigorous and needs regular tying in and pruning to keep it under control, so would not be a wise choice for a small area that you would prefer to be low maintenance. A self-clinging climber such as an ivy would be a better choice.

❀ Although container-grown climbers can be planted at any time when the ground is not frozen, waterlogged, or in extremely hot and dry conditions, fall and spring remain the best times for planting – when the ground is warm, but the sun will not dry the soil out too quickly. It is advisable to plant bare-rooted climbers in fall.

Types of climber

❀ Climber is a term used to describe a wide group of plants. Their common attribute is that they rely on something other than their own stem for support. Some, like ivy, have aerial roots, which attach themselves to solid surfaces, making them easy to grow up walls and fences.

❀ Clematis have leaves that twine around stems, leaves, wires or other narrow supports, while passionflowers have tendrils that coil around their supports, pulling the plant upwards. Ramblers, such as rambling roses, use thorns almost as crampons to attach themselves.

❀ There is also a group of climbers such as ceanothus, which do not actively climb, but which have lax, trailing stems that benefit from additional support.

Types of support

❀ The type of support needed will vary according to the individual plant and its climbing method. Annual climbers with twining tendrils, such as morning glory, need only light support, such as wires, willow, or even netting.

❀ Woody climbers such as wisteria and vigorous, scrambling climbers like honeysuckles need sturdy supports. It is always advisable to consider support at the planting stage; trying to apply support to an out-of-control established climber is a difficult task.

LEAVING A GAP BETWEEN A CLIMBER AND ITS SUPPORT

A common mistake is to plant a climber directly beside its support. The plant needs to be approximately 18 in (46 cm) away from the support so that the ground around the roots receives enough rainfall. Lean the plant gently towards the support and carefully spread out the roots before backfilling with planting mixture.

PLANTING A CONTAINER-GROWN CLIMBER

1 Dig over the site and remove weeds. Add shrub fertilizer to the area to be excavated.

2 Dig a planting hole approximately 12–18 in (30–46 cm) away from the wall, fence or support, following the general guidelines on planting all shrubs. Mix in a generous amount of organic matter with the excavated topsoil and line the planting hole with this mixture.

3 Water the plant well at least an hour before planting.

4 Place the plant, still in its pot, in the hole, and check the planting height with a cane. The soil level in the pot should be level with the surrounding soil. The exception to this rule is clematis, which needs its stems planted approximately 2 in (5 cm) deeper than its soil level in the container, to enable it to grow basal buds. These will give it an opportunity to renew itself if it is attacked by diseases or pests such as slugs.

5 Add or remove soil as needed to bring the plant to its correct height. Gently remove the pot and place the plant in the hole. Lean the climber against the support, and carefully spread out the roots. Add canes to the hole, leaning them towards the support and taking care not to damage the roots of the plant.

6 Backfill the planting hole with the planting mixture, making sure that there are no air pockets in the soil. Water thoroughly and firm in the plant with your heel or hands.

7 Train the stems up individual canes towards the supporting wall or fence. Secure the stems to the canes with purpose-made ties or garden twine. Even self-clinging plants or plants with tendrils will benefit greatly from this initial help. Add a generous depth of mulch around the plant, spread in a similarly generous area around it, leaving the stem itself clear so as not to encourage rotting.

2

3

4

5

7

Training methods

❀ Care in choice, positioning, planting and pruning all help you grow climbers successfully. However, training is also important, particularly on visual grounds, and you should consider training requirements at an early stage, while the plant is young and pliable.

❀ Left to their own devices, climbers will scramble upwards towards the light. Thus a climber that has been left untrained for many years may be very unattractive, with a mass of naked stems patchily covering the support, and a few small flowers way out of sight at the top of these stems. Such climbers will need drastic attention, which as well as being a major task, will temporarily denude the support.

❀ The surface beneath may not be in the best condition to accept new supports either, so in short, plan your training method early in the growing process. Spread out the stems of young climbers and tie them into the supports laterally, rather than letting them grow upwards in a single bunch of stems, which will be difficult to separate without damaging the plant later. Training the main stems horizontally thus allows all stems to reach the light and the plant is encouraged to flower at every level.

Training to control

❀ Although a climber scrambling crazily over an arch or around a doorway looks attractive, you may need to rein it in slightly to allow a smooth passageway for pedestrian access.

❀ Concentrate training efforts on those parts of the plant directly hampering easy movement, perhaps around the inner edge of an arch only, allowing the plant to spill prettily from its supports elsewhere. Some climbers may need training to encourage them to grow across a wall or other supporting surface, rather than outwards.

Training to encourage flowering

❀ When the climber has thrown up some good, long, pliable shoots from the main stems, bend these lateral shoots over in gentle curves and tie them on to the support. Flower buds will appear on the top edges of these curving branches, resulting in a support covered evenly in flowers, rather than just at the ends of the stems high above the support.

❀ As these trained shoots grow, new shoots will develop from them. Bend these over in the same way, while they are still flexible, and secure to the support. Continue in this way so that eventually the whole support becomes covered in an increasing series of arching stems. When training roses in this way, take care to cross over some of the stems rather than fan training, so that there is a good coverage of flowers all over the support.

Training to conceal

❀ Climbers are wonderfully useful for concealing unsightly features such as refuse areas, garden buildings or ugly fences. The same general rules about tying down lateral shoots apply. Depending on the area you

ABOVE: Wall-clothing climbers can soften the edges of a building and make it blend effortlessly with the garden.

are covering, and the plant you have chosen, you may need to install supports in addition to those on the vertical surfaces.

❀ Ivy and other self-clinging climbers are an excellent choice for concealing awkward shapes, as they clamber in all directions, attaching themselves by their suckers or aerial roots. You will need to install a structure, such as a network of wires between the eaves of a building and the wall below the edge of the roof, on to which to tie a less obliging plant.

Choosing ties

❀ In theory, all plant ties should be checked regularly to ensure that they are still holding the plant securely, but are not cutting into the bark as the plant grows.

❀ In reality, particularly on larger, woody climbers, it is not always practical to check every tie regularly. It is therefore best to use natural products for tying in, like raffia or soft twine, which will break under strain as stems thicken, rather than cut into the plant in the way that unyielding plastic or metal would.

TYPES OF CLIMBING PLANT

The particular support required depends largely on the type of climbing plant. Climbing and fixing methods are divided into the following categories:

AERIAL ROOTS: self-clinging climbers such as ivy and climbing hydrangea develop aerial roots from their stems, which clamp on to flat surfaces, making them generally self-supporting.

SUCKER PADS: other self-clinging climber types like Virginia creeper have sucker pads, which stick firmly on to flat surfaces.

TWINING TENDRILS: twining climbers, such as grapevines, climb by wrapping tendrils around other plants or purpose-made supports.

TWINING LEAF STALKS: clematis has leaf stalks, which entwine themselves around their supports.

TWINING STEMS: some climbers entwine their stems around neighboring plant stems or artificial supports. Honeysuckle is the most popular example and needs a sturdy support system.

GROWING CLIMBERS ON WIRES

IF you want to train climbers up a wall, and have not selected a self-clinging climber such as ivy, you will need to plan your support at an early stage. Although it is possible to use trellis, it would detract from the beauty of a particularly nice brick or stone wall, as well as being relatively costly to install. Wires provide a good, unobtrusive support for a wide range of climbers, and can be painted to match the wall for even greater discretion.

Choosing wire and fixings

❀ Although many gardeners simply bang a few nails into the wall and tie in whatever pliable wire is at hand, these measures are inadequate for a climber that is going to occupy an area of any sort of prominence in the garden.

❀ Cheap wire will quickly rust, leaving unattractive rust marks on painted walls, and is also susceptible to breakage. Although your climber may look undemanding when it is first planted, it will quickly grow in both height and weight. Thin wire will simply bend, and possibly even snap, under the strain of a heavy plant.

❀ Choose a strong-gauge galvanised wire. Plastic-coated wire is liable to lose its attractive coating eventually and looks very untidy. Any makeshift measures that need to be renewed later are difficult to replace. The plant will have grown significantly, making access difficult and damage to the plant likely. Therefore it is best to invest in good-quality wire and sturdy, properly applied fixings.

❀ Fixing a tension bolt at one end of the wire is a good idea if you feel that the wire may stretch. The wire may then be easily tightened if necessary.

ABOVE: *This seaside garden makes the most of its situation by growing the old-fashioned bright pink, pompom rambling rose 'Dorothy Perkins' up a pergola so that it is seen almost in silhouette against the blue ocean.*

TRAINING A CLIMBER ON A WIRE

1 First attach vine eyes to the wall. Although it may be possible to hammer these directly into soft masonry, a firmer fixing will be made by first drilling a pilot hole.

2 Insert wallplugs into the wall and screw in the vine eyes. The length of vine eye selected will depend on the type of plant grown. For example, a large-scale climber such as wisteria will need to be held away from the wall on wires, and needs long vine eyes to support the wires at the appropriate distance. Where the demands on a wire supporting system are not so great, for example when you are not planning to clothe an entire wall with a very large-growing, woody-stemmed plant, you could use wedge-shaped vine eyes. These are simply hammered directly into the wall.

3 Continue fixing vine eyes at the same height along the wall or fence, spacing them no more than 6 ft (1.8 m) apart. Fix parallel horizontal runs of vine eyes up the wall at intervals of approximately 20–24 in (50–60 cm). If the wires are too far apart, plants with tendrils may struggle to find the next wire and will need more frequent tying in than if the wires are more sympathetically spaced.

4 Thread galvanised wire through the hole in the first vine eye and wrap it tightly around itself, forming a secure fixing. Pass the wire through all the intermediate vine eyes until you reach the vine eye at the other end of the wall or fence and have completed the first horizontal run.

Pass the wire through this end eye and secure it so that the wire is held taut.

5 Curve over the stems of the climber and attach them in front of the wires using your chosen ties, such as raffia or string. Fix at as many points as necessary to ensure that the climber is held securely.

6 Continue tying in the plant in this way, pulling down and training in lateral shoots as they develop so that eventually the wall or fence is covered in a series of arching stems. These will produce a multitude of flowering buds, as well as clothing the surface evenly.

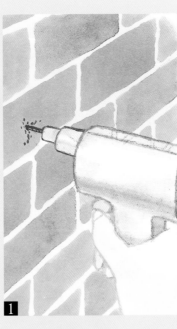

Growing climbers on trellis

- Wooden trellis has much to offer the gardener. Panels of timber battening nailed into squares or diamond formations may not seem very exciting in themselves, but trellis has a multitude of uses, particularly when combined with careful planting.
- It can add height to an existing wall, screen off the less attractive aspects of the garden, such as compost heaps, form part of existing garden structures such as arches, arbors, obelisks and pergolas, or simply be attached flat against a wall or fence to provide a convenient and sturdy support for climbing plants. The grid pattern is perfectly spaced, with the bars not too far apart, so that all kinds of climbers are encouraged to reach upwards without vast amounts of tying in.

ABOVE: *Hanging baskets are a popular way of increasing the growing area of a garden when all the horizontal and vertical surfaces have been filled with plants.*

Choosing trellis

- Trellis is available in many shapes and sizes, for example fan shaped, rectangular or square with an arched top edge. It is also possible to have trellis made to order to fit a particular area.
- It is worth buying the best-quality trellis possible, as the sorts of plants often grown on trellis, such as honeysuckle, can become quite heavy and unwieldy as they mature. Trying to clear a fully grown climbing plant in order to gain access to repair collapsing trellis is not an easy task. Timber that is approximately 1 in (2.5 cm) thick should be sufficiently sturdy, without appearing overwhelming.
- All trellis should be made of rot-resistant wood, or timber that has been treated with wood preservative. A wide range of shades for external wood are now available, which both color and protect the timber.
- Generally, the more subdued shades of slate grey, sage green and dusky blue are the most successful color choices, as they complement planting rather than fight against it visually. If you are attaching trellis to a flat surface, it is easier to paint it before it is fixed in position; but if the trellis is to form a freestanding divider, it is more convenient to paint it *in situ*.

BELOW: *Trellis is an inexpensive and versatile support for all kinds of climbing plants.*

Using trellis discreetly

❀ Because trellis is such a strong graphic shape, with its grid patterning, it can appear quite overwhelming if used in large quantities. In some cases, this may be a problem only initially. For example, where the trellis is being used as a screen, a vigorous climbing plant will eventually conceal the trellis almost entirely. In this instance, annual climbers such as sweet peas could augment the permanent planting until it is established.

❀ If you are planning to grow deciduous climbers over the whole of a house wall, wires may be a more subtle choice than trellis, which would compete with the strong lines of the brickwork when the leaves fall.

Fixing trellis

❀ Trellis may be permanently or semi-permanently fixed to walls and fences. If the wall or fence needs to remain accessible for maintenance, fix the trellis with hinges along its lower edge, and secure with a catch at the top. The whole trellis, with climber attached, may then be gently levered away from the vertical surface to allow repainting of the wall or fence.

❀ Whether permanent or hinged, the trellis needs to be held approximately 1 in (2.5 cm) away from the wall or fence on spacers for ventilation. The main stems of the climber can be trained into this space, and side shoots will grow out through the trellis towards the light, providing good overall coverage of the trellis.

FIXING TRELLIS PERMANENTLY TO A WALL

1 *Mark the position of the trellis on the wall. You will need battening level with the top and bottom of the trellis. If the trellis is over 4 ft (1.2 m) high, have an extra batten across the wall, behind the middle of the trellis. Drill the holes that will take the horizontal battens and insert wooden or plastic wallplugs in the wall.*

2 *Drill corresponding holes in the wooden batten spacers themselves and fix them to the wall. Drill and screw the trellis on to the battens, starting at the top. Use a spirit level to check that the trellis is horizontal.*

3 *Continue fixing the trellis on to the supporting battens, checking that the level remains true. Make sure that the finished trellis is firmly attached to the battening, and that the whole structure is securely fixed to the wall.*

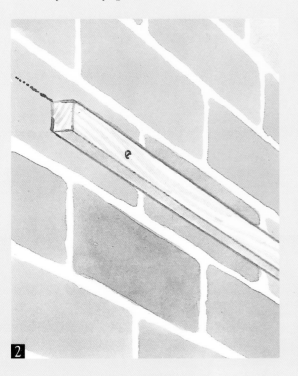

ABOVE: *This beautiful climbing* Rosa Phyllis Bide *decorates the walls of the house with its delicate pink blooms.*

Growing climbers on netting

❀ Netting is an inexpensive way of evenly supporting a climber over a wall or fence. It is, however, not sufficiently strong enough to support a very large-scale woody-stemmed climber such as wisteria over an entire house wall.

❀ Netting is not the most attractive nor the toughest support for climbing plants, but it does have particular uses, such as wrapping around awkwardly shaped objects where trellis would not be an option, and when planting climbers around tree stumps or poles.

❀ Netting is available in a variety of gauges, from quite sturdy rigid square steel mesh, to very flexible, lightweight plastic mesh. The lighter gauges are perfect for fixing between upright posts with straining wire, as temporary supports for annual climbers such as nasturtiums or morning glory, as well as beans, peas, cucumbers and tomatoes.

❀ Although netting is not as good looking as wooden trellis, it can be used as an economical and easy-to-fit support in small-scale applications where it will be quickly concealed by planting, for example when it is fixed to support a vigorous climber over a small fence.

❀ Choose a colored netting that tones inconspicuously with the support, and attach it well above ground level, so that the netting is not visible around the bare lower stems of the plant.

Leaving a growing space

As when attaching trellis, it is important not to simply nail netting directly on to a wall. Apply spacers between the netting and the wall, so that the plant will be able to climb between the two, as well as attach itself freely up and around all surfaces of the mesh, encouraging a good overall coverage of the wall.

Choosing fixings

Netting clips, which are widely available from garden centers and do-it-yourself stores, are not only easy to apply; they also incorporate a spacer, which holds the netting at an appropriate and uniform distance from the wall without recourse to battening. They are therefore an excellent fixing choice.

FIXING NETTING TO A WALL

1 Plan exactly where the netting will be. Position the first clip just below what will be the top level of the netting and hammer in a masonry nail to secure it in place. Alternatively, drill a pilot hole, plug it and fix the netting clip with a screw. Mark the position of the neighboring clip, using a spirit level to ensure that the netting will be horizontal. Hammer or drill, plug and screw the second clip in place as before. Continue applying fixing clips along the wall at roughly 24 in (60 cm) intervals.

2 Position the netting so that a horizontal strand is within the jaws of the clip and push it firmly home. Continue to press the netting into position along the remaining line of clips.

3 Smooth the net down against the wall and mark the position of the next row of clips, approximately 60 cm (24 in) below the first row. Roll the net up out of the way and hold it in place temporarily with string, enabling you to fix the next line of clips. Continue marking and fixing clips in this way, working down the wall. Although you may need to continue a long way down the wall initially to get a climber going, it might be possible to remove some of the netting at the base of the climber, should it prove unsightly when the plant is more established.

4 When all the netting is fixed securely, train the climber into it and tie in place to secure. Even self-supporting climbers with aerial roots, like ivy, will benefit from a little help as they start the ascent, and may need to be trained along canes from their position in the ground, towards the netting.

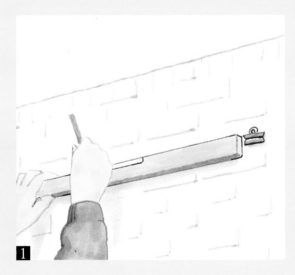

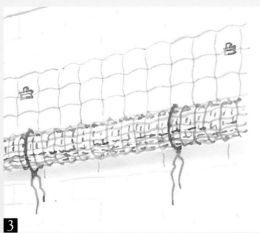
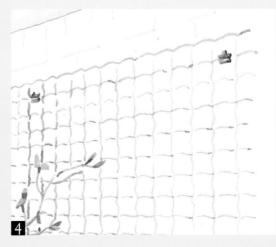

PLANTING BORDERS

THERE is a plant available to suit every space and climate and, with careful research and planning, you can produce borders that are alive with color and interest all year long. Always select plants appropriate to their location in terms of soil, sun and space requirements. Research carefully, to plan for visual interest throughout the year.

Choosing plants

❀ The selection of plants for a border is vast – from shrubs and trees to perennials, biennials, annuals, bulbs, tubers and even vegetables. Most garden borders benefit from a permanent background of shrubs, which provide form and structure throughout the year, supplemented by perennials, which will return year after year to provide their seasonal brilliance.

❀ It is tempting to overplant a new border with many varied specimens, all crammed closely together to cover the bare soil. However, you will achieve a far more cohesive effect if you plant in groups of threes and fives, aiming for a smooth, drifting look rather than the dotted impression created by lots of individual impulse buys scattered randomly throughout the garden.

❀ Remember that what may look like small plants when first purchased can grow at an astonishing rate, so read labels carefully and allow your plants room to grow. Any initial unsightly bareness can be filled with colorful annuals.

Planting perennials and annuals

❀ Container-grown perennials may be planted at any time of year, but to give them the best possible start, avoid planting in very hot, dry, wet or cold weather. Spring is a good time to buy perennials, as their foliage and roots can be thoroughly examined and the plant has an excellent chance of establishing well, provided all risk of frost has passed.

❀ Mix organic matter and fertilizer into the surrounding soil when planting, and the roots will be encouraged to grow out freely into it. Most perennials need to be planted at the same depth in the soil as they are in their pots, although a few plants prefer either deeper or shallower planting, so always read plant labels

carefully before planting. Most annual plants should be planted in late spring, when the danger of frost has passed.

❀ Buy healthy-looking specimens that are not pot bound nor showing signs of having been insufficiently watered. Check that the roots are not congested, and are plump and pale in color, not blackened and thin. The surface of the soil should be moist but not waterlogged, and free of algae and weeds.

Planting bulbs

❀ Although bulbs, rhizomes, tubers and corms are botanically different, they are generally considered together. All should be firm to the touch when purchased, with unblemished exteriors free from insect attack. If growth points are visible, they should not reveal any active growth, and there should be no fresh root development. Always keep this type of plant cool and dry between purchasing and planting.

PLANTING HEIGHT

As a general rule, bulbs are planted at a depth between two to three times their height, but there are some exceptions, so always check the packaging of your bulbs. Bulbs that are planted at the incorrect depth may fail to flower at all, a problem known as bulb blindness.

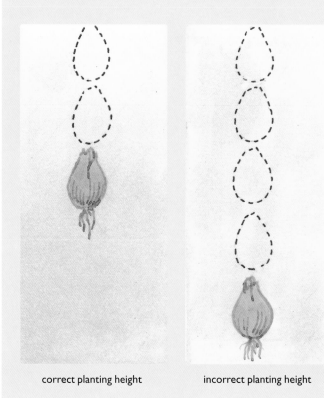

correct planting height   incorrect planting height

❀ After flowering, bulbs need to take in food for the next year's flowering from the dying foliage, so never be tempted to remove it prematurely or tie it off in an attempt to speed the process.

❀ In a border, this decaying foliage is not attractive, so plan your planting so that the leaves will be concealed by plants that begin active growth just as the bulb foliage is dying back. Alternatively, you could plant the bulbs in baskets, allowing them to be lifted out after they have flowered; they can then be moved to an inconspicuous part of the garden as the dieback process is completed.

PLANTING BULBS

1 Plant bulbs as soon as possible after purchase as they deteriorate quite quickly. Dig a planting hole and take care to place the bulbs the right way up.

2 Replace the soil in the hole, mixing it with grit to help drainage if your soil is heavy.

3 Once the hole has been filled, mark the planted area with sticks and water.

PLANTING A PERENNIAL

1 Soak the root ball thoroughly before planting. Tease out the plant without disturbing the root ball.

2 Dig a hole approximately twice the width of the root ball, and deep enough for the plant to sit level with the surface when in the hole. Incorporate plenty of organic matter with the surrounding soil before planting, so that the roots are encouraged to spread.

3 Firm in and water the plant. Continue to water in dry periods until well established. Adding a mulch around, but not quite touching, the plant will help to conserve moisture and suppress weeds.

PLANTING CONTAINERS AND HANGING BASKETS

CONTAINER gardening is a fantastically versatile and enjoyable aspect of gardening, and offers year-round opportunities for bringing color and texture to all areas of the garden. Containers have a place in every garden, whether you live in an apartment with a tiny balcony or window booth, or a house with a sizeable garden and patio. Container planting can visually blur the boundary between the lush greenery of the garden and the hard surfaces of the house itself, as well as paving or other hard external flooring.

The benefits of container gardening

❀ With container gardening, you can indulge your penchant for plants that would not thrive in your garden soil. While it is impractical to transform your garden soil permanently, for example rendering an alkaline border acidic so that you can grow camellias, it is perfectly possible to fill and maintain a container with precisely the right soil type that the plant needs to thrive.

❀ Containers can also be moved around to take full advantage of particular lighting and climatic conditions, which makes them even more adaptable. Plants that are too tender to be grown in the more exposed parts of your garden will appreciate being nurtured in containers close to the shelter of the house, and can be protected easily in extreme weather conditions.

❀ Containers enable you to ring the changes throughout the year. Underplanting containers with bulbs will lift your spirits as the dark days of winter give way all too slowly to spring. Containers come into their own during summer when bedding plants burst into life and blaze away well into fall. Lilies and fuchsias add an autumnal glow, while heather, pansies and berried evergreens provide cheery color all through winter.

Increased options

❀ Container gardening also extends the growing area. When you have planted up every spare inch of soil in the garden and have run climbers up every vertical surface, baskets hanging from wall-mounted brackets or even from the ceilings of pergolas and other structures, contribute yet another level of interest.

❀ It is becoming increasingly fashionable to plant edible plants in containers too, such as tomatoes, strawberries and herbs. Not only is this pretty, but practical, too. There is no need to stray down into the depths of the garden on a winter's lunchtime to collect a sprig of thyme, when you have a well-stocked herb basket just outside the kitchen door. Window boothes and troughs add even more planting opportunities.

ABOVE: *A successful hanging basket requires a subtle and balanced blend of flowers.*

Choosing containers

❀ Almost any type of container is suitable for planting, provided it is weatherproof and can have drainage holes added to it if they are not already present. It is advisable to raise containers slightly off the ground, using purpose-made feet or bricks, so that water can run freely away from the base.

❀ A wide range of purpose-designed containers is on offer at any garden center, in a whole spectrum of shapes, sizes and materials and at all price levels. There is also great satisfaction to be had in adapting containers for planting, for example drilling drainage holes into an old copper wash boiler that has long ceased to serve its original purpose, but which would look wonderful when imaginatively planted.

Planting a hanging basket

❀ As with any form of planting, check that the plants you intend growing will thrive in the site chosen. For example, there is no point planting sun lovers in deep shade – they will grow leggy and not flower well, so read labels carefully before purchasing. Loam-based compost is advised, as it holds moisture well and is easier to re-wet than peat-based products should it dry out completely.

PLANTING A HANGING BASKET

1 Remove the basket chain using pliers. Place the basket on a flower pot to hold it steady as you work. Press the basket liner into position.

2 Combine water-retaining granules with the compost and add water. The granules will swell, making the compost more bulky, so do not fill the basket until the gel has absorbed the water and appears jelly-like. Add a layer of compost to the basket.

3 Trailing plants will soften the lines of the basket and provide all-over interest. Make an X-shaped cut in the liner for each plant.

4 Very gently compress the rootball of each small plant in order to feed it through the liner into the compost.

5 Continue planting the container, building up the layers of compost and plants and firming in well, until the basket is almost full. Plant upright plants towards the center of the top layer, surrounded by trailing plants. Leave sufficient space for watering.

KNOWING THE GROUND RULES OF PLANTING

One of the most important things to understand when starting
to garden is that plants originating from different parts of the world
will thrive in the conditions they have adapted to and will suffer if you
try to grow them in conditions that do not suit them. It is much more
satisfying to grow plants that will enjoy the existing soil, climate and
aspect in your garden than to try and grow plants that would be more
at home elsewhere. If you garden on lime, for example, choose
lime-tolerant plants, and if you live in a frost pocket do not
choose tender plants from warm countries.

Plant associations

❊ Think carefully about plant associations. In fact, this is
made easier by understanding the origins of plants. Those
that come from similar regions of climate and soil will
nearly always associate well together, but trying to grow
rhododendrons, which are acid-lovers, together with the
daisy family will not only be unsuccessful but will not
look good either. Another important thing is to try and
choose plants that will not outgrow their allotted space.

ABOVE: *Gravel is a very good mulch for a dry garden, keeping the moisture in
and preventing weeds from taking hold. Most of the daisy family will respond well
to dry gardens, as will rock roses, both heliathemum and cistus, as well as
alliums and verbascums.*

ABOVE: *Plants that like shady areas include hostas, like this* Hosta undulata
'Univittata', *euphorbias, lilies and the beautiful drooping white flowers of*
Dicentra spectabilis 'Alba'.

Plants for particular aspects

❀ A north-facing wall in total shade will be colder than other parts of the garden. Even plants that tolerate these conditions will grow more slowly than they would in other areas. In the main, plants grown for their foliage are better on north-facing walls than those grown for their flowers. There are a few flowering plants suitable for such walls. They include the evergreen climbing hydrangea (*Hydrangea petiolaris*), which will climb a large wall without help and produce lace-cap hydrangea flowers that turn a pretty tan color as they fade and last into winter.

❀ Shade plants often have bigger leaves than other plants. They include hostas, foxgloves, bergenias, ferns and euphorbias.

❀ The climbing rose 'Guinée', with its deepest red flowers and rather sparse leaves will do well on a north wall, as will the almost thornless white rose 'Madame Alfred Carrière'. This rose has a first flush of flowers in early summer and keeps on flowering, although less profusely, for the rest of the season.

❀ East-facing walls are very difficult. After a frost the early morning sun may damage the buds of otherwise hardy rhododendrons, camellias and magnolias.

❀ Good climbing plants to grow include *Actinidia kolomikta*, which has large heart-shaped green leaves with cream and pink variegations. The color will not show on young plants or old plants grown in too much shade. Virginia creeper is another good climber for an east-facing wall and the feathery yellowy-green flowers of *Alchemilla mollis* will liven up the area nearer to the ground.

❀ South-facing walls are hot and dry. Silver, scented Mediterranean-type plants and plants from Australia and New Zealand will thrive in this sort of area. There is a wide choice of suitable plants, including the asters and other daisies, many herbs and many plants with colorful flowers.

❀ West-facing walls are the kindest. They get the evening sunlight and suffer less from frost. Here you can grow delicate and exotic plants that need shelter. These often come from places like California and include the bright yellow, wall-trained fremontodendron, the Ceanothus family with their clouds of bright blue flowers and *Passiflora caerulea*, the hardiest of the passion flowers with its strange exotic blooms and oval orange fruits.

❀ *Carpenteria californica* is an evergreen shrub from California, which produces an astonishing display of large, yellow-centered white flowers in summer. It may become a little shabby-looking after a cold spell, but soon recovers its good looks.

ABOVE: *Wallflowers, verbena and parsley have all been planted in generous clumps to create this bright and cheerful summer border.*

Beds and borders

❀ By now you will be anxious to choose the herbaceous and colorful plants for your borders. This is the purely decorative part of planting and it is tremendously exciting.

❀ You can work out appropriate schemes, pinpointing which plants and how many are to go where. A dictionary or encyclopedia of plants is invaluable at this stage. A good plant book will describe each plant, tell you how large it will grow, where it comes from and how to cultivate it.

❀ It is best to write down the names of each plant on your plan. You can color in the areas so you appreciate how the scheme will work. Place the large trees and shrubs first to give a good structural basis then work down to the smallest. Remember to allow for plant growth. Flowering times are important too. Mix early and late flowerers in the bed or border so that you get a balance through the summer and fall. List the plants you have chosen separately and the number required of each. This makes it easier when plant shopping or ordering.

Bed or border?

❀ A flower border is a growing area backed by a fence, hedge or wall, whereas a flowerbed is usually something you can walk around and see from all sides. It is important to keep beds and borders in scale with the garden.

❀ In a large garden you can have long, deep borders and allot space to a specific type of plant in the form of a rose garden perhaps or a fernery, whereas in a small garden you may be restricted to narrow beds and mixed planting for year-round effect. Whichever you have, always try to break up the garden into workable units.

❀ Borders should always have a background. Hedges can make good backgrounds but they need maintenance and steal water and nutrients from herbaceous plants. Leave a narrow path or strip wide enough for a lawn mower between the border and the hedge to allow room for weeding and clipping. This should be wide enough to allow you to bend down. Allow, too, for the spread of hedge growth and the eventual width of the hedge.

ABOVE: *This large island bed has been given an informal shape and is planted with low-growing plants at the edges and tall plants in the middle to give it an interesting shape. The color scheme relies very much on reds and purples.*

❀ Fences are also a possibility and again, you should leave a gap between border and fence so you can paint it. The gap can be trampled earth and just wide enough to use. If you are willing to do the maintenance in winter, the space can be quite narrow.

❀ All gardeners use trial and error when planning something as complicated as a bed or a border, but you can eliminate some of the error by researching the plants first. All beds and borders grow and change, so after three years you may want to thin out, move or replant.

ABOVE: *This neat gravel path is edged on either side by upstanding irises, which give it form and color but also a 'marching' quality, taking you swiftly down to the foliage arch.*

Size of borders

❀ The deeper a border, the more plants you can grow in it. In a 4 ft (1.2 m) border you could grow one climber at the back plus two rows of ground cover plants or one of shrubs. Alternatively, you could grow a clipped, trained wall shrub and one row of ground cover plants.

❀ If you try to grow more, the plants will suffocate each other and you will be forever clipping, trimming and cutting back. In a 3 ft (1 m) border you could probably get away with climbing plants at the back and one row of small shrubs but you might decide to concentrate on tiny rock plants instead.

❀ You need nearly 9 ft (2.7 m) to get in three tiered rows of plants comfortably. In a 5 ft (1.5 m) border you could probably just get three rows in, thereby incorporating much color. The tiers should not be planted in strict rows unless the garden is very formal. The plants should be planted in drifts, the taller ones mingling slightly with the shorter ones, so that you get a natural-looking mixture, producing a more varied, patchwork effect.

❀ The maximum satisfactory depth for a bed is 9 ft (2.7 m), unless you have decided on an island bed that you can walk all around. You can create a 12 ft (3.5 m) bed but you need much larger clumps so the size is more suited to a shrub and conifer border or certainly you will want to use some shrubs and conifers to break up the area.

ABOVE: *The cushioned quality of these rounded plants gives the whole of this large bed a quilted quality that is most attractive.*

Plant chart for borders and beds

❀ Designing a border or bed that will look good all summer long and into fall is complex. You need to include plants of different heights, so that the area will have a sculptural and harmonious shape.

❀ A chart that includes all the plants you want to grow will enable you to tell at a glance whether you have enough tall, medium-height and small plants and will help you to place them on your planting plan. Make a grid for each border or bed and as you choose the plants for each, fill them in on the grid.

❀ You will soon see where there are gaps. This will help you to graduate the height only. You will still have to decide on a color scheme, but it is an enormously helpful exercise in getting to know more about plants in general. You can include perennial plants, annuals and shrubs in the chart, and bulbs, too, if you wish.

Ground cover planting

❀ It was once considered aesthetically pleasing to grow each plant in a border individually, leaving an area of bare soil around it so that each plant was treated as a specimen. Nowadays it is considered more attractive to

ABOVE: *Effective ground cover can be given by using different heights of plant and variety in the color of flower.*

allow groups of plants to blend into one another, creating a close blanket of green from which the flowers will rise like Aphrodite from the sea.

❀ This creates a good-looking, colorful result and is also a form of ground cover that helps keep down weeds and reduces the amount of maintenance necessary in the border. Ground cover is also useful under trees where there is not enough light or moisture to support healthy grass. In addition, ground cover plants can be used on steep banks where mowing grass would be difficult or dangerous.

❀ The range of plants that can be grown as ground cover is enormous. Even plants that do not spread of their own

ABOVE: *Skilfully planted marigolds, petunias, hollyhocks and poppies in raised beds framed by a twig fence.*

accord can be used as ground cover if planted densely. Ground cover plants have a practical purpose but they also have a unifying effect in a small garden, especially when one variety of plant is allowed to create a smooth sweep of foliage.

Useful ground cover plants

❀ The best ground cover plants are evergreen. St. John's wort (*Hypericum*) can be grown in a shady part of the garden where its bright yellow flowers will glow out of the darkness. Rose of Sharon (*Hypericum calycinum*) flowers from early summer to early fall. It makes a good specimen plant in non-shady places, too, but if planted in a border it can be invasive.

❀ The periwinkles (*Vinca*) are excellent at covering the ground but can be invasive too, so plant them in woodland where they will have to struggle a little. *Vinca minor* grows to only just off the ground. It normally has pale lilac flowers but white and dusky red forms are attractive and slightly less invasive. *V. major* will reach 12 in (30 cm) and climb into nearby shrubs. It can be difficult to control when grown among other plants.

❀ Ivy (*Hedera*) does well in shade. Irish ivy (*Hedera helix* 'Hibernica') has large green leaves and will grow in dense shade. It is a good maintenance-free plant grown in a north-facing, little-used part of the garden.

❀ Dead-nettles (*Lamium*) make excellent ground cover plants under trees. *Lamium galeobdelon* 'Silver Carpet' has yellow flowers and evergreen leaves heavily spotted with silver. It is invasive but not difficult to pull up where it has outgrown its space.

❀ When planting under trees it is vital to prepare the soil well and to remove all weeds such as couch grass, nettles, and ground elder, otherwise their roots will entwine with your plant roots to disastrous effect.

❀ In a sunny, well-drained spot, the rock rose *Helianthemum nummularium* grows vigorously and makes excellent colorful ground cover. There are many named varieties in pretty shades of red, yellow and white. They should be cut back severely with shears when the flowers are over in summer or they will become leggy and lose value as ground cover. Do not prune in spring or you will remove the flower buds for the year.

ABOVE: *Bulbs can be used to provide a blanket of coloring in the spring months using such flowers as the crocus and the bluebell.*

Alpine and rock garden planting

❀ Some of the most enchanting plants available to the gardener are the tiny alpine and rock plants that originate high up on mountainsides. Gardens created for these little treasures should always be in a light, open, sunny situation to emulate their places of origin as nearly as possible.

❀ The rock garden should face south or west to provide the best and longest light. It should not be near trees, which will cast unwanted shade and damage the tiny plants with drips of water and falling leaves.

❀ It should be on a slope to ensure good drainage. In their natural habitat, alpines receive plenty of moisture from melting snow but the water drains through quickly and the soil does not become waterlogged. All alpines dislike bad drainage.

❀ The main features of a rock garden are terraces and flat areas, well-drained soil behind stone outcrops for growing small plants, and pockets and crevices for plants so that their roots are shaded.

ABOVE: *The pasque flower (*Pulsatilla vulgaris)*, a native of the Carpathian mountains, needs a sunny, open place in the rock garden and associates well with carpeting thymes and sedums.*

Materials and arrangement

❀ Any rocks you use should not lie on the surface of the soil but should appear to emerge from it; as in natural rocky outcrops. Choose local stone if possible. It is less expensive to transport and will look more in keeping. Limestone, sandstone, granite or tufa can all provide a natural appearance by simulating natural rock formations.

❀ A scree is a flat or sloping area of rock fragments with a little soil, plus a few small pools to increase the humidity. In nature, a scree is virtually a river of loose stones found at the foot of a mountainside before the meadow begins.

❀ An increasingly popular way to grow rock garden plants is in a raised bed. This is easy, inexpensive and takes up less space than a purpose-built rockery. A height of $1\frac{1}{2}$–3 ft (0.5–1 m) is recommended. The retaining walls can be of bricks, stone, reconstituted stone or railway sleepers. You can build a series of terraces to create extra interest and a place for trailing plants.

BELOW: Gentiana acaulis *makes a thick cushion of foliage and its beautiful blue trumpet flowers bloom in spring. It should be planted in a sunny position, turned slightly away from the sun in sandy soil that does not dry out.*

Choice of rock plants

❀ Rock plants coming from similar places of origin will associate well together and will thrive if you give them the conditions they are adapted for.

❀ Scree conditions are the most successful for growing plants from higher regions. A few flat stones here and there add interest. To show up against the pebbles, dark green is the best leaf color, although many suitable plants have grey leaves, which also look attractive.

❀ Suitable plants include the tight green hummocks of *Armeria juniperifolia* 'Bevan's Variety', which are completely hidden by bright pink round flower heads in spring. *Asperula lactiflora caespitosa* and *A. suberosa* both make tuffets surmounted by pink tubular flowers with long flowering periods.

❀ *Veronica canescens* has bright blue flowers above silvery tufts and *Edraianthus pumilo* has lavender bellflowers. There are bellflowers (*Campanulas*) for all sorts of garden situations. Some good ones for scree are *C. allionii*, *C. bellidifolia*, *C. saxifraga*, *C. tridentata* and *C. aucheri*, all of which have stemless bells of violet-blue.

❀ There are many plants from Australia that thrive in scree conditions, and *Celmisia coriacea* from New Zealand has white daisy flowers with silvery leaves. *Lewisia tweedyi* needs winter protection from a pane of glass or half a clear plastic water bottle used as a small cloche.

Acid-loving alpines

❀ If you have acidic soil, this is a good opportunity to have a rock garden for a different range of plants. Many of these plants thrive in cool north-facing positions. If your soil is neutral or alkaline, you can build a raised bed 3 ft (1 m) or so above ground level and fill it with ericaceous compost to suit these plants.

❀ Many primulas will grow well in moist acidic soil, including *P. vialii* whose flowers are violet spikes with red tops. *Trillium sessile* associates well with *Anemone nemorosa* and the harebell poppy (*Meconopsis quintuplinervia*) has hanging heads of single pale lavender flowers on slender stems all summer. Gentians, so difficult to grow in ordinary soil, flourish on acidic soils. *Gentiana sino-ornato*, *G. pumila* and *G. verna* all have flowers of a lovely deep blue. Lastly, there are some tiny rhododendrons, such as *R. hanceanum* 'Nanum', which has pale yellow flowers and grows to 6 in (15 cm) tall.

ABOVE: *The carpeting Phlox subulata 'Oakleigh Blue Eyes' will do well in any sandy and stony soil in the sun with adequate warmth and moisture.*

BELOW: *Some species of rhododendron will grow well in a rock garden, particularly one with acidic soil; this type of soil lends itself well to a mixture of plants.*

STRUCTURING YOUR GARDEN

Imagine a garden of separate areas or 'rooms', each one with its own 'look', yet conforming to the overall style of the garden. Each should be hidden from the others so that every new one comes as a surprise. Link these areas with attractive 'gateways' or 'walks', however short. A narrow path between tall hedges will encourage you to walk quickly to the next point of interest; the lower the hedge and the wider the path, the more you are encouraged to wander slowly and enjoy the planting on the way. Creating sudden openings from one area to another is one way to deal with the transition. Some hedges are dense and close-knit, others more open and lace-like, giving glimpses through them.

Backcloths

❀ Clipped shrubs can be used as a backcloth for a flower or shrub border. They can also create a backcloth for a pretty garden seat. A niche can be cut into a yew hedge to hold a sculpture or water feature.

❀ On the whole, dark green varieties of plant are more useful as backcloths than golden ones. Nearly all plants look good against dark green. Box has possibilities as a backcloth, but it takes longer to grow to a good height.

ABOVE: *A disciplined gravel path, marked by curved lines of brick, is flanked by a clipped hornbeam hedge, leading the eye to the open countryside and yellow cornfield beyond.*

ABOVE: *A generous wooden bench is surrounded by color – from the tiny pink and white erigeron and scented thyme at ground level to the two 'Ballerina' rose bushes and silvery Artemisia 'Powys Castle' at the back.*

ABOVE: *In this clever ground cover planting, everything has a positive shape and there are no gaps. The spreading plants are punctuated by the round heads of alliums and the tall spires of yellow verbascums.*

❀ Another good clipped backcloth plant is the Lawson cyprus (*Chamaecyparis lawsoniana*). This is not as dark a green as yew, but an attractive dark blue-green. Like yew, it needs clipping twice in the growing season, but unlike yew it will not rejuvenate from old wood, so if you let it get out of hand, it will not recover. In fact, if you are going to grow a backcloth hedge it must be kept clipped and tidy or it will ruin the effect of any planting or other features in front of it.

Shelter belts

❀ If you are lucky enough to have a garden right next to open countryside, it will probably have the disadvantage of strong winds sweeping in. On the principle that it is usually most satisfactory to keep the formal part of the garden near the house and to allow it to become more informal as it moves away from the house, an informal shelter belt can be made of mixed evergreen and deciduous shrubs.

❀ A hedge is better than a wall because it allows the wind through gently, whereas when the wind hits a wall, the force is severe and can be very damaging. If the wind really tears into the garden, it is advisable to have the double protection of taller trees and then a lower hedge.

❀ The Scots pine (*Pinus sylvatica*), larch (*Larix*), Lombardy poplar (*Populus nigra* 'Italica') and white willow (*Salix alba*) are all good shelter trees for the outer belt. In front of them you can grow dog roses (*Rosa canina*), common hawthorn (*Crataegus monogyna*), privet (*Ligustrum*) and other tough native shrubs, which look attractive and will offer food and protection for small wild animals and birds.

❀ There are several interesting variegated forms of privet; the roses and hawthorn are both pretty when in flower and have bright red hips or berries in fall.

❀ If you live by the sea, you can use *Escallonia macrantha*, which has healthy-looking shiny green leaves, *Olearia* x *haastii* with its grey-green leaves and whitish daisy flowers, *Hippophae rhamnoides*, pyracantha or *Viburnum tinus*, all of which are attractive in an informal situation and can stand salt-laden winds.

ABOVE: *It is easy to divide up your garden with the careful use of plants, shrubs and hedges, creating attractive and verdant areas.*

Divisions

❀ Formal divisions in the garden can be made with evergreen plants such as yew, box, chamaecyparis or holly. These are all easy to shape and are useful for dividing the garden with growing 'walls'. They make strong architectural shapes and can be clipped into pillars or gateways, or given bobbles on top and arches within them. You can make a stunning display by growing the climbing nasturtium, *Tropaeolum speciosum*, with its small flowers of deepest red, up a dark green yew.

❀ For an informal, irregular garden, it may be more desirable to use hedging, which lets a little light through and through which you can just glimpse what lies beyond. Good plants for this sort of hedge are beech (*Fagus sylvatica*) and hornbeam (*Carpinus betulus*). Both are deciduous and make elegant hedges. They have larger leaves than the evergreens, are less closely packed and have an elegant habit of growth.

❀ If your garden suffers from severe winters, you may prefer to use evergreens for all hedges to give protection to other plants during winter. A technique known as tapestry or mosaic hedging combines a number of compatible plants within the same hedge to provide changing visual effects throughout the year.

❀ You can combine deciduous with evergreen species and provide a colorful and varied background. This kind of hedge is probably best only in larger gardens or very informal wild gardens.

Screening

❀ If you want to screen the utility parts of the garden such as the compost heap, the garden shed or an oil tank, you can use a complete blocking off device, such as a tall hedge, or you can use a low hedge or individual shrubs.

❀ You can draw the eye away from the work area with some interesting tree or other feature, or divide the path leading to it, having it curve away from the work area and leading perhaps to a small arbour.

❀ A garden shed can be made much more attractive with a coat of paint. Modern paint ranges include very good positive blues, greys and blue-grey colors, which should be used on anything else you paint, such as fences or doors, if you want to retain a feeling of unity.

❀ Evergreen planting next to the shed can also help disguise its workaday quality. If you want to disguise it during summer only, *Fuchsia magellanica* makes an

ABOVE: *A beech hedge makes a good, dense green garden divider in summer. Its leaves turn a copper brown and remain attached all winter so it is really attractive all year round.*

attractive tallish bush with lots of pendant flowers late into the fall and will retain its leaves during winter. You can then cut it back in spring.

❀ The variegated form has pretty grey-green leaves with darker markings. If you want something taller, *Garrya elliptica* is an evergreen grey-green shrub with slender long catkins. It looks splendid grown next to *Viburnum bodnantense* 'Dawn', which has pretty pink flowers on bare stems in winter and grows its leaves when the flowers are over.

Noise barriers

❀ Hedges can help to screen out unwelcome sounds such as steady traffic. You will not eliminate noise altogether but can muffle it slightly, and the sight of the screen will help psychologically to make the noise less annoying.

❀ If you can do some earth moving and create a bank of earth, and then plant an evergreen shelter belt up the side of it, it should help, although it is difficult to keep out the sound of a nearby highway, no matter what you do. Other penetrating sounds, such as children's playgrounds, workmen's drills and radios are almost impossible to block out.

Using Leyland cypress

❀ The Leyland cypress (*x Cupressocyparis leylandii*) grows very fast, which is why so many people plant it as a screen and perimeter hedge. Unfortunately, it often gets out of hand. If it is not clipped regularly it grows far too tall and if it has been left too long, it cannot be rejuvenated by cutting back hard, as yew can.

❀ However, it does respond well to regular clipping and can be shaped into hedges with interesting shapes. Although the golden form is frequently chosen, the dark green form is often more attractive, especially in association with other planting. If it does get too big and beyond control, the best thing is to cut it down and start again.

BELOW: *The disciplined clipping of this leylandii hedge into a low green 'wall' and gateway demonstrates that there is no need to let this fast-growing hedging tree get out of hand.*

Links

❀ Links between one part of the garden and another can be leisurely, following a path that leads from one to another, or they can be sudden. One area surrounded by hedges or shrubs can let immediately through an opening on to the next.

❀ A path hedged on both sides by tall evergreens such as yew hints at secrets beyond and will lead the visitor quickly from one area to another. A low hedge of box or the shrubby honeysuckle, *Lonicera nitida*, will slow the visitor down, encouraging examination of the flowers and shrubs behind the hedge. A curved path is immediately intriguing and asks to be investigated.

❀ Links need not be made of hedges. A tiny piece of woodland or groups of shrubs on either side of a path can be division enough. Shrubs that make good linking plants are the evergreen *Viburnum tinus*, whose dark green leaves and pretty white flowers are produced in winter when little else is out.

❀ *Choisya ternata* is another useful shrub, with a characteristic smell to its leaves – that you either love or hate – and white flowers in summer. The yellow *C. t.* 'Sundance' can look cheerful grown against a dark foliage shrub.

❀ When grouping shrubs as an informal link you can include a small tree to give height and interest. Some of the hawthorns make pretty little trees. *Crataegus laevigata* 'Paul's Scarlet' has double red flowers in spring but may not produce berries; *C. persimilis* 'Prunifolia' has glossy dark green leaves, which turn orange and scarlet in fall, and lots of dark red berries. They will grow to around 3 m (10 ft).

ABOVE: *From the brightly colored planting of this bed you are invited through an imposing archway of sweet bay (*Laurus nobilis*) to whatever lies beyond.*

ABOVE: *A curved woodland path of slate chippings lined with rounded stones dug up from the garden itself, leads enticingly from the entrance gate to a more open area of the garden.*

Woodland links

❀ Links can open out and become woodland walks. Paths through them should be fairly wide to give a feeling of leisure and encourage people to take time to enjoy the walk.

❀ You can create a tiny bit of woodland in a very small transitional area using forms of birch. If you plant two or three together to keep their growth to a minimum, you will create a little grove in which none of the individual trees will grow too large. Interesting birches to try are *Betula pendula jacquemontii*, which has pure white stems that show up well in winter light with large areas of shaggy brown, peeling bark, an attractive fall leaf color and large catkins.

❀ The paper birch (*Betula papyrifera*) has large leaves and the bark peels off in large sheets to reveal white underneath. It prefers moist conditions. Some birches have orange or brown stems. *Betula albo-sinensis* has red to orange-red peeling bark. All of these look interesting in winter.

❀ The lacy foliage of birches allows a certain amount of light through so they can be underplanted with suitable small plants. Underplanting should be kept simple. Birches underplanted with tiny hardy cyclamen such as *Cyclamen hederifolium* and *C. coum* look enchanting in later summer and winter. The cyclamen grow well under trees, seeming to need little moisture. You can plant them right up to the tree trunks in generous drifts.

❀ Cyclamen need no associates since they look so attractive and dainty on their own. However, if you would like to add a little more greenery to the whole look, you can plant the area with ferns. They should be low-growing varieties because tall ones will dwarf the cyclamen, the true eye-catchers, on the ground. *Athyrium filix-femina* 'Frizelliae' is the tatting fern, found in Ireland about 100 years ago. It is a charming little fern, seldom growing more than 12 in (30 cm) tall.

❀ The Japanese painted fern (*Athyrium japonicum* 'Mettalicum') has soft grey leaves with purple midribs merging to grey-green at the margins. It likes a sheltered spot.

❀ *Blechnum penna-marina* is a tiny creeping species, which creates mats of dark green, roughly textured fronds. Another useful plant for light woodland is *Lathyrus vernus*, one of the sweet pea family. It is a low-growing shrub with matt evergreen leaves and bright blue-pink flowers in spring and summer, which turn almost turquoise as they age.

❀ If you create a narrow archway or perhaps a living gateway of evergreen shrubs at each end, this woodland can become a separate garden enclosure in its own right, as well as forming a transitional area.

BELOW: *A narrow stretch of woodland comprising silver birches, grown in a clump so that they will not grow too tall, leads the visitor to a separate enclosure.*

ABOVE: *This charming little summerhouse or gazebo with its tiled roof and red uprights marks the end of a grassy walk, which itself ends in a statue as a focal point.*

Meeting points

❀ Where two or more paths meet, especially along right-angle axes, you can mark the spot with seats or arbors at each corner. Or you can simply mark the spot with a vertical feature.

❀ You can create a circular or square paved space to give the meeting point some substance. At the center you could place a sundial or a small circular pool or feature tree such as a weeping pear (*Pyrus salicifolia*). If you have chosen a 'built' feature such as a fountain or sundial, you can plant around it using low-growing plants, such as creeping thyme, that will smell delicious if trodden underfoot.

❀ Four tall junipers could also mark the space. The Rocky Mountain juniper (*Juniperus scopulorum*) is a narrow, conical plant with foliage that varies from green to grey-blue in color and consists of fleshy scales. It will grow to about 50 x 20 ft (15 x 6 m), so if your garden is not very big you may prefer to use *Juniperus* 'Blue Heaven', which makes neat, narrow pyramids seldom more than 16 ft (5 m) tall, with very blue foliage and many berries.

❀ The greenish-silvery leaf color and tall, columnar habit of the junipers would contrast well with shrub roses in the borders along the paths, especially silvery-pink ones such as 'Madame Pierre Oger', 'Felicia' and 'La Reine Victoria'.

❀ The junipers would work well in an informal garden. In a very formal one you might prefer to choose box or yew, clipped into obelisks, corkscrews, domes or other geometric shapes. Along the paths you could grow rows of lavender or rosemary, interspersed with regular plantings of standard rose bushes.

❀ The white rose 'Iceberg' looks pretty planted like this, as does 'Ballerina', whose clusters of flowers are pale pink with a white eye. You could interrupt these plantings at intervals with plantings of box clipped into neat balls.

❀ Planting for an informal garden can include low-growing plants such as the blue geranium *Buxton wallichianum* 'Buxton's variety', which has deep blue petals with white centers.

❀ The fiercely puce *Geranium sanguineum* makes a good show. All the geraniums can be interplanted with silver plants such as *Artemisia* 'Powys Castle', as well as old-

ABOVE: *A round hole in a wall can be used to frame a beautiful view. This sort of viewing device is used very effectively in Chinese and Japanese gardens. Here, a brick edging has been used in a flint wall.*

ABOVE: *Four tall, narrow juniper trees mark the meeting point of several axial paths, lending height and interest to an attractive brick-paved area with a large planter placed in the center.*

fashioned roses such as the Portland rose, 'Rose de Rescht', which grows to about 3 ft (1 m) tall and has small rosettes of the brightest purple-red with a delicious scent.

Framing a view

❀ If the garden opens on to countryside, make the most of the view. Any worthwhile view, whether it is a part of the garden created by you or green fields, rolling hills and ripe corn or a pine forest should be incorporated into your plan.

❀ Whatever the view, a path should lead enticingly to the best place to observe it and there should be a seat inviting visitors to do so. You can frame the view with planting to bring it to people's attention, and emphasise its interest by planting shrubs or a hedge along the edge of the garden and leaving an opening to emphasise the transition from garden to 'outside'.

❀ The opening may be wide and generous, with two tall trees such as Lombardy poplars on either side or, in a more formal setting, two obelisks of clipped yew.

❀ Another way of drawing attention to such a view is to create a wide path bordered by pleached limes or a hornbeam hedge leading the eye – and the visitor – directly towards the scene in the distance. A small gate always looks inviting, even if it does not actually lead anywhere.

❀ If the garden is bounded by an evergreen hedge, you can create a 'window' in the hedge by careful training and clipping so that people have a tantalising glimpse of what lies beyond.

❀ Circular 'windows' are not too difficult to achieve with a round template on a stem that you stick into the ground. This works particularly well in a formal rose or herb garden. Even a narrow slit in the hedge can provide a glimpse of the view. Here you could place two seats positioned at an angle so that both the distant view and the enclosed garden can be enjoyed.

Edging and bordering

❀ Edges and borders in a garden function like piping on cushions. They emphasise the shape and neaten the lines. Edging looks most striking when only one plant is used. This is essential for a formal garden and often true of an informal garden as well.

❀ Good bordering plants include the old standby known as elephant's ears (*Bergenia cordifolia*). Many people who have seen this planted in parks think it rather dull but, planted in long rows along a straight path, its large evergreen, dark glossy leaves look attractive and disciplined. *B. cordifolia* 'Purpurea' has bright purple leaves in winter and produces dark purple flowers in spring, while *B.* 'Silberlicht' has tall stems of loose white flowers and bright green leaves.

❀ Box hedges, when clipped low, make excellent edging plants. Their neat formality shows up the flowershapes and colors of plants grown behind them. *Ajuga reptans* is a low-growing plant, good for bordering a narrow path.

❀ The variety 'Atropurpurea' has very dark purplish-green leaves and dark blue flowers in spring. Even when not in flower its leaves are evergreen and attractive.

ABOVE: *Small plants planted near the front of the border are grown to cascade over the brick wall, which softens the line of planting.*

In an informal situation, it can be allowed to creep back into a flowerbed and to creep forward to soften the lines of paving. It is not invasive and is easily controlled.

❀ Geraniums make good informal herbaceous edging plants. They will die back during winter, but some provide a very long season of flowers. Geranium 'Johnson's Blue' has deep blue flowers with pink centres, and flowers prolifically.

❀ Another good geranium is 'Wargrave Pink', which has silvery-pink flowers over a long period. Both these geraniums will line a path very prettily all summer long if you clip the spent flower heads regularly. *Geranium sanguineum* (bloody cranesbill) is a low-growing plant with bright purple flowers from late spring through to late summer and its leaves color well in fall; *G. s.* 'Album' has pure white flowers.

❀ A dark green hedge often looks as though it could do with something to edge its 'feet' but because evergreens are greedy for moisture and nutrients, it is difficult to find a plant that will survive. *Lamium maculatum* 'White Nancy', however, is a low-growing dead-nettle with very pretty white and green leaves and white flowers, which seems to grow almost anywhere and has even been known to clothe the feet of a north-facing yew hedge.

ABOVE: *The yellow peony flowers for only a short time but is worth growing for its wonderful flowers and its attractive leaves.*

Concealing the garden perimeter

❀ In small town gardens particularly, you may want to conceal where the garden ends. A clipped hedge always looks neat but will define and emphasise a garden's narrow shape, whereas informal trees and shrubs will create a less clearly defined outline.

❀ Choose shrubs that give flower, foliage and fruit interest all year round, and the eye will concentrate on the shrubs rather than on what is behind them.

❀ Choose the shrubs carefully for variety of foliage and height. If you are planting a small square area as a garden room, your planting can make it appear oval. Plant the occasional small tree or tall shrub at the back. A smoke bush (*Cotinus coggygria*) can be grown as a small tree or, if you prune it back hard in spring, will throw out new shoots with larger leaves.

❀ The purple forms blend well with blue-green foliage so you can underplant it with *Hosta* x *sieboldiana*. Also at the back, you can plant a variegated weigela. These deciduous shrubs have pretty pink flowers in spring and leaves that contrast well with the dark cotinus.

❀ Next to the hosta, plant as much as you like of *Alchemilla mollis*, whose feathery yellow-green flower heads and pretty fan-shaped leaves go well with almost anything. Bergenia leaves are evergreen and their large size and shiny quality lend body, and will contrast well with the alchemilla. A peony will add color in spring and its foliage will look attractive all summer.

❀ Allow enough space for the plants you choose, particularly for the larger shrubs. The smoke bush, for example, will grow to 6 x 6 ft (1.8 x 1.8 m) in five years and will look best if it can really expand into its allotted place.

BELOW: *Bergenias, or elephant's ears, make good plants for the front of a border with their positively shaped, rounded leaves, which turn good fall colors of red. The crab apple 'Yellow Hornet' and the purple berberis make this a spectacular fall border.*

USING COLOR

Color is very much a matter of taste in the garden as anywhere else. Some people want their garden to be a riot of reds and bright colors; others prefer a more subtle approach of misty blues and pinks in association with silver leaves. Others again will find the variety of colors provided by foliage alone is all the color they need.

❧ Color is not a finite thing. It is affected by all sorts of things, including the other colors surrounding it, the quality of the light shining on it and the texture of the flower or leaf itself.

❧ Colors also appear different in different climates. In Mediterranean areas, the harsh overhead sun creates hard contrasts and shadows. Bright colors are necessary or they will not be noticed at all. The more intense the light, the more saturated the color needs to be.

❧ In more northerly areas, the summer sun is lower in the sky and there is more moisture in the air. The resulting light is always slightly soft and blue, and pastel colors take on a particular glow not found in hotter areas.

Study of color

❧ The science of color was avidly studied by Victorian gardeners. When the French scientist, Chevreul

LEFT: *The subtlest of greens, greys and yellows will pick up the light and transform a garden.*

BELOW: *It is best to restrict pink and red to a few shades in any one bedded area for simplicity and harmony of color.*

ABOVE: *Use color to surprise, like this simple thistle of the deepest purple.*

(1786–1889), published a report on his study of color for the Gobelins Tapestry Workshop in Paris, many British gardeners argued for the use of complementary colors, as recommended by him. Others argued that his color theories took no account of green, which controlled the effect of complementary colors in a garden.

❀ Donald Beaton, head gardener at Shrubland Park, in Suffolk, England, in the 1840s considered that any variegated plant would function as a neutral color and proudly described a bed he had planted with verbena and variegated geraniums, which a visitor had said looked like 'shot silk'. He used to compete with John Fleming, head gardener to the Duke of Sutherland at Trentham Park, in Staffordshire, in the design of spectacular bedding schemes.

❀ Beaton and Fleming both introduced ribbon or 'promenade-style' borders at Shrubland Park and Trentham in the same year. Although the designs were nothing if not bright, the colors were restricted. Each border had three continuous lines of color extending its whole length. Beaton described his like this: 'The first row on each side of the walk is blue, the second yellow and the third on one side is scarlet and on the other, white'.

❀ He used nemophila for the blue, calceolaria for the yellow and geraniums for the scarlet. Gardeners were also well aware that red seems to advance in broad daylight but blue advances in the evening light.

Color complexities

❀ Whatever the complexities of color in scientific terms, most gardeners will observe the effects of colors in their own gardens and decide for themselves which colors work in different parts of the garden at different times of day and in different seasons.

❀ Plant a purple-leaved plant in one place and it will catch the afternoon light so that its leaves become a magical stained glass window display; plant it elsewhere and it will never light up in the same way.

BELOW: *If you want to make a splash in your garden, mingle the perfectly formed flowers of the brightest red and white dahlias in a grand display of color.*

USING THE
COLOR SPECTRUM

The color spectrum is a continuum of infinite gradations of color between the six rainbow colors: red, orange, yellow, green, blue and violet. Colors have other qualities too. They may be very intense; they may be tinged with black (tones) or with white (tints). Examples based on the spectrum give a simplified idea but are a useful guide to the complex interaction of colors in a planting scheme.

THE COLOR WHEEL

THE color wheel shows the colors of the spectrum placed so that each color is opposite the color that it complements. Opposite colors and neighbouring colors both offer pleasing color schemes. Less satisfactory results are usually produced by mixing the yellow-reds and blue-reds.

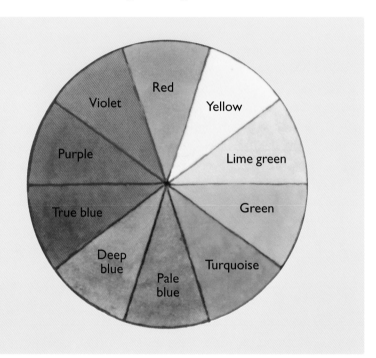

Color in the garden

❀ Colors to choose for the garden are endless. There are dozens of different reds and different intensities of those reds, and the same is true of yellow, blue, green, in fact all the colors. Take red itself. There are blood reds, flame reds, poppy reds, rust, terracotta, wine, crimson, scarlet, beetroot, cerise and rose red, to name but a few.

❀ Green may vary from blue grass to turquoise, emerald, jade, pea green, grass green, olive green, coppery greens and true green, which is more or less epitomised by parsley.

❀ Yellow may vary from the greeny-yellow of many euphorbias to the sunny yellow of *Kerria japonica*. The term 'golden' is often used for yellow-leaved plants, shrubs, conifers and other plants with yellow variegation, as well as for flowers.

❀ However, yellow is brighter than gold and many yellow tones have some blue in them, making them greeny-yellow rather than golden-yellow. 'Egg yolk' or 'buttercup' seems to describe many yellow plants better than 'gold'. The yellows include colors such as buff, sulphur, lemon, maize, saffron, primrose and canary.

❀ Blue is the most misunderstood color of all and true blue is one of the rarest of flower colors. Most blues have some red in them, making them nearer to purple than blue. The shrubs, ceanothus and ceratostigma, are covered in very blue flowers in early or late summer; *Salvia uliginosa* and the Himalayan blue poppy

(*Meconopsis betonicifolia*) are among the true blues.

✤ The purples and violet-blues are easy to find. Many of the herbs such as the thymes, sages and oreganos have violet or purple flowers. Delphiniums, monkshoods, asters and campanulas are all rich in violets and purple-blues, too.

The color wheel

✤ You can experiment very well yourself with different colors and color schemes, but a basic knowledge of color can be valuable, too. The color wheel is a device for demonstrating the relationships between the colors of the spectrum by dividing them into equal segments.

✤ On a wheel like this, colors opposite each other are known as complementary. These colors nearly always go well together. For example pillar-box red is opposite dark green on the wheel and true blue is opposite orange. These colors usually look attractive together in a garden.

✤ Colors next to each other on the wheel usually look good together too, although less arresting. Some adjacent colors are more successful than others. For example, red and purple often associate well but yellow does not always look its best next to another yellow.

✤ The color wheel is useful as a basic guide, but is nevertheless a fairly blunt instrument when choosing a color scheme. Light will affect the colors, depending on the texture of the flower or leaf and depending how bright it is and how it is angled.

✤ Colors will affect each other as well. A particular red may look very bright against a pale color, but become toned down if it is next to a deep color. Orange and cerise may make a brash impression grown together, but if the cerise flower has a black center, for example, it will alter the effect importantly.

ABOVE: *Yellows and reds give a bright, sunny, lively feeling to a border. Here, Gaillardia grandiflora with their yellow and red flowers are mixed with swathes of red lobelia in an informal scheme.*

ABOVE: *Blues and whites are cool and calming. Here, the tall spikes of a range of blue delphiniums combine with white to produce a striking 'cool' scheme, with the pink of the flowers in front adding a little warmth.*

COLORS IN THE SPECTRUM

❦ Red, yellow and blue are described as primary colors. All other colors are produced by mixing these three. Side by side, they produce violent contrasts because they have nothing at all in common.

❦ Children love the primary colors, perhaps because they are so easily distinguishable from each other and so definite. The three colors separating the primary colors on the color wheel are green, orange and violet. They, too, are in contrast but because they are secondary colors – made by mixing two primary colors – they harmonise rather than clash.

❦ Practice in mixing and matching colors greatly increases awareness of color. You can use crayons, felt tips pens, watercolors or simply arrange color samples from paint charts.

❦ In a practical gardening situation you can bisect the color wheel, drawing a line between the green and red sides of the wheel. One side can relate to flowers and leaves with blue in their make-up, the other relates to flowers and leaves containing yellow.

❦ Many effective color schemes have been made by the use of one or other of the two ranges, with only limited use of the other one in the scheme. There are some possibilities below for taking these color associations a little further. Remember, in the garden they will be surrounded by other colors, particularly green.

OPPOSING COLORS ON THE COLOR WHEEL

THERE are some striking possibilities for the garden with these color combinations.

Buttercup yellow and purple

❦ One example of this color combination would be the tall perennial *Filipendula ulmaria* 'Aurea' with the creeping *Ajuga pyramidalis* grown in front.

True blue and orange

❦ Consider growing the funnel-shaped, deep blue flowers with white and yellow centers of *Convolvulus tricolor* with the hardy annual Californian poppy (*Eschscholtzia californica*).

Dark green and pillar box red

❦ This is exemplified by the deep red, semi-double flowers of *Camellia japonica* 'Adolphe Audusson', growing among its own dark green shiny leaves.

Adjacent color combinations

❦ These two-color schemes use colors that are next to each other on the color wheel.

BELOW: *This exciting color combination comprises opposing colors on the color wheel – the deep orange and yellow plates of achillea contrasting strikingly with the purple spikes of* Salvia x sylvestris.

Red and purple

❁ *Rosa* 'Paul's Scarlet Climber' with its fairly small bright red double flowers will give a reliably generous display at midsummer, grown together with Clematis 'The President', whose deep purple flowers with their reddish-purple stamens will flower continuously from early summer to early fall.

Pink and orange

❁ Many annual bedding plants have this mixture of colors. For example, *Dorotheanus bellidiformis* is a low-growing succulent annual with daisy flowers of crimson, orange, pink, red or white, sometimes with petal bases of a contrasting paler color forming an inner zone around the darker central disc. They like a poor, dry soil and associate well with Californian poppies (*Eschscholtzia*) and pot marigolds (*Calendula officinalis*).

Orange and yellow

❁ The Welsh poppy (*Meconopsis cambrica*) is an annual poppy whose bright yellow, tissue-paper petals bloom from spring to mid-fall. It looks even better interspersed with M. *c.* var. *aurantiaca* 'Flore Pleno', which has double orange flowers. If they like the position they will sow themselves and come up again, year after year.

ABOVE: *kimmias are low-growing shrubs with attractive evergreen leaves and good clusters of bright red berries in fall and winter. Here, they contrast highly effectively with the snow-white flowers of the common snowdrop (Galanthus nivalis).*

ABOVE: *Orange and purple are at opposite ends of the color spectrum and produce very positive and exciting planting schemes like this Zinnia 'Golden Sun' with the purple leaves of* Ricinis communis *'Carmencita'.*

Yellow and lime green

❁ The perennial *Euphorbia polychroma*, with its bright lime-green leaves and bracts, can be grown very effectively with the low-growing, front-of-border annual, the poached egg flower (*Limnanthes douglasii*), with its bowl-shaped yellow flowers with white centers.

Green and blue

❁ Baby blue eyes (*Nemophila menziesii*) is a trailing hardy annual with small bright blue flowers, which associates well with *Nemesia strumosa* 'Blue Gem'. Both have the brightest of blue flowers nestling among green foliage.

Blue and purple

❁ Woodland spring bulbs such as the lovely blue scillas and chionodoxas will associate beautifully with the small purple-blue *Anemone blanda*.

Three-color combinations

❁ There are various triads of colors produced by turning an imaginary triangle in the color wheel. Classic examples of successful three-color combinations are sage green/plum/dried grass and citrus green/slate blue/rust red. These bear the same relationships to each other as red/yellow/blue but are easier to combine because they are secondary not primary colors.

❁ This is a simplified view of the color spectrum and there are dozens of combinations to try. Many plants mentioned have other colors in them, such as white or red, and all will be surrounded by foliage of various colors. However, it should help the inexperienced gardener to look at colors with new eyes.

FOLIAGE COLOR

IN general people think of leaves as being green, but look again. Leaves can be all the colors of the rainbow. In itself, green is paramount in the garden. It is the color that induces calm and tranquillity. It has the ability to heighten pale colors and to tone down bright ones, and a pleasant garden can be created with no other color but green. Gardens created entirely with foliage do have a particular quality of unity and peace but they need not be only green. Foliage comprises many other colors besides green, for example blues, silvery-greys, yellows, reds and cream and green variegations. Of course, these plants often have colorful flowers as well.

Blue-leaved plants

🏵 The giants of the blue-leaved plants include *Crambe maritima* and *Thalictrum flavum* ssp. *glaucum*, both of which have blue-green leaves. Medium-sized blue plants include *Euphorbia characias* 'Blue Hills', a rounded compact dome with blue-green leaves, which grows to 3 ft (1 m).

🏵 *Rosa glauca* is a species rose with glaucous purplish leaves and stems. Lower-growing plants include several good blue grasses, including the evergreen *Helicotrichon sempervirens*, 15–18 in (38–46 cm) tall, and *Festuca glauca*, which makes little mounds of blue.

Silvery grey-leaved plants

🏵 There is a really lovely selection of silvery-leaved plants available. They complement dark green leaves, as well as flower and foliage colors from deepest purple to pale pink and blue. They include the artemisias, for example *Artemisia* 'Powys Castle', which grows to 1 x 3 x 6 ft (1.8 m) and A. 'Lambrook Silver', 3 x 4 ft (1 x 1.2 m). *Brachyglottis Dunedin* Group 'Sunshine' (syn. *Senecio* 'Sunshine') grows to 3 x 6 ft (1 x 1.8 m); *Eleagnus* 'Quicksilver' has striking narrow silvery leaves and reaches 3 x 3 ft (1 x 1 m).

🏵 Smaller silver plants include the curry plant (*Helichrysum italicum*) with narrow silver leaves, which grows to 12 in (30 cm). Lamb's ears (*Stachys byzantina*) forms dense mats of thick woolly grey leaves, 16 x 20 in (40 x 50 cm).

🏵 *Convolvulus cneorum* is a charming, low-growing silver plant with white convolvulus flowers. *Artemisia schmidtiana* 'Nana' grows to 12 x 12 in (30 x 30 cm);

ABOVE: *The large, variegated yellow and green leaves of the Hosta fortuneii 'Aureo-Marginata' look extremely interesting against the deeply cut, feathery purple leaves of the Acer palmatum.*

LEFT: *Woodland always provides good opportunities for displaying fall color. Here, a gravel path leads through a variety of shrubs and woodland planting, with colors ranging from the orange of the* Fothergillia gardenii *to the green of the asplenium fern and the deep purple leaves of the heuchera.*

BELOW: Sedum atropurpureum *flowers well into fall and has much deeper colored flowers than the more common* Sedum spectabile, *as well as very dark purple stems.*

cotton lavender (*Santolina chamaecyparisus*) has finely dissected woolly leaves and grows to 24 x 24 in (60 x 60 cm). The woolly willow (*Salix lanata*) is a low, spreading bush for rock gardens, measuring 12 x 12 in (30 x 30 cm).

Red/bronze-leaved plants

❀ Red, bronze and purple leaves can be sensational if carefully placed. The red and bronze colors can complement other plants significantly. They look particularly good with greens and silvers, but may be less successful with variegated and yellow-leaved plants.

❀ *Cotinus coggygria* 'Royal Purple' is a splendid shrub with purple leaves, which turn bright red in fall. *Berberis* 'Bagatelle' is a rounded shrub with bronze-purple foliage, often used as a hedge.

❀ Many roses have deep bronze young foliage in spring, which later turns green. *Cercis canadensis* 'Forest Pansy' is a deciduous tree or large shrub with bronze-reddish-purple foliage, which keeps its color all season. It needs a sheltered, sunny spot and is slow growing but will eventually reach 40 ft (12 m).

❀ The palm-like *Cordyline australis* 'Pink Stripe' has leaves with purplish edges and a rich pink central stripe. It is not hardy so it should be grown outside only in mild areas or in tubs where it can be brought in for the winter.

❀ *Heuchera* 'Palace Purple' has coppery purple leaves and the leaves of *H.* 'Pewter Moon' are heavily marked with silver. *Berberis thunbergii* 'Atropurpurea', also known as 'Crimson Pygmy', is a deciduous berberis with rich purple new foliage. It is good as a colorful low hedge or a rock garden plant.

Yellow-leaved plants

❀ *Berberis thunbergii* 'Aurea' has spectacular yellow leaves and makes a rounded bush 3 x 3 ft (1 x 1 m). The Mexican orange blossom (*Choisya ternata* 'Sundance') is an evergreen shrub with very yellow young growth.

❀ *Cornus alba* 'Aurea' is a deciduous shrub, which grows to about 6 ft (1.8 m) tall. Golden privet (*Ligustrum ovalifolium* 'Aureum') has green leaves with broad bright yellow borders. *Hedera helix* 'Buttercup' is a good bright yellow ivy, which will grow to 7 ft (2 m).

PLANTING FOR COLOR

For colorful beds and borders, a gardener will always be experimenting,
moving plants around and borrowing ideas from other gardens. It's a
wonderfully inexact science. One month the colors in a border will harmonise
beautifully, the next it has all changed and the harmony is lost.
One of the most exciting things about a garden is that it does not remain static
so you must always be rethinking. You may like deep, rich colors to dominate
the whole garden, or a patchwork of pastels or even one dominant single color
such as white or red. Whatever your preference, a disciplined approach is
normally more satisfying in the long run.

Limiting the colors

❀ If you try and grow all the primary colors together, too
many reds, yellows and blues in close proximity can
have a very tiring and confusing effect. They may be
enjoyed in a large space such as a public park where
disciplined formal bedding can make some sense of
them, but they can be really hard on the eyes in a
small garden.

❀ Leave out just one of the primary colors and concentrate
on the reds and blues, say, or the yellows and reds, or the
blues and yellows in any single area of your garden, and
you can make it look as rich as an oriental carpet. There

is an enormous choice of plants and colors even within
this restricted palette.

❀ The successful garden designer, Gertrude Jekyll
(1843–1932), studied first as a painter and
subsequently treated the colors in her gardens as
though she were creating a painting. She would
graduate the colors in her long borders with great skill,
moving from yellows and whites through oranges and
reds to the blues and purples.

BELOW: *The pale yellow of these argyranthemums is a particularly attractive
color, whether used on its own or mixed with other yellows such as lupins and
lilies as here.*

❀ The gardens she designed were large enough, so that these borders could be viewed from a distance and the visitor could get the full effect, as in a painting. In many of today's smaller gardens you could not do this, but you can still concentrate on particular colors in different areas of the garden.

❀ Red and purple are very dominant. White plants such as *Gypsophila paniculata* or Shasta daisies can help to tone them down a little.

❀ Pastel colors such as the violets, pinks or very pale yellows can be planted together. They may need the boost of something positive, perhaps a few black tulips in a spring scheme or some deep velvety-red geranium in a summer patio scheme or the deep colored leaves of a purple cotinus in a mixed border.

Single-color schemes

❀ Of course, no scheme is truly made up of a single color; all schemes are surrounded by the various greens, blues, silvers and bronzes of the foliage. Having single flower color schemes can be effective but it is not wise to give the whole garden over to just one color because of the difficulty in supplying it with enough of the color for the whole season. In just one area or a border or a small front garden, however, you can certainly use a one-color scheme quite successfully.

ABOVE: *Pastel colors are very much in the tradition of the 'old English garden'. Here, low-growing roses, catmint (Nepeta), Geranium 'Wargrave Pink' and stocks are grown in a grand profusion of pink and lilac.*

❀ White is the obvious color choice and probably the most effective. You can get white varieties and cultivars of most plants so you can keep up the effect for a long time and the combination of white and different greens is a particularly charming combination. The structure of the border remains important or it will all begin to look like a bedraggled bridal bouquet.

ABOVE: *It is not often you find such a concentration of color in a water garden, but here, candelabra primulas (Primula bulleyana) in the brightest reds, yellow and oranges are tempered only by a few zantedeschia lilies in the background.*

Suiting the mood of the garden

❀ Choose a color combination that suits the mood of your garden space. Red can be heavy and overbearing because it has the quality of seeming to advance towards you, but it can have a stunning effect in a small courtyard or basement garden.

❀ Harmonious color compositions, rather than strongly contrasting ones, will give unity and a bigger sense of space. If your garden is a cool airy terrace, fresh cream, pink, silver and yellow will complement the atmosphere.

Color ideas for beds and borders

❀ A flower border is an immensely complex thing to design and an all-seasons border is the most complicated of all. For one thing, its shape and form are changing all the time as different plants reach maturity at different times of the year.

❀ The plants that are actually in flower change from week to week and, as the season progresses, plants may outgrow their spaces and begin to look untidy. It is a good idea in spring to rely heavily on bulbs because they tend to be smaller than plants that flower later and, as their leaves die down, new plants growing up nearby will conceal them.

ABOVE: *This pretty example of an informal cottage-style garden mixes the plate-like heads of achillea with cone-shaped echinacea and crosocmia.*

❀ It will help to make a plan of your color scheme. Mark in any evergreens or firmly shaped deciduous shrubs first. Good structure with heights and masses will help integrate all the other plants.

❀ Now divide your bed or border into groups of plants, choosing some for each season. A large showy plant such as a peony can be grown singly but in general most plants give a better effect if planted in groups. Planting in threes or fives is usually best although in a very large border you could increase the numbers.

❀ If you want to include all the colors in your border, arrange them in harmonies or contrasts and make sure the transition from one group of colors to another is marked by a neutral color such as green or white, or that the colors are interrupted by shapely foliage plants.

The yellow side of the spectrum

❀ There are several possibilities if you want spikes in your yellow-based color scheme. *Verbascum nigrum* is a semi-evergreen plant with tall narrow spikes of brown-centered yellow flowers; red hot pokers (*Kniphofia*) are good for providing height.

❀ The hardiest of the plants in the yellow spectrum is *Kniphofia caulescens*, which has coral-red flowers

ABOVE: *The oriental poppy Papaver orientale 'Mrs Perry' is a beautifully shaped plant with superb salmon-pink flowers, which contrast well with the dainty pink spikes of Persicaria bistorta and with pale yellow irises.*

turning yellowish-white; 'Bees' Sunset' has soft orange pokers and the smallest is 'Little Maid', which is a soft yellow. *Crocosmia* can create a splash of color from late summer to early fall. C. 'Lucifer' is deep red, C. 'Jackanapes' is yellow and orange.

❀ For clump-forming plants, try *Achillea* 'Coronation Gold', which has flat heads of tiny golden yellow flowers and silvery leaves for much of the summer and sometimes into fall. *Helenium* 'Moerheim Beauty' is an upright plant for late summer, which has rich reddish-orange flower heads with a dark central boss.

❀ Chocolate cosmos (*Cosmos atrosanguineus*) is a tuberous perennial with single deep maroon crimson flower heads borne singly that make a good contrast with the yellows, and really do smell strongly of chocolate.

❀ For evergreen shrubs consider Halimium ocymoides, a dwarf shrub whose yellow flowers have black or brown spots at the base of the petals from early to midsummer. It reaches 2 x 3 ft (0.6 x 1 m).

❀ If you want to add something on the blue side, *Aster frikartii* 'Mönch' is a bushy perennial with daisy-like, soft lavender-blue flower heads. It goes well with the helenium and flowers continuously from midsummer to late fall. *Phlox paniculata* makes large clumps of fine broad lilac-colored flower heads on tall upright stems.

❀ For the front of the border you could use groups of *Alchemilla mollis*, with its long season of pretty foliage and feathery greeny-yellow flowers and *Eschscholtzia californica*, or pot marigolds (*Calendula officinalis*), whose bright orange flowers will counteract any blue in the alchemilla.

❀ Helianthemum provide a succession of color from late spring through summer. H. 'Wisley Primrose' has pale grey-green leaves and yellow flowers; H. 'Rhodanthe Carneum' has carmine-pink flowers with orange centers and silvery foliage.

❀ In a small garden you may not have room for all these. Remember, if in doubt, it is usually more effective to have larger clumps of fewer cultivars.

A PLANTING DESIGN

Although this sketch is of a summer flowerbed, it has been planted with bulbs as well, so it will only be bare of flowers in the depth of winter. One half of the sketch shows the planting plan, the other gives an idea of the colors and heights of the plants when in flower. The colors are mainly pink and purple, with small touches of yellow and a little deep red here and there. The two shrub roses are pink and flower generously over a long period.

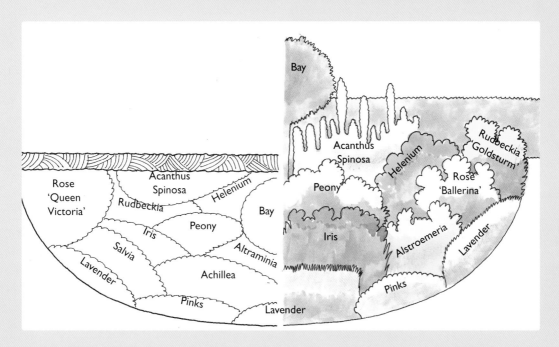

The blue side of the spectrum

❀ For tall spikes you could grow *Delphinium Belladonna* Group 'Cliveden Beauty', a compact variety of delphinium, which produces spikes of sky-blue flowers. It will continue to flower until fall if the old spikes are removed.

❀ Delphiniums in the Black Knight Group are tall with deep violet-purple flowers with black eyes and those in the Blue Bird Group have clear blue flowers with white eyes.

❀ Upright blueish plants include *Campanula lactiflora* 'Prichard's Variety', which has branching heads of large nodding bell-shaped violet-blue flowers from early summer to late fall. *Verbena bonariensis* has wiry stems with tufts of tiny purple-blue flowers in summer to fall.

❀ For clump-forming plants look at *Eryngium* x *oliverianum*, which has large rounded heads of thistle-like blue to lavender-blue flowers. *Geranium psilostemon* is a fairly tall geranium with spectacular magenta flowers with black centers. *Salvia nemorosa* 'May Night' has deep violet-blue flowers, and *Erigeron* 'Serenity' has violet daisy-like flowers with large yellow centers.

ABOVE: *In this informal border, the pinks and reds of the color spectrum have been chosen in the form of the large round heads of dusky red alliums, the tall spikes of* Verbascum phoenicium *and the oriental poppy* Papaver orientale *'Park Farm'*.

Plants for a red and silver fall border backed by shrubs

❀ *Hydrangea villosa* is an interesting and attractive tall shrub for a deep bed. It has large lace-cap flowers of pale purple from midsummer to fall. *Rosa moyesii* 'Geranium' is another tall shrub with bright crimson single flowers and flagon-shaped scarlet hips on arching stems.

❀ In front of these, plant *Sedum* 'Ruby Glow', an upright, fleshy plant with ruby-red flowers suffused with purple. *Artemisia* 'Powys Castle' is a rounded shrub with feathery silver foliage and *Acanthus spinosus* has large, deep green toothed leaves with long spines and spectacular spires of pale mauve and white flowers.

A rich border of reds and greens

❀ This color scheme looks best against a dark green background such as clipped yew. These colors are directly opposite one another on the color wheel so will provide

ABOVE: *This very pretty purple and blue mixture of low-growing spreading flowers such as verbena and geranium is set off beautifully by the silvery leaves of* Teucrium fruticans.

deliberate contrast and startling effect. Ruby chard is a spinach-like plant, grown for its bright red stems and crinkled green leaves with bright red veins.

❀ Penstemons are evergreen perennials with tubular foxglove-like flowers. They will flower all summer long. *Penstemon* 'Garnet' has deep carmine flowers; P. 'Cherry Ripe' is a warm red; and *P.* 'Chester Scarlet' has large dark red flowers with deeper red throats. Dhalia 'Bishop of Llandaff' has bright scarlet flowers with dark purple foliage.

COTTAGE GARDEN MIXTURES

THE charm of a cottage garden is its natural look, which appears to be made up of an unco-ordinated mixture of colors provided by annual and herbaceous plants, often self-seeded. In fact, modern 'cottage gardens' are carefully orchestrated and not as chaotic as is often supposed.

Plants for an early summer cottage garden

❀ This scheme is made up of purple, orange and bright pink. *Geranium magnificum* is a robust clump-forming geranium with deep blue flowers flushed red; *Eschscholtzia californica* is a hardy annual with silky smooth orange upturned flowers on feathery green foliage; *Tanacetum coccineum* 'Brenda' is a perennial with single daisy-like magenta-pink flowers with aromatic feathery leaves.

❀ Violas are well-loved cottage garden plants. Violas in the *Purpurea* Group have flowers of purple and violet and their leaves are often tinged with purple. They associate well with the spiky purple flowers of *Salvia* 'Ostfriesland' and with small silver-leaved plants such as the half-hardy *Senecio maritima* and *Tanacetum densum* subsp. *amani* with its silver-grey mop of feathered foliage.

❀ A midsummer mixture might include *Leucanthemum* x *superbum*, a hardy tall white daisy, more showy and more reliable than the simple marguerite. It associates well with bright red and yellow gazanias and all are easy to grow in a well-drained soil.

Using clematis

❀ Clematises are invaluable for providing color in a garden throughout the year. In winter there are the bright yellow flowering species such as C. *tangutica* and the pale buff C. *balearica*. In spring the vigorous C. *armandii* and C. *montana* varieties can cover a whole wall or fence with white or pink flowers.

Summer-flowering clematis can be grown through many other plants, adding spectacular color.

❀ The starry white flowers of C. *flammula* can be grown over dark green holly. Dusky red and purple clematis look good with silver-leaved plants. Try C. *viticella* 'Madame Julia Correvon' over *Brachyglottis compacta* – you can cut off the Brachyglottis' own yellow flowers.

ABOVE: *There is an enormous choice of colors among the clematis tribe. Here, Clematis 'Niobe' with its deep, velvety-red flowers is mingled with the paler pink of C. 'Comtesse de Bouchaud'.*

PLANNING YEAR-ROUND COLOR

It is impossible to cover the whole garden in bright color all year round, but it is good to have some colorful, eye-catching plants somewhere in the garden at all times of the year. In a larger garden you can allocate particular spaces to specific times of year. Gertrude Jekyll, the famous so, garden writer and designer of the early 1900s, had part of her own garden dedicated to primulas in spring. For the rest of the year it was of little interest and visitors admired the summer border instead. In a small garden, where much of it can be seen at a glance, careful thought must be given to year-round interest and color.

Succession of color

❀ Color is easy to provide in spring and summer when everything is burgeoning with blooms. In a large city the temperature tends to be several degrees warmer than in the surrounding countryside and you can make the most of this by growing flowers for longer in the season.

❀ Fuchsias flower well into late fall; many roses will continue to flower into winter and a choice of different varieties of clematis can bring color into the garden all year round.

❀ It is not difficult to arrange to have color in fall, too, with late-flowering herbaceous plants, red foliage and berries. Tender plants such as geraniums, Impatiens and abutilons will carry on flowering until the first frosts provided you bring them in before then, they can continue to brighten the patio until well into fall.

❀ In winter, colorful stems and bark can add interest. Remember that both white and green can be counted as a color. Your carefully planned framework of evergreen shrubs will give you a structural background.

ABOVE: *Heleniums are tall daisies, which flower over a long period and well into fall. They are in the yellow to browny-red color range and popular varieties include 'Septemberfuchs' and 'Moerheim Beauty'.*

ABOVE: *Among the most welcome of flowers in spring is the hellebore. This attractive form of* Helleborus orientalis *has dark pink petals, paler inside with very dark spots.*

❀ You just need to add colorful highlights to accentuate and brighten the picture. Stems and berries make a fantastic show of color in winter. Some of the dogwoods (*Cornus*) have stunning colored stems, ranging from crimson to orange or even black. They make a really good impact when two or three are planted together along a bank or as a hedge.

❀ Some of the snake and paper bark trees have marvellous colors, ranging from copper to white. Several birches, cherries and maples can also be used for the color of their bark.

❀ Then there are the berries. Hollies, yew, cotoneasters, mountain ashes and many more shrubs retain their berries until well into winter, to attract birds as well as delight us. When choosing a shrub check how fast it will grow and how large. The spindle bush, for example, has fascinating pendent bright pink-red fruits open to display red capsules in fall, but it is fast growing and needs a good 12 ft (3.5 m) spread to do it justice and you may not have room for such a giant.

❀ Skimmias, with their large, bright red berries will not grow to more than about 3 ft (1 m) and pyracantha, although potentially large can be grown up a wall and kept under control by clipping.

❀ Altogether, with disciplined planting, imagination and a choice of plants that will really work for their living by producing interesting flowers, foliage, stems and fruits, you should certainly be able to provide color all year round.

❀ Of course, there are no sudden transitions between the seasons. Snowdrops, the epitome of spring flowers, will appear in winter and carry on to spring; many spring flowers contrive to flower well into summer and many berries start to form in fall but will be retained on the plants well into winter, all helping to create a succession of color.

BELOW: *The leaves of the vigorous decorative vine* Vitis cognetiaea *are a soft, furry green in summer, but become spectacularly colored in fall, creating a long season of color.*

SPRING COLOR BULBS

FROM the first delicate early snowdrops to the late-flowering sturdy tulips and daffodils, spring bulbs provide wonderful color right through from winter to early summer. Many people worry about growing bulbs in a border because of the risk of disturbing them when planting herbaceous plants. However, if the bulbs are happy in their position, they will multiply rapidly, producing far more bulblets than you need, so do not worry if a few get dug up. You can replant some, give some to friends and discard the rest.

ABOVE: *Anemone blanda are among the most enchanting of early spring bulbs. They come in a number of white and blue varieties and can carpet the ground with their bright little faces.*

Snowdrops and aconites

 The common snowdrop (*Galanthus nivalis*) is actually a winter flower but will carry on flowering into spring and is among the most loved of flowering bulbs, naturalising readily in grass, woodland and shady flowerbeds. Snowdrops do best if planted while still in flower. The enchanting G. *caucasicus* has an eight-week flowering period and may start to bloom in late fall or winter.

 Another favorite is the winter aconite (*Eranthis*). With its cup-shaped flowers and little green ruff, it makes a charming yellow clump under trees. Like snowdrops, winter aconites are best planted while flowering in early spring. They need a dry summer dormancy so are most at home under trees.

Crocuses

 Crocuses, with their wide-open flowers welcoming the sun, come in varieties of purple and lilac to yellows and white. Purples and yellows are usually best grown separately, although white will mix with either.

 The very early species are enchanting and delicate-looking planted under specimen trees on a lawn and will multiply freely. *Crocus chrysanthus* is an early-flowering species with over 20 varieties. C. 'Purpureus Grandiflorus' is an intense violet-purple color, very free flowering and among the last to bloom.

Hardy cyclamen

 Elegant and tiny, the hardy cyclamen are essential bulbs for any garden. Like tiny versions of the better-known houseplants, they may be pink or white. They look very pretty naturalised in woodland or in pockets in the rock garden. C. *coum* flowers midwinter to late spring. Others such as C. *hederifolium* will flower in late summer and fall. They thrive in sun or part shade and do not mind drought. They can also be grown in troughs or containers.

ABOVE: *These pale little narcissus appear on the woodland floor while the trees are still bare of leaves, bringing anticipation and color to the garden.*

Erythroniums

❀ The European dog's tooth violet (*Erythronium dens-canis*) is not really a violet but has little pagoda-like flowers of pink, yellow or white on delicate stalks and attractive mottled leaves. It will grow on most soils in sun or shade.

❀ The American erythroniums prefer shade and are best planted among shrubs or trees. They include *E. japonicum* with purple flowers, *E.* 'Pagoda' with pale yellow flowers and *E. tuolumnense* with heads of up to 10 yellow flowers.

Daffodils

❀ You can provide a surprisingly long succession of color with daffodils alone. For example, three months' worth of color can be obtained by planting Narcissus 'February Gold', a cyclamineus type with swept-back petals, which is one of the earliest; 'Dutch Master', tall and vigorous with soft yellow, trumpet-shaped flowers with frilled cups; 'Tête-à-Tête', a dwarf daffodil with masses of multi-headed yellow flowers; 'Carlton', a large cupped, single yellow mid-season daffodil; 'Golden Ducat', a golden-yellow double daffodil; and 'Cheerfulness', with its clusters of sweetly scented creamy-white and yellow double flowers.

❀ It is not necessary to plant all of these in one place. Plant different types separately because confusion will detract from bold simple effects.

❀ 'Golden Ducat', 'Cheerfulness' and other large daffodils are useful grown in large pots in a quiet, sheltered corner of the garden, away from mice. In

ABOVE: Galanthus elwesii *is an attractive snowdrop with strap-like glaucous leaves and honey-scented flowers, which appears in late winter, brightening up the garden with its snow-like white.*

spring, you can place the pots in borders or inside larger pots to bring a splash of spring-time color to a still-dormant area.

Tulips

❀ Tulips can also help to bring a succession of color over a longish period. The kaufmanniana and greigii groups are early-flowering, short-stemmed tulips with handsomely marked leaves in a good range of flower colors.

❀ Single, later tulips include 'Queen of the Night', a deep blackish-maroon color; 'Temple of Beauty', which is salmon rose, and the lily-shaped 'Union Jack', which is raspberry red on an ivory background.

❀ The later tulips stand up tall and straight like soldiers. It is tempting to plant them in serried ranks but they look better grouped naturally among other plants unless grown in a very formal garden.

ABOVE: *These deep red tulips, accompanied by bright red wallflowers and yellow pansies, provide a very cheerful and colorful late spring bed.*

SUMMER COLOR HERBACEOUS FLOWERS AND SHRUBS

THERE is no problem in finding colorful plants for summer. The choice is enormous. In fact the real difficulty is in not overdoing things. The following popular plants can all add color to the flower border. Primulas flower from spring right into midsummer. They form a rosette of leaves, from which grow flowering stems bearing from one to many five-petalled flowers, often with a white or yellow eye. There are species to suit every garden situation, from alpine gardens to bogs and borders. For a bog garden, the candelabra primulas are gorgeous.

For a sunny border

❀ *Convolvulus cneorum* is an evergreen low-growing convolvulus with silver leaves and white flowers carried intermittently for months. Rock roses (*Cistus*) bear papery flowers in white or pink, often with paintbrush marks of dark maroon in the center. C. 'Silver Pink' is hardy with greyish-green leaves and likes a sunny position and poor soil.

❀ Lavender will flower all summer long with spikes of lilac, pink or white flowers above silvery leaves. It is one of the most useful low summer shrubs with the bonus of a lovely scent. Dwarf varieties are especially suitable for underplanting rose beds. Larger types can be planted as an informal low hedge.

❀ English lavender (*Lavandula augustifolia*) has pale lilac flowers on long stems. *L. a.* 'Hidcote' has deep blue, very thick spikes of flowers on grey-green foliage and compact growth. French lavender (*Lavandula stoechas*) has larger flower heads with petals sprouting out like a topknot.

❀ There are many varieties of sage (*Salvia*) worth growing for color. Among the most colorful is *Salvia* x *superba*, a herbaceous perennial with masses of violet-blue flowers in midsummer with crimson-purple bracts that persist after the flowers have faded. *Salvia macrophylla* is a small shrubby sage with deep crimson flowers at the ends of the stems, appearing from early summer to the first frosts.

❀ Achilleas have tiny blooms forming flat-topped clusters of flower heads all summer and sometimes into fall. A. 'Gold Plate' and A. 'Cloth of Gold' both have great platters of bright yellow flowers, which make an impact in a mixed border. A. 'Cerise Queen' has cerise or light cinnamon-colored flowers.

❀ Sea holly (*Eryngium*) has bold, thistle-like flower heads in metallic blues and greens, adorned by spectacular

ABOVE: *Vibrant purples create a beautiful and dramatic summer border, contrasting well with the lush green of the lawns and surrounding plants. The smooth pebbles add to the tidy and well-kept feel.*

ABOVE: *The deep purple leaves of this beech hedge and archway contrast excitingly with the brightly colored planting of red hot pokers (Kniphofia), lythrum and orange calendula.*

spiny bracts and flowers all summer. Many eryngiums are evergreen. *Eryngium* 'Blue Star' has deep blue flower heads and bracts; *E. bourgatii* has rounded flower heads, which change from steely blue and green to lilac blue; *E. variifolium* has small silver-blue flower heads and marbled leaves.

❀ Garden lupins are tall, stately flowers for early summer with astonishing color combinations. The Band of Nobles Series has a range of yellows, pinks, reds, blues and violets.

❀ Rose campion (*Lychnis coronaria*) has handsome grey felted leaves and bold reddish-purple flowers throughout the summer months.

For a clay border

❀ Astilbes are tall, fluffy, plumed flowers in reds, pinks and white, springing from a skirt of fern-like green leaves. They like rich, moist soil and thrive on clay. There is a good range of hybrids, including A. 'Bridal Veil' (white) and A. 'Bressingham Beauty' (pink).

❀ Day lilies (*Hemerocallis*) are available in many colors – from cool yellow to pale creamy-pink or rich burgundy-red. Their strap-like leaves are useful as a contrast to more feathery or rounded plants.

❀ Bergamot (*Monarda dydima*) has a distinctive herby smell and ragged-looking dreadlock flowers in bright pinks, purples and reds. It will grow in part shade and likes a moist but well-drained soil.

❀ Border phlox (*Phlox paniculata*) have fine broad flower heads in blue, purple, pink or white from mid- to late summer. They are tall and upright, and like moisture and full sun or partial shade. They are intensely fragrant. *P. p.* 'Amethyst' has violet flowers, *P. p.* 'Bressingham Beauty' is pink and *P. p.* 'Red Sentinel' has deep red flowers with dark foliage.

❀ The daisy-like flowers of asters, rudbeckias, echinaecaes and heleniums provide color on tall stems in late summer to fall.

❀ Geraniums are essential in most gardens. They flower freely over a long period, especially if you remember to cut off the seed heads. There are many to choose from, including *G. psilostemon* 'Bressingham Flair', which has purple flowers and dark brown centers from early to late summer.

ABOVE: *The silvery-blue pointed leaves of* Artemisia ludoviciana, *with feathery grasses and the flat heads of* Achillea *'Fanal', make a really striking color scheme in this summer border.*

FALL COLOR: FLOWERS, FOLIAGE AND BERRIES

FOLIAGE and berries are the obvious sources of color in the fall garden but there are still plenty of brightly colored flowers to be appreciated at this time of year. If you intersperse them carefully among the earlier flowering plants, they will come into their own when the others are over. Many are tall, so put them at the back of the border and stake them early.

Herbaceous plants

✿ Many of the daisy family give a good show in fall. Michaelmas daisies (*Aster*) offer a lovely selection of colors. *Aster amellus* 'King George' has large violet-blue flowers, while *A.* x *frikartii*, a clear violet-blue color, is free flowering, vigorous and resistant to mildew.

✿ Heleniums specialise in yellows and orange-reds. *H.* 'Moerheim Beauty' has bronze flowers from midsummer. Rudbeckias have brightly colored flowers with dark cone-shaped centers. *Rudbeckia fulgida* 'Goldsturm' is a wonderful yellow with a black center, which glows brightly from green foliage at the back of the border.

ABOVE: *The stem of this black bryony (*Tamus communis*) has obligingly curved itself around the chestnut paling in this wild garden, giving emphasis to its bright red berries, which show up well in front of the ivy.*

Shrubs

✿ Ceratostigmas are low-growing shrubs with bright blue flowers, which bridge the transition between summer and fall brilliantly. They are suitable for the front of a border, a rock garden or for containers. Their leaves turn red in fall.

ABOVE: *Mahonia 'Charity' is an upright evergreen large prickly-leaved shrub, which really earns its keep in summer when it has spikes of bright yellow flowers, and again in fall when its leaf colors and black berries provide winter interest.*

❀ Fuchsias are graceful and pendulous with flowers as elegant or as plump as you like. They start flowering in midsummer and will go on until late fall. *Fuchsia magellanica* is graceful with narrow red flowers and purple calyxes. Its variegated form has pretty pale grey-green leaves with purple markings.

❀ Mop-headed hydrangeas are spectacularly colorful if you have the space. They do well in shrubberies or in large containers. The hortensia varieties have great round heads of red or blue flowers, which can be very spectacular in summer and fall.

❀ As they die, they become 'dried flowers', retaining their colors effectively for a long time. *H.* 'Ami Pasquier' has many vivid crimson flowers (but light blue on acidic soil). It grows slowly, eventually reaching about 3 ft (1 m). *H.* 'Vibraye' is one of the earliest to flower and goes on into fall. Many hydrangea heads will overwinter as a greenish-turquoise color.

❀ Many roses will flower again in fall. The hybrid musks are good value and *Rosa* 'Autumn Delight' and *R.* 'Ballerina', with its pale pink flowers with paler centers, are both excellent value.

❀ The smoke bush (*Cotinus coggygria*) is a large shrub whose inflorescences are just like smoke. The fall foliage of the cultivar 'Flame' is brilliant reddish-orange. It should be planted in a place where the sun will shine through the leaves.

TREES

THE Japanese maples are outstanding for fall color and there is a good choice. *Acer palmatum* 'Dissectum' is a very small pretty tree at any time of year. It has an attractive shape, the leaves are individually enchanting and the fall foliage is a lovely orange-yellow. *Amelanchier lamarckii* again has interest for much more of the year than just fall with snowy-white flowers in spring and coppery young foliage, which turns a rich red in fall.

For acidic soils

❀ *Photinia villosa* has dark green leaves with grey, downy undersides that turn vivid orange yellow. It is slow-growing but will eventually reach 12 ft (3.5 m). It goes well with rhododendrons and azaleas.

❀ For a larger garden, *Parrotia persica* is a tree almost as broad as it is tall, with large leaves that turn vivid orange, yellow and red. Remove the lower branches to reveal the attractive grey, pink and yellow bark.

Berries

❀ Mountain ash trees (*Sorbus*) all have lots of good berries. The rowan (*Sorbus aucuparia*) is a well-known small tree, used freestanding or in a group. It has white flowers, dark green leaves with a grey sheen and clusters of spectacular red fruits. *S.* 'Sir Joseph Rock' has yellow berries and *S. vilmorinii* has interesting mauve berries.

❀ If you want to combine interesting fruits with security, try *Berberis aggregata*, which is very prickly and can be planted as a hedge or in a group. It has deep orange clusters of small fruits on wood that is two years old. *B. wilsoniae* is a very attractive berberis with pink and orange berries.

BELOW: Photinia villosa *is an attractive small tree with bronze leaves when young, turning orange and red in fall. It has heads of small white flowers in spring, followed by red fruits.*

WINTER COLOR

IN the winter garden, green is an invaluable color in its own right and interesting evergreen shrubs make an important contribution. However, there are one or two shrubs that flower exquisitely in winter; there are some trees and shrubs with colorful and interesting stems and bark, and some berries last well into winter.

Stems and bark

❀ The red stems of the red-barked dogwood (*Cornus alba*) glow in the sun on a winter's day. The shrub is attractive all year round, with white flowers in spring, dark green leaves with red veins and silvery undersides and red fall color.

❀ Probably its best feature, however, is the color of its bare stems in winter. Cut it back very hard in early spring to generate strong, well-colored winter stems. Plant two or three together if space allows and make sure they are positioned so that they will catch the sunlight.

❀ The eucalyptuses, tall trees from Australia, are also good value all year round with an attractive growing habit, blue leaves and grey-green stems, often with peeling bark which reveals primrose-yellow underskin.
Use them as ornamental trees or turn them into multi-stemmed shrubs by cutting down to the ground in spring.

❀ A hard frost may cause damage, but the snow gum (*Eucalyptus niphophila*) is a relatively hardy, slow-growing tree with an attractive trunk patched with green, grey and cream.

❀ Other trees worth growing for their bark are *Prunus maackii*, a decorative plum with very striking shiny

ABOVE: Winter can be spectacular in the garden, but only if you do not tidy up too much and cut down all the old flower stems. It is the stems, seeds and old leaves that can come to life in winter frost and sunlight.

mahogany-colored bark, and several birches such as *Betula utilis*, which has pale, papery peeling bark and the very white bark varieties like *B. jacquemontii*. *B. albosinensis* var. *septentrionalis* is one of the finest orange-barked birches.

❀ For a larger garden, *Acer griseum* is a delightful slow-growing tree to grow on its own to get the full effect of its peeling brown bark, which shows a golden-brown underskin.

ABOVE: Helleborus niger is the Christmas rose, and in some areas it will appear by Christmas Day. In others, and particularly in cold clay soils, it will flower in January or February.

Winter flowers

❀ There are more flowering shrubs for winter than many people realise. The mahonias are large evergreen shrubs with small yellow flowers. They are often used rather unimaginatively in public parks but can be a great asset in a small garden. *Mahonia japonica* can be used in a shrub border and is useful in dark, dry places where its evergreen leaves and pale yellow, scented flowers can lighten the gloom.

❀ *Lonicera standishii* is a tall, shrubby honeysuckle with large, cream, highly scented flowers from midwinter and a bonus of red berries in early spring. Use it near the house or next to a path.

❀ *Viburnum* x *bodnantense* 'Dawn' is a tall, narrow shrub with very pretty, small pink and white flowers on bare stems in winter. The leaves follow on later. *Viburnum tinus* has dark green glossy leaves and heads of small flowers in pinkish-white throughout winter.

❀ *Daphne mezereum* is a very popular, attractive scented shrub, flowering from winter to early spring. It will grow to only about 32 in (80 cm) so plant it in a border, a large rock garden or at the edge of a shrub border.

❀ Winter jasmine (*Jasminium nudiflorum*) is not a climber but is good trained up a wall or pergola where its arching stems, carrying small dark green leaves and pretty yellow flowers, can be seen to advantage.

❀ The evergreen *Clematis cirrhosa* var. *balearica* has pretty, divided bronze or purple leaves and masses of creamy-yellow bell-like flowers with maroon spots inside which last all winter.

Winter berries

❀ Many berries last for a long time in winter and can be very cheering. *Skimmia japonica* 'Foremanii' has glossy evergreen leaves and long-lasting, large shiny red berries. They like acidic to neutral soil and dislike any alkalinity or waterlogging, and will tolerate shade.

❀ Choose them for woodland gardens or shrub borders. They also look good in large containers. The female form bears the berries when a male form is planted nearby.

❀ The cotoneasters have berries that last into winter. *C. franchetii* can be grown as a small tree. It has grey-green leaves on long, arching branches. Single white flowers in early summer are followed by dull red fruit, lasting well into winter.

BELOW: Hamamelis mollis *is a small tree with a pleasant shape and habit, whose rounded leaves drop in winter, which is when it produces its spidery, bright yellow or red flowers. Shown here are* Hamamelis x intermedia 'Sunburst' *and* Hamamelis x intermedia 'Diane'.

USING FORM AND TEXTURE

All materials in the garden have a shape, habit and texture.
It is useful to get to know a few plants with different shapes and
habits and see how they can be put together in interesting combinations.
Gardeners whose main interest is in the plants themselves will
want to buy every interesting plant they see, but from the design
point of view, simpler is better and fewer varieties will give
a more cohesive and unified result.

Knowing your plants

❁ It takes time to learn the qualities and characteristics of
different plants. Every garden you visit, whether it is a
stately home or a tiny urban back garden, will have used
plants in a way to interest you. The great skill is in
juxtaposing different forms and textures to create an
interesting complete picture, or rather a three-
dimensional sculpture.

❁ Textures are to do with the leaves and how they are held
on the plant. Feathery textures are soft but have little
structure. They will be most effective next to a plain
wall or planted next to large, leathery foliage plants.

ABOVE: *The contorted hazel (Corylus avellana 'Contorta') has a charming
weeping habit with bright yellow lamb's tails dangling down. This one has been
underplanted with snowdrops, adding to the excitement of spring.*

Clipped plants

❁ The textures of clipped plants should be dense, to give a
clear face or outline, which is why box, yew, hornbeam
and beech are so often used. They make tightly textured
backgrounds for flowers or for sculpting into shapes.
Shrubs used as divisions within the garden can be fairly
small leaved, giving a texture that will conceal what is
the other side but will not seem too forbidding.

ABOVE: *Contrast works well here with the deep green and gentle softness of the
lawn against the chard texture and cool greys of the brickwork step and the
spikyness of the variegated grass.*

ABOVE: *The enormous size of gunnera leaves gives them an open and coarse texture, made more interesting by their hairiness.*

❀ The shapes and structure of the plants used obviously affect the plan of the garden as a whole. In the flower border, feathery or strap-like plants can be offset by round or clipped ones.

❀ Plants with strap-like leaves will provide vertical interest among more undefined or rounded plant shapes. Large vertical plants such as yuccas can be used as focal points among shorter, bushier plants to get their full effect.

Differing shapes

❀ In fact there are few shapes that cannot be found in plants. Umbrella, dome and ball shapes, vertical columns and cones are all good shapes for the formal garden, where their geometrical qualities help to confirm the disciplined design, but they can also be used in the informal garden as 'punctuation marks' or to give height or solidity where needed.

❀ Habit is not so much the shape of the plant as the way in which it holds itself. Shrubs like buddleja have an arching habit, whereas junipers are upright, weeping willows droop and cedars of Lebanon spread.

❀ Roses, which have a rather straggly habit, often need something to cover their bare legs. Rounded shapes like lavender, and geraniums such as 'Johnson's Blue' or 'Buxton's Variety' make good petticoats for roses.

❀ Similarly in a shrub border or shrubbery, you can juxtapose the rounded form of *Hydrangea macrophylla*, especially the lace-cap varieties, with the lightness and elegance of *Cornus controversia* 'Variegata', keeping plenty of space between them so that each can be seen to full effect. When designing a garden, you are creating a kind of living sculpture and all of these textures, shapes and habits have their uses in creating a balanced and interesting whole.

TEXTURE

EVERY plant in the garden has its own individual surface pattern or texture. This textural effect is created by the size of the leaves, their shape and surface features – whether they are shiny, wrinkled, hairy and so on. Texture is also affected by the leaf edges, which may be curled or indented, and whether sunlight can pass through the leaves as it does in an open-textured tree such as birch, or is stopped by the numbers of leaves as it is in most plants. Texture is also affected by the thickness of the leaf, whether it is leathery, fleshy and so on.

Factors affecting leaf texture

❀ Plants draw water and nutrients up through their stems and then release the water vapor through all their aerial parts but mostly through the leaves, via pores known as stomata. This is known as transpiration.

❀ Plants have adapted in many ways to reduce water loss when necessary and these adaptations affect the texture of the leaves. Some grasses roll their leaves lengthways to protect the pores. The leaves of the blue grass *Festuca glauca* do this, giving them a rounded look with a very particular quality of their own. Plants with silver leaves are covered in tiny hairs to protect the stomata from hot sun and drying winds. These catch the light and give the leaves a silvery sheen.

❀ Other plants, such as cacti, have completely replaced their leaves with spines so as to conserve as much water as possible. Plants from humid tropical areas have enormous leaves so that they can transpire freely and the leaves are designed with drainage channels to allow

ABOVE: *Contrasts of texture here include the soft, almost velvety petals of the single French marigolds* (Tagetes) *and the stiff, shiny silvery leaves next to them.*

BELOW: *The wrinkled edges of the leaves of* Asplenium scolopendrium *give this fern a quality all of its own, particularly when edged by a winter hoar frost.*

excess water to run off quickly. All these things affect the texture of the plant and, incidentally, it is easy to see why particular plants will flourish in particular places in the garden and fail in others.

Leaf size

❀ Plants with tiny leaves have a fine texture and include the heathers. Large plants with small leaves such as yew, privet and box are good for clipping. Creeping small-leaved plants such as ajuga or periwinkles are good ground cover.

❀ Plants with medium leaves include trees such as beech and lime, and shrubs such as cotinus and laurel. Large leaves include climbers such as vines and Virginia creeper. Very large plants with enormous leaves, such as gunnera and Rheum palmatum have coarse textures. Some large leaves have a soft and floppy look, while others are very shiny and firm.

Leaf shape

❀ The shape of the leaf itself can also affect the texture. *Bergenia cordifolia* and *Cotinus coggygria* have rounded leaves, which provide a dense blanket of foliage; the grasses with their narrow leaves give a feeling of air and lightness as they are wafted around in the wind.

❀ Conical leaves, as in catalpas, hostas and polygonums, give a graceful look, and dissected leaves, for example *Acer palmatum* 'Dissectum', are also graceful and feathery. Lobed leaves such as those found in hawthorns and figs give a different texture again.

Surface features

❀ Surface features are equally important. They affect the way the plant reflects or absorbs the light. Hairs may give the leaf a velvety appearance, as in *Salvia officinalis*, or they may make it look silvery as in the curry plant. A furry surface such as that of *Stachys lanata* gives the plant a woolly appearance.

❀ Holly has a waxy coating, which makes it very shiny, and prickly leaves, which give it its characteristic look. The heavily veined leaves of viburnum absorb light and make the plant look very dense. *Magnolia grandiflora* has huge glossy leaves, while *Eleagnus pungens* has small matt ones.

ABOVE: *The ornamental cabbage has a leathery texture and a matt finish, which gives density to its attractive dusky pink and blue-green leaves.*

Large leaf textures

❀ If you want to create a dramatic effect in your garden, plants with large leaves are among the most spectacular. Large leaves often indicate that a plant comes from a tropical climate so many of them need to be planted in milder areas or in a sheltered part of the garden.

❀ The foxglove tree (*Paulownia tomentosa*) is deciduous. It originates in China and is an interesting rounded tree suitable for medium and large gardens as a specimen tree and for creating shade. It has 8 in (20 cm) hairy leaves on long stalks with a clammy coating for catching aphids, with the bonus of blue foxglove-shaped flowers in late spring. Its stems may become damaged in very cold winters but this allows the tree to branch more freely from buds below the damage.

❀ The Indian bean tree (*Catalpa bignonioides*) is a large round-topped tree with huge, ornamental, rich green leaves on long stalks, which form a large, shade-giving canopy and turn a good yellow in fall. The spectacular white flowers only grow on 25-year-old trees. Catalpas make good eye-catching specimen trees and grow best in mild areas, away from strong winds but will tolerate urban pollution.

ABOVE: *The large leaves and rosette-like growth of hostas make them very attractive feature plants in garden woodland. This variegated Hosta 'Thomas Hogg' is deeply veined, which adds to its attraction.*

❀ Shrubs with large leaves include *Hydrangea aspera* ssp. *argentiana*, whose velvety, hairy leaves are up to 10 in (25 cm) long. It is a handsome, structural shrub with pretty dusky-pink lace-cap flowers and is good for woodland walks, as a freestanding shrub or a focal point among lower ground covering or as a large wall shrub.

❀ The caster oil plant (*Fatsia japonica*) with its huge palm-like leaves is one of the best shade-loving large shrubs and makes a good freestanding feature.

❀ There are several large-leaved climbers. The crimson glory vine (*Vitis cognetiae*) has heart-shaped leaves, which turn spectacularly yellow, orange, red, purple and crimson, especially if grown on poor soil.

❀ For moist soil there is nothing so spectacular as the giant gunneras. The leaves of *Gunnera manicata* sometimes grow to more than 6 ft (1.8 m) in diameter and the leaves of G. *chilensis* are only slightly smaller. They look majestic growing by the edge of a pond or stream.

❀ The cardoon (*Cynara cardunculus*) has silvery-grey leaves 20 in (50 cm) long and *Acanthus mollis* has dark green, deeply cut leaves 24 in (60 cm) long; both are of great architectural value in a border.

ABOVE: *The ruby-red Swiss chard has become popular for use in flower borders, not only for its spectacular stem color but also for the interesting, deeply wrinkled texture of its leaves.*

Medium leaf textures

❀ There is an infinite variety of plants with medium and small leaves and these make up a large part of the background tapestry of a garden. Medium-leaved plants often create a rather amorphous texture unless they are clipped, and may require the occasional strongly architectural plant to provide structure. Very small leaves, on the other hand, can be so densely arranged on the plant that they create a very definite shape, almost as though clipped.

❀ Medium-leaved plants include many large trees such as beech, ash, lime and poplar. Medium leaves on a large tree will often provide a dense canopy for shade and the leaves move and rustle in the wind. The leaves of poplars in particular can sound like the sea breaking on the shore.

❀ Climbers with medium leaves include evergreen clematis, which can run along a fence or wall for some distance, creating a green blanket of overlapping leaves all shining in the light. Other evergreens with medium leaves include *Choisya ternata*, whose rounded leaves are attractively placed around the branches, and *Magnolia stellata* with its matt mid-green leaves growing on graceful branches.

❀ Roses are so much used in gardens; they deserve some special thought. Some roses have medium leaves, others have small ones. Their habit is often rather open. Only the species and old roses grow more densely and give better coverage, creating a more definite shape.

❀ The large-flowered and cluster-flowered bush roses are covered more sparsely with leaves and rely more on their flowers for interest. From the point of view of garden structure, therefore, roses are better grown together with other plants, unless you are growing a hedge of roses such as *Rosa rugosa* with their bright green, glossy, deeply veined and healthy foliage.

BELOW: *The Indian bean tree has an elegant shape and form, and a texture all of its own created by the large and handsome leaves. There is the added bonus of white flowers and, later, dangling bean pods.*

Small leaf textures

❀ The dividing line between medium and small leaves is not clearly defined. A plant's leaves may seem small when grown next to something like a gunnera, but much larger when grown beside a box bush. The choice here is fairly arbitrary and is intended as a rough guide only.

❀ The shrubby sages with their diamond-shaped, pale green leaves shining in the sun, the hebes with their evergreen compact foliage and the spindle berries (*Euonymus*) all make their own attractive individual contributions.

❀ The daphnes, although usually grown for their flowers, also have attractive small leaves. *Daphne* x *burkwoodii* 'Somerset Gold Edge' has extremely pretty yellow margined, round-edged leaves in rosettes around the stems. Myrtle is an attractive evergreen shrub with small pointed, dark green leaves. It is for mild areas and can be grown as a freestanding or wall shrub, or in a container.

Plants suitable for topiary

❀ Plants suitable for topiary all have small, closely spaced leaves. The most obvious are box and yew but the shrubby honeysuckle *Lonicera nitida* has tiny ovate mid-green leaves with silver undersides, which respond well to clipping; and the culinary bay tree (*Laurus nobilis*)

ABOVE: *The narrow, arrow-shaped leaves of this spiky* Perovskia atripicifolia *give the whole plant an insubstantial feathery look, which shows up well against the rounded, denser purple cotinus behind it.*

with its thin aromatic leaves can be clipped into a mop-head standard. The evergreen *Ceanothus* 'Puget's Blue' has small shiny crinkled leaves, which make a good clipped hedge for mild areas. Clip directly after it has flowered in early summer.

ABOVE: *Here, a number of shrubby plants, all with small leaves, can nevertheless provide variety because some are matt, some shiny, some rounded and some pointed.*

ABOVE: *The tiny leaves of the large shrub* Abies balsamea *give it a fairly solid look; the creeping* Saxifraga moschata *'Densa' makes a dense mat on the ground, and the narrow purple leaves of the nearby grass provide a more open look.*

❀ Conifers are useful with their dense tiny leaves. The western red cedar (*Thuja plicata*) is an evergreen conifer with flattened sprays of scale-like leaves. It will quickly grow into a tall tree but, if trimmed regularly, makes an easily controlled dense hedge.

❀ *Chamaecyparis lawsoniana* 'Pembury Blue' has flattened scale-like overlapping leaves and striking silver-blue dense foliage. It will grow to 4 x 1.2 m (13 x 4 ft) and can be clipped into a hedge or act as a backcloth for a flower border.

❀ Low-growing shrubs with small leaves make good hedges surrounding a herb or rose garden. Box is well known for this but does grow slowly. The lavenders make pretty hedges with their grey foliage and rosemary can also make a good clipped hedge. Less well known is wall germander (*Teucrium fruticans*), a low-growing evergreen sub-shrub for milder areas, with aromatic grey-green leaves covered in fine down.

Feathery textures

❀ Feathery plants do not contribute structurally but can add softness to a scheme that seems too rigid. Such plants include ferns with their regular shuttlecock shapes. Some of the artemisias create soft feathery silver mounds and the curry plant also has a feathery effect, especially grown next to a plant with flat, dark green leaves.

❀ The junipers have tiny leaves giving a feathery effect. *Juniperus scopulorum* with its conical shape contributes structure as well as softness.

❀ The tamarisk is a deciduous shrub with long graceful feathery plumes of dusty-pink flowers. It can be planted as an informal feathery hedge for summer interest and is often used in France to mark the spot where the septic tank is located. Broom (*Cytisus*) is another shrub whose flowers give a feathery effect.

❀ It can be useful in a shrub border, bringing lightness and freshness in spring. Alternatively, it can be used singly but it may begin to look a bit scrawny when the flowers are over so it is best in a place where it can be concealed by other plants.

❀ The white Portuguese broom (*Cytisus albus*) is particularly elegant but there are many, more colorful varieties to choose from. Astilbe is a useful hardy perennial with feathery flowers. The leaves are quite fern-like too.

❀ The flowers are mostly in shades of white, pink, lilac and red. The goat's beard family (*Aruncus*) is made up of tall hardy perennials with elegant feathery plumes of tiny cream flowers in midsummer. *Aruncus plumosus* has 8 in (20 cm) plumes of star-shaped creamy white flowers on tall stout stems. Both astilbes and aruncus thrive best in rich, moist soils.

❀ The cut-leaf forms of Japanese maples are among the most feathery of shrubs or small trees. Yet the positive shape of their trunks and branches makes a good combination of the shapely and the soft, and they make wonderful little specimen trees in a small lawn.

FORM AND HABIT

Having looked at plants as background material and at the way leaves provide different textures in the garden, we now need to look at the form or outline of the whole plant. This is the shape you would see in silhouette. You can see this best in summer with deciduous plants and all year round with evergreens and conifers. As well as its basic natural shape, a plant has its own individual habit. Habit is the way the branches are held on the plant. For example, a weeping habit is where branches hang down from the trunk, while plants with an upright habit have branches reaching upwards.

Structural elements

❧ Some plants are of architectural or structural interest in the garden because they have a strong individuality. They might have large-scale leaves, which is to do with texture; or perhaps there is a well-defined pattern to their growth, which makes them valuable in providing accents. These plants will show up against a simple background or planted somewhere where they will give emphasis to a group of less strongly defined shapes.

❧ Some plants hold their branches horizontally on upright stems and have flat flower heads. Such plants provide an excellent foil to vertical stems in the border and to tree trunks in woodland.

❧ Many are magnificent and will stand alone but they are also good as contrasts to amorphous, rounded plants with less-defined forms. They may give structure to a group of shrubs or a border of perennials, or they may be used to give definition to an avenue or path.

❧ In general, the shapes and forms described on the following pages are those that will add an architectural quality to the garden.

❧ Plant forms are partly inherent and partly created by the gardener. You cannot alter the basic way a plant will grow but you can train many plants to some extent so that they fit in with your scheme.

❧ Others can be cut back and 'molded' to any shape you want. When choosing plants for any structural job in the garden, you must make sure you have left enough space for them to realise their full potential.

❧ You can choose large plants for a hedge and keep trimming it as you will, but if you want a plant because of its particular shape, it must have the space necessary. You do not want to have to move large, expensive plants just when they are coming into maturity and the true beauty of their shapes.

Contrasts

❧ The forms and habits of plants should be used to create interest and all designs need contrast. But if the contrast is too strong it can be distracting. An architectural plant should be placed where it will complement its neighbors, not where it will eclipse them with its magnificence.

❧ The tall, positive shapes of columnar conifers are so emphatically vertical they need to be carefully positioned, especially those with very dark colors. They can eclipse other plants in a border and lead the eye away from other carefully designed plantings.

❧ They can be useful in marking key spaces in the garden, for example a seating area or the meeting place of cross-axis paths. In formal gardens, round, square and conical shapes are in keeping with the geometric layout of the garden.

❧ Form and habit are perhaps most striking in the case of trees. The extreme forms should be used only where special emphasis is needed. These are the fastigiate (plants having erect branches) and plate-like or prostrate shapes. However, every tree and shrub has its own characteristic form, whether grown as an individual or as a group.

BELOW: *This delightful water garden shows many different plant forms and habits, some spreading, some stiffly upright, others prostrate and yet others arching.*

FORM AND HABIT

There are a number of forms and habits to be aware of when designing your garden. Remember that trees and shrubs with their leaves on provide a dense outline, whereas deciduous trees in winter have a more skeletal effect. The size and shape of leaves on a shrub will themselves affect the overall look of the plant.

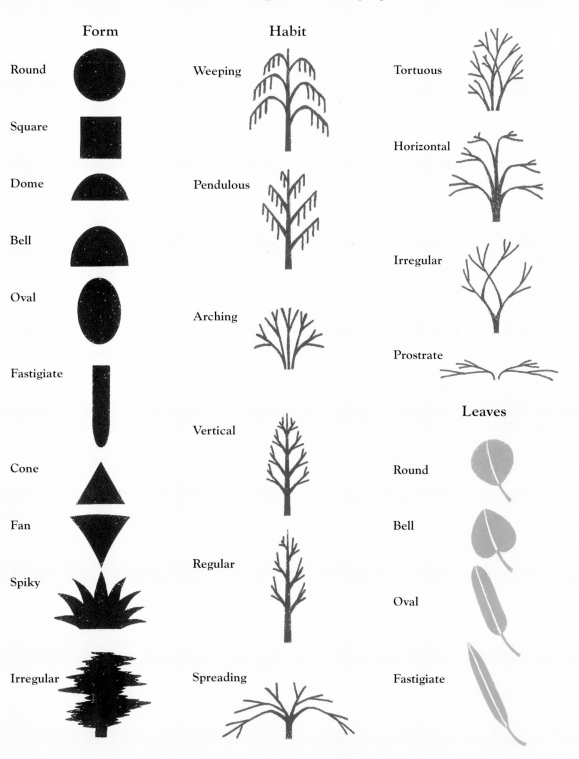

Form

Round

Square

Dome

Bell

Oval

Fastigiate

Cone

Fan

Spiky

Irregular

Habit

Weeping

Pendulous

Arching

Vertical

Regular

Spreading

Tortuous

Horizontal

Irregular

Prostrate

Leaves

Round

Bell

Oval

Fastigiate

FORM

THE shape or form of a plant is its outline pattern seen in silhouette. The plant world has many forms but most can be categorised into a few basic shapes. Each has its own individual value in the garden. Plants with strong forms are valuable in giving strength to a design or as complements to buildings.

❀ All borders need a solid background. When this has been provided, whether as hedge, fence or wall, plants of some solidity can be planted at intervals along it to give a buttressing effect to integrate background and border. For a formal border you could use clipped yew or box. For an informal border you could use plants with solid mass such as choisya, eleagnus or hebes.

❀ Many plants with smallish leaves can be clipped into particular shapes, and these are useful when you want to make a particular statement or create a structural quality in a certain area. Arches, gateways, buttresses and columns can all be created with clipped evergreen shrubs.

❀ When it comes to herbaceous perennials, you may find that the species form is more graceful than modern 'improved' hybrids. Many dwarf cultivars, theoretically ideal for the small garden, have often lost much of their original elegance.

Round shapes

❀ Round shapes are always very formal but will add impact to any garden. Round-headed trees include the black walnut (*Juglans nigra*), a useful quick-growing tree for giving shade to medium or large gardens and avenues.

❀ *Malus floribunda* is a pendulous crab apple with red buds opening to a staggering profusion of pink flowers. It is best grown as a specimen tree. Most of the sorbuses are round-headed and have attractive fruits.

❀ Round shrubs include *Choisya ternata*, a neat shrub that grows quite large but normally needs no pruning unless it outgrows its space when it can be cut back hard and will regenerate. Low-growing hebes such as *Hebe albicans* make neat, round evergreen shrubs for borders, low hedging or containers. Sweet bay, box, standard roses, yew and *Lonicera nitida* can all be successfully clipped into balls, either on long stems or at ground level.

Dome or hummock shapes

❀ These can be like mushrooms or buns or slightly flatter. A dome is a good shape to plant near a building as it softens other shapes. Domed trees are umbrella-like and make good shade trees. They include *Crataegus prunifolia*, a good fall-color form of hawthorn and *Catalpa bignonioides*.

❀ Smaller shrubs include *Erica carnea* and *Salvia officinalis*. Saxifrages, heathers and arbutus make bun-shaped mounds and the flowers of rudbeckias and echinaceas are dome shaped, too.

Bell shapes

❀ These are similar to domes but taller. They can add height in a mixed border and make good background plants and screens. Bell-shaped trees include apples, horse chestnuts and many of the larger trees.

❀ Shrubs include olearia and some evergreen rhododendrons. Bells, domes and round shapes tend to complement each other and can be used well together.

LEFT: *This pretty little clipped tree has been given a bun shape on a slender stalk, which marks it out from its surroundings and gives it a character of its own.*

Oval and fastigiate shapes

❧ Oval shapes are formal bodyguards, adding strength to the garden. They can be used as gateways or in single file along one side of a large lawn. Only a few plants are this shape naturally. One is the fastigiate yew (*Taxus baccata* 'Fastigiata'), but the common yew (*Taxus baccata*) and other shrubs can be clipped into the shape.

❧ Fastigiate plants are tall and thin with erect branches. They can be eyesores if they are not placed correctly, but used as focal points in groups or in a line – not singly – they can be very dramatic. Trees include Italian cypresses, often used to repeat a columnar look, the fastigiate beech (*Fagus sylvatica* 'Fastigiata'), the fastigiate oak (*Quercus robur* 'Fastigiata') and the fastigiate hornbeam (*Carpinus betulus* 'Fastigiata').

Square and rectangular shapes

❧ The square, so often found in human architecture and design, is not found in nature at all. It is particularly suitable for formal situations. Trees in French streets and squares are often pleached into regular blocks, which let light in and integrate well with the geometry of the architecture. The shape is used in pleached hedges, usually of lime, hornbeam, box or yew.

RIGHT: *The spiky leaves of this cordyline, all sprouting from the same point on the stem, create a ball-like form with an interesting open texture.*

BELOW: *The cut-leaved maple,* Acer japonicum *'Green Cascade', has a feathery texture that needs to be seen on its own or with a very plain background for full effect.*

HABIT

MANY plants within the same family have different habits. This is the way the stems and branches are held on the plant. They may be upright or weeping, pendulous, arching or spreading. This not only contributes to the overall shape and form of the plant, but also contributes a quality or mood of its own. This is particularly important in trees but many shrubs have interesting habits, too. Some trees ask to be given a place of honor as single specimens. The Scots pine and the cedar of Lebanon are well known for their stately habit of branching and the beauty of their trunks; weeping trees, too, have particularly attractive forms. Other trees such as hornbeam, ash and alder are best planted in groups or groves.

Vertical habit

❀ Upright plants give a strong line in winter. They include *Salix alba* and *Cornus alba*, whose bare stems in winter can provide superb color.

❀ Similarly, there are several herbaceous perennials that carry the same characteristics into the flower border in summer, including the sea hollies (*Eryngium*), *Thalictrum glaucum*, *Echinops ritro*, *Acanthus speciosus* and *Acanthus mollis*, delphiniums and verbascums. All have a certain rigidity, which gives backbone to plants with less distinctive growth habits.

Spreading habit

❀ Plants with a spreading habit reach out rather than up, often growing wider than they are tall, creating a horizontal effect. It is important to recognise how much space they will need to grow to their full width.

❀ Trees with a spreading habit include *Parrotia persica*, a wide deciduous tree with large leaves that turn a spectacular mixture of reds, oranges and yellows in fall. The medlar (*Mespilus germanica*) makes a wide-spreading ornamental tree with good fall color and is interesting as a specimen plant on a lawn.

Prostrate habit

❀ Prostrate plants reach out rather than up, rather like spreading plants, but they cling close to the ground. They can be useful in rock gardens, or narrow borders where there is no room for tiered rows of plants. Plants such as Juniperus horizontalis make good ground cover.

ABOVE: *All the leaves of these grass-like plants, including the phormium and the palm, have arching habits and together, give a loose, informal look to the garden.*

❀ Several of the cotoneasters have a prostrate habit, including *Cotoneaster cochleatus*, a slow-growing evergreen, and *C. dammeri*, another slow-growing evergreen, which can be used for carpeting banks and bare ground beneath taller trees and shrubs as it has ground-hugging stems that root where they touch the soil.

BELOW: *The alliums and the tall silvery onopordum have upright habits, standing stiffly as if to attention.*

Tortuous habit

❁ These plants, with their strangely contorted stems and branches, are exciting but difficult to place satisfactorily. They really need to be seen against the sky or reflected in water and are best grown on their own as specimen plants.

❁ *Robinia pseudoacacia* 'Tortuosa' is a slow-growing large tree, reaching 50 ft (15 m) with twisted shoots and pea-type leaves. *Arbutus andrachnoides* is a tortuous form of the strawberry tree; *Corylus avellana* 'Contorta' is the corkscrew hazel. It is slow growing but can eventually reach 10 ft (3 m).

Weeping and pendulous habit

❁ This is an appealing habit in which branches 'weep' from the trunk. Weeping plants are usually used as specimen plants on their own and make good focal points. Many weeping trees are smaller than their upright equivalents.

❁ Large trees include the weeping beech (*Fagus sylvatica* 'Pendula'); the weeping willow (*Salix babylonica*), a particularly fine specimen tree to plant beside a large pond; *Prunus pendula*, a weeping ornamental cherry; and the weeping ash (*Fraxinus excelsior* 'Pendula'). Small weepers include the weeping pear (*Pyrus salicifolia* 'Pendula') and the Kilmarnock willow (*Salix caprea* 'Kilmarnock').

Arching habit

❁ Arching plants have branches that grow upright from the ground and then arch over. They are very graceful but may take up more room than expected. Many grasses have an arching habit, as do many old roses.

Strap-like and spiky habits

❁ Strap-like leaves can provide strong contrasts to feathery and other not so well-defined shapes of plant. The fan-like leaves of bearded irises and sisyrinchiums contrast well with plants of horizontal and spreading habit.

❁ Spiky shapes are difficult to use well. They work well with rocks or used on their own, for example at the end of an axis, and if you want to give a tropical look to the garden. They suit urban situations and respond to being planted in relationship to modern buildings, in courtyards and by steps. Spiky plants include *Yucca filamentosa* and *Phormium tenax*.

BELOW: *The silvery-leaved weeping pear* (Pyrus salicifolia) *always seems so sprightly and cheerful for a weeping tree. It can take pride of place in any small garden or stand at the end of a vista in a larger garden.*

GLOSSARY OF GARDENING TERMS

Acidic soil

Soil containing no free lime, and with a pH of lower than 6.5.

Acclimatization

Encouraging plants to develop a tolerance of conditions different from those in which they were originally grown. This usually involves accustoming plants gradually to colder, less sheltered situations, by, for example, placing plants which have been grown on a windowsill indoors, in a cold frame for a few days before planting out; to reduce the risk of growth being adversely affected by a sudden climactic change.

Aeration

Opening up the soil structure and changing its texture by introducing increased air space, for example by spiking the soil with a fork.

Aerial root

A root growing from a plant's stem which absorbs moisture from the atmosphere; not generally rooted into the soil. Some aerial roots, such as those found on ivy stems, may help support the plant.

Alkaline soil

Chalk or limey soil with a pH of higher than 7.3.

Alpine plants

Plants growing naturally in, and adapted to, mountainous conditions by virtue of extensive root systems and a compact, ground-hugging habit. This group of plants is widely used in rock gardens.

Alternate leaves

Leaves which are singly placed on alternate sides of a plant stem, at differing heights.

Annual plants

Plants which germinate, grow, flower, set seed and die within a single growing season.

Aphids

Sap-sucking insects which cause severe damage to fruits, decorative plants and vegetables by attacking the fruits, stems and leaves. Aphids can also cause plant damage by transmitting viral disease. There are many different species, including the greenfly and the blackfly.

Backfilling

Replacing compost or soil around a plant's roots after planting.

Bare-rooted plants

Plants grown directly in soil or compost at the nursery, rather than in a container; dug up and sold with no soil around the roots.

Basal

Buds or shoots which develop from the base of a plant.

Bed

A defined area of cultivated earth.

Bedding plants

Plants, generally annuals, but sometimes perennials or biennials, which are raised in large quantities and used for a temporary display in a bed.

Biennial plants

Plants that complete their life cycle over two growing seasons; germinating and forming leaves in the first year, flowering, setting seed and dying in the next.

Black spot

Unsightly fungal disease causing black spots on affected leaves.

Blanching

Deliberately excluding light from part of a plant, such as the leaves of chicory and the stems of leeks, to prevent the formation of chlorophyll and render those parts of the plant more tender and pleasantly flavored.

Bleeding

Excessive sap loss from a plant after it has been cut.

Blight

A common name for a range of diseases, often fungal, particularly those causing serious, sudden leaf damage.

Blind

Plants which produce no flower bud, such as bulbs planted at the incorrect depth which produce only leaves.

Bloom

A waxy or powdery coating.

Bog garden

An area with permanently wet soil, usually around a natural or artificial water garden or stream. This type of garden is particularly suitable for growing plants such as rushes and water irises.

Bolting plants
Plants which run to seed before they are ready for harvesting. The cause is a check to growth during some stage of the plant's development.

Botrytis
Also known as grey mold, this fungal disease is unsightly and affects both living and dead plant tissue.

Bract
A modified leaf at the base of a flower stalk, which is often mistaken for a flower petal, such as the red bracts of the poinsettia plant.

Brassica
Generic term for plants belonging to the cabbage family, such as turnips, Brussels sprouts, cauliflowers and swedes.

Broadcast sowing
Sowing seeds by scattering them directly onto the soil surface.

Bud
A swelling containing developing petals or leaves.

Bulb
A swollen, underground bud with fleshy scales which are the storage organs for embryonic leaves and flowers.

Bulb fibre
Well-drained planting medium for growing bulbs.

Bulblet
Also known as bulbils, bulblets are tiny bulbs which develop on parent bulbs. They may be grown on separately to increase plant stocks.

Bush
A shrub with no defining leader, and with branches that all emerge close to ground level.

Cacti
Technically referring to the *Cactaceae* plant family, the term is generally used to describe a wide range of succulent and prickly plants well adapted to growing in dry conditions.

Calyx
The outer green ring of a flower comprising numerous sepals which enclose the petals and protect them whilst in bud form.

Capsid bugs
Pale green, sap-sucking insects which damage and distort flower petals and foliage.

Caterpillar
The larval stage of a butterfly or moth; a garden pest which eats holes in leaves.

Chipping
Nicking the outer coating of a hard seed, such as sweet pea, to hasten germination.

Clay soil
A heavy, sticky soil made of minute mineral particles.

Climbing plants
Plants that travel upwards towards the light.

Cloche
Predominantly clear structure of glass or plastic, used to protect plants from inhospitable weather conditions.

Cockchafer
Also known as maybugs, both the adult and larvae of this type of beetle attack many plants.

Codling moth
Small pink caterpillars which are serious, hole-boring pests which burrow into developing plums, pears and apples where they can feed undetected.

Compost
Either sterilized soil for planting, or organic material formed from decomposed animal/vegetable matter used to improve garden soil.

Conifer
Mainly evergreen shrub or tree which bears its seeds in cones.

Contact action
The action of a herbicide, fungicide or pesticide which kills on contact.

Container-grown plants
Plants grown and sold in containers.

Coppicing
Severe pruning method in which trees are cut almost down to ground level to promote growth of new shoots from the base.

Cordon training
Restricting a fruit tree's growth by pruning back to a main, spur-bearing stem, which may be at an oblique angle or upright, and can be single or multiple.

Corm
Swollen, short, underground, bulb-like plant stem, comprising solid tissue, not scales. It shrivels at the end of each season and a new corm grows at the sides or top of the old, withered one. Gladioli, freesias and crocuses are all corms.

Cormlet
Young corm which forms around the parent corm, such as gladioli. Cormlets can be removed for growing on to increase plant stocks. They will

take between two to three years to reach the flowering stage.

Crocks

Pieces of broken terracotta pot placed inside the bottom of a planted container to improve drainage.

Cross bred plants

Plants developed through cross-pollination.

Crown

The point on a herbaceous plant where the stem joins the roots and at which new shoots appear.

Cultivar

A cultivated variety of a plant rather than a naturally occurring type.

Cutting

A piece of leaf, root or stem taken from a plant that is prepared in one of a variety of ways in order to produce a new plant, for example stem-tip, hardwood and softwood cuttings.

Damping down

Wetting the floor of a conservatory or greenhouse in order to lower the ambient temperature and increase humidity.

Damping-off

A fungal disease which infects the stems of seedlings at ground level causing them to collapse and die.

Dead-heading

Removing dead flower heads from plants to give a tidy appearance, but more importantly to make a better display of blooms by conserving the plant's energy that otherwise would go into producing seed.

Deciduous

Plants which shed their leaves in winter.

Deficiency diseases

Plants lacking in one or more nutrients can suffer from a range of problems such as scorched leaves, poor fruit production and spindly, weak growth.

Die-back

Tips or shoots dying, generally because of disease or damage.

Disbudding

Removing unwanted buds in order to direct all of a plant's energy into a few buds. Used to produce exhibition-quality blooms. Fruit trees are shaped by removing buds on young shoots, a process also known as disbudding.

Dormant season

The time when active growth ceases, generally in winter.

Double

A flower with more than the single whorl of petals usual to its type, e.g. double dahlia.

Double digging

A more intensive digging technique than single digging, in which two spits' depth, rather than one, is dug or forked over.

Drill

A shallow, generally straight furrow in which seeds are sown.

Drought

A period of abnormally dry weather.

Dwarf

A plant with a restricted height and root spread, such as dwarf apple trees. Dwarf plants are especially useful for small gardens and dwarf fruit trees may even be grown in containers.

Eelworms

Minuscule, worm-like, soil-dwelling creatures which are invisible to the naked eye. Eelworms attack a diversity of herbaceous and edible crops.

Earwigs

Night-feeding insects which have a distinctive pincer-like rear end. Earwigs shred the leaves of particular plants, such as dahlias, but are not a major threat for most ornamental plants. Earwigs also eat codling moth eggs and some aphids can be useful if your plants are not especially susceptible to earwig damage.

Earthing up

Drawing up soil around plants to provide more covering than they normally receive in level soil, in order to blanch the stems and/or protect against wind and frost damage.

Ericaceous plants

Plants which hate limey conditions; requiring a soil with a maximum pH of 6.5. Rhododendrons and azaleas need ericaceous soil.

Espalier training

Training a tree, often a pear or an apple, into horizontal tiers leading regularly off from a vertical trunk.

Evergreen

Plants which retain their foliage all year.

Exotic

Plants introduced into one country from another.

Fan training

Training a tree, generally a fruit tree, into a fan shape against a wall.

Fertilizer

Plant food, often in a concentrated form.

Foliar feeding
Spraying liquid plant food directly onto the leaves, rather than the soil around a plant.

Forcing
Encouraging plants to develop before their usual time; for example, growing hyacinth bulbs in the dark, then bringing them into warmth and light to produce a colorful display at Christmas rather than waiting until spring.

Formative pruning
Pruning from the early stages of a plant's development to produce a particular shape and branch configuration.

Frost pocket
Area susceptible to trapped cold air in winter; such as the ground at the bottom of a hill. Plants grown here will be at greater risk of frost damage.

Fungicide
A substance used to control fungal diseases.

Fungus
A primitive form of plant life responsible for a range of common infectious plant diseases such as rusts and mildews.

Genus
A number of plant species which share similar characteristics.

Glaucous
Foliage covered with a bloom, or colored grey/blue, for example, the foliage of the Atlas Cedar (*Atlantica glauca*).

Grafting
Joining a bud or stem of one plant onto another.

Graft union
The point at which the topgrowth of, for example, a rose, has been joined on to a different rootstock.

Grease band
A sticky band applied around the trunk of a fruit tree to prevent winter-moth caterpillars crawling up the tree to lay their eggs in early fall. The band is removed and destroyed the following spring.

Greenhouse
Structure of predominantly glass or clear plastic to protect plants from external conditions.

Ground cover
Planting specifically designed to cover the earth, in order to reduce weeding and, if used on sloping areas, to help consolidate the soil. Periwinkles, hypericum and lithsperomum are all excellent ground-cover plants. Ivies and euonymous are especially good soil-binding, ground-cover plants.

Half-hardy
Plants which cannot withstand frost.

Hardening-off
Gradually acclimatizing plants grown under glass to outdoor conditions.

Hardy
Plants which can tolerate average winter frosts.

Heeling-in
Temporarily placing plant roots in soil and lightly firming in with heel pressure until permanent planting can take place.

Herbaceous
Plants producing soft, non-woody growth which usually dies back in winter.

Honeydew
Sticky secretion deposited on plant stems and leaves by insects such as the greenfly.

Hybrid
Plant bred by crossing two genetically different plants.

Hydroponics
Growing plants without soil; usually refers to the practise of growing plants in dilute nutrient solution.

Immune
Plants which are resistant to particular diseases or pests.

Inorganic
Not originating from a substance which has previously lived i.e. one which is of plant or animal derivation.

Insecticide
Substance that is used to destroy insect pests.

Intercrop
A fast-cropping plant grown between the rows of another, more slowly developing plant to best utilise space, especially in the vegetable garden.

Irrigation
Applying water artificially to the ground to increase its fertility.

Lateral shoot
A shoot branching off from a main or leader shoot.

Layering climbers
Propagating climbing plants by growing on sections of rooted stem.

Leaching
The drawing away of chemicals and nutrients from the soil.

Leader shoot
The dominant central shoot of a plant.

Leaf miners

A wide range of pests which 'mine' or burrow within plant leaves.

Leaf node

The point at which a leaf bud or leaf emerges from the stem.

Leatherjackets

Greyish-brown maggots; larvae of the crane-fly which eat the roots of young plants, vegetables and bulbs.

Lichen

Primitive plant growth of algae and fungi often found on old trees and rocks.

Lifting

Digging up plants for storage or planting elsewhere.

Lopping

Severe cutting back of the large, upper branches of a tree.

Mildew

Fungal disease which is unsightly and attacks the vitality of a plant.

Moss

Small, densely growing, non-flowering plant which thrives in stagnant, damp conditions.

Mowing

Cutting down in quantity, as when mowing a lawn.

Mulch

A top-dressing, usually of organic material such as compost; applied to conserve soil moisture and add nutrients to the soil. Inorganic mulches such as gravel are sometimes used to retain moisture within the soil and suppress weed growth.

Naturalize

To establish plants in the garden for a naturalistic appearance; for example, planting snowdrops in drifts within grass.

New wood

Stem growth produced during the current season.

Nitrogen

The most essential element in plant nutrition, promoting dark green foliage and above-ground growth. Nitrogen is used up quickly and needs to be replaced frequently.

Old wood

Stem growth produced prior to the current season.

Opposite leaves

Leaves carried in pairs, rather than at alternating heights, along a stem.

Organic

Substance derived from a source which has once been alive, i.e. a plant or animal. Also a term used to describe a method of gardening that does not use inorganic substances and which respects ecological issues.

Ornamental plants

Plants which are grown purely or predominantly for their decorative attributes.

Oxygenating plants

Aquatic plants which release oxygen through their leaves. These plants are essential to the survival of fish in a pool.

Parasitic plants

Plants which grow on and take their nourishment from another living plant, such as mistletoe growing on apple trees.

Parterre

A formal geometric arrangement of beds, usually edged with low-growing clipped hedges such as dwarf box. A style prevalent in fashionable sixteenth-century Italian and French gardens which is still popular today.

Peat

Dead, partially decomposed vegetable matter often derived from heathland or bogs. Often used as a soil conditioner, planting medium or mulch, due to its moisture-retaining properties and lack of weed seeds and fungal spores.

Perennial

Plants which live and flower for at least two years. Although shrubs and trees are technically perennials, the term is generally used in reference to flowering perennials such as delphiniums and lupins, which die down each winter and produce new growth each spring.

Pergola

A series of arches, straight or curved, which form a covered area. Originally made of brick or stone topped with timber to provide a shaded walkway, pergolas are now generally made of metal or wood and are often installed to define and shade an area for outdoor dining.

Perpetual

Flowering plants such as perpetual carnations which bloom intermittently throughout the year.

pH

A numerical scale used to measure alkalinity or acidity, meaning parts Hydrogen.

Pillar training

Training a plant to grow in a limited space by restricting and encouraging its growth into a pattern of a central trunk approximately 2 m (6.5 ft) high which produces a succession of lateral shoots. Roses and apple trees are often pillar-trained.

Pinching out

Removing the tips of growing shoots to encourage the formation of sideshoots and limit extension growth, i.e. to produce a more compact plant shape and prevent a leggy, spindly effect.

Plunging

Burying potted plants up to their rims in soil, sand, peat or ashes to prevent them from drying out.

Pollarding

Pruning method in which tree branches are repeatedly cut back to the trunk to encourage new shoots to develop from this point.

Pollination

The transfer of male pollen onto the female flower pistil to produce fertilization.

Potbound

A plant is potbound when its pot is full of roots. This is often indicated by a plant draining too quickly or showing checked growth.

Potting on

Transferring a plant from one pot to another, usually because the plant has become potbound.

Pricking out

Transferring seedlings from the container in which they were sown to larger pots or trays.

Propagation

Multiplying plants either vegetatively, i.e. by layering, grafting, budding, dividing and cuttings, or seminally, i.e. from seed.

Prostrate

A plant with a flat, ground-hugging growth habit.

Pruning

Selectively cutting away parts of a plant in order to improve its overall health and performance and/or alter its shape.

Reversion

A highly selected hybrid or plant returning to its prototype, e.g. if suckers are allowed to grow unchecked from an ornamental cherry, the tree may revert from its grafted-on, pink- flowering type to the original white-flowering rootstock.

Rhizome

A thickened, modified stem with leaf buds and roots; a bulbous plant which grows horizontally underground or may be visible just above the ground. Rooted sections of rhizome are easy to propagate. Agapanthus and Canna are examples of rhizomes.

Rock plant

Compact plants suited to rock gardens and growing on walls. Non-invasive plants are specifically chosen in order to prevent the rock garden being overwhelmed by one plant type. Sedum, pulsatilla, saxifrage and gentian are all popular rock plants.

Rootball

The compacted mass of soil and roots at the base of an established, container-grown plant.

Rootstock

Host plant onto which a desirable cultivated variety is budded.

Routine pruning

A program of regular pruning designed to maintain plant health, performance and desirable shape.

Runner

A horizontally extending shoot, e.g. the rooting stems which develop from strawberry plants. These may be removed from the parent plant and grown on.

Rust diseases

Fungal diseases which produce rust-colored pustules on foliage.

Sawflies

The caterpillars of sawflies cause serious damage to ornamental and edible crops.

Scab

Not, as is commonly thought, a specific disease but a term used to describe the damage that a range of fungi causes on plant skins, e.g. the cracked, gum-oozing wounds on peach fruits affected by fungal disease.

Scale insects

Hard-coated, sap-sucking insects which can cause wilt. Many types excrete honeydew which can lead to fungal disease

Scrambling plant

Fast-growing climbers which send shoots upwards through other plants; often supporting themselves using thorns or prickles.

Seedbed

An area of carefully prepared, level soil set aside for seed-sowing.

Seedling

A young plant with a solitary, unbranched, soft stem.

Self-fertilizing

A plant which can set seed when fertilized with its own pollen and needs no pollinating partner. Self-pollinating fruit trees are very useful for situations where space is limited and there is no room to plant a pollinating partner tree.

Semi-evergreen

Plants which retain their foliage in mild winters but which may lose some or all their leaves in particularly harsh winters.

Shrub

A plant with woody branches and stems, with no central trunk.

Snag

A stub of stem left above a bud after pruning. Isolated from the plant's main sap flow, the stub will die, and possibly allow fungal disease to enter the rest of the plant.

Specimen planting

Planting designed to be viewed from all angles, for example, placing a tree centrally in a lawn.

Spot treatment

Applying substances such as weedkillers or fungicides to individual plants, or to a specific part of a plant.

Spur

A short, lateral branch carrying clusters of fruit buds. The term also describes a tube-like, nectar-producing projection from a flower, such as those found on columbine (*aquilegia*) flowers.

Staking

Supporting plants using canes, sticks or other materials to help them maintain an upright habit.

Standard

A trained shrub or tree with a single, bare stem clear of branches from ground level up to a height of approximately 2 m (6½ ft). Half standard trees have a clear stem up to a height of approximately 1.5 m (5 ft).

Stem

The bud-, leaf- and shoot-carrying part of a plant which is above the root system.

Sterile

Unable to breed. The term is widely used to describe plants which produce fertile pollen but no seed. Some plants, such as some fruit trees, are called sterile, but the term is slightly misleading, as they can set fruit with a pollinating partner.

Sterilized compost

Compost treated by chemicals or heat in order to destroy weed seeds, fungi and harmful bacteria. Although known as sterilized compost, it is only partially sterile, as a truly sterile soil would not support plant life.

Stopping

Pinching out or removing growing tips to encourage the development of side shoots and control flowering. A practice often employed to produce better-quality, late-flowering chrysanthemums.

Sub-tropical

Plants of tropical origin which may be grown outside in summer, but which cannot tolerate any hint of frost.

Succulents

Plants with fleshy, water-retaining stems or leaves well adapted to life in arid environments.

Suckers

Unwanted shoots growing from below the ground at the base of a plant, such as the suckers which develop on the original rootstock of hybrid roses. Suckers must be removed at their point of development in order to prevent the plant reverting to its pre-graft origin.

Systemic

The action of a substance such as weedkiller entering the sap stream of a plant through its roots or leaves and being conveyed throughout the whole plant.

Support

Structure, such as trellis or arrangement of poles, which bears the weight and mass of a plant.

Tap roots

Long, sturdy, anchoring roots such as those formed on carrots, which grow straight down from the base of a plant.

Tender plants

Plants susceptible to frost damage.

Tendrils

The fine, curling, modified leaves or stems such as those seen on sweet peas, which emerge from the stems of climbing plants and entwine themselves around available supports.

Thinning out

Reducing the number of seedlings in a seedbed or container so that the remaining plants have sufficient room to grow well with minimal risk or disease and maximum access to light, good airflow, water and nutrients.

Thrips
Tiny elongated insects which attack greenhouse plants and garden herbaceous plants. Affected plants have punctured and torn leaves and are susceptible to virus diseases transmitted by thrips.

Tilling
Cultivating the soil by raking, hoeing, forking or digging either by hand or powered tools such as rotary cultivators or mechanical plows.

Top-dressing
Applying compost, soil or fertilizer to a lawn or the soil around a plant.

Topiary
The art of training and clipping shrubs and trees into ornamental and decorative shapes.

Training
Encouraging and restricting plants to a particular growth pattern by tying them into a framework and by selective pruning, for example, espalier, fan and pillar-training.

Transplanting
Moving a plant from one garden position to another.

Treading
Walking methodically over freshly tilled soil in order to firm it so that it is ready for planting or sowing. Treading encourages good contact of plant roots with the soil for efficient take-up of nutrients and water.

Tree
A perennial plant with a central stem or trunk with branches emerging some distance up this stem away from the ground.

Truss
A loose cluster of fruits or flowers at the end of a stem.

Tuber
A swollen, bulbous, underground stem which acts as a food-storage organ and produces a scattering of buds over its surface. Begonias, anemones and cyclamens are all tubers.

Tuberous root
A swollen, bulbous underground root which acts as a food storage organ and bears buds at the top of the root. Ranunculus and dahlias are tuberous root plants.

Tufa
Porous type of hard limestone popular as the basis of a rock garden because of its ability to absorb and retain moisture.

Turf
Surface soil containing closely planted grass.

Underplanting
Low-growing plants around and beneath taller trees or shrubs.

Variegated
Flowers or leaves of two or more colors. The term is widely used to describe leaves with cream, yellow or white markings.

Vermiculite
A natural substance which is heated until it expands, producing air-filled granules. These lightweight, absorbent granules are often used as part of a planting mixture to encourage good drainage. Tubers lifted from the ground seasonally are also often stored in vermiculite.

Virus diseases
Plant viruses are tiny particles present in plant sap spread throughout all the tissues of a plant. Sap-sucking insects, primarily aphids, suck sap from affected plants and transfer the disease to other plants.

Weeds
Weeds are plants growing in a place where the gardener does not want them. Weeds compete with cultivated plants for food, moisture and light and increase the risk of pest or disease damage to cultivated plants, for example, by leading to the sort of dank, overcrowded conditions that encourage fungal disease. Some weeds host particular pests, e.g. the cabbage root fly found where there is Shepherd's purse.

Weeping
A shrub or tree with branches which have a drooping, pendulous habit.

Wilting
Plants which are drooping, or wilting, may be suffering from a lack of soil moisture, or disease or pest attack. The roots may have been attacked directly, or there may be a fungal disease present attacking the water-conductive tissues of the plant stems leading to collapse.

Wireworms
Orangey yellow, threadlike, click-beetle larvae. These soil-dwelling pests feed on the underground parts of many plants and are of particular threat to root crops.

GLOSSARY OF GARDEN DIY TERMS

To the uninitiated, hardware stores and builder's merchants can seem to use a confusing maze of abbreviations and terminology, understood only by expert construction workers, plumbers and electricians. This glossary will help you navigate the do-it-yourself (DIY) jungle.

Aggregate

A mixture of sand and gravel, combined with cement and water, to make concrete. Types of aggregate are distinguished by the size of the gravel pieces, which range from fine to coarse.

Alkali-resistant primer

A primer/sealer that prevents the attack on subsequent layers of paint by an alkaline substrate, for example, medium-density fibreboard (MDF).

Ballast

Naturally occurring aggregate (sand and gravel mix) used for making concrete.

Bond

The way in which bricks overlap to provide strength and load-bearing capacity.

Capping strip

A timber strip fixed to the top edge of a fence panel, shaped so as to shed rainwater and prevent its ingress into the end grain of otherwise exposed timber.

Cavity wall

Two walls built side by side 75 mm (3 in) apart (a double wall), connected only by 'butterfly' or other galvanized metal ties that are cemented in at regular intervals as the walls are built up. The cavity is for insulation and moisture protection and can be filled with fiberglass or foam insulation.

Coping

The top course of a brick or block wall, often made of shaped concrete slabs designed to shed rainwater from the top of the wall and protect the mortar joints from moisture damage.

Countersink/counterbore

The enlargement of the top of a screw hole to allow the screw head to be driven flush with the surface. Counterboring is where the hole is deep enough for the screw to be driven below the surface; the hole can then be filled with a plug of the same diameter.

Damp-proof course (DPC)

A layer impervious to water, inserted between two of the lower courses in a brick wall to prevent damp rising through the brickwork.

Damp-proof membrane (DPM)

A layer impervious to water, spread beneath a concrete floor to prevent damp rising through the floor.

Efflorescence

The appearance of moisture-borne salts on the surface of brick or plasterwork.

Expansion joint

A flexible joint between large

areas of brickwork or concrete to allow for expansion and contraction with changes in temperature.

Featherboarding

Tapered, section timber, overlapped to make fencing panels.

Footing

A simple foundation to support a wall.

Hard core

Bulky, solid matter such as old bricks or blocks, used to form a sub-base below concrete.

Marine ply

Plywood impregnated and bonded with waterproof adhesive, suitable for use in moist situations.

Masonry bolt

Heavy-duty fixing for brickwork (see 'Wallplug').

Mastic

A flexible, non-setting jointing compound.

Microporous

Allowing the passage of small molecules, i.e. microporous paints allow the wood to 'breathe out', while preventing moisture from passing into the wood.

Pale

A wooden fence upright.

Paver

A brick or block specially made for paved surfaces. Pavers should be water-resistant and therefore frostproof.

Piers

Upright brick columns at the ends and at regular intervals along a run of brickwork.

Prefabricated

Made off-site and simply installed in one or more larger pieces.

Primer

The first coat in a 'paint system', often preservative, which seals and bonds the subsequent paint layers.

Render

A thin coat of plaster; a sand and cement render is often applied to brickwork in a thin layer to form a smooth finish.

Retaining wall

A wall constructed specifically to hold back a weight of soil from an upper level.

Scalpins

Ballast with a clay content, compacted to form a substrate for pathways.

Scratchcoat

An undercoat of sand and cement render, scratched or 'keyed' so that a subsequent layer will bond firmly.

Sett

A small, regular-sized paving block.

Soakaway

An underground pit filled with rubble or sand into which surface water can drain.

Spur

A length of electrical cable connected to a ring main or other main cable.

Subsidence

Sinking of the ground.

Tamp

To compact material, usually concrete, with repeated 'taps', thereby excluding air pockets and forcing the material into cavities.

Wallplug

A fixing for masonry, which works by expanding to a tight fit in a pre-drilled hole as a screw is fastened into it.

Weep hole

A small hole in the exterior of a cavity wall for any accumulated interior moisture to drain from.

INDEX

ACKNOWLEDGEMENTS

❦

BARTY PHILLIPS (design and historical information)

Many people have been generous with their advice and help in writing this book. I would particularly like to thank Graham Cousins, whose garden has been an inspiration, Ruth Chivers for providing many of the photographs, Ken Baker, Michael Clark, Josephine Cutts, Graham Hopewell, John and Dorothy Knight and my editor Katie Cowan, for constant encouragement under pressure.

DEENA BEVERLEY (practical information and advice)
& ANDREW NEWTON-COX (special photography)

Martin Mansfield for his patience in demystifying soil science, disseminating the underlying principles of plantsmanship and general good advice. Pat and Chris Cutsworth for their unfailing tolerance in being used as a garden photography location. Bob Sawyer, manager of the Swindown branch of Jardinerie, for his trust and patience far exceeding the call of duty. Derek Guy for having the trust to allow us to spontaneous access to his beautifully maintained garden for photography.

PUBLISHER'S ACKNOWLEGEMENTS

The publisher would like to thank the following for their kindness in allowing us to photograph their gardens: Anne Birnhack, Ken Baker, Michael Clark, Derek Guy, Graham Hopewell, John and Dorothy Knight and Gae Oaten.

Thanks also to the following companies who have been more than generous in loaning equipment, props and plants for photography: Chairworks, Clifton Nurseries, Draper's Tools Ltd, Idencroft Herbs and Queenswood Garden Center. Extra special thanks to Jardinerie in Swindon, Wiltshire, for allowing us to shoot within the garden center.

PICTURE CREDITS

Andy Keate/Sussie Ahlburg
143 (right), 220 (left), 222 (right)

Amdega Limited
17 (top)

Christie's Images
290

Mary Evans Picture Library
165 (bottom), 291 (bottom), 292 (all), 293 (top), 411

e.t. archive
33 (bottom), 93

Historical Collections Group
204 (top)

Amdega
186 (top), 189

S & O Matthews
2, 8, 14 (all), 16 (all), 29, 43 (all), 44 (all), 46, 50, 52, 53 (top), 58, 80, 89 (left), 90, 94 (right), 95 (all), 96 (all), 97 (left), 98 (all), 100 (all), 108 (right), 111 (all), 113 (all), 114 (left), 118 (left), 128 (right), 130 (right), 131, 138 (bottom), 152 (right), 156, 157 (top), 158 (left), 165 (top left, top right), 170, 179 (all), 183, 185 (top), 186 (bottom), 188, 191, 202 (all), 203 (top), 204 (bottom), 205 (top), 206 (top), 207 (top), 208, 209 (top), 210 (top), 211 (bottom left), 212 (top), 213 (all), 214 (top), 215 (all), 226 (bottom), 227, 231, 240 (all), 241, 242 (all), 244 (all), 245, 246 (all), 247 (top), 250, 255 (bottom), 256 (right), 257 (top), 258 (top), 259 (top), 267 (top), 270 (top),

274, 294 (all), 295 (all), 297 (all), 299 (bottom), 303 (left), 304 (bottom), 305 (all), 308 (top), 324, 326, 327 (top), 326 (all), 331 (all), 332 (all), 333 (bottom), 334, 335 (all), 336, 337 (all), 338(all), 340 (all), 341, 342 (all), 343, 344, 348 (all), 349, 352, 355, 356, 361, 370, 371 (all), 372, 373, 374 (all), 375, 377 (all), 378 (all), 380 (bottom), 381 (all), 382, 383 (all), 384, 385 (all), 387 (all), 388, 389 (bottom), 390 (bottom), 392 (bottom), 393, 394, 395 (bottom), 396, 397 (top), 398 (all), 399 (all), 410, 418, 420, 422, 426, 428, 430 (bottom), 432, 438 (all), 440, 441 (top), 442 (top), 443, 444 (bottom), 445 (top), 446 (right), 447, 449, 450 (right), 452 (all), 454 (bottom), 455, 457 (bottom), 459 (all), 461 (all), 462, 463 (left), 465 (all), 466 (all), 468 (all), 469, 471, 472 (all), 473 (top), 474 (right), 476 (all), 477, 478 (all), 479, 482 (all), 483, 484 (top), 486 (top), 487, 491 (all), 492 (all)

Andrew Newton-Cox
12-13, 15, 20, 21, 23, 25, 26-27, 30 (all), 31 (all), 32, 33 (top), 34 (all), 35 (all), 36 (all), 37 (all), 38 (all), 39 (all), 47 (all), 48, 53 (bottom), 54 (all), 55 (top), 59 (top), 61 (all), 62 (all), 63 (all), 74 (top right), 75, 76 (bottom right), 77, 78-79, 81 (left), 82, 84, 89 (left), 102 (top right), 103, 105, 106-107, 108 (left), 112, 126 (left), 132, 142, 143 (left), 145, 148 (all), 150, 151 (right), 155, 164, 185 (bottom), 193 (top), 194 (bottom), 197, 198, 199, 200-201, 209 (bottom), 216 (top), 217 (top), 228, 229, 230 (right), 236 (bottom), 237 (top), 252 (left), 260 (bottom), 261 (all), 262 (all), 263 (all), 264 (all), 265 (all), 269 (all), 276 (all), 283 (all), 285, 286, 287, 288-

89, 304 (top), 306 (all), 307 (all), 308 (all), 309 (top), 311 (all), 312, 313 (all), 315 (all), 316 (all), 317 (all), 318 (all), 319 (all), 320 (all), 321 (all), 322 (all), 323 (all), 325 (all), 350, 359, 386, 401 (top), 412 (bottom), 413, 415, 430 (top), 436, 448 (bottom), 457 (top), 480 (left)

Scotts of Stow
17 (bottom), 110 (left)

Graham Cousins
18 (all), 19 (all), 71 (left), 87 (left), 114 (left), 122 (top right), 124 (top), 126 (right), 136 (left), 144, 149 (left), 151 (left), 152 (left), 187, 190, 220 (right), 232, 234 (left), 238 (top), 256 (left), 275, 289 (top), 291 (top), 302, 303 (right), 328, 339, 346, 347, 380 (top), 400, 448 (top), 450 (left), 451, 453, 486 (bottom), 488, 490

Ruth Chivers
28, 40 (all), 81 (right), 83 (left), 87 (right), 88 (all), 94 (left), 115 (all), 117 (top), 128 (left), 135, 140 (all), 141, 153, 154, 168 (bottom), 195 (right), 210 (bottom), 212 (bottom), 214 (bottom), 233, 234 (right), 235, 236 (top), 238 (bottom), 239, 243, 252 (right), 273 (bottom), 278 (all), 327 (all), 376, 379, 389 (top), 390 (top), 391, 392 (top), 395 (top), 397 (bottom), 404 (bottom), 439, 441 (bottom), 444 (top), 446 (left), 460, 463 (right), 464, 470 (all), 473 (bottom), 474 (left), 475, 481, 484 (bottom)

Elizabeth Whiting Associates
41, 57, 83 (right), 85, 86, 89 (right), 91 (top), 92 (right), 97 (right), 99 (all), 101 (all), 109,

110 (right), 116, 117 (bottom), 118 (right), 122 (bottom left), 123 (bottom), 124 (bottom), 129, 130 (left), 134 (all), 136 (right), 146, 149 (right), 157 (bottom), 158 (right), 166, 167 (all), 171, 172, 173, 206 (bottom), 221 (top), 222 (left), 223, 224 (all), 225, 226 (top), 230 (left), 247 (bottom), 251 (top), 258 (bottom), 314 (all), 404 (top left and right), 454 (top), 456 (all)

Holt Studios
42, 55 (middle right, bottom right), 60, 62, 63 (all), 64 (all), 65 (all), 66 (all), 67 (all), 68 (all), 69 (all), 70 (all), 71 (right), 72, 73 (all), 91 (bottom), 92 (left), 127, 138 (top), 160, 169, 180, 184, 192 (all), 195 (left), 205 (bottom), 216 (bottom), 248 (all), 249, 251 (bottom), 253, 245-55, 260 (top), 266 (all), 270 (bottom), 271 (all), 272 (all), 273 (top), 277, 279 (all), 280 (all), 281 (all), 282, 296 (all), 298 (all), 299 (top), 300 (all), 301 (all), 303 (bottom), 327 (bottom), 331 (top), 345, 366 (all), 367 (all), 368 (all), 369 (all), 401 (bottom), 402 (all), 403 (all), 405 (all), 416-17, 442 (bottom), 445 (bottom), 480 (right), 485, 493

Mellors Garden Ceramics
168 (top)

Robinson's Greenhouses
174 (left), 176, 178

Jennifer Jones Stoneware
194 (top)

Avon Studios
174 (right)